THE NEGRO IMPACT ON WESTERN CIVILIZATION

THE NEGRO IMPACT ON WESTERN CIVILIZATION

edited by

JOSEPH S. ROUCEK

Queensborough Community College
of the City University of New York

and

THOMAS KIERNAN

author of *Who's Who in the History of Philosophy*

Philosophical Library
New York

Library of Congress Catalog Card No. 72-86509
SBN 8022-2329-X

CONTENTS

v

Foreword

A sudden and quite unsettling curriculum revolution has recently begun to make its impact felt on the teaching of history and the social sciences at all levels of education in the United States. One of the principal causes of this revolution would appear to lie in the unwillingness of today's younger generations to accept without challenge the legacies left to them by preceding generations. So confused and frustrating are some of these legacies that many of the practices and values, as well as educational priorities, held dear in previous decades and centuries have lost validity in the minds and souls of a large part of the current student population.

Another cause of the revolution in history and social science teaching lies in the increasing awareness that traditional history, more often than not, has been a reflection of the point of view—the values, attitudes and assumed verities—of those who write and teach it. That history must by its very nature suffer the consequences of a certain subjectivity has long been accepted as an unavoidable hazard; that it has been too often chauvinistic, doctrinaire and parochial is, in the modern view, its tragic flaw—the source of much of the turmoil the world finds itself in.

Considerable evidence has been developed by contemporary critics of history and history teaching which illustrates the ways in which traditional history has failed us. It remains to be seen whether *what it is* can be transposed into *what it ought to be*. Let it be clear that what it ought to be is not the same as *what it ought not to be*.

What history ought not to be anymore is the almost exclusive domain of the majority. In any nation it is the majority that controls the educational system; it is the established majority point of view that controls the curricula. In the United States, consequently, what history has been is what the majority point of view wished it to be. A third cause of the revolution in history and history teaching, then, resides in the fact that in America there is no longer a clear-cut majority. It has been said that the United States today is a collection of minorities, all joined in a common venture, but each reflecting and expressing its own viewpoints and cultural differences. What an axiom like this fails to say is that there are minorities, and then there are minorities.

That the black minority in the United States is at the center of the revolution should come as no surprise, for it is the black man who has suffered, more than any other minority figure, the consequences of the narrow self-interest inherent in traditional American history and history teaching, and in American education in general. The depressing, almost universal lack of concern on all levels of American society until recently for the educational welfare of the Negro is so well known by now it is hardly worth remarking. Yet it is precisely this lack of concern that has brought the black American to the threshold of despair and has created the social turmoil and racial polarization that have torn seemingly irreparable holes in the fabric of American life.

Alfred North Whitehead once declared that there is no progress that does not grow out of social conflict; and the greater the conflict, the more rapid the progress. One of the self-evident conclusions of current history is that Black America, whether intuitively or rationally, has come to understand this truth and to act upon it. In so doing, it is causing White America to reconsider the situation of the black man in America by putting the white majority "up against the wall."

The possible manifestations and consequences of the present conflict between black and white can take many forms—some destructive, some constructive. As in all profound social upheavals, much time, verbiage and blood will be wasted. But given America's heritage of social conscience and its constitutionally based capacity for decency—of *eventually* being able to do the right thing—and provided that these impulses have not lost their power through the attrition created by the nation's increasingly materialist psychology, the prospects for the success of the black cause are promising.

One of the immediate effects of the black movement, then, has been the curriculum revolution in American education. There has been a headlong rush over the past few years to get what has come to be known as Black Studies into the nation's classrooms. That this movement is controversial goes without saying, and there has been much pedagogical criticism of the sudden and often disorganized introduction of Black Studies into secondary and collegiate curricula that is valid. That Black Studies is an expedient, oil to calm the troubled waters, is just one criticism. That in the educational context it makes little sense is another— why not then have Scandinavian Studies, Jewish Studies, etc.? That Black Studies is elitist, separatist, and evincive of just another form of discrimination is a third criticism that must be considered.

Whatever specialized pedagogical validity these criticisms may have pales before the more profound and acute social question. To properly exercise its responsibility in reversing its disenfranchisement of the Negro in America, white society must apply its full resources to the problem. Before the black American can feel he is an American in the same sense that the white man feels he is one, he must first understand his blackness, just as the white man understands his whiteness.

The problem for the Negro today in America has often been correctly described as a "crisis of identity." The most pressing argument for black history—the one that most white educational leaders fail to understand, mainly because of the security they have in their own whiteness—turns on such questions as developing black identity and pride, creating a sense of black past that is absent in conventional history textbooks, and introducing meaningful ways of teaching black students who, by very virtue of their disenfranchisement, find it impossible to relate to a middle-class Dick-and-Jane portrait of American society—all this within the context of integrated education.

The case for black history for blacks is not a trivial one. Much that is contained in traditional curricula has little significance or meaning for children the majority of whose roots are in the ghetto. The ghetto environment teaches black children to have little respect for themselves or for their possibilities of success. But give them the opportunity to discover something about their past—that blacks were important inventors; that Othello and Augustine were black; that blacks did not accept servitude and that hundreds of thousands died defying slavery; that highly civilized black societies and cultures existed in Africa long before the discovery of America; that black men have been able explorers, soldiers, literary figures, artists and scientists; that the black man had dignity and pride—and they will alter their image of themselves, their motivation and their ability to achieve.

That the emphasis on Black Studies today is perhaps reflective of expediency, that the shortage of qualified teachers of Black Studies is a further weakness in such programs, that there is no general agreement on what courses to offer or what emphases to place within the courses—these criticisms count for very little

ix

when compared with the enormous potential that Black Studies offers in helping the American Negro to liberate himself from the yoke of ignorance about the splendid history of his race.

They count for very little, too, when one considers the yoke of ignorance under which white society lives with respect to the black man. It has often been claimed that there is no such thing as a black problem in the United States; that the problem is a white problem—that the current hostility of Black America toward white is a problem that was created by white society, and so is the white man's problem to solve. And indeed, a significant, well-meaning portion of our white population has recognized the problem in these terms and has begun to deal with its solution. It is almost as important for white students—indeed for all whites—to expose themselves to studies in black history as it is for Negroes. Whites need as much education in the history, traditions and heritage of the black man as blacks themselves do. Black Studies should not be allowed to remain a one-sided educational coin. There is a largesse of cultural riches in black history that can add a whole new dimension to white historical consciousness. With that consciousness thus expanded, the problem will be more available of solution by our future generations.

Black Studies is an investment in the future. The problem of the black-white conflict is not going to be solved overnight, indeed not even by the present generations. The best America can hope for is a hastening of its solution through such social instruments as education. It is in this light that the immediate inauguration of Black Studies programs at every level of the educational process is to be desired. The ends that can be reached through such programs transcend even valid, informed criticism of their present-day educational utility. Criticism aimed at refining and perfecting Black Studies programs should be encouraged; criticism that is merely designed to negate their potential and to kill them while aborning should be treated like all the other well-known rationales against the liberation—the spiritual and moral liberation—of both the black man and the white man.

The purpose of the present book is to make a modest contribution to the liberation process. Victor Hugo's dictum that there is nothing more powerful than an idea whose time has come is illustrated daily in thousands of ways within the context of the black-white confrontation. The editors and contributors of this volume have long believed that the idea of the liberation of the black man from the oppressive and suffocating forces of white supremacy—however subtle or unspoken—is an idea that can no longer be suppressed. The liberation is going to occur, whether White America likes it or not. The white man has three options as he is confronted with the inevitability of the idea. One is to resist, which is to invite ruin and chaos. The second is to remain passive, which is, possibly, to reduce the extent of ruin and chaos, but at the same time to prolong it to a point which would be probably equally as ruinous and chaotic. The third is to help, which would be to minimize ruin and chaos and maximize and hasten the necessary reforms. It is patently clear to all but the most paranoid among us that the only sensible course, if America is to revitalize itself and remain of a piece, is the last.

Contrary to the popular belief that there is a dearth of documentary and other material dealing with black history, the fact of the matter is that there is much in the way of source material having to do with the subject. Until recently much of this material has remained scattered and uncollated, interest in it limited almost exclusively to a handful of scholars of black history dispersed throughout the faculties of the few Negro colleges in the United States. This abundance of source material is evident from the bibliographic and other supporting material cited by the authors in this volume.

The primary practical aim of this book is to synthesize and summarize the knowledge derived from the vast inventory of material relating to the history of the black man in America and throughout the world. The volume represents a collection of studies on various categories of black history by a group of distinguished scholars and authors who have joined together in this common effort to lead the reader from the wilderness of ignorance, through the forest of an ever-increasing but unsynthesized literature of black history, and into the clear where the subject may be perceived with clarity and objectivity. This collection has no pretensions of grandeur; nor can it aspire to exhaustiveness. It is designed simply to serve as an introduction to black history, to outline as many as possible of the details that have made black history what it is, and to put the reader on the road to a more complete interest in and consideration of the subject.

The contributors are leading educators and scholars in the

THE BLACK AMERICAN AND THE NEW
VIEWPOINTS IN BLACK AMERICAN HISTORY*

Joseph S. Roucek

*Queensborough Community College of the
City University of New York (Bayside, N.Y.)*

The stirring events of recent times have led to a renewing and strengthening of the ancient ties to European homelands of American immigrants of the first and second generation. This curious and important phenomenon is commonly agreed to be a result of both world wars and the world situations produced by them. The earlier centripetal forces of Americanization, powerful as they were, have been overcome by these greater forces of the recent past and present.

Yet, how different is the situation with respect to the American Negro, whose history has its primary roots also abroad—in Africa, the second largest continent, four times the size of the United States and three times the size of Europe.[1] It has been only in recent years that the American Negro has begun to show an interest in the past and present problems of his ancestral home. In fact, until recent years, most American Negroes showed no interest in visiting any African countries, preferring, when they travelled abroad, to go mostly to Europe; and it was even more surprising that "Africans visiting this country, in many cases, were not generally accepted by American Negroes."[2]

The roots of the heretofore general lack of interest on the part

---

* This is an expanded version of Joseph S. Roucek's "The Changing Relationship of the American Negro to African History and Politics," which appeared in the *Journal of Human Relations*, XIV, 1, 1966.

of the American Negro in the African continent can be traced to the "climate of opinion" dominating not only the attitudes of most Americans but, in fact, all white men. Africa, perhaps the oldest continent man has known, but also the newest to emerge into worldwide attention, was thought, until quite recently, to have no history, or no history worth speaking of, since it appeared to consist of little more than meaningless tribal rivalries among peoples whom the main current of man's historical development seemed to have left behind. Furthermore, Africans themselves, as they became educated in the ways of the modern West, often turned against their own past and spurned it as unworthy of attention from such "Europeanized" men and women as they, by their efforts, had tried to become. They looked upon Africa's culture as barbarous, and Africa's rich folklore as a collection of old-wives' tales.

On the other hand it is vital that we stress that American and Western historiographical writings, until very recently, offered hardly any information about Africa; and whatever information was available was represented by stereotypes used by motion pictures, cartoons, periodicals, religious organizations (especially those sponsoring missionary work), and those which supported the economic and political claims of the colonizing nations.

ETHNOCENTRISM AND SUPERIORITY COMPLEX

Missionaries came to Africa with a well-defined goal: the conversion of the African people to Christianity. Since most of them came from Europe, they implicitly accepted the superior accomplishments of European civilization. In order to save Africa's souls, they had to promote education. "The object of missionary education was to Christianize the African and to supply him with the moral principles in which he was believed to be deficient. The corollary of this was the elimination from the minds of the young of those elements of African culture, and they were practically the central ones, that were held to be pagan and incompatible with Western Christian ideals."[3] Indolence, polygamy, fetishism, and dancing were all labeled as immoral. It was, of course, "in the interests of missionaries, in emphasizing their undoubted victories, to exaggerate the depravity of the base line from which their ministrations had brought their converts."[4]

(Thus, the Methodist Bishop Walter Russell Lambuth, in his diary of his pioneering trip through the Congo in 1911, listed adultery, polygamy, witchcraft medicine, animism and worship of the fetish as practices of "brutish, shameless immorality." He spoke of "poor, deluded, superstitious, degraded people," concluding that "it will take long and patient work to elevate and purify these people."[5]) Hence, "through primary education, African children received a distorted view of their own depravity and European superiority. While subjugation was never the motivation of Christian missionaries, their implicit acceptance of the superiority of European civilization, expressed through the ideas they taught, contributed to the maintenance of white and black relationships built on white supremacy."[6]

In general, Africa was thus pictured as a land of mystery, full of dense jungles and wild animals, ignorance and danger, full of man-eating savages—and of Tarzan—and where much to his disgust, the colonizer was discharging the "white man's burden," hoping, rather hopelessly, to bring the bright light of Christian civilization to the native heathen. This kind of image was, of course, found to be beneficial to the Europeans engaged in a feverish scramble to grab up more colonies in the last part of the 1800's and the early years of the 1900's, and also to be the most successful way of raising funds for missionary efforts. Even the American Negroes were played upon by such fund raisers—by painting an African geared to the concepts handed down by Livingstone and Stanley nearly a century ago, which presented women being partly or fully nude, with babies fastened to their backs, rings in their nostrils, and practising cannibalism, polygamy, and idol worship.

Such a stereotype of "savage Africa" fitted perfectly into the imperialistic ideology of the colonial powers. This chapter of modern imperialism was, actually, not usually a matter of "trade following the flag" of the various countries involved. Rather, the reverse was true, and traders and other businessmen penetrated Africa, obtained big concessions, and then insisted that their willing governments "protect" them in their business undertakings for the sake of "civilizing missions."[7] Thus, until the end of World War II, the alleged inherent superiority of the white man was accepted almost as an axiom by the peoples of Africa under

3

colonial dependency. This superiority, rationalized by various concepts, such as "the white man's burden," or *La mission civilisatrice*, was frequently impressed upon the African peoples by force of arms.

THE HERITAGE OF SLAVERY

The white man's relationship with the Negro as a slave was eventually rationalized into the most powerful racist doctrine in recent times.[8] The slave trade played a large part in both Arab and European interest in Africa. But it must be noted that neither Arabs nor Europeans introduced the institution of slavery to Africa; it was already there—just as serfdom was a part of Europe's social structure during the Middle Ages.[9]

The first Africans to appear in the English colonies of America's was Portugal. In 1441, when Henry the Navigator's seamen probed the West African coast looking for the sea route to India, they captured twelve men, women and children and brought them back to Portugal as slaves. Within seven years nearly a thousand slaves had been imported and sold at the Lisbon slave market, where, we are told, Henry the Navigator looked upn them with great pleasure, thinking that these people could be converted to Christianity. But whereas the discovery of the route to India made the collection of slaves comparatively unprofitable, Columbus' discovery of the West Indies and America made them the most profitable cargo of all. "By one of the ironies of history the discovery of the continent which now has the Statue of Liberty standing outside its greatest city was responsible for the greatest increase in the slave trade that the world has known."[10]

The first Africans to appear in the English colonies of America's eastern seaboard got to Virginia a little over a year before the Pilgrims landed at Plymouth Rock. A Dutch sea captain sold a group of 20 men and women at Jamestown in the summer of 1619.

Quite often, Negro laborers in the early English colonies were treated much the same as white indentured servants—people who had "sold" themselves for a term of years in order to pay for passage across the Atlantic. But by the mid-1600s, conditions were a great deal harder. Slavery spread to all the English colonies—not just those of the South. (Its failure to take strong root

4

in the North is believed to have been mainly due to the fact that the region had practically no large-scale farms and plantations—the kinds of enterprises most suited to use of slave labor.)

While Northerners held comparatively few slaves themselves, many were deeply involved in the transatlantic slave trade; ships from Boston and other Northern ports would travel around a great triangle—sailing first to Africa, then to the West Indies or Southern U.S. ports, then back home. Their cargo for the first leg of the trip was rum and other items to be traded for slaves on the African coast. The second leg was the infamous "middle passage," with its human cargo. After the slaves were unloaded in southern or West Indies ports, the ships carried such products as sugar, tobacco, and molasses to the North.

Africans who came to this hemisphere as slaves were generally people who had been seized by rival tribes, either in warfare or through kidnapping, and then sold to European and American traders, and at least 15 million Africans actually reached the New World during several centuries of slave trade.

The importance of the institution of Negro slavery in generating race theories can hardly be overestimated. The justification for the slave trade became the evidence of an inherent African inferiority, and there is evidence that there was a caste barrier between Whites and Blacks in America even before the institution of slavery legally came into being.[11]

Thus white men, visiting or living in Africa, developed profound contempt for the moral and intellectual content of the black man's culture. In a nutshell, from the very beginning the English looked on the Negro as something less than a normal human being; the early Negro servants never held quite the same status as white indentured servants, and the temptation to take advantage of these black "heathens" led easily into the idea of life-slavery and a full-blown ideology to support it. This attitude developed into a conviction that the Africans had failed to "grow up" and therefore lacked any ability to achieve a mastery over their environment—characterized interestingly, when described by the white man, as "civilization."

This paternalistic view of Africans as being retarded and reckless children was strengthened by the reports of explorers and missionaries. One colonizer, according to a Belgian center of the

Union Minière copper-mining concern in Katanga, proclaimed that we "must never lose sight of the fact that the Negroes have the spirit of children." Add to this a Portuguese authority on Angola who contended that the "raw native" must be looked upon as "an adult with a child's mentality."[12]

HISTORICAL MISCONCEPTIONS

If, until very recently, Africa was included as a topic in American and British textbooks in "Western" or "World Civilization," or in the growing number of works on international relations and geopolitics, the academic backbone of their approach was almost always the assumption that Africa was quite a problem for the white race—referring, of course, to "Western Civilization" and thus justifying directly or by implication the economic and political exploration of the African continent and its people.

Another factor involved in this deficient historical scholarship was the fact that, until the past few hectic years, Europeans and Americans thought and wrote about Africa—to the extent that they thought about it at all—within a frame of reference which was remarkably simple. It simply described what the white man was doing, or trying to do, there—as a big game hunter, as a missionary, as an explorer, as a mining engineer, or as a colonial administrator who was "developing Africa" or "opening it up." For them Africa was something large, dark and supine, and the African peoples were an amorphous and primitive mass. They were people for whom there would be a future, thanks to the efforts of the white man, but so far as the Europeans and Americans knew, they had no past. As Lord Milverton, a former governor of Nigeria, wrote in 1952: "For countless centuries, while all the pageant of history swept by, the African remained unmoved—in primitive savagery."[13]

A few years ago, Sir Philip Mitchell, former governor of Kenya, in an essay entitled "Africa and the West in Historical Perspective," described what seemed to him to be some of the main characteristics of Africa at the beginning of the Colonial era. He wrote:

The West found itself in control of millions of people who had never invented or adopted an alphabet, or even any form

6

of hieroglyphic writing. They had no numerals, no almanac or calendar, no notation of time or measurements of length, capacity, or weight, no currency, no external trade except slaves and ivory, no plough, no wheel, and no means of transportation except human head porterage on land and dugout canoes on rivers and lakes. These people had built nothing, nothing of any kind, in any material more durable than mud, poles, and thatch. With a few notable exceptions, there were no units of government throughout the area larger than the tribe, and the tribe might amount only to a few thousand people and have half a dozen contending chiefs . . . . Great numbers wore no clothes at all; others wore bark cloth or hides and skins.[14]

This was a classic statement about the dominant view of Africa's cultural heritage, which has produced the image that Africa was the "Dark Continent," a term which symbolically meant not only that there were "Blacks" in Africa, but also that there was lack of information about Africa in the rest of the world. In some respects, this term is still good, for today much of Africa can still be termed "dark"; for, though transportation and communication have improved, ignorance about it is widespread both in and about Africa. Furthermore, the premise involved in this approach has been that the traditional role of Europeans in Africa has been one of civilizers and teachers, a necessary function, a kind of cultural rescue of which, by extension, more and more has been needed—until such time as African culture could absorb Western cultural patterns and remake itself in their image.

The core of this lopsided reasoning has been, however, one fact: that the African has been making his own history, in his own ways and for a very long time. The drama in its earliest phase is unknown to Europe and America because no Europeans or Americans were there to witness it; but it was nevertheless being played; the cast was immense and the action vivid.

This attitude toward everything African and toward the black man has had, naturally, its effect on the mentality of the American Negro. Chick evaluates this brand of ideology:

In brief, American Negroes have been taught over a long

7

period of time that their ancestors were savages, jet black with thick lips, kinky hair, and teeth like the tusks of elephants that roamed the African swamps. Moreover, they were indoctrinated with the belief that they should forever be grateful that the white man took them from the wilderness of savagery and brought them in contact with his civilization because African civilization had never been very far above that of wild animals that roamed the African jungles. Such teachings as the foregoing stripped American Negroes of their cultural heritage. And thus, they grew up believing that black was bad, dirty, poor, and wrong; that Negroes everywhere were treacherous, cruel, impudent, intemperate, with a penchant for stealing, lying, debauchery, and profanity.[15]

HISTORICAL NOSTALGIA

Historically, the Negro has been excluded from the mainstream of American cultural life because of his African ancestry; at the same time, he has been denied the chance to perpetuate an African culture and homeland. By an acquiescence forced upon him, the transplanted Negro in continental America lost his spiritual and meaningful orientation to Africa (the meaning of old gods and languages, myths and legends); whatever meaningful residues of African cultures did to survive, the remnants lived in remote patterns and problems of anthropology and sociology, but did not survive as vital cogent forces in the stream of consciousness of Negro history.[16]

Later, when some Negroes turned their faces toward Africa—for example, in pre-Civil War attempts to colonize Liberia, or in verse, art, and music, or in an intellectual protest against caste, or in the ill-fated Marcus Garvey movement, or in sympathy for Africans living under the yoke of European imperialism—they did so as Americans. "They acted as men who lived in the shadow or light of historical, political, or social forces, but not as true representatives of transplanted Africans seeking to return to a homeland. The student of history looks in vain for serious manifestations and expressions of any kind of African Zionism or Pan-Africanism in the history of the American Negro."[17]

Yet in several important respects, the American Negro, for a long period of years after he had been snatched from Africa and brought as the slave to the United States, retained deep sentiments and feelings for his ancestral continent. This was most clearly shown by the many "Back-to-Africa" movements known to the slavery years and for several decades following that period; and several Negro leaders found responsiveness, to a degree, when promoting them. For instance, in 1815, Paul Cuffe of Massachusetts, the son of an Indian mother and a Negro father, who had sailed his own ships to England, Europe, the West Indies, South America and Africa, took thirty-eight free Negroes to Africa.

Organizers of the American Colonization Society, formed in 1816, sought Cuffe's advice for guidance in its plans to send larger numbers of Negroes to Africa. But Cuffe, shortly before his death in 1817, concluded that migration by Negroes from the United States would be interpreted as an admission of their inability to survive there. At any rate, in 1821, the Society founded the colony of Liberia, although most Negro leaders (and many white abolitionists) opposed colonization because they suspected the aims of the colonizationists. In fact, not more than 25,000 Negroes sought refuge in other countries until Marcus Garvey launched a new "Back-to-Africa Movement" after World War I.

The American Negro's nostalgic appreciation of his African background has been even more definitely symbolized by including the word "African" in many Negro organizations; such names as the "African Methodist Episcopal Church," "The African Episcopal Zion Church," "The African Orthodox Church," "The African Union First Colored Methodist Protestant Church, Inc.," "The Richmond African Baptist Missionary," "The African Benevolent Society" of Boston, and others, indicate this tendency to pay some allegiance to the African roots of the American Negro. The same can be said when the slaves sang spirituals; they were probably thinking as much about their African homeland as they were about their heavenly home, and "Going Home," for example, probably had as much reference to going back to Africa as it did going to heaven.

9

Nevertheless, with the abolition of slavery and with the growing insistence of the Black American on improving his lot within the American's framework as the native sons of this country until about the end of World War II, the American Negro's attitude toward Africa's Negro was, in general, one of indifference, and even sometimes of shame.

Several factors were involved. Many American Negroes, when contrasting themselves to the general image of the Africans, considered themselves quite superior to anything African and as being fully "Americanized" and "Westernized," in spite of the fact that during this period some of the sponsors of the ideology of Dr. W. E. B. Du Bois tried to define their identification as Negroes within the framework of Afro-Americans (just as the various immigrant groups talked about themselves as "Irish-Americans," "Slovak-Americans," and the like). Yet, in spite of the propaganda myths regarding Africa and its people, many American Negroes began to develop a more healthy and favorable attitude towards their ancestral land early in the twentieth century, and especially since World War II.

FORCED RE-EVALUATION

Several elements played definite roles in the changing attitude of the American Negro toward Africa's problems. Probably the most important factor has been the rapid change in the course of the history of Africa.

As one by one of the former colonies have been becoming independent African states, the pendulum of the "inferiority-superiority" complexes has swung to the opposite extremes. Most of the new African nations, eager now to feature their history, have been insistent and enthusiastic in their historic claims (rather than in their choice of accurate historical sources). Thus, when the colony called the Gold Coast had been located to the northwest, far outside the borders of the Gold Coast, its spokesmen also claimed for Africans the invention of architecture, chemistry, the alphabet, and other "modest" achievements.

At any rate, already by 1960 the African Negro race (or races) and its spokesmen had presented themselves as the spokes-

10

men for something which the world had never seen—a major Negro civilization. The trend of historic events has also favored the revived claims to self-assurance of the Negro in Africa. All over Africa, the Negro's homeland, small republics have been springing from the ruins of the old imperialism; the old imperialists themselves, in fact, have been rushing in with technical and financial assistance, partly from smitten conscience, and partly from the self-interest of profits and peace. This has also been a factor related to opportunism within the Cold War. Such is the fear of nuclear holocaust in Europe and the world over, that for the most part, political movements and decisions have ceased to be based primarily upon domestic matters; they have become largely the result of a foreign policy aiming to preserve peace at all costs. In the United States this has also been deemed extraordinarily important: to be supersensitive to foreign opinion. Since the consensus of the United Nations, on the whole, has been pro-African, the American government has swung its policies more markedly in a pro-African (not to speak about the influence of the Negro vote) direction. Added to this has been the guilt-complex of the American conscience. The United States has never been quite able to square its human idealism with its practice of racial segregation. These and other related stimuli have helped to influence the mentality of the American Negro after the much longer, less willing, and more dismal period of separation from his ancestral sources and traditions. Today, when reading a counterpart of his own struggle for equality into Africa's struggle for self-government, he can hardly but draw satisfaction from the sight of African statesmen, capped and robed, being received as equals by the American president and by the reigning sovereigns of the powerful states.

Another important factor in changing the former unfavorable attitude of the American Negro toward the Africans has been personal contacts and acquaintances made during World War II by American Negro soldiers stationed in Africa, and the recent visits by American scholars of African institutions. Similarly, many African Negroes have been influenced by having studied in American institutions of higher learning. Furthermore, this process has been helped by the United States' program of assisting underdeveloped countries to create more chances for American Negroes and Africans to meet on compatible grounds.

In very recent years there has been a revival of the controversy over the "correct" name for Americans of Black African descent and it features an effort to repudiate the term "Negro." Opponents of "Negro" demand its replacement by "Black," or by such hyphenated variants as "Afro-American" or "African-American." In other years, the term "Colored" found much favor.[18]

The contemporary reformers are not satisfied to argue in a context of personal preference or stylistic variety, modes which have largely prevailed heretofore; they insist that the psyche of the race is profoundly implicated, that "Negro" is a white man's term of opprobrium, and that those who continue to use it are guilty of betrayal or, at least, of failure to identify with the masses of black people. This was the burden of a young high school sophomore's letter to the late W. E. B. Du Bois, answered by Du Bois in *Crisis* magazine for March, 1928. Du Bois, who had published *Souls of Black Folk* (1903) and would publish *Black Reconstruction* (1935), said: "'Negro' is a fine word. Etymologically and phonetically it is much better and more logical than 'African' or 'colored' or any of the various hyphenated circumlocutions. Of course, it is not historically accurate . . . [but] 'Negro' is quite as accurate, quite as old and quite as definite as the names of any great group of people."

In fact, according to Morsell, there is simply "no other word we can use if we wish to speak solely and exclusively of persons of black African descent. Black Africans, New Guineans, aboriginal Australians, East Indians (especially the *harijans*) and a host of diverse racial and ethnic strains are all properly called 'blacks,' and 'black' therefore fails the tests of exclusivity and specificity."

"African-American" and "Afro-American" are equally deficient, since Ian Smith of Rhodesia is an African, as are President Nasser, the King of Morocco, and any of the thousands of whites who hold citizenship in Nigeria, Ghana, Kenya, and other black African states. Should any of these, or their descendants, become United States citizens, they too would be "African-Americans."

12

Only "Negro" possesses, by reason of years of wide and continued usage, a clear, specific and exclusive denotation: a person of black African origin or descent. Proponents of other names may object that it is a white man's word; but so is "black" and so is "African-American." All these are white man's words, by virtue of their being English. Moreover, it should be recalled that "Blacks" was the white man's first designation for black Africans; historical circumstance brought into common English use the Spanish word for black, which is "Negro."

But some of the more extreme advocates of the concept of "Black" propound that it is to be more than just an ethnic term. To them it is an elite designation, reserved for only those whom the extremists deem worthy, without regard to skin color or anything else. But this might eventually divide, irrevocably, the Negro population. There could be no more ironic outcome of the generations of struggle against color prejudice than to find Negroes themselves split into rival camps on the basis of skin color.

THE GROWING ACADEMIC SUPPORT

Africa splashed into the consciousness of the rest of the world in July, 1960, with the eruption of the newly independent Congo —all but forgotten since the days of the slave trade. But it was "a profoundly ignorant Western world that Africa was plunged into in 1960. Some colonial governments had mountains of data —almost all of it the wrong kind to cope with the new situation. The professional association in America, the African Studies Association, had far fewer than three hundred fellows in that year and was nevertheless hailed as the largest national organization of its sort. The International African Institute was thirty years old—and it was almost the sole bastion of information and of facts abut Africa; but it was run by a director, a librarian, an executive secretary, and a small editorial and office staff."[19]

Since 1960, all this has changed drastically. The dramatic rise on the world scene of African peoples seeking self-government and independence has been accompanied by a change in the tradition that Africa is without a history. The former neglect, disregard and omission of the African people from history's accounts "contributed to the building of this tradition and to the

13

dilemma created by differences in culture and color. Such people, it was believed, could not have had a history until their continent had been penetrated by Europeans."[20]

These views of Africa were readily propagated, as we have already pointed out, by writers in the years of the slave trade and also under imperialism and colonialism. (Thus the 11th Edition of the *Encyclopedia Britannica* has it: "Africa, with the exception of the lower Nile Valley and what is known as Roman Africa, is, so far as its native inhabitants are concerned, a continent practically without a history and possessing no records from which such a history might be constructed . . . The Negro is essentially the child of the moment; and his memory, both tribal and individual, is very short." And again: "If Ancient Egypt and Ethiopia be excluded, the story of Africa is largely a record of the doing of its Asiatic and European conquerors and colonizers."[21] In fact, even such an eminent historian as Arnold Toynbee writes: "The Black races alone have not contributed positively to any civilization as yet."[22] Tribal and group histories of Africans were not regarded as important by historians, and the history of European expansion in Africa was written as African history; it was, of course, assumed that there was no history of any value among black men prior to the arrival of the white men.

There has been, fortunately, a notable change in information about and attitudes toward Africa in recent years on the part of the general American public. Although the available information is scattered and disorganized, the more recent approach to Africa's history, using the findings of archaeology and social anthropology, has reconstructed a realistic picture of Africa's history, tribal life and cultures. Today's academic research has been stressing, more and more insistently, that the old Africa was seldom, if ever, like the fictional accounts and impressions. Historically, we know that the vast majority of Africa's populations have walked the wending stones of time and social change, lifting themselves from the primitive to the less primitive, in much the same way as everyone else in the world. The scenery and the methods have been different, but not the general course and destination. One by one, our old myths, preconceptions and fairy tales about Africa have been going to pieces.[23]

But not only anthropology, archaeology, and sociology have been playing a role in presenting a more realistic picture of Africa. Historical scholarship has now also taken a definite turn toward being more realistic. The Europe-oriented viewpoint no longer satisfies the contemporary world, and it is essential to study the history of the great cultures not only of the ancient, classical East, but also of India, Indonesia, China, Japan and, above all, Africa. Historical horizons have been broadening, showing that the histories of all the peoples are actually interconnected. Today it is impossible to view the history of Africa as an object of colonial expansion and reduce it to a history of colonial crusades and conquests by imperialistic countries. The Africans had a history before the times of colonial enslavement; now this history must be studied also.

Conversely, "efforts to place the Negroes' role in American history in proper perspective are beginning to bear fruit," according to Negro leaders attending the Sixtieth Annual Convention of the American Teachers Association in Dallas, Texas, in July, 1963. J. Rupert Piccot, Vice President of the Association for the Study of Negro Life and History, reported that "a number of large publishing companies were now 'almost frantically' searching for means to bring their textbooks up to the 'public acceptance level' in dealing with minority groups." And "a better understanding of the Negro heritage has had a profound effect on the Negro himself . . ."

THE BLACK AMERICAN RENAISSANCE

The growing self-awareness of Black Americans—especially among the young—is an unfolding event more dramatic in its own way than man's venture into space. It parallels the development of Black nationhood on the African continent. Spanning centuries and oceans to find a lost past has become one of the prime goals of young Black Americans; African artifacts are treasured, Black history is studied, and African cloths and hair styles are being adopted. Universities and colleges are moving today toward the establishment of special courses in Afro-American studies and toward the granting of degrees in this field, on a par with all other academic disciplines.

Such moves belong to one area of the problems facing most

15

American campuses: how to translate into policy what is legitimate among Black students' demands. Hopeful steps have been taken at three Ivy League schools—Yale, Harvard and Cornell—to offer degree programs in Afro-American studies, as one solution. This is only reasonable. After all, as the Harvard faculty committee on the subject points out: "We are dealing with 25 million of our own people with a special history, culture, and range of problems."[24] And if universities can offer degrees with majors in the culture of classical Greek, Roman, and other defunct civilizations, as well as in Latin-American, Asian and other contemporary regional affairs, why not the same treatment for Africa?

Such a program will have to prove itself, of course. There are few scholars with much of a grasp of the Black's place in America, and no pattern for what should be in such a course of studies. This situation itself comments on America's tardiness in seriously studying the impact of racial thinking.

SELECTED BIBLIOGRAPHY

The best single source of general bibliography on Africa is the published version of the catalogue of Northwestern University's collection of African books. The International Africa Institute of London has issued several volumes of bibliographies, by areas and tribes; some by country; and a few topics (such as maps and labor). *African Affairs for the General Reader: A Selected and Introductory Bibliographical Guide*, 1960-1967, New York, Council of the African-American Institute, (866 United Nations Plaza, New York, N.Y., 10017), 1967, compiled by the African Bibliographic Center, offers a wide range of materials for study and general reading about Africa. The list is an unusually comprehensive one, and includes a vast number of American as well as foreign periodicals, pamphlets, books, etc. The Foreign Policy Association, *Intercom: Handbook on Africa*, New York (345 E. 45 St., New York), Vol. VIII, #3, 1968, contains official sources of information, selected films, a bibliography, and much more on Africa. *A Bibliography of the Negro in Africa and America,*

New York: Ocean Books, 1965, a comprehensive though very expensive guide in the field it covers. Henry L. Roberts, Ed., *Foreign Affairs Bibliography*, New York: R. R. Bowker Co., 1964, "A Selected and Annotated List on International Relations, 1952-1962." *The Negro Year Book*, for 1952, ed. by Jessie Parkhurst Guzman of Tuskegee Institute, offers fairly detailed but scattered biographical information concerning Negroes in such fields as the sciences, athletics and the arts. *The New Africa*, CES (1733 K St., N.W., Washington, D.C., 10006), 1968, a colorful, fact-filled student notebook chart, provides a wealth of historic and geographic information on the world's second largest continent. African Bibliographic Center, *Black History Viewpoint*, Washington, D.C. (P.O. Box 13096), 1969, a new, annotated bibliographical guide, arranged by subject and geographical categories, ranging from print to audio visual aids on black history in the U.S. and Africa. *African Encounter: A Selected Bibliography of Books, Films, and other Materials for Promoting an Understanding of Africa Among Young Adults*, Chicago: American Library Association, (50 E. Huron St., Chicago, Ill. 60611), a handbook for teachers, librarians, and other planning programs to promote an understanding of Africa. Rayford W. Logan and Irving S. Cohen, *The American Negro: Old World Background and New World Experience*, Boston: Houghton Mifflin, 1967, a handy, short text for a course in Negro history, from the background of Negroes in Africa to today's struggle for equality. *Africana*, Catalogue No. 1, "New Books Published January 1967-October 1968," New York (101 Fifth Ave., New York 10003), International University Booksellers, is quite extensive, but, unfortunately, it does not list publishers; the same applies to *Africana Catalogue* No. 2, 1968.

The ever-rising flood of various studies pertaining to our subject can be followed, as reported or evaluated, by such periodicals as: *African Forum* (published by the American Society of African Culture); *Africa Report* (African American Institute); *Africa Today* (American Committee on Africa); *The Journal of Modern African Studies* (Cambridge University Press); *The Journal of African History* (Cambridge University Press); *Africa* (International African Institute); *West Africa* (London); *Drum* (published for and by Bantu South Africans); *Ebony* (monthly, (Howard University, Washington, D.C.); *The Negro Education* (Howard University, Washington, D.C.); *The Negro Educational Review* (Nashville, Tenn.); *Phylon* (Atlanta University, Georgia); *Journal of Negro History* (Association for the Study of Negro Life and History, Washington, D.C.); *Journal of Human Relations* (Central State University, Wilberforce, Ohio); *Africa Quarterly* (The Indian Council for Africa, New Delhi); etc.

In addition to the material cited in the footnotes, and in the subsequent section, see the references pertaining to the chapter on "The Milestones in the History of Education of the Negro in the United States" by Joseph S. Roucek.

SELECTED BOOKS

Broom, Leonard, and Glenn, Norval, *Transformation of the Negro American*, New York: Harper & Row, 1965. Examines the changing of Negroes as a cultural bloc and their relationships with the white majority; see pp. 34, 140, 182-3, for the impact of Africa on the American black man.

Curtin, P.D., *The Image of America*, Madison, Wis.: University of Wisconsin, 1964. Quite erudite, contains material not found elsewhere.

Delafosse, Maurice, *Negroes of Africa*, Washington, D.C.: Associated Publishers, 1931. A substantial survey.

Fagg, William, *African Tribal Images*, Cleveland: Cleveland Museum of Art, 1968. Relatively few art musea recognize African tribal art as an integral part of their comprehensive collections; few art departments of major universities devote any space in their catalogue to list courses or seminars in "primitive" art; some anthropologists still cling to tribal works of art as documents and mere illustrations of the latest assumed configurations of pre-literate cultures.

Herskovits, Melville J., *The Myth of the Negro Past*, New York: Harper, 1951. By a brilliant student of Franz Boas.

Murdock, G.P., *Africa, Its People and Their Culture History*, New York: McGraw-Hill, 1959. A successful attempt to synthesize the available knowledge.

New York City, Board of Education, *The Negro in American History*, New York, 1964. See Chapter 2, "The African Heritage," pp. 11-20. An attempt to promote a better understanding of America's past by developing increased awareness of the history of American Negroes.

Reid, Ira de A., "The American Negro," in: Gitler, J. B. Ed., *Understanding Minority Groups*, New York: John Wiley, 1956. By a well-known Negro sociologist.

Wingert, Paul, *The Sculpture of Negro Africa*, New York: Columbia University Press, 1950. A systematic treatment.

ARTICLES AND PAMPHLETS

Bazziel, W. F., "Correlates of Southern Negro Personality," *Journal of Social Issues*, Vol. XX, April, 1964, pp. 46-53. A valuable study in social psychology.

Chick, C. A., Sr., "The American Negroes' Changing Attitude Toward Africa," *The Journal of Negro Education*, Vol. XXXI, Fall, 1962, pp. 531-535. A valuable analysis; fully documented.

Davidson, Basil, "Africa: The Race Behind the Mask," *Horizon*. Vol. V, March, 1963, pp. 38-59. Quite a readable factual account.

Doddy, H. H., "The Progress of the Negro in Higher Education," *Journal of Negro Education*, XXXII, Fall, 1963, 485-492. Although outdated, still useful.

Green, Gordon C., "Negro Dialect, The Last Barrier to Integration," *Journal of Negro Education*, Vol. XXXII, Winter, 1963, pp. 81-83. A treatment of a rather neglected topic, although a Negro dialect is not "the last barrier to integration."

Harrison, C. H., "Black History and the Schools," *Ebony*, XXIV, 2, December, 1968. No longer accepting historians' efforts to blot out Black History, today black students are demanding the teaching of their past.

Meier, August, "The Emergence of Negro Nationalism: A Study in Ideologies," *Midwest Journal*, IV, Part I, (Winter, 1951-52), 96-104; Part II, Summer, 1952, pp. 95-111. Extremely valuable.

Poinsett, Alex, "Inawapsa Watu Weusi Kusema Kiswahili?" *Ebony*, "Should Black Men Speak Swahili?" is the question confronting Afro-Americans.

Roberts, Launey F., Jr., "Minorities' Self-Identification Through Tests: A Study of Publication Progress," *Journal of Hu-*

19

man Relations, XVI, 3, Third Quarter 1968, 356-367. A study of a distinct degree of change in the editorial, artistic, and over-all publishing views and practices regarding the use of multiracial pictures in elementary school textbooks.

Walden, Daniel, Ed., "The Problem of Color in the Twentieth Century. A Memorial to W.E.B. Du Bois," *Journal of Human Relations,* XIV, First Quarter, 1966. Quite a valuable collection of articles.

NOTES

1. Joseph S. Roucek, "Africa in Geopolitics," Chapter 20, pp. 314-344, in D. P. Rastogi, Ed., *Political Essays,* Meerut (India): Review Publications, 1967; reprinted from: *International Review of History and Political Science,* Vol. IV, 2, December, 1967, pp. 76-96.

2. C. A. Chick, St., "The American Negroes' Changing Attitude Toward Africa," *The Journal of Negro Education,* Vol. XXXI, Fall, 1962, pp. 531-535.

3. Eric A. Walker, *History of South Africa,* London: Longmans, Green, 1960, p. 149.

4. Paul Bohannan, *Africa and Africans,* Garden City, N.Y.: the Natural History Press, 1964, pp. 1-2, 3-4, 22-23, 116, 235.

5. Quoted by T. P. Melady, *The White Man's Future in Black Africa,* New York: McFadden, 1962, p. 48.

6. *Ibid.*

7. A. J. Hanna, *European Rule in Africa,* London: Historical Association, Pamphlet in General Series, Number 46, 1965.

8. Thomas F. Gossett, *Race: The History of An Idea in America,* Dallas, Texas: Southern Methodist University Press, 1965, pp. 28ff.

9. Zoe Marsh and G. W. Kingsnorth, *An Introduction to the History of East Africa,* New York: Cambridge University Press, 1957.

10. Clark D. Moore and Ann Dubar, Eds., *Africa: Yesterday and Today,* New York: Bantam, 1968, p. 107.

11. Gossett, *op. cit.,* p. 30.

12. Quoted by Basil Davidson, "Africa: The Face Behind the Mask," *Horizon,* Vol. V, March, 1963, pp. 38-59.

13. Robert Coughlan and The Editors of *Life, Tropical Africa,* New York: World Library, Time Incorporated, 1963, p. 63, and bibliography, pp. 168-170.

14. *Ibid.,* p. 109.

15. Chick, *op. cit.,* pp. 531-535.

16. Compare with the view by some writers, such as Melvill J. Herskovits, *The Myth of the Negro Past,* New York: Harper, 1961, p. 292; and Miles Mark Fisher, *Negro Slave Songs in the United States,* Ithaca: Cornell University Press, 1953, pp. 43-61.

17. W. A. Low, "The Education of Negroes Viewed Historically," in Virgil A. Clift, Archibald W. Anderson, and H. Gordon Hullfish, Eds., *Negro Education in America: Its Adequacy, Problems, and Needs,* New York: Harper, 1962, p. 28.

18. John A. Morsell, "Topics: Negro, Black or Afro-American?" *New York Times,* July 20, 1968.

19. Bohannan, *op cit.,* p. 2.

20. Charles H. Wesley, "The Changing African Historical Tradition," in Anne O'H. Williamson, Ed., "Down in the Dark Continent: Politics, Problems, and Promises," *Journal of Human Relations,* Vol. VIII, Spring and Summer, 1960, pp. 3-4, 323; see also the bibliographical references, pp. 352-354.

21. *Encyclopedia Britannica,* 11TH EDITION, Vol. I. pp. 325, 331, quoted by Wesley, *op. cit.,* p. 324.

22. Arnold Toynbee, *The Study of History,* p. 54, quoted by Wesley *op cit.,* p. 325.

23. Peter Duignan, *Handbook of American Resources for African Studies,* Stanford, California: Hoover Institution on War, 1967.

24. "Excerpts From Harvard Report on American Negro Studies Program," *New York Times,* January 22, 1968.

JOSEPH S. ROUCEK, Ph. D., is Professor of Social Science at Queensborough Community College of the City University of New York. He received his B.A. from Occidental College, M.A. and Ph. D. from New York University. He was Chairman, Departments of Sociology and Political Science, University of Bridgeport (1948-1967) and has been Visiting Professor in many American, Canadian, Puerto Rican and European universities. Is the author, co-author, and editor of many publications, several translated into Japanese and Portuguese and other languages, among the latest being *The Slavonic Encyclopedia; Behind the Iron Curtain; The Teaching of History,* etc. In recognition of his academic contributions, the royal governments of Rumania and Yugoslavia honored him with the Knighthood of the Star of Rumania and the Knighthood of the Crown of Yugoslavia. In 1955, he lectured at the High School of Diplomacy in Madrid, at universities in Spain, Italy, Yugoslavia, Austria, Germany, Holland and France, and at various U.S. Information Centers in these countries.

DISCOVERING BLACK AMERICAN HISTORY*

JOHN HOPE FRANKLIN

University of Chicago (Chicago, Illinois)

In recent years virtually every organization working for the advancement of Negro Americans, whether militant, moderate or in between, has demanded a more adequate treatment of Negro Americans in books and courses dealing with the history of the United States. Some have emphasized the need for multi-ethnic, racially integrated books and courses, while some have stressed the importance of separate treatments of black history as part of the process of race pride and group identification. Meanwhile, scores of the major newspapers and magazines have devoted many columns to the matter, either discussing the social significance of the demands or recounting some of the more spectacular incidents encountered in "discovering" the history of Negroes in the United States.

This whole phenomenon is as much a part of the Negro revolt as the demand for equality in other areas. It is as though Negro Americans were saying that the past injustices done them in recounting the history of the country are part and parcel of the injustices they have suffered in other areas. If the house is to be set in order, one cannot begin with the present; he must begin with the past.

It is a past that abounds in distortions and misrepresentations, ranging from assumptions of the innate inferiority of persons of African descent to arguments that such persons had no part in the development of the country or even in securing their own freedom. If the past will not die, then the truth about it must be known. And if there is some ambivalence about the best way of doing this—whether through a quite separate account of the history of Negro Americans or by treating the role of Negro Americans in the context of the nation's history—it may well arise from the fact that this type of historical revisionism bears the twin burdens of recovering lost hope and providing a sense of balance.

Many recent writings on the subject communicate an exhilarating sense of discovery that is as refreshing as it is misleading. They possess a quality not unlike that conveyed by Ripley's "Believe It or Not." It is wonderful to discover that 5,000 Negroes fought in the War for Independence, but it is well to recall that the first scholarly book on the subject was published more than a century ago. Within 15 years after the close of the Civil War reputable publishers brought out several thoroughly documented histories of the role of Negroes in the Civil War; but today a surefire way of shocking a reader is to write, "Did you know that 186,000 Negro Americans fought in the Civil War on the side of the Union?" Such "revelations" suggest that we know as little about the history of Negro history as we know about the history of Negroes themselves. If it is important to discover what Negroes have done during their three and one-half centuries in the New World, it is also important to discover what they have done about their history.

In 1841 a 32-year-old fugitive slave, James W. C. Pennington, examined for the first time the history of Africans in the New World, when he published his *Text Book of the Origin and History of the Colored People* (out of print).* In each decade thereafter worthy successors to the slender Pennington volume appeared. Before the Civil War, historical works by William C. Nell (*Services of Colored Americans in the Wars of 1776 and 1812,* o.p.) and Martin R. Delany (*The Condition, Elevation, Emigration and Destiny of the Colored People of the United States,* o.p.) added much to America's knowledge of Americans from Africa. After the war William Wells Brown, Joseph T. Wilson, and George Washington Williams wrote impressive volumes on the participation of Negro Americans, slave and free,

---

* [At the time this paper was written the books indicated as out of print were unavailable. Many works on Negro history are being brought back into print however.]

in the Civil War. The most important historical work of the postwar years was the *History of the Negro Race in America from 1619 to 1880* (o.p.) by George Washington Williams. A treatise of almost a thousand pages and covering virtually every aspect of the New World experience, it was published in both one volume and two volumes by G. P. Putnam's Sons and was widely reviewed in the United States and Europe.

Around the turn of the century, white America was reading Thomas Dixon's *The Clansman* (o.p.), Charles Carroll's *The Negro a Beast* (o.p.), and articles in the leading magazines that gave respectability to the racist doctrines of Dixon and Carroll. No one, except Negroes themselves, defended the claims that they also were Americans, even human beings, who had helped make this country strong and great. In his *Suppression of the African Slave-Trade*, W.E.B. DuBois not only described the barbarism of the trade in men but showed how it persisted for a half-century after it was outlawed by Federal statute. In 1902 he wrote *Souls of Black Folk* which showed, among other things, how the slaves' sorrow songs had greatly enriched the culture of the United States. In the same year W. H. Crogman of Atlanta temporarily dropped his research and writings in the classics to write *Progress of a Race, or The Remarkable Advancement of the American Negro* (o.p.). In 1903 G. F. Richings wrote *Evidence of Progress Among Colored People* (o.p.), which was typical of a veritable spate of books that refuted the arguments of those who said that Negro Americans had no history worthy of attention.

When Harvard-trained Carter G. Woodson organized the Association for the Study of Negro Life and History in 1915, he began what may be termed the modern Negro history movement. The following year Woodson began to edit the Journal of Negro History, now one of America's oldest learned journals in the historical field. Then followed Negro History Week, the Negro History Bulletin, for younger people, and a large number of important monographs written by Woodson and other scholars. Among them were *A Century of Negro Migration* (o.p.), *Free Negro Heads of Families in 1830*, *The Miseducation of the Negro* (o.p.), *The Education of the Negro Prior to 1860*, and *African Background Outlined* (o.p.), all by Woodson; three studies of Negroes in the Reconstruction era in Virginia, South

Carolina, and Tennessee by A. A. Taylor; and a truly significant work, *The Education of the Negro in Alabama: A Study in Cotton and Steel* (o.p.), by Horace Mann Bond. Soon, Charles H. Wesley, Luther J. Jackson Sr., Lorenzo Greene, and Rayford W. Logan, working in labor, political, and social history, added important volumes to the list, while W. E. B. DuBois continued to make his contributions by writing *Black Reconstruction in America* and *Black Folk, Then and Now* (o.p.).

By the middle of the 20th century, there was a large body of historical writing touching on most aspects of the experience of Negro Americans. Gradually it attained a position of respectability, in part because of the impeccable scholarship of many of those who were writing in the field. (Every person mentioned in the preceding paragraph held doctorates from Harvard, Columbia, or Chicago.) In part it was because many of the postwar white historians who dealt with the history of Negro Americans refrained from apologizing for slavery, rejected the ideal of the innate inferiority of persons of African descent, and recognized the injustices that had been done to Negro Americans and to their history. Vernon Wharton's *The Negro in Mississippi, 1865-1890*, Kenneth M. Stampp's *The Peculiar Institution*, Leon P. Litwack's *North of Slavery*, and August Meier's *Negro Thought in America, 1880-1915*, are cases in point. Surely it was also because the effort to determine certain public policies and to settle highly controversial constitutional problems called for a reexamination of the history of Negro Americans. (This examination was made with great care by lawyers and their allies as well as the justices themselves before the Supreme Court spoke out against restrictive covenants in Shelley *v.* Kraemer and segregated public education in Brown *v.* The Board of Education.)

In the past few years there has been a marked increase in the number of works on the history of Negro Americans. At the end of World War II Carter G. Woodson's *The Negro in Our History* was the only satisfactory general history of Negro Americans. Since that time at least ten general histories have been published. They range in scope from the slender paperback by Rayford W. Logan, *The Negro in The United States* and the brief survey by Benjamin Quarles, *The Negro in the Making of America*, to the more extensive treatment in *Before the Mayflower* by Lerone Bennett Jr. and *The People That Walk in*

Darkness (o.p.) by the distinguished Dutch historian, J. W. Schulte Nordhold.

In approach they differ widely, as can be seen in the version by the well-known Communist, William Z. Foster, and the interpretive account by August Meier and Elliott M. Rudwick. The quality is inevitably uneven. Some authors are well-trained historians, and their works show it; others are special pleaders, who labor hard at making their case; still others seek to fill the void created by centuries of neglect, and their good intentions are more praiseworthy than the results.

When Herbert Aptheker's *Documentary History of the Negro People in the United States* appeared in 1951 it was as pioneering as it was unique, for no one had hitherto undertaken to let Negroes tell their own story by the exclusive use of their own words and deeds. The history of Negro Americans, however, is more than what they have said and done; it is also what whites have said about them as well as what they have done to them. Despite objections by some whites that the recent emphasis on the history of Negro Americans is becoming excessive, the fact remains that the preoccupation of white Americans with defining the status and future of Negro Americans has been extensive. This has been true, whether it was the question of how to keep them out of the Continental Army during the War for Independence or how to disfranchise them during the post-Reconstruction years.

Leslie Fishel and Benjamin Quarles recognized this in their *The Negro American: A Documentary History*, published in 1967, which contains the speech in 1890 of Governor Benjamin R. Tillman of South Carolina against Negro suffrage as well as the memorable statement in 1897 by W. E. B. DuBois on racial pride. This is essentially the view advanced by William L. Katz, who published in that same documentary history his "Eyewitness: The Negro in American History." Meanwhile, documentary histories have themselves become rather specialized. Gilbert Osofsky's *The Burden of Race* deals with the knotty problem of Negro-white relations since the 17th century, while James McPherson examines the full range of the problem of how Negroes felt and acted during the war for the Union in *The Negro's Civil War*.

It is in the field of monographs and special studies that one

27

finds the most significant recent contributions to the history of Negro Americans. In the colonial period there are few peers of Frank J. Klingberg's *An Appraisal of the Negro in Colonial South Carolina* and Lorenzo J. Greene's *The Negro in Colonial New England. The Negro in the American Revolution* by Benjamin Quarles is already the standard work on that subject. Slavery and abolition have understandably attracted a large number of historians. In addition to those already mentioned some of the leaders, together with their works, are Stanley Elkins, *Slavery: A Problem in American Institutional and Intellectual Life;* David B. Davis, *The Problem of Slavery in Western Culture;* Richard Wade, *Slavery in the Cities;* Eugene Genovese, *The Political Economy of Slavery;* Herbert Aptheker, *American Negro Slave Revolts;* Martin Duberman and others, *The Antislavery Vanguard;* and Arthur Zilversmit, *The First Emancipation: The Abolition of Slavery in the North.*

For the Civil War and the years following, there is an abundance of studies with fresh points of view, based on new research as well as a reexamination of earlier writings. Benjamin Quarles has done for the Civil War period what he did for the Revolution, while Dudley Cornish has devoted much attention to the activities of Negro soldiers in *The Sable Arm: Negro Troops in the Union Army, 1861-1865.* Meanwhile, William H. Leckie has provided us with much information that is entirely new in his *Buffalo Soldiers,* the story of Negroes in the West with the regular army during the generation following the Civil War.

The Reconstruction period has been re-examined even more than the slave period, with special studies of the Freedmen's Bureau by George Bentley, Martin Abbott, and others. There are numerous state studies, moreover, such as those by Willie Lee Rose and Joel Williamson for South Carolina and Joe Richardson for Florida. Outstanding among the general treatments of the Reconstruction that go far toward revising the traditional interpretations that described Negroes as the ignorant dupes of white politicians are Kenneth Stampp's *The Era of Reconstruction* and Rembert Patrick's *Reconstruction and the Nation.*

The post-Reconstruction years were the period when Negro Americans lost much ground not only in the political and economical spheres but in their very stature as citizens and historical figures. This is the period when white historians began systematically to denigrate them as citizens and as human beings. Recent historians have discovered that the study of this period adds much to our understanding of current policies and practices. Rayford W. Logan covered the entire period in his *The Negro in American Life and Thought, The Nadir: 1877-1901* (o.p.) while C. Vann Woodward's *"The Strange Career of Jim Crow"* shows how racial segregation and discrimination became a way of life in the closing years of the 19th century. George Tindall has studied the situation in South Carolina in his *"South Carolina Negroes, 1877-1900* while Helen Edmonds and Frenise Logan have given attention to North Carolina, the former in *Negro and Fusion Politics in North Carolina, 1895-1901,* the latter in *"The Negro in North Carolina, 1876-1894.*

Historians of Negro Americans are as wary of writing about the recent past as are other historians; and because the numerous and rapid changes of this century challenge both perspective and balance, they have good reason to be cautious. Even so, they have not been able to resist the temptation to describe and explain such highly significant developments as migration, urbanization and its many problems, the persistence of discrimination, and the long, bitter struggle for equality.

The Southern region, where the majority of Negro Americans continued to live until mid-century, has remained an important focal point for study. Louis R. Harlan's *Separate and Unequal* is a shocking revelation of racist practices in the educational programs of the Southern seaboard states in the opening years of the century. Arna Bontemps and Jack Conroy have written of the migration of Southern Negroes in a work significantly titled, *Any Place but Here.* The making of black ghettoes in Northern cities has been the subject of *Harlem: The Making of a Ghetto* by Gilbert Osofsky and *Negro Mecca* by Seth Scheiner.

Some historians have turned their attention to institutional history, an outstanding example of which is Charles Flint Kellogg's *NAACP: A History of the National Association for the Advancement of Colored People.* Current centennial celebrations have stimulated the writing of histories of several predominantly Negro colleges and universities, but they are still in various stages of preparation. Riots and other forms of violence are attracting attention. Arthur I. Waskow's *From Race Riot to Sit-in* and Elliott M. Rudwick's *Race Riot at St. Louis, July 2, 1917* are indications that this is an important field of study for the historian.

It is one thing for the interest in the history of Negro Americans to grow at an unprecedented rate; it is quite another for that interest to be translated immediately into an increased flow of significant works on the subject. The works that have been discussed here have been long in the making, and it will be some time before significant new works, stimulated by the new interest, will begin to appear. Meanwhile, the reading public will be provided with materials that will be as varied in quality as they will be in approach. Some will be the result of joint efforts such as the collection of essays in *The Negro American,* edited by Talcott Parsons and Kenneth Clark and *The American Negro Reference Book,* edited by John P. Davis. Others will be in volumes of essays hitherto published in magazines and journals, such as *American Negro Slavery,* edited by Allen Weinstein and Frank O. Gatell, or in source books containing original speeches and writings, such as *Negro Protest Thought in the Twentieth Century,* edited by Francis L. Broderick and August Meier.

There will be reprints of older works, such as those undertaken by Atheneum, Arno, and Beacon. There will be almanacs, handbooks, and encyclopedias. But major new works will eventually emerge. Scores of scholars and indeed laymen are busy at work on biographies, institutional histories and monographs of a wide variety; and publishers are encouraging their efforts by munificent advances and other blandishments. In time, there will be many new and important works to read. Meanwhile, even the avid and discriminating reader will have much to do if he sets out to discover that which is already available.

JOHN HOPE FRANKLIN, Chairman of the Department of History, University of Chicago, was born in Rentiesville, Oklahoma, on January 2, 1915. He attended Fisk University, where he graduated "Magna cum laude" in 1935. He received his M.A. and Ph. D. in American History from Harvard in 1936 and 1941 respectively, and has been the recipient of honorary degrees from numerous institutions, including Lincoln University, Long Island University, and the University of Massachusetts.

Mr. Franklin was an Instructor at Fisk during 1936-37, and

Professor of History at St. Augustine's College from 1939 to 1943, North Carolina College at Durham from 1943 to 1947, and Howard University from 1947 to 1956. He was Chairman of the Department of History at Brooklyn College from 1956 to 1964 and was Pitt Professor of American History at Cambridge University from 1962 to 1963. Mr. Franklin came to The University of Chicago in 1964 as Professor of American History, and on October 1, 1967 was appointed Chairman of the Department of History.

In 1965 Zenith Books appointed him general editor of Doubleday and Company series intended for use in high school English and social studies classes.

A distinguished author of several books and learned articles, Professor Franklin is a world-renowned scholar of the Civil War and Reconstruction Era. One of his books is *Land of the Free*, an American History text for eighth grade students, co-authored by John Caughey and Ernest R. May. The book brings out of obscurity much evidence about American Indians, American Negroes, immigrants, and other minority groups long ignored by the recorders of history.

He has written many articles, and his other books are *The Free Negro in North Carolina, 1790-1860* (1943), *The Civil War Diary of James T. Ayers* (1947), *From Slavery to Freedom; A History of Negro Americans* (1947, 1956, and 1967), *The Militant South* (1956), *A Fool's Errand* (1961), *Reconstruction After the Civil War* (1961), *Army Life in a Black Regiment* (1962), *The Emancipation Proclamation* (1963), and *The Negro in 20th Century America* (with Isadore Starr, 1967.)

NEGRO CONTRIBUTIONS TO THE
EXPLORATION OF THE GLOBE

Ronald W. Davis

Western Michigan University (Kalamazoo, Mich.)

The role of the Negro in exploring the face of the earth may be portrayed to the satisfaction of most in a simple listing of the individuals who participated in the major European expeditions of discovery, and who also happened to be of African origin. Such a listing is not of inconsiderable magnitude.

SOME INDIVIDUALS

When Vasco da Gama brought the first Portuguese ships into the Indian Ocean in 1498, by way of the Cape of Good Hope, he entered upon a trading network of such complexity as to confound his lieutenants and threaten to frustrate Portuguese ambitions of attaining India. Only through the aid of an East African pilot, Ibn Mādjid, did the tiny fleet realize its goal. Ibn Mādjid is of uncertain ethnic derivation, inasmuch as such distinctions did not find their way into local annals with the depressing regularity with which they are documented in contemporary records, but he was a long-term resident of East Africa. He was the author of one of a collection of *rahmani,* or sets of nautical instructions for negotiating the capricious monsoon winds of the Indian Ocean, the key to successful communication between India and East Africa. Without the aid of such a person, da Gama's voyage almost certainly would not have been successful.[1]

The participation of Africans in early Spanish enterprises in the New World was quite extensive—even more so than might have been the case, owing to peculiar circumstances in the Iberian Peninsula. Historians place much emphasis on the severance of Islamic cultural unity across the Strait of Gibraltar upon completion of the *Reconquista,* but the intermingling of peoples and knowledge, brought about by centuries of relatively unhindered communication between Spain and Africa, did not disappear overnight. The expulsion of Jewish elements from Spain, among them many of the outstanding figures in the fields of cartography and nautical technology in the Western world, perhaps would have been less hasty had the Spanish not had Moorish and African savants upon whom they could draw for such skills and information. Many Africans and persons of the Ibero-Moroccan community thus accompanied the early Spanish expeditions. Their imprint on the Americas of the early sixteenth century was sufficient to lead a writer of the twentieth to conclude that the many Arabic and African language idioms recorded in various sources of the time indicated the presence of a pre-Columbian, African civilization in the Western Hemisphere.[2] Such a hypothesis ignores the fact that Old World slaves very often were among the educated elite, and it is quite as reasonable—perhaps more so—to assume that those of African descent on the Spanish expeditions were literate as it would be to assume that a similar portion of the Spanish themselves were literate in their own language. Moors and Negroes, largely owing to their skills and reservoir of learning, could pass freely to the New World, whereas Jews could not.

Pedro Alonso Niño, high in the chain of command on the first Columbus voyage, is reputed by some scholars to have been of African descent. The expeditions of Balboa, Ponce de Leon, Cortes, Pizarro and Coronado included Africans in many capacities, from the most menial to those of guides and physicians. Perhaps the best known Negro in the saga of Spanish exploration was one Estevanico, who commanded a small expedition in 1538 which first set foot in the lands of Arizona and New Mexico. Estevanico came to the Americas on the expedition of Narvaez some ten years earlier, and wandered about what is now the southern United States for many years before receiving the opportunity to add more lands to the Spanish empire. In the process he became one of the most knowledgeable of men concerning the areas of Florida and points west.[3]

Africa itself, of course, would have proven all but impossible for Europeans to "discover" in the late eighteenth and early nineteenth centuries had not Africans seen fit to guide European expeditions through hostile territories. Mention of such persons in travellers' accounts is parenthetical at best, but no European expedition would have dared attempt to penetrate the interior of Africa without a large complement of Africans who could communicate with the people and who knew the country, as well as carry the Europeans' bags. Such travels were not new to Africans in any case. Even Stanley's epic voyage down the Congo had been anticipated centuries earlier by Africans engaged in transcontinental trade.

Nearly every major expedition to Africa from the beginning of the nineteenth century on stopped on the West coast of Africa to add to their entourages members of the Kru peoples of Liberia. The Kru are perhaps more widely travelled as a people than any other ethnic group in the world. Owing to their willingness to act as lighter operators in West Africa where harbors were all but nonexistent, and as deck hands and intermediaries all along the coast, the Kru quickly became indispensable to European commerce and exploration. They accumulated a vast knowledge of conditions in West Africa and, by settling for years in far-flung ports, usually knew several African languages. Kru communities may still be found today in every West African port from Dakar to Douala, and there is even a small Kru community in Liverpool, a product of Kru service on British steamers.

The Kru served in almost every imaginable capacity on expeditions designed to "open up" Africa to European exploitation. The records of all nations trading in West Africa attest to the value of the Kru, who performed many of the tasks on land, such as trading and victualling, which Europeans dared not do themselves because of the unhealthy environment. Even after medical advances made European habitation of West Africa practical, the Kru continued to be regarded as essential to the development of successful enterprises in exploration and development. Their value to Europeans is demonstrated by the fact that members of the Kru people were almost never enslaved, though

35

their homeland lay athwart one of the major avenues of the slave trade.[4]

In the middle of the nineteenth century the Kru, more than one hundred strong, largely staffed the British Niger Expedition which attempted to open up West Africa through a successful demonstration of the Niger River as a highway to the interior.[5] The Kru did not confine themselves to West African activities, however, and David Livingstone saw fit to add Kru members to his own expedition into more southerly parts of the continent.

The Kru commitment to this type of travel abroad soon permeated their own culture, and appointment to traditional offices came to be reckoned on the basis of the achievements of aspirants on foreign fronts. Those who had been the farthest and away the longest often found themselves appointed to the highest offices, and even in the twentieth century some rulers of Kru towns survived who claimed to have been with Livingstone, or who had spent large portions of their lives in Nigeria or the Gold Coast.[6]

THE QUESTION OF RELEVANCE

In the twentieth century, the foremost Negro in the annals of exploration probably is Matthew Henson. Henson and Commodore Robert Peary became the first Americans to set foot on the North Pole, on April 6, 1909. Henson, however, was but an assistant, and Peary the mastermind. As with the likely fate of the second man on the Moon, Henson's name has nearly faded from popular knowledge of this epic struggle to reach the top of the world.[7]

The names of other individuals of note in exploration might be listed, and doubtless others will come to light as attempts accumulate to ferret out the black skins of the past. One might ask, however, just what is to be proved, or demonstrated, or suggested, by such a compilation. Are we to use the presence of black men on the exploring expeditions of the Western world as an index of Black quality, Black identity, or Black ethos? Such intentions are doomed from the start. The proper names of the great majority of such persons do not appear in the records, either because of deliberate or unconscious omission of a linkage of names and skin color, or often simply because such distinctions were not always made in the normal

36

course of exposition, especially in Classical and Islamic annals. The situation wherein most such names are irretrievably lost must be accepted; the individuality of most Black persons on white expeditions will never be established.

In any case it is a contradiction to approach the Negro role in exploration from the point of view that perhaps some Negro persons ought to share in the glory of these exploits, since perhaps the individuals by whose names the expeditions are known do not deserve all the credit. We can no more parcel out credit for the success of a voyage or expedition to its Negro members than we can to any individuals, and to ascribe a portion of the accolades to a member of a given expedition on grounds of ethnic derivation is sheer foolishness.

No matter how many Negro participants in the voyages of discovery in Western civilization come to light, this method still does not serve the desires of persons of all races to know more of the Negro past. It is at best a foreign *milieu* in which the Black man would thus be judged, and the most that could be hoped for would be an even more consciously parenthetical role than has been accorded him up to now. Judged by the criteria of Western civilization, recognition for great achievements in exploration go to the organization men—those who led the expeditions to success—because this type of evaluation best serves our need to enforce our contexts of individuality. In this respect the Negro role in the explorations with which the Western world is familiar was negligible.

A real appreciation of the Negro achievement in exploration can only be had by taking another approach, one which seeks to establish what is significant in this field within the context of a Negro, or Black, or African civilization. For the "known world" had different boundaries for different peoples, often overlapping, but just as frequently including areas unknown to the West before the Age of Discovery.

Many wonder at the motivations of explorers and travellers. The popular explanation often is that certain men possess a "drive" which causes them to seek the ends of the earth, the peaks of mountains, the depths of the oceans. This suggestion smacks of racism, or at least opens the door to racist judgments, since someone inevitably can be depended upon to speculate that perhaps this "drive" is stronger among whites than among the colored peoples, hence the great white activity in exploration and discovery.

A much more useful explanation of exploration on the part of any people is the desire for trade and commerce. Practically all the major expeditions which resulted in the inclusion of the Western Hemisphere in the known world of Western Europe were economically motivated. The need for spices from the East, and other goods from around the world, as well as precious metals for a European economy expanding faster than its bullion-based currencies—all these factors contributed to the European attempt to widen its horizons from the fifteenth century onwards.

EXPLORATION IN THE AFRICAN CONTEXT

Perhaps in Africa more than anywhere else the promise of trade served as a stimulus to travel and discovery. Beginning with Pharaonic Egypt, nearly every highly organized state in Africa attempted to enlarge its horizons through expeditions beyond its marches. We know of trading expeditions down the Red Sea from Egypt to the land of Punt, generally assumed to be modern Somalia, where Egyptians sought frankincense, myrrh and ivory for their temples. During the Eighteenth Dynasty, around the beginning of the fifteenth century B.C., there came to the throne of Egypt a woman, the famed Hatshepsut, who appears to have been responsible for a new burst of Egyptian maritime energy. There is some evidence to indicate that one Egyptian fleet may have ventured as far as Sofāla, a gold exporting center near the mouth of the Zambezi River in modern Mozambique.

Egyptian expeditions on land also moved far afield, as part of the historic Egyptian ambition to control the lands to the south, whence flows the Nile River. Here the records speak of travel to the land of Yam, which has yet to be identified positively, but lay somewhere in the interior of Northeast Africa.

Around 2300 B.C. several journeys to the south are recorded in hieroglyphs on tombs near Aswān. The principal individual involved in these expeditions was one Harkhuf, who apparently organized and commanded them. There is no certainty as to where in the African interior these expeditions went, but they got at least as far as the provinces of Darfur and Kordofan in what is now the extreme western extent of the Republic of the

Sudan. Ebony, ivory, a little gold and some slaves resulted from these expeditions. The road to Darfur became a well-worn one thereafter. The track which leaves the Nile near Aswān to strike out in the direction of Darfur is known today as the Elephantine Road, and as it enters the area of desert between Darfur and the Nile Valley it becomes the *Darb al-Arba'in*, or Forty Days' Road, along which thousands of caravans have passed, following the trail blazed by such men as Harkhuf.

The fourth and last of Harkhuf's known expeditions to the south of Egypt may have penetrated farther than the others, for upon returning Harkhuf wrote his sovereign that he had captured a black dwarf, whom the Pharaoh commanded he bring to the Egyptian court. In all probability this was an individual from one of the Pygmoid groups now confined to limited areas of the Congo forest. The northernmost extent of Pygmoid habitation probably was closer to Egypt in Harkhuf's time, but even so it appears that some Egyptian expeditions may have penetrated to the edge of the equatorial rain forests.[8]

By the beginning of the Christian era there had developed in the Indian Ocean a major commercial network, with entrepots all along the East African coast, as well as the Red Sea littoral. This growth in commerce prompted two major efforts at bringing the expanses of the Indian Ocean and its commercial hinterland into the bounds of the world known to the men who depended upon this trade. First came the taming of the Indian Ocean and its winds, so that it could be navigated regularly and successfully for purposes of trade with India and the East Indies. Through years of experimentation scores of unnamed seafarers from East Africa and the Arabian Peninsula discovered that the monsoon winds of the Indian Ocean could be depended upon to take them to India, providing that they knew exactly what time of year and precisely which latitudes in which to sail. Negotiating the monsoon winds of the Indian Ocean is still a challenging task; to fail to leave India by a certain time in the era of sailing vessels was to risk being stranded for a year, with the possibility of financial ruin.[9]

One of the products of East Africa most in demand in India was ivory, and to exploit the ivory of Africa there is evidence that in the early centuries of the Christian era the first attempts were made to penetrate the interior, for the purpose of establishing trade routes to the coastal cities. Trade routes emerged along the Zambezi to the gold mines of the Rhodesias, and farther north the traders of Axum, the state which formed the nucleus of modern Ethiopia, probed farther inland each year from the Ethiopian Highlands, regularly penetrating the upper Nile Valley and the Great Lakes region in search of ivory and other products.[10]

THE IMPACT OF ISLAM

The coming of Islam to much of Africa beginning in the seventh century provided new stimuli to travel, discovery and contacts between countries separated by great distances. Built into the Islamic way of life, of course, is the matter of the *hajj*, or pilgrimage—the journey to Mecca which every devout Muslim with adequate means is expected to make at least once in his life. The route to Mecca from the lands of Mali, the greatest of the Islamic states in West Africa, at least in terms of the aristocracy, was over four thousand miles in length, and each time such a journey was made the travellers could have bade fair to receive recognition for a feat rivalling that of Marco Polo. Yet this journey, from deep in the interior of West Africa to the center of Islamic faith, was made not once but hundreds of times, by thousands of Muslim faithful.

Such travels may not be regarded as exploration in the classic sense of the word, except in the case of those who first opened the route. These conditions of travel, however, only demonstrate that many portions of Africa had already passed the stage in which they were accessible only to hardy pioneers by the time that Europeans began to widen their own horizons through systematic exploration. Moreover, links with the center of the Islamic world had many of the same effects upon West Africa in the thirteenth and fourteenth centuries that new contacts were having on Europe at much the same time. A great deal of new knowledge came to Mali through the institution of the *hajj*, knowledge of other countries and peoples which, we may surmise, found ready acceptance within the learned Islamic community of Mali. Exposure to Islamic geographical and cosmographical theories may have prompted attempts at organized exploration by Malians. Certainly the empire of Mali had the wealth to undertake expeditions of considerable size, and there is a record of one project which, if authentic, must stand as one of the most momentous enterprises of all time.

A WEST AFRICAN VENTURE INTO THE ATLANTIC?

In 1323 the then current ruler of Mali, Mansa Mūsa, arrived in Cairo on his way to Mecca. His retinue and the amount of gold carried on the journey mildly excited cosmopolitan Cairo, since it is written that his train may have included as many as sixty thousand camels, each carrying a bag of gold dust. Aside from the unusual wealth brought by Mansa Mūsa, the fact that Cairenes did not regard the journey itself as exceptional is another indication of the regularity of contact over the immense distances separating West Africa from Egypt and Arabia.

Mansa Mūsa received the attention befitting his position, including a number of interviews with learned Egyptian and foreign persons eager to hear of Mali. During one such conversation, the question of succession to the throne of Mali emerged, whereupon Mansa Mūsa, responding to an inquiry as to how he had come to the throne, related a most exciting tale.

Mūsa's predecessor, whose name is uncertain due to differing versions of the Malian king list, had, according to Mūsa, speculated at length about the nature of the world. This particular ruler appears to have become enamored with the conflicting views of the earth held by Islamic geographers, particularly the view that the world-island, or the Afro-Asiatic-European land mass, was surrounded on all sides by water, the so-called Circumambient Ocean. Mansa Mūsa reported that his predecessor refused to accept this view, and determined to mount an expedition to discover what lay beyond the waters.

The ruler of Mali reportedly ordered the assembling of a fleet of scores of vessels, with provisions for a long voyage, and ordered the crews out onto the ocean with instructions not to return until they had discovered what lay beyond the limits of the sea.

Mūsa related that a considerable period of time passed without word of the fate of the fleet, and only after a very long wait did a single ship appear on the coast of Mali. The captain of the ship, summoned to the court, told of his adventures on the ocean. He told how the fleet had sailed for many days without

41

sighting land, whereupon it encountered in the middle of the ocean some sort of river, apparently flowing within the ocean. Most of the fleet sailed into this stream and disappeared, but the captain who returned, apparently last in line, thought better of it and started homeward.

The ruler of Mali apparently was not satisfied with this story, since it did not result in discovery of what lay beyond the Circumambient Ocean. He therefore ordered the gathering of another fleet, supposedly ten times as large as the first, which he himself would command. He delegated power to Mūsa and set out upon the sea with his ships, and was never heard from again. This, stated Mansa Mūsa to his listeners in Cairo, was the story of his own accession to the throne of Mali.[11]

The implications of this story are astounding. Though not widely known even among Africanists, Mūsa's relation has received some attention nonetheless. Speculation has been directed mostly toward the description of a stream, or river of some sort, within the ocean. One writer has suggested that the fleet simply encountered a severe storm, another that it became trapped in a strong current, such as the Guinea Current.[12] Still another is content with the explanation that Mansa Mūsa simply wished to astonish his listeners with a fantastic tale which had no basis of reality whatsoever.[13]

It is difficult to accept the proposition that Mūsa simply invented this story. Too many of the essential elements of Islamic geographical thought appear in it, and unless the court of Mali had had some exposure to these ideas the story would not ring true in this context. We know that the period of Mali's imperial zenith in the fourteenth century was also a time of much scholarship in the empire, largely due to the impact of Islamic learning in many fields. It is fairly well known that a number of mosques, such as the one at Timbuktu, established academic traditions and reputations of considerable merit. We know of many manuscripts produced in the Western Sudan, and it seems improbable at best that all this activity would overlook Islamic geography, one of the most important areas of Arab achievement.

Islamic geographers were at odds over the nature of the earth, having incorporated the conflicting views of Strabo and Ptolemy into their thinking. The principal point of dissension lay in the matter of Africa itself, Strabo claiming that the continent terminated far to the south, allowing the Circumambient Ocean to exist, since the waters of the Atlantic and Pacific Oceans would have to mingle to realize this situation. Ptolemy, on the other hand, believed that Africa extended indefinitely to the south, until it merged with a vast Antarctic continent, which in turn enclosed the Indian Ocean and made it an enormous inland sea, thus also making impossible the Circumambient Ocean.[14]

It may well have been that local and foreign scholars in Mali discussed this and other points of controversy, and that such disputes led to efforts to prove or disprove certain points through exploitation.

We know that Mali, although essentially an inland empire, did have an outlet to the sea in the Senegambia region during parts of the fourteenth century.[15] There is no better point of departure for the Americas than this particular portion of the African coast, for here expeditions may take advantage of the Northeast trade winds, which blow steadily and evenly almost year round in a vast arc skirting the northwest coast of Africa and curving toward the great eastern bulge of South America. Columbus himself, for reasons not yet certain, chose to drop from Spain to latitudes comparable to those of Senegambia before starting the ocean crossing.[16] Even today the British Admiralty advises that sailing vessels crossing the ocean use these latitudes as the fastest and most dependable means of reaching South America. With such sailing conditions, it is hardly surprising that one writer has ventured to suggest that the "river" encountered by the Malian fleet in the open sea might have been the fresh water current of the Amazon, which often penetrates into the Atlantic as much as one hundred miles or more.[17]

Mali possessed far more in the way of resources for such an expedition than simply speculative wonder induced by exposure to Islamic manuscripts. Ships capable of a transatlantic voyage existed in West Africa by the thousands in the fourteenth century, and riverine craft in the Niger, Senegal and Gambia rivers continued to impress Europeans by their size well into the nineteenth century. The burthens of some of these vessels ran into the hundreds of tons, far larger than the frail craft which carried Columbus on his first voyage.[18]

43

Sheer size of vessels is not the most important prerequisite for exploration, of course. Had this been the case, Columbus himself might have used some of the larger ships available in Western Europe, where freight carriers approaching one thousand tons burthen had been in use for two centuries before Columbus' time. More important are considerations of mode of locomotion and maneuverability. Columbus used the caravel, a Portuguese development blending the nautical technology of the Christian and Islamic worlds into a craft which could maneuver in far superior fashion to any sailing ship before it.

Mali, however, might have relied on other developments, particularly the type of vessel propelled by ordinary square sails but equipped with auxiliary oars, which may still be seen on the Niger. This combination of propulsion systems was most successful for the Norsemen, in areas where the winds were hostile to westward penetration. West African vessels of the fourteenth century were certainly equal to anything put on the water in Scandinavia, and for the Malians the winds would have been fair.

Navigation itself was a problem in early transatlantic endeavors, for although the Portuguese quickly learned the relatively simple means of determining precise latitudes, the matter of longitudinal calculation was not fully solved until the nineteenth century. Perhaps Columbus and the Malians did not sail into completely unknown seas, since there is a growing body of evidence that numerous pre-Columbian transatlantic attempts may have been undertaken. It is still sheer speculation to speak in terms of these attempts having some effect on the cosmography of Old World civilizations, but this is a line of research which deserves a great deal of attention, for Western Europe as well as West Africa.

The skills of navigating by the stars were in use in West Africa at least as long as in Western Europe. It would be completely misleading to suggest that Mali was a maritime state in any sense of the word, but technology of a comparable sort evolved in the trans-Saharan trade network, with caravans crossing the desert navigating in much the same way as the early European mariners probing the West African coast, although across uncharted lands rather than uncharted seas. The analogy of the camel as the "ship of the desert" can hardly be carried too far.

Africa has been treated as a passive partner in the matrix of expanding knowledge of the world during the European Renaissance. Yet, if one considers the motivations of European explorers, there is reason to believe that many of the same stimuli affected West Africa, particularly the dominant inland empire of Mali.

ECONOMIC STIMULI TO EXPLORATION IN MEDIEVAL WEST AFRICA

We have suggested that European motivations to exploration were primarily economic. Efforts to gain access to the riches of the East without depending upon the Islamic world or Italian cities prompted much early Portuguese activity. In the early years of the fifteenth century, when the Portuguese began their cautious probes down the West African coast, a much more immediate goal was in mind, that of securing a direct channel to the gold of West Africa, which grew dramatically in importance as the medieval "gold drain" from Europe to the Orient forced the burgeoning, proto-capitalist economies of Western Europe to look beyond domestic sources of precious metals upon which to base their currencies.

The increased demand for gold may have manifested itself in a general increase in the price of gold across the whole complex of the trans-Saharan trade structure, eventually reaching Mali in the form of higher prices for the gold caravans, since Mali realized much of its wealth through duties levied on the gold trade. The increased demands for gold apparently prompted Mali to seek to open up whole new sources of gold for itself, in order to meet the market. To this end, the empire turned to bringing the Akan gold fields of what is now southern Ghana into regular production and some form of regulation. This meant entering the forest zones of the West African Guinea coast for the first time, since the grassland empires of the Western Sudan traditionally could not bring the forests under their sway, owing to their dependence upon cavalry in the open grasslands, and the debilitating effect which the forest environment had on their horses. The advance into the forest had to be of a different sort, requiring a whole new system of exploration, which eventually took on a sort of frontier aura.

Again the individuals are nameless, and most will remain so.

But it seems fairly certain that, early in the fifteenth century, when the Portuguese began their movement down the West African coast, most of the forest zone of West Africa was brought within the larger West African trading complex through the energies of largely independent "prospectors," so that by the time the Portuguese reached the Gold Coast in the 1480s they found agents of the trade awaiting them, having covered hundreds of miles of hostile environment on land just as the Portuguese had done on the seas.[19]

CONCLUSION

Africans, then, opened up their own continent. Europeans followed in their footsteps. Bringing the greater part of a continent more than three times the size of the United States into a single, enormous commercial network is an achievement which should stand alongside the opening up of other parts of the world by Europeans. Both processes took centuries. Both processes were interrelated. Perhaps, then, as Prince Henry speculated on the contrasting views of the ancient and medieval geographers of many civilizations, so also did the predecessor of Mansa Mūsa, and with comparable results.

The question of the Negro contribution to the European process of exploration is a dubious and limited one. What is important for any civilization are the contributions within it to the improvement of its own segment of the human experience. The African process of discovery is a matter of first consideration in this context. Indeed, while persons of African descent were on many of the great European expeditions of discovery, Europeans attempting to "open up" Africa merely trod upon routes centuries old, opened by Africans long before them.

In this time of racial turmoil we can only begin to appreciate the achievements of those of African descent within contexts more meaningful to them than our own. This, however, should be our prime task, not the incidental addition of Africans or Black Americans within our own historical experience. Only by widening our perspectives, as peoples everywhere have extended the horizons of their known worlds, can we eliminate racial problems through a better understanding of the nature of Man.

SELECTED BIBLIOGRAPHY

BOOKS

Bovill, E. W., *The Golden Trade of the Moors*. London: Oxford University Press, 1968. The most recent of many editions of this work provides an insight into the complexity of the trans-Saharan trade and the contacts it made possible.

Cauvet, G., *Les Berbères en Amérique*. Alger: J. Brignau, 1930. An example of many such attempts to attibute the discovery of the Americas to Africans, this work suggests the term "Brazil" derives from a Berber tribe in North Africa called Banu Birzalah. Despite its almost certainly fictitious nature, the work points out the many instances of unexplained references to lands across the Atlantic in pre-Columbian days.

Davidson, Basil, *The African Past*. Boston: Little, Brown, 1964. One of the most valuable collections of readings illuminating all aspects of African history.

Franklin, John Hope, *From Slavery to Freedom: A History of American Negroes*. New York: Alfred A. Knopf, 2nd ed., 1965. A standard attempt to add Black men to their rightful places in American history.

Mauny, Raymond, *Les navigations médiévales sur les côtes sahariennes antérieures à la découverte portugaise (1434)*. Lisboa: Centro de Estudos Históricas Ultramarinos, 1960. An inventory of pre-Portuguese maritime activity on the West African Coast.

Mauny, Raymond, *Tableau géographique de l'Ouest africain au moyen âge*. Dakar: Institut Français d'Afrique Noire, 1961. A monumental study of medieval West Africa. The bibliography alone is an imposing guide to early West African history.

Terrell, John Upton, *Estevanico the Black*. Los Angeles: Westernlore Press, 1968. A somewhat romanticized version of the life of this Black explorer of the American Southwest.

al-Umari, Ibn Fadl Allah, *Masālik al-Absar fi Mamālik al-Amsār*. Trans. Gaudefroy-Demombynes. Paris: Paul Guethner, Tome I, 1927. The original story of the Malian expeditions onto the Atlantic is found on pp. 74-75.

Wiener, Leo, *Africa and the Discovery of America*. Philadelphia: Innes, 3 Vols., 1920-1922. An attempt to construct a case for a pre-Columbian African civilization in the Americas from apparent linguistic and archeological evidence.

Bloch, Marc, "Le problème de l'or au moyen âge," *Annales, d'histoire économique et sociale,* Vol. V, 1933, pp. 1-34. A brief look at the problem of gold in medieval European economies. Also important in this respect is Lombard, M., "L'or musulman du VIIᵉ au XIᵉ siècle: les bases monétaires d'une suprématie economique," *Annales, Economies, Sociétés. Civilisations,* Vol. II, 1947, pp. 143-160.

Hamidullah, Muhammad, "L'Afrique découvre l'Amérique avant Christoph Colomb," *Présence Africaine,* 1958, pp. 173-183. An attempt to gain a wider audience for the story of the Malian voyages. The story is used here in an early attempt to balance the scales against previous Eurocentric ideas about Africa.

Hui-Lin Li, "Mu-Lan-Pi: A Case for Pre-Columbian Trans-atlantic Travel by Arab Ships," *Harvard Journal of Asiatic Studies,* Vol. XXIII, 1960-1961, pp. 114-126. Rumors of ventures into the Atlantic from the Afro-Islamic world may have got as far afield as China.

Issawi, Charles, "Arab Geography and the Circumnavigation of Africa," *Osiris,* Vol. X, 1952, pp. 117-128. A summary of Arab views about the nature of the African continent. Also see Kumm, H. K. W., "The Arab Geographers and Africa," *Scottish Geographical Magazine,* Vol. XLI, 1925, pp. 284-289.

Jeffreys, M. D. W., "Pre-Columbian Negroes in America," *Scientia,* Vol. LXXXVIII, 1953, pp. 202-218. A claim for pre-Columbian discovery of the Americas by Africans, based on alleged evidence of pre-Columbian maize remains in West Africa. Also see Jeffreys, "Pre-Columbian Maize in Africa," *Nature,* Vol. CLXXII, 1953, pp. 965-966.

Wilks, Ivor, "A Medieval Trade Route from the Niger to the Gulf of Guinea," *Journal of African History,* Vol. III, 1962, pp. 337-343. A possible example of Africans reacting to greater European demands for gold by opening new areas of West Africa to exploitation.

Wright, R. R., "Negro Companions of the Spanish Explorers," *American Anthropologist,* N.S. Vol. IV, 1902, pp. 217-228. A listing of recognized and possible Negroes on the Spanish expeditions to the New World.

Zéki Pacha, Aḥmad, "Une seconde tentative des musulmans

pour *découvrir* l'Amérique," *Bulletin de l'Institut d'Egypte*, Vol. II, 1919-1920, pp. 57-59. Another description of the Malian voyages. The first attempt to discover the Americas, incidentally, refers to a story of eight brothers in Cordoba who set out to discover their fortunes in the Atlantic.

The reader is also referred to several valuable articles in the *Encyclopaedia of Islam*, which deal with the oceans and Islamic knowledge of them. Some of these occur under the titles "Bahr Muhit" and "Bahr al-Maghrib."

NOTES

1. See T. A. Shumovskii and M. Malkiel-Jirmounskii, *Três roteiros desconhecidos de Ahmad ibn-Mādiid, o piloto árabe de Vasco da Gama* Moscow: n. p., 1957-1960, *passim*.

2. Leo Wiener, *Africa and the Discovery of America*, Philadelphia: Innes, 1920-1922, 3 Vols., *passim*.

3. John Upton Terrell, *Estevanico the Black*, Los Angeles: Westernlore Press, 1968, *passim*.

4. Ronald W. Davis, "Historical Outline of the Kru Coast, Liberia, 1500 to the Present," Unpublished Ph.D. dissertation, Indiana University, 1968, *passim*.

5. *African Repository*, Vol. XXXVII, 1861, p. 95.

6. Walter B. Williams and Maude W. Williams, *Adventures With the Krus in West Africa*, New York: Vantage Press, 1955, p. 78.

7. John Hope Franklin, *From Slavery to Freedom: A History of American Negroes*, New York: Alfred A. Knopf, 2nd ed., 1966, p. 554.

8. Basil Davidson, *The African Past*, Boston: Little, Brown, 1964, pp. 47-48.

9. For a description of contemporary sailing in the Indian Ocean world, see A. H. J. Prins, *Sailing from Lamu*, Assen: Van Gorcum, 1965, *passim*.

10. Jean Doresse, *Ethiopia*, New York: Frederick Ungar, 1959, *passim*.

11. Ibn Fadl Allah al-'Umari, *Masālik al-Absār fi Mamālik al-Amsār* (trans. Gaudefroy-Demombynes), Paris: Paul Geuthner, Tome I, pp. 74-75.

12. Ahmed Zéki Pacha, "Une seconde tentative des musulmans pour découvrir l'Amérique," *Bulletin de l'Institut d'Egypte*, Vol. II, 1919-1920, pp. 57-59.

13. See translator's note in al-'Umari, *op. cit.*, p. 75.

14. Charles Issawi, "Arab Geography and the Circumnavigation of Africa," *Osiris*, Vol. X, 1952, pp, 117-128.

15. Raymond Mauny, *Tableau géographique de l'Ouest africain au moyen âge*, Dakar: Institut Français d'Afrique Noire, 1961, p. 410.

16. Samuel Eliot Morison, *Christopher Columbus: Admiral of the Ocean Sea*, Boston: Little, Brown, 1942, pp. 265 ff.

17. Muhammad Hamidullah, "L'Afrique découvre l'Amérique avant Christoph Colomb," *Présence Africaine*, 1958, pp. 173-183.

18. Raymond Mauny, *op. cit.*, pp. 234, 409.

19. Ivor Wilks, "A Medieval Trade Route from the Niger to the Gulf of Guinea," *Journal of African History*, Vol. III, 1962, pp. 337-343.

RONALD W. DAVIS was born in Cleveland, Ohio in 1943. He received the B.A. from Bowling Green University, and the M.A. and Ph.D. from Indiana University. A member of the Department of History at Western Michigan University since 1966, he is also a member of the Faculty of African Studies, and became Chairman of the African Studies Program at Western in 1969. He has done field work in Liberia and is the author of a number of articles dealing with the Kru peoples and problems of medieval West African geographical knowledge. He is a member of the African Studies Association.

THE NEGRO IN SCIENCE

Lewis H. Carlson

Western Michigan University (Kalamazoo, Mich.)

THE AFRICAN AND HIS SCIENCE

The evolution of the term "science" in Western civilization has burdened the concept with many connotations. Surely "science" implies as much in the realm of cultural arrogance as in the more proper sphere of empirical thought. The term as it now stands cannot be applied fairly to the world of traditional Africa, or, for that matter, anywhere else beyond the restrictive bonds of Western civilization.[1]

It is true, of course, that the ancient Egyptians developed many of the basic skills of mathematics and geometry, that the portion of North Africa in the Islamic world contributed mightily both to the preservation and transmission of earlier learning, as well as contributed important advances of its own. To count these elements among African scientific achievements, however, is to run afoul of two major problems. In the case of the Egyptians, the nature of Pharaonic society and the gap of millennia between that time and the present have served to erase the names of the scientific "heroes" of the day. In any case, to seek the "inventor" of the pyramid as applied mathematics is akin to seeking the "inventor" of fire or the wheel. The great irony of Western science, founded as it is upon experimentation, which implies legions of men and women toiling for years on end toward a single goal, is that it seeks out individuals for places on pedestals. This is nothing less than a perversion, and cannot be expected to have operated outside the Western world.

51

The case of the Islamic world is somewhat different, in that the problem here is we expect Muslim chroniclers to practice our own racist concepts and pick out the different men of color among their intellectul leaders in all fields. Many North African savants may have been of Black Africa, many not.

If we seek individual scientific achievements "south of the Sahara," so to speak, we shall be disappointed. All but a tiny handful of African peoples, for example, developed the techniques of iron smelting before the end of the first Christian millennium, but this is again a matter of unnamed and frightfully numerous "experimenters;" and in any case we hardly call this science in the Western world, where men also at one time pondered the nature of iron ore, and it would be a matter of the most callous racism to laud those Africans who, in a sense, played with blocks, simply because we cannot transfer our own concepts of scientific achievement to other societies with successful results.

The term "science" remains, to us, part of our definition and categorization of the world and the universe. The definitions of these elements in Africa are totally alien to our own; it follows that our concepts of science cannot apply. A great deal has been done, for example, in the field of herbalogy by Africans, yet most is still oral tradition and yet to become part of the Western pharmacopoeia.

The greatest problem in looking for our kind of "science" in Africa is the inextricable relationship between the physical and metaphysical realms among African peoples. The two are almost violently separated in Western civilization; in Africa they are one. We cannot isolate African concepts of the physical from their concepts of the metaphysical. All physical phenomena, according to Father Placide Tempels, really reflect natural forces, which are in a sense the ties that bind the physical and metaphysical together. The immense difficulties of comparison between two such alien concepts, according to Father Tempels, lie in the fact that both civilizations arrive at accepted, rational conclusions, vastly different, through totally different paths of logic and ontology. In sum, "We understand causality in terms of our static metaphysics, the Bantu in terms of their philosophy of forces."[2]

In the fall of 1949, Charles R. Drew, the renowned Negro physician who gained fame for his work in perfecting blood plasma, delivered a paper on the subject of "Negro Scholars in Scientific Research."[3] Drew concluded that "our opportunities and our contributions as scientists have been meager." It was an observation that was to be echoed by other well-known Negro scientists. Dr. Herman Branson, chairman of the Physics Department at Howard University and a recognized scholar in the field, admitted some two years later that the "overall performance of the Negro in science is not too impressive."[4] And Samuel M. Nabrit, President of Texas Southern University and well published in the field of biological regeneration, opined as late as 1957 that "the history of the Negro in science is of the future rather than in the past."[5]

Quite clearly these three scientists were emphasizing the present at the expense of the past to focus attention on the critical need for updating the Negro's opportunities in the sophisticated world of mid-century science. Yet they could not afford to neglect the past. In 1955 Morgan State College Press brought out a book entitled *The Negro in Science,* which was an open plea for recognition of future possibilities for the Negro scientist based upon past promise.[6] In the preface, Dr. Branson noted that there were other identifiable groups whose scientific contributions were not commensurate with their numbers—Catholics and women, for example—but that the Jews had contributed far more than their numbers would seemingly warrant. Branson concluded that it was a tradition of research and an atmosphere of scholarship that resulted in scientific contributions.

A few years earlier, however, Branson had written, "I know of no [Negro] college where research is considered as the characteristic function of a professor or where research and teaching are actually on a parity;"[7] furthermore, he saw the problem exacerbated by the fact that increasing numbers of Negroes were entering Negro colleges, thereby leaving even less time for the instructors to engage in personal research. The day was past when the black scientist could work in his outdated, ill-equipped laboratory and win the white world's accolades for research in the peanut. Negro scholarship in the sciences, as elsewhere, had to be updated and intensified; and the past achievements of black scientists, hitherto unknown, with the exception of the ubiquitous George Washington Carver, would suggest what the Negro could be expected to accomplish in an expanded world of opportunity. In addition, the successes illuminate the obstacles which must be overcome in a world not always ready to welcome the black scientist. Who were these men and what allowed them to make their contributions to our scientific and technological growth?

What we know about the Negro inventor before 1900 is due almost entirely to the tireless efforts of Henry E. Baker. As Assistant Examiner in the United States Patent Office in the early years of the twentieth century, he compiled the inventions of American Negroes into four massive volumes. Baker's task was made particularly difficult by the fact that though the first Negro to receive a patent, Henry Blair for his 1934 corn harvester,[8] was so designated by race this was not subsequently done. In 1900 and again in 1913 Baker sent out several thousand circular letters to prominent patent lawyers, large manufacturing firms, and various newspapers, soliciting information. The response was gratifying, as several thousand replies came back to his office. From this information Baker concluded that, indeed, many Negroes had consulted patent lawyers, but unfortunately not all these attorneys had kept records of patents granted. In addition, many patents had been taken out by attorneys for Negro clients who preferred to protect the commercial values of their inventions by remaining anonymous. Finally, Baker was able to draw together more than 1000 authentic cases in which he fully identified the inventor, the date and number of the patent, and the title of the invention. His four volumes were replete with drawings of the respective inventions.[9]

SLAVE DAYS

The particular problem facing a Negro inventor during the slave years was that as a slave he had no right to take out a patent. In 1858 Jeremiah S. Black, the Attorney General of the United States, confirmed a decision of the Secretary of the Interior which refused patents to slaves or their masters on the grounds that not being a citizen, the slave could neither contract with the government nor assign his invention to his master.[10]

Thus Jo Anderson, a Negro slave in the Cyrus McCormick family, could receive no credit for the reaper though McCormick's grandson later wrote: "Above all the name of his Negro helper, Jo Anderson, deserves honor as the man who worked beside him in the building of the reaper."[11]

Even Jefferson Davis was unable to register a patent for a boat propeller invented by one of his slaves. It was perhaps with this in mind that he suggested that the constitution of the Confederacy recognize slave inventions.[12]

This restriction did not apply to "free persons of color;" thus James Forton was able to patent his device for handling sails in the early 1800's and Norbert Rillieux in 1846 received credit for his vacuum pan, which revolutionized the refining of sugar.

Forton, born in 1766, worked in a sail-making factory which he later came to own after his successful invention; in fact, he became one of the richest men in Philadelphia, greatly aiding the abolitionist movement, and was one of the Negroes who helped finance William Lloyd Garrison's *Liberator*.[13]

Norbert Rillieux's name has been scattered through textbooks on evaporation and reference works on sugar, but it was not until midway through the twentieth century that his work was to regain its deserved recognition.[14] Born a *quadroon libre* in New Orleans in 1806, the young Rillieux was sent to Paris for his education, where, by the age of twenty-four, he was teaching applied mechanics at L'Ecole Centrale. In 1830 he published a series of papers on the steam engine and steam economy, which led to his invention of the multiple-effect evaporator, on which he received American patents in 1843 and 1846. This invention led to a cheaper, better, and more automated process for crystallizing sugar, and its basic concept is also used in the manufacturing of condensed milk, soap, gelatine, and glue and in the recovery of wastes in distilleries and paper factories.

Rillieux also designed a plan for the drainage of the lowlands of New Orleans and the implementation of a city sewerage system. This was blocked, allegedly because "sentiment against free people of color had become sufficiently acute to prohibit the bestowing of such an honor upon a member of this group."[15]

When the atmosphere for free men of color became unbearable

in the years before the Civil War, Rillieux returned to France where for years he immersed himself in the study of Egyptology, though continuing to publish papers on steam engines. When he was almost seventy-five, Rillieux "returned from his pyramids," as one French colleague phrased it, to again concentrate on the problems of evaporation and sugar machinery. His last great invention, aimed at reducing fuel consumption in sugar processing, was lost to him, ironically enough, because of French patent conflicts.

As late as 1946 the name of the man who had revolutionized the sugar industry could not be found on a reference card in the public libraries of New York or New Orleans; nor had early Negro historians like Carter Woodson given him much attention. Yet Charles Browne, then a sugar chemist with the United States Department of Agriculture, wrote in the 1940's: "I have always held that Rillieux's invention is the greatest in the history of American chemical engineering and I know of no other invention that has brought so great a saving to all branches of chemical engineering."[16]

EMANCIPATION

After his emancipation from slavery the Negro was allowed to take out patents in his own name, but recognition was still difficult. White inventors have often experienced problems in protecting their inventions, but the black inventor, often without competent legal assistance, was even more at a disadvantage. Nevertheless, the number of inventions by Negroes greatly increased in the last third of the nineteenth century and many of these were of considerable significance.

Jan E. Matzeliger, born in 1852 in Dutch Guiana of a Dutch father and a native black mother, came to the States as a young man, worked in a shoe factory, and patented a lasting machine that greatly affected the entire industry. His machine held the shoe on the last, pulled the leather around the heel, guided and drove the nails into place, and then discharged the completed shoe. Matzeliger sold his patent to Sidney W. Winslow who used it to help expand the United States Machinery Company into a multi-million-dollar enterprise. Within twenty years Matzeliger's lasting machine had helped to reduce the cost of shoes by more than fifty percent and to double their production.[17]

Better known than Matzeliger, who died young and unrewarded in 1889, was Granville T. Woods. Woods was born in 1856 in Columbus, Ohio, where without the benefit of much formal education he sufficiently educated himself to gain a job as an engineer on the Danville and Southern Railroad in 1880. Four years later he marketed his first invention and used the profits to open his own factory in Cincinnati. The Woods Electrical Company took over by assignment many of his earlier patents, including inventions for electrical railroads, automatic airbrakes, and a telegraphic device for transmitting messages between moving trains. In spite of the fact that his company won two court cases against the Edison Company on disputed patents, most of his 150 patents were later sold to firms such as General Electric, Westinghouse Air Brake, and American Telephone and Telegraph. The *Catholic Tribune* of Cincinnati, with understandable local pride, had predicted in 1886 that Woods was "destined to revolutionize the mode of street car transit," and a year later the same paper concluded that he was "the greatest electrician in the world."[18]

Elijah McCoy was almost as prolific in his work as was Woods. The son of runaway slaves, McCoy was born in Canada in 1843. When still in his teens he moved to Ypsilanti, Michigan, and there began experimenting with lubricators for steam engines. By his death in 1929 he had received over fifty patents and had organized the Elijah McCoy Manufacturing Company in Detroit to help market his inventions. He is regarded as the pioneer in devising means for supplying oil to running machinery. His lubricating cup was in use for years on locomotives, steamships, and various factory machines.[19]

Two other Negro inventors who received at least financial recognition in the late nineteenth century were Andrew J. Beard and Lewis Howard Latimer. Beard reportedly received $50,000 in 1897 for the rights to his automatic car-coupling device, making him one of the best rewarded of the Negro inventors.[20] Latimer, on the other hand, worked with two of the best known inventors of the day, Alexander Graham Bell and Thomas Edison.

Born in Boston in 1848, Latimer has been cited as the man responsible for the preparation and drawing of Bell's telephone patents;[21] and his work on an incandescent electric light led to his joining the engineering staff of the Edison Electric Light Company as the only Negro member of the "Edison Pioneers," a group of select individuals formed in 1918 who had worked with Edison before 1885. In 1890 he wrote a layman's explanation of the use and workings of the electric light and in his twilight years published a volume of poetry.[22]

THE TWENTIETH-CENTURY INVENTOR-ENGINEER

The twentieth century saw a gradual expansion of opportunity for the Negro in many fields, and predictably, from the earliest days of flight to the age of interplanetary rockets, increasing numbers of Negroes were able to develop and market their inventive and engineering talents.

As the Wright brothers experimented with their theories of flight, so too did men like J. L. Pickering of Haiti, James Smith of California, W. G. Madison of Iowa, and H. E. Hooter of Missouri, all of whom were granted patents for early inventions on airships. Other Negroes moved into fields of electrical and mechanical engineering: Shelby J. Davidson invented an adding machine; Charles V. Richey developed several devices for registering calls and for detecting the unauthorized use of the telephone; Benjamin F. Jackson of Massachusetts invented a heat apparatus, a gas burner, an electrotypers' furnace, a steam boiler, a trolley wheel controller, a tank signal, and a hydrocarbon burner system; and J. W. Benton walked from his home in Kentucky to the Washington Patent Office, hand-carrying his model for a derrick.

Carrett A. Morgan was perhaps the most successful of this group of early twentieth-century inventors. In 1923 he patented an automatic stop signal which he sold to General Electric for $40,000. Earlier he had won an international prize for his invention of a smoke inhalator, a prototype for the World War I gas mask.[23]

The best known Negro construction engineer of the first half of the twentieth century was Archie A. Alexander. Born in 1887, Alexander spent a lifetime building tunnels, viaducts, bridges, roads, airports, and various industrial plants. Before he died in 1958, Alexander owned his own engineering firm where he once removed racial signs over the toilet facilities and substituted "skilled" and "unskilled."[24]

Alexander was joined by increasing numbers of engineers: David N. Crosthwait Jr. became a specialist in the engineering of heating and ventilating systems and patented many related devices; Cornelius Langston Henderson and Joseph L. Parker, like Alexander, became noted for their building and designing of bridges and tunnels; and Adolphus Samms, a sergeant in the U.S. Army, developed an "air frame center support" which has stripped rockets of unnecessary dead weight, thereby making greater payloads possible.

Sergeant Samms is perhaps the most noteworthy of the above group, for in addition to the above invention he now has four patents on various aspects of rocketry. Perhaps it appears strange that a lowly sergeant should be making such lofty contributions, but so it has always been; and such achievements have given rise to an excitement of anticipation of the day when black opportunities become at one with black potentialities.

THE NEGRO AND SCIENTIFIC RESEARCH

Black contributors in the realm of pure science are even less known than those who made their mark through the practical application of their talents. If we eliminate the name of George Washington Carver, and perhaps that of Benjamin Banneker, we are hard pressed to think of a famous Negro scientist. To be sure, the barriers confronting the Negro in research were higher than those for the man who could tinker with his inventions in the privacy of his own garage; but as late as 1950, Dr. Charles Drew could count only seventy-five Negro doctorates in the natural sciences—and he found this to be a great improvement over earlier years. However, as with the inventor, those who have risen to the top are significant not only for their contributions but as examples of the vast potential that has been left largely untouched.

Edward Bouchet was the first Negro to earn a doctorate at an American university, receiving it in physics at Yale University in 1876. But it is necessary to go back to colonial times and Benjamin Banneker to discover the first major Black-American scientist.

Banneker did more than research the heavens and predict eclipses and the cycle of the locust plague. Lerone Bennett calls him "the first black man of national stature to give vent to the Negro protest."[25] Banneker stood out in magnificent profile for whites and blacks alike and forced thoughtful men to reconsider their basic racial assumptions at an important time in our young history. His almanacs won the grudging admiration of Jefferson and the general praise of his contemporaries, and his contributions to the planning of Washington, D.C., have only recently been recognized.[26]

Banneker was born a free man in the early 1730's in Baltimore County, Maryland. His slave grandfather, allegedly the son of an African chief, had his freedom and hand bought by one Molly Welsh, whose own unsolicited trip to America had been the result of a stolen pail of milk in her native England. The issue of this marriage, Mary Banneker, married a slave, Robert, whose freedom she also purchased and who retained her family name.

The young, Bible-educated Banneker inherited a farm, but appeared to have spent more time on the precision instruments and books lent to him by a Quaker neighbor.[27] His study of astronomy allowed him to predict eclipses, and his observance of nature resulted in a learned dissertation on bees as well as his series of almanacs that were published between 1791 and 1802. He was also reputed to have invented the first clock made in America and unquestionably played an important role in the laying out of Washington, D.C. Yet he is perhaps best remembered for the letter he wrote to another scientist of the day taking issue with the latter's racial views. Thomas Jefferson was later to qualify his praise of Banneker, but there can be little question that he was impressed with his words:

> How pitiable it is to reflect, although you are convinced of the benevolence of the Father of Mankind—that you should at the same time counteract His mercies in detaining by fraud and violence so numerous a part of my brethren under groaning captivity and cruel oppression.[28]

James McHenry, Secretary of War in the Cabinet of Washington and Adams, was unstinting in his praise of Banneker and the significance of his work:

This Negro [is] fresh proof that the powers of the mind are disconnected with the color of the skin, or, in other words, a striking contradiction to Mr. Hume's doctrine, that the Negroes are naturally inferior to the whites and unsusceptible of attainments in arts and sciences.[29]

Though the record of Banneker is now known, there were undoubtedly others during the slave years who not only marveled at the world about them but actively studied its natural phenomena. Unfortunately, with few exceptions, they left no traces of their discoveries.[30]

One who did leave his work for posterity, in addition to the aforementioned Rillieux, was Martin R. Delany. If Banneker was the first man of national prominence to insist on Negro rights, Delany had to be among the first to take pride in his own blackness. Born a free Negro in 1812 in Charleston, West Virginia, Delany's medical and scientific studies at Harvard University led to his practice of medicine in both Chicago and Canada; but he was to become better known for his studies in race and his exaltation of racial pride. It was after he had helped Frederick Douglass bring out his *North Star* that the latter made his famous pronouncement on Delany: "I thank God for making me a man simply, but Delany always thanks Him for making him a black man."[31]

In 1859 Delany led an exploratory party of American-born Negroes to Africa where in the region of the Niger River they carried out scientific studies and made agreements with several African chiefs concerning the treatment of prospective emigres from America. His scientific observations were then presented in a paper given to the Royal Geographic Society in London. He later summed up his feelings on race in his *The Origins of Race and Color*, published in 1879, some six years before his death.[32]

THE TWENTIETH-CENTURY SCIENTIST

One of the most interesting Negro scientists of the early twentieth century was Charles Henry Turner. Perhaps second only to Ernest E. Just in the field of biology, no testimony better typifies the restrictive nature of the Negro scientist's world than does his. Born in 1867, Turner earned his doctorate from the University of Chicago in 1906. Though he did pioneering studies in the field of entomology, publishing over fifty papers in scientific journals on the subject of the behavioral patterns of ants and bees, Turner never held a position higher than that of biology teacher in a St. Louis high school. Even in his secondary teaching Turner felt he was not advanced as rapidly as he should have been because of his interest in research rather than in selling tickets or doing the ordinary extra-curricular chores of the high school teacher. In his twilight years he was to be called back to the University of Chicago, but the professor responsible for the invitation died, and shortly thereafter, in 1923, so did the disappointed Dr. Turner.[33]

Contemporary Negro scientists like Herman Branson and Samuel M. Nabrit consider Ernest E. Just the greatest of the Negro scientists, though throughout his life he was overshadowed by the fame of George Washington Carver and remained almost totally unknown outside the scientific community. Just was born in 1883 in Charleston, South Carolina, and received the benefit of an excellent education. He graduated Phi Beta Kappa and *magna cum laude* with his bachelor's degree from Dartmouth and received similar honors in zoology and physiology from the University of Chicago, where he received his doctorate in 1916.

The only university he was ever affiliated with was Howard University, though he worked for many summers at the Woods Hole Marine Biological Laboratory in Massachusetts where he became a leading authority on the embryological resources of marine fauna. Just was to author over sixty scholarly papers and two monographs, which included pioneering studies into the mysteries of egg fertilization, artificial parthenogenesis, and cell division. He is the only Negro to receive a star beside his name in *American Men of Science*, the badge of excellence that can only be given by other colleagues in the field. Yet Ernest Just never achieved security or satisfaction in the country of his birth. Extremely sensitive on the subject of race, he shied away from students and society, totally immersing himself in his research, and seemed happiest when working in the freer racial climate of Europe. Samuel M. Nabrit, a former student of Just's, later commented on why Just refused to push young Negro students into the world of science: "He wanted no bitterness for others of his race, and so did not encourage them to greater attainment."[34]

In spite of the fact that he was made vice president of the American Society of Zoologists, Just felt he was never really accepted, even by his fellow scientists; and the fact that he was refused admittance to the Rockefeller Institute and never courted by one of the great white universities of the day further embittered him. Dr. Frank R. Lillie, a white colleague and friend of his at Woods Hole, understood his racial torment and penned a fitting epitaph upon the occasion of Just's death in 1941:

> Just's scientific career was a constant struggle for opportunity for research, the breath of his life. He was condemned by race to remain attached to a Negro institution unfitted by means and tradition to give full opportunity to ambitions such as his . . .
>
> An element of tragedy ran through all Just's scientific career due to the limitations imposed by being a Negro in America, to which he could make no lasting psychological adjustment in spite of earnest efforts on his part. The numerous grants for research did not compensate for failure to receive an appointment in one of the large universities or research institutes. He felt this as a social stigma, and hence unjust to a scientist of his recognized standing. In Europe he was received with universal kindness, and made to feel at home in every way; he did not experience social discrimination on account of his race, and this contributed greatly to his happiness there. Hence, in part at least, he prolonged self-imposed exile on many occasions. That a man of his ability, scientific devotion, and of such strong personal loyalties as he gave and received, should have been warped in the land of his birth, must remain a matter for regret.[35]

George Washington Carver, who seemingly was never troubled by the fact of his color, makes an interesting contrast with Ernest Just. One of the most famous scientists of his day, partly because of his work on crop diversification and soil conservation and partly because of his passive attitude toward race, Carver was often held up by white America as the shining example of the Negro race—proof that anyone could achieve in America if he had the determination. Unlike Just, Carver never aspired to take his place alongside the great scientists of his day in their well-equipped, well-financed research facilities. To his death in 1943, Carver was quite satisfied to work in his small laboratory at Tuskegee, unraveling the mysteries of the peanut and the sweet potato and encouraging other young Negro students to follow in his footsteps.

It is difficult to evaluate Carver's real scientific contributions. Richard Bardolph writes that his "reputation in the scientific community fell far short of his stature as a Negro curiosity."[36] Contemporary Negro scientists like Nabrit and Branson seem to support this contention. While both agree that part of the difficulty in assessing Carver's work is the fact that in his long life he never published a single paper in a standard professional journal, Branson does acknowledge that Carver's fame unquestionably did stimulate interest in scientific work among Negroes.[37] Nabrit later penned a particularly illuminating comment on his early impression of Carver the scientist:

> I heard a lecture by Carver when I was in high school. The row of bottles was impressive. He was mystical and frequently referred to these mechanically different forms of the peanut or potato products as the results of Divine revelation. His humbleness and his willingness to accept humiliation made him a Southern hero, but not a scientist.[38]

There can be no question that Carver made white America feel good with his refusal to criticize racial injustices—not even when he was expelled from the public parks near Tuskegee when he wandered in to look at the flowers did he object—but he also made significant contributions to the science of agronomy in the South. Discovered by Booker T. Washington after he had completed his master's degree at Iowa State College in 1896, he returned with him to Tuskegee Institute. There he gained fame by extracting literally hundreds of products from the peanut, sweet potato, and soybean. From the peanut he produced meal, instant and dry coffee, bleach, wood filler, metal polish, paper, ink, shaving cream, rubbing oil, linoleum, synthetic rubber, and plastics. From the soybean he obtained flour, breakfast food, and milk; in addition, he developed some 100 products from the sweet potato.

Carver's work on scientific techniques to improve the land was also applauded, and when upon his death he was fittingly laid to rest beside Booker T. Washington, he left his life's savings to Tuskegee for the establishment of the George Washington Carver Foundation to assist the education of young Negro scientists. Perhaps Carver's personal world of science can most fittingly be summed up by his own explanation of how he worked:

> I have made it a rule to get up every morning at four. I go into the woods and there I gather specimens and study the great lessons that Nature is eager to teach us. Alone in the woods each morning I best hear and understand God's plan for me.[39]

Black scientists in the pre-World War II period were similar to both Just and Carver in that they were usually restricted to Negro colleges and universities: Hyman Y. Chase, a student of Just's at Howard, made important studies on the effect of radiant energy upon animal cells; Samuel M. Nabrit, later President of Texas Southern University, published the results of his studies on biological regeneration in the leading scientific journals; Thomas Wyatt Turner, chairman of the Department of Biology at Hampton Institute, critically studied the effect of mineral nutrients upon seed plants, the physiological effects of nitrogen and of phosphorus upon plants, and experiments in cotton breeding; Charles Stewart Parke, the chairman of Biology at Howard during the 1930's, discovered and described thirty-nine species of plants and became the author of some sixty scholarly papers; and Elmer Samuel Imes, a physicist, did original work in infra-red absorption bands while at Fiske. This list of those who contributed significantly to the sciences while usually carrying heavy teaching loads at their respective schools could be extended, but there were also a few Negro scientists by World War II who had worked their way into private industry.

Lloyd Augustus Hall, born in 1894, received his secondary

education in Aurora, Illinois, and his college training in chemistry at Northwestern University and the University of Chicago. During World War I he served as a research chemist in explosives for the Ordnance Department of the U.S. Army. Later he became the chief chemist and director of research for Griffith Laboratories in Chicago, and in this capacity he was responsible for great changes in the meat-packing industry with his development of a curing salt for the preserving and processing of meats.[40]

The best known Negro scientist in the world of white industry in the pre-World War II days was Percy L. Julian. Julian was to rise to the heights of industry, eventually owning his own laboratory, but his background struggle well depicts the difficulties confronting the Negro scientist in America.

Julian was born in Montgomery, Alabama, in 1898, the grandson of a slave who ironically lost part of his hand for daring to learn to read, and the son of a railroad clerk who sent his wife and entire family northward to receive a better education.[41] The young Percy graduated valedictorian from DePauw in 1920, and after a short teaching interim at Fiske, won a scholarship to Harvard University. At Harvard his genius was quickly recognized but, unfortunately, so was his color. Paul deKruif later wrote: "Harvard usually appointed men of that [scholastic] rank as teaching assistants, but the authorities explained that they feared Southern white students might not accept him as a teacher."[42] Accordingly, he remained at Harvard for four years in minor fellowships before returning to teaching at West Virginia State College for Negroes where, according to deKruif "His laboratory had next to no apparatus. He was the one-man chemistry faculty, and a laboratory storekeeper and janitor as well."[43]

From West Virginia State Julian moved on to Howard University where he planned and built a million-dollar laboratory. He might have remained at Howard indefinitely, but a former white friend from Harvard days offered to finance his doctoral work; this was completed at the University of Vienna in 1931. He returned to resume his teaching at Howard, moved on to DePauw, and received his first real acclaim when he synthesized the drug physostigmine, used in the treatment of the dreaded eye disease, glaucoma. Dean William Blanchard of DePauw recommended that Julian be made chairman of the chemistry department, which would have made him the first Negro professor of chemistry in any white institution in America. But the appointment was deemed "inadvisable," and in 1936 Julian left the world of academe to join the research department of the Glidden Corporation in Chicago.

At Glidden, Julian's first task was to work with soybeans, from which he extracted the protein to be used in coating paper. His soya protein was also used in creating the foam fire extinguishers used during World War II, called Aero-foam or "bean soup." But his most outstanding achievement was his successful isolation and synthesis of male and female hormones.

After the war Julian opened his own Julian Industries where, in addition to making hormone preparations, he succeeded in making the drug cortisone available to consumers at a reasonable cost. But even in this most successful period of his life, Julian exemplified the peculiar duality of life confronting the Negro genius. On the one hand his scientific achievements continued to be applauded—in fact, he was named man of the year by a Chicago newspaper—but when he moved into Oak Park, an exclusive Chicago suburb, his home had to be guarded for over a year.[44]

During World War II the necessity of the times further widened opportunities for the Negro scientist. At least two Negroes worked on the Manhattan Project to develop the atomic bomb. William J. Knox, a chemist with his doctorate from Massachusetts Institute of Technology, worked on the project at Columbia University between 1943 and 1945;[45] and J. Ernest Wilkins, who received his doctorate from the University of Chicago at the tender age of nineteen, applied his mathematical genius to the project at his alma mater.[46]

The list of Negro scientists in the postwar era is an increasingly long one, and what is perhaps more important than a further listing of names is the recognition of the promise for the future. It is true that most of our predominantly white universities have now opened their laboratories to people of color and it is likewise a fact that industry can no longer afford to use color as a substitute for talent in its hiring practices, but perhaps the greatest promise for the future is exemplified by a twenty-five-year-old Negro who, while serving a life sentence in a Missouri prison, has been trying to publish his manuscript on "Science and Africa: Essays on the Part Which Folk of Color Have Played in the Development of the Natural Sciences."[47] Surely the undiscovered potential of this young lad, as well as the recognized genius of a Percy Julian or a J. Ernest Wilkins, hold the key to the future for the Black-American man of science.

SELECTED BIBLIOGRAPHY

BOOKS

Adams, Russell L., *Great Negroes Past and Present,* Chicago: Afro-American Publishing Co., 1963. A collection of short, somewhat superficial sketches of famous Negroes; it includes some of the men of science described in this paper. It does cite additional sources for further reference.

Baker, Henry Edwin, *The Colored Inventor,* New York: The Crisis Publishing Co., 1913. It is Baker who is responsible for most of the information we have on the pre-twentieth-century Negro inventors.

Bardolph, Richard, *The Negro Vanguard,* New York: Random House, Inc., 1959. Bardolph's book includes sketches of prominent Negroes from all walks of life whom he succeeds in placing into historical perspective. His "Essay on Authorities" is excellent and comprehensive.

Bennett, Lerone, *Pioneers in Protest,* Chicago: Johnson Publishing Co., 1968. Bennett includes a good, readable chapter on Banneker.

Block, Maxine, ed., *Current Biography,* New York: H. W. Wilson, 1940. This 1940 edition includes a sketch of George Washington Carver; the 1947 edition, Percy Julian; the 1963 edition, Samuel M. Nabrit.

Cattell, Jacques, ed., *American Men of Science,* Tempe, Arizona: Arizona State University Press, 1960. A "Who's Who" of American science, but it does not designate race.

Graham, Shirley and Lipscomb, George D., *Dr. George Washington Carver, Scientist,* New York: J. Messner, Inc., 1944. Written on the inspirational level with a young audience in mind.

Graham, Shirley, *Your Most Humble Servant,* New York: J. Messner, 1949. A moving, adulatory biography of Benjamin Banneker written in the "I was there" style.

Holt, Margaret Van Vechten (Rackham Holt, pseud.), *George Washington Carver, an American Biography,* 2d ed. revised. Garden City, New York: Doubleday, 1963. A well-received, sympathetic study of Carver and the prejudiced America in which he worked. Though this is perhaps the best biography of Carver, it still does not include a good analysis of the real scientific significance of his work.

Katz, William Loren, *Eyewitness: The Negro in American History,* New York: Pitman Publishing Corp., 1967. Written for a young audience, Katz contains sketches on many famous Negroes.

Malone, Dumas and Johnson, Allen, eds., *Dictionary of American Biography,* New York: Charles Scribner's Sons, 1933. The *DAB* has sketches of McCoy, Matzeliger, Delany, and Forton but overlooks many prominent Negroes in science.

Robinson, Wilhelmena. *Historical Negro Biographies,* New York: Publishers Co., Inc., 1967. Short, superficial sketches of many famous Negroes.

Taylor, Julius, ed. *The Negro in Science,* Baltimore: Morgan State College Press, 1955. Contains an excellent introductory essay by Herman Branson on "The Negro Scientist." The rest of the book is made up of essays by prominent Negro men of science on their particular field of study; hence these essays are of a highly technical nature, written in the hope of attracting attention to the work being done by Negro scientists.

Tempels, Father Placide. *Bantu Philosophy,* Paris: 1959. This small book is especially helpful in distinguishing the different concepts of science in the Bantu mind.

The Negro Handbook, compiled by the editors of *Ebony.* Chicago: Johnson Publishing Co., 1966. The *Handbook* contains brief samplings of some of the more recent Negro inventors, as well as the more famous ones of the past.

ARTICLES

Baker, Henry E. "The Negro in the Field of Invention," *Jour-*

nal of Negro History, II, January, 1917, 21-36. This article is based on his long and thorough research on Negroes who might have listed their inventions with the U.S. Patent Office.

Branson, Herman. "The Negro and Scientific Research," *Negro History Bulletin*, XVI, April, 1952, 131-136, 151. A good introduction into the role of the Negro in science, past and present.

Chapman, Frank E., "Science and Africa," *Freedomways*, VI, Summer, 1966, 235-245. Excerpts from Chapman's unpublished manuscript by the same title.

deKruif, Paul, "The Man Who Wouldn't Give Up," *Readers Digest*, XLIX, August, 1946, 113-118. A brief account of Just's achievements and the obstacles he faced because of his race.

Downing, Leslie K., "Contributions of Negro Scientists," *Crisis*, XLVI, June, 1939, 167-169, 187. Contains a considerable list of contemporary Negro scientists.

Drew, Charles R., "Negro Scholars in Scientific Research," *Journal of Negro History*, XXXV, January, 1950, 135-149. Presents the problems and hopes of Negro scientists, as well as sketches of contemporary scientists.

Lillie, Frank R., "Ernest Everett Just," *Science*, XCV, January 1942, 10-11. Written upon the occasion of Just's death, the white Dr. Lillie discusses the contributions and problems of his black friend and colleague.

Meade, George, "A Negro Scientist of Slavery Days," *Scientific Monthly*, LXII April 1946, 317-326. It was this article by Meade which renewed the all-but-forgotten reputation of Norbert Rillieux.

Nabrit, Samuel M., "Ernest E. Just," *Phylon*, VII, 2d Quarter, 1946, 121-125. Nabrit describes the racial torment of his former teacher as well as his achievements.

————, "The Negro in Science," *The Negro History Bulletin*, XX, January, 1957, 84-86. A brief evaluation of the contributions and limitations of the Negro in science.

————, "Negroes Distinguished in Sciences," *Negro History Bulletin*, II, May, 1939, 67-70. Contains sketches of Banneker, Turner, Just, and Carver.

Oliver, Vernell McCarroll, "Historical Significance of Benjamin Banneker," *Negro History Bulletin*, XV, May, 1952, 155, 159. Emphasizes the need to place Banneker in his rightful place in

American history.

Tubbs, V., "Adjustment of a Genius," *Ebony*, XIII, February, 1958, 60-62. A brief sketch of the mathematical genius, J. Ernest Wilkins.

NOTES

1. These pages on "The African and His Science" are the work of Dr. Ronald W. Davis, the Director of African Studies at Western Michigan University.

2. Father Placide Tempels, *Bantu Philosophy,* Paris: 1959, p. 61.

3. Charles R. Drew, "Negro Scholars in Scientific Research," *Journal of Negro History,* Vol. XXXV, January, 1950, p. 135.

4. Herman Branson, "The Negro and Scientific Research," *Negro History Bulletin,* Vol. XVI, April, 1952, p. 131.

5. Samuel M. Nabrit, "The Negro in Science," *Negro History Bulletin,* Vol. XX, January, 1957, p. 84.

6. Julius Taylor, Ed., *The Negro in Science,* Baltimore: Morgan State College Press, 1955.

7. Branson, *op. cit.,* p. 133.

8. Some sources say Blair's first patent was on a seed planter; however, in 1836 Blair received a second patent and this could well have been the seed planter.

9. Baker's four bound volumes are located in the Moorland Foundation Room of the Howard University Founders Library in Washington, D.C. Baker described his work and the results in an article: "The Negro in the Field of Invention," *Journal of Negro History,* Vol. II, January, 1917, pp. 21-36.

10. Baker, *op. cit.,* p. 24.

11. Cyrus McCormick, *The Century of the Reaper,* New York: Houghton Mifflin, 1931, p. 11.

12. Baker, *op. cit.,* p. 24.

13. *Dictionary of American Biography,* Dumas Malone and Allen Johnson, Eds., New York: Charles Scribner's Sons, 1933, Vol. VI, p. 617; see also Richard Bardolph, *The Negro Vanguard,* New York: Random House, Inc., 1959, p. 40.

14. The belated recognition for Rillieux's work is due largely to a fine article written by George Meade on the 100th anniversary of the invention of Rillieux's multiple-effect evaporator: "A Negro Scientist of Slavery Days," *Scientific Monthly,* Vol. LXII, April, 1946, pp. 317-326. This article was reprinted with valuable notes by Sidney Kaplan, *Negro History Bulletin,* Vol. XX, April, 1957, pp. 159-164.

15. Charles Rousseve, *The Negro in Louisiana,* New Orleans: Xavier University Press, 1937, p. 52.

16. Kaplan, *op. cit.,* p. 163.

17. Dictionary of American Biography, *op. cit.,* Vol. XII, pp. 426-427; Bardolph, *op. cit.,* p. 124; see also Wilhelmena Robinson, *Historical Negro*

Biographies, New York: Publishers Co., Inc., 1967, p. 99; and Russell L. Adams, *Great Negroes Past and Present,* Chicago: Afro-American Publishing Co., 1963, p. 51.

18. Adams, *op. cit.,* p. 52; Bardolph, *op. cit.,* pp. 257-258; see also Benjamin Brawley, *Negro Builders and Heroes,* Chapel Hill, North Carolina: University of North Carolina Press, 1937, pp. 227-228.

19. *Dictionary of American Biography, op. cit.,* Vol. XII, p. 617; see also Carter Woodson, *The Negro in Our History,* ninth ed. Washington, D.C.: The Associated Publishers, 1947, pp. 465-466.

20. "The Negro Inventor," *The Negro Handbook,* Compiled by the editors of *Ebony.* Chicago: Johnson Publishing Co., 1966, p. 322.

21. As cited in a statement issued by the Edison Pioneers upon the occasion of Latimer's death in 1928; cited in William Loren Katz, *Eyewitness: The Negro in American History,* New York: Pitman Publishing Corp., 1967, pp. 300-301.

22. Katz, *op. cit.,* pp. 289-290.

23. Robinson, *op. cit.,* p. 230 and Katz, *op. cit.,* p. 292, both include an interesting anecdote. They credit Morgan with being on the scene of a 1916 Ohio mine disaster with his gas mask with which he was able to save several trapped miners; however, the *New York Times* of the day mentions the disaster but neither Morgan nor his gas mask.

24. Bardolph, *op. cit.,* p. 258.

25. Lerone Bennett, *Pioneers in Protest,* Chicago: Johnson Publishing Co., 1968, p. 14.

26. Vernell McCarroll Oliver, "Historical Significance of Benjamin Banneker," *Negro Historical Bulletin,* Vol. XV, May, 1952, pp. 155, 159.

27. Much of the information on Banneker dates back to Martha Ellicott Tyson's *Banneker, the Afric-American Astronomer* (1884). Tyson was a descendant of the Ellicott family which befriended Banneker in his youth and later, through Thomas Jefferson, obtained for him his Washington commission.

28. Oliver, *op. cit.,* p. 159.

29. *Ibid.*

30. John James Audubon has been referred to as a man of colored blood. This debate over his parentage stems from the fact that his mother, a Mlle. Rabin, was simply referred to as a "Creole" by the delivering doctor; but the word "Creole" in Spanish and French means only of European descent. In any case, Mlle. Rabin died shortly after the illegitimate birth of John, taking the mystery of her ancestry with her to the grave. See Alexander B. Adams, *John James Audubon,* New York: Putnam's, 1966, p. 489.

31. Russell Adams, *op. cit.,* p. 54; *Dictionary of American Biography, op. cit.,* Vol. V, pp. 219-220.

32. Earlier Delany had written *The Condition, Elevation, and Destiny of the Colored People of the United States Politically Considered* (1852).

33. Samuel M. Nabrit, "Negroes Distinguished in Sciences," *Negro Historical Bulletin,* Vol. II, May, 1939, pp. 67-70.

34. *Ibid.,* "Ernest E. Just," *Phylon,* Vol. VII, 2nd Quarter, 1946, p. 121.

35. Frank R. Lillie, "Ernest Everett Just," *Science,* Vol. XCV, 2 January 1942, pp. 10-11.

36. Bardolph, *op. cit.,* p. 248.

37. Branson, *op cit.,* p. 131.

38. Nabrit, "The Negro in Science," *op. cit.,* p. 84.

39. *Current Biography,* Maxine Block, Ed., New York: H. W. Wilson,

1940, pp. 148-150.

40. Leslie K. Downing, "Contributions of Negro Scientists," *Crisis,* Vol. XLVI, June, 1939, pp. 167-169, 187.

41. Eventually the six Julian children received fourteen degrees. Each boy in the family received his doctorate; each girl, her masters.

42. Paul deKruif, "The Man Who Wouldn't Give Up," *Readers Digest,* August, 1946, p. 114.

43. *Ibid.*

44. Bardolph, *op. cit.,* p. 432; Robinson, *op. cit.,* p. 218; *Current Biography, op. cit.,* 1947, pp. 338-340.

45. *American Men of Science,* 10th ed., Jacques Cattell, Ed., Tempe, Arizona: Arizona State University Press, 1960, p. 2202.

46. *Who's Who in Atoms,* 4th ed. London: Harrap Research Publications, 1965, p. 1402; see also V. Tubbs, "Adjustment of a Genius," *Ebony,* Vol. XIII, February, 1958, pp. 60-62.

47. A review of Frank E. Chapman Jr.'s "Science and Africa," appears in *Freedomways,* Vol. VI, Summer, 1966, pp. 235-245.

LEWIS H. CARLSON was born in 1934 in Muskegon, Michigan. He received his B.A. and M.A. from the Universtiy of Michigan and his Ph. D. from Michigan State University in 1967. His doctoral dissertation was "J. Parnell Thomas and the House Committee on Un-American Activities, 1938-1948." Dr. Carlson is now an Assistant Professor of History at Western Michigan University, where he teaches courses in Recent U.S. and Afro-American history. He has published articles in the field of Afro-American history.

THE AMERICAN NEGRO'S CONTRIBUTIONS
TO RELIGIOUS THOUGHT

J. Deotis Roberts

Howard University (Washington, D.C.)

The Negro's contribution to religious thought in America is considerable. But due to neglect of treatment and the often unsystematic character of presentation, his contribution has not been widely known. The comprehensive nature of the subject assigned to me allows for a variety of approaches to religious thought. Is Joseph Washington correct when he asserts that there is an absence of theology among blacks?[1] He sees this as an explanation as to why brilliant laymen and clergy are not attracted as spokesmen for the faith. There is little intellectual endeavour in religion and, thus, no place for creative and independent thinkers. Washington concludes that blacks can only boast of leaders (and we may add—writers) in the field of race relations. Notwithstanding this judgment, it is my view that many black writers have reflected upon religion as artists, poets, philosophers, psychologists, ethicists and mystics.

The Negro's contribution to theology as a specialty has been insignificant, even though several prominent Negroes have earned doctorates in this field. Among those who have such distinction are Martin Luther King, Jr., B. E. Mays and Samuel Proctor. In most instances the racial crisis and its pressures on the personal lives of Blacks, together with a fellow-feeling for all members of their suffering race, has led them from theology as an academic pursuit. Even at the present time all advanced degree programs in theology are supervised by Whites. To my knowl-

75

edge, no major appointment of a Negro in the field of theology has ever been made. Nathan Scott, who is at Chicago University, is more of a literary critic with religious insights than a theologian, even if he is known as professor of theology and literature. Advisors have often "stereotyped" black[2] students for ethics and practical theology. Most job opportunities and even seminary appointments are limited to such areas of specialization. Even those who fight the issue through their graduate studies programs find opportunities for employment and development almost non-existent and bow to the inevitable.

The province of our concern is limited to the Negro's contribution to religion in the United States. Historically, we move securely only in this century. We do not deny a heritage that began before the Mayflower. This period does provide a more reasonable historic framework within which to discuss our subject. Many of the contributions discussed come from persons within the memory of the present writer, who has been inspired personally by several of his noted black brothers.

There will be certain broad categories under which we will present the material. This does not imply that other ways of organizing the material could not have been found. The reader will observe that this writer is closely tied to theological education, since the schema of my essay emerges from the seminary curriculum. This is a convenient way to provide sub-topics for our discussion. My choice of representative thinkers is limited to men of considerable formal education, though I am aware that others have made their mark. Most have written at least one substantial work which may serve as a tangible basis for evaluation. What cannot be done in this brief study concerning the Negro's contribution to religious thought needs to be done at another time and in future writings.

THE NEGRO IN CHRISTIAN ETHICS

It is in the field of ethics that the Negro has made his most signal contribution to religious thought. The most celebrated contributor to this field, perhaps in the history of the American Negro, was Martin Luther King, Jr. This was witnessed to in his life and even by his death. His field was ethics, even though he studied intensely in philosophy and theology. He was deeply influenced by the personalism of the Boston School and was greatly impressed by his teacher, Harold DeWolf. But scarcely did King complete his study before he was plunged to the hilt in the Montgomery racial crisis as leader of a bus boycott under the sponsorship of the Montgomery Improvement Association. As the minister of the Dexter Avenue Baptist Church, King was drafted as leader of the movement. The racial problem had haunted King from childhood. He had observed patterns of segregation in Chester, Pennsylvania and Boston, Massachusetts, as well as in Atlanta, Georgia. During summers, while studying in the North, he had assisted his father at Ebenezer Baptist Church in Atlanta. Thus, he could speak and act knowingly against segregation wherever he confronted it.

It became clear to King, as he became the acknowledged leader in Montgomery, that ethics rather than theology must claim his thought and life. He looked again at Gandhi's understanding of non-violence but he preached the Christian ethic of love. According to King, "Jesus gave him the message while Gandhi gave him the method." What he really sought was social justice. In some ways King was closer to Amos than to Jesus. Better still, King combined ethical traits of both Amos and Jesus. He conceived of the Christian God as one who is lovingly just. He believed, therefore, that love and justice must somehow be reconciled in the Christian's experience. Because of King's deep involvement in the racial struggle, almost to the point of a messianic consciousness, he did not have the time, nor did he sense the need, to formulate a constructive and well-organized statement of his thought. Under the pressure of "black power" there was a type of desperation toward the end of his life to prove the pragmatic validity of his non-violent approach to better race relations. In his militant crisis-precipitating approach to race relations, he sought to provide a viable alternative to "black power". At this point King moved further away from any significant contribution to Christian ethical thought. Since he died on the eve of what he called an ultimate attempt to vindicate non-violence, we shall never know what goals he would have offered after the Poor People's Campaign. King was a charismatic leader and thus it is not possible to assess his total impact upon religious thought and life. His was a great life which defies an accurate, detached judgment.

His contribution was immense and it is not yet time to fully appreciate it.[3]

George D. Kelsey is a different breed of black moralist. He is more rational and more precise in his reflections upon Christian ethical principles. His is not an ethic completely detached from life. Indeed, it would almost be impossible for a Negro to write such a work. He would need to be insensitive to his own sufferings and those of his loved ones. As far as it is possible for a black man to write an "ivory tower" ethic, Kelsey's is representative. During much of his life he has lived above the fray, both as a student and, later, as a professor. Kelsey has long been recognized as a Christian ethicist, but an ethicist of a different stamp from the "involvement" approach of Martin Luther King, Jr.

Kelsey was born in Georgia and trained at Harvard and Yale. He taught at Morehouse College and from there moved to Drew University, where he is at this writing Professor of Christian Ethics. His definitive work is *Racism and the Christian Understanding of Man*. In this book Kelsey promises "to provide a Christian criticism of racism as a faith system."[4] His prescription is the overcoming of racism through faith in Christ, through whose grace self-centeredness, evident in the pride of race, is replaced. Man is renewed and God becomes the center. Kelsey has read Brunner with great care. Theologically, he stands securely within the camp of Neo-Reformation thought. There is little evidence that he has reacted critically to this tradition but has embraced it fondly. The recent changes in both theology and ethics seem to have passed him by and left him unmoved.

Kelsey does show more hopeful promise in his expert analysis of social, economic and political materials. But one is disappointed that even the "black revolution" has not really grabbed him. As one of the few mature scholars in Christian ethics of his race, he has not provided sufficient guidelines. His confrontation with the "counter-racist," the Black Muslims,[5] is too little and too late, since many black separatists now reject both Allah and Jehovah with impunity, saying that they do not desire to be "hung up" on either. In all fairness to Kelsey, we must add that Black Power has gained momentum most recently and it is very difficult to reverse or to reassess the work of a lifetime momentarily.[6] One does have to bear in mind, however, that "new occasions teach new duties." Is Joseph Washington correct? He says, "Kelsey is most relevant when he is least theological."[7]

C. Eric Lincoln is an ethicist whose specialization is the sociology of religion. At the present time he is Professor of Sociology and Religion at Union Theological Seminary. In this post he was among the first members of his race to be appointed to a major teaching position in any non-black theological seminary, notwithstanding the strong figures in ethics at Union and at other liberal seminaries. Lincoln is recognized as one of the most perceptive and respected authorities on race relations in the field of religion. Lincoln was born in Athens, Alabama. He was educated at LeMoyne College, Fisk University, The University of Chicago and Boston University. Three factors have catapulted him to his present standing in the scholarly world: 1) he is in the field of race relations, which has been conceded by the white society as the Negro's territory as a scholar; 2) he is competent in the field of sociological research; and 3) he is recognized as a gifted and prolific writer.[8]

His book, *The Black Muslims in America,* launched him as a recognized sociologist of religion. Lincoln struck upon a very important and timely subject. He published his findings; this is important. I am aware of other studies by Negro scholars which are just as important but which gather dust in seminary and university libraries around the country. Lincoln, however, has put us in his debt in this regard. He became aware that many Negroes were despairing of the Christian faith as a way of life capable of affording them the respect and dignity they seek and deserve. They have concluded that Christian love is the white man's love for himself and for his race. It seemed natural for the black man to look for a more relevant faith.

For black men disillusioned with Christianity, the Black Muslim message has real appeal. In my view, the Black Muslim movement is more a "Christian heresy" than it is a "Muslim sect." It is tailored to answer the legitimate gripes of Negroes in a racist society. Its strongest contributions to Negro life are social, economic and political. For example, it is to be commended for rehabilitation of criminals, improvements in family relations and economic betterment. The Black Muslims hold to a Puritan ethic which is highly legalistic. The Bible is quoted more often than the Koran. The theology is a mixture of surface insights from Islam as well as from Christianity. God is called Allah rather than Jehovah. To my knowledge, no leader in the movement has been schooled in classical Islam. Those who have studied Islam seem to drop out of the movement. The ties with Islam (mainly Egyptian, perhaps because Egypt happens to be in North Africa) appear to be more diplomatic than theological.

Lincoln's work remains one of two definitive studies of the Black Muslims.[9] Even though he has written since about the race problem in general, it was this study which launched his career. As a sociologist of religion, Lincoln was not equipped to delve into a critical evaluation of the phenomenological and theological pre-suppositions of the Black Muslims, especially the disparity or affinity between this phenomenon in America and the world-wide Islamic religion, which is indeed one of the great religions of man.[10] All who perceive the importance of this phenomenon called the "Black Muslims" realize the magnitude of Lincoln's contribution. This contribution increases as one observes the affinity between the Black Muslims and the more widespread Black Power movement. The anticipations of Black Power in the Black Muslim movement extend far beyond any prophecy which Lincoln might have made in the early 1960's.

Yet another contributor to ethics is Joseph R. Washington, Jr. Washington is a native of Iowa and is at present Dean of the Chapel at Albion College. He was educated at the University of Wisconsin, Andover Newton Theological School and Boston University. Unlike most black writers in the field of religion, he is not a native of the South. This may explain his "honeymoon" with integration, followed by a radical re-assessment of his earlier position. For a very brief period he was Dean of the Chapel at Dillard University in New Orleans. This limited acquaintance with the South did not provide him with a sufficient orientation to identify with the racial situation in that part of the country. Most of his concern for the problem has been from the North and in "integrated" teaching posts. This may explain his first controversial book, *Black Religion.* What happened in the dark ghettoes of the North in the last few "long, hot summers," and the "black power" and "black awareness" that has been aroused, has confronted all Negroes with a stark realism. This may explain the revisionism in Washington's thought as he moves from *Black Religion* to *The Politics of God.*

In *Black Religion* Washington makes several bold assertions about deficiencies in the Negro's religion: 1) an inadequate sense of the historic church; 2) insufficient roots in the Christian tradition; 3) the absence of a meaningful theological frame of reference; 4) no real longing for renewal; 5) a weak ecumenical impulse; and 6) no true commitment to an inclusive Church.

It is Washington's belief that the Negro in America is only a partial member of either the secular or the Christian community. The Negro develops sub-cultures and sub-religions. His non-acceptance in the Christian mainstream produces a preference for an ethical religion which endeavours to provide some relief from the tensions of being a Negro in America, but also tends to exclude other equally indispensable dimensions of the Christian faith. The socio-economic forces excluding the Negro from full participation in the society also exclude him from full participation in the Christian faith.

In *Black Religion* Washington suggests that Negroes be converted from their Jesusology and folk religion into mainstream Protestantism. This is where they will find salvation. It is the responsibility of white Christians to integrate Negroes *en masse* until they have been assimilated in this august white body. Negroes are potentially Protestant, though not historically or theologically so. Initiative must be from white Christians. They must risk all for the sake of this minority. The Negro should close his house of worship and exist only as a defensive operation.

In *The Politics of God* Washington has made what appears to me to be a radical change in outlook. Whereas *Black Religion* sought to urge Negroes to join the mainstream of white religion, *The Politics of God* concludes that white religion is bankrupt. What he calls "white folk religion" is antithetical to the Kingdom of God. He sees the Negro Church as existing on a separate basis for the indefinite future. He now feels that Negroes should question rather than accept "white-folk theology." He distinguishes between the Church and churches. The true Church is the servant of the Kingdom of God. It now seems probable that Negroes can be, as Christians, "suffering servants" and "chosen people." He sees the need to combine the biblical promise and the Negro's experience. He now pleads for "a conscious rejection of white theological and ecclesiastical double-talk and

81

a conscious acceptance of their black promise."[11]

The Negro is said to be "an involuntary suffering servant," whereas whites who *choose* to suffer are not to suffer *with* the Negro. The suffering of the Negro is not of his own choosing and cannot be escaped.[12] He desires an affirmative and constructive understanding of the suffering servant role—not one of deprivation, defensiveness and escapism stemming from an inferiority complex. The Negro Church must now take on the reconciling role which white churches were asked to perform in *Black Religion*. The Negro Church has the responsibility to enter black politics and release all men from the sin of "in-groupness." Black politics are good politics—the politics of God.

It is very difficult to explain such a radical about-face in a few years. But it is often true that one major traumatic experience in a Negro's life in America—North or South—is sufficient to change an extremely optimistic outlook on race relations into a more realistic one. I have no knowledge as to why Washington's strong "integrationist" position should change suddenly into a militant "separatist" view.[13] Perhaps the "black consciousness" which has seized the Negro community has been for Washington a new inspiration.

My final example in the broad field of Christian Ethics is William A. Banner, who is Professor of Philosophy at Howard University. He has been for more than a decade a beloved associate of mine. Banner was educated at Pennsylvania State, Yale and Harvard. His skills as a teacher have been widely recognized and thus he has taught at Smith College, the University of Colorado and the University of Rhode Island. It was during his year as a visiting professor of philosophy at Yale that he prepared his most recent work, *Ethics: An Introduction to Moral Philosophy*.

In this book Banner attempts to be existential and realist at once and to relate social and metaphysical issues. He is concerned with the unity of personal and public morality. His selection of moral philosophers and questions from Socrates to the present is representative and noteworthy. Banner taught Historical Theology in the School of Religion at Howard University before joining the faculty of Philosophy. It is not surprising that great Christian moralists like Augustine, Aquinas and Reinhold Niebuhr are given large-scale treatment. Banner's contribution to philosophical ethics is unique for a black scholar. Few black men possess either the philosophical, historical or theological skills needed for such a contribution to the field of ethics. We hope that Banner will find it possible to provide scholars and laymen alike with needed guidance for these troubled times. Banner is basically a philosophical and religious "thinker," and it is in the province of "thought" that the present racial revolution is most poverty-stricken.

This brief but representative coverage of the Negro's contribution to Christian ethics indicates several points of view. Martin Luther King represents an ethical stance which is informed by philosophy and theology but is not intensely indulgent in either discipline. George Kelsey's views are informed by Biblical faith and neo-Reformation theology, but he is much stronger in his use of humanistic sciences. Eric Lincoln approaches religion from the sociological point of view. He applies sociological theories and methods to religion. He is not really concerned about intense theological interpretation of his subject matter. Joseph Washington, though similar to Lincoln in orientation, has given more attention to biblical and theological questions. Calvin appears to be his master theologian in *The Politics of God*. In the ethical field he appears to be seeking both a method and a message. Since he has raised such important questions, it is important that he find his way. Last, but not least, William Banner has made his mark as a contributor to philosophical ethics. His work represents the blazing of a new trail for Negroes in the field of Christian Ethics. The following comment remains to be said: upon examining the rich heritage of the Negro in this field, one wonders why most if not all books in Christian Ethics have either ignored the Negro's insights or given them inadequate treatment. This limited but timely recognition is long over-due.

HISTORICAL AND THEOLOGICAL ANALYSIS

Miles Mark Fisher combined a vigorous intellectual pursuit of knowledge and an active ministry for many years. He was at once Professor of Church History at Shaw University in Raleigh, North Carolina, and minister of the White Rock Baptist Church of Durham, North Carolina. He brought honor and distinction

83

to both institutions. His teaching and ministry were a great inspiration to me during my early theological studies. His knowledge of the Negro Church was extensive. His ability as a preacher was awe-inspiring to his students, to whom he also taught homiletics. His work as preacher and pastor was greatly enriched by his lifetime of study in reference to the history of the Negro Church and the meaning of Negro spirituals.

Fisher's father was Elijah Fisher, who was for many years the distinguished pastor of the Mt. Olivet Baptist Church of Chicago. Elijah Fisher was a great inspiration to his son. One published book by Miles Mark Fisher treats of the life and ministry of his father. During his childhood in Chicago, as a son of the pastor of a large black church in a Northern ghetto, he became aware of racial patterns outside of the South. During his own ministry to a large and very prestigious "bourgeois" congregation in the South, his experience in the church life of Negroes was varied and complete.

Miles Mark Fisher's most important work for our purpose is his *Negro Slave Songs in the United States,* which was published by the American Historical Society. While studying the Psalms at the University of Chicago's Divinity School, Fisher became excited over the idea that the spirituals might be more than folk music. He was allowed to investigate Negro songs for his doctoral dissertation. The same manuscript was later updated, re-written and published.

In his *Negro Slave Songs in the United States* Fisher has provided a completely new approach to spirituals. He started with the use made of songs in Africa and interpreted the Negro songs in that light. The songs conveyed veiled messages between the Negroes, the meaning of which was not known to their slave masters. The Negro developed a vocabulary and means of expression that was entirely his own. Some songs may have carried two messages, depending upon the purpose for which they were being used. "Heaven" for example, could refer to Canada or the Future Life. Whether one feels that Fisher's research and arguments have justified his conclusions or not, his book is never dull and creates a desire for further knowledge of the meaning of the spirituals beyond their artistic beauty. "Never before," says Fisher, "have the songs of a people woven such charms."[14] He concludes that the spirituals provide the

Negro with "uncommon strength" in their suffering and troubled lives. They permitted pent-up energies to escape.[15] Fisher made great use of the spirituals in preaching and in worship at his church. Those who seek to establish a relationship between Black Religion and Black Power at the present time should explore his contribution. It may be that he anticipates what would be designated today as "black liturgics" and "black hermeneutics."

Another expert analyst of Negro writings of the past is Benjamin Elijah Mays. Whereas Fisher used history as his method, Mays uses theology. Both men completed their Ph.D. degree programs at the University of Chicago. Mays made an intensive study of the "idea of God" as portrayed in Negro literature. It was published later under the title of *The Negro's God*. He was, at one time, Dean of the School of Religion and Professor of Christian Theology at Howard University. From Howard University he moved to the Presidency of Morehouse College in Atlanta. A native of South Carolina and a world traveler, Mays became an expert in race relations and in higher education, as well as an international religious figure.

In his brief work *Seeking to Be Christian in Race Relations*, Mays attempts to state a Christian basis for human relations in the area of race. He states what he considers to be some essential Christian beliefs as they relate to race. He takes up the Christian understanding of God, Man and Sin. He insists that love is central to the Christian ethic and that love of God and love of man are inseparable. He deals with prejudice as a sinful manifestation. This work was published in 1957.

The most important work by Mays for our purpose here is his *The Negro's God*. He attempts in this work to present the historical development of the idea of God in Negro literature from 1760 to 1937, both in its "mass" and in its "classical" expressions. In Mays' own words: ". . . This book represents the first attempt to study the development of the idea of God in Negro literature."[16]

Mays discusses three areas in which the idea of God has developed. They are: 1) an other-worldly or compensatory idea of God; 2) an idea of God as an ethical means to social change; and 3) an extremely pragmatic idea of God. All ideas grow out of social crises. Mays does not attempt a normative job on his

85

subject matter. His is an analytical and descriptive task. In other words, his method is phenomenological.

Jupiter Hammon, according to Mays, was the author of the first poem produced by a Negro in the United States. Hammon felt that God did not sanction slavery but that God does permit it. Negroes should wait on God. If God wants them to be free, He will free them. His ideas are compensatory and serve as an opiate for the people. Hammon presents this conception of God in his "Dialogue Between the Master and Slave."[17] Both slave and master could be good Christians and inherit the Kingdom of God. Hammon was more concerned about salvation in Heaven than he was in any form of social reconstruction. This other-worldly emphasis is different from the ethical emphasis which emphasizes the "impartiality of God and the unity of Mankind." Another way of expressing this latter view is the "Fatherhood of God and the Brotherhood of Man." W. E. B. DuBois sums up this position in his "God made of one blood all nations."[18]

It is surprising that one finds in Negro literature ideas of God involving frustration, doubt, God's impotence and even His non-existence. There is a threat to abandon God as a useful instrument for social change. This mood leads to a denial of His existence in some cases. In his poem, "Heritage", Countee Cullen expresses a view which anticipates Cleage's *Black Messiah*.[19] At times, Du Bois seems to favor this doubtful outlook.[20]

Mays concludes that the Negro used ideas that were compatible with the needs and hopes of a suppressed group. God is just, God is on the side of the right, God is love, God is beauty and God and humanity are one. According to Mays, "the Negro is on an errand for God—they employ the ideas of God that embody the values the Negro seeks."[21]

Mays' book is analytical scholarship at its best. Though he completed this work years ago, its message is fresh and vitally relevant at present. This type of careful and scholarly study of the Negro's experience is greatly needed to overcome some of the harmful effects of some of the materials now being published.[22]

MYSTICISM AND RELIGIOUS PHILOSOPHY

In this category, Howard Thurman has no rival and no second

among his black brothers. It is surprising to me that he has been ignored almost completely in anthologies and works on mysticism. He is, indeed, one of the great mystics of all times. His mysticism is not "introverted," nor is it a mysticism of withdrawal from human problems. His mysticism is practical and urges us toward involvement and engagement in the real world where social and ethical issues are at stake.

Baron von Hügel has said that all vital religion has a mystical element. Thurman has given his life to the exposition of this important aspect of religious experience. Thurman was greatly influenced by Rufus Jones, the distinguished Quaker philosopher of Haverford College. The deep appreciation which Quakerism has for the workings of the Spirit permeates all of Thurman's messages. He visited India early in his professional life and fell under the spell of *Bhakti* mysticism.[23] His upbringing in the Deep South is the best explanation of his outlook. He has a close acquaintance with Negro folk religion and undeserved suffering has often been his lot.

Thurman brought a measure of refinement and sophistication to all strands of thought and experience which fed his genius. As Dean of Chapel and Professor of Philosophy of Religion at Howard University, as Minister of the Church for the Fellowship of All People in San Francisco, and as Dean of Chapel at Boston University, his ability as thinker and his deep mystic sensitivities flowered. In his combination of mysticism and ethics, he resembles the Quakers who are notorious for their "practical mysticism."

Thurman is not a theologian. His contribution is mainly to philosophy of religion in its broadest sense. He is informed by the Christian message—especially the Holy Spirit and the teaching and example of Jesus. He brings an expertise and refinement to "spiritual disciplines" which is unique and deserves the attention of all who sense the importance of mysticism as a vital aspect of religion.

In his *The Luminous Darkness*, Thurman is concerned with what segregation does to the human spirit. The book is "a personal interpretation of the anatomy of segregation and a testimony as to the grounds of hope for the individual."[24]

Thurman, a grandson of slaves, adds this personal word: "The fact that the first twenty-five years of my life were spent in

Florida and in Georgia has left its deep scars in my spirit and has rendered me terribly sensitive to the churning abyss separating white from black."[25]

And finally he clinches the point this way: "There is no waking moment or sleeping interval when one may expect respite from the desolation and despair of segregation."[26]

This statement is both alarming and shocking. It comes from one who appears to "have made it." If he feels this way, then segregation is a cancerous growth throughout American society. Even if "black power" is not the answer, surely some radical changes in race relations in this country are now very much overdue.[27]

According to Thurman, the Negro Church has had a strategic position as an institution in Negro life, making it a rallying center for the civil rights movement. But this is not true because of its religious and ethical teaching. It happens to be the one autonomous institution in the Negro community which is comparatively free from interference from the white community. Here every Negro is somebody.[28]

In *Jesus and the Disinherited,* Thurman tells of how his grandmother's rejection of St. Paul led him away from this Apostle to Jesus himself.[29] Thus he sees a need to treat the life and teachings of Jesus for the benefit of those "with their backs against the wall."[30] Thurman sees a real affinity between the circumstances of Jesus and all disinherited people. While Paul was in many ways an aristocrat who interpreted the Gospels so as to maintain his Roman citizenship, Jesus took his place among the poor and despised common people. Jesus meets the needs of the fear-stricken and hated. He made the love-ethic central.[31] He taught that men are made for one another and that love of God is manifest through love of neighbor.[32]

Deep is the Hunger is a collection of meditations in prose and poetry. Through this book we get a glimpse of the faith of Howard Thurman together with penetrating thought. Thurman the mystic and philosopher are one.[33]

A classic statement by Thurman sums up his religious philosophy: "Human life, even the life of a slave, must be lived worthy of so grand an undertaking. At every moment a crown was placed over his head that he must constantly grow tall enough to wear."[34]

The thought of Howard Thurman appears to be his own in a unique sense. Among the writers discussed in this essay, Thurman's thought seems to be the most warm and personal. His mysticism is deep and has been forged out of the pain of undeserved suffering. His philosophy is profoundly religious and is filled with flashes of insight into the realm of the spirit.

THEOLOGY AND LITERATURE

In his *Modern Literature and the Religious Frontier*, Nathan Scott tells us how he moved into a concern for a "theology of culture." He moved from theology to a consideration of aesthetic and literary problems. He became interested in the role of theology as an interpretation of real life situations. Scott believes that a relation between Christianity and culture is implicit in the faith itself.

In stating that the relationship between the questions of man's cultural existence and the answers given in the *kerygma* are interrelated, Scott reminds us of existential theology in general and Paul Tillich in particular. Scott feels that theological thought must be anthropological. His approach to theology requires an inter-disciplinary method. To this end the literary intelligence is best in its creative self-interpretation of man's culture. He holds that writers like Joyce, Lawrence, Kafka and Eliot have "ventured" in the "centers of our distress" more than the rest of us.[35]

Scott is an enlightened critic of theology as well as literature. A case in point is when he criticizes Karl Barth for creating a chasm between theology and culture through his narrow doctrine of revelation. The problems appear, according to Scott, on the literary side in T. S. Eliot and Cleanth Brooks.[36] Much of Scott's interest has centered in poetry, drama and the novel. His goal is to create a dialogical relationship between the Christian faith and modern literature, "so that art may speak to religion and religion to art."[37] He believes that this engagement may lead to a renewal and deepening of both.

His *Broken Center* carries on the discussion begun in *Modern Literature and the Religious Frontier*. In the *Broken Center*, Scott observes that "the anchoring center of life is broken and . . . the world is therefore abandoned and adrift."[38] This is what underlies most of the modern representative poetry, drama and fiction. There is "a lament that has often been heard as a deep, resounding undertone in the literature of this century."[39] Modern literature has a negatively theological character that compels the critic to turn to theological discourse for evaluation. What was anticipated in his earlier writings has now been validated. He concludes that theological inquiry into the major poetry, fiction and drama can lead to mutual enrichment.

Scott, as a black writer, seems to be relatively unmoved by the racial crisis. As Professor and Chairman of the Theology and Literature Department of the Divinity School at the University of Chicago, he has become the number one specialist in theology and literature at that institution and ranks high in the field throughout the nation. It is obvious that to become a specialist in both theology and literature is almost impossible today. Even though Scott shows considerable acquaintance with philosophical and theological literature, it is as a literary critic with an informed religious outlook that he excels.

The theme of the "tragic vision," which is closely associated with suffering and death, seems to haunt him. Could this be associated with a pre-conscious, perhaps involuntary identification with a suffering people? Scott has much to offer both as a theological interpreter and a literary critic. In this period of "black consciousness," one wonders if he is prepared to aid us through careful and skillful criticism of Negro literature to a personal, social and religious identity. He has done this to some extent but not to the degree that the times demand.

THE HISTORY OF RELIGION

Charles H. Long of the University of Chicago stands alone, among black men, as a specialist in history of religion. It is interesting to note that both Nathan Scott and Charles Long, who have become experts in fields other than religion and race, are located at the same university. Whereas Scott received his earlier grooming at Howard University, Long came up under Wach and Eliade as a student and has continued to grow in his chosen field as a professor. My point is that Chicago University has pioneered in the development of Negro scholars on the faculty level. A great university like Chicago offers opportunities for development that are not available in the best Negro institutions. Against this background, we understand the incentives which have led Scott and Long and Franklin as well to excel in their chosen fields. While these men are gifted and have become worthy examples of what a Negro scholar can become in the best situations, the institutions of higher education must share the blame for thousands of potential Negro scholars who have "withered on the vine" because no suitable opportunity for growth was open to them. The theological schools, which have been most vocal on civil rights, may be seen as the most hypocritical, for they have the worst record of all. The Divinity School of the University of Chicago did not wait for a "caucus of black power students" to apply the necessary pressure for this important move. While the seminarians at this divinity school may not be pleased with things as they are, they are fortunate to have these two distinguished black scholars from whom they may receive inspiration to excel in their chosen field.

Charles Long interprets myth in the field of history of religion. It is his belief that the contemporary discussion centering around the adequacy of myth as a meaningful form of expression for religious experience should be informed by the interpretations which this form of human expression has had in the greater part of history.[40]

The myth is a true story—the myth is a story about reality. It is impossible to understand the reality and being of these people, unless one understands their reality in relationship to the myth. Myths are not true in the literal sense. Myths are not logical, though not illogical or prelogical either. Myth is a type of thinking which represents man's initial confrontation with the power in life. The myth is a symbolic ordering which makes clear how the world is present for man.

Myths have many subjects, but Long is concerned with "What started it?" and "How was it done?" In a word, he is concerned with cosmogonic myths or the myths of creation. He pleads for an overcoming of the conflict between scientific and mythological explanation. Scientific thought cannot do justice for the life of man as he experiences it. Symbols are expressions of man's historical concreteness. Man's true history is the history of his religion.

91

Much of the symbolic expression of man's historical situation has to do with his natural environment, but there is a dimension of the real which is other than the environment. This is the transcendent pole of the symbol. It is the task of the history of religion to interpret human reality in relation to this type of symbolic expression. The symbols which express these meanings to the highest degree are those found in the cosmogonic myths. These are the myths of creation found in almost every culture.

With these premises before him, Long turns to various examples of creation myths found in many lands and among many peoples. He has attempted to make the point that acquaintance with "religion" is the basis for an understanding of "religions." This is one of the best collections of myths available to the student of world religions. In this book and in shorter essays,[41] Long has emerged as an expert interpreter of primitive religions as well as a specialist in methodology and hermeneutics in the field of the history of religion.

As a black man trained in theology and the history of religion, Long is in a unique position to treat the relation between African traditional religion and Afro-American religion. He has shown some interest in meeting this need. Still a young man, he has served as friend and counselor to many black students. Some would not have "made it" without his encouragement. Many students who are not interested in his field admire his ability as a teacher, his integrity as a scholar, and the warmth of his friendship. I have not heard from his white students, but there is inherent in his experience as a Negro in America a dimension which must enrich the outlook of all who study under him.

RELIGION, BLACK NATIONALISM AND BLACK POWER

An essay on the Negro's contribution to religious thought in the United States would not be complete without reference to Black Nationalism and Black Power. The black "revolt" or "revolution" is so closely associated with these movements that even Negro religious institutions and spokesmen of the Church have been greatly influenced by them. Perhaps the most open evidence of the widespread impact of the new mood of the Negro is found in the emergence of "black caucuses" in all major integrated Protestant denominations and, most recently, in the Roman Catholic Church as well.

It is my impression that much of the new emphasis was pre-figured in the Black Muslim movement of which Malcolm X was the most brilliant and eloquent spokesman for about twelve years. Malcolm has left in his *Autobiography*[42] a moving account of his contribution to this movement. No one reading this work can doubt that in this dynamic leader we confront an unusual man whose prophetic views must now be reckoned with.

Malcolm Little was the son of a free-lance Baptist preacher who was a dedicated organizer for Marcus Aurelius Garvey. Garvey sought to lift up black pride and race purity by urging Negroes to return to Africa. Malcolm's father was born in Georgia, but was married to a light-skinned woman from the British West Indies. Malcolm's skin-color came from his mother. Most of Malcolm's uncles and his own father died violent deaths at the hands of white men in both South and North.

The family moved many times—from Philadelphia to Omaha, from Omaha to Milwaukee, and from Milwaukee to Lansing, Michigan. Everywhere he went his experiences with whites were the worst possible. There was a constant tension between his parents. When he was only six years old, his father was killed at the hands of a white man. After this the family fortunes were even worse than before. He lived with relatives in many urban ghettos—in Boston, in Detroit and in Harlem. He saw life in the raw in his teens and became a hoodlum in the worst sense of that word.

He was placed in prison very early in life. There he learned to read, write and debate. The wide range of his study and his comprehension of what he read may only be explained by the gift of a brilliant mind which had not been exposed to formal education.

He was converted to Elijah Mohammed's Black Nationalist Movement while in prison. After release from prison, he rose swiftly to the position of a loyal and dynamic aide and organizer of the movement throughout the country. Malcolm X's attachment to this movement may be explained by the unfolding of his past in the nature of a conversion experience. As Eric Lincoln puts it: "To the various black nationalist fronts in Harlem and elsewhere. Malcolm was a potential 'liberator', a man on a

Black Horse who would some day lead them in a revolutionary struggle against the hated blue-eyed devils."[43]

In his *Autobiography*, Malcolm X outlines many of the basic beliefs and practices of the Black Muslims. The work with criminals and addicts, as well as the overall socio-economic program aimed at the "dark ghetto," is admirable. But when one is asked to accept Elijah Mohammed as "The seal of the prophets," together wih a puritan ethic that it is humanly impossible to fulfill, and I believe unnecessary, the movement becomes odious to most thinking people. This is perhaps why Malcolm X did his "fishing" among members of store-front churches. In fact, it was because Malcolm X found Elijah Mohammed unfaithful to his own teachings as required of others that he became disenchanted with the movement and his role in it.

His famous "chickens coming to roost" statement upon the assassination of President John F. Kennedy provided the excuse for his being silenced. Soon thereafter he took his pilgrimage to Mecca and travelled through several Afro-Asian countries. This trip confirmed his belief that the Black Muslim Movement is not consistent with Islam. Upon his return, his views reflected a significant change. He had been Elijah Mohammed's spokesman in the intellectual centers of this country. Therefore, when he defected and founded his own mosque and the Organization for Afro-American Unity, many Negro professionals joined him. He now accepted all men at face value. Whites were not able to join, but could support his work and were urged to work in their own community for human rights. He saw the United Nations as an instrument for procuring such rights. He sought to broaden the program of the Black Muslims. He moved from "black nationalism" to a "third world" outlook. Allah became his God and Mohammed of Arabia, the founder of Islam, was now his true example. He did not advocate wanton violence, but did stress the right, even the duty, of men to defend themselves by violence if necessary.

Malcolm X rose above his youth. Even if we do not agree with his solution, we must admit a radical transformation in his life. His past gave him a unique insight into the nature of the problems with which he sought to deal.[44] Lincoln sums up his life as follows:

94

"Malcolm X must be taken for what he was. He was a remarkably gifted and charismatic leader whose hatreds and resentments symbolized the dreadful stamp of the black ghetto."[45]

Albert B. Cleage, Jr., is a clergyman of the United Church of Christ and is at present the minister of the Shrine of the Black Madonna in Detroit. He was educated at Wayne State University and Oberlin Graduate School of Theology. He came to the ministry from the field of social work. He was at one time co-pastor of the Interracial Fellowship Church of San Francisco. He left his interracial work to assume leadership in the Black Freedom Movement. He felt that the "integrationist" approach was too slow and that a program is needed to transfer power to the black community.

Cleage's *Black Messiah* is a controversial book and in many ways quite disturbing. If there is any theology in it, it is primarily biblical. He has completely re-interpreted biblical history, his motive being to undergird his message of Black Power. His program of re-interpretation of the Old Testament and the teachings of Jesus is as radical as Bultmann's demythologizing program. We must admire Bultmann's careful scholarship. Cleage only provides us with sermons and addresses. Careful exegesis and documentation are conspicuous by their absence.

In keeping with his purpose, the Old Testament is said to contain the history of Black Jews whose "blackness" is explained by miscegenation between Israelites and Egyptians. All this is intended to provide a "black" genealogy for Jesus, the Black Messiah. While accepting Jesus on these terms, Cleage rejects Paul because he associated primarily with Gentiles and spiritualized the message of Jesus in order to win favors from Rome. Most of Cleage's discussion is clearly a historical one. It is hard to believe that he expects anyone to take his arbitrary interpretation of scripture seriously without any effort to provide a shred of evidence for his radical views. His obvious purpose is the creation of a Bible-based "myth" to support the religion of black power. Since a myth does not have to be true, merely believed in order to be effective, the use of the Bible has been very useful in his service.

According to Cleage, there are no personal principles of morality—only the collective ethic of the black nation matters. All black men belong, or should belong, to this black nation. Love

95

binds those inside together, but strict justice is the basis for any relationship with those outside. Most of his message has to do with the mundane arena of power politics and he reveals a remarkable and intimate acquaintance with the black community. Religion is seen as a powerful force in the black community. The Negro Church is his only autonomous institution. It is the means for the fulfillment of the rightful objectives of the black community. He is willing to use the Bible and the Church under the assumption that the end justifies the means.

This point of view may be "religious," but whether it is Christian is questionable. It is clear that Cleage does not provide the kind of evidence to make this point. The book is not a real contribution to theology, "black" or "white." Cleage has provided a pious dress for the same type of message one may receive from a Stokely Carmichael or a Rap Brown. Our suspicions are confirmed by Cleage's suggestion that such brothers should be accepted and ordained to the ministry. In some ways Cleage, as a "man of god," may be more inflammatory than the more "secular saints" of the Black Power movement. It is in religion that the "cult of personality" is most pronounced in the black community. An exponent of a Black Messiah, he may even become, in the eyes of the black masses, a messiah himself.

Nathan Wright, Jr., though different from Cleage in many respects, has, in common with him, a zeal for a religion of black power. Wright was the 1967 chairman of the National Conference on Black Power. He is an education and urbanization consultant. He has served as Executive Director of the Department of Urban Work of the Episcopal Diocese of Newark, New Jersey, and as a Field Secretary for CORE at one time. He holds a doctorate in education from Harvard University and lectures in Urban Sociology at New York City Community College. He has produced some very careful scholarly works in religion, including *One Bread, One Body*.

In his definitive work on religion and black power, *Black Power and Urban Unrest*, Wright speaks of the absence of power on the part of Negro Americans to fulfill or to realize *in life* as well as *in law* the promises of America.[46] Negroes have been led to believe that their right of appeal is only through the agency of conscience. White people, on the other hand, may enlist power to secure their ends.[47]

A great deal of what Wright has to say in this work is a commentary on the July 22, 1966, session of the National Committee of Negro Churchmen. This was soon after the cry "Black Power" had first been heard in the South. This cry summed up the mood of many Negroes who had long been aware of their powerlessness and the need for "some new form of power in the service of justice" to confront the "unabated abuse of power."[48] Love can be acquiescence. Power alone may address itself to power.[49] White churches have often sentimentalized love while the claims of justice have not been met. This is why Negroes founded their own churches and why integration has been unmeaningful.[50]

Wright sees the first glimpses of "Black Power" in Frederick Douglass, W.E.B. DuBois, Marcus Garvey, John Brown, A. Philip Randolph, and even in Howard Thurman's *The Luminous Darkness*. All these men have been witness to "the Negro's recognition and aggressive assertion of his fundamental dignity, integrity and worth."[51]

There are many vital insights in *Black Power and Urban Unrest* concerning economics, self-development, self-respect, education, black leadership and black awareness. But what he has to say about the religious opportunities arising from Black Power merits some consideration.

We are told that all men need the power to become; according to Wright, power and life are interrelated. Power is basic to life. Without power, life cannot become what it must be. Black Power opens up new possibilities for self-awareness among the churches. The Negro must be brought into the mainstream of free competition in every field. Negro equality in America becomes meaningless unless led by Negroes, whether this equality be sought in the churches or in the community. "In religious terms, a God of power, of majesty and of might, who has made man to be in His image and likeness, must will that His creation reflect in the immediacies of his life His power, His majesty and His might."[52]

It was unfortunate for me that my one and only encounter with Nathan Wright was some two years after his authorship of *Black Power and Urban Unrest*. My evaluation of him is colored by this meeting. Several riots and two very "hot summers" had passed. Much of the reason and sanity of his earlier writings was not evident. It would have been good to have known him before. When I met him, he wore a flowing African robe and beads. There was in his manner an air of "pomp and circumstance." He now spoke of "honkies" and "blacks" rather than of "whites" and "Negroes." He resembled in many ways a self-appointed messiah. I sensed in his hypnotic hold over his audience a potential for good or ill in the racial crisis. Because of his sacramental upbringing, there was an obvious, though perhaps an unconscious attempt, to introduce certain cultic rights into the movement. Examples were his personal greeting and what he described as a "black power handshake." Nathan Wright is a learned man with the knowledge, experience, writing skills and charisma to give a constructive direction to black power. Will his over-reaction neutralize his influence? Will his unusual gifts be put to constructive or destructive ends? For an answer to these questions, we must await the verdict of history.

Vincent Harding is one of the most sober analysts of the relation of religion to "Black Power." Harding is Chairman of the History Department at Spelman College. He was educated at the University of Chicago. Harding is widely known as a writer and spokesman on the theme of "religion and black power" throughout the nation.

Harding is critical of what he calls the "American Christ." He says that Americans "have kidnapped the compassionate Jesus and made him into a profit-oriented, individualistic, pietistic cat."[53] It is Christians who have made the universal Christ into a puppet blessing all American acts.

In his essay on "The Religion of Black Power" in Donald R. Cutler, *The Religious Situation 1968*, Harding seeks to make a meaningful examination of the religious elements of Black Power. When he asserts that the "gospel of blackness" is necessary for self-love (self-respect), Harding refers to the power to develop to the full stature of a human being. Such self-esteem is the basis of community. Black Power, then, is that which calls black people to the self-love which is the stuff of all fulfilled relationships. True love can exist only among equals. There is, says Harding, a sense in which both love and hate are irrelevant until all men are considered equal. Even if we cannot love whites, just to be able not to hate them is an achievement.

Things being as they are and have been, the natural response would be hate or revenge.

Black men must build a black community even if it falls short of the universal community. Such a community can be an improvement over the disdain of the black community as it now is. In the type of community of which Harding speaks, black and broken men will be able to see themselves as the Creator sees them.[54] This would be the beginning of true corporate health and integrity for black people. Black Power calls for an ultimate identification between black people here and all the non-whites of the earth.

Harding is somewhat critical of the type of messianism associated with Marcus Garvey, Malcolm X and Nathan Hare. He might have added, as we have tried to point out, Nathan Wright and Albert Cleage, as he makes the following point: "Is it given to black men any more than to whites to be self-commissioned executors of divine judgment on evil-doers?"[55]

According to Harding, black love and resurrection are ways of speaking about and discovering the incarnation where it is most needed today. The "glorification of blackness" is part of a healing process for those who have been ashamed of their blackness.[56] The Negro is in search of manhood and therefore the right to self-defense arises. It is difficult for a black man to take up yet another cross when confronted by his enemy, when he has been bearing crosses all his life.[57] At any rate, the quest for true manhood, true community and true humanity are important. Political, economic and social power are means to these ends. It is not surprising that the Negro's God is becoming a God of power in the writings of Nathan Wright, as well as in the speeches of Ron Karenga.

Ever since Marcus Garvey, black nationalists have found religion one of their modes of expression. The Negro Church has always had a pragmatic function in the black community. This is one reason why Carmichael attends church and why some black revolutionaries remain in the ministry. Harding believes that there is also a deeper reason: "There is a sense of religious ferment on the path of Black Power . . . Mixtures of old and new approaches to the essential issues of life are being attempted."[58]

We cannot conclude that Harding is an absolute exponent of

Black Power in all its aspects. He is a "fellow-traveller" in some sense. He is listening creatively to black students and leaders with great understanding. Harding has strong religious sensitivities and feels that religion has great importance in the racial crisis. He is a good historian of the Negro's past and a competent observer of the sociology of Negro life. In addition, one must admire his use of words. He is a skillful journalist and knows how to get the most freight out of words and ideas. He chooses a middle way between black revolutionaries and the exponents of non-violence. He has not formulated a clear ideological or theological position. He is seeking for the best answers and solutions. For all his scholarship, eloquence and influence, we cannot expect real direction from him. For this reason, to hear or read what he is saying is disappointing. He is, however, providing good contextual information and raising the right issues.

❋   ❋   ❋

In this essay we have been able to provide only an introduction to the Negro's contribution to religious thought in the United States. Our selection does not cover the gamut of all black writers of importance in the field of religion. We have tried to be varied and representative in our choice of authors and their works. I believe that we have sufficient evidence here to indicate that the Negro's contribution to religious thought is both considerable and worth examination. One wonders why Negro scholars, whose experience has provided them with so much valid religious data, are such reluctant authors. Perhaps the greatest surprise to the reading public will be that they have written so much against overwhelming odds and that what they have written is so vital.

SELECTED BIBLIOGRAPHY

BOOKS

Banner, William, *Ethics: An Introduction to Moral Philosophy*, New York: Scribner's, 1968. Banner's book is both historical and interpretative. It is for the general reader and not for the specialist. For a survey of ethics in the West, this book is very good.

Cleage, Albert B., Jr., *The Black Messiah,* New York: Sheed and Ward, 1968. This is one of the most radical statements of "the religion of black power". The author gives no scholarly justification for his conclusions. The work is a popular interpretation of the black revolution. As sermons, most messages are set in the context of the author's understanding of the Bible. The Bible is *used* and not *understood.* The real value of the book is the author's awareness and concern for what is happening and his intimate knowledge of the Detroit racial situation.

DuBois, W.E.B., *The Souls of Black Folks,* Greenwich, Conn.: Fawcett Publications, 1961. This soul-searching work by DuBois is unusually contemporary considering the date when it was first published. This account of the Negro's struggle and self-awareness should be read and re-read by all Americans.

Fisher, Miles Mark, *Negro Slave Songs in the United States,* Ithaca, New York: Cornell University Press, 1953. This is one of the best interpretative works on the Negro's spirituals from the point of view of religious history. The author also reveals his gifts as a preacher and liturgist. It is one of the most valuable contributions to the subject-matter available.

Lincoln, Eric, *The Black Muslims in America,* Boston: Beacon, 1961. This is one of the few authoritative accounts of the Black Muslims. It is scholarly and candid. This work introduced Lincoln and launched him as one of the best interpreters of the Negro's experience in the United States.

Long, Charles, *Alpha, The Myths of Creation,* New York: Braziller, 1963. The author is a specialist in methodology in the history of religions with special reference to primitive religions. This work dealing with cosmogonic myths is among the most comprehensive available.

Kelsey, George, *Racism and the Christian Understanding of Man,* New York: Scribner's, 1965. This is one of the few works on race relations cast in the mold of theological ethics. The theology of Emil Brunner is here applied to the race question together with extensive knowledge of the behavioral sciences. The book is a real contribution.

King, Martin Luther, Jr., *Stride Toward Freedom,* New York: Harper, 1958. This is perhaps the most important book written by Dr. King. This is his own story concerning his call to leadership in the racial struggle. The spiritual and intellectual autobiography of Dr. King as well as the early history of the movement he led is included in this book.

Malcolm X, *An Autobiography*, New York: Grove Press, 1966. This is Malcolm's own story and he tells it like it is for millions of black Americans North and South. The work is an intimate account of his tortured life as well as the history of the Black Muslim Movement. This is an unusual story, but it casts light upon America's number one problem in the social field.

Mays, Benjamin Elijah, The *Negro's God, As Reflected In His Literature*, Boston: Chapman and Grimes, 1938. This is, according to Mays, the first attempt to give a theological interpretation of the idea of God in Negro literature both classic and popular. The work has not been surpassed by any comparable study and stands as an invaluable resource for understanding the faith of the American Negro.

Scott, Nathan, *Modern Literature and the Religious Frontier*, New York: Harper, 1957. This is a work which introduces Scott who is recognized today as one of the best interpreters of religious insights in modern literature. This book should be read in order to gain an understanding of the program of this important writer.

————, *The Broken Center*, New Haven, Conn.: Yale University Press, 1966. This more recent work by Scott continues to search for religious meanings in poetry, fiction and drama. It is a collection of essays and lectures gathered over several years on many occasions.

Washington, Joseph, Jr., *Black Religion*, Boston: Beacon, 1964. In this controversial book, Washington is highly critical of Negro folk-religion. It is known for its absence of theology, extreme emotionalism and lack of moral sensitiveness. In this book, Washington sees the white church as the place where the true religion is to be found. This book is interesting both for its point of view and the half-truths it contains.

————, *The Politics of God*, Boston: Beacon, 1967. In this latter volume, Washington almost reverses the position held in *Black Religion*. Now we are told that Negroes are the chosen people and that they must seek to convert white people from their "folk religion". One wonders if Washington is able to make up his mind. By putting the two works together we discover that both white and black religion are in trouble. On the whole *The Politics of God* is more realistic and mature than *Black Religion*.

Wright, Nathan, *Black Power and Urban Unrest*, New York: Hawthorn Books, 1968. This is a good sociological and theological study of an important initial statement of the National Committee of Negro Churchmen. This committee is a kind of ecumenical coordinator of the numerous "Black Caucuses" in most major integrated Christian bodies in the United States.

ARTICLES

Bond, Julian, "The Negro and Politics," *Motive*, May, 1968, pp. 16-20. A young Negro journalist, civil rights worker and politician speaks with real authority concerning politics. He speaks out of experience, describes the present scene and makes valuable suggestions as to how political action may be employed by Negroes to win their rights. As a member of the "now generation", mainly in reference to his youth, Mr. Bond should be heard by young and old alike.

Etzion, Amitai, "The Sins of Commission", *Motive*, May, 1968, pp. 22-27. Those who have little faith in studies and reports that gather dust in Washington, know that the political failure of the Kerner Report is no exception. All may read this article with profit. We are challenged to find ways to activate such reports for the solution of human problems.

Grinshaw, Allen D., "Lawlessness and Violence in America and Their Special Manifestations in Changing Negro White Relationships", *The Journal of Negro History*, Vol. XLIV, no. 1, January, 1959, pp. 52-72. This article places violence in America in sociological and historical perspective. The author establishes the fact that "ours has been a lawless and violent nation". Lawlessness and violence has permeated every area of civic life. "Real Americans", usually White-Anglo-Saxon-Protestants, have punished other religious, cultural and social groups. Inter-racial violence must be seen in this context. Only thus may we discover the *cause* and find the *solution*. This article is necessary reading for all concerned Americans.

Harding, Vincent, "Black Power and the American Christ", *The Christian Century*, January 4, 1967, pp. 13-14. This is a scathing criticism of the misuse and misunderstanding of Christ as the center of the Christian message. Whether one agrees with his point of view or not, what he has to say about this subject should provoke serious thought.

————, "The Afro-American Past". *Motive*, April, 1968, pp. 6-11. This is an excellent brief account of the Negro's heritage in sociological as well as historical perspective.

————, "The Religion of Black Power" in Donald R. Cutler, editor, *The Religious Situation 1968*, Boston: Beacon, 1968, pp. 3-38. In this statement Harding presents a helpful interpretation of religion in relation to black power. Perhaps the most helpful part of his discussion is his evaluation of Dr. M. L. King's life and work.

Ianni, Francis, "Teaching Violence As a Means Towards Social Justice", *The Catholic World*, January, 1968, pp. 160-164. This is an important and timely statement for it provides the type of reflection needed for those who have grown weary with alternative means to social justice. The questions of means and end, of the self-defeating nature of blind rage and all related issues are put in perspective. The issues raised in this article are crucial.

Lincoln, Eric, "How Now, America?" *Christianity and Crisis*, April 1, 1968, pp. 56-59. This is a prophetic call to America to make a choice about the race question. It is an urgent plea to eradicate the "black Ghetto" and to implement the Kerner Report.

————, "The Meaning of Malcolm X", *The Christian Century*, April 7, 1965, pp. 431-433. This article describes the conditions which produced Malcolm X for the black ghetto explains his life to a great extent. Malcolm X must be accepted for what he was. He was in some sense a revolutionary even though he made a radical change in his life. Lincoln closes with the warning that unless conditions change, the ghettos of America will produce many others like him.

Long, Charles H., "Primitive Religion" in Charles J. Adams, editor, *A Reader's Guide to the Great Religions*, New York: The Free Press, 1965, pp. 1-30. This excellent chapter is a description of what is going on in the study of primitive religions. The descriptive reading list is invaluable.

————, "Archaism and Hermeneutics" in Joseph M. Kitagawa, editor, *The History of Religions—Essays on the Prob-*

lem of Understanding, Chicago: At the University Press, 1967, pp. 67-88. This essay reveals Long's wide knowledge both in the area of primitive religious thought and in methodology in the history of religions. This is a good introduction to the outlook of this important writer.

Miller, Robert M., "The Attitudes of American Protestantism Toward the Negro, 1919-1939", *The Journal of Negro History*, Vol. XLI, no. 3, July, 1956, pp. 215-240. White churches were found to be segregated and segregating institutions. Color of skin has been more important than purity of heart. Miller asserts that the main reason why Negroes do not feel welcome in white churches is because they are not accepted as equal. He is too optimistic about improvements. It is because so little progress has been made that we are now confronted with the "Black Caucus".

Poussaint, A. F. and Ladner, Joyce, "Helping Hands Were Out of Touch," *The National Observer*, August 12, 1968. This is one of the best explanations given as to why the "black power" movement was born out of the failures, frustrations and mistakes of the civil rights movement. The approach is from the medical and behavioral sciences.

Roberts, J. Deotis, "The Christian Conscience and Legal Discrimination", *The Journal of Religious Thought*, Vol. XIX, no. 2, 1962-63, pp. 157-161. In this article an attempt is made to provide a careful examination of the nature of the "christian conscience" both in thought and life. The issue of legal discrimination, mainly in the South, is discussed in relation to the manner in which the christian conscience "ought" to give direction in race relations. In view of the recent more nationwide spread of the racial crisis, the discussion in this article is incomplete and is in need of updating.

Ross, Sherwood, "The Kerner Report", *The Christian Century*, April 3, 1968, pp. 416-419. This is a good analysis of the conclusions of this very important report, together with a summons for its implementation.

NOTES

1. Joseph R. Washington, Jr., *Black Religion*, Boston, Mass.: Beacon Press, 1964, p. 143.
2. In this essay "black" and "Negro" are used interchangeably.

3. See M. L. King, *Stride Toward Freedom*, New York: Harper, 1958.

4. George D. Kelsey, *Racism and the Christian Understanding of Man*, New York: Scribner's, 1965, p. 9.

5. *Ibid.*, p. 126.

6. I met Professor Kelsey for the first time during the summer of 1968 and was deeply impressed by the logic and force of his lectures. He did not, as I understood him, speak meaningfully to the new challenge presented by "the black caucus" movement in the churches or of "black power" in the larger society.

7. Joseph R. Washington, Jr., *The Politics of God*, Boston: Beacon Press, 1967, p. 45.

8. C. Eric Lincoln is the author of at least five books. In addition, he has contributed chapters to textbooks and anthologies and has written numerous articles for popular magazines and scholarly journals.

9. The other study is by E. U. Essien-Udom, a Nigerian, who studied at the University of Chicago. His work is called *Black Nationalism*. Chicago: at the University Press, 1962. The Nigeran, having direct knowledge and contact wth Islam in his own country, has an advantage over Lincoln in evaluating the affinity of the movement with Islam. Lincoln, on the other hand, has greater knowledge of the Negro problem in the United States which is the ultimate explanation for the Black Muslims.

10. This is my opinion in spite of a brief chapter in Lincoln's book on "The Black Muslims and Orthodox Islam." See, *The Black Muslims in America*, Boston: The Beacon Press, 1961, pp. 210-226.

11. Joseph R. Washington, Jr., *The Politics of God*, Boston: Beacon Press, 1967, p. 185.

12. *Ibid.*, p. 186.

13. In a conversation at Washington's home in Albion, Michigan, he referred to *The Politics of God* as a "bad" book. At the time, I had not read it. Consequently, it was not possible for me to react to this judgment. After reading the book, it is my impression that this latter book is a much more realistic assessment of the religious dimensions of the current racial crisis than his *Black Religion*.

14. Miles Mark Fisher, *Negro Slave Songs in the United States*, Ithaca, New York: Cornell University Press, 1953, p. 191.

15. *Ibid.*, p. 190.

16. Benjamin E. Mays, *The Negro's God: As Reflected In His Literature*, Boston: Chapman and Grimes, Inc., Mount Vernon Press, 1938, preface.

17. *Ibid.*, p. 100.

18. From Dubois, *Dark Water*, New York: Harcourt, Brace and Howe, 1920, pp. 3-4. Quoted by Mays, *Ibid.*, p. 163.

19. From Countee Cullen, *Color*, New York: Harper, 1925, pp. 39, 40. Quoted by Mays, *Ibid.*, pp. 219-20.

20. DuBois, *Dark Water*, pp. 275, 276. Quoted by Mays, *Ibid.*, p. 220.

21. Mays, *Ibid.*, p. 254.

22. Some years ago, in the summer of 1965, while attending a Danforth Conference at Lake Miniwanca, near Muskegon, Michigan, it was my privilege to discuss a number of important subjects with Dr. B. E. Mays. His personal experiences at our school as dean were of great interest to me. The most traumatic statement, however, resulted from a conversation at lunch after one of Van A. Harvey's exciting lectures on contemporary theology. I had just recalled my theological upbringing among the so-called "giants" of Neo-Reformation Theology. Mays remarked that one's

theological position matters little since the politicians rule the world. Whether this statement resulted from his long involvement in race relations or whether it was an expression of complete disillusionment with theology, in view of Christianity's ethical failures, I do not know. This is a statement which I have recalled many times since. Does theology need to be abandoned or does it need to be re-written by black men in keeping with their experience? I have accepted the latter challenge. A good place to begin is with Mays' *The Negro's God.*

23. During a brief visit to Madras Christian College at Tambaram, a town near Madras City in India, I met a professor of philosophy who remember Thurman as a visitor to that college many years ago. He did not remember Thurman's name, but the professor's description suited only one man, Howard Thurman.

24. Howard Thurman, *The Luminous Darkness*, New York: Harper, 1965, p. ix.

25. *Ibid.*, p. x.

26. *Ibid.*

27. Those who desire full acquaintance with the life of Howard Thurman are referred to Elizabeth Yates, *Howard Thurman: Portrait of a Practical Dreamer*, New York: The John Day Company, 1964.

28. *Ibid.*, p. 21.

29. Howard Thurman, *Jesus and the Disinherited*, New York: Abingdon, 1949, pp. 30-31.

30. *Ibid.*, p. 11.

31. *Ibid.*, pp. 108, 89.

32. *Ibid.*, p. 112.

33. Howard Thurman, *Deep Is The Hunger*, New York: Harper, 1951.

34. Howard Thurman, *The Negro Spiritual Speaks of Life and Death*, Being the Ingersoll Lecture on the Immortality of Man, New York, Harper, 1947, pp. 54-55.

35. Nathan Scott, *Modern Literature and the Religious Frontier*, New York: Harper, 1957, p. xi.

36. *Ibid.*, pp. 18-19.

37. *Ibid.*, p. 115.

38. Nathan Scott, *The Broken Center*, New Haven, Conn.: Yale University Press, 1966, p. ix.

39. *Ibid.*, p. ix.

40. Charles H. Long, *Alpha, The Myths of Creation*, New York: George Braziller, 1963, p. 1.

41. Charles H. Long, "Archaism and Hermeneutics," in Joseph M. Kitagawa, *The History of Religions: Essays on the Problem of Understanding*, Chicago: University Press, 1965, pp. 67-88. See also, his, "Primitive Religions" in Charles J. Adams, *A Reader's Guide to the Great Religions*, New York: Free Press, 1965, pp. 1-30.

42. Malcolm X, *The Autobiography of Malcolm X* (with the assistance of M. S. Handler and Alex Haley), New York: Grove Press, 1964.

43. C. Eric Lincoln, "The Meaning of Malcolm X," in *The Christian Century*, April 7, 1965, p. 432.

44. *Ibid.*

45. *Ibid.*, p. 433.

46. Nathan Wright, *Black Power and Urban Unrest*, New York: Hawthorn Books, 1968, p. 5.

47. *Ibid.*, p. 4.

48. *Ibid.*, p. 2.
49. *Ibid.*, p. 5.
50. *Ibid.*, pp. 8-9.
51. *Ibid.*, p. 14.
52. *Ibid.*, p. 136.
53. Vincent Harding, "Black Power and the American Christ," *Christian Century*, January 4, 1967, p. 13.
54. Vincent Harding, "The Religion of Black Power," Donald R. Cutler, editor, *The Religious Situation 1968*, Boston: Beacon Press, 1968, p. 15.
55. *Ibid.*, p. 15.
56. *Ibid.*, p. 18.
57. *Ibid.*, pp. 21-22.
58. *Ibid.*, p. 31.

J. DEOTIS ROBERTS was born in 1927 and studied at Johnson C. Smith University (B.A., 1947), Shaw University (B.D., 1950), Hartford Seminary Foundation (B.D., 1951; S.T.M., 1952), University of Edinburgh (Ph. D., 1957). He has pursued post-doctoral studies in the history of religions at Harvard, Michigan, Chicago, Wisconsin, California and Michigan State Universities; professional study in Theology at Cambridge University, travel study in Asian Religions for the Society for the Study of Religion in Higher Education (1964-65). He has been Associate Professor and Chaplain, Shaw University (1953-55, 57-58), and is presently Professor, History of Religion and Christian Theology, Howard University. He is Visiting Professor of Religion, Swarthmore College, 1969-70.

AFRICAN CONTRIBUTIONS TO
WORLD RELIGION

JAMES D. TYMS

Howard University (Washington, D.C.)

Any attempt to write about the abiding religious values among a people of a bookless religion may seem to be an exercise in futility. World cultures in which religions of the book have emerged have hardly been disposed to show the openness that would admit the possibility of genuine value in a bookless religion. The peoples of Africa have for centuries been objects of pursuit by Christian and Islam missionaries, to be claimed for Jesus or Allah. The style of life of these non-literate peoples was, from the perspective of Western religious dogma, far too long viewed as one in which savages bowed down to sticks and stones. Their religion offered at best nothing more than a few specimens, long since discarded by the peoples of the book, to be viewed as showcase relics of man's long trek toward high religion.

The underlying assumption of the writer of this article, however, is that inherent in the conscious and subconscious religious and cultural strivings of the African in the remote past is a value content and thrust of life which transcend cultural limitations.

The writer does not overlook the fact that certain aspects of African religion have for a very long time embraced what may be termed book religion (Egypt and Ethiopia). The preferred task here, however, is that of focusing upon the African of the bookless religion — central, east, south and west. An intensive analysis of religion within the areas chosen is too great a task to be covered adequately within the limits of an article. So certain main emphases on aspects of African culture and religion in a somewhat general fashion will meet the need for marking out areas of contribution. Now, the emphasis on religion and culture serves the purpose of noting the fact that African religion embraces the total sphere of life. This seems to be true whether the religious orientation is said to be positive (subsumed under the dynamics of the kinship group tradition) or negative (the sacrifice of human beings upon the death of a chief). This lack of a dichotomy between African religion and culture suggests that aboriginally the races of mankind have much in common. Melville Jean Herskovits, for example, has stressed the fact that when certain indigenous religious patterns, African or otherwise, are abstracted certain general principles emerge which do not differ markedly either from Christianity or Islam to an extent that would preclude a measure of accommodation under contact.[1]

The distinctively religious categories under which some general principles are grouped and indicating areas of compatibility between African religion and religions of the book are fourfold: (1) the Great God along with subsidiary beings to whom executive powers have been delegated; (2) the collective powers of antecedent generations, manifested most often in ancestor worship; (3) human destiny as it relates to problems which can be clarified by divination or discovery of the will of God; and finally, (4) magic which is characterized by devious human efforts to control destiny.[2]

The first two of the aforementioned categories are germane to the subheadings of this article. The latter two, indirectly, are relevant and may be subsumed under different headings. It is assumed that the value significance of African religion, in the light of world religion, may be seen, then, in the following subheadings: The Great God and Subsidiary Beings, The Collective Powers of Antecedent Generations (Ancestor Worship), Art and Religion, African Proverbs and Religious Values, and African and Other Religions.

THE GREAT GOD AND SUBSIDIARY BEINGS

Religion is without exception a common possession of the races of mankind. The points of difference in a people's religion may be found to be rooted in the cultural matrix, the unique way in which a people has carved out its life style in interacting with the material and spiritual content of its existence. It is thus our assumption that the word — concept — God is a mental construct which has emerged out of man's struggle to derive a sense of ultimate meaning from the experience of living. A given people — Hebrews, Arabs, Indians, Greeks, Romans and Africans — came to its idea of God against the background of antiquity. The former sought to clarify the God idea in books; the latter had no books in which to record and systematize a doctrine of God or its affirmation of faith. They who have given unstinted time and energy to the study of African culture and religion have nevertheless apprised the world of the fact that the African in his isolation from world culture nurtured into being an idea of the Great God, along with subsidiary beings whose role in the divine order was determined by the Great One. This God among the Africans is the Creator, the Moulder, the Creator of souls, the Giver of breath, the God of destinies.[3] Viewing the idea of God against the screen of natural phenomena, the African, as averred by Edwin William Smith, gave to the world a God concept as the manifestation of Power: He is the Giver of rain, the Maker of thunder and sunshine; rain and food imply that He is kind, though pain and death occasion real doubt; and refreshing indeed are the thoughts that the Great One desires good hearts in men and that He helps men in being good or that He saves them from sin.[4]

Typical names for the supreme spirit are found among Africans of the Congo, East and West Africa. Among Congo tribes (Ngombe), the supreme spirit is known as *Akongo,* the chief God of the tribe and their ancestors, the Creator of the universe, the "Moulder and Maker of men like a potter." He is the Beginner, Unending, Almighty and Inexplicable. This God is closely related to each individual as a guardian spirit, giving good or bad fortune. He has no idols or temples, yet He is easily approached by man.[5] The Kikuyu of Kenya call the supreme spirit *Murungu* whose habitat is on the four sacred mountains. The "Possessor of Whiteness," this God is the creator of all things. He shows His power in the sun, moon, stars, storm and rain. All men direct their prayers to *Murungu* at night and in the morning at the rising of the sun.[6] The name *Leza* is given to the God of Rhodesia, Tanganyika and the Upper Congo. In the event of rain and wind, "God falls" and "God blows," terms to express God's action. Exceptionally unexpected good harvest evokes the response (Rhodesians and Tanganyikans), "God is our Father."[7]

The Ashanti of West Africa call God *Onyankopon* or *Onyame*. In all the earth *Onyame* is the Wise One.[8] *Nyankopon* manifests His creativity under diverse appellations. For example, as *Abommubuwafre* it is He who is called upon in times of distress, so He is "a Counselor or Comforter who gives salvation"; addressed as *Tetekwaframus*, He is the one who is there now as from ancient times, who endures forever; and known as *Nana*, He is the grand ancestor. Commenting on the name *Nana*, J. D. Danquah says, "This gives Him the full title for religious purposes of *Nana Nyankopon Kwaame*, 'the Great Ancestor Nyankopon whose day is Saturday,' a description which entitles Him to the honorific or strong name of Amen, . . ."[9]

These four designations of names to convey the idea of God among the peoples of the Congo, Kenya, Rhodesia, Tanganyika and West Africa (Ghana, Gold Coast up to 1957) serve our purpose for pointing out certain characteristics of the Great God among Africans. The lesser gods now come into focus as they perform their intermediary role between the Great God and man. Here attention is called to the fact that in prayer, generally, Africans by-pass God Himself, choosing in times of distress and need to address their prayers to the lesser gods. Among the Akan people of Ghana, for example, *Abosom* are the chief representatives of *Onyame* on the earth, being sons who came down to earth.[10] *Orisha-nea* of Yorubaland is the god who was sent down from above to bring the first earth, and with the help of the hen and pigeon to spread earth abroad. Another task was that of planting trees. Later *Orisha-nea* was delegated the task of creating human bodies into which God placed breath.[11]

Another example of the role of a lesser god is that of the god *lubare* of East Africa. Among the Ganda *Katonda* (the Great One) ruled the Unseen. *Lubare* was under him and aided him in ruling. It was he whose place of worship was a small house; viewed in the plural, the *lubare* are the working-managers, they keep their fires burning the year round.[12]

The tendency to by-pass the Great God in prayer and to

effect communion with the lesser gods suggests that God was conceived as being too far away for urgent contact. His sons were close at hand, so to speak, and could be expected to respond to the needs of man. Should they fail, however, the devotee could turn to the Great God. The Ashanti are an exception. They have altars near their houses and daily put upon them offerings for *Nyame*.[13] The emphasis on altars is a reminder of Edward Goeffery Parrinder's observation that Africans built temples to the Great God (Akan) and especially the lesser divinities. Generally, the temples were not places for the assembly of large congregations. Like many Hindu and Buddhist temples and pagodas, the African temples were mostly shrines to enclose relics or sacred objects. This is a marked contrast to Christian churches and Mohammedan mosques specially designed to be houses of God for the assembly of the people of God.[14]

In summary, then, a review of the literature on the idea of God among Africans reveals a hierarchy of an all-pervasive power force above which is the Great God who is the Creator, the Giver of existence and the increase of life. He is the Founder of the clan and is, therefore, linked to man in between whom are the lesser gods and the so-called 'dead' of the tribe. A bond of relations is actualized (links in the chain) through "which vital force influences the living generation." In connection with their vital power, it is observed, the living are motivated to form a hierarchy in which the eldest of the group or clan may bridge the passage between ancestors and their descendants. So the chief, when duly installed in accordance with tradition, reinforces the life of his people and all other minor forces, animal, vegetable.[15] In fine, the idea of God, summed up as a doctrine of God by J. B. Danquah, "is a cult of God as the Great Ancestor with all other ancestors in between as Mediators."[16] Extended still further, the doctrine implies a God who is the "Father of all the diverse men of one blood and the good chief of the tribe is exemplar of the chief good."[17]

There is, then, in spite of all cultural differences among the varied African tribes, spread over a large geographical area, a sense of cohesion in the ideas of God. This cohesive element transcends cultural differences. One Great God is the Creator of the world and man, and lesser gods — his sons and servants —

and human destiny are organically related to the quality of relationship sustained between God and man. It may, therefore, be affirmed that religion embraces that style of life in which man tries to conduct the affairs of life in accordance with the Will of God. The discernment of the Will of God, however, is colored conditionally. That is to say, the creativity of the human mind, the dynamics of its stimulation and motivation condition the ideational construct which gives rise to the God-concept and it also conditions the style of life man seeks to perpetuate as he affirms the meaning of God in human experience. The African, isolated from the cultural influences of the world, evidences a depth of mental creativity and inner stimulation that gave to the world an idea of God as Creator, Father, the Sustainer of life and values needed in human conduct. Put in the words of Galbraith Welch,

> . . . it was a startling discovery to Christian visitors to Africa of the pagans to find splashed across the continent a sort of monotheism, a belief in a big boss god, and a god-in-chief who was often believed to have been their Creator.[18]

Furthermore, it may be admitted that in a sense the African idea of God tends to isolate Him from an all-inclusive practical religion. He is nevertheless a reality of transcending significance. What is affirmed of God, however nebulous, bears marks of the purest religious thinking in the making and of religious experience. In fact, Diedrich Westermann who spent a large portion of his life in Africa and in studying African life and thought, is not far from the mark in contending that many African sayings about God might be applied to the God of the Bible.[19]

THE COLLECTIVE POWERS OF ANTECEDENT GENERATIONS
(ANCESTOR WORSHIP)

We have observed that God is so conceived in African culture, religion and life as to symbolize the ancestor. The Akan appellation *Nana Nyankopon Kwaame*, The Great Ancestor, stresses this fact. The given dynamic for perpetuating an undergirding sense of the collective power of antecedent generations inheres in this God-concept and it is symbolically kept alive in the rite of ancestor worship in which is implicit, according to Meyer Fortes, the delimitation of the group of worshippers by rule of kinship, descent and marriage.[20] One thing must be kept in mind, Fortes tells us, is that ancestor worship, consisting descriptively as it does of "a ritual relation with dead forebears, is not coterminous with the worship of the dead."[21] In this ritual the spirit of ancestorhood is conferred upon persons who are of the parental generation who have jural authority in living social relations.[22]

So, in observing the ritual ceremony of ancestor worship, the African has traditionally sought to keep alive the time-binding influence of the lineage as a social, religious and moral obligation. The observing of the ceremony has been the means of providing the climate for expressing the family feeling, intense sense of loyalty to the health, vitality, aspirations and beliefs of the family tree, reinforced by the clan's philosophy and desire to keep alive and productive.[23] Thus to fail to share in the experience of ancestor worship is (was) to fail to show reverence and respect for the antecedent generation, the dynamics of their experiences which made possible the present experiences and achievements of the lineage. Galbraith Welch has stated the case thusly:

Ancestor reverence was the confirmation to an established social pattern: parents should breed many children; the children they breed should carry along the honored memory of the parents—an endless chain of procreation.[24]

The family element in ancestor worship has merit in its own light. Though no exhaustive treatment is aimed at here, it helps to mark out the fact that the stress on the collective and patriarchal character of lineage is grounded in such a way that "each group coming from the same line constitutes a cell at once individual and impermeable" in principle.[25] In ancestor worship, therefore, not just any man's soul is deified, but only he who has during his lifetime belonged to the cellule, who has demonstrated tangible signs as an asset to the clan, is capable of making that impact upon life rise to the point of making ancestor worship the motif of the cult.[26] Religion among the Africans, then, has been declared to be primarily family religion, for in ancestor worship the ancestors are the intermediaries between the God and the tribe. As for the gods and their status in the ritual, Maurice Delafosse has observed that "the gods, whether or not they be of human essence, are members of the family, and the divinities of one family have no part in the worship of members of another family."[27] A question that arises here is what is the status of divinity conferred upon ancestors? The answer seems to be that ancestors are spiritual beings whose status is likened to that of saints. They exist in a spiritual realm and from their deified status seek to influence the life of the tribe. In ancestor worship within the kinship group the ancestors are accepted as being just. Their justice, according to Meyer Fortes, "is directed to enforcing moral and religious norms and values on which the social order rests."[28] They, therefore, exert power on the kinship group in line with the value thrust of the antecedent generation.

The deification of ancestors gives them a status of divinity but does not make them gods. The Reverend St. John Evans, Anglican Archdeacon of Ashanti, supports this contention. In his view and experience reverence for ancestors and worship in no sense seeks to raise the 'asamanfo' (practical ancestors) to the status of gods. Their sphere of influence is limited to the particular family or clan group; reverence for ancestors—the ritual—may not be regarded as worship in the strict religious sense. The cult rather reinforces the recognition of the essential unity of all who descend from a common ancestor or ancestors. In the rite the individual is imbued with the fact that he owes his duties and obligations to the clan. He comes to know also that he can expect help from the larger group during crises. The kinship group makes up the larger society.[29]

Ancestor worship as a means of firming up the collective power of antecedent generations includes the offering of prayers to the ancestors who are asked to aid the corn to grow, the rain to fall, to provide food and to help in the safe return home of those who have gone away on a journey. Prayer further reveals the fact that the tribe depends on the ancestors for aid to those of child-bearing age that they may bear children and so perpetuate the clan. The movement of the ritual, centered around a significant person—chief, priest or headman—also includes offering food and drink to the ancestral spirits and the pouring of libation, food and drink to the end that the ancestors might share with their descendants in taking of food and drink. Libation serves to effect real contact with the ancestors—those deified spiritual beings—whose aid is requested in prayer.

The total thrust of the rite of ancestor worship is social and religious, two parts of a whole in African culture. It keeps alive a dynamic relationship between the living and the departed; it gives collective expression to the "sentiments on which the social solidarity of the group depends."[30]

K. A. Busia, following the theory of Durkheim and others, holds that ancestor worship functions so as to recreate the social order by "reaffirming and strengthening the sentiments on which the social solidarity and therefore the social order itself depends."[31]

There is an element of non-creativity in the story of ancestor worship which, to be ignored here, would distort the ritual values of cementing ties within the kinship group. This is the practice of human sacrifice. It is thus noted that among African tribes there was a practice of offering not only the blood of victims such as chickens, goats, and sheep but the most prized victim of all, human beings. Often at the death of a revered one —chief or queen mother—human victims were sacrificed, for the revered person needed servants to attend his needs in the world of spirits.[32] Ancestor reverence and worship, grounded in the kinship group, is viewed as being honorable for it implies that the dynamic of merit which impinges upon ancestors in this life was a condition to be met in order to qualify to be raised to a level of ancestor (ancestorhood). The condition of merit being met, the deceased ancestor's demise was celebrated in such a way as to demonstrate the quality of reverence and respect for ancestors that would not fail to incur their good-will. The human victim, then, was the *great* sacrifice, variously illustrated in African culture by impaling a young female annually to secure plenty, rain and good crops (Lagos, Nigeria); by offering a young girl each year to the Niger (Bamanko, capital of the Republic of Mali), by building live children into the walls of a town to secure the defense of the town (Lake Chad region); by sacrificing one hundred and fifty persons at the obsequies of a sixteen-year-old prince and three thousand at the death of a queen (Kumasi, Ghana); and by burying alive the wives of princes at their death (Zandeland).[33]

These shocking experiences of sacrificing human beings force one to say religiously that they reveal a distorted view of God and the Will of God. Seeing through a glass darkly and not having a Micah to thunder out against human sacrifice, the African missed having fed into his pagan religious culture the idea that human sacrifice was an offense to God. For all the power accredited to deified ancestors, they seem to have failed to break through from their spiritual abode and direct the people to new heights of sacrifice.

It must be remembered, however, that the offensiveness of ancestor worship notwithstanding, Africans in this respect were not unlike other peoples in the stride toward an enlightened creative comprehensive view of the Will of God. For indeed, Abraham's being foiled in the attempt to offer Isaac as a burnt offering in response to God's orders, a test of faith, can hardly be understood independently of a context of human sacrifice; Jephtha's keeping of the vow of offering his daughter as a burnt offering can hardly be understood except within a cultural setting in which human sacrifice was accepted as a cultural and religious phenomenon; and the prophet Micah could hardly have raised the question of burnt offering pertaining to the immolation of first-born sons (the fruit of the body for the sin of the soul) except in a context in which such sacrifice was practiced.[34] The practice of human sacrifice in the religious rites of the Egyptians and the Romans is also a part of the record, all as a means of incurring the favor of the gods.

There is the story of human sacrifice, on the other hand, which may be termed "human sacrifice in the reverse." That is the murder of human beings, not as an offering to God but because man, in his nearsighted concept of God, assumed that to kill him who dissented from an approved dogma or rejected the God offered, was in harmony with the Will of God. The devotees of both Christianity and Islam have been guilty of this type of "sacrifice in the reverse." The adventurers of Mohammed and then the Califs have the bloody record of having carried the "long sword hidden under a religious banner,"[35] views of the death of the slaughtered as motivation to win souls to Allah.

Christians, acting from a zeal of God and faith in Jesus Christ, have done their "human sacrifice in the reverse." Examples of such experiences are seen among the Crusaders who captured Jerusalem, removed their shoes and sang Hosannahs: "Jerusalem, lift up thine eyes and behold thy liberators." They then proceeded, we are told, to slaughter the pagans, to herd all the Jews they could capture into the synagogue of Jerusalem and burn them alive.[36] Reacting against those who dared to depart from approved dogma and teachings of the church, Christians (?) are seen participating in "human sacrifice in the reverse" also by instigating the burning of persons at the stake: John Hus burned as a heretic on July 6, 1415; John Resby in 1407 and Paul Craw in 1432; Michael Servetus in 1453. These examples of violence under God illustrate the fact that the Africans have not stood alone in the non-creative approach to religion. This fact, nevertheless, fails to blot out the abiding values of the religions of men—Hebrew, Islam, Christian, African.

In close proximity to the abiding values of African religion is the given situation of community, fellowship, the kinship group. The experience of worship, and all the elements pertaining thereto, has served the purpose of cementing social relations around the kinship ideal. To this end K.A. Busia has noted that "Man, and the social relations of men, comes first; the things to serve the needs of men come second. This is the quintessence of African traditional culture."[37]

African religion, undergirded by the essential cultural aspirations of the people under the aegis of ancestor worship, has been functional in keeping alive the value of an abiding sense of social unity among members of the clan. Therefore, the value ascribed to the collectivity is given in the security provided individual members of the tribe and the moral stability of the corporate community. Something of the true dynamics of religion and ancestor worship is implied in K.A. Busia's argument that the disintegration of the social structure and the "decay of the ancestral cult appear to proceed together."[38]

In like manner the genuine value thrust of African religious life and thought is revealed by a member of a Nyasaland tribe, following his exposure to Christian convictions and practices between 1884 and 1904. Under the title, "The Religion of My Fathers," he offers a most cogent account of the built-in value of ancient African religion. We learn from this African that the social and religious life is lived as one; that in social troubles one appeals to the living family head, in spiritual crises appeal is made through the same family head and through him to the spirits of the ancestors whose abode is in the realm of the spirit, on to the God-spirit; and that the sum total of the health and good fortune of the living is contingent upon messages from the Supreme Being, mediated through ancestral spirits to the living clan.[39]

In fine, a genuine sense of value, religiously, is found in the dynamics of the kinship group which has traditionally tended to give Africans a sense meaning, understanding and reality. Herein has resided a regulating principle for the moral and social stability of the members of the kinship group. This is that which has served the purpose of eliminating from society many ills that haunt society generally. And, moreover, as Galbraith Welch has stated the case, "destitute widows and orphans, unloved, lonely spinsters and uncared-for elderly people" have been reported to be traditionally unknown in the cultural and religious setting thus described. Africans therefore anticipated in their bookless religions and cultural struggles a most profound religious truth, accentuated in the kinship group. This is that the eternally inherent value thrust of religion is to be found in a quality of fellowship created and maintained in intergroup relations and in mutual service to the corporate community.[40]

Closely related to ancestor worship, and geared to the same common ends, are other rites too numerous for treatment here. It is enough therefore just to name the rites and describe the same in a brief statement. These are the birth rite (generally shown in outdooring in which the new born is brought out and presented ritually in such way as to symbolize the desires of the kinship group to have the qualities of the ancestors to live and come to fruition in the new born); puberty rite (an initiation of youth into the mature tribal society and into certain safeguards of moral conduct); death rite (a ritual in which music, drumming, and dancing become means of coping with grief and expressing gratitude for the life of the deceased);[41] harvest festival (a time for thanksgiving, communal meal, pouring libation, purification of the stool); and the stool rite (a ritual in which the cult-group expresses its reverence for the ancestors of the chief, their deified ancestors).[42] In all of these rites the religious, social, political and social aspirations of the Africans are symbolized. From these rites we turn now to the artistic motif of African religion—Art.

ART AND RELIGION

Aesthetic sensitivity may be represented or symbolized in all spheres of life. Such a statement finds ample support in the painstaking job done by R. S. Rattray in his *Religion and Art in Ashanti,* for in this volume hardly any expression of African life is omitted. Art and religion embrace life in such comprehensive manner in this document that at one level or the other the total community is seen as a participant. The aesthetic life, therefore, is by no means the concern of a favored upper class. In a very real sense, then, art among the Africans may, in the spirit of Leo Tolstoy, be dubbed a spiritual blessing in which all the people participate.[43] So when art is made accessible to all the people it is a genuine means of transmitting a fresh flow of feeling from man to man, the creative upsurge of which gives life a new sense of depth and weds man to the essence of that which is symbolized, the positive side of which tends to lift man up to the ideal envisioned; the negative, the vulgar level of living, as implied in bad art. The fresh flow of feeling, moreover, transmitted by way of the religious motif in art, moves toward experience of value, truth, beauty, and the fullness of human well-being.[44]

Art in religion among the Africans (special art forms of carving, painting, pottery, etc. may be exceptions) has traditionally been accessible to all the people as participants. Aspects of such participation are implied in Rattray's review of the varied experiences of African life from birth on through the life cycle to the burial of the dead in which music, drumming and the dance allow for total clan participation.

In the special art forms (wood carving, stone, fired clay—terra cotta—, iron, bronze, brass formed by a lost wax method, pottery and basket making) the African has been credited with "working across the sub-Sahara" over a period of from twenty to thirty centuries and giving the world, in the estimation of Galbraith Welch, an "original art of vibrant vitality and queer searching images which have been of world import."[45] And Vernon Blake reinforces this evaluation of primitive African art in stating that

> the really appreciated part of their artistic effort is its representation; not perhaps quite as we recognize representation, that is, to a considerable degree, by estimating its value according to its degree of photographic 'likeness', but simply as being a kind of fixation of the idea.[46]

When the carved stools of Ashanti are taken as examples of art objects (the Golden stool symbolizes the highest expression of art of this form) of form, one learns, or is helped to catch a true glimpse of what is represented. That is, the stool "is not supposed to be like a soul." The African comes, has come, to recognize the stool to be an abiding place of the soul,[47] that is, the soul of deified ancestors. R. S. Rattray, in fact, holds that wood-carving, represented on a high level in stools, owes its origin to demands made pertaining to religious functions. The varied shapes and forms of the stools are assumed to have appeared to serve the need of the various spirits—living chiefs and departed ancestral spirits.[48] Of all the art forms, however, African artists seem not to have reached a high level in architecture. This does not obviate the fact of genuine achievement in art among Africans. So convincing has this achievement been shown to be that scientists have been compelled to revise their estimates of the cultural contribution of Africans.[49]

Generally, African art which represents scenes in which human beings are variously portrayed is often dubbed grotesque—men and women on bended knees, singularly short limbs with respect to the trunk, enormous heads, masks of terrifying expressions. Concerning these factual art expressions (representations) Maurice Delafosse reminds us that in these art pieces the artists had in view not the representation of living beings but the deified dead ancestors; they who imagined these likenesses sought to express symbolically a redoubtable divinity to those who are not initiated into the mysteries: both are believers, comparable to the anonymous artist to whom our old Gothic cathedrals owe those extraordinary gargoyles, those grimacing heads of demons, those statues of saints or the dead conventionalized in hieratical and formal attitudes.[50]

In the light of this insight we may conclude that at the point at which the artist transmits to the believers, members of the clan, something of his feeling and sentiment or the collective power of the antecedent generation—beliefs, feelings and aspirations—at that point a work of art has been wrought. If in a pre-theological setting the artist were able to project the feeling and treasured belief of the kinship group into "a variety of religious experiences having a scale of values," apprehended even if not clearly comprehended, then he did for his time and generation what the artist aims to do.[51] This seems to be the main thrust of religious art objects among the Africans.

Art among Africans in the remote past was interwoven into the same aspirations as those of the clan. In truth, R. S. Rattray has hinted that primitive man could hardly divorce the mythical, mystic, and religious from his handiwork.[52] So in stools, pottery, basket making, and in various objects capable of artistic treatment—spoons, combs, calabashes, doors, sticks, pots, pipes, and tools, etc.[53]—the African projected his religious and aesthetic delights. Appreciation for the artistic and a sense of awe are represented in names of the stools—the big spirit stool (gin or rum) and Golden Stool (shrine and symbol of the national soul).[54] The religious motif in the art of pottery which achieved a high level of perfection among the Ashanti is uniquely tied into a tradition which says that the art was learned from the God *Odomankoma* by a woman pottress called Osra Abogyo.[55] Even the Golden stool of Ashanti was believed to have descended from the skies, thus validating its being accepted as the sacred vehicle of the presence of the spirits of the ancestors and so the source of the moral, religious and social destiny of the people, and also the symbol of the politico ritual office.[56]

The foregoing representations of art and religion in Africa cover specialized art forms. The all-inclusive emphasis suggests that the people as a whole organized life around the religious and artistic impulse in these art forms. One could go on, as Basil Davidson has hinted, from the famous golden death-masks of the Ashanti King, representing achievements in highly skilled metal work, found in the Wallace Collection, London, England, to an almost endless number of wood-carvings of equatorial Africa, work in wood and metal of the upper Niger, etc., in search for manifestations of African consciousness and cosmogony and care for the decorative arts of life that comprise a world of their own.[57] Our purpose will be served here, however, by giving a summary statement on African art which includes drumming, dancing and singing in which full participation is the given phenomenon.

Addressing himself to the tradition of enstooling a king in Ashanti, K. A. Busia reminds us of the fact that when a chief is enstooled his person becomes sacred and that at the ceremony *Adae* the spirits of the departed (the chief becomes the intermediary between the living and the dead) are propitiated, names are called, favors and mercy solicited.[58] This is a religious rite which is experienced under the leadership of the chief. Marked features of the ceremony are characterized by drumming and dancing which have been traditionally employed as a means of invoking the spirits to bless the seeds at planting and to represent thanks at harvest festivals. The drums communicate something of the brave deeds of the ancestors of the chief and the people dramatize the same in the dance.[59]

A rather creative summary is given on art and religion by Jack Mendelshon. A synopsis of his appraisal of African culture will satisfy the need to see art and religion in perspective. Here it is noted that whether the art product is sculpture, carved objects, painting, pottery, the dance, singing or drumming, something of the religious affirmations of the people is implied. For in handicraft and bodily activity is encompassed an affirmation of a spiritual universe; the objects made bear the imprint of the sacred with a sacred role to play. The African is thus seen to be "expressionistic" in that his efforts in art form the essence of the spirit of deified ancestors, which could not be accomplished merely by reproducing the likeness of human beings. "The sacred purpose is to evoke only the essence, the vital force, the innermost rhythm."[60]

Art in religion, then, achieved a level of creative significance. It served the purpose of facilitating tribal participation in the religious meaning symbolized and the aspirations engendered. Finally, art has been a spiritual blessing in which the African has traditionally identified and participated in obedience to what has been affirmed to be the spirit and expectations of the ancestors, the intermediaries between the kinship group and the High God.

AFRICAN PROVERBS AND RELIGIOUS VALUES

Besides the values implied in an examination of ancestor worship and art in African religion, there are proverbs in which the value of the wisdom of the sage or wise man is set forth. This does not mean that aboriginal African life and thought are set before us in systematic thought. There is in the proverb, rather, the distilled essence of the human spirit, carved out of incisive observations on the experiences of living. The interest in African proverbs and their implied values, for our purpose, is limited to the section of Africa that was known as Gold Coast up to 1957.

In 1879 the Reverend J. G. Christaller had published the results of his intensive study of African language in Gold Coast, West Africa. This was part of the result of a rather long effort, made by German missionaries, to reduce African oral literature into written literary form. The result of Christaller's labors appeared under the title, *"Twi Mmebusem Mpensa-Ashansia Mmoaao,"* given the English title, "A Collection of Three thousand and six hundred Tshi Proverbs in use among the Negroes of the Gold Coast speaking the Asante and Fante (i.e. the Akan) language."[61] J. B. Danquah made use of about two hundred and twelve of these proverbs in his *Akan Doctrine of God.* [62] A selected number of the proverbs, plus an idiomatic English translation as given by J. B. Danquah will serve our purpose of marking out the religious values in African proverbs. The comments which follow each proverb are suggestive of the potential of the proverb to stimulate value responses. Each proverb is given the original number by Christaller and recorded by Danquah:

1.227 — *Obi Nkyere Abofra Onyame.* "God needs no pointing out to a child."

The validation of the reality of God in human experience is not contingent upon arguments about God or in attempts to point at an object of the senses which may be called God. This is to say, God is not a thing to be manipulated as a condition of establishing his reality, but a mental construct involving a transcending quality of being and symbolizing the rarity of the creativity of the human mind in its search for ultimate meaning. J. B. Danquah records the fact that Christaller understood *Onyame* to refer to Heaven or Sky, because the term refers to the high expanse firmament, the place of the sun, shining and glorified. Now when R. S. Rattray looked at the meaning here implied he came forward with the idea that the word *Onyame* pertains to Sky or luminous place, and so the proverb suggests that little children lying sprawling on their backs, looking into the sky do not need anyone to point it out to them. The fuller meaning of the term *Onyame,* however, suggests that he is not to be identified with the sky, moon, or stars[63] even though he is associated with them. Danquah thus holds that the genius of the human mind attributes to *Onyame* intelligence, personality, qualities of being which transcend the impersonal sky or firmament.[64]

This interpretation of the word *Onyame* lends further strength to the proverb. God, who needs no pointing out to the child, is a spirit who broods upon the stuff of experience and creates order, light, which dispels the darkness; God is spirit whose reality must be validated in spirit and truth. Man, any man, affirming faith in the reality of God, is ever challenged to commit himself to the pursuit of values as essences of God's creativity. So the spirit of the African sage breaks in upon every God-fearing people: "God needs no pointing out to the child"; the reality of God must be validated in the quality of life which is shot through with the spirit of God. The quality of life that is grounded in the creativity of God gives man, the clan, a foundation for growing up in the reality of God, the base of operation which helps man to become truly man. Although the ancestral spirits, mediating between the living and the dead, and also the High God in African life and thought functioned in such way as to sensitize the living to the will and reality of God, the fuller implication of our proverb communicates the truth that living man in dynamic interaction with living men alone can create the climate for communicating the reality of God in human experience.

2.301 — *Obi nnyaw astuten nkonom otare.* "No sensible man would leave a stream to drink from a pool."

The law of consistency is a test of sanity and moral integrity. A sensible creative mind, stimulated to think without confusion, wills to differentiate between value and disvalue, and also levels of value. Having done this, the sensible man wills always to make a choice of the best possible. Now to choose to leave a flowing stream and drink from a stagnant pool is utterly inconsistent with being sensible. The moral implications of this proverb stand out in bold relief: Man ought always choose the best possible of given alternatives. How does man know what is the best possible alternative? The insights of the African wise man suggest that the individual and the tribe follow the guidelines hewn out by the ancestors; the insights of the current age suggest that the individual and the community seek to become morally sensitive to those values which alone can deepen and enhance life in harmony with the will and powers of the ancestors.

3.1471 — *Woanhye Woho a, wonhye wo.* "Unless you control yourself, nobody would."

True discipline wells up from the inner potentials of human personality as the person interacts with the moral and religious content provided by society and as he internalizes the essences thereof as guidelines for inner and outer control. Unless man is controlled, disciplined, guided by inner self-imposed creative content he remains loose at both ends. True moral integrity, made meaningful in inter-personal and intergroup relations. arises and comes to fruition out of the inner moral and religious sensitivity of man. Whatever may be the limitations of the kinship group among Africans, all of the members of the clan were expected to develop the inner resources and disposition, to regulate the life of private desires and ambitions in accordance with the expectations of the kinship group in deference to the wishes of the ancestors who, from their abode in the spirit world, communicate with the clan. It may be assumed, then, that unconditionally man becomes man in community in which he is obliged to internalize the values, attitudes, and sentiments traditionally espoused by the kinship group, the condition to be met for full participation in the life of the tribe.

4.1996 — *Oman rebebo a, efi afi mu.* "The ruin of the city comes from the home."

This proverb has great value and undergirds a most profound insight relative to the dynamics of the home as an influence for good or evil influences in the larger community. It bears that which ought to be etched on the consciences of every member of the household or its substitute. The crime of the city, the violence of the city, and also the creative potentials of the city come from the home. Herein is suggested the awesome task that is given the home: it is given the task of becoming the type of community in which creative energy is distilled in such terms as to imbue the members of the household with a meaningful sense of self and reverent regard for values human and divine. For, indeed, coping with the spiritual malaise of any city demands the growth and development of healthy sentiments, refined feeling, right attitudes, respect for persons, property and the rights of others. The city is the home written in capital letters.

5.2436 — *Nnipa nyinaa ye Onyame mma; obi nye asase ba.* "All men are the offspring of God, no one is the offspring of Earth."

One great God, a cohesive principle running through African religious affirmations, is the creator of heaven and earth. It is no minor tribute to the human spirit, cultural circumstances notwithstanding, to ruminate upon the stuff of existence—man, animal and the sum total of the natural orders—and conclude that a dynamic creative spirit is, has been, at work in bringing into existence everything that is. No, not Earth, but *"Onyame."* He who is the Creator of all things and who never ceases to create.[65]

6.2453 — *Amo-bone ye okrabiri.* "A foul mouth is an affliction of soul."

Participating in the universal insights of the ages, reflected in the Old and New Testaments, and that of wise sages generally, the African communicates an eternal truth in this proverb. It compares favorably with the truths given in like statements found in the Gospel of Matthew and the Epistle of James: "The tongue is an unrighteous world among our members, staining of the whole body . . . (James 3:6)." "But what comes out of the mouth proceeds from the heart, and this defiles a man (Matthew 15:18)." A truth of universal import comes out of all these wise sayings: A pure heart is the remedy for a defiled soul.

7.2825 — *Wuse wobesom Nyankopon a, som no preko, na mfa biribi mmato ho.* "If you would serve God, be thorough, attaching no conditions."[66]

Such a proverb as this calls to mind Satan's challenging question to Job's God: "Does Job fear God for naught? (Job 1:96)." Both the proverb and the question asked call attention to a critically deep dimension of the religious life—unconditional loyalty and service to God. It is a difficult lesson that must be learned, provided religion is to reach the height and depth desired in the affairs of men. Pure religion and undefiled challenges the devotee now as always to be thorough in serving God, attaching no conditions.

AFRICAN AND OTHER RELIGIONS

The religions of the book, severally, have been enriched and refined by virtue of the cross-fertilization of world cultures. The people of Israel grew up to a high level of God-consciousness; from a God circumscribed by the land to a God who transcends time and space; from a God of a peculiar people to a God of all the people; from a God who rained down fire of the enemy to a God who willed that the enemy might be enveloped in the circle of his divine love; and from a God who agreed to covenant with his people in terms of what was written on tablets of stone to a God who accepted covenant agreement only in terms of what was written on the fleshy stones of the heart. These insights were posited as contents of the nature of the divine being by a people who interacted with the Egyptians, Canaanites, Babylonians, Syrians, Persians and Greeks, to name a few.

The Christian faith, emerging as it did out of the rich heritage of the Hebrew people, came to a level of maturity and intellectual respectability as the devotees and followers of Jesus Christ rubbed shoulders with the sophisticated representatives of the Graeco-Roman world. And, Mohammed, having been stimulated both by the genius of the Hebrew faith and the religion of Jesus, then, and only then, came and gave utterance to the idea of one God, Allah and Mohammed as his true prophet. In this affirmation he evidences reaction against implied monotheism in Christianity as he saw the situation in the dogma of the trinity. These three religions are undergirded by the principle of monotheism. It must be said of the Hebrew faith, however, that the full-grown monotheism came as a result of a long struggle and battle waged by the great prophets. For in the more primitive life of the people the gods are plentiful.[67]

The African, in contrast to the three religions mentioned above, and so far as the record has been able to show, on the basis of his own inherent resources and isolated from the cultures of the world, emerged with a God-concept as the Great One, impregnant with creative dynamics not unlike the three faiths considered here. The subsidiary divine beings delegated with special powers are real in African religion, but they are still subsidiary and, in a sense, sons or daughters of the Great One. For, indeed, the Great God alone exercises power of transcending import—the Creator, the Great Ancestor of ancestors.

In a rather real sense, the African who studies the *Old Testament* and the New Testament against the background of a penetrating knowledge of primitive African religion finds many parallels to his own religion: natural phenomena are symbolical of the presence and reality of God—pillar of cloud by day, pillar of fire by night as seen in Exodus 13:21 somewhat parallels the concept of *Onyame*, the God personified by the sun or bright firmament in Ashanti or *Shango*, the God of lightning and thunder of Yorubaland.[68] Subsidiary beings delegated with special powers among Africans are not unlike or far removed from the angels of the Lord among the Hebrews and the messengers of the nativity in the New Testament and also the communication of God's concern for Cornelius.[69]

Then, there is the situation of worship among the Africans which bears a content that closely resembles that of other religions. In ancestor worship, rites pertaining to birth, puberty, stools, harvest festivals, and death, the African makes use of prayers, hymns, sacrifice, libation, drumming and the dance. All of these are accentuated by movement, spontaneity and gaiety hardly matched by devotees of any other religion.[70] It is here that some real tensions are had between African religion and Christianity. Increasingly Africans who are Christians are nonetheless convinced that in African culture are values that ought to be honored and respected by the missionary be he of the Christian faith or Islam. For he knows that the Christian religion has not come to him free from the garb of primitive Western culture—the Christmas season and the Easter season.

As pertains to the quality of community that is sustained by way of worship in African culture, it has been observed that the sum total of the various ceremonials aid the process of keeping in focus a sense of the collective power of antecedent generations. The rites dealing with birth (outdooring) and puberty (initiation into adulthood) may thus be averred to be grounded in social and religious values comparable to christening and confirmation in certain communions of the Christian faith. And, by virtue of the binding power of the kinship group, these two rites may possess a dynamic of permanence lacking in the latter two.

Now when we critically examine the aesthetic principle which undergirds African religion and culture, we find it tempting to conclude that African art defies being put in second place to that of world religions. All art forms—carving, pottery, sculpture, basket making, painting, drumming, music and dancing—may be accepted as sacred media for communicating the feeling, sentiment and attitude intended.

Finally, we may conclude that when African proverbs (maxims) are placed alongside those of other religions they stand in no inferior position, the absence of a book notwithstanding; that despite cultural isolation the African caught a glimpse of reality in projecting an idea of God as Creator and who continues to create, even as does the God of Israel or of the Christian theologian; and that to know primitive African religion is to honor and respect the African as a significant contributor to world religious thought.

SELECTED BIBLIOGRAPHY

BOOKS

K. A. Busia, *The Position of the Chief in Ashanti*, London: Oxford University Press, 1951. This African author, Christian and sociologist, gives an analysis and description of the spiritual and political role of the chief in Ashanti.

————, *The Challenge of Africa*, New York: Frederick A. Praeger Publishers, 1962. Here one may observe something of the challenge of African culture and religion to western culture and religion.

J. B. Danquah, *The Akan Doctrine of God*, London: Lutterworth Press, 1944. From the perspective of what may be termed philosophical theology, the author of this volume interprets the doctrine of God as this doctrine emerged among a people without a book.

Basil Davidson, *The Lost Cities of Africa*, Boston: Little, Brown and Co., 1959. The story of what Africa has been in history is vividly portrayed in lost cities of long ago, symbolizing a culture of antiquity.

Maurice Delafosse, *The Negro of Africa, History and Culture*, Washington, D. C., 1931. A most penetrating analysis of African life, history and culture, also the religious life of the African is seen in this book.

Meyer Fortes, and Dieterlen, G., *African Systems of Thought*, London: Oxford University Press, 1965. Both in English and French the reader will find this book, a symposium; one finds a careful delineation of the African systems of thought within the culture that is African.

Melville Jean Herskovits, *The Human Factor in Changing Africa*, New York: Alfred A. Knopf, 1962. In this volume the reader will find a rather comprehensive treatment of African culture, religion and the changes that have been in process under the influence of new insights and African nationalism.

Jack Mendelshon, *God, Allah, and Ju Ju*, New York: Thomas Nelson and Sons, 1962. Viewing the dynamics of religion in world culture, the author opens up to view the significance of the God-concept as it is seen in Christian, Islam, and traditional African thought.

Geoffrey E. Parrinder, *African Traditional Religion*, London: Hutchinson House, 1954. He who wants to understand traditional African religion will find this volume to be an invaluable source of information.

————, *West African Religion*, London: Epworth Press,

1961. West African religious thought, practice, and cultural peculiarities are well marked out in this book. The reader will find it to be an objective approach to the problem of West African religion.

R. S. Rattray, *Religion and Art in Ashanti*, London: Oxford University Press, 1954. The all inclusiveness of the art motif in religion among the Africans of Ashanti is documented and interpreted from dimensions of depth in this book.

Dagobert D. Runes, *Despotism, A Pictorial History of Tyranny*, New York: Philosophical Library, 1963. The story of despotism and tyranny in religion and in nationalism is pictorially told in this volume. Though not a book on Africa, it will not let the reader forget the horrors wrought in the name of faith.

Edwin William Smith, *African Beliefs and Christian Faith*, London: The United Society for Christian Literature, 1937. The implications of African religious beliefs, viewed from the perspective of the Christian faith, are well marked out in this book. One will find it to be a real help in viewing religion comparatively.

John V. Taylor, *The Primal Vision*, Philadelphia: The Fortress Press, 1963. There are several helpful hints in this volume for creative encounters between African religion and culture and the Christian faith.

Galbraith Welch, *Africa Before they Came*, New York: William Morrow and Co., 1955. He who desires to know something about Africa before the coming of European influence will find this book to be of great value.

Diedrich Westermann, *The African and Christianity*, London: Oxford University Press, 1937. Many of the inherent values of African religion and culture are marked out in this book, and the points of their challenge to the Christian faith are indicated.

Carter G. Woodson, *The African Background Outlined*, Washington, D. C.; The Association for the Study of Negro History, 1936. A broad overview of the contributions of the Negro to world culture is provided the reader in the book.

ARTICLES

W. E. Abraham, "Mind of Africa", *Review Spectator*, Vol. 209,

December 14, 1962, p. 937. The African mind is seen at work in this article, as observed by the author.

K. A. Busia, "Ancestor Worship, Libation, Stool, Festivals", *Christianity and African Culture*, Accra, Gold Coast, Christian Council of the Gold Coast, 1955. A pamphlet of seven articles and a summary, based on a conference on African culture and the Christian faith. Each article contains information and deep insights pertaining to African religion and Christian thought.

——————, "The Conflict of Cultures, A Plea for Patience", *The Atlantic Monthly*, Vol. 203, April, 1959, pp. 81-84. An African sociologist critically examines and interprets the cultural conflicts between Africa and the West. He pleads for patience.

P. D. Fueter, "Theological Education in Africa", *International Review of Missions*, Vol. 45, October, 1956, pp. 377-395. An attempt made to propose a creative curriculum procedure for a Christian theology, designed to aid African students in making Christians of Africans.

Edmund C. O. Ilogu, "Religion and Culture in West Africa", *Theology Today*, Vol. 20, April 1963, pp. 53-60. Helps the reader to see and understand something of the dynamics of African culture and religion.

R. A. Kennedy, "West Africa in Prehistory", *History Today*, Vol. 8, Sept., 1958, pp. 646-653. Against the background of oral history, the writer provides a content that will help the reader to understand West Africa.

Melville F. Lagos, "Polygamy in West Africa", *International Review of Missions*, Vol. 12, June, 1923, pp. 403-411. an interpretation of African family life, its cultural habits in marriage, plus problems for Christian missions.

W. H. Lewis, "Islam: a rising tide in Tropical Africa", *Review of Politics*, Vol. 19, October, 1957, pp. 446-461. Islam is a great missionary contender for the soul of the African. Adjusting to African cultural patterns in a unique way, she challenges Christian missions at every turn.

E. Torday, "Curious and Characteristic Customs of Central Africa", *National Geographic*, Vol. 36, October, 1919, pp. 342-368. A critique in story and portrait.

T. Cullen Young, "The Religion of My Fathers", *International Review of Missions*, Vol. 19, July, 1930, pp. 362-376. A good account of African religion as told by an African who is not named. His story is given to the reader through the effort of T. Cullen Young.

NOTES

1. Melville Jean Herskovits, *The Human Factor in Changing Africa*, New York: Alfred A. Knopf, 1962, p. 178.
2. *Ibid.*
3. E. Geoffrey Parrinder, *African Traditional Religion*, London: Hutchinson House, 1954, p. 39.
4. Edwin William Smith, *African Beliefs and Christian Faith*, London: The United Society for Christian Literature, 1937, p. 79; Parrinder, *loc. cit.*
5. Parrinder, *op. cit.*, pp. 34 ff.
6. *Ibid.*, p. 35.
7. *Ibid.*, p. 36.
8. Smith, *op. cit.*, pp. 49 ff.
9. J. B. Danquah, *The Akan Doctrine of God*, London: Lutterworth Press, 1944, p. 55.
10. Smith, *op. cit.*, p. 50.
11. Edward Goeffrey Parrinder, *West African Religion*, London: Epworth Press, 1961, pp. 20, 27. Though *Orish-nea* is called the Great God, his function puts him in the role of a lesser god for he was sent to perform roles he did not design.
12. Smith, *op. cit.*, p. 50 f.
13. *Ibid.*, pp. 69, 79.
14. Parrinder, *West African Religion*, pp. 60 ff.
15. John V. Taylor, *The Primal Vision*, Philadelphia: The Fortress Press, 1963, p. 80. The summary is from a passage quoted by Taylor from Edwin William Smith's *African Ideas of God*, p. 18.
16. J. B. Danquah, *op. cit.*, p. 19.
17. *Ibid.*
18. Galbraith Welch, *Africa Before They Came*, New York: William Morrow and Company, 1955, p. 169.
19. Diedrich Westermann, *The African and Christianity*. London: Oxford University Press, 1937, p. 73.
20. Meyer Fortes, "Some Reflections on Ancestor Worship in Africa" in *African Systems of Thought*, London: Oxford University Press, 1965, p. 123.
21. *Ibid.*, p. 126.
22. *Ibid.*, p. 130.
23. Welch, *op. cit.*, p. 191.
24. *Ibid.*, pp. 191 ff.
25. Maurice Delafosse, *The Negro of Africa, History and Culture*, Washington, D.C.: The Associated Publishers, 1931, p. 227. Translated from the French by F. Fligelman.
26. *Ibid.*
27. *Ibid.*, p. 228.

28. Meyer Fortes, *Oedipus and Job in West African Religion,* Cambridge: University of Cambridge Press, 1959, p. 56.

29. K. A. Busia, "The Conflict of Cultures, A Plea for Patience," *Atlantic Monthly,* Vol. 203, 1959, pp. 81-84.

30. K. A. Busia, "Ancestor Worship, Libation, Stools, Festivals," in *Christianity and Culture,* a series of lectures. Accra, Gold Coast: Christian Council of the Gold Coast, 1955, pp. 17-23.

31. *Ibid.,* p. 20.

32. Delafosse, *op. cit.,* p. 230.

33. Welch, *op. cit.,* pp. 190-201. This resume of human sacrifice, according to Welch, is what appears in the literature on the subject, based on observation of Europeans in Africa up to as late as 1899. Britain and French did much during their colonial rule to stamp out human sacrifice.

34. *Genesis* 22:1-4; *Judges* 11:19; *Micah* 6:7. The judgment of God on human sacrifice among the people of Israel was kept alive by the prophets.

35. Dagobert D. Runes, *Despotism: A Pictorial History of Tyranny,* New York: Philosophical Library, 1963, pp. 2 ff.

36. *Ibid.,* p. 177.

37. K. A. Busia, *The Challenge of Africa,* New York: Frederick A. Praeger Publishers, 1962, p. 108.

38. K. A. Busia, "Ancestor Worship, Libation, Stools, Festivals," in *Christianity and African Culture,* Accra, Gold Coast, 1955, p. 22.

39. T. Cullen Young, "The Religion of My Fathers," *International Review of Missions,* vol. 19, 1930, pp. 362-376.

40. Welch, *op. cit.,* 169.

41. Westermann, *op. cit.,* p. 102; R. J. Figures, "Summary of Group Discussion," in *Christianity and African Culture,* Accra, Gold Coast, 1955.

42. K. A. Busia, *The Position of the Chief in Ashanti,* London: Oxford University Press, 1951, p. 364.

43. Leo Tolstoy, *What is Art?* London: Oxford University Press, 1959, pp. 148-149.

44. *Ibid.,* p. 288.

45. Welch, *op. cit.,* p. 216.

46. Vernon Blake, "The Aesthetic of Ashanti," in *Religion and Art in Ashanti,* by R. S. Rattray, London: Oxford University Press, 1954, p. 355.

47. *Ibid.*

48. R. S. Rattray, *Religion and Art in Ashanti,* London: Oxford University Press, 1954, p. 269.

49. Carter G. Woodson, *The African Background Outlined,* Washington, D.C.: The Association for the Study of Negro History, Inc., 1936, p. 165.

50. Delafosse, *op. cit.,* p. 257.

51. R. R. Maratt, "Some General Aspects of Ashanti Religion," in *Religion and Art in Ashanti,* R. S. Rattray, London: Oxford University Press, 1954, p. 392.

52. Rattray, *op. cit.,* p. 217.

53. *Ibid.,* p. 270 ff.

54. *Ibid.,* p. 130.

55. *Ibid.,* p. 301, *Odomonko* is the Creator God.

56. Meyer Fortes, "Some Reflections on Ancestor Worship in Africa," in *African System of Thought,* London: Oxford University Press, 1965, p. 138.

57. Basil Davidson, *The Lost Cities of Africa,* Boston: Little, Brown and Co., 1959, p. 144.

58. K. A. Busia, *The Position of Chiefs in Ashanti,* London: Interna-

tional African Institute, 1951, pp. 26 f. As set forth by R. S. Rattray, *Ashanti*, Chapters v-ix.

59. *Ibid.*, pp. 27-29.

60. Jack Mendelshon, *God, Allah, and Ju Ju*, New York: Thomas Nelson and Sons, 1962, pp. 88-89.

61. Danquah, *op. cit.*, p. 188.

62. *Ibid.*, pp. 188-197.

63. *Ibid.*, pp. 38 ff.

64. *Ibid.*

65. *Ibid.*, p. 39.

66. *Ibid.*, pp. 188-194.

67. See examples of gods in Genesis 22:28; 35-2, 4; Deuteronomy 32:17.

68. Parrinder, *African Traditional Religion*, pp. 45-47.

69. Psalms 91:11; Genesis 24:7; I Kings 19:3; Luke 2:10-12; Acts 10:3-7.

70. J. H. Nkitia, "The Contribution of African Culture to Christian Worship," *International Review of Missions*, vol. XLVII, 1958, pp. 265-278.

JAMES D. TYMS received his A.B. degree from Lincoln University, Missouri, his B.D. and M.A. degrees from Howard University School of Religion and Graduate School, and his Ph.D. from Boston University, where he continued his theological studies. He holds an honorary D.D. from Western Baptist Seminary, where he took his early teacher training. He has been a pastor and for five years served as a teacher and counselor at Morehouse College. His present position at Howard University dates from 1947. In 1956-57 he was a Fulbright Senior Research Scholar in the Gold Coast (Ghana), West Africa. Earlier he had been a General Education Board Fellow for Studies in Human Development. In 1957 he toured Europe and in 1959, Europe and Russia as a member of a peace seminar. Dr. Tyms has been published in many scholarly and religious publications, and he is a well-known lecturer.

AFRO-AMERICAN MUSIC AND DANCE

Mohan Lal Sharma

Slippery Rock State College (Slippery Rock, Pa.)

"We are the music-makers/And we are the dreamers of dreams,/Wandering by lone sea-breakers,/And sitting by desolate streams;/World-losers and world-forsakers,/On whom the pale moon gleams;/Yet we are the movers and shakers/Of the world forever, it seems."
—Arthur O'Shaughnessy

If we would know the Negro, let us study his songs. Who can say to what extent the Negro's life has been sung in his songs, or how much they have influenced it?[1]

In any discussion of Negro music and dance the question of inborn talents is sure to come up. It has been a cliché, not altogether dispelled by anthropologists and ethnomusicologists, that the Negro's sense of music is instinctive, or, at least, biologically derived from his African ancestors. That there is a Negro inheritance is undeniable, but perhaps it is not so much biological as cultural. Negroes who have grown to maturity out of reach of Negro cultural influences may have no more sense of counterpoint and blue tonality, and no greater ability to give out a rich, raspy, sandy, but withal "full-throated" cry, than, say, the average Hudson Bay Eskimo.[2] Conversely, a non-Negro reared in a Negro community could be expected to possess, at least, average awareness and feeling for Negro music.

Which brings us to the question-cum-claim: Has any minority group ever started out with greater handicaps and made more

139

significant progress in a shorter time in the history of man than the American Negro?[3] After listening spellbound to Marian Anderson's Salzburg recital, the renowned Toscanini said: "What I have heard today is not heard once in a hundred years." Everyone should know, or have the opportunity to know, the thrilling story of the achievements of the Negro in many a field, especially, in dance and music, which (fields) are uniquely stamped by "the beauty of the genius" of the Negro, to use a golden phrase of W. E. B. Dubois.[4] Such a story, made available to and in every school and library, would show his "Soul Music"[5] as one of the prime examples of "the beauty of holiness" and "the holiness of beauty," involving what Gerardus Van der Leeuw has perceptively designated as *Vom Heiligen in der Kunst* in his famous book bearing the same title.[6] Here is a strong refutation of the infamous dictum of Kant put, in his book *Beobachtungen über das Gefühl des Schönen und Erhabenen* of 1764: "The Negroes . . . have, by nature, no feeling which transcends the silly (das Läppische)."[7]

The term "Negro music" is no less inapt and imprecise than "white music," and, for reasons that are readily apparent, the once favored term "Afro-American music" can be both inadequate and misleading. Yet, there remains the necessity of having an expression by which to refer to the musical and the musico-literary traditions of the Negro community in the United States of America. The term "Afro-American" in relation to Negro custom—musical or otherwise—seems to imply that African tradition is supremely significant and that Negro music-making in the United States has an essentially African core. Few scholar-critics entertain this position, even though the paramount importance of the African contribution has become increasingly clear. "Negro music," on the other hand, suggests, perhaps unwittingly, that race has something to do with tradition, a concept that is rather untenable in the light of modern, scientific knowledge. Influences that played a part in the development of music in Negro communities (African as well as American), as has been noted in the opening remarks of this article, were not racial. Thus, different settings, different local histories, and different juxtapositions in America produced different kinds of "Negro," or "Afro-American" music.[8]

O I'm gonna sing, gonna sing
Gonna sing all 'long the way,
O I'm gonna sing, gonna sing,
Gonna sing all 'long the way.

The Negro slave from Africa, with his "bent and lash-scarred back" (in Alain Locke's sensitive and compassionate parlance), was introduced into an alien culture and was constantly modifying and being modified by it. In the new American environment it is indeed remarkable that the Negro music or dance, in such a relatively short period of development, could and did retain its special character and become so prolific.

Music played so vital a part in African—civilized or jungle—life that it is natural that the Negro continued singing after reaching America. Of course, the Negro "has always been a great singer, but the Caucasian peoples have had to be reminded of this fact again and again before they were convinced, or attached any importance to the conviction." Ironically, the Negro himself was convinced last of all.[9]

The calamity of his cruel enslavement perhaps stirred the Negro's "inner self," if not his whole being, to sing more than he did before. Paradoxically, then, Southern America, by culturally rejecting the "poor whites" but patriarchically accepting the Negro (on its own terms, which, surely, included keeping him "in his place"), paved the way for Negro folkways to become the peasant culture of nearly three-fourths of its geographic area. (If American civilization had absorbed instead of exterminating the American Indian, his music and culture would have been the folk music and culture of this land.) This fate (no less awesome than the one in Greek dramaturgy) or *kismet* (as the Arab concept goes), which was and to an extent still is the Negro's unfortunate ordeal, had one lone compensation, as Emerson would have put it. The immobility, reinforced by the psychological weight of prejudice, developed an unusual degree of group solidarity, fostered folk values, thus intensifying the Negro's traditional modes of expression—music and dance, particularly, serving as cathartic, emotional exhausts and safety-valves for successful survival. By virtue of unique folk qualities and their perennially fresh artistic manifestations, the foundations of which were well laid before the end of slavery, the Negro has made America and the entire world, considerably, his cultural debtor.[10] Strange mockery of destiny this, that the group in the American population most subject to oppression, suppression and repression should provide so large a share (in effect, the "lion's") of the American people's joy and relaxation. A brilliant ex-slave, Frederick Douglass, metaphorically called slavery "the graveyard of the mind," but happily, thanks to the Negro genius for song and dance, it did not turn out to be the tomb of the Negro spirit.

How much of the African idiom remained in the New World's Negro song is hard to measure. Complete separation of the Africans from their native land and from their kith and kin, and their sudden and forced introduction into and exploitation by an utterly alien culture, brought about an inevitable interruption of African culture and mores in America.

Opinions among experts vary considerably regarding the amount of African culture surviving in American Negro life. Some rate it negligible. Others, including Dr. Lorenzo D. Turner, who sees the situation linguistically, contend, however, that the survivals are extensive.

THE SPIRITUAL

Lord, I want to be a Christian
In my heart, in-a my heart
Lord, I want to be a Christian
In-a my heart.

The largest number of Negro (folk-) songs collected thus far are spirituals. They were first presented to the world at large by the Fisk Jubilee Singers, who toured America and Europe from 1871 to 1878.

Spirituals are shy, elusive things; they defy notation. If you wish to capture them, you have to steal up behind them unbeknownst, and sprinkle salt on their tails, listening, all the time, with your "heart in your ears." For lack of fitting symbols, it is impossible, however, to set down on paper many of these songs as they are sung in their native setting. Extravagant postamenta, slurs, and free use of extra notes serve to mystify the ardent collector who strives for accuracy, too.

Of much interest are the scales of the Negro employed in the spirituals. He unconsciously avoids the fourth and seventh major scale steps in many songs, thereby using the pentatonic scale. But there are employed notes foreign to the conventional major and minor scales with such frequency as to justify their being regarded as distinct. The most common of these are the "flatted third" (the feature note of the blues) and the "flatted seventh."

Spirituals, though orally transmitted, were actually history. Allen, Ware, and Garrison's *Slave Songs of the United States* (1867), a "landmark,"[11] was widely advertised and speedily sold, like hot cakes and loaves, as illuminating the history of the American Negro. Collectors justified their generalizations with contemporary data, although internal evidence attests that all the songs were developmental.

At least eight kinds of material went into the making of spirituals.

1. First came the *African* or rather the Gulf Stream of African musical influence.[12]

2. Among those who noted the influence of *nonhymnal European airs* upon Negro spirituals was Fanny Kemble, who mentioned Scotch and Irish tunes.

3. *Hymns* were introduced among slaves in the eighteenth century.

4. *White songs* of the North American possibly influenced spirituals.

5. Christian and Jewish *theology, mythology,* etc.

6. The *pilgrim,* the chief actor of Bunyan's *Pilgrim's Progress.*

7. *Representative Christians* and leaders such as the great Lincoln.

8. The great spiritual events of *American history* were frequent subjects of spirituals. Slave songs throw light upon camp meetings, African colonization, the oral instruction of Negroes after 1831, work and leisure-time activities of Negroes, the Civil War with its soldiers, education, and evangelism, and the Reconstruction. How Negroes accepted Americanization is told with some color. Had every spiritual been preserved, a complete story of every emotion of American Negroes would be available.[13]

More than one person has expressed doubt that Negro spirituals were primarily music.[14] At Leipzig, musicologists did not publicize the singing of Negro spirituals by Roland Hayes as music "at all."[15] But, the considered opinion, today, is that the spirituals reflect the most serious and intimate aspects of the slave Negro. Under the crucible-like pressures of slavery, with semiliterate but deep absorption of the essentials of Christianity, the slave Negro found with amazing intuition and insight his two main life-sustaining aspirations: the hope of salvation and that of freedom. This was a creative action (or reaction) of the highest magnitude; it saved his sanity and built up his inner strength.[16] It was also a rare triumph of folk art. From the episodes and imagery of the Bible, the Negro imaginatively reconstructed his own versions in musical and poetic patterns both markedly original and of immense emotional vitality. The borrowed materials were given new life and a magical mysticism, issuing surprisingly from a naïve and literal acceptance of biblical truths and their translation into homely but withal most strikingly concrete imagery that can be conceived. Serious hymns became rhapsodic chants, and the biblical lore came alive again in such new startling colloquialisms as the "deep river that chills the body but not the soul," "Dese bones gwine to rise again," "Bright sparkles in de churchyard give light unto de tomb," and "My Lord is so high you can't get over him,/He's so low you can't get under Him,/You gotta come in an' through de Lamb."

From Old Testament sources, the slaves' *free* imagination singled out the episodes most relevant to their plight, using Jewish parallels to feed their flame-like or flickering hopes of liberty, chiding shrewdly and challenging their *unfree* (slaves of MAMMON) masters with their own beliefs. There was social pointedness, as also religious faith, to such exclamations and exhortations as "Go down, Moses, tell ole Pharaoh to set my people free" and "Didn't my Lord deliver Daniel and why not every man?" "Steal away to Jesus" was, sometimes, a plea for revival conversion, at others, a password for camp-meeting assemblies, and occasionally, so goes the story, a signal for fugitives. Rescued from the stigma and disesteem of slavery and judiciously appraised, these first-crop folk creations fully endorse James Weldon Johnson's estimate: "The Uncle Remus stories constitute the greatest body of folklore America has produced, and the spirituals are its greatest single body of folk-song." Although reactions to the Negro's own specific situation and experience, they are so profoundly intense as to become significantly universal; there are no finer expressions than these Negro folk utterances of the belief in freedom and immortality or of the emotional essences of Christianity native to the American soil.[17]

THE BLUES

Woke up dis mornin' feelin' sad an' blue
Woke up dis mornin' feelin' sad an' blue
Didn't have nobody to tell my troubles to.

The blues differ radically from the spirituals. The spirituals are choral and communal, the blues are solo and individual. The spirituals are passionately religious and intensely other-worldly, the blues are just as intensely worldly. The spirituals sing of heaven, and of the shining hope that after death the singer may enjoy the celestial joys to be had there. The blues singer has no interest in heaven, and little hope on earth. Suffering from a kind of an existential *angst*, he is a thoroughly disillusioned fellow, akin to the proverbial cynic, who, by (standard) definition, is "one who knows the price of everything and the value of nothing." The spirituals were made in and for the church; the blues sprang from daily, hard existence. The lofty words of many spirituals could be read and sung from the most exalted pulpit, while the blues are not even, or often, print-worthy. The spirituals needed no accompanying musical instruments, but these go well with the blues. Nevertheless, one could scarcely imagine a convention of any kind in connection with this Negroid free music. It is partial to the three-line stanza instead of the customary one of four or more, though not insisting on it, and it ends with a high note that has the effect of incompleteness. The close of a stanza comes with a shock like the whip-crack surprise at the end of an O. Henry story, for instance —a gimmick, but not ineffective as a novelty. It sings of themes remote from those of the old religious, or spiritual "staples," and, above all, its skimpiness of the stanzaic form makes the listener gasp, suspecting some odd trick beyond the censor's province and power.

As is well recognized, the Negro normally is a person of strong religious impulse, and the spirituals are justly famous as expressions of his religious moods; but, they do not exhaust his nature nor fully "mirror" it. The Negro, like any human being, has longings, regrets, despondencies, and hopes that sway him strongly, but are not connected with religion. The blues may, therefore, be said to voice his secular interests and emotions as sincerely and effectively as the spirituals do the sacred ones.

"Blues" originated during the first quarter of the nineteenth century. The black masses used them "as a vehicle for expressing the individual mood of the moment."[18] It has been admitted that the blues are woven from the same stuff as work songs, love songs, and other songs. They are all, in effect, developments from the spirituals. A teenager once remarked (the keen-ager would perhaps concur) that jazz made one pat his feet and swing on the outside while a spiritual might evoke the same emotion "on the inside."

W. C. Handy has put it rather well. He says that the blues express the Negro's twofold nature, the grave and the gay, and reveal his ability to appear the opposite of what he is.

"Most people think that the Negro is always cheerful and lively," Handy explains. "But he isn't, though he may seem that way sometimes when he is most troubled. The Negro knows the blues as a state of mind, and that's why this music has that name.

"For instance: suppose I am a colored man, and my rent is due. It's twenty dollars, and my landlord has told me that if I don't pay him today he'll put me and my things out on the sidewalk. I haven't got twenty dollars, and I don't know where to get it. I've been round to all my friends, and asked them to lend me that much, but they haven't got it, either. I have nothing I can sell or pawn. I have scraped together ten dollars, but that's positively all I can get and that's not enough.

"Now when I know the time has come and I can't get that twenty dollars, what do I do? The white man would go to his landlord, offer him the ten, and maybe get the time extended. But what do I do? I go right out and blow in that ten dollars I have and have a gay time. Anybody seeing me would think I

146

was the jolliest darky in town, but it's just because I'm miserable and can't help myself.

"Now, if a Negro were making a song about an experience like that, it would be a genuine specimen of blues."

And so the blues go on, singing of all conceivable interests of the Negro, apart from his religious interests, which are well taken care of in his spirituals and other religious songs. These fleeting stanzas (called *verses*), rhymed or in free verse that might fit in with the most liberated of *vers-libertine* schools of poetry, these haunting tunes that are albeit so hard to capture within bars, have a vibrancy and vitality lacking in more sophisticated metrical movements. One specimen speaks of its own tune, saying: "the devil brought it but the Lord sent it." This kind of music is very much here and has its own interest and value, as music and as a sociological phenomenon of great momentousness.

Isaac Goldberg suggests, following no less an authority than W. C. Handy, that the spirituals, ragtime, and jazz form one continuous sequence of Negro music; that ragtime, essentially, is nothing more than a "pepped-up secular version" of the Negro spirituals. As Goldberg later says, "Ragtime, then, is, in part, the pagan release of the Negro from his addiction to holiness, and his rhythms brought to us something of that—deliverance. . . . The spirituals translate the Bible; ragtime translates the other days of the week."

In spite of the obvious development of ragtime and jazz from Negro sources and the pioneer wizardry of Negro dancers and musicians, the question frequently pops up: "How Negro is jazz after all?" No one will deny that the elements of ragtime and jazz can be found elsewhere in the world, not only in other folk music, but as a device of syncopation in some of the most classical music, Beethoven's for example. But jazz and ragtime are, nonetheless, distinctively, Negro. Original jazz is more than syncopation and close eccentric harmony: it has a distinctive intensity of mood and a peculiar style of technical performance. Of course, these can be copied but their original pattern was Negro. Inborn with the folk Negro, this is a quality detected in a stevedore's swing, a preacher's cadenced sermon, a bootblack's flick, or the "amen" emitted in a church.

This can be said, however, only of the early jazz, which remains not only the most racial, but also musically the most powerful of the species.[19]

Captain, Captain, you must be cross
It's six o'clock an' you won't knock off!

By nature rhythmical, the Negro works better if he sings at his labor. He can work not only more pleasurably to himself, but more profitably to his employer, for he moves faster and accomplishes more if he sings. This is well recognized by those who employ bands of Negroes at various types of work, as on construction gangs, and the like, and the fact is taken advantage of. Singing is encouraged—not as an art, but as an economic factor in efficiency. Song leaders are chosen, formally or informally, their responsibility being to speed up the efforts of the workers.

SONGS ABOUT ANIMALS

Monkey sitting on the end of a rail,
Picking his teeth with the end of his tail.

The Negro is perhaps at his "creative best" when he is making songs about animals. The living creatures around him are very real to him, and perennially interesting, even inspiring at times. He makes them the objects of his amused observation, his philosophic study, and he loves to rhyme their antics and tricks, traits and characteristics; for the Negro is closer to nature than most people, say the ancient Greeks and Romans, ever have been. A small Negro boy drives a cow to pasture with the air of a Hindu devotee escorting a sacred personality; while an old woman converses with her cat, hen, "horny ox," "mulie," "Bre'r Rabbit," "blue-tailed fly," "po' inch-worm," "the boll weevil," "the picaresque rattler," and other friends, on affairs nearest her golden heart.

Of course, the Negro sings about the animal world because he likes animals as God's creatures—ALL THAT LIVES IS HOLY. The Negro may deal with his subjects impersonally, as figures in a universal comedy. Or, he may compare his lot, his *Historia Calamitatum* (to use the historic phrase of Pierre Abelard) to theirs in songs which arouse deep compassion rather than mere passion.

> Oh, the wind is in the west,
> And the guinea's on her nest,
> And I can't find any rest
> For my baby.

No figure of the old South was more vivid or more beloved than the "black mammy," with her white apron and her gay bandana, or *tignon*, on her head, tending her small charges and singing them to sleep.

Here too, the cruel conditions of Slavocracy made the Negro lavish love—or demonstration of affection—on her white charges rather than on her own kids. Thus, in her peculiar job situation tears and smiles ran together. While she made the children laugh, her predicament, nonetheless, fitted like a glove the well known poetic complaint uttered by William Blake in one of his greatest humanitarian moods:

> And because I am happy and dance and sing,
> They think they have done me no injury,
> And are gone to praise God and His Priest and King,
> Who make up a Heaven of our misery.

These simple, homely songs have a touching charm characteristic of folk songs lacking in professionally composed lullabies; for as H. E. Krehbiel has well said, folk music constitutes "the most truthful and the most moving music in the world."

DANCE-SONGS OR "REELS"

Down through the years the old dance tunes tinkle gaily. They have a vitality to match that of the boll weevil proverbially sung of in the Negro ballads, surviving not only time's onslaughts but those of man.

An early folk gift of the African Negro to America was, indeed, rhythm. Of the many reasons advanced for this unmatched skill, the most likely is *the* fact that the Negro has had such long, unbroken contact with dance. Dancing for the Negro has always been a spontaneous and normal mode of expression rather than an artificial and formalized one. The Negro dancer

149

improvises not only in solos, but quite often in group dancing. Seemingly a matter of foot movements, rhythm in Negro dancing begins from within as a body vibration and throughout the entire dance the body vibrates in coordination, sympathetically. The Negro dancer's capacity to elaborate on a basic rhythm by changing, doubling, and skipping beats bewilders those less expert in rhythmic patterns. Along with this, the Negro dance has the features, common to Russian, Polish, and other Slavic folk dances, of sudden and startling changes of pace, of daring climaxes of tempo. Such subtle ways of varying the simplest rhythmic patterns are the secret of their extraordinary and basic musical appeal. Many critics consider the Negro rhythm inimitable in its naturalness, its lack of self-consciousness, and its freedom and technical assurance.

To retell "the dizzying tale" (Melville's language) of the Negro: When the Negro was first imported into North America as slave, he brought with him the religious and ritualistic dances of his African tribal culture. Over a period of time, however, with the Negro's adoption of Christian beliefs and practices, the African forms were modified—at times, absorbed by the dominant culture, at others assimilated.

In her essay, or rather scholium, entitled "The Negro Dance," Katherine Dunham points out that England (and, by extension, America) is more prone than, say, France, to impose its own culture on a minority. Says she: ". . . the integrity of African culture and the sanctity of African religious tradition persists to a greater extent in, for example, Haiti and Martinique than in Jamaica or Trinidad." She concedes, nonetheless, that, although "a direct retention of African forms in North America is certainly the exception rather than the rule," there is clear evidence of assimilation of African modes into Christian religious expression. She cites hand-clapping, foot-stamping, the "confession" and "conversion," the jumping and leaping that characterize many church rituals as carry-overs from Africa's Old World (tribal?— not a satisfactory word really) to the New World.

Inasmuch as the dance is concerned, "the transition from tribal to folk culture expressed itself in three ways," Miss Dunham notes. She points out: "1. the use of African ritual patterns for the expression of Christian ideology; 2. the degeneration of religious ritual patterns by virtue of the degeneration of the ideology which sustained them into secular use; and 3. the combination of secular African patterns with the secular patterns of whatever European nation happened to dominate the territory." Here, in America, the "Juba" dance, well described by Thomas Talley in *Negro Folk Rhymes* as a dance involving a large number of participants, is a fine instance of a secular.[20]

In "Juba" the big group maintains hand-clapping and foot-tapping, and dances singly or in pairs. Talley's explanation—plausible enough—is that the foot-tapping is a substitute for the drum beats of jungled Africa, which Mungo Park, David Livingstone, and other stalwarts were fortunate and brave enough to enjoy in person.

There being no drums in America, foot-tapping was naturally resorted to and instituted. From this point on, the story or the rest of it is that of the Negro genius for "passionate inwardness" (in Kierkegaard's illustrious phrase) and for inspired, inspiring expressiveness of the highest distinction.

Emotion, Aime Césaire, the poet from Martinique, claims, is at the heart of négritude: Emotion *is* Negro. Sings he:

My négritude is neither a tower nor a cathedral
It plunges into the red flesh of the earth
It plunges into the burning flesh of the sky
It pierces the opaque prostration by its upright patience.[21]

Simple, humble words these, but they are charged with the power of music to which all art aspires. Music is, surely, the one "god that did not fail" the Negro. It is high time (and high space) that America and the whole world appreciated—properly—the Afro-American's unique gift and through this sublime medium the splendorous soul of the Negro. *SIC DEUS DILEXIT MUNDUM* (FOR THOSE WHO LOVE THE WORLD)—as Pierre Teilhard de Chardin has it, epigraphically, in *The Divine Milieu: An Essay on the Interior Life.*[22]

To put the matter in a philosophico-critical nutshell, it might be safely said that even if Afro-American Music and Dance are not quite analogous to an eagle's nest built over an abyss, they, surely, are incomparable for impromptu musicianship, extraordinary techniques, mystically spontaneous harmony, forceful rhetoric,[23] spectacular imagery, brilliantly dramatic projection, and, above all, felicity and facility in controlling and improvising rhythm which defy trite analyses and pseudoscientific explanations.

May these great gifts of the Negro light many a candle, small and big! May their refreshing currents reach even the most unresponsive ears, and through the ears all the hearts! Thus will part of the dream of the great Negro leader King come true, cancelling the curse of "darkness," using the word with its cluster of literal and metaphorical connotations. Thus will the deeply moving story of the Negro's song and dance come alive as the story of his "life-blood," of his "master-spirit," charismatically combining Apollonian lucidity with Dionysian, "primal" unity.

SELECTED BIBLIOGRAPHY

BOOKS

Bailey, T. A., *The American Pageant: A History of the Republic.* D. C. Heath & Company, Boston, 1956. A standard, well-documented *opus*, which in its 1007-page treatment is comprehensive in scope touching on every fact, including the black American's contributions. A big mirror with many smaller mirrors reflecting and refracting the multiple images of the American identity, entity and reality.

Beard, Charles A. and Mary, *The Rise of American Civilization*, Vols. I-II. Macmillan Company, New York, 1930. Excellent for an overall view.

Brawley, Benjamin, *A Social History of the American Negro.* Macmillan Company, New York, 1921. Useful to begin research on anything pertaining to the Negro's special situation in America.

————, *The Negro Genius.* Biblo & Tannen, New York, 1966. An intriguing discussion that directs the reader's attention and interest toward the American blackman's solid achievements. It is not just effervescent talk, which, like a bottle of coke, leaves "nothing" behind.

Brown, Ina C., *The Story of the American Negro.* Friendship Press, New York, 1936. Chapter ten has, among others, sections entitled "The Negro's Gifts to America" and "The Negro's Achievements," which objectively and fairly eulogize great Negro entertainers and sportsmen.

Drake, St. Clair & Cayton, H. R., *Black Metropolis.* Harcourt, Brace & Company, New York, 1945. Carrying an Introduction by Richard Wright, the book is a socioeconomic mine of agonizing information which explains why the Negro finds a cathartic release, or escapist exhilaration in song and sport.

Henderson, Edwin B., *The Negro in Sports.* The Associated Publishers, Inc., Washington, D. C., 1939. A pithy, in effect, to-the-point, report on the subject by a Negro sportsman of considerable prominence.

Jennings, H. S., *The Biological Basis of Human Nature.* W. W. Norton, New York, 1930. Explodes some "lovely and ugly nonsense" about the Negro's allegedly special biological traits endowing him with magical athletic ability.

Locke, Alain (ed.), *The New Negro.* Albert & Charles Boni, New York, 1925. A landmark that gave the Negro a much-needed "new image" and boost.

Meany, Tom & Tommy Holmes, *Baseball's Best.* Franklin Watts, Inc., New York, 1964. This is "the all-time, all-star team of baseball history," which, like all human history, repeats itself, signifying, in the case of the Negro a great deal, rather than the "sound and fury" summed up in the famous Shakespearean cliche.

Robinson, Jackie, *Baseball Has Done It.* J. B. Lippincott Company, Philadelphia & New York, 1964. A Negro star tells his story in his own words, often speaking out freely à la "the good grey poet" Whitman quoted epigraphically, "And why should I not speak to you?" An intriguing Odyssey that challenges the perceptive as well as the superficial reader to sit up and read on and on.

Rose, Arnold, *The Negro in America.* The Beacon Press, Boston, 1961. The classic condensation of Gunnar Myrdal's famed *magnum opus The American Dilemma,* this is a study in depth of the Negro problems. By no means a substitute for cigars, alcohol, and drugs, this is a basic tool for research on the Negro in every important field. Sports, with their paramount importance, are no exception.

Stobart, J. C., *The Glory That Was Greece*. Sidgwick & Jackson, London, 1960 Reprint. This is a "stunningly" scholarly treatment of the sunrise, twilight, and sunset of Greece's gloriously humanistic values, one being the harmonious physical-cummental development and improvement of her citizens. The implications for America and other lands are there for anyone to fathom.

Thompson, Daniel C., *The Negro Leadership Class*. Prentice-Hall, Inc., Englewood Cliffs, N. J., 1963. This book carries an inseminating foreword by Martin Luther King, Jr. and a chapter entitled "The Negro Leadership Class: *Occupational Characteristics*," which is highly relevant to the gifted Negro sportsman's herculean efforts to raise himself by the bootstraps in a highly complex and competitive world.

Work, Monroe N. (ed.), *Negro Year Book*, 1931-   Negro Year Book Publishing Company, Tuskegee Institute, Ala., 1932-   Useful.

———, (ed.), *A Bibliography of the Negro in Africa and America*. H. W. Wilson Company, New York, 1928. Even though outdated, it remains a handy source for the researcher looking for early material on the subject.

ARTICLES

Backus, E. M., "Negro Songs from Georgia," *Journal of American Folk Lore*, vol. X, 1897, pp. 116, 202, 216; vol. XI, pp. 22, 60. Six religious songs.

————, "Christmas Carols from Georgia," *Journal of American Folk Lore*, XXII, 1899, p. 272. Two songs.

Barton, W. E., "Hymns of Negroes," *New England Magazine*, Vol. XIX, pp. 669 et seq., 706 et seq. A number of songs with some musical notation and discussion.

Bergen, Mrs. F. D., "On the Eastern Shore," *Journal of American Folk Lore*, vol. II, 1889, pp. 296-298. Two fragments, with a brief discussion of the Negroes of the eastern shore of Maryland.

Brown, J. M., "Songs of the Slave," *Lippincott*, vol. II, 1868, pp. 617-623. Several songs with brief comments.

Cable, George W., "Creole Slave Songs," *Century*, vol. XXXI, 1885, pp. 807-828. Twelve songs with some fragments, music of seven.

Clarke, Mary Almsted, "Song Games of Negro Children in Virginia," *Journal of American Folk Lore,* vol. III, 1890, pp. 288-290. Nine song games and rhymes.

Garnett, L. A., "Spirituals," *Outlook,* vol. CXXX, 1922, p. 589. Three religious songs. However, they appear to have been polished considerably by the writer.

Haskell, M. A., "Negro Spirituals," *Century,* vol. XXXVI, 1888, pp. 577 et seq. About ten songs with music.

Hentoff, Nat. "Jazz and Jim Crow," The *Commonweal,* vol. LXXIII, 26, March 24, 1961. Useful.

Higginson, T. W., "Hymns of Negroes," *Atlantic Monthly,* vol. XIX, 1867, pp. 685 et seq. Thirty-six religious and two secular songs with musical notation.

Lemmerman, K., "Improvised Negro Songs," *New Republic,* vol. XIII, 1918, pp. 214-215. Six religious songs or improvised fragments.

Lomax, J. A., "Self-pity in Negro Folk Songs," vol. CV, *Nation,* 1917, pp. 141-145. About twenty songs, some new, others quoted from Perrow and Odum, with discussion.

————, Negro Hymn of Day of Judgment," *Journal of American Folk Lore,* vol. IX, 1896, p. 210. One religious song.

Odum, Anna K., "Negro Folk Songs from Tennessee," *Journal of American Folk Lore,* vol. XXVII, 1914, pp. 255-265. Twenty-one religious and four secular songs.

Odum, Howard W., "Religious Folk Songs of the Southern Negroes," *Journal of Religious Psychology and Education,* vol. III, pp. 265-365. About one hundred songs.

————, "Folk Song and Folk Poetry as Found in the Secular Songs of the Southern Negroes," *Journal of American Folk Lore,* vol. XXXIV, 1911, pp. 255-294; 351-396. About 120 songs.

Parrish, Lydia. "The Plantation Songs of Our Old Negro Slaves," *Country Life,* Vol. LXIX, 1935. Useful.

Perkins, A. E., "Spirituals from the Far South," *Journal of American Folk Lore,* Vol. XXXV, 1922, pp. 223-249. Forty-seven songs.

Perrow, E. C., "Songs and Rhymes from the South," *Journal of American Folk Lore,* vol. XXV, 1912, pp. 137-155; vol. XXVI, pp. 123-173; vol. XXVIII, pp. 129-190. A general collection containing 118 Negro songs, mostly secular.

Redfearn, S. F., "Songs from Georgia," *Journal of American Folk Lore*, vol. XXXIV, 1921, pp. 121-124. One secular and three religious songs.

Robinson, Louie. "Charles White: Portrayer of Black Dignity," *Ebony*, vol. XXII, 9, July, 1967. Useful.

Speers, M. W. F., "Negro Songs and Folk Lore," *Journal of American Folk Lore*, vol. XXVIII, 1910, pp. 435-439. One religious and one secular song.

Speight, W. L. "Notes on South African Native Music," *The Music Quarterly*, vol. XX, 1934. Good.

Steward, T. G., "Negro Imagery," *New Republic*, vol. XII, 1918, p. 248. One religious improvisation, with discussion.

Thanet, Octave, "Cradle Songs of Negroes in North Carolina," *Journal of American Folk Lore*, vol. VII, 1894, p. 310. Two lullabies.

Truitt, Florence, "Songs from Kentucky," *Journal of American Folk Lore*, vol. XXXVI, 1923, pp. 376-379. Four white songs, one of which contains several verses often found in Negro songs.

Webb, W. P., "Notes on Folk Lore of Texas," *Journal of American Folk Lore*, vol. XXVIII, 1915, pp. 290-299. Five secular songs.

NOTES

1. Dorothy Scarborough, *On the Trail of Negro Folk-Songs*, Hatboro, Pennsylvania: Folklore Associates, Inc., 1963, p. 96.
2. Harold Courlander, *Negro Folk Music, U. S. A.*, New York: Columbia University Press, 1964, p. 11.
3. P. H. Lotz, Ed., *Rising Above Color*, New York: Associated Press, 1946, p. vii.
4. *Ibid.*, p. 26.
5. Nat Hentoff, "Jazz and Jim Crow," *The Commonweal*, Vol. LXXIII, 26, March 24, 1961, p. 658.
6. Gerardus Van der Leeuw, *Sacred and Profane Beauty: The Holy in Art*, New York: Holt, Rinehart & Winston, 1963, p. vii.
7. Quoted by Hans Nathan, *Dan Emmett and the Rise of Negro Minstrelsy*, Norman: University of Oklahoma Press, 1962, p. 4. On another occasion, in rejecting the argument of a Negro, Kant allowed himself to remark, "This chap was entirely black from head to toe, a clear proof that what he said was stupid." (Quoted by Nathan, *op. cit.*, p. 4.)

8. Courlander, *op. cit.*, pp. 13-14.

9. Newman I. White, *American Negro Folk-Songs*, Hatboro, Pennsylvania: Folklore Associates, Inc., 1965, p. 3.

10. For Negro influences on artists, for instance, Pablo Picasso, see William Fleming, *Arts and Ideas*, New York: Holt, Rinehart & Winston, Inc., 1966, p. 505; Robert Coughlan, *Tropical Africa*, New York: Time Inc., 1962, pp. 109-123. See also Louie Robinson, "Charles White: Portrayer of Black Dignity," *Ebony*, Vol. XXII, 9, July, 1967, pp. 25-36.

11. R. E. Spiller *et al.*, *Literary History of the United States*, New York: The Macmillan Company, 1963, p. 714.

12. Margaret Just Butcher, *The Negro in American Culture: Based on Materials left by Alain Locke*, New York: Alfred A. Knopf, 1966, p. 50.

13. Miles Mark Fisher, *Negro Slave Songs in the United States*, New York: The Citadel Press, 1963, p. 180.

14. *Ibid.*, p. 17.

15. *Ibid.*

16. Cf. Mahatma Gandhi's experiences lovingly described by Vincent Sheean, *Lead, Kindly Light*, New York: Random House, 1949, pp. 363-364.

17. Butcher, *op. cit.*, pp. 38-39.

18. Fisher, *op. cit.*, p. 188.

19. Butcher, *op. cit.*, p. 70.

20. *Ibid.*, pp. 45-46.

21. Coughlan, *op. cit.*, p. 110.

22. Pierre Teilhard de Chardin, *The Divine Milieu: An Essay on Interior Life*, New York: Harper & Row Publishers, 1965, p. 11.

23. The Negro's words sing themselves. A great example is the Reverend Martin Luther King's speech entitled "I have a dream . . ." See D. E. Saunders, Ed., *The Day They Marched*. Chicago: Johnson Publishing Company, Inc., 1963, pp. 81-85.

MOHAN LAL SHARMA received his M.A. in English from Punjab University and his Ph.D. in English and American Literature from Ohio State University. He has taught in the Punjab State Colleges and at Ohio State University. He is at present Professor of English at Slippery Rock State College, Pennsylvania. He has published numerous articles. Some of these fall in the general category; examples are "America: the Tripod of Plenty, Progress, Prosperity," and "The Soviet Woman's Stirring Saga"—both—Contest, Prize-Winning Essays. Most are, however, literary, pertaining to American, English, and Comparative Literatures. A recent one is "Martin Luther King: Modern America's Greatest Theologian of Social Action," published in the *Journal of Negro History*, Summer, 1968.

THE BLACK AMERICAN'S PROWESS ON THE PLAYING FIELD

Mohan Lal Sharma

Slippery Rock State College (Slippery Rock, Pa.)

"Far and wide shineth the glory of the . . . Games . . . where swiftness of foot contends, and feats of strength, hardy in labor. All his life long the victor shall bask in the glory of song for his prize. Daily continued blessedness is the supreme good for every man."—Pindar

"To set the cause above renown,
To love the game beyond the prize,
To honor as you strike him down,
The foe that comes with fearless eyes,
To count the life of battle good,
And dear the land that gave you birth,
But dearer yet the Brotherhood,
That binds the brave of all the earth."
                                   —Sir Henry Newbolt

Unless it be the ancient Greeks, or modern Sikhs, Gurkhas, Pathans *et al.*, no group of people can favorably compete or compare with the American Negro in the world of sports. Black and white boys alike, together with many of their elders, experienced a whole set of new thrills *par excellence* when Eddie Tolan smashed one track record after another, and when Jesse Owens and Joe Louis took championship status in track and the prize ring,[1] displaying to the whole world *arete,* the quality of the perfect man,[2] as the Greeks named it, philosophically and pedagogically. Today, besides being a potential escape from poverty, sports have become, in Jesse Owens's perceptive and democratic phrase, "the great equalizer"—the one area where black youngsters can confront their white peers and prove their equality (or even superiority). The dedication of ex-heavyweight champion Floyd Patterson, "to Wiltwyck School For Boys, which started me in the right direction," pinpoints the "happy escape from poverty and delinquency" aspect; whereas, Jackie Robinson's words emphasize the discovery of the "equalizer": "When I was eight, I discovered that in one sector of life in Southern California (Pasadena), I was free to compete with whites on equal terms—in sports . . . Sports were the big breach in the wall of segregation about me."[3] And, although he knows about the special problems and handicaps faced by today's Negro, Olympic trainer Buddy Taylor, without being an "Orpheus of Optimism" (which Martin Luther King was on the highest level), "is too busy trying for crying."[4] The saga of the American Negro on America's, and international, playing fields is neatly epitomized in Buddy's pithy observation: "The game is tough, but I've got my stuff. Now something has to break, right?" The black sportsman's golden achievements are an eloquent answer to Buddy's rhetorical question.

Early in America's annals, sports and games and systems of physical training and athletics became an integral part of national life. In the Colonial era, play and some athletic events were common to almost all settlers barring the Puritans. Many, indeed, are the anecdotes concerning sports engaged in by George Washington and his contemporaries. Before the Civil War, the really striking development in this sphere was the beginning of the great American game, when in 1839 Abner Doubleday of Cooperstown, N. Y., is credited with having started the ball and base running combination which is now known as baseball.

THE FIRST COLLEGE PHYSICAL DIRECTOR, A NEGRO

It is significant that the first director of Harvard University physical education was a black man, A. Molineaux Hewlitt. He was appointed as an instructor and director of the first gymnasium built in 1859 and remained in charge, as a highly regarded man, until 1871, when he died. Said a writer in the *Harvard Magazine* of October, 1859: "It is with feelings of pleasure and pride that we record the completion of the Harvard Gymnasium; of pleasure, in anticipation of the good effects of regular and varied exercise; of pride, that 'Conservative Harvard' should be the first of the colleges in this country to incorporate into its course of education an organized system of physical training . . ."[5]

About 1890 Negro athletes began to appear and, in effect, loom large on the college scene. From Alexandria and Norfolk, Virginia, two young Negro men went to the Virginia Normal and Collegiate Institute, at Petersburg, and thereafter to Amherst College. Their exploits on the gridiron and on the tracks of Amherst and Harvard made headline copy for press. W. T. S. Jackson was known for his track and football career, whereas W. H. Lewis earned immortal fame as one of the great football centers of the game. Lewis eventually became a prominent political figure under President Taft. When Coolidge was in the White House, he invited Jackson to spend many pleasant informal evenings to relive the days when the colored boy was the college idol, and the President just a plodding freshman.

BOXING

Boxing is an ancient sport, for Homer records it as one of the events of the celebration at the fall of Troy. Not much is on record after the sun set on glorious Greece and resplendent Rome until 1716, when (a certain) John Figg announced himself "A teacher of boxing, fencing and singlestick to the nobility of the British Empire."

The first American Negro to receive pugilistic honors was "Bill" Richmond. That he was well known to Lord Byron is attested by the references given him in the *Life and Journals of Lord Byron,* edited by Thomas Moore.

One of the first writers of *Fistiana* says, "Richmond may be pointed to as one of the men who never lost sight of the situation in which he was placed in society. In the elevation of the moment, he always bore in mind that, however the Corinthian fancier may connect himself with milling, there are times when he has a different character to support, and must not be intruded upon. Would that many of our white-faced boxers would take a hint on this point from Bill Richmond, the Black."[6]

Perhaps the most exemplary boxing figure, in fact, a king of the ring, is Joe Louis, whose story matches the exploits "of any national hero in the hearts of young America."[7] Even pugilism, "with its long background of bare-knuckle brutality, gained a new and gloved respectability"[8] at his good and powerful hands.

Gifted with the physique of a Greek god, Joe also had great courage. Knowing that nearly a hundred thousand pairs of eyes were on him, and that millions over the world were listening in, he permitted no whit of trepidation to unnerve his neuromuscular mechanism when he engaged in the primal business of outsmarting to beat the most worthy and redoubtable contenders who faced him under the lights.

Joe Louis bears comparison with today's heavyweight titlist Muhammad Ali. Joe's frustrations were never unleashed outside the ring. He did not identify himself with unpopular causes, although there were plenty. His image blended perfectly with what the white public thought the heavyweight champion should be. When World War II threatened, Joe willingly offered "to serve his country." His benefit fight against Buddy Baer for the Navy Emergency Relief Department in 1940 revealed every black man's dilemma of national loyalty versus pent-up racial bitterness. "I knew that the Navy at the time didn't give our boys much of a chance," declared Joe. "But I didn't hold that against them. I just hoped that some day things would be better," he optimistically added.

Twenty-nine years later, despite improvement in all the services, Muhammad Ali *does* hold it against the entire American nation that Negroes are not free. Instead of following ("aping" mimetically, as some might say) the great ex *champ*, Ali resolutely, militantly, refuses to "do what the white man says and go fight a war against some people I don't know nothing about to get some freedom for some other people when my own people can't get theirs here."[9] A black Muslim, a lover of poetry, a believer in a kind of a self-mystique, Ali is withal a colorful Negro boxer possessing a lot of nerve and coolness.

The earliest black lad to break into the "fastest human" class was Howard P. Drew of the Springfield High School in Massachusetts around 1912. He elicited romantic press comments. For instance, the New York *Tribune* wrote about him, "It seems incredible that a man running without fear of life and not the slightest desire to catch a train can impel himself to such prodigious speed. The sight of Drew hurtling along inevitably suggests a concealed motor. Anybody who saw Drew run last night cannot doubt his supremacy among American sprinters."[10]

In August, 1932, a Negro's name crashed front page head lines of the New York *Times* and those of a thousand journals around the world. Eddie Tolan, the phantom flier of Detroit, Michigan, raced his colored American, Ralph Metcalfe of Marquette University, to a photo-finish in the finals of the coveted Olympic 100 meter dash at Los Angeles, California. Black America and men of color around the globe had never before been so stirred emotionally. It was the first time a Negro had won the premier event.

Four years later, a greater miracle occurred. When in August, 1936, before Germany's Fuehrer Hitler in Berlin, the charismatic Jesse Owens led that long line of American Negroes to victory after victory in events that many men would have died willingly to achieve; he not only won Apollonian praise for America and his race, but he spiked many heavy guns of Nazi Nietzschean and Rosenbergian doctrines of racial superiorities and inferiorities. Thrice Jesse mounted to the rostrum of individual victory; thrice the American flag topped all others and the American anthem resounded in the ears of a hundred and ten thousand spectators at the games, and then again, as one of the four members of the sprint (400 meters) relay team which included Metcalfe, he helped establish a new record of forty seconds.

When Jesse returned from his triumphant Olympic feat, (most of) America paid tribute to his stunning achievements. In old Greece, many an Olympic winner entered his home city through a specially made breach in the walls and his statue was copied in marble, and frequently he was given a pension. In modern America, ticker-tape showers and a stately reception by Mayor La Guardia met Jesse's entry to New York and America. Seeking to gain by his fame, the Republican Party used Jesse in the political campaign; and, of course, Ohio State University gladly and gratefully planted the oak trees won by him at Berlin.

FOOTBALL

Centuries before Christ, the Spartans played "Harpaston," which involved kicking a ball. Early in the 10th century football came to England and in time became so popular that Henry II banned it, a ban that endured for 400 years, and was lifted by James I.

Until 1823 football was a kicking game only. In that year one William Webb Ellis deliberately, or "pulling a boner," picked the ball up and ran with it. Someone tackled him and the world of sports had something new.

In the United States football did not amount to much until about 1868 when Princeton and Rutgers adopted a set of rules for a kicking game. Columbia acquired a team in 1870, Yale in 1872, Michigan and Cornell in 1873 and Harvard in 1874.

Negro football players on white teams were first seen on the liberal college teams of New England. The two gridiron athletes who claimed the attention of the earliest fans and writers were William H. Lewis and W. T. S. Jackson, who were teammates on the Amherst College elevens of 1890 and 1891. According to the Boston *Globe* "Lewis was a wizard at fathoming plays and . . . a deadly tackler."

Brown University's outstanding contribution to football was Fritz Pollard. His great day was the afternoon of Saturday, October 27, 1916. This day Brown beat Yale; the score was: Brown 21, Yale 6. Reported the New York *Times* the day after: "Individually, Fritz Pollard, a lithe, dusky, six-foot halfback, displayed the cleverest all around backfield success attained on a Yale field this season. In end running, forward passing, in executing a bewildering criss-cross and delayed pass run, which was Brown's trump card, in running back punts, in side stepping and dodging Yale tacklers in a broken field, Pollard gave a peerless performance. His head-line exhibition brought the crowd of 25,000 spectators up with a roar in the opening minutes of the final playing period . . ."[11]

Since those first glorious days, many Negro boys have thrilled the hearts of thousands at Eastern and Western college games. Their most recent and glowing performance is part of the story of the Ohio State Buckeyes' victory in the traditional Rose Bowl game on New Year's Day in Pasadena. Well may Woody Hayes of Columbus, Ohio, have great expectations and dreams of his crew gathering "back-to-back" crowns and wreaths.[12]

The bar sinister has operated many times to placate the caste or class prejudice of Southern schools when matched with football teams with black players—Sidat-Singh, Dave Meyer, Charles West *et al.* The Southwest has, however, been fast growing more American; and America in sports has been growing multi-racial. The happy result has been more and more All-Americans among Negroes and other minorities. This is a good augury indeed, betokening a great athletic future for this great land, which is also the youngest in the comity of (sizable) nations.

BASKETBALL

Most people know that Dr. James A. Naismith, while instructor at the Springfield Young Men's Christian Association in 1891, used two peach baskets and had his boys play the first game of basketball. Today, millions in the United States and abroad play basketball.

Basketball was, at first, considered a "sissy" game, as was tennis in the rugged days of football, which (game) seemed to evoke—as it still does—gladiatorial trends from overexcited spectators so much so that sophisticated foreigners complained that the American nation was getting sports "on the brain."[13] But, the great indoor game caught on.

By 1906, a league of basketball teams had developed in Washington, D. C., and by 1911 nearly every elementary school and high school had teams.

Actual basketball in Negro colleges began about 1909 or 1910. Until then, the brief basketball scene was dominated by the clubs. Prior to 1910 there were but few Negro colleges engaging in the sport. Hampton Institute was probably the only college that had a gymnasium large enough to accommodate a game on a regulation court and seat a thousand spectators. Howard University had the strongest team of the collegiate class after the disbanding of the champion Young Men's Christian Association team of Washington. Since then, basketball has come along extremely well in a land which likes to perfect everything.

Negro college players of the first rank, fortunately many in number, find, after graduation, the lure of the game still pretty strong, and easily affiliate with alumni, fraternity, or club aggregations. Soon, however, they lose the brilliance of college days and become by-gone heroes. The wonder or star-player of ten or even five years ago lives only in the memory of contemporary worshippers of his all-too-brief scintillating scene in the limelight. His picture hung on the walls of his Alma Mater, his name on a cup, a book of clippings, and the record of his team connect him with the string of those gone to live in the limbo of past reminiscences. Alas, soon, too soon, "the day ends, the play ends," to use the philosophical words of T. S. Eliot. For those who would know the champion basketeers whose names were rolled on the tongues of the fannish thousands (as the Elizabethans rolled Shakespearean lines on their palates, or as mystics do the name of God on theirs) during their careers at Negro schools, it will be imperative to get the bound copies of the splendid annual journals of proceedings of Colored College Conference Athletic Associations. Thus will sports reach the category and status as well as function of great Art: conferral of deathless, dateless immortality on man as the Greek Plato conceded centuries ago, and as the French Andre Malraux (in *The Voices of Silence*) has claimed recently.

BASEBALL

It is supposed—some say apocryphally—that America's national game baseball, or cricket with a base, was started in New York in 1839 by Abner Doubleday. Anyway, the game, has developed from a two-player, pitcher-catcher team to the present four base, nine-player team.

It is not known to what extent Negroes played baseball during slavery and slavocracy, but after freedom the game was copied from the soldiers who frequently played in camp during Civil War days. But, in the late eighties most country towns and crossroads had baseball teams, from the Gulf of Mexico to the Mason-Dixon line.

The first Negro team composed of paid members is recorded as a playing aggregation that, at first, was a team of waiters of the Argyle Hotel at Babylon, New York. This club of hotel waiters and bell-hops was organized in 1885 by Frank Thompson, head waiter of the hotel. During that summer, the team played ten games with the best of the white *semi-pro* clubs around New York and Long Island, winning six and losing four. In September Thompson gave them an onomastic boost by designating them as the "Cuban Giants," and gave them a professional career push. Why the name "Cuban Giants?" This "important why" merits a reply.

Knowing the growing "Pride and Prejudice" (with apologies to Jane Austen for this alliterative but expressive phrase) that had infiltrated and insinuated into the arteries of the body-politic of the North and the East, the management realized that to pass off the boys as Cubans or Spaniards would enable them to play in places where as native Negro boys they would not have a ghost of a chance to make business contacts and contracts. On the playing field, a few of the Negro players would put on an act and talk "a gibberish" to each other. Because the New York Giants were a popular team of players, the Cubans added the titular appellation "Giants." The name "Giants" became attached to nearly every prominent colored team for a quarter of a century. One still remembers the Brooklyn Royal Giants, the Bacharach Giants, the Mohawk Giants, the Chicago American Giants, and others. "What's in a name," bard Shakespeare might well ask. "A lot," perhaps would be the sportsmannish and sports-fannish answer.

The Negro teams have had many a knotty problem to solve. The depression caught quite a few baseball ventures and, siren-like, pushed them towards the deep waters or the rocks. Greenlee's field, one of the best in the land, blossomed and faded like a frail flower out of existence. Competing leagues and outlaw clubs weakened the holding power of player-contracts and the disciplinary control of players. Slippery players would frequently leave a club in the lurch in mid-season. The craze of entertaining the fun-loving as well as the sophisticated baseball crowd led to clownish antics and clap-trap by players—in effect, to much un-orthodox behavior—which often was distasteful to the genuine fans.

Today, in commercialized America and to the hedonistic crowds, "sports," much like "show biz," constitute big business controlled by mighty magnates and a vast, intricate machinery wherein fabulously paid coaches and players and referees play rather robot-like roles. It is high time (and high space) "the tail stopped wagging the dog." A campus palaestra must be kept a sacred and character-building spot, rather than a money-making transaction dedicated to Machine and Mammon. Gold must not be permitted, even symbolically, to replace God; cynicism should not dethrone idealism in the hearts of athletes and on the playing fields of America.

Of course, there is no place for stuffiness in today's non-Puritanical America; but, nor is there much room for commercialized amorality—using men as things—and complacencies of ante-diluvian notions of caste, creed, color, and chauvinism. Nor can anyone put the clock of history back or unwind it—it would be like trying to clap with one hand, as the Zen Buddhist would say. The forces of history are moving so fast—none ever puts his foot twice in the same river anyway—that the black athlete in America is being whirled about at a dizzying pace. Myriad are the "sporty" avenues open to him in modernistic America; to name a few, there are all kinds of competitions held in bicycling (a "new type of spinning wheel"),[14] motor-racing, horse-racing,[15] cowboy-bullriding,[16] jiujitsu,[17] golf, tennis, even karate,[18] in all of which (and other) fields[19] the Negro is giving a fine account of his well-coordinated body and mind. This is all to the good.

And, militancy or no militancy, gone or going is the spectre of "sporty segregation," as the confessions and sacrificial endeavors of Jackie Robinson, Ray Robinson, Willy Mays, Bill Russell, Jim Brown, Lew Alcindor, Richie Allen, Willie Horton, and other current marvels among Negro sportsmen amply prove.

Since World War II, near-revolutionary changes in sports have had a marked impact on Negro youth. Baseball has replaced boxing as the sport with the greatest lure for black youngsters. Boxing is no longer the proving ground for the poor black kid from a broken home who does not "make it" in school and cannot find (or hold) a steady job. The sport slid downhill in the '50s because of overexposure on television, "gangland" influences, and the miserable plight suffered by ex-pugs like Johnny Bratton and Johnny Saxton. Speaking in terms of economics (not quite "a dismal science," as Winston Churchill would have it, for the professional player), there was just not enough money in it.

As boxing went down—money-wise—baseball's open door policy gave scores of Negro kids chances for fame and fortune they never dreamed of before.

No fewer than 27 Negroes, 25 years old and under, are in the big leagues. Some receive fabulous bonuses for signing. Major and minor league rosters are bulging with talented tan prospects. With scouts lapping up every black and white kid with promise, the influx is as heavy as ever.

Like the decade of the '60s, that of the '70s seems to offer the existential paradox for Negro youth—more and more opportunities for the talented middle-class Negro boy, less and less for the ghetto gamin whose gurus and talents lie unexplored and hidden like the biblical "talents" sung about by Milton in his famed sonnet entitled "On His Blindness." Sports, the "great equalizer," seemingly emulates the way of the world by giving more to the "haves" at the cost of the "have-nots." Where will they go? How will they survive in a "dog-eat-dog" world (not just in America) of nature wherein, according to a naturalistic-Darwinian image, "the strongest snake in the pit eats up the rest?" If the population explosion in America's black man's ghettos continues, the question may pass the rhetorical-academic stage by the '80s and go beyond the solutions to be now sought in the arenas and stadia.

That there is extravagance in the cult of the athlete, black or white, today is not likely to escape a critical-sympathetic eye. Long before Christ's coming, the Bernard Shaw-like brainy Euripides of ancient Greece fulminated against the brawny athletes in his satiric play *Autolycus*: "It is folly for the Greeks to make a great gathering to see useless creatures like these, whose god is in their belly . . ." Twenty-three centuries later, Kipling passed Mark-Twainian strictures on "The flannelled fool at the wicket, the muddied oaf at the goal." I fear the wiry, weak-kneed Euripides and the sickly, hypochondriac Kipling (spreading his plumage as the Victorian peacock) got no more attention than do modern America's egg-heads, who, by immoderately and immodestly lampooning athletes in and out of season, merely manage to "lose their yolks," as the late and witty Adlai Stevenson would have agreed.

Playing is, after all, naturally instinctive to man. So, no lover of sport can help saying: "Play on, America! Play the game!" In this sense and context, the black American's agile, wiry, and lithe limbs will continue to experience cathartic *agony*, giving the entire world the free gift of breathtaking, albeit vicarious *ecstasy* and bliss that are beyond human understanding. Like the Negro dancer and singer (there is more than gold in that throat, to borrow a colorful phrase from Fitzgerald, the typical author of the Jazz Age and the Lost Generation), the black American sportsman has a date with destiny—more worlds to conquer and better and Brave New Worlds to inaugurate.

Thus the great Negro player will ever regale and touch the heart and that "fiery particle," the soul of America, that will surely and warmly laud the black brother's heroic achievements at home and abroad. To use the immortal Keatsian line: "For ever wilt thou love, and she be fair!" Herein would lie the essence of the Golden Rule.

SELECTED BIBLIOGRAPHY*

ARTICLES

Sports Editor, "Female Black Belt Holder," *Ebony*, Vol. XXII, 6, April, 1967, pp. 107-110. An article on the Negro woman who is a judo expert.

Sports Editor, "Iowa U. Coed Pool Star," *Ebony*, Vol. XXII, 10, August, 1967, pp. 63-68. This issue carries a decently presented picture entitled "Today's tan athletes get more money, opportunities."

Sports Editor, "Negro Youth In Sports," *Ebony*, Vol. XXII, 10, August, 1967, pp. 130-133. An excellent and clean article.

Sports Editor, "Champion On Wheels," *Ebony*, Vol. XXII, 11, September, 1967, pp. 108-113. This speaks well of the Harlem youth "who becomes star cyclist after four years."

Sports Editor, "Eight Seconds On A Barrel Of Dynamite," *Ebony*, Vol. XXIII, 12, December, 1967, pp. 35-40. This essay

---

*For Books see bibliography previous article.

deals with a "bullrider who holds on to vie for rodeo champion-ship." This issue has two more articles of considerable interest—"New Football Stars In The Old South," and "Chicagoan Makes Horse Sense Pay Off." The captions are self-explanatory.

Sports Editor, "Medicine Man To Olympic Stars," *Ebony*, Vol. XXIII, 6, April, 1968, pp. 86-89. The subtitle "Tennessee's A & I trainer gets ready for Mexico Event" explains the value and meaning of the article. The issue has another piece entitled "Exploring The Underworld: Young Spelunker seeks adventure in Kentucky Cave," which has curiously Mark Twainian touches combined with a scientific zest for the quest of knowledge.

Sports Editor, "College Prof Spurs Karate Boom In Virginia," *Ebony*, Vol. XXIII, 7, May, 1968, pp. 144-150. This is an account of Professor Hulon Willis's building "enthusiastic support for the Oriental sport."

Sports Editor, "School Of The Equestrian Arts," *Ebony*, Vol. XXIII, 11, September, 1968, pp. 44-50. This is an eye-and-mind catching story of the "D. C. family that teaches youngsters the fine points of show riding."

Sports Editor, *The Harvard Magazine*, VI, October, 1859, p. 38. An old piece of "historic" proportions and value.

Journal of Negro Education, The (a quarterly). Howard University, Washington, D. C., 1932—Good for basic information.

Journal of Negro History, The (a quarterly). Association for the Study of Negro Life and History, Washington, D. C., 1916—A respectable and reputable journal of worldwide circulation and decent standard.

Ohio State University Letter. Columbus, Ohio. This letter put out by the Ohio State University carries news about sports and related items.

Opportunity, A Journal of Negro Life (a monthly). National Urban League, New York, 1923—Some promising material is featured here.

Donald Young, (ed.), "The American Negro," *Annals* of the American Academy of Political and Social Science, Vol. 140, November, 1928, Philadelphia. An insightful essay.

FOR FURTHER INFORMATION

Several articles on Negro sports and sportsmen in *Time, Sat-*

urday Review, Christian Century and other American journals and magazines, newspapers, etc. are surely of real value to the meticulous researcher. To use the current saying of Marshall McLuhan, with a slight variation, "the message" is right there in the medium.

(For the author's "Who's Who," see Chapter on "Afro-American Music & Dance").

NOTES

1. E. B. Henderson, *The Negro In Sports*, Washington, D.C.: The Associated Publishers Inc., 1939, p. 49.
2. J. C. Stobart, *The Glory That Was Greece*, London: Sidgwick & Jackson, 1960, Reprint, p. 84.
3. Sports Editor, "Negro Youth In Sports," *Ebony*, Vol. XXII, 10, August, 1967, pp. 130-131.
4. Sports Editor, "Medicine Man To Olympic Stars," *Ebony*, Vol. XXIII, 6, April, 1968, p. 86.
5. Henderson, *op. cit.*, p. 4.
6. Quoted by Henderson, p. 14.
7. *Ibid.*, p. 33.
8. T. A. Bailey, *The American Pageant: A History of the Republic*, Boston: D. C. Heath & Company, 1956, p. 564.
9. Quoted in "Negro Youth In Sports," p. 131.
10. Quoted by Henderson, p. 45.
11. *Ibid.*, p. 45.
12. Dick Mall, "The Ohio State University Association Letter," February, 1969.
13. Bailey, *op. cit.*, pp. 563-564.
14. Sports Editor, "Champion On Wheels," *Ebony*, Vol. XXII, 11, September, 1967, pp. 108-113.
15. Sports Editor, "School Of The Equestrian Arts," *Ebony*, Vol. XXIII, 11, September, 1968, pp. 44-50.
16. Sports Editor, "Eight Seconds On A Barrel Of Dynamite," *Ebony*, Vol. XXIII, 2, December, 1967, pp. 35-40.
17. Sports Editor, "Female Black Belt Holder," *Ebony*, Vol. XXII, 6, April, 1967, pp. 107-110.
18. Sports Editor, "College Prof Spurs Karate Boom In Virginia," *Ebony*, Vol. XXIII, 7, May, 1968, pp. 144-150.
19. Sports Editor, "Iowa U. Coed Pool Star," *Ebony*, Vol. XXII, 10, August, 1967, pp. 63-68.

CONTRIBUTIONS OF THE NEGRO PRESS
TO AMERICAN CULTURE

WILLIAM C. SPRAGENS

Bowling Green State University (Ohio)

One of the more important elements in the contributions of black intellectual leadership to American culture may be found in the development of the Negro press.

In the 142 years since publication of the first Negro newspaper in the United States, the "black press" has become an important element in the struggle of black Americans for full equality in our national life and culture.

EARLY DEVELOPMENT OF THE NEGRO PRESS

Although many persons tend to think of William Lloyd Garrison's newspaper, *The Liberator,* as the first publication to champion militant abolitionism in the nineteenth century, the honor really belongs to a newspaper known as *Freedom's Journal,* founded in 1827 in New York City by two Negro editors, John B. Russwurm and Samuel E. Cornish.[1] This newspaper was published from 1827 to 1830, when Russwurm returned to Africa as an expatriate. In 1837 Cornish, the co-editor of *Freedom's Journal,* became editor of *The Weekly Advocate,* just being started by Phillip A. Bell of New York. By 1861 and the outbreak of the Civil War, perhaps a score of Afro-American periodicals of this type had been launched and were being published. Most of these were started in the 1840's and 1850's. Perhaps the best known of these is the newspaper published by Frederick Douglass, the *North Star,* which was first published in 1847 and was renamed *Frederick Douglass' Paper* three years later. Douglass' newspaper was published until 1864, thus lasted longer than most of those of the ante bellum period. In the same era four new "black" magazines were started.

The first issue of the nation's first Negro newspaper, *Freedom's Journal*, stated editorially, "We wish to plead our own cause. Too long have others spoken for us." Douglass expressed the same sentiment in launching the *North Star*. In Vol. I, No. 1 of that newspaper, Douglass published the following editorial:

"We solemnly dedicate the *North Star* to the cause of our long oppressed and plundered fellow countrymen. May God bless the undertaking to your good! It shall fearlessly assert your rights, faithfully proclaim your wrongs, and earnestly demand for you instant and even-handed justice. Giving no quarter to slavery at the South, it will hold no truce with oppressors in the North. While it shall boldly advocate emancipation for our enslaved brethren, it will omit no opportunity to gain for the nominally free complete enfranchisement. Every effort to injure or degrade you or your cause—originating wheresoever, or with whomsoever—shall find in it a constant, unswerving, and inflexible foe. . . .

"Remember that we are one, that our cause is one, and that we must help each other, if we would succeed. We have drank to the dregs the bitter cup of slavery; we have worn the heavy yoke; we have sighed beneath our bonds, and writhed beneath the bloody lash;—cruel mementoes of our oneness are indelibly marked on our living flesh. We are one with you under the ban of prejudice and proscription— one with you under the slander of inferiority—one with you in social and political disfranchisement. What you suffer, we suffer; what you endure, we endure. We are indissolubly united, and must fall or flourish together. . . .

"It is scarcely necessary for us to say that our desire to occupy our present position at the head of an Anti-Slavery Journal, has resulted from no unworthy distrust or ungrateful want of appreciation of the zeal, integrity or ability of the whole noble band of white laborers in this department of our cause; but, from the sincere and settled conviction that such a Journal, if conducted with only moderate skill and ability, would do a most important and indispensable work, which it would be wholly impossible for our white friends to do for us.

"It is neither a reflection on the fidelity, nor is it a disparagement of the ability of our friends and fellow-laborers, to assert what 'common sense affirms and only folly denies', that the man who has *suffered the wrong* is the man to *demand redress*,—that the man STRUCK is the man to CRY OUT—and that he who has *endured the cruel pangs of Slavery* is the man to *advocate Liberty*. It is evident we must be our own representatives and advocates—not exclusively, but peculiarly—not distinct from, but in connection with our white friends. In the grand struggle for liberty and equality now waging it is meet, right and essential that there should arise in our ranks authors and editors, as well as orators, for it is in these capacities that the most permanent good can be rendered to our cause. . . ."[2]

Lerone Bennett Jr., Martin Luther King's biographer, suggests that the establishment of the first American Negro newspaper, along with the Negro convention movement of the 1830's, represented "tremendous leaps forward in Negro group consciousness." He also notes that this marked the first time in American history when black men saw themselves reflected in the pages of journals dedicated to their own interests. Along with Negro conventions, Negro newspapers welded black men into a common unit and served as "sounding boards and mirrors." They also helped to define the bounds of permissible dissent from group values of the American Negro. Even in this early stage, Negro leaders were noticeably more militant than the white abolitionists, many of whom were "gradualists."[3]

FREDERICK DOUGLASS' EDITORIAL CAREER

A leading role in the early history of the American Negro press was played by Frederick Douglass. Bennett has suggested that with Douglass, the Negro had "come of age." In this leader's speeches and books can be found analyses of every aspect of the American racial problem. If one wished to understand the agony, pain and joy of the American Negro soul, he could do worse than to read a copy of Douglass' collected speeches, the manifestoes of W. E. B. Du Bois, Richard Wright's novels, and James Baldwin's essays.

During the period from 1845 to 1895, Douglass' voice commanded the public ear. Over this era, Douglass laid the foundation and helped establish the borders and limits of the Negro's freedom right and thus earned the title, "Father of the Protest Movement." While Douglass did not always urge men to take up arms against a sea of troubles, he did always suggest that it was their duty to cry out in protest. He felt that men who supinely accepted oppression would never lack for oppressors.

Douglass undertook a program of continuous agitation. He maintained that every Negro should challenge every case of bias and discrimination he met with. This great abolitionist also practiced what he preached in this regard. Bennett describes him as "perhaps the first systematic 'sit-inner'." He always made the assumption that every door open to a human being was open to him; if he was turned away, he made an issue of the matter. If he was told to leave a "white" restaurant or a "white" railroad coach, he would refuse to do so. Conductors of Jim Crow coaches usually responded by summoning several burly men who would drag Douglass out of the car along with several seats he usually held onto. Always, wherever possible, Frederick Douglass defied the Jim Crow system.

Douglass maintained that struggle, strife and pain were prerequisites for the Negro's progress. In an address at the West India Emancipation Celebration at Canandaigua, New York, August 4, 1857, the Negro editor and leader gave a definitive analysis of one of his favorite topics, the philosophy of reform. He stated on that occasion:

"The whole history of the progress of human liberty shows that all concessions yet made to her august claims, have been born of earnest struggle. . . . If there is no struggle, there is no progress. Those who profess to favor freedom and yet deprecate agitation are men who want crops without plowing up the group, they want rain without thunder and lightning. They want the ocean without the awful roar of its many waters. This struggle may be a moral one, or it may be a physical one, and it may be both moral and physical, but it must be a struggle. Power concedes nothing without a demand. It never did and it never will. . . . Men may not get all they pay for in this world, but they must certainly pay for all they get. If we ever get free from the oppressions and wrongs heaped upon us, we must pay for their removal. We must do this by labor, by suffering, by sacrifice, and if needs be, by our lives and the lives of others."

What appears to distinguish Douglass most of all is the hopeful attitude associated with him. It might be said of Booker T. Washington what one conservative French historian said about Louis XIV: "He did not know how to wish." Frederick Douglass did know how to wish; he wished for immediate, total and complete integration of the Negro into American social, economic and political life.

Since this prize was such an outstanding one, Douglass demanded advocates worthy of it. No other Negro, with perhaps the exceptions of Martin Luther King Jr. and A. Philip Randolph, has asked so much from Negro men with such great insistence. Douglass argued that freedom could not be granted; rather, in his view, it was necessary to seize it. Douglass maintained that for success in this undertaking, it was necessary to have unity, organization and sacrifice.

Douglass' career can be divided into three major periods: the abolitionist era, the Reconstruction era, and the post-Reconstruction era. In the first, he was a champion of direct action and continuing agitation. With the approach of the Civil War, his stance became increasingly militant; he advocated ballots if possible, and bullets if necessary. He next led a brilliant campaign for adoption of the Fourteenth and Fifteenth Amendments following Emancipation. Finally, he became after Reconstruction an advocate of political action and protest within the existing system.

Douglass was not only an editor and social engineer. He can also be described as a reformer, agitator, orator, author, abolitionist and philosopher. In the nineteenth-century history of the American Negro, he was one of the leading foes of prejudice and oppression. He had a background which had prepared him for this long, hard battle. Born on the Eastern Shore of Maryland in February, 1817, as Frederick Augustus Washington Bailey (he assumed the name Douglass later on), he worked as a slave in and around Baltimore until he was 21. During this early phase of his life, two experiences changed his whole life. As a boy of 10 or 11, his mistress taught him the alphabet and a few words and his master objected, saying that "learning would spoil the best nigger in the world." But Douglass wanted to be spoiled; he became his own teacher, at times hiding dirty pages in his pockets and painfully spelling out words in the dark recesses of the attic.

While he was still a slave, Douglass learned that power has its limits. This extraordinary discovery opened his eyes to a whole new horizon of struggle. It happened in this fashion. Refusing to knuckle under to the slave regime, he was sent by his master to Edward Covey, a "professional Negro-breaker" whose specialty was wearing down the spirit of trouble-making slaves. Covey kept Douglass at work until he was nearly ready to drop from exhaustion, then whipped him until he would bow and smile. Douglass decided, however, to turn and make a desperate last stand one day. After the two men grappled with each other and had an indecisive draw, Covey walked away and never afterwards touched the slave. Douglass drew a moral from this incident and applied it to numerous situations after he had gained his freedom. It was: "He is whipped oftenest who is whipped easiest."

Four years after this incident, at the age of 21, Douglass escaped from slavery. He joined the ranks of both Negro and white men who were waging a moral crusade against slavery. On the speaker's platform during the abolitionist years, Douglass had a striking posture. A good-looking man, he was tall and athletic with olive skin and hair worn long in the natural African style. His physical presence and booming voice were capable of moving people. William Wells Brown wrote of him, "White men and black men had talked against slavery, but none had spoken like Frederick Douglass." In a matter of a few short years, Douglass was widely known on both sides of the Atlantic. He had just completed a triumphant tour of England in 1847 when he set forth on his own, establishing his famous newspaper, the *North Star*, which was published in Rochester, New York. From the year of its founding until the Emancipation Proclamation, he was a leader in the Freedom movement.

One of the most famous of Douglass' orations was his Fourth

of July speech which indicates the passion and brilliance he brought to this Freedom movement. He indicted every power structure in American life when he spoke at Rochester July 5, 1852. He said in part:

"What, to the American slave, is your 4th of July? I answer: a day that reveals to him, more than all other days in the year, the gross injustice and cruelty to which he is the constant victim. To him, your celebration is a sham; your boasted liberty, an unholy license; your national greatness, swelling vanity; your sounds of rejoicing are empty and heartless; your denunciation of tyrants, brass fronted impudence; your shouts of liberty and equality, hollow mockery; your prayers and hymns, your sermons and thanksgivings, with all your religious parade and solemnity, are, to him, mere bombast, fraud, deception, impiety, and hypocrisy—a thin veil to cover up crimes which would disgrace a nation of savages. . . .

"You boast of your love of liberty, your superior civilization, and your pure Christianity. . . . You hurl anathemas at the crowned headed tyrants of Russia and Austria and pride yourselves on your democratic institutions, while you yourselves consent to be mere tools and bodyguards of the tyrants of Virginia and Carolina. You invite to your shores fugitives of oppression from abroad, honor them with banquets, greet them with ovations, cheer them, toast them, salute them, protect them, and pour out your money on them like water; but the fugitives from your own land you advertise, hunt, arrest, shoot, and kill. You glory in your refinement and your universal education; yet you maintain a system as barbarous and dreadful as ever stained the character of a nation—a system begun in avarice, supported in pride, and perpetuated in cruelty. You shed tears over fallen Hungary, and make the sad story of her wrongs the theme of your poets, statesmen, and orators, till your gallant sons are ready to fly to arms to vindicate her cause against the oppressor; but in regard to the ten thousand wrongs of the American slave, you would enforce the strictest silence and would hail him as an enemy of the nation who dares to make those wrongs the subject of public discourse!"

It was Douglass who dared to make "the ten thousand wrongs" a subject of public discourse. Week in and week out, year in and year out, during the critical decade preceding the Civil War, he went up and down the North, pleading the Negro's case.[4]

While I have digressed to discuss the career of the famous editor, Frederick Douglass, the ante bellum development of the Negro press must not be neglected. The original *Freedom's Journal* mentioned above was renamed *Rights for All* in 1828; it ceased publication altogether in 1830. From 1827 until 1863, the year of the Emancipation Proclamation, approximately 30 Negro newspapers began publication, but few of these lasted for more than a year or two. The only one which has continued publication to the present time from this period is the *Christian Recorder,* founded in 1852. Circulation of these Negro newspapers at this time was largely limited to the free Negroes of northern cities, and this was not a large readership. Despite the brief existence of individual newspapers, together they performed a worthwhile service: they were a medium through which the wishes and desires of the free Negroes could be given voice. Indeed, they were often instrumental in developing race pride or race consciousness among Negroes. Papers with considerable impact in this regard were the *Colored American* (New York, 1837); the *Elevator* (Albany, 1842); *Genius of Freedom* (New York, 1842); the *Ram's Horn* (New York, 1847); the *North Star* (Rochester, 1847), and the *Alienated American* (Cleveland, 1852).[5] In 1850 Frederick Douglass changed the name of the *North Star* to *Frederick Douglass' Paper* "in order to distinguish it from the many papers with 'Stars' in their titles."

Not surprisingly, Negro newspapers published prior to Emancipation devoted considerable space to the abolition of slavery. But they were not unaware of the problems of free Negroes as well. A number of individual Negro newspapers also showed strong political leanings, taking sides on the political issues of the day. Typical of the Negro press in this era were the aims of the *Colored American*—"to promote the moral, social, and political elevation and improvement of the free colored people and the peaceful emancipation of the enslaved."[6]

180

From Emancipation to the close of the nineteenth century, Negro newspapers were only moderately more successful than they had been in the ante bellum period. The reading public increased only slightly in size, for Emancipation was unaccompanied by any immediate increase in Negro literacy.

Because most of the masses of Negroes were poor and illiterate, their cultural level was low; to most of them, newspapers of any kind represented a luxury they could scarcely afford. The Negro press carried meagre advertising; therefore, income was inadequate to meet operating expenses, since circulation was usually limited to a few hundred copies. Thus financial troubles continued to plague many editors and publishers, and were frequently more than they could overcome. Sympathetic and philanthropic white friends sometimes helped subsidize Negro newspapers. Despite all these financial difficulties, 50 Negro newspapers were launched between 1861 and 1900, and several of these are still being published.

From 10 Negro periodicals in the nation in 1870, the number grew to 20 in 1880 and to 154 by 1890. Leading papers in 1890 included the Philadelphia *Tribune*, the Washington *Bee*, the Cleveland *Gazette* and the New York *Age*. As in the case of newspapers edited by white editors, the Negro press had editors with colorful personalities and strong opinions.

With the Negro press, poor training, education and poverty of the editors were reflected in the frequently sensational slanting of the news, use of cheap paper, poor pictures, faulty grammar and proof reading, and an odd assortment of advertising. These defects also reflected the similar conditions which were fairly typical of the Negro reading public for which these newspapers were intended to be sources of race pride and militant awakening. Editors everywhere thought of themselves as racial leaders and spokesmen. In his modern classic work, *American Dilemma*, Gunnar Myrdal erred in taking these editors at their own word when he concluded that the Negro press is "the greatest single power in the Negro race." What Myrdal apparently overlooked is the fact that until recent years, southern Negroes often have been afraid of the militancy and outspokenness of their editors. Lower class persons have regarded these editors on some occasions as "overly intellectual" and self-seeking men who wished to make money by capitalizing on racial problems, while the more sophisticated, frequently made more conservative by the fact that they held public positions, wished editors would take time to tone down their protests and militant demands—that they would not "stir up trouble."

The Negro press has usually been almost exclusively concerned with news involving Negroes directly; it often has somewhat exaggerated the importance of this news. Even in coverage of sports, white athletic teams have been noticed only when they either had Negro members or when they were in competition against Negroes. In the case of the Lindbergh kidnaping, the Negro press did not pay great attention to the case until a Negro woman found the body of the Lindbergh baby. Especially since the First World War, the increased international outlook of the Afro-American has tended to broaden the "colored community" to a world setting; it was this fact which prompted Frederick G. Detweiler to conclude that the Negro editor's horizon is "at least as wide as that of the small-town white editor and often wider." Such a world-focus on the problem of race has caused the Negro press to join in sympathy with colonial peoples everywhere as they have attempted to overthrow European rule. The Negro press has constantly reflected the belief that not even northern whites were free of prejudiced attitudes and false notions regarding the black man. The first Negro editorial commented, "Our friends are actually living in the practice of prejudice, while they abjure it in theory, and feel it not in their hearts." This was given as a reason why there ought to be a segregated Negro literature and separate action by blacks.

The following newspapers were established during the year indicated: *California Eagle,* Los Angeles, 1870; *Savannah Tribune,* Georgia, 1875; *The Conservator,* Chicago, 1878; *The Planet,* Richmond, Virginia, 1884; New York *Age,* 1885, and the Cleveland *Gazette,* 1883. The fact that northern Negroes felt freer and more able to protest than those in the South seems to be reflected in that of the approximately 30 newspapers existing in 1880, only 17 were published in the South, despite the fact that more than 80 per cent of all American Negroes lived there. The two decades between 1890 and 1910 saw the most successful of all race newspapers established. In 1884 the Philadelphia *Tribune* was founded, the Baltimore *Afro-American* in 1892, the Norfolk *Journal and Guide* in 1900, the Chicago *Defender* in 1905, the *Amsterdam News* in 1909, and the Pittsburgh *Courier* in 1910. By 1948 the total circulation of the Chicago *Defender*, the *Afro-American*, Pittsburgh *Courier*, and *Journal and Guide* was near the million mark. By 1959 there were almost 400 Negro periodicals being published across the nation. The journalist P. L. Prattis says the traditional function of the race press has been "to speak up for the rights of Negroes, to wage war against those who would have kept Negroes in chains." He finds this "is, and always has been a necessary" service, but he believes that twentieth-century progress in race relations is causing some Negro Americans to lose interest in "their" papers. He feels these newspapers, in order to survive, must change their objectives and "be for and of the people, white people and black people."

In summing up the role of the Negro press, Earl E. Thorpe suggests:

"On the tendency of the Negro press to sensationalize news of such matters as segregation and instances of Jim Crow, one observer has pointed out that this tendency 'acts as a kind of counter-weight to the tendency of many white papers to highlight the reverse situation—Negro crimes against whites.' This same writer analyzed two Harlem newspapers of the post World War II era, the *People's Voice*, formerly edited by Adam Clayton Powell Jr., who founded it in 1942, and the *Amsterdam News*. From this analysis he concluded that the most common techniques used by the colored press 'to assert the Negro's fundamental right to equal opportunity and socio-economic status' have been:

1. Protest (attacks on discrimination, Jim Crow, etc.);

2. Playing up achievements of Negroes, both past and contemporary, and

3. Identifying Negroes with liberal and progressive movements, both among white Americans and the world's rising masses and colonials. In their volume *Black Metropolis*, Horace Cayton and St. Clair Drake present similar conclusions from their study of the Chicago *Defender*, while studies

made by Howard University graduate students have revealed that the New York *Age,* long a leader in the Afro-American press, fitted (sic) these generalizations. The *Age,* too, emphasized news about affluent and otherwise successful Negroes. The same was true of the Washington *Bee* and other papers."[7]

Since 1900, the growth of the Negro press has been great, due in part to the better economic status of many Negroes, their increased rate of literacy, growing race consciousness, and growing urbanization of Negroes. Various estimates suggest that some 500 Negro newspapers have been published in the United States since 1827. Probably some 60 per cent of these have ceased publication, as there are now something like 210 weekly and semi-weekly Negro newspapers published in 32 states and the District of Columbia. These 210 newspapers in 1950 had a combined weekly circulation estimated at 2,500,000. The 20 leading newspapers accounted for 47.7 per cent of the total weekly circulation. Leaders with circulation figures listed in parenthesis were: Pittsburgh *Courier* (274,329); Baltimore *Afro-American* (203,594); Chicago *Defender* (161,008); New York *Amsterdam Star-News* (64,797); Norfolk *Journal and Guide* (63,428), and Kansas City *Call* (40,231). The leading Negro daily newspaper, the Atlanta *Daily World,* had a circulation of 29,000 (combined daily and Sunday) in 1950.[8]

The Negro press has at times been criticized for alleged partisanship in news coverage. It has been accused of radicalism, bias, inaccuracy and sensationalism, even of subversion. The forthright stand of Negro editors in ferreting out discrimination against Negroes and their militancy in demanding full equality of opportunity for all have caused the Negro press to be accused of distortion and propaganda as well as scandal-mongering.[9]

Most Negro publications spoke out against segregation in the armed forces during World War II and some members of the white press joined in this criticism.[10] Because of its outspokenness and insistence on immediate reform, the Negro press was accused of being subversive; it was even charged that

184

the Negro press was subsidized by Japanese sources, but an FBI investigation proved these charges groundless.

Many critics of the Negro press appeared to ignore two important considerations in evaluating the Negro press and its role in American cultural and political life. These factors are (1) reporting and interpreting of news stories about Negroes, or of interest to Negroes, in the dominant white press, and (2) the Negroes' historical minority status in American society, the real reason for existence of the Negro press.

The Negro press' basic function, in the light of the first factor above, is to report news of interst and concern to Negroes about Negroes, to report events occurring in Negro society and to report and interpret news of national and international significance as it specifically affects the Negro in American society. Without the Negro press these events and their significance would remain unknown to most Negroes. It is also the Negro press' function to voice opinions of a minority group that would not otherwise be heard. By its very nature, the Negro press is a crusading and a reform press.[11]

NEWSGATHERING AND EDITING FOR THE NEGRO PRESS

Besides reporting news about Negroes, the Negro press also looks for Negro-oriented angles of news about national and local events that will have an important impact on the lives of Negroes. Court decisions on segregation or discrimination, exploits of Negro athletes, scientists and educators are the kinds of matters of special interest to Negroes that are covered by the Negro press.

Unlike the editor of the metropolitan daily, the typical Negro newspaper editor is usually the owner and publisher as well. Few Negro editors have had extensive training as a reporter. Less than 3 per cent of them had had formal journalism training as recently as 1950, though the proportion may be slightly higher today. To a considerable extent the personal journalism of the white dailies of an earlier era may still be found in many Negro newspapers.

Perhaps 90 per cent of the open space in the news sections and on the editorial pages of Negro newspapers is devoted to (1) attacks on segregation and discrimination; (2) endorse-

ment of federal and state laws and city ordinances to guarantee
civil rights for Negroes; (3) interpretation of court decisions
and legislation dealing with civil rights; (4) coverage of activities of prominent Negro personalities and institutions; (5) encouragement of Negroes to use political, economic and social
opportunities to improve their status, and (6) deploring of the
fact that Negroes have failed to take advantage of all opportunities made available to them.

Several larger weeklies, including the Pittsburgh *Courier*, the
Chicago *Defender* and the Baltimore *Afro-American*, maintain
foreign correspondents who keep their papers informed at first
hand on world events occurring abroad. Negro columnists have
seldom been traditionally trained journalists; instead they are
usually college professors, or recognized leaders with a large
personal following; some better known Negro columnists in the
past have been Arthur P. Davis and Rayford W. Logan of
Howard University, Gordon B. Hancock of Virginia Union University, and Benjamin E. Mays, president of Morehouse College
in Atlanta.

Several developments have reflected improving quality of the
Negro press in recent years. For one thing, Negro newspaper-
men are now eligible for the Nieman Awards for excellence in
journalism. For another, white daily newspapers have begun to
hire Negro journalists on their regular staffs, rather than as
special writers. For still another, editorials in the Negro newspapers are more widely quoted in the white daily press.

While there are 14 Negro newsgathering agencies, only two
are of major importance. These are the Associated Negro Press
(ANP), and the Negro Newspaper Publishers Association
(NNPA). Negro newspapers do not receive the services of the
Associated Press and United Press International, and Negro
reporters were long barred from press clubs in major cities.
Since 1946, Negro reporters have been admitted to presidential
press conferences and in 1947, the first Negro correspondent,
Louis Lautier of the Atlanta *Daily World*, was admitted to
Senate and House press galleries in Washington.

Negro newspapers have also shown considerable progress in
recent years in advertising. Increased circulation of Negro newspapers came along with improvements in quality and increased
volume of advertising. For many years practically all adver-

tising in Negro newspapers consisted of real estate advertisements of rooms, apartments, and houses for rent or sale; good luck charms, love potions, and the like for the superstitious and uneducated, and hair straighteners guaranteed to make the hair wavy or straight, and beauty preparations for lightening the skin. Much more national advertising now goes to the Negro newspapers, and this has become a less significant portion of the total advertising except in the case of the smallest papers. More than $500,000 worth of national advertising now goes to Negro newspapers annually.[12]

NEGRO MAGAZINES AND JOURNALS

Negro magazines and journals appear to have much the same function as the Negro newspapers. They describe life in the Negro community as it is lived by Negroes, and they afford an additional medium for black self-expression. Except for the fact that they deal chiefly with Negro life, Negro journals and magazines tend to be the counterpart in many ways of the white magazines after which they are patterned. There are some 60 Negro magazines and journals in the United States, exclusive of church and fraternal periodicals. These vary in content from scientific and scholarly writing to fiction and picture magazines. For purposes of analysis, this content can be categorized as educational and scientific, social action, and pictorial.

Among the scholarly Negro journals may be included the *Journal of Negro Education, Journal of Negro History, Negro College Quarterly, Negro History Bulletin, Phylon,* and the *Quarterly Review of Higher Education Among Negroes.* Most of these journals are published by Negro colleges or universities; their function is to provide a medium through which the scholarly and creative efforts of Negroes can be brought to the public's attention. The number of Negro scholars and scientists has increased considerably in recent years, and as the number has risen the contributions of Negro scholars in the fields of science, education, and the arts have likewise increased. Men like Justice Thurgood Marshall and Ralph Bunche have gained prominence in the fields of law and political science, and other examples could be cited. Although Negro scholars also publish the results of their researches in older and better known journals, Negro journals are often more easily accessible. Perhaps the feeling of race pride and race consciousness also compel the young Negro author to publish where he can become known more quickly.

As a result of the specialized nature of these journals, their circulation is chiefly limited to school and college libraries, and to members of organizations that sponsor their publication. They usually carry no advertising and follow the pattern of white journals with similar functions. Occasionally white scholars are asked to contribute to them, and this practice is growing. In most cases the articles, whether scientific, learned, creative, or otherwise, describe some phase of Negro life.

Social action journals deal primarily with the social, economic, and political welfare of the Negro; they usually express the policies and programs of the organizations that publish them. This group of periodicals includes *Crisis*, official organ of the National Association for the Advancement of Colored People, and *Opportunity*, official organ of the National Urban League. Like the *New Republic* and the *Nation*, these journals are immediately interested in social and political reform, particularly in civil rights. Despite the relatively small circulation of each of these journals, their influence in the Negro community has been considerable, perhaps partly due to the influence of the sponsoring organizations.

Another group of Negro magazines, with a strong racial slant, may also be included in the classification of social action and reform. These include the *Negro Digest, Negro Quarterly,* and *Racial Digest*. The former and the latter resemble the *Reader's Digest* in size and format. Few of the articles appearing in these magazines are original; rather they are condensations of articles that have been published elsewhere. All the articles deal with Negro life or some phase of race relations, and authors are both white and Negro. The *Negro Quarterly* carries all original articles.

A recent and successful development in Negro journalism is the pictorial magazine. Some examples of these magazines, which resemble *Look* and *Life* in format, are *Brown American, Color, Criterion, Ebony* and *Our World*. All have become prominent in the Negro press since 1945, and in 1966, *Ebony*, the most successful, had a circulation of 872,535, compared with

317,574 in 1950. In 1966 *Jet,* another picture magazine, had a circulation of 355,122. They are printed on slick paper and carry advertising. The subject matter includes social activities of upper and middle class Negroes, home life and entertainment of prominent Negroes, and success stories of Negro business men and women, scholars, and sports personalities. In photography and editorial writing they have shown great and rapid progress.

The Negro press is rapidly coming of age and improving in its journalistic standards—in terms of organization, special features, news reporting, and editorial writing, as well as in format. It is predictable that when Negroes have become fully assimilated into American society and culture, the Negro press as we know it will disappear with the disappearance of its reasons for existence. Thus we can expect it to survive for many years, since the end of racial conflict and discord does not yet appear to be in sight.

In sum, the Negro press and Negro editors have made an important contribution, not only to Negro cultural life in the United States, but also to the broader American cultural life. To promote interracial understanding and the cause of civil rights advancement for the Negro and other racial minorities, it appears to have a worthy purpose for many years to come.

SELECTED BIBLIOGRAPHY

BOOKS

Baldwin, James, *The Fire Next Time,* New York: Dial Press, 1963. A Negro spokesman urges all Americans to examine the dangers of racial conflict a century after the Emancipation Proclamation.

Bennett, Lerone, Jr., *Confrontation: Black and White,* Baltimore: Penguin Books, 1965. See especially the chapter on "The First Freedom Movement", pp. 38-56, which carries an account of the editorial career of Frederick Douglass and the *North Star.*

—————, *Before the Mayflower: A History of the Negro in America, 1619-1964,* Chicago: University of Chicago Press, 1964. A detailed history of the American Negro from his origins in Africa through the Negro revolt of the 1960's.

Broderick, Francis L., and Meier, August, *Negro Protest Thought in the Twentieth Century,* New York: Bobbs-Merrill Co., Inc., 1965. A study of the writings of protest editors and leaders.

Brown, Francis J., and Roucek, Joseph S., Eds., *One America: The History, Contributions, and Present Problems of Our Racial and National Minorities,* New York: Prentice-Hall, 1952 (Third Edition), Chapter 14, "The Negro Press", by Clifton Jones, pp. 401-415. Although now somewhat dated, this is a good brief discussion and analysis of the Negro editors' and journals' contributions to American culture.

Douglass, Frederick, *Life and Times of Frederick Douglass, Written by Himself,* Boston: De Wolfe & Co., 1895. An autobiography of the famous Negro leader.

Du Bois, W. E. Burghardt, *The Souls of Black Folk,* New York: Fawcett Publications, Inc., 1961. A famous statement of black militant beliefs and doctrine.

Franklin, John Hope, *From Slavery to Freedom* (Second Edition), New York: Alfred A. Knopf, Inc., 1967. A history of the Negro's progress since slavery to the civil rights movement.

Fishel, Leslie H., Jr. and Quarles, Benjamin, *The Negro American: A Documentary History,* Glenview, Ill.: Scott, Foresman & Co. and William Morrow & Co., 1967. This excellent collection contains material from the writings of Frederick Douglass, W. E. B. Du Bois and other prominent Negro leaders of the past, as well as such recent leaders as Martin Luther King Jr. and Malcolm X.

Foner, Philip S., *Frederick Douglass,* New York: Citadel Press, Inc., 1964. A biography of the Negro editor.

Garfinkel, Herbert, *When Negroes March,* Glencoe, Ill.: The Free Press, 1959. An account of the civil rights protest movement and its organizational and interest group activities.

Grant, Joanne, Ed., *Black Protest: History, Documents, and Analyses, 1619 to the Present,* Greenwich, Conn.: Fawcett Premier Books, 1968. A valuable collection of documents in the history of slavery, emancipation and civil rights as well as other aspects of the history of Afro-Americans. See especially the Frederick Douglass editorial from the *North Star,* pp. 83 and 84. This book contains a great deal of documentary material on the current civil rights movement of the 1960's.

Hughes, Langston, *Fight for Freedom, the Story of the NAACP*, New York: W. W. Norton & Co., Inc., 1962. A history of the well-known Negro interest group and its crusade for civil rights.

Malcolm X, with the assistance of Alex Haley, *The Autobiography of Malcolm X*, New York: Grove Press, Inc., 1964. Autobiography of the Black Nationalist leader who was assassinated in 1965.

Myrdal, Gunnar, with the assistance of Richard Sterner and Arnold Rose, *An American Dilemma: The Negro Problem and Modern Democracy*, Vols. I and II, New York, Harper & Bros., 1944. A classic academic study of the American Negro and his place in American society.

Redding, Saunders, *The Lonesome Road: The Story of the Negro's Part in America*, Garden City, N. Y.: Doubleday & Co., 1958. An excellent history of the American Negro up to the 1954 school desegregation decision of the U. S. Supreme Court. For a good account of the editorial and other aspects of Frederick Douglass' career, see especially Chapter Three, "Born Slave", pp. 39-62.

Report of the U. S. National Advisory Commission on Civil Disorders, New York, Bantam Books, 1968. The report of the famous Kerner Commission on the urban riots of the 1960's, including material on the Detroit and Newark riots of 1967.

Silberman, Charles E., *Crisis in Black and White*, New York: Vintage Books, Random House, Inc., 1964. Describes the Negro's need for political and economic power and means by which he seeks to achieve them.

Thorpe, Earl E., *The Mind of the Negro: An Intellectual History of Afro-Americans*, Baton Rouge, La.: Ortlieb Press, 1961. As part of a broader discussion of Negro authors and editors, Thorpe discusses the history of the Negro press in the United States in a brief but informative summary.

Zinn, Howard, *SNCC, the New Abolitionists*, Boston: Beacon Press, 1964. A history of the Student Non-Violent Coordinating Committee.

ARTICLES

Bell, Howard H., "Expressions of Negro Militancy in the

North, 1840-60", *Journal of Negro History,* January, 1960. Negro protest and opinion during the ante bellum era.

Bunche, Ralph J., "The Negro in the Political Life of the United States", *Journal of Negro Education,* X, July 1941. Role of the Negro in politics.

Clark, Septima P., "Literacy and Liberation", *Freedomways,* IV (First Quarter, 1964), pp. 113-124. Contemporary views of the Negro role.

Douglass, Frederick, "Reconstruction", *Atlantic Monthly,* XVIII, December, 1866, pp. 761-765. Views of a famous Negro editor.

Ebony. "Special Issue in Commemoration of the 100th Anniversary of the Emancipation Proclamation", September, 1963.

Harlan, Louis R., "Booker T. Washington and the White Man's Burden", *American Historical Review,* LXXI, January, 1966, pp. 441-467. An account of one Negro leader.

Johnson, Guy B., "Negro Racial Movements and Leadership in the United States", *American Journal of Sociology,* XLIII, July, 1937, pp. 57-71. A study of Negro leadership in interracial affairs.

Marvick, Dwaine, "Political Socialization of the American Negro", In Lawrence H. Fuchs, Ed., *American Ethnic Politics,* New York, Harper Torchbooks, 1968, pp. 247-273. Negro political socialization.

McWilliams, Carey, "How the Negro Fared in the War", *Negro Digest,* IV, May, 1946, pp. 67-74. Role of the Negro in World War II.

Meier, August, "Negro Protest Movements and Organizations", *Journal of Negro Education,* Fall, 1963. Leadership of Negro protest movements.

Miller, Loren, "Farewell to Liberals: A Negro View", *The Nation,* CXCV, Oct. 20, 1962, pp. 235-238. A Negro view of protest tactics.

Reed, Ira De A., "Negro Movements and Messiahs, 1900-1949", *Phylon,* Fourth Quarter, 1949. Negro leadership in the 20th century.

Rudwick, Elliot M., "Du Bois versus Garvey: Race Propagandists at War", *Journal of Negro Education,* Fall, 1959. A study of two famous Negro leaders.

Wilson, James Q., "The Negro in Politics", in Lawrence H.

Fuchs, Ed., *American Ethnic Politics*, New York, Harper Torchbooks, 1968, pp. 215-246. The Negro role in contemporary politics.

Wish, Harvey, "American Slave Insurrections Before 1861", *Journal of Negro History*, July, 1937, pp. 299-320. The Negro in the abolitionist era.

NOTES

1. For accounts of *Freedom's Journal* and other early Negro-edited newspapers, see Earl E. Thorpe, *The Mind of the Negro: An Intellectual History of Afro-Americans*, Baton Rouge, La.: Ortlieb Press, 1961, especially pp. 461-464 in Chapter XXI, "The Mind of the Negro Writer and Artist," pp. 451-495; also Clifton R. Jones, "The Negro Press," pp. 401-415 in Francis J. Brown and Joseph S. Roucek, *One America* (Third Edition), New York: Prentice-Hall, 1952; and Lerone Bennett Jr., *Confrontation: Black and White*, Baltimore, Md.: Penguin Books, 1965, p. 47.

2. Joanne Grant, ed., *Black Protest: History, Documents, and Analyses, 1619 to the Present*, Greenwich, Conn.: Fawcett Premier Books, 1968, pp. 83-84.

3. Bennett, *op. cit.*, pp. 47-48.

4. Bennett, *op. cit.*, pp. 56-59. For another account of Douglass' career as editor and abolitionist activist, see Saunders Redding, *The Lonesome Road: The Story of the Negro's Part in America*, Garden City, N. Y.: Doubleday, 1958, especially Chapter Three, "Born Slave," pp. 39-62. An account of the *North Star* may be found on pp. 47-57.

5. See I. Garland Penn, *The Afro-American Press and Its Editors*, Springfield: Willey & Co., 1891. This is a treatise on the history of the American Negro press, with individual biographies of leading Negro editors.

6. Quoted in Frederick G. Detweiler, *The Negro Press in the United States*, Chicago: University of Chicago Press, 1922, p. 39.

7. Earl E. Thorpe, *The Mind of the Negro: An Intellectual History of Afro-Americans*, Baton Rouge, La.: Ortlieb Press, 1961, pp. 462-464.

8. See Clifton R. Jones, "The Negro Press," in Brown and Roucek, *op. cit.*, pp. 401-404.

9. See Virginius Dabney, "Press and Morale", *Saturday Review of Literature*, Vol. XXV, 27 (July 4, 1942), p. 25; Warren H. Brown, "A Negro Warns the Negro Press," *Saturday Review of Literature*, Vol. XXV, 51 (December 19, 1942), pp. 5-6.

10. See Walter White, "It's Our Country Too," *Saturday Evening Post*, Vol. CCXII, 24 (December 14, 1940), pp. 27 ff.; "The Negro's War," *Fortune*, Vol. XXV, 6 (June, 1942), pp. 76-80.

11. See Thomas Sancton, "The Negro Press," *New Republic*, Vol. CVIII, 16 (April 26, 1943), pp. 557-560; Frederick G. Detweiler, "The Negro Press Today," *American Journal of Sociology*, Vol. XLIV, 3 (November 1938), pp. 391-400. For a fuller discussion of the role of the Negro press,

see Clifton R. Jones, "The Negro Press," in Brown and Roucek, *op. cit.*, pp. 404-407.

12. See Clifton R. Jones, "The Negro Press," in Brown and Roucek, *op. cit.*, pp. 407-412.

WILLIAM C. SPRAGENS, received his Ph.D. degree in Political Science in 1966 from Michigan State University, where he completed his dissertation on "Press Coverage of Congressional Campaigns." He received the degree of AB in Journalism in 1947 from the University of Kentucky, which awarded him the MA degree in Political Science in 1953. He had daily newspaper experience as an editor and reporter from 1947 to 1960. A specialist in ethnic politics, public opinion and American political parties, Dr. Spragens is Assistant Professor of Political Science at Bowling Green State University, He previously taught at the University of Tennessee Michigan State University; and Millikin University, Decatur, Illinois and Wisconsin State University, Oshkosh. Has published book reviews and articles in the *Western Political Quarterly, Political Science Quarterly, Midwest Journal of Political Science, The Journal of Negro History, Wisconsin Review and Wisconsin Law Enforcement Journal*. Has done extensive research into the activities of civil rights interest groups and is a contributor to *The Slow Learner*, edited by Joseph S. Roucek. He is also doing research on the presidential nominating process and presented preliminary findings at the 1969 annual meeting of the American Political Science Association in New York.

MILESTONES IN THE HISTORY OF THE
EDUCATION OF THE NEGRO IN
THE UNITED STATES*

Joseph S. Roucek

*Queensborough Community College of the
City University of New York (Bayside, N. Y.)*

Much has been written, especially lately, both in the United
States and abroad, about the problems connected with the education of the American Negro; most of it is influenced by strong
emotions, hot-headedness, ignorance of facts, sympathy, anger,
and fear.

The difficulty is that the whole problem is presented along
ideological lines, although the issues concerning segregated education lie within the framework of a wider, more pressing problem of the United States: the need to provide adequate education
opportunities for all American citizens.[1]

Furthermore, the problem of the American Negro is inseparable from other sociological factors relating to the Negro's
existence in the United States as citizens born in the United
States; it is not just a problem of the South, as often supposed,
since racial tensions that have exploded in Northern cities in
recent years had been taking place also in the past. The fact
remains that the problem of the American Negro looms larger
in the United States than ever before; and one of America's
most enduring moral, social and political problems has been
shaped, or at least influenced by, the presence of the black man—

---

* This is an expanded version of an article originally published in
International Review of Education, X, 1964, pp. 162-175.

and it so far remains unsolved. In fact, it seems clear that the greatest problem facing the United States today is interracial relations. (The President's National Advisory Commission on Civil Disorders, headed by Governor Otto Kerner of Illinois, issued on March 1, 1968, a critically important report. The Commission discovered that behind the many diverse and complex factors causing the urban violence which erupted across the nation in the summer of 1967, the one fundamental and universal feature was the racial attitude and behavior of white Americans toward black Americans. It states: "White racism is essentially responsible for the explosive mixture which has been accumulating in our cities since the end of World War II.")[2]

In fact, the great majority of American Negroes have been concentrated in the Southern states, and obviously the major determinant in the white Southerner's life—at least insofar as it was distinguished from the white Northerner's life—has been his relations with Negroes. Thus, until recently, the Negro problem dominated American life mainly within the framework of southern traditions. We must note that the Civil War was not fought on the issue of the freeing of the Negro, although it culminated with his Emancipation; the step taken on his behalf by President Lincoln was one of the emergency measures designed to weaken the fighting power of the South.[3] The basic issue of the Civil War was what we might call the "self-determination of the states" within the Federal Union; another issue was rivalry between the slave-owning South and the "capitalist" —industrialized—North.

EDUCATION OF THE NEGRO IN THE COLONIES

The early English settlers, upon their arrival in America, sometimes showed interest in the religious education of the Indians. When the number of slaves increased, they became also interested in educating these "black heathens." The first public school to educate Indians and Negroes was established in Virginia in 1620; this school, however, was destroyed by the Indians a couple of years later. Another attempt to educate them was made in 1701; a Missionary Society was founded and Samuel Thomas became its first missionary, taking it upon himself to instruct 20 Negroes to read. In fact, the Anglican Society for the

Propagation of the Gospel in Foreign Parts outshone all groups in its services to Negro education, establishing schools and teaching slaves and freed Negroes not only Christian doctrine but also reading, writing, and simple arithmetic. Meanwhile, Puritan slave-owners in New England sometimes also gave religious instruction to their household servants, and the Quakers as early as 1693 advocated religious training as a preparation for emancipation and had established schools for Negroes by the third quarter of the 18th century. In 1738 the Moravians established missions exclusively for Negroes. Other such schools were founded by different denominations in the Southern colonies to instruct Negroes in Christian doctrines, and sometimes the English language.[4]

In the North, the history of the education of the Negro is traced as far back as 1704 when the Anglican Society for the Propagation of the Gospel in Foreign Parts undertook the religious training of the slaves in New York City; the work was carried on for nearly two decades by Elias Neau, a Frenchman.[5]

In general, the dominant white view of formal instruction for Negroes in the Colonies crystallized slowly.[6] In the interest of efficiency, masters started early to teach Africans the English language, vocational skills, and concepts of obedience and subordination. As the slave status became legalized, masters were reluctant to Christianize colored people since this could open the way for freeing the slaves. But the Bishop of London proclaimed that conversion need not affect slave status and this opened the way in the Colonies to instruct Negroes in Christian doctrine. The Rev. Thomas Bray of the Anglican Society, and his "associates," founded schools and taught hundreds of slaves and free Negroes not only Christian doctrine but also the elements of reading, writing, and simple arithmetic.

Nevertheless, in spite of these efforts, progress was slow because of the cultural background of the Negroes and the fear of the slave-owners that the knowledge of reading might promote Negro unrest and make white control more difficult. Thus a South Carolina law of 1740 prohibited whites to instruct Negroes in reading and writing. In fact, there was hardly any time for "learning," since most Negro slaves worked on plantation-sized units in 7 states of the Deep South, which were a combination factory, village and police resort.[7]

As we had already indicated, religion has always played an important part in the education of the American Negro. During the colonial days, most religious groups in America sanctioned slavery, while at the same time endorsing policies of Christianization. Such policies were likewise endorsed by the Crown, which ruled that the conversion of slaves would not change their status. But many slave-owners opposed this effort, believing that Christianity would eventually mean freedom of slaves.[8]

The Church of England made efforts at conversion through the Society for the Propagation of the Gospel in Foreign Parts, organized in London in 1701; an early catechizing school was founded in New York City at Trinity College in 1704.[9] Rev. Thomas Bray in Maryland was another who encouraged instruction and conversion; his followers, known as Bray's Associates, continued his work, notably in Philadelphia and North Carolina, until the 1760's.

Early efforts to teach the Negro were made by Catholics in New Orleans. The Ursuline Nuns tried to teach Negroes and Indians in 1727 and, a few years later (1734), a school for Negroes was conducted on Chartres Street.

The most conscientious efforts, however, were made by Quakers. In the face of considerable opposition, Quakers permitted slaves to attend their meetings, even before they had decided to stop buying or to free them.[10] Paul Cuffe, a prosperous Negro, set up a school in Massachusetts in the 18th century.

While the Society for the Propagation of the Gospel in Foreign Parts sent more than three hundred missionaries to the Colonies from the beginning of the eighteenth century to the Revolution, and established a number of parish libraries, in some instances they seem to have done more harm than good. Stephen B. Weeks, historian of Colonial North Carolina, declared that the backwardness of the colony in education was directly attributable "to the pernicious activities" of the missionaries. The missionaries themselves were often unhappy over their reception and some felt being "plagued" by the Quakers, and in Georgia, various humanitarian efforts to make good Anglicans out of the Negro slaves, and to teach them to read and write, met with meager success.[11]

On the whole, then, before the end of the colonial period, at least a few Negroes were sufficiently trained, or on the way to being trained, to instruct the sons of the white gentry in the higher as well as in the elementary branches of knowledge. In fact, instruction in reading for Christian uplift gave some Negroes a considerable body of the white man's knowledge, and exceptional members of the black race achieved distinction in the white man's realm: the poems of Phyllis Wheatley (1773) and of Jupiter Hammon (1761) may be cited for their feeling and versification, and the almanacs of Benjamin Banneker for their mathematical skill.

THE COLONIAL HERITAGE

While the Negroes were slowly becoming familiar with some of the white man's ideas and even his intellectual skills, the whites were influenced by the Negroes. In areas where their numbers were considerable, the Africans influenced the folklore, idiom, pronunciation, and food habits, and possibly the music and dance, of the whites.

The influence of the Negro on American intellectual life was even a greater factor in the colonial legacy. In the South, the presence of a host of abjectly ignorant slaves deepened the traditional Old World gulf between the classes, who shared the great body of humane and scientific knowledge, and the masses, whose world was governed largely by lore and superstition. The problem of slavery and a related race issue bequeathed a stubborn legacy to the new nation. The concept of the dignity of manual labor, which was to become a characteristically American idea, was lacking in the slave-holding communities of the Old South, where physical toil was related to slavery.

In the latter part of the seventeenth century, as the whites slowly crystallized their ideas about the slave status of the Negro (at first regarded as servants in more or less temporary bondage), it became necessary to rationalize the dominant position of the white race. The blacks were looked upon as "accursed" and "inferior." At the same time, the pitiful condition of the blacks fed the springs of Christian and humanitarian sentiment and gave rise to the idea that the Negroes must be free and enlightened.

Efforts toward the education and freedom of the Negro were

curtailed, of course, by the rapid rise of slave power in the cotton South. This is clearly illustrated by the fact that the South became frantic over a slave insurrection of 1831, led by a Virginia Negro, Nat Turner; thereafter, "black" codes were passed, curtailing the movements of Negroes, forbidding the teaching of Negroes. The codes were not, however, always strictly enforced, and Negroes continued to learn somewhat clandestinely. Some schools for Negroes operated in Danville and Richmond (Virginia) as late as a decade before the Civil War, and Berea College in Kentucky pioneered during this period in admitting Negro students — even though repercussions from John Brown's raid were to close its doors to Negroes. The Ursulines in New Orleans, furthermore, were still conducting a school for free *gens de couleur* in 1838. In general, legacies from the earlier work of religious and civic groups, mainly in the North and Upper South, provided sporadic incentives for the academic education of the Negro during the generation prior to the Civil War.

On November 1, 1787, the Manumission Society opened the African Free School in New York City. In 1824, the City of New York took over the support of its 7 African Free Schools; thus colored children had free education available to them in New York 7 years before there were similar public schools for white children. (The African Free School became the precursor of the New York free public school system). In 1858, all the Negro schools of New York City, taught at that time entirely by Negro teachers, were taken over by the newly organized Board of Education; many distinguished persons were graduated from them, including Patrick Reason, Henry Highland Garnet, and the actor Ira Aldridge.

In 1849 Sarah C. Roberts sued the city of Boston for its discrimination in refusing to admit a colored child to its school. Her lawyer was Charles Sumner (who became a noted abolitionist Senator, and Sumner's assistant was a young Negro attorney, Robert Morris); their cause was lost, but Sumner's legal brief for desegregated schools was a forerunner of the 1954 Supreme Court desegregation decision. But in 1855 the Massachusetts legislature declared that "no person shall be excluded from a Public School on account of race, color or religious opinions."

Before the Civil War, all Negroes interested in college educa-

200

tion went to white colleges or travelled abroad. The first black student to graduate from an American college was John Russwurm, who received a degree from Bowdoin College in Maine in 1826. Oberlin was one of the first colleges in the West — although Ohio, from 1829 to 1849 excluded Negroes from the public schools — to enroll (in 1834) not only Negroes, but also women; it had been founded by abolitionists who had withdrawn from Lane Theological Seminary in Cincinnati after free discussions of the evils of slavery had been curtailed there. In 1855, an antislavery editor and an abolitionist minister founded Berea College; it freely admitted Negroes as well as white; its charter began with the phrase; "God hath made of one blood all nations that dwell upon the face of earth." But by 1860 the grand total of Negro graduates was only 28; they had attended Oberlin, Franklin and Rutland Colleges and the Harvard Medical School.[12]

There were a few experiments made with Negro education before the Emancipation Proclamation. In 1840, the Avery "College" for Negroes opened in Allegheny City, Pennsylvania. In Washington, the Miner Academy for Negro Girls opened in 1851. A year later, an Institute for Colored Youth started functioning in Philadelphia; these were all only elementary and secondary schools, and not colleges. Two denominational institutions that were founded during that period began with work on a somewhat higher level; Wilberforce University in Ohio was founded by Methodists in 1855 and Ashmun Institute in Pennsylvania was sponsored by the Presbyterians in 1854. (Ashmun Institute was granted aid from the Presbyterian Church for the purpose of training missionaries for Africa; it eventually received a college charter as Lincoln University in 1866).[13]

THE POST-CIVIL-WAR PERIOD

After the Civil War the roads of the South became choked with clusters of Negroes wandering aimlessly, with no clear-cut idea where they were going or what they should do. The former slaves were mostly illiterate, thanks to the deliberate policy of the planters to keep their slaves illiterate and in ignorance of the most basic fundamentals of how to manage their own affairs. The whites received them as a horde of locust and tried to combat the problem by including in the new state constitutions what came to be known as "Black Does." These were laws which were necessary, in the view of the Southerners, to maintain order; from the standpoint of Northerners these laws were simply an insidious way of reinstituting slavery. In some states, a Negro was required to contract his employment a year in advance, and his employer had virtually the same power over him that "de massa" would have exercised in slavery days. Negro artisans were required to buy expensive licenses to do business, not required of the whites; Negro orphans could be bound to their former masters as "apprentices" until they were 18; and the penalties for a Negro found guilty of committing a crime were far more stringent than those for a white for the same offense. Thus, thousands of Negroes simply wandered.

In this chaos came, however, a period which witnesses the first great program of organized education for the Negro. There was, for instance, the program of the Federal Government as conducted by the War Department. As refugees and "contraband," Negroes were early cared for and given some instruction under the military commands of General Rufus Saxon in the Sea Islands and vicinity, under Colonel John Eaton in Mississippi, and under General N. P. Banks in Louisiana.

Then there was the work of one Northern organization whose name was to become anathema to the ex-Confederates: the Freedmen's Bureau.[14]

Congress had passed a law establishing the Freedmen's Bureau before the war ended. In the beginning, its purpose was "to aid these helpless, ignorant, unprotected people . . . until they can provide for and take care of themselves." Operating as an agency of the War Department, the Bureau set up shop in the South immediately after the cessation of hostilities and began the Herculean task of trying to feed, clothe and provide gainful labor for the newly freed Negro masses; it also issued rations to destitute whites.

In the beginning — and throughout its history in fact — its affairs were to some extent in the hands of idealists; but the Radical Republicans were to make it a political football and a roosting place for sharpeyed profiteers (carpetbaggers), its brand of idealism, verging often into fanaticism, and pure chicanery, greediness, fraud, inefficiency, graft, and political opportunism, marked the conduct of the Bureau and thus earned it the contempt and hatered of the Southern whites. Next to giving the vote to Negroes, nothing offended the South more than efforts to give them schooling; the slogan, "School ruins the Negro," expressed this popular attitude.

At any rate, the Bureau helped in the foundation of a system of schools for Negroes, giving "central organization, encouragement, protection, and financial support to the efforts of philanthropists, freedmen, and states." Although between 1865-67 many Negro schoolhouses were burned down, the Bureau operated, during its peak period, some 4,000 primary schools, 74 normal schools, and 61 industrial schools for Negroes.[15]

The Freedmen's Bureau also cooperated, for a brief period, with northern philanthropy. One of the first civic and religious groups was the Boston Educational Commission (later known as the New England Freedmen's Aid Society); in the same year (1862), the National Freedmen's Relief Commission of Philadelphia and New York was founded. Later these organizations formed temporarily the U.S. Commission for Relief of National Freedmen with headquarters in Washington, D.C.; by 1865 this consolidated body was replaced by the American Freedmen's Aid Union, which eventually ceased to exist in 1869. Other organizations formed to help freedmen were the African Civilization Society, the Baltimore Association for the Moral and Educational Improvement of Negroes, and a similar organization in Delaware. Churches also made valuable efforts in the institutional history of Negro education. The American Missionary Association created schools for Negroes in Newport News, Portsmouth, Suffolk, and Yorktown in Virginia, Washington, D.C., and Columbus, Ohio. In addition, the Friends Association for Aid to Freedmen, the Board of Freedmen's Missions of the United Presbyterian Church, and the Freedmen's Aid Society of the Methodist Episcopal Church gave important help to freed slaves; significant work was also done by the American Baptist Home Mission Society, the American Church Institute of the Episcopal Church, and the Conferences of the African Methodist Episcopal Church.

Philanthropy was financed mainly by wealthy Northerners, whose fortunes came from the nation's industrialization; two major funds, the Daniel Hand and Anna T. Jeanes, were set aside exclusively for Negroes. But it must be also noted that "Northern philanthropy inadvertently perpetuated an old tradition of paternalism as a philosophy in solving the Negro 'problems'."[16]

The formal education of the Negro in the South during the Civil War is traced to Mrs. Mary S. Peake, a black woman, who taught the first school, opened on September 17, 1861, in Hampton, Virginia.[17] Soon after the Union forces gained control of a city or a sizable rural community, freedmen began to learn their three R's; by 1869, there were 9,502 teachers in these schools. Many of the teachers were Northern white women who, as well as men, suffered ostracism, insults and violence.

Most singular, it appeared to scoffers, was the founding of "universities." Edmund A. Ware, a graduate of Yale, was the first President of Atlanta University, Georgia; Erastus M. Cravath, a graduate of Oberlin, 1857, headed Fisk University in Nashville, Tennessee, which opened in 1866. General Oliver O. Howard, a graduate of Bowdoin, who was Commissioner of the Freedmen's Bureau, was the first President of Howard University, founded in 1867 in Washington, D.C.

While these so-called "universities" for many years had more elementary, high school, and normal school than college students, they had goals inspired by those of the best northern institutions.

A period of rapid growth for Negro colleges occurred during the decades following the Civil War, the period dominated by the benevolence, zeal, and humanitarianism of northern Christian churches, especially Congregationalists, Presbyterians, Methodists and Baptists, which sent "Yankee schoolmarms" down South to staff common schools for the newly emancipated colored people. They also showed a great deal of interest in Negro higher education. An example was the Baptist Home Missionary Society of New York, which organized (1867) the Augusta Institute (later Morehouse College), or the American Missionary Society of New York, which founded Atlanta University in Georgia and Talladega College in Alabama. In fact, prior to 1900, nearly all of the faculty members in southern Negro colleges were idealistic educational missionaries trained in northern colleges.[18]

These institutions, along with 30 other universities and colleges founded in the South during Reconstruction, graduated many teachers and others who formed a segment of what William Edward Burghardt Du Bois called "The Talented Ten."

Vocational education, which best suited the needs of most Negroes then, was started by General Samuel C. Armstrong, a graduate of Williams College, Williamstown, Mass., at Hampton Institute, Virginia, in 1868. Both white and Negro leaders had come to realize that so long as the ex-slave remained illiterate, he would remain a slave in fact, if not before the law. Vocational education would equip him for better jobs, increase his self-respect, and develop his natural aptitudes.

The most famous graduate of Hampton Normal and Agricultural Institute was Booker T. Washington, who became the head of a normal school at Tuskegee, Alabama, in 1881, and was soon recognized as the educational leader of the Negro. Tuskegee was to become a pioneer example of an independent industrial school. Washington's agricultural and industrial projects, his part in establishing small business by and for Negroes and in the practical rehabilitation of the rural South, and his efforts toward Negro-white cooperation under existing conditions made his name almost a household word by the early twentieth century.

He propounded to the Negro to abandon, for the time being, any claims to equal treatment: to look up to the substantial southern whites as friends; and through the cultivation of practical skills in trade and agriculture to make themselves economically self-sufficient and indispensable to the prosperity of the white South. Yet, his docility infuriated militant Negroes, and today his attitude toward Negro-white relations is repudiated by the majority of his people. Nevertheless, his service to his people cannot be minimized. If Washington prepared his people for agriculture, domestic service, and the lower-paid factory jobs, it was simply because better jobs were not open to them then.

Booker T. Washington's approach to the problem resulted in debates carried on for several decades over industrial education of the Negro which, for some people, meant "practical" public education, and for others, "industrial training." Booker T. Washington's influence on the rise of the industrial school movement was important; but actually this form of education for the Negro was "little more than a slogan to cover poor, cheap, and ineffective Negro education."[20]

This movement expired in the subsequent decades, due to the gradual reduction of Negro illiteracy and the realization on the part of the public and philanthropic foundations and Negroes themselves that they needed the same varieties of education as the white man.

The general antagonism of the South to the more educated Negroes fitted into the need of the region to keep Negro labor cheap. But this attitude began to be modified at the turn of the present century when the larger industrial concerns (especially those in the coal and iron business in Alabama) started to elevate Negroes slightly in the socio-economic scale. Yet, during this period, the situation in the rural districts was especially miserable, since there existed a close relationship between the operation of the Negro schools and of the agricultural system. The dates for the opening and closing of the school in the cotton belt were, in fact, decided by the landlords watching the crops, and the internal school program had to accommodate itself to the farming needs.[21]

Nevertheless, the first definite advances in organized education for the Negro took place. Civic and religious organizations started to cooperate with the Freedmen's Bureau and developed programs of their own (such as the Boston Educational Commission, later known as the New England Freedmen's Aid Society, 1862). The American Missionary Association set up schools for Negroes in Newport, Portsmouth, Suffolk, and Yorktown in Virginia, Washington, and Columbus, Ohio, as early as 1863. Philanthropy was another great source of support, although northern philanthropy inadvertently perpetuated an old tradition of paternalism as a philosophy in solving the problem. The Peabody Education Fund, whose donations eventually amounted to about $3,500,000, began in 1867. Andrew Carnegie gave $10 million in 1902, establishing libraries on the campuses of many Negro schools and colleges. There was also the General Education Board enriched by John D. Rockefeller, the Rosenwald Fund and the Anna T. Jeanes Fund.

Southerners also began to make some of their first provisions for public education. Maryland, for instance, made its first provisions for organized public education in 1864 and 1867. States farther south followed: Arkansas and Louisiana in 1864; Florida in 1865; North Carolina in 1868 and 1876; Virginia in 1869 and 1870; South Carolina in 1877.

Yet public education for Negroes, and for many white Southerners, was condemned as a "misnomer" and "totally and radically inadequate."[22] In many southern communities only about half of the children of school age attended any school at all, and only about half of those enrolled attended with a fair degree of regularity. The Southern states were spending an average of $4.92 per year on a white child in 1900 and $2.71 on a Negro child.[23]

As the last century wore on, some groups started to emphasize the need of more adequately trained ministers, teachers, or tradesmen at scores of schools, variously styled as "normal," "institute," "academy," "seminary," "college," or "university." Some of these appellations were surely misleading. Many of these schools survived; some changed their names or purposes; some were absorbed by the states. And some lived as landmarks. In Alabama the American Missionary Association supported the establishment of a school at Talladega in 1867; later it became Talladega College. Fisk University (1866) in Nashville, Tenn., and Tougaloo University (1869) in Mississippi were also set up by the American Missionary Association.[24]

Federal aid was an important factor in this development, mainly under the Morrill Act of 1862 and 1890.

THE EFFECT OF THE ATLANTA COMPROMISE

It was at the Atlanta Cotton States and International Exposition in 1895 that Booker T. Washington, in a memorable speech, gave persuasive sanction to the course of southern sectionalism in the New South and the role assigned therein to the Negro; the surrender has been called the "Atlanta Compromise."[25]

Washington's plea was that the Negro, a loyal Southerner, deserved a place of recognition in the rising progress of the South. Looking upon questions of social equality as "extremist folly," he advised southern Negroes to "Cast down your buckets where you are," educating the "head, hand, and heart" through "the shop, the field, the skilled hand, habits of thrift, and economy, by way of the industrial school and college."[26]

Washington fell under the spell of Samuel C. Armstrong, a founder of Hampton Institute, a former Union General, and a student of Mark Hopkins while at Williams College. Armstrong's emphases were that Hampton students should have a high regard for the dignity of labor; he built his program on the foundation blocks of skilled labor and moral character.

Negroes found a measurable sense of success and pride in their segregated schools, churches, homes, and businesses. Endorsement of the Compromise was also written into law. The U.S. Supreme Court case of *Plessy* v. *Ferguson* gave sanction to both the theory and practice of segregation if accommodations were equal.

But some Negro leaders challenged the Compromise, especially W. E. B. Du Bois, who barely missed taking a teaching job at Tuskegee. He went to Atlanta University in 1896, having there a brilliant and distinguished career in scholarship and letters. He favored a program of education that would teach the Negro to think and recognized the need of higher learning in the Americanization of the Negro. He led the "Niagara Movement," the spiritual ancestor of the National Association for the Advancement of Colored People.[27]

The controversy continued until Washington's death in 1915. A realist, he really favored the ultimate equality of the Negro.[28] Du Bois, on the other hand, was far less a materialist and far greater an intellectual and scholar; he stood openly and unequivocally, but at times bitterly, upon the timeless belief of Americans in freedom. History may yet in its perspective accord him a greater stature, without bitterness, for not compromising the moral challenge which he plainly recognized as underwriting the so-called problem of the Negro in American life.[29]

THE GENERATION BETWEEN 1900 AND 1936

The Negro generation of 1900-1936 began with the Tuskegee idea in the ascendancy: purchasing peace for their time by deferring social and political aspirations. In the Negro institutions, the standards were still low, and a "college" was still mostly an elementary and "normal" school with a "collegiate department" plus a few feeble theology courses. Courses were largely taught by self-taught Negro "professors" and white missionary teachers "who (with notable exceptions) had more zeal than competence." But among the 50-odd church leaders were also some of the earliest Negro Ph.D.'s — J. W. E. Bowen, Sr., Boston University

(1882); Richard Robert Wright, who got his degree in sociology at Pennsylvania, but such higher academic and professional degrees were unusual, "for education of most of the group fell short of junior-college levels and theological training was even more modest."[30] These were still days when whites were convinced that education "spoiled" a Negro and that there were no suitable vocations for college-bred Negroes anyhow. About 50 persons in the period between 1900 and 1936 were in the category of educators identified with Negro higher education.[31]

By 1900, institutions calling themselves colleges or universities numbered about 99; in 1936 the number was about the same. Founded in the post-Civil War decades by Northern philanthropy, missionary enterprise, the Freedmen's Bureau and state authority, as well as by denominations, one group was under public control, another under white sectarian boards, and one cluster in the hands of Negro denominations.

As of 1922, 85% of the enrollment in the so-called "colleges" was in the elementary and secondary department, for all but three or four of the colleges were in the South, where common-school provision for Negro children was still minimal and public high schools wholly absent. But at the end of the period (1936), more than three-fourths of the enrollment was in the collegiate departments (which often afforded only a 2-year course).[32]

Opportunities for Negroes to rise to prominence as educators were extremely small. There were only 23,000 students, most of them ill-prepared, in the Negro colleges in 1932, and the supply of adequately trained professors and administrators was microscopic. Most of the best Negro colleges were in the hands of white trustees, faculties and administrators; the most notable exceptions were the schools founded by Negro denominations. Howard (60 years old) acquired its first Negro president in 1926; Hampton was still run by whites in the early 1940's; Fisk, then 80 years old, inaugurated its first Negro president in 1947.

Of the 52 educators in the roster, all but a tiny minority were college presidents (or, in a few cases, deans), and resident in the South. All but two were born in the South (the only exceptions being Du Bois and Locke). Negroes distinguished in fields other than religion and education, by contrast, were nearly all residents of the North.

Concludes Bardolph: "At the end of the era (1936), the institutions were still seriously deficient as to library facilities, equipment, preparation of instructors, administrative skill and all the other indices of academic status. Their symbol was the begging bowl; they were from the beginning dependent upon alms, first from religious and relatively unorganized benefactors, and then from foundations and philanthropic agencies."[33]

THE CHANGING EDUCATIONAL PATTERN

Ever since the Reconstruction period, Negro education suffered from the handicap of starting from nowhere. Literacy was estimated at about 5% among Negroes in 1860; by 1890 nearly 60% were still illiterate; by 1910 illiteracy had been reduced to 30%. While a few lower schools in four or five southern states had been opened on a mixed basis by the Negro "carpetbag" governments of the immediate post-war era, most of the southern states established separate schools for whites and blacks. For many years, there were no local school taxes in the South, the funds being distributed from state sources to counties on a per capita basis; thus the heavily populated counties with large numbers of Negroes received more money than those counties with smaller Negro populations. White groups in smaller counties were angered by these provisions and it was not long before funds due to Negro schools were being diverted in various ways to white schools. By 1930 Negro schools were still on the average getting only 37% of the amount due them on a per capita basis. Having no political voice, being a particularly weak economic force, and remaining largely uneducated, Negroes were the unfortunate victims of one of America's greatest national tragedies and blights.

Although a considerable amount of aid was given Negro education by private foundations during the late 1890's and early 20th Century (Peabody, Slater, Jeanes, Rosewald, Carnegie, Phelps-Stokes funds and the General Education Board), they made only a limited dent, important though it was, in the local morass. By 1900, according to a report of the U.S. Commissioner of Education, out of over 1,000 public high schools in the South, less than 70 were provided for Negroes. The years of the Great Depression further strained Negro education as increased thousands of black youngsters, squeezed from the labor market, bulged the school. Generally in the South, the Negroes still had ramshackle buildings, more poorly trained teachers, near starvation salaries, and "benefited" from discarded white school desks, books, and decrepit buses.[34]

Several key factors brought the long overdue improvements that have marked the recent history of Negro education. An important factor was the changing "climate of opinion" developing among the Negro leaders.

As we have seen, Booker T. Washington, in essence, wanted Negroes to prepare for jobs which were open to them; the Negro must first become literate and learn skills which might help him to be economically independent; then, perhaps, he would be ready for political and social equality.[35] On the other hand, W. E. B. Du Bois, a Negro sociologist and educator, attacked Washington for accepting the Negro caste position and for remaining silent and asking other Negroes to remain silent in the face of injustice; he and his group demanded no less than equality of opportunity in education at the higher levels as well as in elementary and vocational training. This group argued that, in the struggle for equality, training for inferior positions will not be of much help. What was needed was a large number of highly literate and capable Negro leaders who could only come into existence if equal opportunities in higher education become a reality.[36] The controversy between Washington and Du Bois continued until Washington's death in 1915.

A great migration of Negroes from the farm to southern and northern cities came after Washington's death. "In an important sense the movement was flight from poverty, oppression, and the boll weevil. The unprecedented urbanization and industrialization of the Negro was thus under way."[37] And, in spite of disenfranchisement, discrimination, poverty, and lack of opportunity, which had been the black man's lot, the Negro's situation had improved in many ways after 1900. For instance, 30% of the Negroes had been illiterate in 1910; only 8% were thus handicapped in 1940.[38] As late as 1915 there had been only 64 Negro high schools in this country; by 1940, the number had risen to 2,500. Almost 20,000 Negroes were graduated from colleges during the decades of the 1930's—more than twice the number of the more prosperous twenties. After World War II, these educational trends were accelerated.

More specifically, between World War I and World War II,

there was a significant growth of Negro public high schools, especially in large urban areas, both in North and South; there were enormous increases in both the relative and actual sizes of the enrollment, supply of teachers, number of graduates, and capital outlay; many Negro colleges dropped their high school programs, added graduate instruction, and many degree-conscious Negroes graduated in ever-increasing numbers from Negro and northern colleges; state supported and land grant institutions surpassed the private Negro colleges in enrollment and financial support; and "the most profound change was the quest for equality."[39]

THE STEPS TOWARD DESEGREGATION

One domestic event during Eisenhower's first term can be considered a revolutionary advancement at any period of American history — the U.S. Supreme Court's decision on segregated education.[40]

In 1883 the Supreme Court decision on civil rights sanctioned the segregation of Negroes by individuals in all states; in the *Plessy* v. *Ferguson* decision of 1896, which upheld the constitutionality of state laws providing "separate but equal" accommodations for Negroes, a precedent was set which greatly aided the spread of segregation on public carriers and in public places. On May 17, 1954, the Supreme Court of the U.S. unanimously outlawed racial segregation in the public schools, setting aside the "separate but equal" doctrine which the Court had upheld in 1896. 'Separate educational facilities are inherently unequal. . . . Liberty under law extends to the full range of conduct which an individual is free to pursue, and it cannot be restricted except for a proper governmental objective. Segregation in public education is not reasonably related to any proper governmental objective."

Chief Justice Earl Warren read two decisions a year later, the first of which affected 17 states in which there was legal segregation and the other the District of Columbia. Implementing these decisions a year later, the Court directed on May 31, 1955, that educational integration be achieved with "all deliberate speed," based on equitable principles and a "practical flexibility." And one year after that, on March 5, 1956, the Supreme Court ruled that its ban on segregation applied also to tax supported colleges and universities.

In spite of the decision, the application of the rulings has had its ups and downs — although, on the whole, mostly ups. During 1955-1956, more than 500 black students enrolled in formerly all-white colleges and universities in the South. In Washington, D.C., in 1955, the complete integration of the District of Columbia public schools began. By 1956, Baltimore, the population of which is 41% Negro, had integrated 11,000 out of its 51,000 black pupils (but in the rest of Maryland not more than 8 counties had begun to mix the races).

Symbolic of the Deep South's defiance of the Supreme Court's desegregation decisions was the incident that occurred in Tuscaloosa, Alabama, when Autherine Lucy, a Negro, had been trying for 3 years to enroll as a student; riots took place and eventually she was expelled. As of January, 1963, the University had enrolled no other Negro applicants. Mississippi was the scene of brutal murders, and Montgomery, Alabama, saw an example of the Negroes' use of mass passive resistance. In fact, school desegregation in America became front-page news in papers throughout the world and remained headlines for several years: Clainton, Nashville, Atlanta, Little Rock, and Oxford. In many communities resistance took various forms, ranging from inaction, less than "deliberate speed" and token integration, to blatant official defiance of federal edicts, riots at schools to which Negroes applied, violence against black students and the bombing of educational institutions, churches and homes. Both Negro and white schools were bombed in Atlanta and other cities. In Nashville, Z. Alexander Lobby, a member of the National Association for the Advancement of Colored People's Legal Committee, was blown from his bed by a bomb.

It is only fair to say that the swift and accelerating pace of desegregation events, including the cases of dramatic federal-government intervention and the wave of sit-ins, eat-ins, kneel-ins, and other types of non-violent demonstrations, has thus far outstripped the demonstrated ability and resources of researchers "to study them from the viewpoint of the comparative causation of particular outcomes." And it must be also noted that the whole question of Negro desegregation is inseparably related to the whole problem of civil rights, which covers all minorities and all Americans.[41]

Since the U.S. Supreme Court decision of 1954, the Negro situation has improved considerably — and even more improvements can be expected in the future. At the time of that decision 17 southern and border states, in addition to the District of Columbia, had complete segregation in their elementary and secondary schools, with the exception of a few communities with only a few Negro children to educate. Four states outside this region (Arizona, Kansas, New Mexico, and Wyoming) allowed some local segregation contrary to law. Sixteen states prohibited by law any segregation, although not all of them enforced these statutes. Eleven other northern and western states had no laws dealing with this matter.

The current status of school segregation-desegregation in the southern and border states, according to the latest figures, shows that in six states there was between 50 and 100% integration, in six states there was 10 to 50% integration, and in the five states (Louisiana, Mississippi, Alabama, Georgia, and South Carolina) there was only 2 to 10% integration.

As of December 1966, in 11 southern states an average of only 12.5% of Negro school children were attending schools with less than 95% Negro enrollment, the range being from 2.4% in Alabama to 34.6% in Texas; at the same time, 75.6% of the Negro school children, or 2,571,540, were enrolled in all-Negro schools.

In the five border states, as of December 1966, an average of 45.1% of the Negro pupils were attending schools with less than 95% Negro pupils, the range being from 40.5% in both Maryland and Oklahoma to 88.5% in Kentucky. In the border states there were only 32.2% of the Negro pupils attending all-Negro schools.[42]

Residential segregation in large cities generally means that, in both the North and the South, many schools are in fact segregated. Because pupils are required to attend schools in the neighborhoods in which they live, the schools in Negro areas virtually have all-Negro pupils. Even Negro teachers are generally assigned in the North to schools located in the Negro areas. But the effects of segregated schooling have been amply demon-

214

strated through special studies made of pupils in desegregated schools; in Washington, D.C., for instance, it was found that when Negro students were integrated with whites, their educational level, in many cases, was generally inferior.[43]

It is interesting to observe significant changes that have taken place in the status of the American Negro in American life since the 1954 U.S. Supreme Court decision. Although Negroes are still far from attaining the goals which their leaders have set for them, significant progress has nevertheless been made. Slowly, they have gained entrance into a number of the professions — education, law, medicine, and the like — and have succeeded also in securing membership in a considerable number of professional organizations in the South as well as in the North. For example, in 1948, the Missouri State Teachers Association admitted Negroes to its fold, and since 1947 more than 27 state and county medical societies, including those in southern states, have either admitted Negro physicians or amended their rules so as to make this possible.

Professional recognition prior to May 17, 1954, reflected an attitude shared by an increasing number of Southerners. Speaking of the great mass of Southerners in the early 1940's Professor Howard W. Odum stated they identified the Negro "as a Negro and nothing more." They "did not appraise the Negro as the same sort of human being as they themselves are."[44] But once this attitude is changed, and the Negro is recognized as a *person*, the groundwork is laid for a new attitude toward the restrictions that have kept him as a thing apart. This change, in turn, depends upon the improved educational, economic, and cultural status of an increasing number of Negroes, which is also characteristic of recent years. Deplorable as conditions of Negro education still are in most of the southern states, the progress of recent years has been marked. (Considering the South alone, Negro school attendance in the period of 1940 to 1950 increased twice as fast as the total population).

Moreover, on the higher levels of education in the South, as well as in the North, a steadily increasing number of white people, through their association with Negroes in institutions of higher learning, have come to appreciate qualities of intellect and character strikingly different from the conventional stereotype.

When the U.S. Supreme Court outlawed school segregation, some educators began writing obituaries for the nation's 120 Negro colleges — most in the South. Since integration was to be just around the corner, black institutions seemed sadly out of date. But the obituaries proved premature. Today, despite acute financial problems, most of these Negro colleges are thriving, surviving because they changed with the times.

The majority of Negro college students, either in the North or in the South, still attend Negro colleges.[45] In Alabama white colleges in 1967, for example, there were only 296 Negroes; in Arkansas, 303; in Mississippi, 131; and in South Carolina 169. On the other hand, there were 39,612 Negro students attending 28 predominantly Negro colleges. In the border states and the District of Columbia, 34,890 Negro students were attending predominantly white colleges and universities, with a total enrollment of 289,264. In the combined southern and border states, there were 1,078,494 students enrolled in predominantly white colleges and universities, while there were 85,362 Negroes enrolled—34,890 in predominantly white schools and 50,472 in predominantly Negro colleges and universities.[46]

In their new role, the black colleges cater to the needs of Negro students who, because of poor school preparation and impoverished lives in city ghettoes or rural areas, cannot make it to predominantly white institutions. They have been designing programs for the whole spread of students — remedial programs, reinforcement programs, enrichment program, helping bright but unqualified students reach the college level. The graduates of these new programs have been getting good jobs. In the spring of 1968, businesses were invited to send recruiters to the campuses of the black colleges. At most of these colleges, the recruiters outnumbered the graduates for positions that could lead to the executive level.

But, amid their successes, the black colleges face several grave problems. First, money. Predominantly Negro colleges make up 6% of all U.S. colleges and universities, but they carry on with less than 2% of the total college expenditure. (And this despite expensive new special programs. The United Negro College Fund, 55 East 52nd St., New York, is spearheading a fund drive for the colleges; by 1970, it hopes to reach the goal of $11,-000,000 annually).

Second, there is the image problem. The Negro colleges have worked hard to remove the "Uncle Tom" image which some critics — justifiably or not — have tried to pin on them. On the campuses of the colleges, there is a new emphasis on black pride, black accomplishment and, in the constructive sense, black power. Violence to foster these ends, however, is rejected flatly by the administrations of the colleges, although not always by all students.

As a result of the new image, the Negro colleges attracted in 1968 some 1,500 students who lived in the ghettos of New York City. Attracting this many black youths from the city is remarkable when one considers that many of the colleges are located in redneck country of the South.

In recruiting big city students, college representatives generally point out that graduates of black colleges have always been in the forefront of the civil rights and black power movements. For example, the late Rev. Martin Luther King attended Morehouse College in Atlanta; James Farmer, former national director of CORE, is a graduate of Wiley College in Texas; Stokely Carmichael, the black power activist, attended Howard University in Washington (sometimes regarded as the Harvard of black colleges).

Another problem black colleges face is the brain drain. Black colleges in the main cannot compete on a financial level with white colleges and, therefore, are losing many of their best teachers. In addition, white colleges are skimming off the top black high school students and offering them tempting scholarships. Black students who manage to overcome the economic and social handicaps and who display intellectual ability are solicited from all sides by white schools, North and South. Many black students decide to accept the generous scholarships and grants-in-aid these white institutions do offer.

Black colleges are under fire from critics who think it unwise to encourage the solvency of black institutions when white colleges are opening their doors to black students in ever increasing numbers. But Negro colleges can provide inspiration and encouragement to discouraged youths on a one-black-man-to-another basis that predominantly white colleges simply are not geared to provide. "In a black college, a student can make the transition from high school to college in a world that is not hostile and where his psychological insecurities are muted," says Stephen Wright, head of the United Negro College Fund. "He has a climate of learning where he does not have to carry the burden of the race problem on his back every day. He finds a college where he can concentrate on studying and growing as a person, where he can shape his future as a student — not just a Negro student." Black colleges also supply financial aid to poor students who could not get it anyplace else.

Wright also rejects the notion that Negro colleges are helping to perpetuate *de facto* segregation. "These schools are meeting a need during this time of transition in the fight for equal rights. There is more integration on the boards and teaching staffs of the fund colleges than in the predominantly white colleges. And in some cities where there are fund colleges and predominantly white colleges, cross-registration, faculty exchange and cooperative teaching methods involving both white and black students and teachers are the trend."

Eventually, the Negro colleges may become part of a national, integrated college system. But, until society makes this possible, they intend to continue fulfilling their special mission.

THE CHANGING BRAND OF NEGRO COLLEGE PRESIDENCY

Of America's 120 Negro colleges, most are in the South and most have, traditionally, ministers as Presidents — often men of intellectual distinction but with no training as educators. However bombastic in the pulpit, they made a point of being obliging to white authority. They demanded little, and they got little. The result was what sociologists David Riesman and Christopher Jenks have denounced as an "ill-financed, ill-staffed caricature of white higher education."

Lately, however, reflecting both the new pride and the new competence of the American black community, a number of more militant Negro presidents have risen to power. They appear to be "all professional educators with substantial records of academic achievement. (They) are committed to integration but are nonetheless convinced of the permanent need for stronger Negro institutions. Responding to the surge of black consciousness among their students, they have added Negro-oriented courses in history, sociology and psychology, and are determinedly trying to make their schools more relevant to the problems and opportunities facing young blacks today," reports *Time.*[47]

Outstanding among the new Negro Presidents noted by *Time* are: James E. Cheek, 36, Shaw University (Raleigh, N.C. 1,078 students), the campus where the Student Non-Violent Coordinating Committee got its start in 1960; he took this Baptist institution from virtual bankruptcy, doubled faculty salaries, expanded the curriculum to include courses on black culture and history, and is planning to launch a new School of Urban Science to attack the problems of ghettos.

Vivian W. Henderson, 45, Clark College (Atlanta, Georgia, 1,006 students), a longtime consultant to the U.S. government on Negro affairs, helped to develop the federal poverty program, is Chairman of the Task Force on Occupational Training in Private Industry for the U.S. Departments of Labor and Commerce, and has doubled Clark's budget since becoming President in 1965. Like Cheek, he puts a high priority on urban studies and is establishing a Southern Center for Studies in Public Policy with a $25,000 planning grant from the Field Foundation; he is also using grants to pay for an upcoming seminar on the economic development of black ghettos and a program to upgrade Negro college newspapers.

George A. Owens, 49, Tougaloo College (Tougaloo, Mississippi, 712 students), the son of a sharecropper, he earned a Master's degree in business administration at Columbia on the G. I. Bill, established a cooperative program with the Ivy League's Brown University that includes the exchange of both students and faculty, and has also started a remedial course in reading, writing and speaking that is taken by 25% of the students, and a program that he calls a "poor man's Antioch plan," in which students are helped to find course-related summer jobs, many of them in urban ghettos.

Norman C. Francis, 37, Xavier University of Louisiana (New Orleans, 1,362 students), was the first Negro ever to earn a law degree at nearby Loyola. He served in a variety of administrative posts, and organized the school's recent $10 million expansion program. In June, 1968, he became Xavier's President, a job that throughout the school's 43-year history had been held by white nuns. Francis' declared aim is "to steer students into the mainstream of American life," and he has very little patience for radical students; students must be taught pride, but they must also be taught the tools with which to compete.

THE FUTURE OF "BLACK STUDIES"

The last few years have witnessed the introduction of a new approach, born not in the legislatures but in the black communities across the nation, designed to rebuild in the black man his lost sense of worth, of value, or human dignity. One of the important measures being taken to create a growing self-awareness is the teaching in the public schools (as well as in the institutions of higher learning) of the history, culture, and achievements of Negro Americans — generally known as "Black Studies." By providing an acquaintance both with the important Afro-American figures of the past and with the critical facts of history which explain his present position in American society, it is hoped that the sense of citizenship and social potency will be enhanced and enlarged in Negro youth.

The call for the teaching of black history in the schools is not new. Reasons for its inclusion in the curriculum were advanced many years ago by the earliest of the Afro-American historians, George Washington Williams, who in 1880 wrote *The History of the Negro Race in America;* he suggested such a history was needed ". . . because Negroes had been the most vexatious problem in North America from the time of its discovery down to the present day; because that in every attempt upon the life of the nation . . . the Colored people had always displayed matchless patriotism in the cause of Americans; because such a history would give the world more correct ideas of the Colored people, and incite the latter to greater effort in the struggle for citizenship and manhood. The single reason that there was no history of the Negro race would have been sufficient reason for writing one."[48]

Other Afro-Americans, including the two best-known early twentieth century historians, W. E. B. Du Bois and Carter G. Woodson, have also urged the study.[49] But serious problems do confront the teaching of Black Studies. For instance, in the ghetto

220

schools, the underprivileged status of the children has produced harmful teaching attitudes; these attitudes declare that the children are "unteachable," for reasons based on their home environments. Thus the children are evaluated as inferior and this limits the effectiveness of any subject matter in creating confidence and self-esteem. Negative teaching attitudes must obviously be eliminated for Black Studies programs to benefit ghetto children. This also demands the call for more black teachers in the ghetto schools.

Then there is the rest of the society — the white majority — for which the teaching of Black Studies in the schools has a different meaning. Since the major problem in American race relations is white racism, the eradication of notions of racial superiority in white children is a critical task, and accurate and representative information about the Black Man's role in the making of American society must be made a part of every school curriculum. But this depends also on the revision and correction of most of the historical materials supplied to the schools in the past.

SELECTED BIBLIOGRAPHY

See the references pertaining to the chapter on "The Afro-Americans and the New Viewpoints in Afro-American History" in this volume; the works published by the Associated Publishers (1538 Ninth St., N.W., Washington, D.C.); the list provided by "The Ebony Bookshop" (1820 S. Michigan Ave., Chicago, Ill., 60616); the "References" in Louis R. Harlan, *The Negro in American History*, pp. 26-29, Publication Number 61, Service Center for Teachers of History, American Historical Association (400 A Street, S.E., Washington, D.C., 20003), 1965; Meyer Weinberg, Ed., *School Integration: A Comprehensive Classified Bibliography of 3,100 References*, Chicago: International Education (343 S. Dearborn, Chicago, 60604), 1967; Charlemae Rollins, Ed., *We Build Together*, Chicago: National Council of Teachers of English, 1967; *The Black Experience in America*, series, New York: Negro Universities Press (211 E. 43 St., New York); "Negro History Materials," *Civic Leader* (1733 K St., N.W., Washington,

D.C., 20006), Vol. XXXXVII, 16, February 3, 1969; Joseph E. Penn, Elaine Brooks Wells, and Mollie L. Berch, *The Negro American in Paperback: A Selected List of Paperback Books Compiled and Annotated for Secondary School Students,* Washington, D.C.: National Education Association, 1968; Elizabeth W. Miller, *The Negro in America: A Bibliography,* Cambridge, Mass.: Harvard University Press, 1966; St. Clair Drake, Introduction, *Negro History and Literature: A Selected Annotated Bibliography,* New York: 165 E. 56 St., New York 10022, n.d.; *Black History Viewpoints,* Washington, D.C.: African Bibliographic Center, P.O. Box, 13096, Washington, 20009, 1969; The Association for the Study of Negro Life and History, *1969 Negro History Study Kit,* Washington, D.C. (1538 9 St., N.W., Washington, D. C., 20001), 1969; The Negro Bibliographic & Research Center, Inc., *Bibliographic Survey: The Negro in Print,* Washington, D.C. (117 R St., N.E., Washington, 20002), African-American Institute, *African Affairs for the General Reader: A Selected and Introductory Bibliographical Guide, 1960-1967,* New York (866 United Nations Plaza, N.Y. 10017), 1967; E. K. Welsch, *The Negro in the United States: A Research Guide.* Bloomington, Ind.: Indiana University Press, 1965.

BOOKS

Adoff, Arnold, Ed., *Black On Black: Commentaries by Negro Americans,* New York: Macmillan, 1968. A superb anthology; some of the voices are bitter, some moderate — all are articulate, thoughtful and pertinent.

Aptheker, Herbert, Ed., *A Documentary History of the Negro People in the United States,* 2 vols., New York: The Citadel Press, 1968. A valuable collection; Vol. I presents documentary material from 1661 to 1865, together with editorial comments and notes; Vol. II covers the period from the Reconstruction years to the founding of the NAACP in 1910.

Board of Education, City of New York, *The Negro in American History,* New York Board of Education, 1964. Quite useful, although also criticized by some Negro specialists; a good bibliography on pp. 151-158.

Broderick, F. L., *W. E. B. Du Bois*: *Negro Leader in a Time of Crisis*, Palo Alto, California: Stanford University Press, 1959. A scholarly survey.

Cuban, Larry, Ed., *The Negro in America*, Chicago: Scott Foresman, 1964. A short collection of source materials around the role of Negro played in U.S. history.

Franklin, John Hope, *From Slavery to Freedom*. New York: Knopf, 1956. Probably the best survey of Negro history in the United States.

Frazier, E. Franklin, *The Negro in the United States*, New York: Macmillan, 1957. Detailed, by an outstanding Negro sociologist.

Fishel, Leslie H., Jr., and Quarles, Benjamin, Eds., *The Negro American*: *A Documentary History*, Chicago: Scott Foresman, 1967. A valuable collection of documents showing the primary role of the Negro in American history and the importance of the Negro's own history.

Meier, August, *The Negro in American Thought, 1880-1915*. Ann Arbor, Mich.: University of Michigan Press, 1964. Brilliant.

Mendelson, Wallace, *Discrimination*, Englewood Cliffs, N.J.: Prentice-Hall, 1962. Based on the report of the U.S. Commission on Civil Rights.

Myrdal, Gunnar, *An American Dilemma*. New York: Harper & Row, 1944. Condensed in: Arnold Rose, *The Negro in America*, New York: Harper & Row, 1948. A classic in race relations.

Pettigrew, Thomas F., *A Profile of the Negro American*, Princeton, N.J.: D. Van Nostrand Co., 1964. One theme of this volume is that racism, in addition to its vulgarity, is simply not supported by the empirical findings of the biological and social sciences.

Quarles, Benjamin, *The Negro in the Making of America*: *Today's Civil Rights Struggle & Its Three Century Background as Seen by a Famous Historian*, New York: Collier-Macmillan, 1964, bibliography, pp. 267-272.

Rudwick, Elliott M., *W. E. B. Du Bois*: *A Study in Minority Groups Leadership*, Philadelphia: University of Pennsylvania Press, 1960.

Spencer, Samuel R., *Booker T. Washington*, Boston: Little, Brown, 1955.

Thompson, Daniel C., *The Negro Leadership Class,* Englewood Cliffs, N.J.: Prentice-Hall, 1963. A good report on the neglected aspect of Negro's behavior.

Wish, Harvey, Ed., *The Negro Since Emancipation,* Englewood Cliffs, N.J.: Prentice-Hall, N.J., 1964. A valuable collection of the thinking of such authorities as Frederick Douglass, Booker T. Washington, William E. B. Du Bois, James Weldon Johnson, Carter G. Woodson, Langston Hughes, Ralph Johnson Bunche, Martin Luther King Jr., James Baldwin, Elijah Muhammed; selected bibliography, pp. 183-184.

ARTICLES AND PAMPHLETS

Conway, Alan, *The History of the Negro in the U.S.A.,* London: The Historical Association, 1968. The problem as viewed from the English viewpoint.

Doddy, Hurley H., "The Progress of the Negro in Higher Education," *Journal of Negro Education,* Vol. XXXII, Fall, 1963, 485-492. Factual.

Glenn, Norval D., "Negro Prestige Criteria: A Case Study in the Bases of Prestige," *American Journal of Sociology,* LXVIII, May, 1963, pp. 645-657.

———, "Occupational Benefits to Whites from the Subordination of Negroes," *American Sociological Review,* XXVIII, June, 1963, pp. 443-448. Both sympathetic to the Negro cause, although based on empiric research.

Green, Gordon C., "Negro Dialect, the Last Barrier to Integration," *Journal of Negro Education,* Vol. XXXII, Winter, 1963, pp. 81-83. An introduction to a very important factor.

Harlan, Louis R., *The Negro in American History,* Washington, D.C., American Historical Association, 1965. A short, but a very valuable concise survey; references pp. 26-29.

Rosen, Bernard C., "Race, Ethnicity, and the Achievement Syndrome," *American Sociological Review,* Vol. XXIV, February 1959, p. 47-60.

Thompson, D. C., "Career Patterns of Teachers in Negro Colleges," *Social Forces,* Vol. XXXVI, March, 1958, pp. 270-276. A competent survey of a rather neglected subject.

Vander Zanden, James W., "The Non-Violent Resistance Movement Against Segregation," *American Journal of Sociology,* Vol. LXVIII, March, 1963, pp. 544-550.

Weinberg, Meyer, Ed., *School Integration: A Comprehensive Classified Bibliography,* Chicago: Integrated Education Associates, 1967. Helpful.

NOTES

1. The literature now available on the problem of segregation in the education of the Negro in American history, and on the recent problems related to the 1954 Supreme Court decision declaring segregation in public schools inherently unequal and unlawful, is growing daily by leaps and bounds. Probably the best recent available study of the history of Negro education in the United States is Virgil A. Clift; Archibald W. Anderson, and H. Gordon Hullfish, Eds., *Negro Education in America: Its Adequacy, Problems and Needs,* New York: Harper & Row, 1962, and especially therein, W. A. Low, "The Education of Negroes Viewed Historically," pp. 27-59; William H. M. Martin, "Unique Contributions of Negro Educators," pp. 60-92; and Regina M. Goff, "Culture and the Personality Development of Minority Peoples," pp. 124-152. Of great value are the numerous articles and reviews in the quarterly *Journal of Negro Education* (Howard University, Washington, D.C., 20001). Among numerous other studies and references, see especially Robert M. Frumkin and Joseph S. Roucek, "Contributions from Minorities, Elites, and Special Educational Organizations," Chapter X, pp. 365-422, in Richard Gross, Ed., *Heritage of American Education,* Boston: Allyn & Bacon, 1962; Francis J. Brown and Joseph S. Roucek, Eds., *One America,* New York: Prentice-Hall, 1952; Harry S. Ashmore, *The Negro and the Schools,* Chapel Hill, N.C.: University of North Carolina Press, 1954; Margaret Just Butcher, *The Negro in American Culture,* New York: Mentor Books, 1956; E. Franklin Frazier, *The Negro in the United States,* New York: Macmillan, 1957; Eli Ginsberg, et al., *The Negro Potential,* New York: Columbia University Press, 1944; Edward A. Suchman, et al., *Desegregation,* New York: B'nai B'rith, 1958; Barbara Dodds, *Negro Literature for High School Students,* Champaign, Ill.: National Council of Teachers of English, 1968; Henry Allen Bullock, *A History of Negro Education in the South: from 1619 to the Present,* Cambridge, Mass.: Harvard University Press, 1967; Christopher Jencks and David Riesman, *The Academic Revolution,* Garden City, N.Y.: Doubleday, 1968 ("Negro Colleges," pp. 56 ff, 417-479 ff); E. K. Welsh, *The Negro in the United States: A Research Guide,* Bloomington, Indiana: University of Indiana Press, 1965; Margaret Anderson, *Children of the South,* New York: Farrar & Straus, 1966; E. J. McGrath, *Predominantly Negro Colleges and Universities in Transition,* New York: Columbia University, Teachers College, 1966; Philp T. Drotning, *A Guide to Negro History,* Garden City: Doubleday, 1969; Erwin A. Salk, Ed., *A Layman's Guide to Negro History,* New York: McGraw-Hill, 1967.

2. *Report of the National Advisory Commission on Civil Disorders,* New York: E. P. Dutton, 1968, p. 203.

3. Lerone Bennett, Jr., "Was Abe Lincoln a White Supremacist?" *Ebony.* Vol. XXIII, 4, February, 1968, pp. 35-42. According to the author "Abraham Lincoln was *not* the Great Emancipator . . . There is abundant evidence to indicate that the Emancipation problem was not what people think it is and that Lincoln issued it with extreme misgivings and reservations. . . ."

4. The continuing research in the history of the Negro, and thus also of the education of the American Negro, has been too extensive to summarize here. A good survey is from the pen of Horace M. Bond, "Negro Education," pp. 746-772, in Walter S. Monroe, Ed., *Encyclopedia of Educational Research,* New York: Macmillan, 1941. See also Harry Ashmore, *op. cit.;* Horace Mann Bond, *The Evolution of the Negro in the American Social Order,* New York: Prentice-Hall, 1934; Virgil A. Clift, et al, *op. cit.,* pp. 27-59; Carter G. Woodson, *The Education of the Negro Prior to 1861,* New York: G. P. Putnam's Sons, 1919; Paul S. Pierce, *The Growth of Southern Civilization,* 1790-1860, New York: Harper & Row, 1961, especially Chapter 3, "Profits and Human Slavery," pp. 49-71, and Chapter 4, "Danger and Discontent in the Slave System," pp. 72-97.

5. James Weldon Johnson, "The American Negro," Chapter IV, pp. 56-66, in Francis J. Brown and Joseph S. Roucek, *op. cit.*

6. Winthrop D. Jordan, *White Over Black: American Attitudes Toward the Negro, 1550-1812,* Chapel Hill, N.C.: University of North Carolina Press, 1968. A thorough-going monograph, derived from unpublished and printed source materials, on Negro-white contacts in colonial times and in early America; excellent bibliographical material.

7. For the social structure and processes of the slave system, see Lerone Bennett, Jr., *Before the Mayflower: A History of the Negro in America, 1619-1962,* Chicago: Johnson Publishing Co., 1962, Chapter 4, "Behind the Cotton Curtain," pp. 70-95, and Chapter 5, "Slave Revolts and Insurrections," pp. 97-126. For the social aspects of slavery, see Dwight Lowell Dumond, *Antislavery Origins of the Civil War in the United States,* Ann Arbor: University of Michigan Press, 1939, and bibliography, pp. 131-134; William Summer Jenkins, *Preslavery Thought in the Old South,* Chapel Hill, N.C.: University of North Carolina Press, 1935, and bibliography, pp. 309-358.

8. Marcus W. Jornegan, *Laboring and Independent Classes in Colonial America, 1607-1783,* Chicago: University of Chicago Press, 1931, pp. 39-40.

9. A general and reliable reference to the early academic education of the Negro is Carter G. Woodson, *op. cit.;* a good reference to later years is Horace Mann Bond, *op. cit.*

10. Thomas E. Drake, *Quakers and Slavery in America,* New Haven, Conn.: Yale University Press, 1950, pp. 1-33, 71.

11. Wright, *op. cit.,* p. 115.

12. Charles S. John, *The Negro College Graduate,* Chapel Hill, N.C.: University of North Carolina Press, 1938, p. 7.

13. Ruth D. Wilson, "Negro Colleges of Liberal Arts," *American Scholar,* Vol. XIX, Autumn, 1950, pp. 462-463.

14. Paul S. Pierce, *The Freedmen's Bureau,* Iowa City: University of Iowa Press, 1904. Henry Allen Bullock, *op. cit.,* reflects the viewpoint that the influence of the schools is pervasive. Bullock ranges from the portrayal

of a literary movement, such as the Harlem Renaissance, to a description of the social mechanisms employed to make the Negro think of himself as a lesser being; Bullock has his materials well in hand.

15. Pierce, *op. cit.*, p. 83. See also: George Bentley, *A History of the Freedmen's Bureau*, Philadelphia: University of Pennsylvania Press, 1955; John LaWanda Coc, "General O. O. Howard and the Misrepresented Bureau," *Journal of Southern History*, Vol. XIX, November, 1954, pp. 427-456; W. E. B. Du Bois, "Reconstruction and Its Benefits," *American Historical Review*, Vol. XV, July, 1910, pp. 781-799; Francis B. Simkins, "New Viewpoints on Southern Reconstruction," *Journal of Southern History*, Vol. V, February, 1939, pp. 49-61; Howard K. Beale, "On Rewriting Reconstruction History," *American Historical Review*, Vol. XLV, July, 1940, pp. 807-827.

16. Ullin W. Leavell, *Philanthropy in Negro Education*, Nashville, Tenn.: George Peabody College Press, 1930; Jesse B. Sears, *Philanthropy in the History of American Education*, Washington, D.C.: Government Printing Office, 1922.

17. Low, *op. cit.*, p. 41.

18. Dwight O. W. Holmes, *Evolution of Negro College*, New York: Columbia University Press, 1934, and "Seventy Years of the Negro College," *Phylon*, Vol. X, 1949, pp. 307-313; Ruth D. Wilson, "Negro Colleges of Liberal Arts," *American Scholar*, Vol. XIX, Autumn, 1950, pp. 462-463; Willard Range, *Rise and Progress of Negro Colleges in Georgia*, Atlanta, Georgia: University of Georgia Press, 1951, p. 21; Charles S. Johnson, *The Negro College Graduate*, Chapel Hill, N.C.: University of North Carolina Press, 1938, p. 286.

20. Gunnar Myrdal, et al., *An American Dilemma*, New York: Harper, 1944, p. 894; Merle E. Curti, *The Social Ideas of American Educators*, New York, Scribner's, 1935, pp. 28 ff.

21. Myrdal, *op. cit.*, pp. 897-899; Charles Johnson, *Patterns of Negro Segregation*, New York: Harper, 1943, p. 21.

22. Edgar W. Knight, *Public Education in the South*, Boston: Ginn, 1922, p. 422.

23. Low, *op. cit.*, p. 44.

24. A general survey of the origin of Negro colleges is told in D. O. W. Holmes, *The Evolution of the Negro College*, New York: Columbia University Press, 1934. The question of the oldest Negro College in the U. S. is debatable; Lincoln University in Pennsylvania, formerly Ashmun Institute, claimed that honor at a centennial observance in 1954.

25. See C. Vann Woodard, *Origins of the New South 1877-1913*, Baton Rouge, La.: Louisiana State University Press, 1951, pp. 250-268.

26. Quoted in Booker T. Washington, *Up from Slavery*, Garden City, N.Y.: the Sun Dial Press, 1900, pp. 218-225, from an address before the Harvard Alumni in 1896 after receiving an honorary Master of Arts degree, as cited in Lewis Copeland, Ed., *The World's Great Speeches*, Garden City, N.Y.: Garden City Publishing Co., 1942, p. 332.

27. Du Bois tells the story of his fight against the "Tuskegee Machine" in his autobiographical *Dusk of Dawn*, New York: Harcourt, Brace & Co., 1940, pp. 72-96.

28. Basil Matthews, *Booker T. Washington*, Cambridge, Mass.: Harvard University Press, 1948, p. 302.

29. See: "The Problem of Color in the Twentieth Century, A Memorial to W. E. B. Du Bois," special issue of *Journal of Human Relations*, Vol. XIV, No. 1, First Quarter, 1966.

30. Richard Bardolph, *The Negro Vanguard*, New York: Rinehart, 1959, p. 115.

31. For their list, see *ibid.*, p. 120.

32. *Ibid.*, p. 120.

33. *Ibid.*, p. 121; for more details, see: p. 121-135.

34. Among the well-documented histories, see especially: Edgar W. Knight, *Public Education in the South*, Boston: Ginn, 1922; Truman M. Pierce, et al., *White and Negro Schools in the South*, Englewood Cliffs, N.J.: Prentice-Hall, 1955; Horace M. Bond, *op. cit.*

35. See: William Wise, *Booker T. Washington*, New York: Putnam, 1968, and bibliography; Basil J. Matthews, *Booker T. Washington, Educator and Interracial Interpreter*, Cambridge, Mass.: Harvard University Press, 1948.

36. The first Ph.D. American Negro was apparently Patrick Francis Healy, S.J., who had to go to Belgium to win his degree; in 1874, he was inaugurated as President of Georgetown University, the oldest Catholic University in the United States. The first Negro to win a Ph.D. in an American institution was Edward Bouchet, who received his doctorate in physics from Yale in 1876, according to *Parade, Bridgeport (Conn.) Sunday Post*, December 29, 1968.

37. W. A. Low, *op. cit.*, p. 52.

38. Oscar Heedore Barek and Nelson Manfred Blake, *Since 1900; A History of the United States in Our Times*, New York: Macmillan, 1959, p. 747.

39. Low, *op. cit.*, pp. 53-54.

40. The roots of the U.S. Supreme Court decision can be found in Murray and Gaines cases; see Low, *op. cit.*, pp. 54-56.

41. Milton M. Gordon, "Recent Trends in the Study of Minority and Race Relations," *The Annals of the American Academy of the Political and Social Sciences*, Vol. CCCL, November, 1963, pp. 148-156. Two major summary reports of the U.S. Commission on Civil Rights, established as an investigatory and advisory agency by Congress in the Civil Rights Act of 1957, provide indispensable information on discrimination in such areas as education, housing, voting, employment, and the administration of justice. See *The United States Commission on Civil Rights: Reports*, Books 1-5, Washington, D.C.: Government Printing Office, 1961, and the earlier *Report* of 1959. An unofficial resumé of the 1961 *Report* by its editor-in-chief will be found in Wallace Mendelson, *Discrimination*, Englewood Cliffs, N.J.: Prentice-Hall, 1962. The most recent survey, covering all these points, is offered in: *Report of the National Advisory Commission on Civil Disorders*, Washington, 1968.

42. U.S. Office of Education's National Center for Educational Statistics, December 9, 1966.

43. Marshall B. Clinard, *Sociology of Deviant Behavior*, New York: Holt, Rinehart & Winston, 1968, p. 662.

44. Harry S. Ashmore, *op. cit.*, p. 130.

45. For the background details, see: Nelson H. Harris, "Desegregation in Institutions of Higher Learning," Chapter IX, pp. 235-251, in Clift, *op. cit.*; Milton M. Gordon, "The Girard College Case: Desegregation and a Municipal Trust," pp. 53-61, in *The Annals of the American Academy of*

Political and Social Science, Vol. CCCIV, March, 1956; Abram J. Jaffe, Walter Adams, and Sandra G. Meyers, *Negro Higher Education in the 1960s,* New York: Praeger, 1968; F. J. Barros, "Equal Opportunity in Higher Education," *Journal of Negro Education,* Vol. XXXVII, 3, Summer, 1968, pp. 310-315; Russell H. Barrett, *Integration at Ole Miss,* Chicago: Quadrangle, 1965, a firsthand account of the legal maneuverings and violence attending the 1962 integration at the University of Mississippi.

46. *A Statistical Summary, State by State, of School Segregation-Desegregation in the Southern and Border Area from 1954 to the Present,* Nashville, Tenn.: Southern Education Reporting Service, February 1967, p. 3.

47. "Colleges: The New Black Presidents," *Time,* Vol. XCII, 26, December 26, 1968, pp. 48-49.

48. Quoted by: Sherill Harbison, "Negro History: What Should be Taught in School, and Why?" *Vital Issues,* Vol. XVIII, Number 5, January, 1969.

49. Carter G. Woodson, who received his Ph.D. from Harvard in 1915, founded the Association for the Study of Negro Life and History, which began publishing the pioneering *Journal of Negro History* in 1916; in 1925 it added a less technical publication, *The Negro History Bulletin,* designed for high school use. Both are still published today.

THE NEGRO'S CONTRIBUTION TO THE WORLD OF ENTERTAINMENT

CALVIN A. CLAUDEL

West Virginia Wesleyan College (Buckhannon, W. Va.)

By the rivers of Babylon, there we sat down, yea, we wept, when we remembered Zion.

We hanged our harps upon the willows in the midst thereof.

For there they that carried us away captive required of us a song; and they that wasted us required of us mirth, saying, Sing us one of the Songs of Zion.

How shall we sing the Lord's song in a strange land?

—Psalm 137: 1-4

HIS CLOWN ROLE

The above verses of the Psalmist, relating the captivity and persecution of the Jews, who were required even in their suffering to sing and entertain their captors, also describes somewhat the role of the Negro in Western civilization, for while much of his creative activity was for his own diversion and recreation, it was more often, in his state of subjugation, to entertain and amuse the white man by whom he was held in bondage.

It was very difficult for the Negro to escape from his clowning part that was already cut out and required of him. Emanuel tells of this in "A Clown at Ten."[1] Tinker aptly said that Southerners detested Cable for depicting the Negro as a human being and not as a clown: "The very reasons that make Cable famous in the North made him infamous in the South. Not one of its authors had ever before dared to write of the Negro except as a loyal, humble family retainer, or as a black-face buffoon. The Negro as a flesh-and-blood human being, as a living problem in adjustment, was so sore a subject that by tacit agreement southern society ignored the existence of this aspect and, on pain of ostracism, permitted no one to discuss it . . ."[2]

Cable's humanitarian efforts among hostile whites cannot be over-emphasized. Another writer adds: "Cable also had the courage to write of Negroes as human beings, as representing a problem in the South, and as having minds that might be the equal of the whites about them, as well as sensitive natures and talents. Until then Southern writers had written of them only as minstrels . . ."[3]

In Tinker's statement that there was an entirely different opinion of the Negro in the North, we see that the Western World, especially America, was destined to help free the Negro and help him realize his own talents and potentiality, which are basically equal to those of the white man. The concept of equality and justice for Negroes was expressed very early by our Founding Fathers who, being influenced strongly by western philosophy from France and other enlightened countries, generally did not relish slavery and looked toward freedom for all mankind as the final fulfillment of the American dream.

In writing to Benjamin Baneker, a Maryland freeman who was a self-taught mathematician and astronomer, Thomas Jefferson said: "Nobody wishes more than I do to see such proofs as you exhibit, that nature has given to our black brethren talents equal to those of other colors of men, and that the appearance of a want of them is owing merely to the degraded condition of their existence, both in Africa and America."[4]

It is indeed impossible to cover in one chapter the numerous and far-reaching contributions of the Negro to the field of entertainment. These cover the various kinds of music and allied arts, including folk and jazz music, religious and classical music; these likewise cover acting and performances in the drama and cinema, on radio and television, to mention only a few. In the broad sense entertainment should also include the Negro's contribution to the world of sports, which is no small one when we consider his vast accomplishments in boxing, baseball, basketball, tennis and finally in the Olympic games, wherein he has shown himself not only to be outstanding, but no doubt superior in many aspects.

Let us first consider some of the many contributions the Negro has made to the world of music with its many related areas, about which many volumes have already been written. It is first of all in the field of music that the Negro especially distinguished himself, for like the Biblical captives of old, he sang and danced to amuse his captors or to lull his own pain as he toiled in the fields or elsewhere.

Jefferson was one of the first Americans to note that Negroes are talented musically. "In music, the Negroes are more . . . gifted than the whites . . . The instrument proper to them is the *banjar*."[5]

Thus it has been rightly said that Negroes are natural-born musicians, dancers and entertainers. No doubt since primitive times they danced and chanted to the beat of musical instruments. They must have also had seasonal ritual festivals, similar to other peoples elsewhere, in which they danced and chanted. Even today we may witness various dances in the heart of African forests.[6] We also find examples of festival celebrations with ritual dancing, no doubt of primitive religious significance.

However, let us hasten to note that most African nations of today are fast coming or have already come into the civilization of modern times and are absorbing and adopting western entertainment by way of music and sports. For instance, the Bantus have both their traditional as well as imported Western entertainment, the former being found especially in the country areas and the latter in urban localities. Some of their traditional instruments, often very similar to those of the whites, are the drum, used in most of their folk dances; the cow horn, used as a bugle or trumpet; the *ghoro*, a one-string instrument; the *lesiba*, a sort of horn; the *mbira*, a piano-like instrument, etc. In the city Bantus have all forms of Western amusement—waltzes, balls, ballet, radio and recordings of all kinds. Curiously enough, these people have readopted jazz music with syncopated rhythms and dances, which somewhat originated in African music.[7] Besides loving and participating in music and dancing of all kinds, Bantus join in all Western sports and recreation—football, tennis, basketball, golf, swimming, bowling, cycling, etc., etc.[8]

The Negro possessed in Africa a stock of folklore, especially folktales, which he brought with him to the New World. These tales were rich in lore about clever and stupid animals as they were known in Africa.[9] As a form of daily entertainment, slave nurses told these to white children.[10] We have but to cite Joel Chandler Harris' *Tales of Uncle Remus*. Louisiana and all its widely related regions were permeated with this strong influence.[11]

In reality, however, the Negro slave had very little time for amusement and entertainment. Depending on his master's mood, on Sunday or holidays he might have some time for rest and recreation. At plowing, harvest or work time, which was generally always, he had no surcease. Yet he would sing then his sorrowful work chants, another part of his rich folklore, reflecting his undaunted spirit of gaiety. The back-breaking toil of cane-grinding time is expressed in the Creole songs of Louisiana Negroes:

Cane grinding began, bad weather came.
Ah me! young folk, no more Sunday for me.
No more Saturday for us, just cane upon our backs![12]

The Negro brought with him from Africa his music by way of dances and songs. In the early days of New Orleans, which affords an excellent example of a melting pot of both African and European traditions, Negroes sang their folksongs and danced their dances, such as the Calinda and the Bamboula. After their weary hours of toil, at night Negro men and women, while beating and playing on their musical instruments, danced and chanted in the celebrated Congo Square.[13] Saxon also gives a good description of this Negro entertainment.[14]

FOLK MUSIC

Among the countless Negro folksingers, "Leadbelly" or Huddie Ledbetter, born in Mooringsport, Louisiana, was one of the most outstanding and colorful. He played the accordion and a twelve-string guitar, singing and composing songs that have been recorded for the Library of Congress. Although he played before world-wide audiences, Leadbelly spent many years in Louisiana's notorious Angola penitentiary for various crimes. While the latter was accused of catering to whites, a critic said: "Among the finest Negro work songs recorded outside of the prisons are those sung by Leadbelly."[15]

While the Negro quickly absorbed much of white European culture and entertainment, he also contributed to the latter his own traditions and creative genius, especially by way of music. Louis Moreau Gottschalk underwent and spread the influence of early Creole Negro music. Hector Berlioz said: "Mr. Gottschalk was born in America, whence he has brought a host of curious chants from the Creoles and the Negroes; he has made from them the themes of his most delicious compositions . . ."[16]

There is a folk saying in New Orleans, "The blacker the berry, the sweeter the juice!" This proverb reveals the attraction of the Negro woman for the white man. Despite laws and social taboos against amatory relations between whites and blacks, from ancient times to the present, many children have been born from these illicit affections.[17]

Lyle Saxon tells elsewhere how women of mixed color were used for sporting pleasure and entertainment by idle Creole men. Beautiful quadroon and octoroon women, mixed and re-mixed with whites, became the concubines and dancing partners of Creole gay blades. He gives us a vivid description of the abodes or cribs of these mistresses along the Ramparts of New Orleans, as well as the festive quadroon balls.[18]

JAZZ MUSIC

Kmen tells of white and Negro balls and dances in early New Orleans, where music and entertainment were furnished by Negro musicians. His chapters "Quadroon Balls" and "Negro Music" give a full account of this period.[19]

Saxon's mentioning the Ramparts, on the outskirts of New Orleans near Congo Square, is interesting, for this very section later became Rampart Street, close to the area around Basin Street, which finally grew into the notorious Red-Light District of Storyville, containing block after block of houses of assignation.[20] In this section prostitutes went from varying shades of color, from the white ones on and near Rampart Street to the black and tan ones at a distance, calling out from their doors to their potential white customers looking them over, "Come in, Daddy, I'll show you a good time." In the "high-toned" houses, Negro musicians entertained with bawdy and racy jazz music. The very word "jazz" seems to have originally been a verb, meaning "to copulate." The words of "Old Basin Street Blues" reveal the atmosphere of this area:

Oh, Basin Street is the street
Where black and white always meet.
In New Orleans, land of dreams,
You'll never know how sweet it seems,
Or how much it really means! . . .[21]

As pointed out by numerous writers, the now world-famous Negro jazz music had its beginnings in New Orleans from the above sordid environment, illustrating again how the Negro was able to create beauty and harmony out of these conditions of moral depravity and spiritual captivity. Williams gives us a touching and often bitter story of these early jazz masters of New Orleans.[22]

One of the first jazz geniuses, Buddy Bolden or Buddy the King, had a truly depraved and tragic life, ending up by spending many years in the state mental institution where he died.[23] Ferdinand Joseph la Menthe Morton, known as "Jelly Roll" Morton or simply "The Roll," was a great New Orleans jazz musician, who won international fame. Williams says: "There are reasons to call this man with the clown's obscene nickname important. In him, New Orleans Jazz produced one of its only theorists. Most important, in him jazz produced one of its first and most durable artists."[24]

However, jazz music has earned world-wide respectability and recognition, as entertainment and dance music. No doubt the greatest of these jazz entertainers has been Louis Armstrong, or Little Louie, who was reared in an orphanage.[25] At the present age of 68, he has won international fame. For his playing, he was recently wildly cheered and acclaimed at the sedately conservative Savoy Hotel in London where he was feted at a luncheon given in his honor by Britain's Beaverbrook news-papers.[26] Moreover, he is very beloved and popular in New Orleans, where he is called "Satchmo" (a contraction of "Satchel Mouth") because of his widely-flapping mouth as he sings in his somewhat derisively croaking voice.[27] Commemorating his fiftieth anniversary in show business, in 1965 Armstrong returned to New Orleans to give a concert at the Loyola Field House, the proceeds going to the Fund for the Expansion of the Jazz Museum there.[28]

Another example of this Negro music from the Crescent City appeared recently in London: "A bit of old New Orleans came to this city's streets Friday when the Olympia Brass Band played on the steps of St. Paul's Cathedral for a cheering and appreciative crowd."[29] A musical program of "Jazz and Its History" ("El Jazz y su historia") was recently celebrated in the Palacio de Bellas Artes in Mexico City.[30]

Among the many, many jazz celebrities we should mention Duke Ellington, born in Washington, D. C., for his great musical talent, compositions and productions, among which is "My People," his contribution to the Century of Negro Progress held some five years back.[31] Ellington and other well-known Negro jazz musicians are biographized in the series *Kings of Jazz.*[32]

In celebrating the recent 250th anniversary of New Orleans, one of this city's oldest and most respected newspapers said that "volumes have been written, and rightly so, about Negro musicians who contributed tremendously both to this city's fame and fortune in the entertainment world . . ."[33] This same article adds: "In music Annabelle Bernard and Debria Brown, both products of the Xavier University Music Department, are enjoying tremendous success and are appearing in the great opera houses around the world."[34]

The Negro not only entertains himself but also others in New Orleans during the Mardi Gras Season. A colorful description is given of one of the bands improvised during carnival by Negro youths. One is called "The Spasm Band": "Not in one of the parades, the Spasm Band goes, perhaps, down Royal Street and lingers near a crowd that looks happy. The leader gives the beat, and the washboard rhythm, from tin cans, wires, and homemade percussion instruments, begins. These boys pass the hat too."[35]

In New Orleans the whites celebrate Mardi Gras or Fat Tuesday with a parade at high noon, led by Rex, the Carnival King. In their usual satirically comic vein, Negroes have a parody of this ceremony in the parade of King Zulu. "He is the serio-comic King of the Negroes, a man of jest and satire. His scepter is a ham bone."[36]

Bolden was reared a Baptist and had learned very early the spirituals and hymns of the Negro religious music, which was considered God's music by Negroes. The gay and ribald jazz music that Bolden later played to entertain whites in houses of ill-repute was considered the Devil's music. It was said that when he went mad, carrying his cornet and a bottle, he withdrew into his room where he began playing at first softly and sadly, later mingling in his blues notes jazz and hymn music. The belief was expressed that there was a battle then between God and the Devil in Bolden's playing.

SPIRITUALS, MINSTRELS AND BLUES

Indeed hymns and spirituals represent the deeply personal side of the Negro's life, apart from white people, reflecting his profound spirituality that unifies him to his suffering brethren. "By 1871 the Negro Fisk-Jubilee Singers were touring, and so true Negroes on the stage were accepted enough to make well known 'Deep River'; 'Go Down, Moses'; 'Swing Low, Sweet Chariot'; and 'Little David, Play on Your Harp.' From these came the true blues."[37]

Such hymns and dirge-like music are played at colorful funeral processions. Yet, reflecting the Negro's resilience and gaiety, often on the return of such processions, jazz pieces are played, such as "Didn't He Ramble!" so aptly described in the poetry of Alice Claudel:

... When the grieving surged back home,
The corpse was gone.
The jaunty trumpets ribalded heaven's throne.
"Didn't he ramble? Didn't he ramble?"
... Wasn't there time to dance
And time to savor?
"He rambled till the Butcher cut him down."[38]

Negro musicians of the famous Eureka Brass Band played for funeral corteges in New Orleans and its environs. However, these splendid players are growing old and passing on, this century-old tradition disappearing with them.[39] There is perhaps not a more stirring experience than to hear and join in the compelling rhythm of the tune, "When the Saints Go Marching In," or "Oh! For a Closer Walk with Thee" played by such a band.

It is impossible to cover the countless number of Negro spiritual singers, whose music varies from presently very secular to deeply spiritual tunes. Following somewhat the traditions of the late Bessie Smith and other famous Negro blues singers, Aretha Franklin is winning wide acclaim.[40] The same article cited above says, "Nobody has more vividly evoked the kind of super-charged evangelist-gospel atmosphere of Aretha Franklin's childhood than Black Novelist James Baldwin (a one-time Harlem storefront preacher). In his novel, *The Fire Next Time*, he wrote: "There is no music like that music, no drama like the drama of the saints rejoicing, the sinners moaning, the tambourines racing, and all those voices coming together and crying holy unto the Lord . . ."[41]

The Negro's church remains the center of his life, offering him both spiritual edification and recreational release. From his traditional religious singing and music have come such great singers as Mahalia Jackson. Hodding Carter, in speaking about the tremendous progress of the Negro, says, "And what of New Orleans' Mahalia Jackson who made gospel singing a modern musical art form? The biographies of such people could fill a sizable volume . . ."[42]

However, Mahalia Jackson has refused on numerous occasions to commercialize her spiritual singing, which she identifies with a deeply divine mission. She and others, especially centered around the great Martin Luther King, have kept in the great tradition of the oppressed people of Israel, expressed in such deeply moving folk spirituals as the following:

When Israel was in Egypt's land,
Let my people go,
Oppressed so hard they could not stand
Let my people go!

Go down, Moses,
Way down in Egypt's land,
Tell old Pharaoh
To let my people go!

Among the many forms of entertainment that Negroes gave the American public we should mention the Negro minstrel shows presented on showboats along the rivers and in the many amusement halls and centers throughout the country, especially during the last century. One of the minstrel greats was the celebrated W. C. Handy from Florence, Alabama, who was a songwriter, cornet player and band leader. Handy earned fame for noted blues compositions, among which are "Saint Louis Blues," "Memphis Blues," "Careless Love," and many others. In memory and honor of this great Negro musician the Post Office Department recently issued a postage stamp with his picture.

Perhaps one of the best blues singers and minstrel performers was Bessie Smith, born in Clarksdale, Mississippi. She was known as "Empress of the Blues" and has been described as "the greatest artist American Jazz ever produced."[43] She lived much of her early life in Chattanooga, in a grim Negro ghetto through grinding poverty and unimaginable squalor. The life of Bessie Smith, like that of so many other outstanding Negro artists, is a living testament of courage and enthusiasm against great odds. Her biography is well presented by Paul Oliver.[44]

In the world of classical music Negroes have made and are increasingly making contributions not only in composition but also in symphony directing and conducting. Samuel Coleridge-Taylor, born in London in 1875, attended the Royal College of Music and composed *African Suite, Songs of Slavery, African Dances*, and numerous other outstanding pieces.[45] A prolific composer and arranger of religious music was Harry T. Burleigh of New York.[46] Another great name in American Negro music, famous not only in America but also in Europe, is that of John W. Work, founder of the Jubilee Singers of Fisk University. Another outstanding Negro musician and composer was R. Nathaniel Dett, a graduate in music from both Oberlin and Harvard.[47]

An article, describing the great progress of the Negro in music, from the difficult days of Roland Hayes' appearance in Nazi Germany to the present day, has been written by Galkin.[48] Dean Dixon, born in New York, is perhaps the first Negro to have gained world renown as a conductor, for he has conducted in most of the world's capitals and "at once captivated players and audience alike . . ."[49] In 1967 Dixon was directing the Sydney Orchestra on an A. B. C. tour. A promising young conductor of 22 is Alfred Morris.[50]

In the field of popular and classical singing appear other important entertainers. Some of these are Harry Belafonte, Lena Horne, and Marian Anderson. As a contralto singer, Marian Anderson, born in Philadelphia, has won international renown and countless honors. She was just recently awarded an honorary doctor's degree by Tulane University for her great contributions to the world of entertainment. In a touching story Marian Anderson tells about the shock and hurt she felt on being rejected to attend a music school because of the fact of being colored. She also narrates in a poignant fashion the humiliations and indignities she went through because of racial discrimination. Yet through all this, like so many of her people, she was able to maintain an uncomplaining feeling of pride and dignity.[51] In a current article in *Redbook*, this great woman, now retired, shares her touching thoughts of the Christmas season.[52]

As a great opera singer Leontyne Price has won world-wide renown. Like so many of these Negro musicians, singers, actors and celebrities of the entertainment world who come from segregated southern towns, she was born in Laurel, Mississippi, where racial discrimination has been at its worst and accomplishment of any sort most difficult to achieve. She appeared as Bess in *Porgy and Bess*, performed in Vienna, Berlin, Paris, London, and at La Scala in Milan. She was also a soloist at the Metropolitan Opera.

Negroes have earned a notable record in drama, motion pictures, radio and television. A noted nineteenth-century Shakespearean actor was Ira F. Aldridge. Both Charles Gilpin and Paul Robeson gained fame in *The Emperor Jones* and *Othello*. Richard B. Harrison distinguished himself in *The Green Pastures*. These are but a few of the Negroes who have contributed much to the dramatic world.[53]

In a series of articles Dworpin gives a good account of the Negro's activities on the screen.[54] We should remember Hattie McDaniel as a pioneer who won an award for her playing in *Gone with the Wind.* Other distinguished Negro movie actors have been Bill Robinson, Clarence Muse, Louise Beavers, and Lena Horne. However, from the stereotyped "mammy" role of Hattie McDaniel and the inarticulately blundering clown role of "Step-and-Fetchit," the Negro is truly coming into his own with such great movie actors as Sidney Poitier and many others.

On radio and television as well, from the somewhat demeaning roles of Amos and Andy, Negroes have leapt ahead in a multiplicity of outstanding performances. At first we have the celebrated Mills Brothers, who began singing as a barbershop quartet, appearing in *The Big Broadcast* in 1933. Today colored persons are playing serious and heroic roles on television.[55] Everyone is familiar with Bill Cosby's interesting *I Spy* program. In fact, many of TV's new stars are black.[56] A glamorous television star today is Diahann Carroll.[57] The professional performances of such splendid actors as Percy Rodriguez are described in a recent article.[58]

These names with their outstanding contributions here and there have only scratched the surface of the daily and ever-increasing performances of the Negro. We have seen that in the old days he was consigned to the role of the clown, having to pander to the tastes and whims of white masters, often to the degradation of his own integrity. Placed beyond the pale of human life, the Negro was sometimes regarded as a tom-tom-beating savage. On the other hand the only way he might gain the condescending sympathy of the white man was "to keep in his place" and behave in the self-pitying role of an "Old Black Joe." In conclusion, not only in the entertainment field but in all other areas, the Negro has come a long way indeed and can be justly proud and hold up his head high because of his great accomplishments against great odds, especially in the world of entertainment.

SELECTED BIBLIOGRAPHY

BOOKS

Behrend, Jeanne, Ed., *Notes of a Pianist, Louis Moreau Gottschalk*, New York: Alfred A. Knopf, 1964. Has interesting sections showing the influence of Negro music on his own music and compositions.

Chatelain, Heli, *The Folktales of Angola*, Memoirs of the American Folklore Society, Vol. I, New York: The American Folklore Society, 1895. A collection of folktales gathered from Angola and translated into English.

Crum, Mason, *The Negro in the Methodist Church*, New York: The Editorial Department of the Board of Missions and Church Extension of the Methodist Church, 1951. Not only gives the story of the Negro in the Methodist Church but also the account of his contributions to various fields, including entertainment.

Delavignette, Robert, *Afrique Equatoriale française*, Paris: Librairie Hatchette, 1957. Tells of Negro life and entertainment in a region of Africa.

Emanuel, James A., "A Clown at Ten," in *Dark Symphony: Negro Literature in America*, James A. Emanuel and Theodore L. Gross, Eds., New York: The Free Press, A Division of the Macmillan Company, 1968. An important contribution to the study of Negro literature.

Feather, Leonard, *The New Edition of the Encyclopedia of Jazz*, New York: Bonanza Books. An indispensable volume showing the tremendous contribution of the Negro to the world of music and entertainment.

Fortier, Alcée, *Louisiana Folk Tales*, Memoirs of the American Folklore Society, Vol. II, New York: The American Folklore Society, 1895. A collection of tales gathered from Negro informants with an African background.

Kmen, Henry A., *Music in New Orleans*, Baton Rouge: Louisiana State University Press, 1966. A very scholarly work showing the great contribution of the Negro to the world of entertainment.

Lambert, G. E., *Kings of Jazz: Duke Ellington*, New York: A. S. Barnes and Company, Inc., 1959. Gives a good story of the life of Duke Ellington.

Les Peuples bantous deviennent des nations, Pietermaritzburg, la République d'Afrique du Sud: 1961. Tells of the traditional and western background among the Bantus.

Longstreet, Stephen, *Sportin' House, New Orleans and the Jazz Story* (*A History of New Orleans Sinners and the Birth of Jazz*), Los Angeles: Sherbourne Press, Inc., 1965. Shows that jazz compositions were the "flowers of evil," so to speak, growing out of a sordid environment.

Longstreet, Stephen, *The Real Jazz, Old and New*, Baton Rouge: Louisiana State University Press, 1956. Gives a good account of the Negro's contribution to the world of jazz.

Oliver, Paul, *Kings of Jazz: Bessie Smith*, New York: A. S. Barnes and Company, Inc., 1961. Gives the sad and fascinating story of the life of Bessie Smith.

Saxon, Lyle, *Children of Strangers,* Boston: Houghton Mifflin Company, 1937. The story of a love relationship between a white convict and a Negro woman, from whom a child was born. Saxon as well as other Southern writers shows the deep suffering and onus that these "children of strangers" had to bear.

Tallant, Robert, *The Romantic New Orleanians*, New York: E. P. Dutton and Company, Inc., 1950. A worthwhile contribution not only to the history of New Orleans but to the history of the Negro.

Tinker, Edward Laroque, *Creole City: Its Past and Its People*, New York: Longmans, Green and Company, 1953. Not only supplies a better understanding of New Orleans history but a true and sympathetic account of the role Negroes played.

Wickiser, Ralph, Durieux, Caroline, and McCrady, John, *Mardi Gras Day*, New York: Henry Holt and Company, 1948. Tells of Mardi Gras Day in New Orleans, including interesting accounts of the entertainment of Negroes there.

Williams, Martin, *Jazz Masters of New Orleans*, New York: The Macmillan Company, 1967. Gives each story of the great jazz masters of old New Orleans.

ARTICLES

Anderson, Marian, ". . . My Deepest Ties to People," *Redbook*, Vol. CXXXII, 2, December 1968, pp. 48-49, 136, 138. Marian

Anderson tells here of her great love for spirituals.

"Armstrong Celebrates 68th," *The Houston Post,* July 5, 1968, sect. 3, p. 1. This article tells of Louis Armstrong's enthusiastic reception abroad.

Cable, George W., "The Dance in Place Congo," *The Century Magazine,* Vol. XXXI, 40, February 1886, pp. 517-532. This excellent article tells of the entertainment of Negroes in New Orleans in early days.

Carter, Hodding, "The Negro Heritage and Green Power," *New Orleans,* Vol. II, 9, June 1968, p. 8. This is an article favorable toward the activities of the Negro in New Orleans, written by a man who has always been a great friend to colored people.

Claudel, Alice Moser, "A Southern Memory," *Experiment,* Vol. IV, 4, p. 109. This is one of a number of poems, written by this splendid poet, describing beautifully and sympathetically the singing and music of Negroes.

Claudel, Calvin, "Louisiana Folktales and their Background," *The Louisiana Historical Quarterly,* Vol. XXXVIII, 3, pp. 35-36. Analyzes the folktales of Louisiana, showing the influence of Negroes.

Claudel, Calvin, "The Syrup Mill," *The Georgia Review,* Vol. XVI, 1, Spring 1962, p. 88. Tells how Negroes contributed not only to the working economy of Louisiana but also to the folklore.

Dworpin, Martin S., "The New Negro on Screen," *Progressive,* Vol. XXV, 1, January 1961, pp. 36-38. This writer tells in several articles about the contributions of the Negro to the screen.

Galkin, Elliott W., "Musical Recognition comes Slowly to Negro," in *Spectator of The Sun,* Baltimore, September 28, 1968, sect. D, pp. 1-3. A splendid article on the contribution of the Negro to the field of music and entertainment.

Kirkley, Donald, "Next Season's Shows Closing the Color Gap," *TV Week, The Sun,* August 25, 1968, p. 2. Tells how the Negro is coming into his own in the show world.

"Lady Soul: Singing It Like It Is," *Time,* Vol. XCI, 26, June 23, 1968, pp. 62-68. Reports on the singing and popularity of Aretha Franklin.

Lemon, Richard, "Black Is the Color of TV's Newest Stars," *The Saturday Evening Post,* Vol. CCIXL, 24, pp. 42-44, 82-84. About the many new Negro TV stars.

Moody, Sid, "Funeral Brass Band Heads Toward Own Grave in New Orleans," *The Times-Picayune*, April 12, 1964, sect. 2, p. 6, cols. 1-3. Gives an account of the Eureka Jazz Band and its playing for funerals and other occasions in New Orleans.

Neustader, Marcus, Jr., "Negro Has Made Great Strides in Louisiana since Eighteenth Century," *The Times-Picayune*, April 16, 1968, sect. 4, p. 30, cols. 1-8. Narrates the great achievements of the Negro in the history of New Orleans.

Padover, Saul K., "The World of the Founding Fathers," *The News*, Mexico, D. F., July 5, 1959, sect. 3, p. 10-C, col. 3. Reveals some important facts about the idealism of our Founding Fathers and their liberal attitudes toward the Negroes, especially that of Jefferson.

Rink, Janet, "Satchmo Comes Home," *Dixie, The Times-Picayune*, October 31, 1965, pp. 7-9. This write-up tells how Louis Armstrong is a man of great credit and acclaim in his own city.

Ross, Ruth M., "Diahann Carroll Wins Title Role in New TV Series 'Julia,'" *Urban West*, Vol. I, 6, July-August 1968, pp. 16-17. Tells of the fine acting of Diahann Carroll and other Negroes associated with her in their family role.

Saxon, Lyle, *Fabulous New Orleans*, New Orleans: Robert L. Crager and Company, 1958. A fine account of the fascinating history of New Orleans with the role of the Negro sympathetically presented.

Swetnam, George, "Up-and-Coming Conductor," *The Pittsburgh Press*, November 17, 1968, Magazine Section, p. 3. This write-up tells about the accomplishments of Morris and other Negro conductors.

"The Duke at 64," *Newsweek*, Vol. LXII, 19, August 26, 1963. The achievements of Duke Ellington at the age of 64.

The Times-Picayune, New Orleans, July 27, 1968, sect. 1, p. 14, cols. 3-4. "Olympia Brass Band Plays in London." The visit of this great jazz band in London.

Thomas, Bob, "Room for Black Heroes as Well as for Villains," *TV Week, The Sun*, August 25, 1968, pp. 4-5. How the Negro is taking his rightful place in the entertainment world.

Tolchard, Clifford, "The Music Makers," *Walkabout: Australia's Way of Life Magazine*, Vol. XXXIII, 4, April 1967, p. 22. The great achievements of Dixon in music and symphony conducting.

NOTES

1. James A. Emanuel, "A Clown at Ten," in *Dark Symphony: Negro Literature in America*, James A. Emanuel and Theodore L. Gross, Eds., New York: The Free Press, 1968, p. 504.
2. Edward Laroque Tinker, *Creole City: Its Past and Its People*, New York: Longmans, Green and Company, 1953, p. 214.
3. Robert Tallant, *The Romantic New Orleanians*, New York: E. P. Dutton and Company, Inc., 1950, p. 161.
4. Saul K. Padover, "The World of the Founding Fathers," *The News*, Mexico, D. F., July 5, 1959, sect. 3, p. 10-C, col. 3.
5. Stephen Longstreet, *The Real Jazz, Old and New*, Baton Rouge: Louisiana State University Press, 1956, p. 25.
6. Robert Delavignette, *Afrique Equatoriale Française*, Paris: 1957, plate 28.
7. *Les Peuples bantous deviennent des nations*, Pietermaritzburg, la République d'Afrique du Sud, 1961, pp. 127-129.
8. *Ibid.* pp. 143-144.
9. Heli Chatelain, *The Folktales of Angola*, Memoirs of the American Folklore Society, Vol. I, New York: The American Folklore Society, 1895.
10. Alcée Fortier, *Louisiana Folk Tales*, Memoirs of the American Folklore Society, Vol. II, New York: The American Folklore Society, 1895.
11. Calvin Claudel, "Louisiana Folktales and their Background," *The Louisiana Historical Quarterly*, Vol. XXXVIII, No. 3, pp. 35-56.
12. Calvin Claudel, "The Syrup Mill," *The Georgia Review*, Vol. XVI, No. 1, Spring 1962, p. 88.
13. George W. Cable, "The Dance in Place Congo," *The Century Magazine*, Vol. XXXI, No. 40, February 1886, pp. 517-532.
14. Lyle Saxon, *Fabulous New Orleans*, New Orleans: Robert L. Crager and Company, 1958, p. 157.
15. Leonard Feather, *The New Edition of the Encyclopedia of Jazz*, New York: Bonanza Books, p. 308.
16. Jeanne Behrend, Ed., *Notes of a Pianist, Louis Moreau Gottschalk*, New York: Alfred A. Knopf, 1964, p. XXII.
17. Lyle Saxon, *Children of Strangers*, Boston: Houghton Mifflin Company, 1937.
18. Lyle Saxon, *Fabulous New Orleans*, pp. 178-186.
19. Henry A. Kmen, *Music in New Orleans*, Baton Rouge: Louisiana State University Press, 1966.
20. Stephen Longstreet, *Sportin' House, New Orleans and the Jazz Story* (*A History of New Orleans Sinners and the Birth of Jazz*), Los Angeles: Sherbourne Press, Inc., 1965.
21. Stephen Longstreet, *The Real Jazz, Old and New*, Baton Rouge: Louisiana State University Press, 1956, p. 2.
22. Martin Williams, *Jazz Masters of New Orleans*, New York: The Macmillan Company, 1967.
23. *Ibid.*, pp. 1-25.
24. *Ibid.*, p. 76.
25. *Ibid.*, pp. 162-177.
26. "Armstrong Celebrates 68th," *The Houston Post*, July 5, 1968, sect. 3, p. 1.
27. Janet Rink, "Satchmo Comes Home," *Dixie, The Times-Picayune*,

New Orleans, October 31, 1965, pp. 7-9.

28. *Ibid.*, p. 8.

29. *The Times-Picayune*, New Orleans, July 27, 1968, sect. 1, p. 14, sols. 3-4.

30. "Música: Jazz en la Sala Ponce," *Excelsior*, July 13, 1968, p. 30A, cols. 7-8.

31. "The Duke at 64," *Newsweek*, Vol. LXII, 19, August 26, 1963.

32. G. E. Lambert, *Kings of Jazz: Duke Ellington*, New York: A. S. Barnes and Company, Inc., 1959.

33. Marcus Neustader, Jr., "Negro Has Made Great Strides in Louisiana Since Eighteenth Century," *The Times-Picayune*, New Orleans, April 16, 1968, sect. 4, p. 30, cols. 1-8.

34. *Ibid.*, col. 6.

35. Ralph Wickiser, Caroline Durieux and John McCrady, *Mardi Gras Day*, New York: Henry Holt and Company, 1948, pp. 18-19.

36. *Ibid.*, p. 13.

37. Martin Williams, *op. cit.*, p. 76.

38. Alice Moser Claudel, "A Southern Memory," *Experiment*, Vol. VI, 4, p. 109.

39. Sid Moody, "Funeral Brass Band Heads Toward Own Grave in New Orleans," *The Times-Picayune*, April 12, 1964, sect. 2, p. 6, cols. 1-3.

40. "Lady Soul: Singing It Like It Is," *Time*, Vol. XCI, 26, June 23, 1968, pp. 62-68.

41. *Ibid.*, p. 64.

42. Hodding Carter, "The Negro Heritage and Green Power," *New Orleans*, Vol. II, 9, June 1968, p. 8.

43. Leonard Feather, *op. cit.*, pp. 422-423.

44. Paul Oliver, *Kings of Jazz: Bessie Smith*, New York: A. S. Barnes and Company, Inc., 1961.

45. Mason Crum, *The Negro in the Methodist Church*, New York: The Editorial Department of the Board of Missions and Church Extension of the Methodist Church, 1951, p. 117.

46. *Ibid.*, p. 117.

47. *Ibid.*, p. 118.

48. Elliott W. Galkin, "Musical Recognition Comes Slowly to Negro," in *Spectator* of *The Sun*, Baltimore, September 28, 1968, sect. D, pp. 1-3.

49. Clifford Tolchard, "The Music Makers," *Walkabout: Australia's Way of Life Magazine*, Vol. XXXIII, 4, April 1967, p. 22.

50. George Swetnam, "Up-and-Coming Conductor," *The Pittsburgh Press*, November 17, 1968, Magazine Section, p. 3.

51. Marian Anderson, "Shock," in *The Outnumbered*, Charlotte Brooks, Ed., New York: Dell Publishing Company, 1967, pp. 122-129.

52. Marian Anderson, ". . . My Deepest Ties to People," *Redbook*, Vol. CXXII, 2 December 1968, pp. 48-49, 136, 138.

53. Mason Crum, *op. cit.*, p. 117.

54. Martin S. Dworpin, "The New Negro on Screen," *Progressive*, Vol. XXV, 1, January 1961, pp. 36-38.

55. Bob Thomas, "Room for Black Heroes as Well as for Villains," *TV Week*, *The Sun*, August 25, 1968, pp. 4-5.

56. Richard Lemon, "Black is the Color of TV's Newest Stars," *The Saturday Evening Post*, Vol. CCIXL, 24, pp. 42-44, 82-84.

57. Ruth M. Ross, "Diahann Carroll Wins Title Role in New TV Series 'Julia,'" *Urban West*, Vol. I, 6, July-August 1968, pp. 16-17. See also

"Diahann Carroll: A New Kind of Glamour on TV," *Look*, Vol. XXXII, 22, October 29, 1968, pp. 66-69.

58. Donald Kirkley, "Next Season's Shows Closing the Color Gap," *TV Week, The Sun*, August 25, 1968, p. 2.

CALVIN CLAUDEL was born in the small village of Goudeau, Louisiana, where at an early age he saw Negroes toiling in the fields for a pittance from sunup to sundown and whose children had very little or no educational advantages. When he was ten his family moved to New Orleans, where he attended the public schools, in which he later became a teacher in 1931. Along with Mrs. Sarah Towles Reed, a dedicated worker for Negro rights and education, he helped organize Negro teachers there so that they might have equal pay with white teachers and other similar advantages.

He holds a B.A. and M.A. with Phi Beta Kappa from Tulane University, a Ph.D. in Romance languages and literature from the University of North Carolina, a diploma from the Sorbonne, the French Academic Palms, and numerous other honors and achievements. He was formerly Chairman of the Department of Romance Languages at West Virginia Wesleyan College and now is Professor of Modern Languages at Salisbury State College, Salisbury, Maryland.

He wrote his doctor's dissertation on "A Study of Louisiana French Folktales in Avoyelles Parish," University of North Carolina, 1947, in which he tells about the Louisiana Negro's contribution to folklore there. He touches on the plight of the Negro in his translations of Creole Negro folksongs and poetry, found in *Quarterly Review of Literature, The New Quarterly Review, The Louisiana Historical Quarterly, The Southern Folklore Quarterly* and elsewhere.

THE NEGRO IN WORLD POLITICS

Daryl R. Fair

Jersey City State College (Jersey City, New Jersey)

Elevation of a black man to high public office is still likely to cause much comment in predominantly white countries. While some, perhaps much, of the comment will be favorable in this increasingly enlightened age, a great deal continues to be derogatory. Likewise, white attitudes toward black attempts at self-government in Africa tend to be condescending. After all, the detractors say, black people are but recently sprung from savagery; they have no history, no political experience, and thus cannot be expected to succeed at statesmanship, either in Africa or elsewhere. Unfortunately, even friends of Negroes sometimes tend to accept black men in public office primarily as a means for the education of the race in the art of government. Thus, friend and foe alike frequently accept the notion that black men have no historical background for political participation. This view ignores the fact that black men have been involved in politics and government for thousands of years, sometimes as rulers of empires larger than most of the nations of the world today. Too many persons of both races have been cut off from this cultural heritage, consciously or unconsciously. Yet this heritage has important lessons to teach about both the capacities and contributions of black men. It is important that individuals of all colors begin to learn these lessons.

Before turning to the story of Negroes in politics, however, we must be clear about whom we are considering. The statement of W. E. B. Du Bois on this matter is as good a guide as any:[1]

"... we are studying the history of the darker part of the human family, which is separated from the rest of mankind by no absolute physical line and no definite mental characteristics, but which nevertheless forms, as a mass, a series of social groups more or less distinct in history, appearance, and in cultural gift and accomplishment."

While this statement may not be a scientific definition of "Negroid," it certainly matches the notion of "Negro" held by much of the white world, including the United States. It is the political record of this "darker part of the human family" in which we are interested.

AFRICA

African political history can be divided, for our purposes, into three broad periods. The first is the ancient period centered in the Nile Valley; the second is the period from the start of the age of metals (roughly the time of Christ) to the "discovery" of sub-Saharan Africa by Europeans; the third is the post-Colonial period.

In the ancient period three civilizations must be noted; these are Egypt, Kush, and Axum. While none of these were purely Negro kingdoms, they were not "white" in the current sense of the word. They likely had mixed peoples, racially, and they all had substantial numbers of blacks in their populations. From the vantage point of the twentieth century it is impossible to isolate the contribution of the Negro elements in these countries to their political development. Nevertheless, the conclusion seems inescapable that blacks, like other groups, had an impact on political events in these kingdoms; these were, after all, African states, and the pattern of government that emerged there seems entirely compatible with later sub-Saharan forms.

The pattern of government found throughout the Nile Valley in the ancient period was that usually associated with Egypt. Near the end of the Fourth Millennium B.C. Egypt emerged as a unified nation under one ruler, a god-king, Pharaoh. Before the Third Millennium before Christ ended, a black, Ra Nehesi, was on the Pharaoh's throne. Others of at least part-Negro descent ruled Egypt throughout its history. One honored figure was

Nefertari, wife of Ahmose I, who founded a new Egyptian empire in 1703 B.C. She was a black who gave a decided Negro appearance to her descendants, such as Amenhotep I. Close relationships with the upper Nile Valley helped bring about a cultural unity of the region. The exile of many Egyptians to this region during the Hyksos invasions accelerated the process. Following the expulsion of the Hyksos, blacks regularly occupied the most important and honored positions in the Egyptian government.

The Kingdom of Kush was founded about 750 B.C. and shortly thereafter ruled Egypt for a century. Kashta, the King of Kush, conquered Thebes and most of upper Egypt during his reign. His son Piankhy then brought much of lower Egypt under his control during the years 751-730 B.C. The taking of Memphis was one of his greatest achievements. Piankhy's brother, Shabaka (707-696 B.C.) completed the conquest of Egypt by taking the Nile Delta. He and his successor, Shabataka, both experienced trouble from the Assyrians, but were able to keep the peace through negotiations. When Taharka took the throne he led a revival of Egyptian culture and styled himself "Emperor of the World." By about 660 B.C, however, he had been driven out of Egypt by the Assyrians. These, and subsequent, conquerors did not share and protect Egyptian culture as the Kushites had; as a result ancient Egyptian civilization declined precipitously following their takeover.

Following their defeat in Egypt by the Assyrians, the Kushites continued to rule in their homeland for approximately 900 years. The capital of Kush, originally at Napata, was moved to Meroë. At these two cities a long line of kings ruled over a culture which continued to employ political ideas developed in the multiracial society of Egypt. The kingdom reached its zenith during the period from about 250 B.C. until the early years of the Christian era, and remained the major power of the upper Nile until it was overthrown by Axum in the fourth century A.D.

Settlement of Axum, the ancestor of modern Ethiopia, began about 500 B.C. and continued until a strong state emerged in the second century A.D. Legend has it that the Ethiopian dynasty dates from the visit of the Queen of Sheba with King Solomon in the eleventh century B.C. The result of this visit became Menelik I, ruler of Axum and founder of the Solomonid line.

Solomonids led Axum to the height of its power in the ancient period during the fourth century. It was at this time that Axum defeated Kush. At this time also the strongest ruler of the period, Ezana, was converted to Christianity. The rise of Islam, which cut Ethiopia off from Mediterranean contacts, coupled with invasions from non-Christian peoples from the South, led to a decline of Axum shortly after the heights of its glory.

The ancient period clearly passed on an important political heritage to subsequent generations. From the Valley of the Nile came traditions such as a unified political state located on a specific territory and ruled by one man under a written law and through a hierarchy of officials. Originated and developed in part by black men, these traditions were spread in many directions through the wide contacts of the Nile Valley civilizations with other peoples of Asia and Africa.

Africa was clearly in the vanguard of political development during much of the ancient period. Europe forged forward during the heights of Greek and Roman civilization, but during much of the period from the start of the age of metals in Africa until European "discovery" of Africa south of the Sahara, Africa was at least the equal of the European civilizations. Some African states clearly surpassed the European ones in terms of political sophistication. The three great states of the Western Sudan — Ghana, Mali and Songhay — were the outstanding African political achievements of the period. These states were governed by a proto-feudal system of which the essential features were a powerful monarch, a court hierarchy which may or may not have been part of the council of state, a council of state composed of territorial governors and princes, an influential queen mother, and a large army sometimes as loyal to the council of state as to the king. The Mossi states, founded in the eleventh and twelfth centuries, displayed this pattern almost exactly, as did old Kanem, Ghana, and Mali.

Ghana, the first of the great Sudanese kingdoms, flourished from 700 to 1200, reaching its heights during the last two centuries of its existence. At his capital of Kumbi, the King ran a luxurious court financed by revenues derived from the trans-Saharan salt-for-gold trade. The downfall of the empire resulted from the holy war proclaimed by the Almoravids in the eleventh century. In 1076-77 a segment of the Almoravid force under Abu

Bakr conquered the capital of Ghana and subdued the empire for a short time. While the Almoravids soon withdrew, Ghana never regained its strength and passed from the scene in the thirteenth century.

Following the demise of Ghana, Mali emerged as the power of the Western Sudan. Although Mali existed both before and after its imperial period, it was during the years 1200-1500 that it flourished. After the Almoravid withdrawal, the Kingdom of Soso became a small power in the area formerly governed by Ghana for a brief period. The Soso emperor, Sumanguru, defeated Mali and on the death of its king in 1230 assassinated all of his sons except the youngest, Sundiata, who was an invalid. In time Sundiata recovered, assumed the throne, and met and defeated in battle Sumanguru, who was killed in the engagement. Sundiata ruled until 1255, expanding Mali and consolidating its independence during his reign. Mali then fell into some disarray until Mansa Mūsa assumed the throne in 1312.

He made Mali one of the greatest states of its time. He expanded its boundaries, reorganized its government, increased its trade, and spread its fame by means of his famous pilgrimage to Mecca. The Arab scholar Ibn Batuta visited Mali during the reign of one of Musa's successors, Sulaiman, and commented favorably on various aspects of its government: the efficient administration, the courtesy and discipline of public officials, the excellent public finances, the prosperity, the respect accorded the decisions and authority of the sovereign, and the luxury and ceremony of royal receptions. The law was also administered efficiently and the army was well organized. Clearly, Mali at its height was a remarkable kingdom; at the point of its greatest expansion, it was as large as Western Europe. Unfortunately, a series of weak rulers and civil wars after the death of Sulaiman in 1360 led to a decline which saw much of the area formerly governed by Mali slip away by 1500. King John II of Portugal, unaware of Mali's troubles and under the impression that it was still a major power, started sending ambassadors to the court of the *Mansas* in 1484, but by that time Songhay had begun to outstrip Mali in importance.

Songhay reached its height from 1350 to 1600. It had existed before that with its capital at Gao and was defeated by one of Mansa Mūsa's generals while the Emperor of Mali was in Mecca.

Mansa Mūsa was so pleased by this that he visited the captive city on his way back to Mali. He took home with him the two sons of the King as hostages. They escaped from his successor, however, and the eldest established the *sonni* dynasty at Gao.

Sonni Ali (1464-1492) was the greatest ruler in this dynasty, and was the architect of a great empire. After a reign of twenty-eight years, he drowned crossing a stream while returning from one of his campaigns. He was succeeded by his son, who apparently was even less faithful a Muslim than Sonni Ali had been. The alarmed Muslim group supported a move by Mohammed Touré, one of Sonni Ali's generals, to overthrow the Emperor. This attempt succeeded and in 1493 Mohammed became the first and greatest of the *askia* dynasty.

Askia Mohammed was an able military leader; he led numerous campaigns and expanded Songhay to the size of all Europe. His genius, however, was as an administrator. He made a pilgrimage to Mecca at least partially to learn about modernization of government, law, taxation and administration. Upon his return he instituted many reforms. He established a professional army and a secretariat for bureaucratic functions. He appointed provincial governors himself, as Sonni Ali had done, thus diminishing the independence of the council of state. Each important town had its own municipal government. This efficient government enabled Mohammed, assisted by his brother and chief lieutenant, Omar, to rule over a stable kingdom for thirty-six years.

Old and blind, Askia Mohammed was forced to abdicate by his son in 1529. He spent the last years of his life in exile and as a prisoner in the palace from which he once had ruled Songhay. After a period of intrigues and assassinations, Songhay's fortunes were revived under Ishak I (1539-49) and Daoud (1549-82). Thereafter Songhay was brought to her knees by a succession of weak rulers during a time of Moroccan invasions. Judar Pasha, the Moroccan general, overthrew the *askias* in 1591. Although subsequent *askias* claimed the throne, they were either powerless or puppets of the local pashas, who had taken over portions of the empire largely to war among themselves.

To the east of Songhay, in the Central Sudan, the empire of Kanem-Bornu was the greatest state in the middle period of African political development. Kanem, north of Lake Chad, existed as a fairly traditional Sudanese state from the eighth through the thirteenth centuries. The first foothold of the *mai* dynasty in Bornu, south of Lake Chad, was gained in the thirteenth century. The rulers of Kanem re-located their seat of government to Bornu at the end of the fourteenth century. Early in the sixteenth century Kanem was recaptured and the empire of Kanem-Bornu emerged. Mai Idris Alooma (1571-1603) was the greatest of the rulers of this kingdom. He replaced customary law with Islamic law, appointed his own ministers, unified Kanem-Bornu, and in general exercised control over the functions of government. He was a strong, perhaps even authoritarian ruler, more like the great kings of Songhay than earlier emperors in his own country. After his death Kanem-Bornu declined in importance, although it remained independent until conquered by the soldier-of-fortune Rabah in 1893 and annexed by the French in 1896.

One group of states, the Hausa states of the Central Sudan, deserve mention as the African counterpart of the European city-state. Originally there were seven Hausa cities, but as many as 100 independent cities existed at various times. These cities seem to have emerged approximately the eleventh century. Their greatest prosperity followed the decline of Bornu in the seventeenth century. The original ones were Kano, Biram, Katsina, Gobir, Zaria, Rano and Kaura. A balance of power kept any one from conquering the others, but forced all of them to fight fiercely to avoid conquest by their neighbors. They were once united under a Fulani empire during the nineteenth century. Ousman dan Fodio declared a holy war in 1801 and conquered most of Hausaland, which he and his successors then ruled until the British took the area in 1909.

In general, then, the Western and Central Sudan during the middle period was a succession of great states governed by elaborate political organizations. These were the equal of most states of the time and were considerably more advanced than many. These states represent a considerable political achievement by the black man.

South of the Sudanese states just discussed lay several smaller kingdoms just as advanced politically as their larger northern neighbors. The most important of these were Benin, Oyo, Dahomey, and Ashanti. In existence from 1300 to 1897, Benin reached its heights in the period 1450-1800. Ewuare the Great (1440-1473) was the most noted of its kings. Benin established diplomatic relations with Portugal in about 1486 and maintained them for a century. Ohen-Okun was the first ambassador from Benin to Portugal. The King (*oba*) of Benin was an absolute monarch, but ruled through a state council and a regularized administrative structure, inasmuch as his many ceremonial duties occupied a great deal of his time. Eventually Yoruba replaced Benin as the most powerful kingdom of the Niger delta region.

The Yoruba state of Oyo was founded perhaps as early as the thirteenth century and lasted until the nineteenth. Its period of greatest influence was from about 1600 to 1799. Oyo was ruled by a god-king (*alafin*) who was, in principle, all powerful. The *alafin* was elected by provincial councilors and ruled through court ministers and military commanders. In the provinces there were locally elected officials who exercised the *alafin's* authority. In the various towns there were councils which expressed their views on both local and national matters. Although in principle absolute rulers, the *alafins* were not. Their exercise of authority was hampered by the tradition that they not allow themselves to be seen for fear that certain of the myths (e.g., that they could live without eating) surrounding their sacred persons be dispelled. Furthermore, if the locally elected officials presented the *alafin* with certain symbols of rejection, he was expected to commit suicide. This extraordinary version of the "vote of no confidence" was actually used in Oyo.

Dahomey, farther to the west than Oyo, existed from 1500 to 1894. It originated to the north of the forest region, but invaded and conquered the coastal region under one of its greatest kings, Agadja (c. 1720-1735). The country was well organized and administered and had a complicated revenue system controlled by one of the King's wives.

Ashanti, still farther to the west, was the most remarkable of the late pre-colonial West African states. For this reason it is included here even though its origins lie in the period after European "discovery." It existed about 1675 to 1900. An early king (*asantehene*) and hero was Osei Tutu who ruled from the late seventeenth century until about 1720. His successor, Opuku Ware, consolidated the kingdom and made it the strongest on the Guinea Coast. Ashanti had a strong state with a good administrative bureaucracy. There were six wars between Ashanti and Britain during the nineteenth century; the British found Ashanti a stubborn foe. Finally Western technology prevailed and Britain took over the country in 1901. It has been said that Ashanti had one foot in the modern world at the time, however.

Another kingdom of some note in the middle period was Kongo. Founded in the fourteenth century its kings exchanged diplomatic correspondence with Portugal, and Kongolese went to Portugal for education. The Royal Family became Christians and Afonso I (1505-1543) made valiant attempts to maintain good relations with Portugal while developing his country. The interest of Portugese merchants in the slave trade prevented this, however, and largely destroyed Kongo.

The history of southern and eastern Africa is less well known than that of West Africa, particularly that of the period before the coming of the Europeans. There were, however, a series of trading states along the coast which amazed Vasco da Gama's sailors with their luxury. These cities were based on a mixture of Bantu and Arab cultures and peoples, but the Swahili culture that emerged was basically African. Ambassadors and gifts from the East Coast of Africa likely reached China as early as the eleventh century. The greatest of these states probably was Kilwa. Sultan Ali bin al-Hasan (c.1150-1225) was its first ruler; his father was Persian and his mother a black African. Kilwa captured other trading cities and reached its heights in the twelfth and thirteenth centuries. It, along with other coastal cities, were destroyed by the Portuguese in the fifteenth century.

An inland empire that suffered somewhat the same fate was Monomotapa. It was brought into being by a Rozwi king, Mutota, in about 1440. In 1485 a split between the King (*monomotapa*) and one of his subordinates, Changa, led to the creation of the rival Changamir empire. Monomotapa lasted until about 1700, at which time rivalries with other empires, pressure from the Portuguese, and migrations from the South combined to bring about its collapse. Located in what is now Rhodesia and Mozambique, Monomotapa was at its height as large as Mali had been at the start of Mansa Mūsa's reign. The unity of the empire seems to have depended very much on the personal qualities of the ruler; that is, a strong ruler could hold it together, but a weak one had difficulty in doing so. It is likely that the empires of

Monomotapa and Changamir were in some sense descendants from the peoples who built the Zimbabwe stoneworks.

Another notable East African state is Buganda. It was one of two Lwo states (Bunyoro was the other) founded in the area formerly ruled by the Cwezi kings of Kitari, between Victoria Nyanza and Lakes Albert and Edward, during the fourteenth and fifteenth centuries. During the seventeenth century Buganda became the more important of the two states. The King (*kabaka*) was an absolute ruler who had the help of a centralized administrative structure in governing. Mutesa, one of the greatest *kabakas*, substituted regional officials responsible to him for the former clan heads, upgraded the court hierarchy, and made upward mobility of commoners easier. Buganda was annexed by the British in 1899, but the leader of the force that subdued the country paid it the tribute of saying that no African state had a better-developed political or legal system.

There are other African political systems and leaders of great importance in the history of the continent. Many of the more significant of these belong to the period between European "discovery" and European annexation of Africa, however, and will therefore be merely mentioned here.

Chaka (c.1787-1828), the great Zulu military leader, also made a contribution to the political life of his people. He brought together a great empire subsequently headed by such men as Dingaan, Cetewayo and Dinizulu. One less favorable political fact about Chaka is his status as one of the few real tyrants in the pre-Colonial period of African history. Most of the other rulers found it necessary to operate within the customary law of their tribes and courted trouble when they strayed beyond it.

A contemporary of Chaka who founded the state of Basutoland to escape the Zulu wars was Moshesh (c.1790-1870). He was widely respected as a wise leader and great statesman. Another contemporary of Chaka who founded a state was Moselikatze, who had been one of the Zulu leader's generals. In about 1828 Chaka turned on Moselikatze, who escaped with about 15,000 followers. They eventually settled in an area south of the Zambesi River (1838); this state was known as Matabeleland. When Moselikatze died in 1870, Lobenguela succeeded him. The state was destroyed and taken over by the Europeans in 1893, after the discovery of gold there. Bechuanaland, governed later in its history by the Christian King Khama II (c.1830-1923), was another notable southern African state.

How, then, could black people, who had such an extensive background of political experience, have been regarded as savages who lived in a condition bordering on anarchy? There seems to have been a number of factors in explanation of this. One was the advanced state of European technology. Europeans reached the erroneous conclusion that because Africans were less advanced in technology, they were less advanced in everything else (including politics). A second factor was the religious difference between Europeans and Africans. Because Africans were not Christians, Europeans regarded them as generally backward heathens. A third factor, probably the most important, was the slave trade. In order to carry it out, Europeans had to convince themselves that it was being inflicted upon inferior peoples who had no culture, no civilization, no religion, law or politics; thus the "savages" were better off as slaves, in which condition they would at least have the benefits of contact with more enlightened European ways. In addition, the slave trade wreaked very real havoc in many African states. It brought about continuous intertribal wars, depopulation, economic dislocation, and eventual chaos. Thus, many of the African states eventually were weakened or destroyed by the slave trade, and, because of the Europeans, they began to resemble the anarchies that Europeans thought they intrinsically were. In any event, after about four centuries of trade and exploitation Europe began in earnest the annexation of African territory, shortly after 1879. By the First World War the partition of Africa was complete; only Ethiopia and Liberia remained outside the firm control of European powers. (The Union of South Africa, granted dominion status in 1909, is not included with Ethiopia and Liberia because self-government there was for descendants of Europeans only.)

Ethiopia emerged from the ancient Kingdom of Axum, which had been in a state of decline since the rise of Islam. The country began to rise again under the Zagwe kings, who usurped the throne from the Solomonids early in the twelfth century and ruled until about 1270. Despite their contribution, the Zagwes are remembered today primarily as usurpers; only Lalibela (c.1190-1225) is highly regarded, and he primarily for his religious dedication. During the period of decline, Muslim trading states on the Red Sea coast had expanded inland, occupying former Axumite territory. When the Solomonids and national strength had been restored, Ethiopia began to take the offensive against these Muslim states. The area was conquered in the fourteenth century and consolidated under Ethiopian rule in the fifteenth. The Muslims countered with a holy war, something which had not been directed against Ethiopia before. The state of Adel, supported and armed with firearms by the Ottoman Turks, almost surely would have defeated Ethiopia had Portugal not responded positively to an Ethiopian appeal for help in the sixteenth century.

European help proved to result in long-range problems, however, although it did enable the country to solve the short-range crisis by driving the Muslims out of the country. Subsequent assistance from Spain brought into the country Jesuit missionaries who tried to "cleanse" Ethiopian Christianity. This resulted in popular revolts, factionalism, attempts to purge the nation of foreign influence, and eventual disintegration of the empire into largely independent provinces. In this confusion an adventurer, Ras Kassa, had himself crowned emperor as Theodore II in 1856. He reunited the country to some extent, but eventually shot himself in 1868 when a British expedition invaded his realm to free British subjects he had imprisoned out of pique over the failure of Queen Victoria to answer a letter he had sent her. John IV succeeded him and ruled somewhat uneasily as Menelik of Shoa gained considerable independence from central authority. When John IV was killed in 1889, Menelik took the throne despite the Emperor's deathbed nomination of another man to succeed him. As Menelik II, he ruled until 1913. He concluded the Treaty of Uccialli with the Italians, but differences in interpretation of it led to a war in which Menelik prevailed at the battle of Adua in 1896 and saved his country from the same fate that had befallen most of the continent.

When Menelik, who had nominated his grandson Lij Jasu as his successor in 1907, became paralyzed in 1909, a power struggle ensued. Empress Taitu, Menelik's fourth wife, who had led a portion of the Ethiopian army at Adua, maneuvered for power by nominating Zauditu, a daughter of one of Menelik's previous wives, for the throne. Ras Tafari, a powerful political figure, was also a factor in the contest. Lij Jasu won the first round; he began to exercise power in 1911 and succeeded to the throne in 1913. He subsequently lost his position by encouraging a feudal kind of political pattern in his country, by becoming a Muslim, and by toying with support of the Turks and Germans in World War I. While on a trip in 1916 he was deposed. Zauditu was elevated to the throne and Ras Tafari became regent and actual ruler. He led Ethiopia into the League of Nations in 1923 and had consolidated his power by 1928. He became Emperor as Haile Selassie I on the death of the Empress and continues to rule Africa's oldest independent state today. He was Emperor in Exile for some time, however; war with Italy broke out in 1934 and he had to flee the country when it was defeated following the refusal of the League of Nations to assist Ethiopia. He returned in 1941 when the British drove the Italians out of the country. As dean of African heads of state, he has attempted to modernize his country by founding a civil service, by revising the laws, and by other means.

Liberia, which came into existence in 1821 as a colony to receive Negroes repatriated to Africa from the United States, was governed at first by whites. The first black governor, Joseph Jenkins Roberts, who had emigrated from Virginia, declared the colony independent in 1847. It was recognized at once by most great powers, but the United States withheld recognition until 1862. Roberts was elected the first president of the republic and served until 1856. He was called back to office from 1871-1875 following the deposing of an unpopular president who seemed to be developing a dictatorship. Liberia's independence has at times been precarious. Her financial affairs were administered for a time by the United States early in the twentieth century, and the Firestone Rubber Company has exercised a great deal of influence in Liberian affairs. A difficult period followed the resignations of the President and Vice President in 1931 during an investigation of shipment of Liberians for forced labor on Spanish plantations. Edwin Barclay was elected president in that year and conducted an enlightened administration until 1944 when he was succeeded by William V. S. Tubman, who is still in office today. The political system of the country is modeled after that of the United States, but the True Whigs remain the only effective political party in the country and descendants of Negroes from the United States continue to have disproportionate influence in national politics.

Although a number of African states became independent before 1957, they were for the most part not black-controlled governments (e.g., Union of South Africa, Egypt, Libya, Sudan, Tunisia and Morocco). The rush for independence in black Africa began when the Gold Coast assumed independence under the name Ghana in 1957. The independence movement there was originally led by J. B. Danquah, but by 1957 Kwame Nkrumah had assumed leadership. He eventually became president and remained in power until overthrown in 1966.

There are now 40 independent states in Africa. Two of these (Union of South Africa and Rhodesia) are white-ruled countries in which blacks are allowed no part in political life; in addition, Britain, France, Portugal and Spain still have dependencies and protectorates in Africa. About 88% of the people of Africa now live in political systems controlled by native Africans, however. These African states have assumed an important role in the General Assembly of the United Nations and in other international forums.

Among the outstanding of the black African states are Tanzania, Kenya and Nigeria. Tanzania is made up of Tanganyika on the mainland plus Zanzibar, off the coast. Tanganyika became independent in 1961 and joined with Zanzibar in 1964 to form Tanzania. Its President, Julius Nyerere, is recognized as one of the leading statesmen of Africa.

Kenya became independent in 1963 and Jomo Kenyatta became President. He had been a leader of the Kenya independence movement for a long time and was imprisoned by the British for a time as a suspected Mau Mau leader. Assisted by such men as Tom Mboya, Kenyatta has provided able leadership for Kenya since her independence.

Long thought to be one of the more stable African political systems, Nigeria experienced political troubles in 1966. A multi-tribal state, Nigeria became independent in 1960 as a realm within the Commonwealth of Nations. Nnamdi Azikiwe, a noted leader of the independence movement, was Governor-General, and Sir Abubakar Tafawa Balewa Prime Minister. The country became a federal republic in 1963 with Azikiwe as President; Tafawa Balewa continued as Prime Minister. Following difficulties in 1965, they were overthrown early in 1966 by a military group from the Eastern Ibo Region led by Major General Johnson T. U. Aguiyi-Ironsi. Tafawa Balewa and several others were killed in the revolt. He was ousted about six months later by Lieutenant Colonel Yakubu Gowon from the Northern Region. In 1967 Lieutenant Colonel Odumegwu Ojukwu led the Eastern Region in secession; it became Biafra and continues its fight for independence at the time of this writing.

Some outstanding individual post-Colonial statesmen in Africa deserve mention. Sékou Touré of Guinea, who led his country into independence and has led it since, is, like Nkrumah, somewhat left-leaning, but an important political figure. Felix Houphouët-Boigny of the Ivory Coast was a leader of the independence movement in French Africa and served as a representative in the French National Assembly before becoming President of his country after its independence. President H. K. Banda of Malawi returned to lead his country's independence movement after many years abroad; he later became President. Léopold Senghor, the poet-president of Senegal, is another black African statesman of note. Milton Obote, fighter for independence in Uganda and later President and Prime Minister, is another example of competent political leadership in independent Africa. Kenneth Kaunda, President of Zambia, is highly regarded also. Other leaders of independence movements who later became heads of state in their countries were Leon M'ba of Gabon and Sylvanus Olympio of Togo; both are now dead. There are many other African political figures who could be mentioned. Some of these (e.g., Patrice Lumumba, Joseph Kasavubu, Moise Tshombe, Joseph Mobutu, to mention only those associated with Congo—Kinshasa are more controversial, however. Perhaps it would be fitting to close this listing with one who never was a head of state, yet was winner of the Nobel Peace Prize: the late Chief Albert Luthuli. He became chief of his tribe in 1935 and soon thereafter was a leader of the African National Congress. The government of the Union of South Africa responded by depriving him of his chieftainship, placing him under house arrest, and barring him from political activity. In 1960 he received the Nobel Prize in recognition of his efforts on behalf of his people.

What, generally, can be said, then, about African politics? First, it seems clear that African political ideas may have influenced those of Europe somewhat through ancient Egypt. Second, the isolation of black Africa from Europe since the rise of Islam prevented interchange during the Middle Ages. Third, the slave trade and its aftermath kept Europeans from taking African politics very seriously once Afro-European relations were established. Fourth, the Colonial period helped cut Africans off from their political heritage, which was largely proto-feudal and monarchical in nature, but nonetheless impressive in many respects. (The slave trade had already done much to demolish African political culture in many areas.) Finally, the post-Colonial African states, under the influence of the Colonial powers and foreign-educated independence leaders, are almost uniformly intended to be democratic republics. These have neither widespread popular support nor foundations in the traditions of the continent. It is not surprising that military coups have taken place in a large number of African states. These may well be a phase in the evolution of an indigenous form of government based upon the African past and present combined with modern political ideas. If Africa can evolve such a system of government, her political future may be as impressive as her past.

LATIN AMERICA

The first black people to reach Latin America apparently did so by way of Europe. African slaves were first sent to Europe in the late fourteenth century; in less than a century approximately 700-800 per year were being taken to Portugal. Descendants of this group accompanied many of the explorers from Spain and Portugal to the New World. It is said that a pilot for Columbus, Pedro Alonzo Niño, was a Negro. Blacks also were with Balboa, Cortés, Pizarro, Cabeza de Vaca, Coronado, and others. In 1501 Madrid authorized the introduction of African Negroes into the New World as well. The slave trade was formally opened in 1517, and within twenty-five years 10,000 slaves per year were arriving in the West Indies. The status of Negroes has never been as much of a problem in Latin America as it has been in the United States, however. On the Latin American mainland, assimilation proceeded rapidly, so that today racial distinctions have been all but physically obliterated in many places. In the West Indies, Negroes were the numerical majority on many islands; in a great many such locations, they took over the reins of government when self-government was achieved.

French San Domingo was the first place in Latin America where blacks rose to political power. Like other colonies, it had been troubled by runaway slaves (Maroons). Several Maroon leaders presided over the colony of runaways on the island. One of these leaders, Macandal, threw quite a scare into the white population with a plot to poison the island's water supply. He was captured and executed, but predicted his return, inasmuch as he had called himself the Black Messiah. Later, many people regarded Toussaint as his reincarnation. Macandal's death did not eliminate the Maroon colony. It became so strong that it was recognized by the Colonial government in 1784.

In 1789 trouble of another sort developed. Following the start of the French revolution, the free Negroes of San Domingo sent a delegation composed of Julien Raymond and Vincent Ogé to Paris with a petition for their citizenship. This request was refused by the French government and Ogé returned to lead, with Chavannes, a revolt. This failed and the two leaders were brutally executed in 1791. Later that same year the French government made free Negroes citizens and enfranchised them. A new colonial assembly was set up based on this electorate; it met, then recessed to await the arrival of three French commissioners sent to pacify the colony, which had been in turmoil since agitation by the free Negroes had begun. Before their arrival, however, the slaves of the colony suddenly rose in revolt, beginning a ten-year period of war which led to independence for the colony. The revolt was planned and led by Pierre Dominic Toussaint, although Jean François and Biassou were leaders in the early stages of the uprising. Toussaint controlled much of the colony by the time the commissioners arrived, unaware that the revolt had even taken place. Toussaint was able to reach terms with neither the white planters of the colony nor the commissioners, nor their replacements, sent later. When Louis XVI was beheaded, Toussaint entered the service of Spain, united the island, and held off the British, who were attempting a take-over. However, when France affirmed the emancipation of slaves in 1794 Toussaint re-entered French service. When Toussaint finally conquered the British invaders, France sent a colonial governor to deal with them because they did not trust the black leader. The British continued to deal with Toussaint in an attempt to embarrass the French, however. The treaty arrived at recognized the independence of San Domingo; Toussaint thereupon proceeded to draw up a constitution for the country. Napoleon later decided to reconquer the island. He sent his brother-in-law Le Clerc on the mission. Failing to accomplish his mission by force, Le Clerc won the confidence of Toussaint's principal advisors: his brother Paul, Jean Jacques Dessalines and Henri Christophe. Although Toussaint remained suspicious, a treaty with the French was signed. One month later, Toussaint was kidnapped by the French and banished to Europe, where he died shortly thereafter. Dessalines now determined to drive out the French. In this he was greatly helped by an epidemic which hit the French troops and almost wiped them out. Le Clerc himself died and his successor surrendered in 1803. White rule thus became extinct in French San Domingo (the Spanish portion reverted to Spain), which Dessalines renamed Haiti. As French power died in Haiti, so did Napoleon's dreams of an empire in the Americas. For this and other reasons, he sold Louisiana cheap to the United States. Thus the United States owes something to the greatest of American Negro political leaders, Toussaint L'Ouverture (Toussaint the Savior) and his successors.

Independent Haiti has had a stormy existence. Its first ruler, Dessalines, was overthrown and killed by his own men in 1807. Following his death, Christophe and Alexandre Pétion fought for the right to succeed him. Neither really won; although Christophe declared himself emperor in 1811, he was unable to subdue the part of the country controlled by Pétion. Christophe reorganized the government in his part of the island along African tribal lines with an emperor, chieftains and clans. Christophe eventually became unpopular because he, like Dessalines, was inclined to be tyrannical. He committed suicide in 1820 after being partially paralyzed by a stroke. In all, seventeen governments were overthrown between 1803 and 1914. The current Haitian ruler, François Duvalier, has been in office for over ten years and now holds the position for life. His regime is a dictatorial one and the country is not in very sound economic condition; it would seem, therefore that Haiti is not on the verge of breaking with the Latin American tradition of governmental change by revolt.

Negroes have been significant in several other Caribbean island states as well. Maroon colonies existed in many of them, with the one in Jamaica being perhaps the most troublesome. The freedom of this Maroon colony, led by Juan de Bolas, was acknowledged in 1663. Fighting erupted again in 1795 and peace was eventually made on the understanding that no Maroons were to be deported. Six hundred were promptly sent to Nova Scotia, and subsequently to Sierra Leone, the African colony founded by the British for the repatriation of African slaves. Slave revolts also figured in the history of these areas. Farcel led one in Dominica, Washington Franklin in Barbados, and José Aponte in Cuba. After emancipation there were further revolts. Antonio Maceo, one of Cuba's most honored revolutionists during the Spanish colonial period, was of African descent. In Jamaica, George William Gordon, a mulatto who had tried to help the island's blacks, was hanged after the 1861 riots although there was no proof that he was involved.

Several predominantly black countries in the Caribbean have achieved independence in recent years. Among these are Jamaica (1962), Trinidad and Tobago (1962), and Barbados (1966). Dr. Eric Williams has been Prime Minister of Trinidad and Tobago since its independence. Sir Alexander Bustamante served as Prime Minister of Jamaica until his retirement in 1967; his successor, Sir Donald Sangster, died after a few months in office and Hugh Lawson Shearer assumed the leadership of the country. Errol Walton Barrow became Prime Minister of Barbados when it became independent in 1966.

Some Caribbean states which are not predominantly black have involved blacks importantly in governmental affairs nevertheless. The Dominican Republic became independent in 1821 (it had been independent earlier for a brief period), and one of its early political leaders was Ulisse Heureaux, a mulatto. Negroes have held various political positions since, including that of chief justice as early as 1873. In the early days of Cuban independence, Martin Delgado was an important behind-the-scenes political leader. Unsatisfied with this status for black leaders, Esteñoz founded the Independent Colored Party in 1907. Riots resulted and parties based on color were outlawed; black political officers – judges, police chiefs, etc. – began to appear in Cuba, however. Fulgencio Batista, who twice ruled the country prior to the Castro revolution, was a mulatto.

On the mainland of Latin America Negroes are politically important in Brazil and Guyana more than elsewhere. In the other countries blacks number generally less than ten percent of the population. In many of these areas, Negroes have been so well assimilated that achievements, political or otherwise, by them are not remarkable but expected. In this regard John Hope Franklin has said: "The acceptance of the Negro into the life of the community presented few new problems to the Latin American."[2] In Guyana and Brazil, where blacks are more numerous, however, their activities are easier to trace.

Guyana has been independent only since 1966. Its prime minister since that time has been Forbes Burnham, who accomplished what his fiery East Indian predecessor Cheddi Jagan was unable to: independence for British Guiana under the new name of Guyana.

Brazil is one of the nations of the Western Hemisphere which has been most influenced by Negroes. Africans were first brought to Brazil by the Portuguese in 1538; by 1800 they made up nearly two-thirds of the population. One significant role played by Brazilian blacks was that of slave rebel. There were outbreaks in 1756-1757 at Sapuchay, and in 1772 at São Thomé and San José. The most serious were those from 1807 to 1835 at Bahia, however. More than a half-dozen revolts took place during the period; they were principally revolts of Muslim Hausas against both whites and non-Muslim blacks. Among the leaders of these outbreaks were Luiza Mahin (who was an African princess), Arrumá, Pacifico, Elesbão do Carmo, Belchoir, Gaspar da Silva Cunha, Luiz Sanim, Manoel Calafate, and Aprigio. The 1835 outbreak was the most serious and was so well planned and led that its leaders were shot with full military honors rather than being hanged as common criminals.

Another role of the Negro in Brazil was that of leader of rebel governments. The *balaiada*, a revolt which broke out in 1823, is named for its principal leader, Manoel Francisco dos Anjos Fereira (nicknamed Balião). These rebels controlled the province of Maranhão for three years. There were numerous colonies (*quilombos*) set up by runaway slaves in Brazil. The most important of these was Palmares, which existed as a state-within-a-state for over sixty years. From 1630 to 1644 it consisted of two settlements which were eventually destroyed by the Dutch.

These were rebuilt after 1644, but were leveled by the Portuguese in 1676. Up to this point the colony had been governed by a king called Ganga Zumba, with his capital at Cerca Real do Macaco. The King's brother, the Zona, was also important, as were the Minister of Justice and other officials. The Portuguese expedition which had destroyed several Palmares settlements in 1676 took numerous captives, including two sons of the Ganga Zumba. As a result, a pact of peace was made. Zambi, the nephew of the Ganga Zumba, was unhappy with the situation. A brave man who had excelled in the war against the Portuguese, he revolted, killed his uncle, proclaimed himself King, and re-opened hostilities against the Portuguese. He remained in power until Palmares finally fell in 1697. The Portuguese were able to overcome Zambi only after a long siege of his capital city; when they finally entered the city, Zambi and his lieutenants committed suicide by leaping from a cliff. Palmares was truly a remarkable political achievement. It consisted of numerous settlements, with perhaps 20,000 people bound together into a single community by a working legal and political system. It demonstrated talent for political leadership, public administration and legislative procedure.

Another role of the Negro in Brazil has been that of abolitionist leader. Among these was Chico Rei, a minor African king sold into slavery. He purchased his son's freedom, then his own, then that of all members of his tribe. He led a colony of his people in Villa Rica and continued to purchase the freedom of slaves. Others who fought slavery through the press and through politics were Luiz Gama (the son of Luiza Mahin), Antonio Bento, André Rebouças, José Ferreira de Menezes, Theodomiro Pereira, Manoel Querino, Castro Alves, and José de Patrocinio (the greatest of the abolitionists).

Following emancipation, Negroes played important roles in the political life of Brazil. Some of the abolitionists (Gama, Rebouças, Patrocinio) did party work, wrote legislation, or held office. Eliseu Cesar and Monteiro Lopes were noted political orators. Cardoso Vieira and Evaristo Ferreira da Veiga were important members of the Chamber of Deputies. Nilo Peçanha served as a member of the Constituent Assembly, as a deputy, as a senator, as Vice President, and, following the death of the President, as President of the Republic in 1909-1910. He later went back to the Senate, served as President of the state of Rio de Janeiro, and as Minister of Foreign Affairs beginning in 1917. Other Negro political leaders in Brazil were Domicio da Gama, Alcebiades Peçanha, João Mangabeira, and Octavio Mangabeira. It is impossible to go much beyond this in discussing specific Negro political leaders in Brazil. Because of the Brazilian attitude toward intermarriage, the situation has developed in such a way that Sir Harry Johnston was led to write in 1910: ". . . at the present moment there is scarcely a lowly or highly placed federal or provincial official at the head of or within any of the great departments of state that has not more or less Negro or American-Indian blood in his veins."[3] Brazil deserves the title of "The Melting Pot" perhaps more than the United States.

THE UNITED STATES

During the years through the end of the Civil War in the United States, the Negro was more a political issue than an active participant in the process of government. There were two principal roles which Negroes inclined toward political activism could play during this period: that of slave revolutionist and that of abolitionist. Although not as numerous as slave revolts in places to the south, slave rebellions did take place in the United States. Three of the most significant were those led by Gabriel Prosser (1800), Denmark Vesey (1822), and Nat Turner (1831). The first two were betrayed by informers and did not materialize despite intricate planning and organization. Turner's rebellion was carried past the planning stages and was responsible for the death of a number of whites. It was eventually put down and its leader captured. All three rebel leaders were hanged.

The degree of activism of the abolitionists varied widely. Some did little more than escape from slavery and serve as the subjects of pamphlets written by white abolitionists. Others were quite active, and several were leaders of the anti-slavery movement. Undoubtedly the most prominent was Frederick Douglass. An escapee from slavery, Douglass became a noted and effective orator in the abolitionist cause. His autobiography also served as an effective tool for the opponents of the peculiar institution. Douglass eventually became one of the leaders of the American Antislavery Society. Others high in the councils of the Society were Robert Purvis, David Ruggles, Charles Bennett Ray, and

John B. Russworm. The most radical of the abolitionists was David Walker, whose *Appeal* called upon slaves to engage in violent resistance against their masters.

The first real political opportunity of Negroes in the United States came during the Reconstruction period. During the time when reconstruction policy was being formulated by the executive, the southern states were allowed to set up political systems dominated by whites, in many cases by former Confederate officials. Congress became increasingly disenchanted with this situation, however, and assumed control of the matter with the Reconstruction Acts of 1867. Many white Southerners were disenfranchised by these statutes, which directed the calling of constitutional conventions to design new governmental structures for the former rebel states. Slightly more than half of the voters enrolled under these statutes were black; Negro registration was encouraged by the Union League, which was attempting to build up the Republican Party in the South. As a result of this situation, all of the conventions contained Negro members. In South Carolina, a majority of the delegates were black; in Louisiana whites and blacks had equal numbers of delegates. In the other states the percentage of Negroes in the conventions ranged from ten percent in Texas to forty percent in Florida. In all, roughly twenty-six percent of the delegates to the ten conventions involved were black. These conventions produced generally good results. The constitutions were forward-looking and progressive. When white supremacy was re-established, the whites did not hasten to rewrite these documents, except for the portions having to do with voting rights for blacks. In some states these constitutions are even today the basis for government. Many people, including some contemporary Southern newsmen, commented favorably on the contribution of the Negro delegates to the work of these assemblies.

During Congressional Reconstruction, hundreds of blacks held local and state political office in the South. Never was any state under Negro rule, however. In the first Reconstruction Legislature in South Carolina, there were eighty-seven blacks and forty whites, but the whites controlled the State Senate. In Mississippi forty Negroes served in the first Reconstruction Legislature, in Virginia twenty-seven. In Louisiana there were 133 Negro legislators between 1868 and 1896. Negroes also served in the legislatures of Alabama, Florida, Tennessee, Arkansas, Texas, and other states, but not in as large numbers. Three — Samuel Lee and Robert Elliott of South Carolina and John Lynch of Mississippi — served as Speakers of the House. While the ethical conduct of these legislatures may not always have been of the highest order, neither was that of most other lawmaking assemblies during this period. North and South, this was a period of considerable malfeasance in public office; it would have been surprising if Southern legislators had not taken part, along with their brethren elsewhere. Despite some chicanery, the legislative output of these groups was better than is generally recognized. Legal codes which still form the basis of Louisiana law were enacted at this time. When South Carolina was attempting to disenfranchise Negroes in 1894-95, Senator Ben Tillman charged that blacks had shown no capacity for government; an opponent of white supremacy replied by pointing out that the state's laws on finance, building of penal and charitable institutions, the establishment of the public school system, and reform of most state and local agencies had been enacted by Reconstruction legislatures in which Negroes had played a leading role. As state lawmakers in the Reconstruction period, blacks thus made a significant contribution.

Negroes held other important state posts during this period. Six served as Lieutenant Governor: Alonzo J. Ransier and Richard H. Gleaves in South Carolina; A. K. Davis in Mississippi; and Oscar J. Dunn, C. C. Antione, and P. B. S. Pinchback in Louisiana. Pinchback also served as Governor for a short time after the removal of the previous incumbent. Francis L. Cardozo served as Secretary of State and as Treasurer in South Carolina. James Hill was Secretary of State and T. W. Cardozo Superintendent of Education in Mississippi. Jonathan Gibbs was Secretary of State and Superintendent of Public Instruction in Florida. Jonathan J. Wright was an Associate Justice of the South Carolina Supreme Court. In Louisiana Antoine Dubuclet was State Treasurer, P. G. Deslonde Secretary of State and W. G. Brown Superintendent of Public Education. In addition there were important Republican Party officials, such as Norris W. Cuney of Texas who headed the party there for twenty years and served as national committeeman for ten; James C. Napier of Tennessee also served twenty years on the state Republican committee and four times as a delegate to national conventions.

The best known of the Negro public officials during the Reconstruction period were undoubtedly those who served in the United States Congress. Twenty-two men achieved this distinction. Two served in the Senate: Hiram Revels and Blanche Bruce, the latter for a full term. The others served in the House. Eight were from South Carolina, four from North Carolina, three from Alabama, and one each from Georgia, Mississippi, Florida, Louisiana, and Virginia. The largest number to serve at any one time was seven. Half of them served only one term; six served two terms, two were elected for three terms, and two represented their districts five terms in Washington. The ablest probably were Robert Elliott, John Mercer Langston, James C. Napier and John R. Lynch. The others were Robert Smalls and J. H. Rainey (who served five terms each), Jefferson Long, Alonzo J. Ransier, Robert C. DeLarge, Richard H. Cain, Thomas E. Miller, G. W. Murray, John A. Hyman, James E. O'Hara, Henry P. Cheatham, George H. White, Benjamin S. Turner, Jeremiah Haralson, Josiah T. Walls and Charles E. Nash. When White left the House in 1901, no Negro served again until Oscar DePriest was elected from Illinois in 1928. These men did not make an outstanding record in Congress, but then they were not assigned to the most important positions by their party. All in all, they served as effective spokesmen for civil rights causes and remained above the scandals which touched some of their white colleagues.

During the period from the end of Reconstruction to the end of the nineteenth century, Negroes did not fare too well as public office holders, especially when the offices were elective. They were forced out of most public offices in the South, sometimes by terrorist tactics. Except for a brief period during the Populist Movement in North Carolina when numerous Negroes held public offices, most of the southern states named only whites as officials. In the North Negroes had never held large numbers of public offices. John Mercer Langston was probably the first elected Negro official in the United States; he was elected township clerk in Ohio in 1855. Later George Washington Williams served a term in the Ohio legislature and John Jones was twice elected Cook County Commissioner.

However, the bulk of Negro officeholders during this period

were appointed by Republican administrations either to local positions with the Internal Revenue Service or the Post Office Department in the South, or to a number of national posts reserved for Negroes until the Wilson Administration. These positions and some of their better-known incumbents included: Minister to Haiti (Ebenezer Bassett, John Mercer Langston, John E. Thompson, Frederick Douglass, John S. Durham, William F. Powell and Henry W. Furniss); Minister to Liberia (James M. Turner, John H. Smyth, Henry Highland Garnet, Moses A. Hopkins, Charles Taylor, Ezekiel Smith, William McCoy and William H. Heard); Register of the Treasury (Blanche Bruce and James Napier); and Recorder of Deeds for the District of Columbia (Douglass). Many of the people appointed to these posts were prominent Negro Republicans. In addition to Norris Cuney and James Napier, such men as Ebenezer Bassett, John H. Smyth, Charles T. Walker and Richard T. Greener were important Republican leaders of the period. Greener served as a U.S. commercial agent in Russia prior to 1900. Very few appointments of the time were unconnected with race. That is, they were either made to offices reserved for Negroes, or they were to positions with which race was thought to be related (e.g., Archibald Grimke and Henry Furniss were named consuls at Santo Domingo and Bahia, Brazil, respectively).

From the turn of the century until the New Deal there were not large numbers of Negro office-holders. Many of the Negro positions had been eliminated by the Wilson Administration (e.g., (e.g., Minister to Haiti, Register of the Treasury, Recorder of Deeds for the District of Columbia). Furthermore, many Southern Republican parties were going "lily-white" and blacks were losing local patronage jobs in the South as a result. Nor were Negroes being elected to public office. A few diplomatic appointments were still made. Seven blacks held the position of Minister Liberia during the early years of the twentieth century. Five, including James Weldon Johnson, held consular appointments in Africa or Latin America. Perhaps symbolic of the position of the Negro in politics during this era was Booker T. Washington. Although not a public office holder, he was, according to Richard Bardolph, ". . . the most powerful national politician in the South in his day, with an immense influence on the patronage system . . ."[4] In both this period and the previous one Washington was an influential advisor to several presidents. While not in public office, he was not divorced from politics; he attempted to make his wishes felt despite his lack of official position. This, essentially, was the status of the black people as a whole from 1900 to 1936.

Prior to the start of the New Deal there was some political resurgence among blacks. During the years between the outbreak of World War I and the start of the New Deal there had been heavy Negro migration to northern urban centers. In these cities the black residents were concentrated in ghetto areas which, while they had numerous disadvantages, had one political advantage—they made possible the election of Negroes to political office. By 1936 there were black members of at least twelve state legislatures and numerous city councils. A few municipal judgeships were also secured by blacks in this fashion. In Illinois, there was a Negro member of the state legislature as early as 1876, and after 1882 not a team went by in which there was no Negro legislator. In 1914 two Negroes were sent to the state capital, and in 1918, three. In 1924, the number increased to four in the Lower House, and one in the State Senate. By 1929 the Negro delegation numbered five in the House and one in the Senate. In Chicago Oscar DePriest was elected to the city council in 1914. He was replaced by Louis B. Anderson a few years later, and Anderson was joined by Robert R. Jackson in 1918. In Cook County, John Jones had served as Commissioner from 1871-76. No other Negro was elected until 1894 when Theodore Jones won a seat. Edward H. Wright was then elected in 1896 and 1898, Oscar DePriest in 1904 and 1906, and Frank Leland in 1908. No Negro was elected to a court in Chicago until 1924 when Albert B. George won a six-year term; he was not re-elected in 1930. It was also from Chicago (and before the New Deal) that a black man re-entered the United States House of Representatives: Oscar DePriest was elected in 1928 and served three terms.

Much of the resurgence prior to the New Deal was in the traditional partisan context—Republican. The black politicians from Chicago who achieved political office in this period were true to the party of Lincoln. Many of them were identified at one time or another with Mayor Big Bill Thompson of Chicago, who has been called "the Second Lincoln." Chicagoans hostile to Thompson's appointing large numbers of blacks (for the time) to public office in the city called City Hall during his administration "Uncle Tom's Cabin." Negro loyalty to the Republican Party survived the first Roosevelt victory in 1932. Many blacks apparently felt that a Democratic vote would strengthen the hands of southern racists in Congress. Furthermore, the presence of "Cactus Jack" Garner on the ticket did little to attract black voters, particularly because of some doubts about Roosevelt's physical ability to exercise the Presidency.

By 1934 things had changed. In that year Arthur Mitchell, who had until recently been a Republican, became the first black Democrat to sit in Congress by defeating Oscar DePriest. From that time on Negro conversions to the Democratic Party increased rapidly, and from 1936 to the present time, black voters have remained, for the most part, with the Democrats. Roosevelt's actions in appointing numerous Negroes to the executive branch of the federal government helped along the conversion process. Known as the Black Cabinet, these people often served as advisors on Negro affairs in whatever agency they served. The group included, at various times, Robert Vann, William Hastie, Robert Weaver, Eugene K. Jones, Lawrence Oxley, Mary McLeod Bethune, Edgar Brown, Frank Horne, William Trent, Crystal Bird Fauset, Ted Poston, Col. Campbell Johnson, Abram Harris, William Dean, Ralph Bunche, Rayford Logan and Ira Reid. The work of many New Deal agencies also produced beneficial results for black citizens and aided in the conversion process. Among these agencies were the National Youth Administration, the Civilian Conservation Corps, the Federal Public Housing Authority, the Public Works Administration, and the Work Projects Administration. The Social Security Act and the Fair Labor Standards Act also aided Negroes, although many of them worked in occupations exempted from the coverage of these pieces of legislation.

Since the New Deal, Negro participation in politics has proceeded more rapidly than before in the United States. When William L. Dawson replaced Arthur Mitchell in Congress in 1943, he was still the only Negro member. In 1945 he was joined by Adam Clayton Powell, Jr., who had previously served on the New York City Council. In 1954 Charles C. Diggs, previously a state senator, was elected from Detroit. In 1958 Robert N. C.

Nix of Pennsylvania joined the delegation, and in 1963 Augustus F. Hawkins of California. John Conyers, Jr., became the second Negro Congressman from Detroit in 1965. All of these men were re-elected in 1966 and 1968, and three more Negroes won election in 1968 (Louis Stokes of Ohio, William Clay of Missouri, and Mrs. Shirley Chisholm of New York). In 1966 Edward Brooke became the first Negro elected to the United States Senate since the Reconstruction era. Elected as a Republican from Massachusetts, Brooke had previously served as Attorney General of his state. A number of these black Congressmen have accumulated enough seniority to reach positions of power in Congress. Both Dawson and Powell have been committee chairmen. Powell was denied his seat in the Ninetieth Congress, but was re-elected by the voters of his district both in a special election and in the regular election of 1968.

Numerous Negroes have served in the executive branch since the days of the Black Cabinet. William Hastie served as Governor of the Virgin Islands; J. Ernest Wilkins as Assistant Secretary of Labor; E. Frederic Morrow as Administrative Assistant to President Eisenhower, Andrew Hatcher as Associate Press Secretary to President Kennedy, Robert Weaver as Secretary of Housing and Urban Development (the first Negro Cabinet member), and Thurgood Marshall as Solicitor General. Blacks have served regularly in recent years as high officials of such agencies as the Agency for International Development, the Office of Economic Opportunity; the Department of Labor, the Department of Agriculture, the United States Information Agency, the Department of State, and the Department of Health, Education and Welfare. Andrew Felton Brimmer was named to the Federal Reserve Board in 1966; Howard Jenkins, Jr., to the National Labor Relations Board in 1963; Samuel Nabrit to the Atomic Energy Commission in 1966; and Hobart Taylor, Jr., to the Board of Directors of the Export-Import Bank in 1965. Negroes have held numerous ambassadorial appointments in recent years. Among these have been Mercer Cook (Niger, Senegal and Gambia); Patricia Harris (Luxembourg); Clinton E. Knox (Dahomey); John H. Morrow (Guinea); Carl Rowan (Finland); Elliott P. Skinner (Upper Volta); Hugh H. Smythe (Syria); Clifton R. Wharton (Norway); and Franklin H. Williams (Ghana). The traditional Liberian post was manned by ministers until 1946, at which time it was given embassy status. Since then ambassadors to Liberia have included Edward R. Dudley, Jesse L. Locker and Richard Lee Jones.

Negroes have also made headway in the judicial branch in recent years. William H. Hastie served as Judge of the District Court of the Virgin Islands, as did Herman E. Moore. Hastie was appointed Judge of the U.S. Court of Appeals in 1949, and Thurgood Marshall also served on the Court of Appeals prior to becoming Solicitor General. United States District Court judges have included William B. Bryant, Walter A. Gordon, A. Leon Higginbotham, Wade H. McCree, Jr., James B. Parsons, Constance Baker Motley and Spottswood Robinson, III. Irvin Mollison and Scovel Richardson have served on the U. S. Customs Court. The first Negro member of the United States Supreme Court was Thurgood Marshall, appointed by President Johnson in 1967.

Negroes have been appearing in state and local offices in increasing numbers as well. More than 100 black people now occupy seats in state legislatures. (Only Alabama, Arkansas and South Carolina have no black legislators.) Perhaps the best known of these is Julian Bond, who was denied his seat in the Georgia legislature because of his statements on the Vietnam war until the United States Supreme Court ruled in his favor in a suit he brought to force his admission into the lawmaking body. Other state legislators well known for their later achievements include Carl Stokes, Constance Baker Motley and Mrs. Shirley Chisholm.

On the local scene, black faces have also been more in evidence. Hulan Jack was elected borough president of Manhattan in 1953. Constance Baker Motley also held this seat later. Robert C. Henry became the first Negro mayor of a city of significant size when he achieved that office in Springfield, Ohio, on January 3, 1966. Floyd J. McCree became mayor of Flint, Michigan, later that same year. In 1967 Carl Stokes was elected mayor of Cleveland and Richard Hatcher of Gary, Indiana. In the same year Walter E. Washington was appointed chief executive of Washington D.C. by President Johnson. There are many other Negroes in local offices of other kinds as well. It is estimated that approximately 700 blacks hold elective offices of all kinds in the United States today. The vast majority of these are local offices. There are, of course, many Negroes in appointive offices at all levels as well.

No major party has ever run a Negro for nationwide public office. Channing Phillips was placed in nomination for the Democratic presidential nomination in 1968, and Julian Bond for the Democratic vice-presidential candidacy. Several Negroes have run for national office on minor party tickets. James Ford was three times the Communist Party candidate for Vice President. Charlotta Bass held the second spot on the Progressive Party ticket in 1952. In 1964 the Socialist Workers ran Clifton DeBerry for the Presidency; in 1968 the Communist Party ran Mrs. Charlene Mitchell. Two other Negro presidential candidates in 1968 were comedian Dick Gregory and Black Panther leader Eldridge Cleaver. Dr. Martin Luther King, Jr., had been mentioned as a minor party candidate for one or the other of the top offices prior to his assassination.

To one agency Negroes, both from the United States and elsewhere, have made a very important contribution in recent years —the United Nations. Black Africa has of course been represented before the UN by black delegates who have done well in seeking to achieve the objectives of their governments. The United States has also sent a number of Negroes to the UN. Alternate delegates have included Marian Anderson, Robert Brokenburr, Archibald J. Carey, Zelma George, Edith Sampson and Channing Tobias. C. C. Marr and Frank Montero were advisors to the U. S. Mission to the UN. Charles H. Mahoney was the first permanent Negro delegate to the UN, while Franklin Williams served as representative to the Economic and Social Council. James M. Nabrit, Jr., became the highest-ranking Negro to serve the United States before the UN with his appointment as Ambassador in 1965.

Several Negro Americans have served the United Nations itself, rather than acting as United States' representatives to the UN. William H. Dean was Chief of the African Unit, Division of Economic Stability and Development, in 1949-52. The best-known Negro American serving with the UN undoubtedly is Dr. Ralph Bunche. An academician who worked with Gunnar Myrdal on *An American Dilemma,* he served with the Office of Strategic Services during World War II and with the State Department after the war. He then went to the Trusteeship Division of the UN. In 1948 he was chief assistant to the UN mediator of the Palestine crisis. When the mediator was assassinated, he carried on and eventually worked out a cessation of the hostilities between the Arabs and Israel. For this he received the Nobel Prize in 1950. In 1955 he became Undersecretary of the United Nations and in that capacity has been assigned to such difficult crises as the Suez, the Congo, Kashmir, and Cyprus. Like the other Negro American Nobel Prize winner, Dr. Martin Luther King, Jr., Dr. Bunche has displayed remarkable qualities of statesmanship which few can match. Both of these men, along with the others mentioned above and many not mentioned, have had an unmistakable impact on the course of events in the world.

SELECTED BIBLIOGRAPHY

BOOKS

Adam, Thomas R., *Government and Politics in Africa South of the Sahara*, 3d ed. New York: Random House, 1965. A good introduction to the post-colonial scene in Africa.

Bardolph, Richard, *The Negro Vanguard*, New York: Random House Vintage Books, 1959. A study of famous Negro men and women in America; contains a wealth of information on people in all fields of endeavor.

Davidson, Basil, *African Kingdoms*, New York: Time, Incorporated, 1966. A fine introductory work with many excellent illustrations and pictures.

————, *The African Slave Trade*, Boston: Little, Brown, 1961. A fine telling of the story of the trade in men; includes good chapters on the Congo, East Africa, and the Guinea Coast.

————, *A History of West Africa to the Nineteenth Century*, Garden City, New York: Doubleday Anchor Books, 1966. A comprehensive and interesting study of pre-colonial West African history.

DuBois, W. E. B., *Black Folk, Then and Now*, New York: Henry Holt and Company, 1939. Contains some very good chapters on Africa prior to the coming of Europeans.

Franklin, John Hope, *From Slavery to Freedom*, 3d. ed. New

York: Alfred Knopf, 1967. The outstanding book on Negro history, contains excellent chapters on Africa and Latin America, incomparable ones of the United States.

————, *Reconstruction After the Civil War*, Chicago: University of Chicago Press, 1961. Contains an original and challenging analysis of Southern politics under Reconstruction which sets right many misconceptions.

Gosnell, Harold F., *Negro Politicians*, Chicago: University of Chicago Press, 1935. A study of pre-New Deal Negro politics in Chicago; it is unique in its thoroughness and thoughtfulness.

Labouret, Henri, *Africa Before the White Man*, New York: Walker and Company, 1962. Broad coverage with much basic information.

Oliver, Roland, and Fage, J. D., *A Short History of Africa*, 2d ed., Baltimore: Penguin Books: 1966. A fine short work covering the entire period from ancient to recent times.

Ploski, Harry A., and Brown, Roscoe C., Jr., eds., *The Negro Almanac*. New York: Bellwether Publishing Company, 1967.

Ramos, Arthur, *The Negro in Brazil*, Richard Pattee, trans. Washington: Associated Publishers, 1939. A fine study of the Negro in Brazilian culture with good chapters on politics.

Rogers, J. A., *World's Great Men of Color, 3000 B.C. to 1946 A.D.*, 2 Vols. New York: J. A. Rogers, 1947. Contains good information on a number of personages, but should be used cautiously.

Rotberg, Robert I., *A Political History of Tropical Africa*, New York: Harcourt, Brace and World, 1965. A fine text with very detailed information.

Wilson, James Q., *Negro Politics*, New York: Free Press, 1960. A study of Negro political leadership in Chicago, and, to a lesser extent Detroit, Los Angeles, and New York.

Woodson, Carter G., *African Heroes and Heroines*, 2d ed. Washington: Associated Publishers, 1944. Intended for public school use, it nevertheless contains much information, especially on nineteenth century Southwest African figures.

ARTICLES

Abramowitz, Jack, "The Negro in the Populist Movement,"

Journal of Negro History, XXXVIII, 1953, 257-289. Deals with the impact of the Populist Movement on Negro political participation in the South late in the Nineteenth Century.

Bunche, Ralph J., "The Negro in the Political Life of the United States," *Journal of Negro Education*, X, 1941, 567-584. A review of Negro political participation in the United States between the end of Reconstruction and the beginning of World War II; emphasizes the situation in the South.

Gosnell, Harold F., "The Negro Vote in Northern Cities," *National Municipal Review*, XXX, 1941, 264-267, 278. Analyzes the shift of Negro votes from the G.O.P. to the Democratic Party in the New Deal era.

Houston, G. David, "A Negro Senator," *Journal of Negro History*, VII, 1922, 243-256. A study of Senator Blanche K. Bruce's term in the United States Senate.

Lloyd, P. C., "The Political Development of West African Kingdoms," *Journal of African History*, IX, 1968, 319-329. A discussion of the Guinea Coast states in the Nineteenth Century.

Padgett, James A., "Diplomats to Haiti and Their Diplomacy," *Journal of Negro History*, XXV, 1940, 265-330. Deals with the Negroes who served the United States in the diplomatic service to Haiti.

————, "Ministers to Liberia and Their Diplomacy," *Journal of Negro History*, XXII, 1937, 50-92. A study of Negro diplomatic service in Liberia.

Porter, Dorothy B., "The Negro in the Brazilian Abolition Movement." *Journal of Negro History*, XXXVI, 1952, 54-80. Story of the role of the Negro in the fight against slavery in Brazil.

Ramos, Arthur, "The Negro in Brazil," *Journal of Negro Education*, X, 1941, 515-523. Discusses ethnic origins of Brazilian Negroes and their integration into Brazilian society.

Reid, Ira DeA., "The Negro in the British West Indies," *Journal of Negro Education*, X, 1941, 524-535. Describes the British West Indies during the colonial period and the emergence of a nationalist movement there.

Robinson, George F., Jr., "The Negro in Politics in Chicago," *Journal of Negro History*, XVII, 1932, 180-229. A study of Negro office-holders in Chicago.

Skinner, E. P., "The Mossi and Traditional Sudanese History,"

Journal of Negro History, XLIII, 1958, 121-131. A brief history of the Mossi with emphasis on government and politics.

Taylor, Alrutheus A., "Negro Congressmen a Generation After," *Journal of Negro History*, VII, 1922, 127-171. A very valuable article on the twenty-two black members of Congress who served between 1871 and 1901; contains biographical material and an evaluation of these men as legislators.

Williams, Eric, "Trinidad and Tobago; International Perspectives," *Freedomways*, IV, 1964, 331-340. The Prime Minister of Trinidad and Tobago speaks about his country.

Wood, Forrest G., "On Revising Reconstruction History: Negro Suffrage, White Disfranchisement, and Common Sense," *Journal of Negro History*, LI, 1966, 98-113. Challenges the notion that "Carpetbag" governments were made possible by mass disfranchisement of whites and shows that Negroes never "ruled" any state during Reconstruction.

NOTES

1. W. E. B. DuBois, *Black Folk, Then and Now*, New York: Henry Holt and Company, 1939, p. 1.

2. John Hope Franklin, *From Slavery to Freedom*, 3d ed. New York: Alfred A. Knopf, 1967, p. 350.

3. Harry Johnston, *The Negro in the New World*, London: Methuen, 1910, p. 109.

4. Richard Bardolph, *The Negro Vanguard*, New York: Random House Vintage Books, 1959, p. 113.

DARYL R. FAIR is Associate Professor of Political Science and Assistant to the President at Jersey City State College, Jersey City, New Jersey. Previously he was on the faculty of Rider College, Trenton, New Jersey, for five years. He has also been a visiting faculty member at Lehigh University, Bethlehem, Pa. He holds the degree of B.S. in Education from Millersville State College, Millersville, Pa., and the M.A. and Ph.D. from the University of Pennsylvania. His area of specialization is the contemporary political system of the United States. He is the author of several articles, primarily on political parties and constitutional law, which have appeared in such journals as the *Southwestern Social Science Quarterly* and the *Wisconsin Law Review*.

THE BLACK LATIN AMERICAN IMPACT
ON WESTERN CULTURE

Franck Bayard

West Virginia Wesleyan College

(*Buckhannon, W. Va.*)

Over its almost five centuries of immigration, miscegenation, acculturation and assimilation, Latin America has evolved as a unique continent of pluralistic ethnicity and cultural diversity. Multiracialism and multiculturalism differentiate its modern national societies and the social classes within each of its countries.

From the first slave cargo which disembarked in Hispaniola in 1502 to the end of the slave traffic by mid-nineteenth century, at least fifteen million uprooted Africans have been transplanted into the Latin American colonial settlements. They, their hybrids, and their descendants, are largely accountable for Latin America's mosaic of races and cultures. Although imperceptible in some areas, the Negro's presence has touched all the Latin American countries, each of them having received, at one time or another of the slave trade period, its small or large contingent of African slaves. However, the Negro's preferred home and area of greatest influence has been and remains centered in Northern Brazil and the Caribbean region, which developed a plantation economic system and a distinctive Creole culture of Negro-Caucasian derivation.

Initially debased and humiliated in the New World's slavocracies, the Latin American Negro took advantage of his strong biology, of some non-material aspects of his ancestral cultures, and of his rich artistic and musical heritage to contribute biologically, economically, socially, culturally and artistically to changing Latin America's life patterns and ideals. He also pervaded his new continent with a passion for liberty, and heroically fought, alone or with other racial groups, for its political transformation. Colonial emancipation or freedom in sovereign states came for most in the first half of the nineteenth century. Abolition was won in the remaining countries in the second half of the same century, although several Caribbean islands achieved independence only in the 1960's, and even today a few remain with colonial status, however loose it is.

Generally, freedom or citizenship did not mean the termination of the Negro's troubles. They failed to suppress the social inequities in societies which remained colonial or inherited the colonial and plantation complex, and were not freed from the racist views of the past. The Negro elites, mostly light-skinned and a black minority, gained a lot. But the dark ones remained, usually alone, at the bottom of the social strata, doomed to misery, illiteracy, superstitions and other associated evils. The socio-economic and educational disadvantages left in the slavery heritage had strong and persistent effects on their life and selves. Even today, the Negro's growth continues to be handicapped by enormous obstacles.

With new methods, and in a generally more friendly world, the black Latin American's struggle continues. It now tends to attain world-wide proportions with the Negritude, which originated in the Caribbean area, and other contemporary Negro theories, driving at a global redemption of the Negro race. In this instance, as in his other great achievements, the black Latin American is showing his dynamism and creativeness. Throughout his Western Hemisphere's existence, he has been remarkably effective, not only as a culture modifier and a political factor within his own national society, but also as a partner in the continent's destiny and as a contributor to world history and culture.

This paper, limited to the space of an article, cannot hope to unfold all the numerous and various achievements of the Negro groups and distinguished Negro sons of Latin America. Much will probably remain unsaid, particularly since those worthy actions extend throughout the long Negro presence in the region and are distributed over more than thirty particularized national areas. It can only be hoped that the most original and far-reaching contributions will be revealed.

The Deculturation Antecedent

Associated to the slavery enterprise was a deculturation scheme which aimed at stripping the Negro slaves of their traditional cultures and human personality. The methods included their embarkment from the African ports without the material artifacts of their ancestral cultures, dispersion at destination of members of the same kinship affiliation, brutalizing work schedules and conditions, bodily punishments, and denial of any formal education, except for a token christening not followed by true Christianization in most of the cases.

But this plan failed because of its false assumptions. Inspired by racist traditions in Europe's cultures, originating perhaps from the Noah's curse story, it rested on an erroneous belief in the Negro's inborn and insuperable inferiority, based itself on the preconceived premise that Negroes are without history, skills or arts, and are incapable of developing any. The truth is that behind a great number of Latin America's Negro slaves, there was a long cultural history in the course of which magnificent empires, influenced by the Islamic penetration, were built in Ghana, Mali, Songhay, Dahomey, Benin and Timbuktu. Among the others who came from less cultured societies, many had acquired in their African existence skills in agriculture, cattle-raising, wood sculpture and iron-making. All had languages and traditions. All used to pray, sing and dance to the dazzling rhythms of their thrilling African beats. These human attributes resisted the ways that attempted to break up their human nexus.

Negro's Participation in the Colonial Bio-Socio-Cultural Dynamics

The Negroes in Latin America were not long in asserting their human nature. Soon they won a *de facto* recognition of it from the other races encountered in the new environment. The biological urge was stronger than certain cultural prohibitions. From their entry onwards, they blended their genes and cultures with those of the other racial stocks. Mixing their blackness with the whiteness of the Caucasian colonialists, they produced the Mulattoes. With the redness of the equally enslaved aboriginal Amerindians, they generated the Zambos, while their biological cross with the Mestizos (white-Indian offsprings) gave birth to another variation. Widespread and never-ending miscegenation of the Negroes with all these racial types has resulted in Latin America's gamut of skin color shades, for which an abundant and varying taxonomy exists in the countries.

As an effect of white-Negro biological exchanges, the initially tight bilateral organization of the slavocratic societies was gradually undermined.[1] They created an intermediate free stratum for the usually born-free Mulattoes and their often-freed black mothers. The free Negro group was subject to some politico-legal restrictions. Yet, its members had large, although not total, access to the white culture. Doors to a number of economic, social and educational pursuits were open to them. For many, acculturation into the European life patterns was almost complete.

At the same time, the Negro slaves were impressing the environment with their extraordinary vitality and genial disposition. In each land, and perhaps under the worst conditions ever experienced by any other human group, they were extracting the minerals, raising the cattle, tilling the soil, serving the master's households, and doing artisan works. However, with their sense of fatality, unfathomable gaiety, and love of life, they were filling the air with the intensely rhythmic music of their religions and dances.

Exceptional physical proficiency demonstrated at work brought to many Negro slaves manumission and entry into the free group, with the much greater acculturative opportunities involved. Elements of class stratification, based on personal merits, were thus being slowly added to the prevalent racial caste stratification system.

Even among the non-manumitted Negroes, social distinctions existed. The social leveler of slavery had erased their tribal identity and their differential African statuses, but not the personality variations among them. As in any human grouping, some were skillful, talented, hard-working and teachable. Many were good mannered, tractable and light-hearted, and a few had leadership qualities. But, others had such attributes at a much lower degree, or showed opposite character traits. In the first group, the slaveholders picked up the urban artisan helpers, the domestic servants of the *casa-grande*[2] (the big house), the semi-skilled workers needed for the mining or processing industries, and the overseers of field slaves. The latter were generally included in the second and larger group. Higher occupational statuses were usually associated with greater acculturative opportunities. The more acculturated slaves were those likely to receive manumission or to be among the "Maroons of the alphabet"[3] who occasionally and secretly acquired reading and writing skills from some humanitarian priests or a few compassionate masters.

All those developments related to miscegenation, acculturation, and Negro adaptability, were slowly but steadily introducing some measure of mobility in the colonial societies. They were also providing the Negro groups increased opportunities to infiltrate the white culture.

There are two major reasons for the extraordinary adaptiveness demonstrated by the New World Negroes in the course of their long and infamous plight. Firstly, they constituted a biological elite.[4] This, rather than any congenital physical superiority, explains the Negro slaves' greater strength and greater productivity compared to the Indian slaves, whose price was five times less than theirs. The selective standards applied by their buyers in the African slave markets, and their 20% kill rate during the painful journey to America, guaranteed their biological fitness.

Secondly, having been deprived of their traditional life patterns related to economic life, government, property, education or marriage, which could not outcrop in the slavery set-up,[5] the slaves resolutely clung to their non-material Africanisms. In their souls, they had brought Africa's animistic beliefs, cosmic metaphysics and occult magics; and in their selves, a love of life and a sense of dignity, of equanimity, and of destiny. They had also transported to America their onomatopoeic languages, unwritten literature, aesthetic forms, and the complex cadence of Africa's sensuous songs and dances. From this ancestral heritage they drew the supernatural comfort and stoic patience needed for survival, as well as a Zionist-like hope of ultimate return to Mother Africa. Moreover, they found in it charms to withstand humiliations and diseases, alienative escapes, and recreational diversions.

However, none of those major African retentions continued unaltered. To forge their cultural cohesion, the tribally different slaves created their own cultural amalgams.

In each colonial area, they homogenized their different cults and languages on the basis of those of the numerically dominant tribal group. The unified religions also borrowed from the Christianism of the masters some symbols, rituals and dogmas, such as the sign of the Cross, part of the Roman liturgy and litanies, a few Biblical parables and concepts, and the names and personalities of many Catholic saints to whom were identified their African gods. A few elements were also incorporated from the equally animistic religions of the aborigines. In such syncretized forms, the Yoruba-Bantu religions of Sudan, Ghana, Guinea and Angola became the *macumba* and *candomble* of Brazil, the *lucumi* of Cuba, and the *shango* of Trinidad, Tobago. The Fanti-Ashanti sects of the Gold Coast were maintained in almost pure form by Surinam's "Bush Negroes," but were modified into the *cumina* of Jamaica and other islands. The Ewe-Arada cults of Dahomey, Nigeria, and the Congo Basin were transformed into the *Rada* and *Petro* rites of Haiti's *vodun*.

Similarly, to improve the inter-slave and master-slave communication system, they formed linguistic blends, mingling the European language with African terms, syntactic forms and phonetic sounds. Departures from the metropolitan languages varied in extent from one instance to another and from one area to another. Relatively small in the Spanish-speaking and English-speaking areas, they were a little more pronounced in Brazil where the Portuguese pronunciation was much truncated and agglutinated. Even wider differences existed between the Creole patois and the French from which it derived three-fourths of its vocabulary, while the syntax was prevalently West African. More than any such vernacular, the Creole patois has shown its capacity to endure as a separate linguistic form. It remains today the unique language of the illiterate masses in Haiti, Guadeloupe and Martinique, where it is also spoken about half of the time by the French-speaking elites. It is still partly used in Trinidad, St. Lucia, and other British-cultured islands once occupied by France. Only recently has it been disappearing from Louisiana in the United States, after about two centuries of decolonization from the French.

The slavery milieu also modified certain traits of the Negro's traditional character. His original equanimity, good-natured character and fatalistic mood often gave way to volatility, restiveness and aggressiveness. He became distrustful, fierce and unpredictable, alternating deceitful postures of extreme submission with restive and fierce attitudes. In challenging their degradation and oppression, some used all defensive means, including dissimulation, lie and disguise.[6] To the violence of slavery, they opposed in their revolts equal if not greater violence. Always present was the never-abandoned hope for liberty and the removal of the socio-cultural barriers against the free Negroes.

Of all the traditional heritage, the African artistic background was the part that has been least withered by slavery. Instead, it has substantially pervaded the other racial groups. Whites and Mestizos were little impressed by the African-derived religions and used selectively the distorted linguistic forms of the Negroes. On the psychological front, the cross-cultural transferences of the Negroes seem to have been more important. The Negro's passion for freedom and his stubbornness in fighting for it have probably influenced Mestizos and White Creoles in their secession and independence struggles in Spanish America. But the influence of the Latin American Negro has been and is evident and substantial in the arts. His artistic and musical talents soon became widely recognized in all the colonial areas. None of the races could resist the enchantment and contagion of the simple and short melodic line, repeated phrases, spontaneity of emotion, power and poetry of African music. Many white and Mestizo composers, in both their social dance and higher music, have taken inspiration from the Negro's exotic melodies and borrowed from his genius for artistic expression.

Latin America's Racial and Cultural Dichotomy

African-derived populations and traditions have influenced most Latin American countries. But they tended to cluster in Northern Brazil, the Caribbean islands, and several coastal strips of mid-America. This resulted from the economic plantation system that prospered in the geographical region where the climatic

293

conditions fitted the cultivation of sugar, cotton, indigo, tobacco, coffee and other tropical crops, for which demands were rising in the then mercantilistic and economically booming Europe. The abundant slave force, required by the large-scale and labor-intensive agricultural techniques applied in the plantation zone, was supplied solely by massive Negro importation as early as 1600. Unable to bear the overwork, rigid work discipline, the other exigencies of plantation slavery, the Amerindian race had vanished by that time from the plantation region. Its genes have since been diluted into those of the whites and Negroids. At the same time, cold winters and particularly intensive miscegenation were causing the decrease of Negro populations in the small-scale farming areas of the mid-American highlands and all southern South America. In the southernmost countries, they have long been completely absorbed by the other races.

As a result of these socio-cultural changes brought about by the interacting forces of geography, biology, ecology and culture (in both its economico-technological and its ideological aspects), Latin America has been racially and culturally dichotomized. In the "greater Caribbean" plantation area blossomed a Creole race and culture of white-Negro derivation, which is quite distinct from the Mestizo race and culture of white Amerindian origin that grew in the rest of Latin America.

Appendices I and II give an approximate idea of Latin America's color mosaic, as well as a delineation of its two distinctive areas in relation to race and culture, as they appeared in the 1960's. The figures are only conjectural, because modern Latin American nations do not any more count their populations by racial types in their censuses, and tend in their unofficial reports to "overwhiten" their populations. This is why the statistics recorded tend to underestimate rather than overestimate the Negro percentages. Based upon them, in the Creole area, Negroes and their derived populations account for nearly one-fourth of Latin America's total population, now estimated at nearly two hundred million. They number forty-eight million, of which roughly thirty-four million live in Brazil alone.

Race Relations History and Variations Among Creole Countries

By the sheer arithmetical law of large numbers, it is in the

Creole countries that the Negro's role as co-maker of society, culture and history has been more pronounced and his contributions more abundant. Throughout the Creole area, the economic performance, the political structure, the psychological temper, the artistic production, the recreational life, and the ideological ethos in general, bring persuasive testimony of the heavy Negro presence. The common Creole culture has been structured by the similar historical patterns of the nations, conquest, colonization, slavery, racial and cultural intermixture, abolition and independence struggle, certain cultural continuities, and persistence of a neo-Colonial social structure in spite of decolonization and politico-cultural changes.[7]

However, looking at today's Creole countries, one can hardly consider them as a homogeneous unit. Variance can be observed in their population density and growth, ethnic and color distribution, resource availabilities, land-population ratio, per capita income and its growth rate, economic organization from very commercialized to almost subsistence agriculture, industrialization level, religion, degree of racial prejudice, amount of social mobility and educational opportunities for the dark-skinned Negro masses, political status and rule (a few remain colonies, and the free-state rulers range from very democratic to police-state dictators).

These variations are rooted in their differing slavery history and mainly came out of their past metropolitan affiliation. Although sharing the same white culture, the four major colonial powers and slaveholders differed as to the intensity of their racial prejudice, their treatment of the slaves, attitude toward people of mixed genes, and restrictions against free Negroes. They also varied with regard to the extent of their greed for quick and large monetary profits, their technological abilities, and the sharpness of the mercantilistic taxation pressure exerted by the metropolis and always passed on to the slave labor force. In general, the Iberians showed more racial permissiveness, the French less, and the English the least. They also had lower technical skills, and lesser success in their plantation agriculture, compared to the two other nationalities; and once their gold greed had almost exhausted Latin America's rich gold mines in less than one century of exploitation, Spaniards and Portugese tended to moderate their mercantilistic appetite.

Modern students of race relations and cultural variations in Latin America disagree on the causes of such differentials.[8] For the ideologico-institutional school of Freyre, Ramos, Tannenbaum and Elkins, differences in the slave nations' religion and pre-New World experience with the Negro (the Iberians were Moorish ruled from 711 to 1030) were the key factors that always prevailed over counter-tendencies in the material setting. For the ecologico-economic school of Frazier, Williams, Harris and Wagley, predominance rather goes to the material factors related to divergences in the colonialists' mercantilist goals, their industrialism and ecological adaptiveness, the demographic ratio of the races in the colonies, and the financial pressures of the metropolitan centers on the plantation economies which were geared to world markets.

Each of these theories sheds light on many cases, but not all the cases. For example, the first school cannot explain why the French's extreme brutality in eighteenth-century St. Domingue (Haiti) contrasted to the relative benevolence of master-slave relations in British-ruled Trinidad at the same period,[9] and even to seventeenth-century St. Domingue; nor why the usually mild Spanish treatment of the Negro worsened in Cuba during the nineteenth century compared to what it was in the eighteenth. It is historically verified that racial prejudice and discrimination strengthened whenever and wherever the large-scale plantation system was instituted, and was even stronger when it became particularly successful. It has been so all along its expansion path from Northern Brazil, where plantations came into existence by the end of the sixteenth century, but did not assume very large size, to Barbados, the Leewards and the Virgins in early seventeenth century, then to Jamaica, Martinique and St. Domingue, where it attained its maturity in the eighteenth century, thence to Trinidad, Puerto-Rico, Santo Domingo and Cuba, where it reached its peak in the nineteenth century. In all the lands it pressured for the rising financial needs of Europe's Commercial Revolution or later Industrial Revolution, it brought "a powerful instrument of differential cultural growth,"[10] creating a severely handicapped population segment, darker in color than the rest of the people.[11] Nevertheless, technological-economic reasons alone are not enough, because the cultural history aspects, stressed by the ideological school, often tempered the rigors of the plantocracies. The racial permissiveness and promiscuity of the Portuguese, and the full citizen rights they granted to free Brazilian Negroes, strikingly contrasted with the racial intolerance, constraints and hypo-descent rule[12] of the English. Likewise, even at the height of Cuba's plantation system, the Spanish never approached the French violence and repressiveness in eighteenth-century Haiti and Martinique.

Therefore, the Balanced-Approach school of Bastide, Finley, Mintz and Rubin sheds better light on these questions. It combines and reconciles the two former schools in concluding that both sets of factors—the colonizer's institutional history and his technology—have interactingly produced the Caribbean Creole diversity. The solution, in Bastide's words, lies at the "intersection of traditions and economic milieu,"[13] and in Mintz' equivalent language, at the "intersection of ideology and economics."[14]

Slavery History, Negro Progression and Negro Contributions

A close correlation exists between colonial race relations history, the circumstances that attended Negro emancipation and progression, and the quality and orientation of his achievements and contributions. The same major factors of ideology and economics interacted, jointly or conflictingly depending on the time and the place, to determine the temper of the Negro, the form of his protest against oppression, the amount of violence put into it, the manner and timing of his emancipation or independence struggle, and the militancy or lack of it in his non-political achievements, literary or artistic.

Rare, if any, were the Latin American Negroes who accommodated themselves to their slavery status or their inferiority in freedom. But the expression of their will for liberty varied. The most fierce, refractory, or impatient, and those who were most mistreated or neglected by the white culture, said "no" to acculturation and assimilation, and preferred to run away from the plantations and to isolate themselves individually or collectively, in Latin America's *selvas*, bush, mountains, and other open spaces. They were the *cimarrones* of Spanish America, the *maroons* of British America, *les marrons* of French America, and those who formed their *quilombos* in Portuguese America. Large-scale Negro revolts occurred everywhere in Latin America. But their frequency and violence coincided with the intensity of racial and work rigors in the plantations. The tradition started as early as 1520, when in a show of interracial solidarity of the two victimized races, Negro and Amerindian maroons in Hispaniola (Haiti and the Dominican Republic) fought together under the leadership of the young but fierce Cacique Henri and challenged the Spanish power for thirteen years. Unsuccessful Negro uprisings occurred in Colombia in 1529 and 1550, in Panama in 1531, in Cuba in 1533, in Venezuela in 1550 and 1773, in St. Domingue (Haiti) in 1758 and 1784, in Jamaica in 1722, in British Guyana in 1749 and 1763. The dates and frequency coincide with either the first shocks of slavery, or the strengthening of the plantation structure. Three assumed particular significance for their organization, prenationalistic inspiration, or long duration. In Brazil in 1627, deserting slaves founded their independent and well-organized "Republic of Palmares" and held it for seventy years.[15] In Surinam, the "Bush Negroes" escaped from the plantations in the seventeenth century and formed free societies in which they lived in almost complete isolation until the 1950's. The most violent of all was the general slave uprising of 1791 in St. Domingue; it was also the most successful, as it made in 1793 of Haiti the first colonial area to achieve emancipation and culminated in the country's early independence in 1804.

The long revolt tradition nourished and fortified the rebellion spirit of the Negroes and their hopes to get out of bonds and subordination. More significantly perhaps, this propensity to resistance and will to live independently may have convinced the socially superior Mestizos, against whom certain restrictions nevertheless existed, and even many white Creoles who resented the metropolitan arrogance and tariff abuses, that an alternative to colonial life may be found. More assuredly, their hit-and-run tactics against the plantation centers initiated the guerrilla and scorched-earth tactics that the Latin American independence wars utilized and that the modern world thinks it has invented.

However, the great majority of Negroes decided to quiet down their rebellious dispositions to get the most they could from the superior white culture and to postpone their explosion until appropriate circumstances favored it. This majority comprised those who were more tractable, more patient, less frequently humiliated, and those to whom the doors to acculturation and assimilation were wider open, such as the miscegenated, the freemen, the household and other better-placed slaves.

While waiting, they cleverly took advantage of any socio-economic opportunities granted to them to improve their own position or to help the less fortunate ones. In some areas, the free Negro class owned up to one-fourth of the colonial property, including slaves; many acquired substantial education; and a few graduated in the metropolitan universities. Some slaves working on a partial wage basis made enough money to buy their manumission, other slaves clandestinely got some rudimentary education. More generally and under their cosmic impulse inherited from Africa, many freedmen and slaves used their relatively privileged status to assist those seeking manumission or to give refuge to the hiding or fleeing slaves. The rigidities of the plantation system were progressively increasing racial awareness and racial cohesion among the Negroes, creating a sort of "blood block"[16] that would eventually be used to break down the slavery enterprise.

The Negroes as Carriers of White Culture

Also in the meantime, the Negroes were asserting themselves as agents of the civilization imposed upon them or their ascendants, but in which they wanted to exercise sharing rights. At the onset of their New World existence, they started adding their part in the making of Latin America's "crucible of civilizations," whatever the ultimate consequences for them or for the continent.

One or two Negro slaves, in slavery in Spain, probably accompanied Columbus in his first trip in 1492. But more certain is the fact that Latin American Negroes did participate in the exploration and conquest of the continent.[17] Thirty were with Balboa, discovering the Pacific Ocean in 1513, and several with Cortes in his 1519-1521 conquest of Mexico, one of them planting the first wheat crop of the new continent. Many participated in the shipwrecked expedition of Narvaez along the Texas Coast in 1527, and some in the French conquest of the Mississippi River by Jolliet, Marquette and La Salle in 1673. In the first half of the sixteenth century, the Spanish often assigned Negro freedmen or slaves as *calpisques* (overseers) of the Indian *encomien-das* (villages for Indians in serfdom).[18] Speaking of the civiliz-ing effects of fugitive slaves upon the Indians, Freyre affirms "all Negroes interned in the forests and the backlands played a use-ful part as bringers of civilization,"[19] and he adds that in Bra-zil's colonization, the Negro was "an active, creative, and one must add, a noble element."

The Negro's capacity for military bravery and leadership, demonstrated in their slave revolts, also served the colonial powers in the defense of their colonies against intruding Euro-peans. One of the heroes of the mid-seventeenth-century Portu-guese war against the Dutch invaders was a Brazilian Negro, Henrique Dias. For his brilliancy and leadership, he was en-nobled and accepted in the Order of Christ. Many Negroes fought bravely in the Spanish-Portuguese border wars along the Brazilian frontiers with Uruguay and Argentina during the sev-enteenth century. The Mulatto and Negro leaders who dis-tinguished themselves in the Haitian revolutionary war were career officers in the French army who bravely fought the Eng-lish and Spanish intruders.

The Negro was also "the white man's greater and most plastic collaborator in the task of agrarian civilization."[20] Although more anonymous, their economic contributions to Latin America were as substantial as their artistic contributions. The Negro slaves were the sinews of the plantation economy, and with the free Ne-groes, provided most of the services and the artisan skills. By their physical resistance, their skills imported from Africa, and their adaptability to the master's technology, they gave vitality and success to the plantations. Besides, iron-making and dia-mond and gold-searching in Brazil and Colombia largely de-pended on the Negro. Thanks to them, Latin America remained for centuries the almost imaginary continent yielding its rich-ness to the small band of *conquistadores* and to the rising bour-geois class of Europe.

Furthermore, in Brazil, they were builders of towns, church prelates, elementary teachers of white boys, and the musicians of the colonial era. A woman Negro, Jacintha de Siqueira found-ed the town Villa Nova do Principe in 1714, after discovering a rich gold deposit. Dom Silvero Gomes Pimenta, a Mulatto, was an Archbishop in Colonial times. Several were instructors of

300

young Portuguese. The altar boys in the churches were Negro lads, a number of plantation chapels had Negro choruses, and bands of Negro musicians and circus acrobats performed for the pleasure of the whites.[21] Everywhere, the whites were fascinated by the Negro's rhythm, his excitements, his sheer joy in the movements of his body. Negro themes were translated into Spanish, Portuguese, French and English melodies. The Afro-American folk music was born, and it was played throughout the territory of the Creole culture complex by white and Negro bands alike, to the accompaniment of African derived instruments such as drums, tumbas, marimbulas and marimbas.[22] More sophisticated works in literary and artistic fields, done by Negroes during colonial times, are later listed.

The Creole Negro was getting increasingly Latin-Americanized, and losing more and more, on all planes, his pure Africanism. As Frazier has maintained, against Herskovits' opinion,[23] in the Negro's modern behavior and accomplishments the marks and scars left by the slavery heritage are more apparent than the original African inheritances. With a sense of belonging to his new habitat, acquired through three centuries of residence and participation, of sweat, blood, and laughs, he was, by the end of the eighteenth century, about ready to claim his ownership rights and to ask for justice and liberty in Latin America.

THE BLACK MAN'S CONTRIBUTIONS TO
LATIN AMERICA'S DESLAVERIZATION AND DECOLONIZATION,
TO CONTINENTAL AND UNIVERSAL NEGRO SOLIDARITY
AND TO THE WESTERN WORLD'S CULTURE AND POWER STRUCTURE

As Freedom Fighters and Political Engineers in Latin America

Negro emancipation and endowment with full politico-legal rights in Latin America came as a backlash of the tremendous changes that occurred in both the technology and ideology of Western Culture during the second half of the eighteenth century. The associated political events that took place in Europe and North America by the end of the century have also been influential. Technological breakthrough, institutionalization of capitalism, diffusion of the trilogy of liberty, equality, and fra-

301

ternity, coined by English philosophers and French Encyclope-
dists, the 1776 American War of Independence, the 1789 French
Revolution, the emergence of a number of abolition campaigners
in England and France, and finally, rivalries and wars among
Europe's colonial powers, were the interacting dynamisms which
found repercussions throughout Latin America.

However, they attended, but did not directly cause either
the breakdown of slavery or the blooming of sovereign states
in the half-continent. For that, considerable struggle was necessary, in which the Negro resolutely and commendably put all
his resources. His major assets were his biological strength, his
cultural apparatus as it developed from an acculturation conducted on his own terms, his sense of pride and dignity as it
was modified by Colonial plantation slavery, the Negro cohesion
that resulted from his detribalization and cultural history in the
New World, and his extraordinary military bravery and sense
of leadership, as was already proved both in his revolts and his
past cooperation in Colonial defense. Whether the local conditions required military action or political campaigning, whether
the fight was conducted by Negroes alone or jointly with the
other racial entities, and regardless of the area's amount of racial
stratification and prejudice, the Negro was always the decisive
factor for final victory. It is increasingly recognized today that in
all parts of Latin America he has been the major artisan of his
liberation and a valuable element in Latin America's nation
founding process.

It is in Haiti that he struck his first victorious blows, when
Napoleon attempted to rob the Haitian Negro of the emancipation he won in 1793. Mulattoes and blacks, putting aside the
rivalries that the enslavers stirred up between the two groups,
united in arms and routed the Napoleonic armies sent to destroy
their revolution. They fought fiercely, professionally and heroically to break up the injustices of the greatest hell on earth
for the Negro that eighteenth century St. Domingue was.[24] Under
the leadership of dozens of outstanding Negro strategists, they
matched or superseded the skills and ferocity of the French
troops. Among their military leaders, four were exceptional by
their mastery of organized warfare and their sense of vision.
The greatest of all was "the Precursor," Toussaint L'Ouverture,

who dared to militarily antagonize and diplomatically outwit the master of the world at that period. Napoleon Bonaparte. A slave during his first forty years, a plantation veterinarian and coachman, a maroon of the alphabet, Toussaint had "unusual qualities of the art of command, of leadership, political sagacity and astuteness."[25] This permitted him to exercise for ten years supreme power in the colony. Auguste Comte put him and Washington among the greatest men who ever lived, and Wendell Phillips put him above Cromwell, Washington and Napoleon. Speaking of Toussaint, Lamartine, in his lyrical accent, said, "This extraordinary man was more than a nation." Among other famous world authors who extolled him were Chateaubriand, Hugo, Wordsworth and Cesaire. Still, an exiled and enchained Toussaint died in a French jail nine months before Haiti's independence in 1804. His task was completed by three other titans.

Another ex-slave, less educated but a more eminent strategist than Toussaint, General Dessalines, became the prominent avenger. He led the band of slaves and quasi free men to final triumph and gave them a nation, at least five years before any other Latin American country attained sovereign existence. Also born in slavery, General Christophe was indomitable in combat and showed brilliance and aggressiveness in his tactical maneuvers. Later he built a glittering kingdom, at the top of which he erected his Citadel, a fascinating piece of architecture designed to signify his defiance of the enslaver's world. But in his broad perspective, he showed concern not only for defense, but also for economic and educational development that he made efforts to promote after the ravages of the independence war. Cesaire recently eulogized Christophe in an excellent drama. Last but not least comes the skilled artillery gunner and able Mulatto commander, General Petion. Well educated and a man of great vision, Petion proved, in the republic he instituted, that a substantial amount of democracy may fit even an emerging nation. His systematic land distribution program anticipated by more than a century the agrarian reform schemes of modern development economists. Besides, he believed in and practiced Panamericanism before the word itself was invented.

Latin American Negroes were less successful in other Creole

areas, where their longing for liberty and recurrent revolts pressured for but did not immediately bring emancipation. The blacks of Guadeloupe and Martinique had been emancipated by a law passed in 1795 under the insistence of the liberals at the French Convention. But they were put back into slavery by an expedition sent by Bonaparte, despite their heroic defense; in the end many preferred suicide to submission. Nevertheless, their constant thrust, in addition to the assistance given in France by abolitionists such as Victor Schoelcher, brought emancipation to slaves of all French colonies in 1848. Since 1946, the two islands have had the status of French departments.

In the British West Indies, the story was about the same. Frequent revolts helped to convince England of the truth and pracicality of what Adam Smith's "new economics" was theorizing since 1776: that in the new capitalistic structure, free labor is more productive than forced labor, serfdom or slavery.[26] The English Parliament voted in 1834 an abolition law which took effect in 1839. Once emancipation was achieved the thrust was toward independence. A dreadful revolution in Jamaica in 1865 failed. For it, as for Trinidad and Tobago, Guyana and Barbados, independence came only in the 1960's.

In Brazil, the methods and timing for emancipation differed widely from the usual Creole patterns. Brazil's racial permissiveness and equal liberties for all free people permitted dark and light-skinned free blacks to exercise their anti-slavery pressure through peaceful means. They did it through ardent campaigning, journalistic propaganda and parliamentary action. Moreover, it was done with the active and ardent cooperation of white and Mestizo abolitionists, the most conspicuous of whom were the positivists Ruy Barbosa (1843-1923), Sylvio Romero (1851-1914) and Joaquim Nabuco (1849-1910), who opposed slavery because of its incompatibility with scientific progress and human well-being. But in the political arena, the Negroes of Brazil were as effective as the Brazilian white Creoles and as impassioned as their counterparts in arms in the other Creole areas. Many distinguished themselves in this struggle patiently fought over five long decades with pen and articles rather than weapons. Among the most outstanding that can be listed in this article are the dark-skinned liberal journalist and leading politician, Evaristo da Veiga, whose articles in his newspaper "Auroro Fluminense" were so strong that he is given great credit in the 1831 downfall of the corrupt and despotic Emperor, Pedro I; the two romantic Mulatto poets, Goncalvez Dias and Castro Alvez, who devoted much of their verse to denouncing slavery; and those who carried on the abolition propaganda—the Bahian Mulatto mathematician, Dr. Francesco Alvarez dos Santos, the freed Negro and leading scientist-engineer in the Brazilian Empire, Andre Reboucas, the born-slave Mulatto and historian journalist, Luis Gama, and above all the champion of the 1888 emancipation, the Mulatto editor Jose de Patrocinio. The Brazilian Negro was also instrumental in the establishment of the Republic in 1890. In 1909, the almost white Nilo Pecanha, President of Brazil, showed pride in acknowledging his Negro ancestry and openly praised his *Mae Preta* (Black Mother).

In Cuba, where violence was required, the Negro brought his full weight on the side of the revolutionists, fighting hand in hand with white patriots in the combined abolition-independence struggle which began in 1868. On the abolition promise of the nationalist Creole leader, Cespedes, they fought courageously. The long ten-year war failed, but the Negro had shown his muscle, and Spain had to decree abolition in 1886. When the war raged again in 1895, Negro soldiers fought fiercely. A Mulatto general, Antonio Maceo, was on the side of the white "Apostle" Marti, commanding and leading the revolutionary army to its final victory.

It is, however, in Mestizo Spanish America, where the armed struggle took place in the early nineteenth century, that the Negro politico-military cooperation with white Creoles and Mestizos started. The latter's promise of manumission helped to induce Negroes into the ranks of the patriot armies, and their fighting qualities won general recognition. In the judgment of the white Argentine general, San Martin, whose 30 to 40 Percent Negro army liberated Chile, "the best soldier we have is the Negro and Mulatto, whereas the whites are good only for the cavalry."[27] In the Great Colombia, where Negroes were fighting simultaneously on the side of royalists and patriots, who both made the manumission promise, the "Libertador" Bolivar finally achieved triumph only after persuading in 1817 "two Mulatto Generals, Jose Antonio Paez and Manuel Piar, to join the patriots instead. From that moment the savage heroism was in the service of the Criollo revolution."[28] However, because of the opposition met by Bolivar in his effort to fulfill his promise, general emancipation occurred only one or two decades after victory.

In all the nations whose founding was achieved by or largely due to the Negroes, emancipation provided them with full legal and political personality. But it failed to remove the pre-emancipation socio-cultural disadvantages of the ex-slaves for whom equal rights remained more theoretical than real. Remaining in the lowest social strata, they continued to be economically and educationally deprived and quasi isolated culturally. This was aggravated by the inclination of many of them to equate freedom with a right not to work, or to work little on the small plots of land that they occupied right after obtaining freedom, raising subsistence crops and cash crops on a small scale. These adverse circumstances to further Negro growth were compounded by other detrimental factors, internal and external to the countries. The war-ravaged economies, and the capital and technology losses incurred in expelling the Europeans, offered little chance for employment on a free wage basis to the masses of liberated slaves. In addition, the military heroes who became the political rulers were ill-equipped for the difficult task of nation-building, for which no model fitting the new countries' socio-cultural circumstances existed at that time. They rather showed a tendency to *personalismo* and *caudillismo*, whose roots may be traceable to their Negro or Amerindian antecedents or to the past colonial methods of government. Externally the trend was toward a strengthening of race prejudice, which in the nineteenth century acquired academic respectability through such writings as those of Macaulay, Lord Acton and Count de Gobineau, whose ideas gained popularity over those of such anti-racist thinkers and abolitionists as Clarkson, Abbe Raynal and Abbe Gregoire. This new surge caused abroad a denigration of the new countries and nationally affected the psychology of the people and the social relationships of the different racial types.

By the end of the nineteenth century, expanding trade with Europe and the United States permitted industrialization to begin in several South American countries, including Brazil, and in Cuba. Negroes benefited from the rise in employment opportunities, high wage levels, and somewhat greater amount of social mobility. These expanding opportunities tended to weaken the African-derived inheritances and to reduce the Negro's ingrained frustrations and feelings of insecurity. However, in most of the Caribbean, where development was harder to come by, Negro progress was slower; ancestral beliefs and superstitions kept much of their strength reined. This particularly held true for Haiti, which soon became a country of too many people on too little land, with meager development potentials, and which suffered throughout the nineteenth century from a sort of cultural quarantine enforced by the white powers to protect their remaining slave areas from the "bad example" of its slave revolution. Its lack of development and strong African survivals remain exceptional even today, despite the pronounced relaxation of racial prejudice in Western culture and the rising trends toward international development assistance which have much benefited the other countries and their Negro communities during the twentieth century, and especially in the last three development decades.

As Contributors to the Cause of Freedom in the Continent

The already noted African belief in the cosmological nature of man that the Afro-Latins inherited is accountable for the sense of mission demonstrated in their desire to expand liberty in other lands. Once Haiti's independence was won, its leaders made efforts to force emancipation throughout Latin America. They failed in their attempts to export their revolution to Cuba and Martinique by sending men and money to local Negro revolutionists; and the methods they used for emancipating Santo Domingo's slaves in 1822, and their subsequent occupation of the country until 1844, were senseless. But more generously and more effectively, they contributed to Spanish America's independence. Firstly, Emperor Dessalines provided funds and encouragement to Miranda when the Venezuelan precursor went to Haiti in 1806 to ask aid. When for the same reason the South American liberator, Simon Bolivar, went twice to Haiti in 1816 and 1817, President Petion generously provided him with men, weapons, supplies and funds to launch his final assaults against the Spanish fortresses. It was for no personal or national profit, but it was on the condition that right after victory abolition would be decreed. As already seen, through no fault of his, Bolivar was unable to realize his promise. Yet, Bolivar cannot be excused for not inviting Haiti to the first Pan American conference, which he organized in Panama City in 1826. Having showed the way to continental cooperation by assisting the blooming of freedom in so many Latin American countries, no country other than Haiti deserved more the honor of attending the birth of Pan Americanism.

In addition, Haiti offered its land as a refuge to oppressed Negroes of other countries. An article in the nation's first constitution provided the Haitian nationality to any person with Negro genes. Many United States Negroes, wanting to escape racial persecution, explored the offer, and several took it. President Boyer in the 1830's distributed land to 13,000 of them who settled in Haiti and Haiti-occupied Santo Domingo. But given the low economic social standards of the Haitian peasants—so much lower compared to theirs in the United States—most of them returned home. In 1861, President Geffrard's plan to import Negroes from the United States, in order to ease up the formation of a skilled Haitian middle class, met the approval of President Lincoln. But only 110 wanted to migrate, of whom only a few stayed.

As Artisans of Universal Negro Solidarity

The Afro-Latin Americans did not confine their concern for inter-Negro solidarity to the continent, but directed it also to assisting the then colonized Africans and to defending universally the Negro race. Three distinguished Haitian intellectuals, Antenor Firmin, Louis Joseph Janvier and Hannibal Price, published respectively and successively in the last third of the nineteenth century, *De l'Egalité des Races Humaines, L'Egalité des Races,* and *De La Rehabilitation de la Race Noire,* to refute such French racist authors as de Gobineau, Renan and Le Bon. Another Haitian, Benito Sylvain, founded in 1889 a paper in Paris to protest Africa's colonialization, then in 1896 put his pen at the service of Ethiopia's Emperor, whose armies were repelling an Italian invasion, and later extended to the whole world his crusading voyages for the Negro cause. In 1900 a

Trinidadian lawyer, Henry Sylvester Williams, was the first to launch the concept of Pan Africanism; he convened in London the first Pan-African conference, which was attended by many British West Indians and the Haitian Sylvain. At the second London Pan-African conference, convened this time by the well-known United States Mulatto, Du Bois, 20 British West Indians participated. In 1935, the second and crushing Italian invasion of Ethiopia stirred up international Negro solidarity, and the Afro-Latin Americans were not inactive. In denouncing that aggression at the League of Nations, Haiti's delegate, Alfred Nemours Auguste, uttered to the Assembly this prophetic and notorious warning: "Let us fear and avoid to become tomorrow somebody's Ethiopia." In the inter-war period, a Jamaican immigrant in the United States, Marcus Garvey, gave to the North American Negro masses, on which he exercised a charismatic influence, their first dynamic feel for Africa,[29] and established at Harlem his "Universal Negro Improvement Association." In his own debatable ways, the contemporary West Indian immigrant to the United States, Stokely Carmichael, seems to be following Garvey's path.

The black Latin American intellectuals did not limit themselves to racial defense and occasional cooperation. Some representatives of the elite also constructed Negro theories aimed at total Negro redemption and national as well as international integration of the large Negro masses. However, their works were preceded by breakthroughs, made in the fields of cultural anthropology and social psychology by the positivist school to which Latin America remained culturally tributary in Europe, and by Mestizo America's *indigemismo,* which urged the integration of the Amerindian heritage into the life patterns of the Mestizo countries. In Creole Cuba, *indigemismo* became *Afrocubanismo* after Fernando Ortiz, a white sociologist, recognized the immense and worthy contributions of the Negro race to Cuba's formation and framed, in 1905, a theory of cultural nationalism emphasizing the social rather than the racial character of the Negro problem. He concluded: "Since there exists no pure race, then there is no Cuban race, and Cubanity is the peculiar quality of Cuba formed by the intermixture of the Indian, the white, the Negro, and the Chinese."[30] In Brazil, the white social scientists Freyre and Ramos advocated in the 1920's the full acceptance and recognition of the Brazilian Negroes in the country's life. Giving continental and even world proportions to the urge for interracial integration, the Mexican Jose Vasconcelos expounded in the 1930's his idealistic "cosmic race" theory, envisioning for the future the fusion of all mankind's races and cultures. Cosmic race, for the time being at least, sounds unrealistic and utopian, but the other theories, based on transculturative and integrative racial fusion, have found substantial although not complete application in many Latin American countries where the historical "bleaching" process has been very intensive. But, given the world's persisting although narrowing cultural gap in matters of race relations, they can hardly apply to overwhelmingly black countries whose history of differential cultural growth, mainly based on a "pigmentocratic" social stratification setup which provided opportunities only to a small number of dark Negroes, has resulted in the continuity of the socio-cultural impediments affecting the dark populace. For the further growth of this social category and of such countries, other theories had to be found. Several have been offered by remarkable black Latin American scholars.

An eminent ethnologist, historian, diplomat, and a member of Haiti's black elite, Jean Price-Mars, introduced in 1919 his brand of black Indigenism in his *La Vocation de L'Elite*, which blamed the Haitian elites of all color shades for their failure to accept their share of African heritage, their "bovaristic" and alienating propensity to French imitation, and their lacking sense of social responsibility vis-a-vis the poor black peasants and low-income urbans. In *Ainsi Parla L'Oncle,* published in 1928, his recipe of national culturalism consisted in a soul-searching quest for national identity, a reassessment of the mixed French-African content of Haitian culture and personality, a balance between the two, keeping the best of both, and an intellectual pilgrimage to Mother Africa for inspiration and for re-securing the lost virtues of the race. The theory rapidly spread, brought enthusiasm and hopes, gave rise in the 1940's and 1950's to a rich artistic renaissance movement based on the folklore, and inspired a 1946 political uprising that put in power a predominantly black ruling group. After two decades of such changes, Haiti has changed little and has worsened in certain aspects. Whatever the merits of the suggested ideological cure, the theory obviously neglected the technology component of culture, so crucial in modern times.

Similar to Price-Mars' theory which inspired it, Negritude is a doctrine which originated from the Caribbean Basin, where it was conceived by the brilliant poet and philosopher Aime Cesaire of Martinique and his associate, Leon Damas of French Guiana. But while the former theory was limited to a Haitian cultural nationalism, Negritude looks at world Negro cohesion, redemption and welfare. Its black internationalism, at least within the confines of the French cultural empire, was enhanced when Leopold Senghor, the great poet and president of Senegal, concurred and diffused Negritude in Africa. World acclaim followed the encouragement and praise given by the leading French intellectuals Breton and Sartre. Cesaire's theory is a myth calculated to recapture the African glories of the past in order to regenerate the Negro's intrinsic pride, self-respect, heightened sensibility and strong emotional expression, qualities that have been threatened by slavery and Colonial degradation. Negritude asserts the predominance in human life of emotion and intuitive reason over rationalism, and proclaims that it is through the use of the former cognitive tools that the Negro will regain his lost personality and attain world importance. Here again, excessive emphasis is put on the racial aspects of the Negro problem to the neglect of the socio-cultural requirements. Although Negritude can hardly solve the current development needs of the black nations, it has contributed to the alleviation of the Negro's feelings of frustration and insecurity, and has been a powerful instrument in the post-war decolonization of Africa. For all these, credit must be given to the meritorious Caribbean scholars who shaped it.

Another theory, born again in the Caribbean shores but in the English-cultured islands, views the Negro's troubles and arrives at an opposite solution, stressing economic and educational development for the removal of the bottlenecks left by the ancestral, plantation slavery or Colonial heritage. This group of academicians and statesmen, mainly represented by the clever social scientist and Prime Minister of Trinidad and Tobago, Eric Williams, shows its relations to the already noticed ecologico-

311

economic school by giving precedence to economic forces over tradition forces in the growth process. According to them, an obsession with Africa is a divisive factor that can only hinder rather than help national and Negro development. "There can be no Mother Africa for those of African origin, and the Trinidad and Tobago society is living a lie and heading for trouble if it seeks to act under the delusion that Trinidad and Tobago is an African society."[31] Although not internationally-intended as Negritude, this theory coincides with the views of English-cultured Africans such as the Ghanaan writer Busia, who refutes Negritude in these terms: "When they talk of African culture, of African personality, they seem to be harking ominously to an anachronistic, primeval Africa . . . A scientific age demands a scientific mind. This is a task of education."[32] Once again, it seems that a balanced approach combining the French-West Indian Negritude with the English-West Indian theory could best reconcile the psychological and socio-economic needs of the Negro, and perhaps lead to the universal Negro salvation so ardently contemplated by so many outstanding Afro-Latin Americans.

The Black Latin American Impact on Western World Culture and Power Structure

Beyond their impact on regional cultures, nation-building, national and continental politics, and the universal Negro struggle, the Negro achievements in Latin America have to a large extent affected Western culture itself in both its technology and ideology aspects, as well as the modern world power structure.

The contributions of his arduous work in Colonial times on the economies and the technology of Western Europe are well known. It has fed Europe's commercial revolution and the attendant rise in urbanization, technical progress, factory system, financial capitalism, and entrepreneurial industrialism. By doing so, it has helped England, then France, to promote their Industrial Revolution in the second half of the eighteenth century, creating the required capital accumulation from two sources—the slave traffic and slavery. Two partial figures give an idea of such a contribution. By conveying from 1783-1793 303,000 slaves. Liverpool slavers had made a profit of £2,360,000.[33]

Around 1789, the annual exports and imports exchanges of France with its St. Domingue colony, which represented two-thirds of French foreign trade, exceeded $140 million, employed more than 700 ocean-going vessels with as many as 80,000 seamen.[34] Of course, with or without African slavery in Latin America, the Industrial Revolution would have taken place, but probably at a much later date.

Less well known are the contributions made to Western thinking by black Latin America. Given the dynamic relationship of technology and ideology, it may conjecturally be inferred that the big hand given by slavery in Latin America to Europe's economy has also helped its institutional strides with regard to national unification, scientific revolution, the breakdown of feudalism, capitalistic social structure, and the rise of democracy. However, in spite of such striking progress, Western culture continued to rely on and practice the shameful labor system of slavery. Even the laissez-faire arguments of Adam Smith and the point of view of social justice advocated by liberals and abolitionists were not convincing enough to change the slavery frame of mind. Indeed the Afro-Latin American's revolts and emancipation wars have rendered a great service to Western culture by removing the slavery disgrace that was tarnishing it. Western culture is also in debt to black Latin America for the contributory role played by the Caribbean Doctrine of Negritude in the removal of the other blemish that Africa's colonization was.

Almost unknown, except by a few specialists of international affairs, is the black Latin American's worth in the determination of modern world power structure and the current leadership of the United States. In this connection, the token although valiant contribution to the birth of the United States of 600 free blacks and Mulattoes from Haiti, who shed their blood at the Battle of Savannah in 1779, may not have been quite significant; but the side effect of the Haitian independence struggle was of greatest relevance. The relatively small country formed in 1776 by the thirteen original Colonies would probably not have attained that strength and influence had not the courage and heroism of half a million Haitian Negroes driven out Napoleon's army from St. Domingue and at the same time crushed his dream of a huge American empire. The monarch's ambitious plan was to use St. Domingue as a base for securing the Louisiana territory ceded to him by Spain in 1801. The threat was such that President Jefferson said: "The day that France takes possession of New Orleans we must marry ourselves to the British fleet and nation."[35] The young nation did not have to do it, because the Haitian victories decimated Bonaparte's troops and deprived him of the launching base of St. Domingue, compelling him to sell the French territories in North America to the United States. The Louisiana Purchase in April 1803, for the insignificant sum of $15 million, roughly two pennies an acre, almost doubled the size of the United States, adjoining to it the Mississippi Valley and extending it to the Rocky Mountains, and gave it fourteen new states. Wendell Phillips in 1863 was right in saying: "Toussaint was indirectly responsible for doubling the area of the United States and spreading the greatest democracy in the world from ocean to ocean."[36] In effect, the Haitian deeds and the Louisiana deal may well have changed the course of history.

THE BLACK LATIN AMERICAN'S CONTRIBUTIONS TO WORLD LITERATURE, SCIENCES, ARTS AND ENTERTAINMENT

The least contested and most readily visible contributions of the black Latin Americans are those related to the fields of arts and letters. Nearly everybody agrees that the development and current maturity of the Creole aesthetics have enriched world literature, architecture, sculpture, music, choreography and painting. Placed at the crossroads of the Americas, the Eurafro or Creole culture has produced a distinctive form of literary and artistic expression. It is characterized by its powerful rhythm, structural plasticity, creativeness, predominance of emotion, psychic tension and symbolic imagery. These are features common to all Negro-derived arts and part of the complex entity of Negritude.

However, Creole art does not only reflect the initial African inspiration, themes, cadence, sounds and contours, it also mirrors the European verses, melodies and shapes captured during the enculturation process as well as the times and conditions of the now-long Latin American existence of the Negro. In its versatility, it conveys the pains and frustrations as much as the joys and hopes experienced in slavery, then in freedom. This is

314

why the Creole national arts, as the corresponding national cultures, present both similarities and dissimilarities. They are the products of different histories and varying environments, natural and social. Thus, each national art has its oneness, and this variety gives an additional originality and attractiveness to the Creole region.

The uniformities consist in the identical amalgamating process of the rich African aesthetic inheritance with the equally rich European artistic heritage; an artistic dualism consisting in each country in the coexistence of fairly sophisticated artistic forms, even in the fields of popular song and music, with almost primitive Africanist modes (a reflection of the dualistic socio-economic structure); the simultaneous presence of three artistic attitudes related to the Latin America-made polyvalent Negro psychology, one of anxiety, complaint and lamentation, another of defiance and protest, and a third of accommodativeness, each prone to unrestrained gaiety, however, when relief is found in popular Creole recreations such as dances, soccer, cricket, cockfight and carnival; and finally, constant observance and imitation, avowed or not, of the arts and letters as they develop in the European mother country. The disparities come from the varying size, shape and fertility of the land to be praised; differences in languages; artistic variations among the different European models; varying psychic dispositions resulting from different slavery and emancipation history; differing length of the colonization period; and overall prevalence of racial protests and nationalism in the literature and arts of certain countries.

In spite of these distinctions, the history of the development of Creole art can be divided into three specific periods: a formative phase, a maturation stage, and the era of maturity. As any classification, this serialization is arbitrary and may not always fit certain countries. However, it is suitable for the Creole area as a whole, and besides it serves this paper's last purpose, which is to search for literary and artistic accomplishments of particularly-gifted Negroes throughout the Latin American historical record. The search will also include the area's Mestizo, or white, or East Indian individualities whose works have been strongly inspired and influenced by *Criollismo*, meaning the complex mentality and set of psychomotor reactions distinctive of the White-Negro mixture.

315

The Formative Phase

It stretches from the Negro arrival to the 1820's, a period of slow modification of the African artistic heritage through the integration of new forms and shapes. These were drawn upon the arts of the other cultures met (European, Arawak, Carib, etc.) in the acculturative period, or were impelled by the new environment, natural and social. Negro literature remains unwritten, and its legends, proverbs and lore are orally transmitted. It is the period *par excellence* of the story tellers mixing the African past with the plantation experiences, the mythical uncle Remus of Brazil, the Anansi stories in several British colonies, the Haitian tales narrating the cognitive discussions between Malice the wise and Bouqui the foolish (brain over brawn), and other similar ways by which the Negro's informal socialization and indoctrination were conducted. This was the origin of the Afro-Latin American folkloric traditions. The African music and dances were also being altered by observance of the master's social events, with the use of European fiddles, tambourines, and triangles, side by side with the powerful African drums in modulating the African beat, or the assimilation of stately figures of the French minuet or the European square dances to the African movements. But in the two-way process of acculturation, the master's music, whether from Castille, Portugal, France or England, was being modified by the Negro tunes, giving rise to plaintive melodies, or to European reels, jigs, quadrilles and tangos, danced to the accompaniment of African marimbas, drums and bongos. Even at this early stage, a number of Negro artistic talents were discovered and acknowledged. Many slaves played violin, mandolin, guitar, or performed stylized dances for the *casa grande's* guests. Some free blacks and Mulattoes were showing skills in execution or composition of serious music, in dance characters, or in the theatre. But very few were really conspicuous in their arts. It was true also for the other races. In general, the colonial period did not make any substantial contribution to the arts, except for some sophisticated achievements in sculpture, architecture and music in Spanish America and Brazil.

Nevertheless, by the end of the period, a few Negroes were outstanding in Brazilian arts. The most prodigious was Antonio Francisco Lisboa, nicknamed O'Aleijadinho (the Crippled), a

316

Mulatto craftsman, sculptor and architect, remembered as the greatest artist of colonial Brazil and one of the world's best architects at his time. He built several of Brazil's loveliest churches in Minas Geraes, using mainly the baroque style but mixing it with elements of his own. Other talented Brazilian artists were the Mulatto Mestre Ataide, who did excellent paintings on Aleijadinho's panels in the Churches of Ouro Preto; a black slave by the name of Sebastae who did excellent paintings on the ceilings of several churches in Rio; and Mestre Valentin (1750-1813), a free black who was well known in Rio for his sculpture and architecture. Conspicuous in other fields were the Mulatto priest Jose Mauricio (1767-1830), a great singer and musician, who excelled on viola and clavichord, was a great composer, and founded the first real school of music in Brazil; the Mulatto poet Jose Natividade Salandha, who led a revolt in Recife in 1824; and Jose Basilio de Gama, who won a name in literature for his epic poem "Uruguay," published in the 1830's; and Dom Silvero Gomez Pimento, a Mulatto Archbishop during the Colonial time.

Even less numerous but worthy to be noted were some Negro achievements in Haiti by the end of the period. In the 1780's, two Mulatto sisters, Minette and Lise, were outstanding theatrical performers who won the loudest applause at the opera, and their success opened the way to other Negro performers, namely Pierre Flignau and Dupré.[37] The flaming Independence Proclamation, written in 1804 by Dessalines' gifted secretary, the Mulatto Boisrond Tonnerre, was a literary masterpiece which inaugurated at the same time the new country and its brilliant literature. The architecture of Christophe's gorgeous Citadel, with its dungeons and lofty galleries, has been commended abroad in three famous dramas, Eugene O'Neill's "Emperor Jones," J. W. Vandercook's "Black Majesty," and Cesaire's "La Tragedie du Roi Christophe," played in premiere at the musical festival of Salzburg in 1964, and acclaimed at the World's Negro art festival of Dakar in 1966.

The Maturation Stage

During the period which extended from the 1820's to the "Negro Renaissance" of the 1920's, Brazil and Haiti remained the only countries of importance with respect to intellectual and artistic

317

Negro works of significance and sophistication. However, in the rest of Creole America, the maturation of Negro art was also progressing, although slowly and almost imperceptibly, with no works of great relevance until the 1930's. As for the Brazilian and Haitian Negro intellectuals, they not only maintained their early lead, but showed extraordinary vitality and talent in a number of articulate and valuable works. There, as in the other Creole countries where Negro art was advancing more slowly, the small but influential Negro intellectual elites heavily committed themselves to defending the Negro populations, advocating their rights, protecting these rights after they had been conquered, providing thoughts and guidance for action, and participating in the nation-building tasks in countries which attained independence.

It is no wonder that black Latin American literature and arts tend generally to display two simultaneous tendencies, although at varying levels in different countries or at different times. The first tendency aims at the universal and borrows its themes, forms, feelings, and ideas from the European model followed. The other emphasizes national history and local life situations, exhibiting strong racial overtones and sensitive nationalism. In these two orientations both the Brazilian Negroes, who manifested more often the former tendency, and the Haitians (practically all Negroes), who more frequently followed the second tendency,[38] brought during the period their contributory store to the enrichment of the continent and world knowledge and aesthetics.

In Brazil's nineteenth century literature, the most gifted of all poets was undoubtedly the Mulatto Machado de Assis. He has been recognized as the greatest writer in Portuguese of that time, and his novel *Dom Casmuro* won him a well-deserved reputation abroad. However, it is pointed out that although he had Negro ancestry he sided against the abolitionists. By contrast, most of the other Negro writers were ardent abolition campaigners; for example, the two remarkable and already-cited poets Goncalves Dias and Castro Alves, as well as Luis Gama, the black son of an African princess, poet, journalist and great political leader. Other brilliant scholars of African ancestry were Antonio Goncalvez Texeira, a novelist, poet and playwright of romance and fantasy; Farias Brito, whose *German*

Studies placed him as the utmost Brazilian philosopher of all times; and Tobias Barreto, distinguished writer, scientist and philosopher. In music, compositions of excellence were written by the great violinist Joaquim Manuel Augusto, and by Francisco Braga, Jose Raymundo da Silva and Paulo Silva. Caldas Barbosa was a great singer of popular songs in the 1830's. In painting, the two greatest names were the black Chrispian de Amiral, who was praised as the best painter of nineteenth-century Brazil, and the Mulatto Pedro Americo (1843-1905), who painted the impressive "Independence Panel" at the Ypiranga Museum. Before leaving the Brazil of the 1920's, the names of two non-Negro but essentially Creole authors must be recalled, the eminent sociologists Freyre and Ramos. More than the writings of any single Brazilian Negro, their passionate sociological works led to further improvements in Brazil's "racial democracy." Their merits are comparable only to those of another non-Negro but basically Creole sociologist who should also be recalled at this point, the white Cuban Ortiz. It is his work in the 1900's which laid the foundation for Afroamericanism and for world acceptance of *Criollism* in the literature and the arts.

In Haiti, the period witnessed tremendous growth in letters and arts. The country's 5000 books from Independence to the 1950's placed it, as recently as 1951, ahead of any other Latin American country with respect to intellectual production.[39] Most of these works are racial theses or social studies analyzing the country's poorness, social maladjustments, African inheritances, and perpetual strife among the black and mulatto elites. Several were outstanding works, written in the best French language and style. The French Academy bestowed its highest recognition to several historians, namely Beaubrun Ardouin, Emile Nau, Beauvais Lespinasse, Celigny Ardouin and Thomas Madiou, and to the greatest among a number of Haitian poets, Etzer Vilaire. His poem *Les Dix Hommes Noirs* is a philosophical dissertation of great depth and also of despair and helplessness. Other poets who won wide reputation were Edmond Laforest, whose style is Parnassian, the original playwright and poet Massillon Coicou, and the imaginative and sensible Oswald Durand, considered as the initiator of a Haitian-Creole mode of expression and classified as next only to Vilaire for that period.[40] In the field of the social sciences, which blossomed after 1860, the names of the able authors Antenor Firmin and Louis Joseph Janvier have already been mentioned. Other brilliant writers were the sociologist Demesvar Delorme, who had friendly relations with Lamartine and Hugo while in Paris, and later in the early twentieth century the historian Pauleus Sanon and the ethnologist and philosopher J. C. Dorsainvil. But the two intellectual giants were, firstly, J. Price Mars (1876-1969), whose work has already been mentioned above and who dominated the field and exercised great influence in the country, in scholarly circles abroad, and in World Negro movements; and secondly, Dantes Bellegarde, who expressed views that contrasted the Marsian approach and gave priority to the French over the African heritage. Prominent for the social realism of their novels were Frederic Marcelin, Fernand Hibbert and Antoine Innocent.

Haiti was not lacking in the arts either by the end of the period. Two prominent sculptors were Louis Laforesterie and Normil Ulysse Charles, both well known for the artistic purity of their busts. In music, four Haitians made a name in the high musical forms: Justin Elie took inspiration for his wonderful compositions "Babylon" and "Danses Tropicales" from the rich folkloric motifs of Peru, Cuba and Haiti; Theramene Manes studied the folk dances of Haiti; Occide Jeanty was the brilliant composer of the fiery Haitian March "1804"; and Ludovic Lamothe composed waltzes in which the slow melody reflects the nostalgic melancholy of the Negro.[41]

Three exceptional Caribbeans of that period achieved top fame in the literature of France. The two Alexandre Dumas, father and son, were Haitian Mulattoes. The father (1802-1870) born in St. Domingue of a black mother, raised in France by his white father, wrote romantic novels still popular today, such as *Les Trois Mousquetaires*, in which the exaggerated imaginativeness is perhaps attributable to his Negro affiliation. The son (1824-1895) won great reputation in the French social drama. The third, Jose Maria de Heredia (1842-1905), was a Cuban and a light-skinned Creole. Although his Negro ancestry is doubtful, his Creole inspiration and warmth is certain. He showed it in his passionate revolt poetry against Spanish Colonialism during the abortive Cuban revolution of the 1860's, and after he migrated to France in his deep-toned sonnets, *Trophee*, which gave the Creole flavor to his best expression of the French Parnassian School.

In the meantime, in all the Creole countries, the compelling and contagious music of the Negroes continued to keep alive the African musical beat, made of brief melodic phrases repeated throughout a piece with little or no variation.[42] However, it was increasingly blended with motifs, elements, and instruments inspired by the Creole ecology. The still powerful but now enriched rhythm animated the colorful pre-Lenten Carnivals and other social recreation of the Negroes, which the other racial groups increasingly liked and shared. In the streets and public places of the Creole capitals and towns, it provided the catalyst uniting at least once a year people of different race or income groups and providing them with exuberant joy and psychological relief. Moreover, its constant enrichment throughout the period was building the folkloric base of the Creole culture and foundations for the artistic and intellectual explosion that pervaded all the Creole areas in the subsequent period.

The Era of Maturity

This period, starting from the 1930's, has been called the era of black Latin American art renaissance, in fact a naissance in several countries. It also witnessed the world-wide vogue of Negro Creole poetry and arts. Both climbed with clearer and more articulate expression. But the drive to maturity is still underway, as black Latin American expression continues to search for new modes and *raison d'etre*. In addition to the already mentioned factors that led to this epoch, it has also resulted from the lagging effects of other past occurrences, within and without the Creole nations, and from the direct effects of more recent ones. In several British and Dutch colonies, thousands of East Indians and Chinese imported for indentured plantation work to replace the Negroes after emancipation had increased even more the area's racial and cultural intermingling. Inversely, many of the unemployed Negroes were migrating to the Panama Canal, thence to the banana countries of Costa Rica and Honduras, and lately to Great Britain. Likewise, thousands of Haitians settled in the early decades of the twentieth century in Cuba and the Dominican Republic where they were wanted for sugar cane cutting. Steady mass migration from most of the Caribbean has been directed to the United States, in particular over a million Puerto Ricans since Puerto Rico achieved commonwealth status in 1942, and more than 400,000 Cubans since Castro's revolution. Other external events influenced the Creole ethos, way of life and temper, some favorably, others unfavorably. All found reflection in Creole arts. Among those events, the most consequential were the American interventionist policies from the 1890's to the 1930's, the Mexican Revolution, World War I, the Russian Revolution, which gave leftist leanings to the area's political nationalism, the 1930's World Depression, World War II, the 1949 UNESCO report which stressed the predominance of culture over race, the Assistance programs in favor of the LDC's and the Alliance for Progress in particular, and finally, Castro's Revolution, which practically took Cuba out of the Creole orbit as national attention became mostly focused on the task of building a communist set-up and spirit whose constraints altered the themes and inspiration of Afrocuban art and limited its previously unrestrained inventiveness, redirecting it to other horizons.

At the same time, the dynamic Creole arts and letters were not only receiving ideas. After climbing with clearer and more definite expression, they were carried to other lands by the carriers of culture that black Latin Americans have proved to be. All the Creole lands have propagated to the world their indigenous variants of Negro poetry, novel, drama, painting, music and sculpture. The Negro religious music and dances, which had left the *lucumi*, *macumba* and *shango* temples to animate the folk and social dances within nations, were now assaulting Broadway, the French cafes, Piccadilly Circus, and music halls and ballrooms throughout the world. The Creole beats have penetrated the pop music of South America, North America, Europe and Africa. Greatest world acclaim went to the compelling rhythms of Cuba's rhumba, danzon, son, conga, mambo and cha-cha-cha; Brazil's samba; Martinique's beguine; the calypso and the famous steel bands of Trinidad and Jamaica; the boleros of Puerto Rico; and the meringues of Haiti and the Dominican Republic. But Colombia's chuchumbe and jarabe, Venezuela's joropo, and Peru's zamba and marinero are not unknown abroad either. The music popularized by the Cuban orchestras of Perez Prado and Tito Puentes, by the fascinating Brazilian singer Carmen Miranda, and by many other prominent Creole entertainers, is familar to foreign ears. Today,

American jazz, also of African derivation, is being more and more enriched by Caribbean folk music and themes. Both the former and the latter are now making inroads into the Communist world, despite efforts made in that area against the entry of such so-called "decadent bourgeois and capitalist influences."

In more refined forms, the Creole folk dances have reached the theatre stage in the form of plastic dances executed by marvelous choreographers from Haiti, Jamaica and other islands. Research work made in the 1930's by the creative American Negro dancer Katherine Dunham, together with a Haitian composer, Lina Mathon Blanchet, led to the stylization of several Haitian folk rhythms and dances. Such plastic dances have been brilliantly performed by the internationally known Haitian Jean Leon Destine, who was praised at the 1951 National Folk Festival and the 1959 World Dance Festival, both in Washington; and by great Jamaican dancers, such as Ivy Baxter, Louise Bennett and Noel Vaz, who harvested applause in a tour of the United States in 1961. These black dancers are remarkable by their morphologic flexibility and their puzzling gestures and acrobatics in expressing the astounding rhythms of the Vodun, and other African, drums.

African and Creole folk music has also inspired leading composers of chamber and classical music. Among these, the white Brazilian Hector Villa-Lobos (1881-1959) has been outstanding. Using the melodies that reflected the sufferings and joys of the Negroes, he composed more than 1,400 works. His "Dansas Africanas" and "Macumba" stress the African music's polytonality and polyrhythm. Puerto Rico's classical music compositions have the distinctive flavor resulting from their reflection of the rich folkloric wealth both in their forms and themes. This trend has been accentuated during the long stay in the island of the famous Spanish cellist and composer, Pablo Casals. It is manifested in the musical achievements of such talented Mulattoes as the Figueroa-Sanabia family, and the prolific composer, Rafael Hernandez, whose works have won world-wide renown.

Painting is another field in which the introduction of black Latin American folklore and of Creole nature gave rise to top-notch contributions which obtained world success. In modern times, among those who mastered such themes, the most eminent

323

names have been the white Brazilian Candido Portinari, whose best works deal with Negro life, and the cubist Cundo Bernandez and the surrealist Wilfredo Lam, both Cuban Mulattoes who produced works expressing with subtle colors and entangling shapes the country's scenery and Negro imagery. Haiti's primitive paintings have acquired fame abroad for their splendid colors and naive techniques in depicting the country's tropical green and blue, and the people's gaiety and underlying sorrows. The most astonishing and spectacular are those of a Vodun houngan (priest) Hector Hyppolite, of Philome Obin, whose mural "Calvary Scene" taking place in a Haitian street decorates the capital's Episcopal Cathedral, and others of C. Bazile, W. Bigaud, D. Cedor and A. Joseph. More elaborate are those of R. Dorcely, P. Savain and, in particular, the surrealist M. Pinchinat. In Jamaica, the young painters W. Francsi, Benjamin Campbell and Mallita Reynolds, a survivalist priest, are noteworthy. In Guyana, a promising painter is Donald Locke.

The African-inherited sculptural skills have assisted the imagination and fame of some Creole sculptors, both in traditional and in terra-cotta sculpture. Most formidable are the Cuban Ramos Blanco and the Jamaican Edna Manley, who obtained top press acclaim in several countries. The Haitians J. C. Garoute and Frido Vilaire have produced interesting ceramic works.

It is in the field of letters that the black Latin Americans of this period have brought more numerous contributions. In their verse, prose, novels, essays and short stories they have shown remarkable originality, power of expression and highest aesthetic forms in communicating their socio-racial protest, their painful self-searching analysis, or their feelings on more conventional and universal themes.

In his "Orphee Noir," Jean-Paul Sartre described the Negro poet as "an intuitive seeker, plumbing into the dark void, using his instinct as a kind of radar to discover a fresh vision of the truth." In similar ways, the modern Afro Latin American writers, with their spirit and fire, have built their own mode of literate expression, their own poetry of universal emotion, their own humanism, and thereby have impressed and influenced the world. In the sensitive and uniquely warm verses and prose of many of them can be felt the excitement and cadence of the Creole music, while the feelings and content squeeze out the

Negro's martyrdom and a sense of cosmic mission for Negroes and other victimized people everywhere. For them, the Muse does not care too much for aesthetic refinements and strictly philosophical motives, but principally for the song of the land and for portraying real life, particularly that of those who suffer.

In Brazil, outstanding among such black or Mulatto poets are the powerful Jorge de Lima, the musicologist M. de Andrade, the unpredictable O. de Andrade, and the sensible B. M. Labato, all of whom are internationally appreciated.

In Haiti, a rich but exceptionally militant and explosive literature sprang up as a result of the country's occupation from 1915 to 1934, and the spreading of Price Mars' ideas. The period's best poet is the versatile L. Laleau, who masters both the traditional verse and the "indigenist" expression; his "Le Choc" and "Musique Negre" won him in France his membership at Edgar Ronsard Academy, and the Allan Poe prize in 1962. Among many other remarkable Haitian poets of that period, the worthiest were C. Brouard, E. Roumer, A. Vieux, L. Diaquoi, J. Brierre, R. Camille and F. Morisseau Leroy. All have expressed the heart and soul of the Haitian masses. More special are M. St. Aude and R. Belance who brought the surrealist touch to their picturing of Haitian reality; R. Depestre, whose poems reflect his pronounced leftism; and three younger poets, R. Philoctete, A. Phelps, and Davertige, trying to reach the heights of their elders. In the social protest novel, the greatest and internationally recognized names are J. Roumain, who brilliantly interprets the hopes as well as the pre-logic mentality of the peasants who incriminate invisible forces for their misfortunes in his *Gouverneurs de la Rosee* now translated in more than a dozen foreign languages; and the two brothers P. and Ph. Thoby-Marcelin, whose *Canape Vert*, reproducing the rhythm and tempo of Haitian peasant life, has received the highest honors abroad, particularly in the United States; and J. S. Alexis who revealed his fastuous language, marvelous imaginative expression and revolutionary ideas in his masterpieces *Compere General Soleil*, *Les Arbres Musiciens*, and above all *Romancero aux Etoiles*, published in France in the 1950's and applauded by Haitians and foreigners alike.

In Cuba, the Afrocuban inspiration and racial rhythm are particularly strong in the original verses of N. Guillen, D. Bellagas, Cabrera and A. Carpentier.

Similar expression is found in Puerto Rico in the wonderful poetry of P. Matos, A. D. Alfaeo, J. L. Morales, J. M. Santiago, D. R. Arellano, J. de Burgos, C. R. Nieves, J. M. Lima, and in the novels of E. D. Laguerre.

In the Dominican Republic, Negro themes inspired the fine verses of T. H. Franco, M. del Cabral, H. Cabral, J. Bosh and A. Avelino.

Martinique and Guadeloupe have not only produced A. Cesaire, whose poems are of passionate beauty, and who, according to French critics, "handles the French language better than any white Frenchman,"[42] these two islands are also the home of other good poets, such as St. John Perse, whose wonderful verses won him the Nobel prize for literature in 1940; R. Gordon, to whom the Grand Prix des Antilles was awarded in 1949 for his good poetry; the promising R. Lardon, and the delicate F. Morand. Also from those islands came the imaginative novelist C. Richer, who won the Paul Flat prize in 1941 and 1948; J. Zabel who specialized in the slavery novel; and F. Fanon, whose revolutionary novels are well known abroad.

In the emerging English-speaking nations of the West Indies, which are not Latin in any sense but are considered as such because of their location and their historical experience with the Latin American countries, intellectual production has been rising both in quantity and in quality. The racial overtone in literature is also pronounced there. In Jamaica, the poems of Morris and Hearn are well known, as well as the social novels of R. Mais and O. Patterson. The best known writers of Trinidad and Tobago are the poets W. Cartey and B. Jones, and two East Indian Creoles, S. Selvon and V. Naipaul. In Guyana, E. Mittelhozer and M. Carter are poets of great reputation, while J. Carew and W. Harris write exciting novels. Finally, in Barbados, the names of G. Lamming, F. Collymore, L. E. Braithwate and H. A. Vaughn are prominent in the verse; while K. Sealy, A. Clark, P. Marshall, A N. Forde and G. Drayton have published novels or short stories of great interest.

Literature has also flourished in the Dutch possessions of Surinam and Curacao, where C. Detrot, A. Helman, T. Marugg and R. de Rooy have produced original works.

Like the rest of Latin America, Creole America has continued to be poor in the natural sciences. But among its intellectuals, there are important social scientists. The Jamaican A. Lewis is a world authority in the field of economic development; the development theory he has constructed is honored and taught in the United States and England. In the field of modern sociological and historical research, the names of G. Padmore, C. R. James, B. Davidson and of course, E. Williams, all from Trinidad, are honored both at home and abroad. The Barbadian L. Hutchinson, the Haitians L. F. Manigat and H. Trouillot, the Martiniquese P. Dupray, and the Trinidadian W. Rodney, have also made appreciable historical work. Even the field of pure philosophy has been explored by several Caribbeans; among the best is the Dominican mulatto Andres Avelino in the 1940's and 1950's.

Conclusion

At the end of this long historical excursion, the certain conclusion is that the Negro in Latin America has gone a long way from his initial transplantation from Africa to the present. In the New World, he has been an active culture-maker, a liberty bearer, a nation-founder, and an art-enricher. His abundant and meritorious contributions have transcended the national scene and the racial plane. They have generously been projected over the whole of Western culture and have assisted mankind's pains to increase human knowledge and mastery of this earth as well as the constant drive of the world toward more justice, liberty, and happiness to all human beings. Yet, the largest number of black Latin Americans are found in the *bidonvilles* (slum areas) of Latin America's cities or in the deprivation of peasant life. In spite of the politico-civil rights conferred on them more than a century ago, most have been unable to enter the orbit of today's technological world. One of the most crucial unfinished tasks of the over fifty million black Latin Americans, of the countries where they live, and of the world, is to foster and hasten the socio-economic development of that socio-racial group which did so much in less than five centuries. Given the constant lessening of ostracism against blackness in the white nations, and the rising importance of the black Latin American, the solution to his remaining problems consists in his obtaining more and more access to equal life opportunity—increasing employment, better incomes and education. Thus, there is a need for greater assistance to the black Latin American from the segments of the world which owe so much to him. Based on his sweat which enriched others, his blood which provided the leaven for freedom in Latin America, his music and arts which infused with gaiety and happiness all the continents of the world, and his proven attachment to his adopted continent, the Creole Negro is right in repeating, after the Nicaraguan Mulatto poet, Adalberto Ortiz: "I am the Negro brother; I also am America."

APPENDIX I

POPULATION SIZE AND ETHNIC COMPOSITION
OF CREOLE LATIN AMERICA
IN THE 1960's

Country	Population (million)	White %	W. Indian %	Mestizo %	Black %	Mulatto %	E. Indian %
Barbados	0.41	5.0	0.0	0.0	77.0	18.0	0.0
Brazil	85.70	41.0	2.0	17.0	11.0	29.0	0.0
Br. Honduras	0.10	3.9	24.0	12.3	38.0	21.8	2.0
Cuba	7.80	72.8	0.0	0.0	12.4	14.5	0.0
Dom. Rep.	3.90	39.0	0.0	0.0	11.0	50.0	0.0
Fr. Guiana	0.04	3.0	4.0	0.0	80.0	10.0	3.0
Guadeloupe	0.32	1.0	0.0	0.0	83.0	15.0	1.0
Guyana	0.70	3.1	4.3	0.0	38.1	10.0	44.5
Haiti	4.70	0.1	0.0	0.0	90.0	9.9	0.0
Jamaica	1.90	1.0	0.0	0.0	78.0	17.5	3.5
Martinique	0.33	1.0	0.0	0.0	82.0	16.0	1.0
Puerto Rico	2.70	50.7	0.0	0.0	20.2	29.1	0.0
Surinam	0.35	1.0	0.0	0.0	50.0	10.0	39.0
Tr. & Tob.	1.00	2.7	0.0	0.0	46.8	14.4	36.1

Notes: In Creole countries, the total Negro population is larger than the Amerindian-Mestizo population.

The population size figures are for 1967.

Sources. 1. *Encyclopedia Britannica*, 1968.

      2. A. G. Horton, *An Outine of Latin American History*, Iowa: Brown Book Co., 1966.

      3. M. G. Smith, *The Plural Society in the British West Indies*, Univ. of California Press, 1965.

328

POPULATION SIZE AND ETHNIC COMPOSITION
OF MESTIZO LATIN AMERICA
IN THE 1960's

Country	Population (million)	White %	W. Indian %	Mestizo %	Black %	Mulatto %
Argentina	22.1	92.0	0.0	8.0	0.0	0.0
Bolivia	3.8	4.0	63.0	33.0	0.0	0.0
Chile	8.9	40.0	0.2	59.8	0.0	0.0
Colombia	19.2	20.0	5.0	59.0	4.0	12.0
Costa Rica	1.6	60.0	0.3	37.6	0.6	1.5
Ecuador	5.5	10.0	40.0	40.0	5.0	5.0
El Salvador	3.1	3.0	21.0	76.0	0.0	0.0
Guatemala	4.7	5.0	53.6	37.4	2.0	2.0
Honduras	2.5	5.2	6.7	86.0	0.5	1.6
Mexico	45.7	8.5	28.0	61.5	0.5	1.5
Nicaragua	1.8	17.0	4.0	69.0	3.0	7.0
Panama	1.3	10.0	11.0	40.0	13.3	25.7
Paraguay	2.1	19.2	0.8	80.0	0.0	0.0
Peru	12.4	11.4	47.5	36.1	1.0	4.0
Uruguay	2.8	89.0	0.0	11.0	0.0	0.0
Venezuela	9.4	20.0	1.0	59.0	3.0	17.0

Notes: In Mestizo countries, the Mestizo-Amerindian population is larger than the Negro population.
The population size figures are for 1967.
Sources: 1. *Encyclopedia Britannica*, 1968.
2. A. G. Horton, *An Outline of Latin American History*, Iowa: Brown Book Co., 1966.

SELECTED BIBLIOGRAPHY

BOOKS

Busia, K. A., *The Challenge of Africa*, New York: Praeger, 1962. Offers a good background of both Africa's past and current mentality.

Davidson, Basil, *Black Mother*, Boston: Little, Brown & Co., 1961. Abundantly exposes the glory of past African Empires from which the Black-Latin American derived.

Fouchard, Jean, *Le Theatre a Saint Domingue, Port-au-Prince*: Imprimerie de 'lEtat, 1955. A survey of the surprisingly active theatrical life in colonial Haiti.

————, *Les Marrons du Syllabaire*, Port-au-Prince: Editions Deschamps, 1953. A passionate work stressing the ways by which

Negroes in Saint Domingue were proving their humanity and trying to secretly acquire education for a more conscious liberty fight than that of the maroons.

Frazier, E. Franklin, *Black Bourgeoisie,* New York: Collier Book Ed., 1962. Although mainly destined to an analysis of the American Negro middle class and its shortcomings, this book emphasizes predominance of slavery experience over the African antecedents in current Negro behavior.

Freyre, Gilberto, *The Masters and the Slaves,* New York: Alfred A. Knopf, 1967. This master work is essential for the understanding of the special Negro situation in Brazil, and is an impassioned plea for the complete recognition and acceptance of the Negro in Brazilian society.

Harris, Marvin, *Patterns of Race in the Americas,* New York: Walker & Co., 1964. Short but important, this study brilliantly summarizes the plantocratic system to which priority is given in the determination of national variations in Creole America today.

Herring, Hubert, *A History of Latin America,* New York: Alfred A. Knopf, 1965. Contains a remarkable chapter (Chap. 4) on the African background, the assets brought by the Negroes to the New World, and some of their contributions.

Horton, Arthur G., *An Outline of Latin American History,* Iowa: Brown Book Co., 1966. It is, with Herring's book, one of the rare history books on Latin America, giving due relevance to Negro role in the formation of the sub-continent's patterns.

Howes, Barbara, *From the Green Antilles,* New York: Macmillan, 1966. Although very incomplete, this anthology of good poets from the green Caribbean gives in its introductory remarks a few worthwhile ideas on the literary potentials of the Creole islands.

Leyburn, James H., *The Haitian People,* New Haven: Yale University Press, 1941. Many of the observations and conclusions of this rather old book continue to be valid and usable today.

Logan, Rayford W., *Haiti and the Dominican Republic,* New York: Oxford University Press, 1968. Short but well-documented, this comparative study of the two republics sharing the same island concludes that "opportunity, not the percentage of Negro blood is the determining factor" in the differential development levels of the two countries.

Morner, Magnus, *Race Mixture in the History of Latin Amer-*

ica, Boston: Little Brown & Co., 1967. Offers profound insight on racial history and Negro evolution in Latin America.

Pan American Union, *Haiti,* Washington, D.C.: Pan American Union, 1954. Very brief but quite factual pamphlet on Haiti's past achievements, particularly in the literary and artistic fields.

Mars, Jean Price, *Silhouettes de Negres et de Negrophiles,* Paris: Presence Africaine, 1960. A less dogmatic book, compared to the other publications of the great doctrinaire, these interesting profiles of selected world Negroes are nevertheless written to convey some of his essential ideas.

Pierson, Donald, *Negroes in Brazil,* Chicago: University of Chicago Press, 1942. Presents a careful and detailed analysis of the role and contributions of Brazilian Negroes.

Pompilus, Pradel, *Manuel Illustre de la Litterature Haitienne,* Port-au-Prince: Editions Deschamps, Editions 1961. It is one of the best attempts so far to logically sort Haiti's abundant and various literary production.

Ramos, Arthur, *Las Culturas en el Nuevo Mundo,* Fondo de Cultura Economica, Mexico, 1943. (The first edition in Portuguese was published in 1937). Written more than three decades ago, much of this book seems now obsolete; but the insights it provides on the Afro-Latin American transculturation process maintain some relevance.

Smith, Michael G., *The Plural Society in the British West Indies,* Berkeley: University of California Press, 1965. A meticulous sociological work which insists that the study of the Negro background should not be confined to the slavery history but should extend to the post-emancipation period during which many additional adjustments have taken place.

Williams, Eric, *History of Trinidad and Tobago,* Trinidad: PNM Co., 1962. A clear and objective examination of Trinidad and Tobago's history and present by its current leader, stressing the need for technological strides rather than obsession with past African traditions.

————, *British Historians and the West Indies,* Trinidad: PNM Co., 1964. The first part offers a good classification of British writers among those friendly and those inimical to the Negroes.

Antoine, Jacques C., "Haiti and the Louisiana Purchase", *Haiti Today,* Haiti Government Tourist Bureau, No. 3, Aug. 1954, pp. 16-17. This article provides detailed information regarding the circumstances of the Louisiana Purchase, and the ways in which the Haitian Negroes contributed to it.

Bastide, Roger, "Race Relations in Brazil", *International Social Science Bulletin,* Vol. IX, No. 4, 1957, pp. 495-512. A keen sociological work stressing the impact of both institutional background and economic setting on Brazil's racial permissiveness.

Bastien, Remy, "Vodun and Politics in Haiti", *Religion and Politics in Haiti,* Institute for Cross-Cultural Research, Washington, D.C., 1966, pp. 39-68. Recognition is given in this article to the contributory role of Vodun in Haiti's independence and rich artistic background; however, the author insists that Vodun today is the country's "bane and arch-enemy".

Bobrowska-Skrodzka, Helina, "Aime Cesaire, Chantre de la Grandeur de L'Afrique", *Presence Africaine,* Paris, No. 59, 3rd Trimester, 1966, pp. 34-56. A thorough review of Cesaire's ideas and works.

Carpio, Campio, "Emocion Universal de la Poesia Negra", *Journal of Inter-American Studies,* Vol. VI, No. 1, Jan. 64, pp. 105-110. In presenting the book *Poesia Negra* of the Nicaraguayan author, Juan Felipe Toruno, this study gives a good account of the universalism and cosmicity of Negro poetry.

Cartey, Wilfred, "The Rhythm of Society and Landscape", *New World,* Guyana Independence Issue, May 26, 1966, pp. 97-104. Summarizes the talents of some modern Guyanese writers and their apprehensions, but hopes, regarding the new country's future.

Genovose, Eugene D., "Materialism and Idealism in the History of Negro Slavery in the Americas", *Journal of Social History,* Vol. 1, Summer, 1968, pp. 371-394. A systematic analysis and criticism of all the three major schools on race-relations and cultural variations in Latin America.

Gillian, John P., "Possible Cultural Maladjustment in Modern Latin America", *Journal of Inter-American Studies,* Vol. V, No. 2, April 1963, pp. 149-160. Attention is drawn on four possible maladjustments in the mixed Latin American culture that Latin

Americans should try to eradicate if fullest development is the goal.

Godoy, Gustavo G., "Fernando Ortiz, Las Razas y los Negros", *Journal of Inter-American Studies,* Vol. VIII, No. 2, April 1966, pp. 236-244. This excellent article exposes and supports Ortiz' humanistic ideas on the question of races.

Hill, Adelaide Cromwell, "The Impact of Africa on the American Negro", *Papers Contributed to the 26th Annual Spring Conference of the Division of the Social Sciences,* Howard University Press, Washington, D.C., 1964, pp. 75-102. Mainly designed to narrate the historical relations of American Negroes with Africa, this short sketch nevertheless provides interesting information about the attitudes of certain Caribbean Negroes toward World Negro solidarity.

Isaacs, Harold R., "Color in World Affairs", *Foreign Affairs,* Vol. 47, No. 2, Jan. 1969, pp. 235-250. A brilliant analysis of the new aspects and importance of race or color cleavages in the late 1960's politics of a world where "white dominance no longer exists, certainly not in its old forms."

Mintz, Sidney W., "Review of Stanley M. Elkins' book, Slavery", *American Anthropologist,* Vol. LXII, June 1961, pp. 579-587. Mintz criticizes Elkins' institutional approach and suggests that both ideology and economics have determined race relations in Latin America.

Scofield, John, "Haiti—West Africa in the West Indies", *National Geographic,* Vol. 119, No. 2, Feb. 1961, pp. 226-259. Provides a picturesque, but generally objective, analysis of Modern Haiti and its arts.

Williams, Eric, "Race Relations in the Caribbean Society", *Caribbean Studies: A Symposium,* Vera Rubin, ed., University of Washington Press, Seattle, 1960, pp. 54-60. In this article, Williams somewhat departs from his previous economic determinism and recognizes the effect of historically-developed ideas on racial relations. Besides, a few Afro-Latin American contributions are cited.

NOTES

1. Magnus Morner, *Race Mixture in the History of Latin America,* Boston: Little, Brown & Co., 1967, p. 45.

2. Gilberto Freyre, *The Masters and the Slaves,* New York: Alfred A. Knopf, 1967, Ch. IV. Originally published as Casa Grande e Sensale, Rio de Janeiro, 1939.

3. Jean Fouchard, *Les Marrons du Syllabaire,* Port-au-Prince: Editions Deschamps, 1953, p. 96.

4. Magnus Morner, *op. cit.,* p. 19.

5. James Leyburn, *The Haitian People,* New Haven: Yale University Press, 1941, p. 136.

6. Jean Price Mars, *Silhouettes de Negres et de Negrophiles,* Paris: Presence Africaine, 1960, p. 17.

7. Michael G. Smith, *The Plural Society in the British West Indies,* Berkeley: University of California Press, 1965, Introduction.

8. Eugene D. Genovese, "Materialism and Idealism in the History of Negro Slavery in the Americas," *Journal of Social History,* Vol. 1, Summer 1968, pp. 371-394.

9. Eric Williams, "Race Relations in Caribbean Society," *Caribbean Studies: A Symposium,* Seattle: University of Washington Press, 1960, p. 54.

10. Marvin Harris, *Patterns of Race in the Americas,* New York: Walker & Co., 1964, p. 53.

11. *Ibid.,* p. 64.

12. *Ibid.,* p. 56.
  Harris' hypo-descent rule refers to the English rigid classification of any person of Caucasian-non Caucasian derivation on the exclusive basis of his "lower race" (as a Negro or an Indian), regardless of the dosage in his mixed composition.

13. Roger Bastide, "Race Relations in Brazil," *International Social Science Bulletin,* IX, No. 4, 1957, pp. 495, 496.

14. Sidney W. Mintz, "Review of Stanley M. Elkin's Book on Slavery," *American Anthropologist,* LXIII, June 1961, pp. 579-587.

15. Hubert Herring, *A History of Latin America,* New York: Alfred A. Knopf, 1965, p. 113.

16. Jean Fouchard, *op. cit.,* pp. 101-107.

17. Arthur G. Horton, *An Outline of Latin American History,* Iowa: Brown Book Co., 1966, pp. 22-25.

18. Magnus Morner, *op. cit.,* p. 46.

19. Gilberto Freyre, *op. cit.,* p. 271.

20. *Ibid.,* p. 261.

21. *Ibid.,* p. 364.

22. Arthur Ramos, *Las Culturas Negros en el Nuevo Mundo,* Mexico: Fondo de Cultura Economica, 1943, p. 125; First edition in 1937 was in Portuguese.

23. E. Franklin Frazier, *Black Bourgeoisie,* New York: Collier Books ed., 1962, p. 197.

24. Eric Williams, *British Historians and the West Indies,* Trinidad: PNM Co., 1964, p. 177.

25. Rayford W. Logan, *Haiti and the Dominican Republic,* New York: Oxford University Press, 1968, p. 91.

26. Eric Williams, *op. cit.,* p. 4.

27. Magnus Morner, *op. cit.* p. 85.

28. *Ibid.,* p. 81.

29. Adelaide Cromwell Hill, "The Impact of Africa on the American Negro," *Papers Contributed to the 26th Annual Spring Conference of the*

Division of the Social Sciences, Washington, D. C., Howard University Press, 1964, p. 91.

30. Gustavo G. Godoy, "Fernando Ortiz, Las Razas y los Negros," *Journal of Inter-American Studies,* Vol. VIII, No. 2, April, 1966, p. 241.
The Chinese mentioned in Ortiz' quotation originated from the large number of those who migrated to Cuba in the nineteenth and early twentieth centuries.

31. Eric Williams, *History of the People of Trinidad and Tobago,* Trinidad: PNM Co., 1962, p. 178.

32. K. A. Busia, *The Challenge of Africa,* New York: Praeger, 1962, p. 7.

33. Basil Davidson, *Black Mother,* Boston: Little Brown & Co., 1961, p. 68.

34. James Leyburn, *op. cit.,* p. 15.

35. Jacques C. Antoine, "Haiti and the Louisiana Purchase," *Haiti Today,* Haiti Government Tourist Bureau, No. 3, 1954, p. 6.

36. Wendell Phillips, *Speeches and Lectures,* Boston, 1863.

37. Jean Fouchard, *Le Theatre a Saint-Domingue,* Port-au-Prince: Imprimerie de l'Etat, 1955, pp. 345-349.

38. Pradel Pompilus, *Manuel Illustre de la Literature Haitienne,* Port-au-Prince: Editions Deschamps, 1961, Introduction.

39. Barbara Howes, *From the Green Antilles,* New York: Macmillan, 1966, p. 147.

40. Pradel Pompilus, *op. cit.,* p. 109.

41. Pan American Union, *Haiti,* Pan American Union, Washington, D.C., 1954, p. 18.

42. E. Williams' article, V. Rubin, *op. cit.,* p. 58.

FRANCK BAYARD was born in Haiti. He studied law at the University of Port-au-Prince before earning his graduate degree in Economics at Howard University and American University in Washington, D. C. He spent several years in the military, civil and diplomatic service of Haiti before teaching Social Science and Economics at Howard University from 1961 to 1967. He is currently an associate professor of Economics at West Virginia Wesleyan College. Bayard has done much socio-economic research on Latin America and has contributed to Rayford Logan's book, *Haiti and the Dominican Republic* (1968).

THE BLACK MAN AS A SOLDIER

JACK J. CARDOSO

State University (College at Buffalo)

The Negro has always been a warrior. In Africa his personal and tribal survival depended on his ability to both defend against and suppress his enemies, whether they were opposing blacks or European whites bent on imperial aggrandizement. The essence of African manhood was preparation for the life of the warrior, who was, as in all military units, the basic fighting factor. Survival, though not indigenous only to blacks, was nevertheless primely important to them even through the dismal centuries of international slavery. The warrior individuality persisted throughout the suppressive conditions that servitude imposed, and its character remained distinct both personally and collectively in the Western world. The essence of the warrior instinct is pride in the essential quality of one's nature as a person, and even in the most oppressive institutional slavery frameworks, the prideful quality of individuals was always in evidence. Those nations whose slavery practices included provisions for recognition of the essential worth of slaves as persons fared better socially and historically than those which structured their society so as to preclude black participation.[1] In the latter societies the stresses of existing in a state of constant tension demanded a displacement of energies and resources which in turn compelled an internalization of political and economic development, thus forcing them to absorb regressive philosophies which isolated them from the trust of world advances. The Americas are an essential laboratory example of comparative slavery systems which took into account the natures of their blacks in radically different ways.

South American slaves were allowed and even encouraged to retain their individual proud natures to an extent radically contradictory to that of their North American brothers in bondage. The inculcation of Spanish and Portuguese cultural traits by South American slaves was a structured personal and collective process, with the denial of the personality of the individual seldom even a moot concern. Within this process of cultural transplanting the blacks retained their individuality, thus allowing them to persist in attaining warrior identities.[2]

THE BLACK SOLDIER IN THE UNITED STATES

The North American experience was one of a denial of both personality and cultural identity. The factors of cultural and physical suppression were as intense as the whims of slaveowners might determine. Existence as chattel, rather than life as persons, became the mode of survival generally, despite individual paternalisms which in their own nature were perhaps more destructive to the independent psyche than regimented suppression. To an extent that is a testament to the soldierly nature of the Afro-American slaves, the accounts of individual and group rebellions against bondage declare emphatically the integrity of the blacks as persons in even the most oppressive of conditions.[3] The essential warrior nature of blacks in bondage is seen especially in the Revolutionary War in North America, as blacks participated in both British and Colonial armies, each of which held out the promise of freedom as a reward for service. The opportunity for enlargement of personality and independence led blacks to join militias despite the strictures of the Continental Congress which would deny them service. Only when Lord Dunmore of Virginia offered freedom to the blacks for service in the King's Army did General Washington and the Continental Congress hold a third meeting in 1776 and provide for the recruitment of black soldiers.[4] The quality of such service stands in bold relief in an otherwise disjointed struggle.

Ironically perhaps, the individual heroism of black volunteers becomes more pronounced historically as increasing attention is paid to Afro-American development. Peter Salem's killing of the British Commander, Major Pitcairn, at Bunker Hill was an achievement of moment in any war; and the valor of Salem Poor during the battle of Charlestown brought him commendations from fourteen Colonial army officers. After General Washington adopted a policy of allowing individual commanders to determine their own recruitment policy, black soldiers from every colony except Georgia and South Carolina were recruited. Even in these latter two colonies, blacks left in alarming numbers to join either the British or Colonial forces in the field.[5] South Carolina alone was believed to have lost 25,000 blacks while Georgia saw over 9,000 of their 15,000 blacks run away. The war provided an opportunity for blacks to assert their independence, both as men and as Americans participating in a national struggle for freedom. Of the 300,000 regular soldiers who served the Colonies, one-sixth were black, and they participated in every major engagement of the Revolution. In the Battle of Rhode Island under Lafayette, 144 blacks under attack by seasoned British regulars served so valiantly that one official declared: "Had they been unfaithful or even given way before the enemy all would have been lost."[6] At Point Bridge, New York, a detachment of blacks sacrificed themselves to the last man while defending Col. Greene's position in 1781. The counter-intelligence activities of the black soldier, Pompey, contributed immensely to the victory of Mad Anthony Wayne at Stony Point; and one black contingent serving the British as "The King of England's Soldiers" caused such harassment along the Savannah River that Georgia feared a general insurrection of blacks. In this same colony the French allies utilized hundreds of black freedmen from the island of Haiti during the siege at Savannah, one of the blacks being the notable Christophe, who became one of the most valiant fighters in his own island's quest for independence.[7] The revolution in America as a crusade for freedom stirred blacks to assert themselves and was a beginning for blacks who would shape their own destiny.

However, the contributions of blacks as soldiers were not to be institutionalized, as the proceedings and developments of the Constitutional Convention proved. Congress in 1792 limited national militia service to whites and the states adhered to the established criteria—except, ironically, South Carolina, Georgia and North Carolina, all of which accepted free blacks, and Louisiana, which accepted free men from the Creoles.[8] The Georgia and South Carolina experience during the Revolution, in which they suffered slave losses mentioned above, had apparently convinced these states that their actions had been folly and also that absorption of the free blacks into the military would provide an alternative institutional control. In view of these proscriptive laws, black service in the American military became a limited one. However, the War of 1812 proved to be more than a quasi-confrontation for black men, who again were courted by Great Britain in the South. Southerners in Louisiana, sensitive to the possibilities of internal revolution by black aspirants to freedom, acceded to General Jackson's rational thoughts on black identity: "Distrust them and you make them your enemies."[9] Some six hundred black troops joined the Jackson lines along with 150 Santo Domingo fellows to build the cotton-bag fortifications and lay the field of fire which broke the British attack at New Orleans.

The indomitable spirit of the black soldiers in battle and under conditions where their essential worth was acknowledged was further evident in the naval engagements on the Great Lakes. Black men had turned to the sea throughout early American history in pursuit of that individuality and worth that seafaring seemed to connote. Despite earlier qualms about blacks, Captain Perry found his black sailors to be "insensible to danger" and John Johnson, a black seaman serving with Commander Nathaniel Shaler, lay on the decks of his ship, *Governor Tompkins*, his body shattered, and exhorted his mates with, "Fire away my boys; no haul a color down."[10] These essential sacrifices in a dubious struggle were the rule rather than exceptions, and in any national experience stand as heroic hallmarks.

But General Jackson's wartime challenge to civilian authority was a sometime thing applicable to the exigencies of the moment. The myth of the "Era of Good Feelings" in American national life was brought home to the blacks on February 18, 1820, when the United States Army issued general orders declaring that "No Negro or Mulatto will be received as a recruit of the Army."[11] With this pronouncement the expanding South was pacified in her increasing commitment to slavery. Therefore, the expansionist war with Mexico became essentially a white man's venture and more specifically a pro-slavery Southern move for territorial acquisition. The internecine doings of the Whigs and the vacillation of the Democrats had allowed Southerners to preempt the political sphere, and the Mexican War held little for blacks in the way of either liberation or nationalism.

In America it was to be the Civil War that opened for blacks new avenues for liberating a dormant heritage. The resulting destruction of the Southern Democratic Party, compromise and cleavage of sections through consolidation of the agents of abolitionism and divergent antislavery, forced by 1862 a holy war against the Southern institutions. President Lincoln, pragmatically holding to the letter of his party's platform, bent by military failures and the South's intransigence turned toward a new and irrepressible commitment. Of the blacks he mused, "Why should they do anything for us, if we will do nothing for them?"[12] Ideas were thus joined and the reality of the past set the military policies of 1863, and the character of the war following this date changed dramatically. The announcement of the Emancipation Proclamation meant there was no turning back; it was the death knell of slavery.

Adjutant General of the Army Lorenzo Thomas, aided by the indomitable Frederick Douglass, who contributed two sons of his own, pursued his mission to recruit black soldiers with vigor. By 1865 some 186,000 blacks had seen organized service, and of this number 68,178 gave their lives. Desperation compelled America to learn emphatically the fallacy of the decision of the Supreme Court on Dred Scott: the blacks were indeed men. Confronted by the obstacles of prejudice, the reality of death or impressment if captured, infantile discriminatory practices as to pay and duty, and deprivations not equally shared by their fellow whites in arms, the battle for individual survival often fused with the larger struggle for freedom.[13] The Union forces, possessing little valid information as to climate and terrain, used indigenous blacks extensively for such intelligence. General McClellan's "wait and see" strategy, which was perhaps too greatly criticized by contemporaries, was in part attributable to estimates of enemy strength provided him by black guides. And though he decried the lack of more sophisticated means of ascertaining Southern forces and their deployment, his use of black guides continued. Still another item of note is the fact of Union materiel superiority which was a constant; much of the labor necessary for the construction of fortifications and for the lending of efficiency to matters of supply and engineering were black contributions.[14]

Further, General Sherman, following complaints from General John Hood of the Confederacy on the use of blacks against his troops, replied that the Union had used blacks to drive General Wheeler out of Dalton and had stationed them as guard units in Chattanooga. This latter activity allowed Sherman to consolidate his march of liberation through the South by protection of his rear.[15] The harried South also learned their lesson dearly, as reflected in the comment by Henry Allen, Governor of Louisiana, who said, ". . . we have learned from dear bought experience the negroes can be taught to fight."[16] Sherman too, reacting to criticism that he had been harsh with straggling slaves who trailed his sweeping forces, credited his pioneer (engineering) blacks with excellent service. He further suggested that enlisted black companies be established within white regiments and that politicians consider guaranteeing blacks homestead rights.[17]

It has been further estimated that one of every four Union sailors was a black man, among whom four won Congressional Medals of Honor along with sixteen from the Army who received the same high honors. There were 166 all black regiments in addition to blacks who served with predominantly white units. Louisiana, Kentucky, Tennessee and Pennsylvania led Union states in contributing black men for the war.[18]

Following the Civil War, demobilization was the rule; however four black regiments continued service with about 13,000 men. The 9th and 10th Cavalry and the 24th and 25th Infantry were recruited to serve in the Western territories. In the frontier they lent their energies to the stabilization of national control. By garrisoning outposts, protecting and guiding wagon trains, aiding in road-building and telegraph installation, and scouting Indians who called them "Buffalo soldiers," these black soldiers lent themselves to national expansion.[19]

Many of these same men contributed effectively to the United States effort in the Spanish-American War and took part in the capture of the enemy at San Juan Hill. Further, they won awards for braving the Spanish fire at El Caney and sacrificing themselves as hospital workers during epidemics of yellow fever. The four regiments of blacks mentioned above later went to the Philippines to fight the protracted guerilla war of Aguinaldo. Proud and resolute, the men later were stationed in Texas where they again encountered white social antagonism. Five blacks had earned Congressional Medals of Honor in 1898, and fourteen others had gotten the same award while serving with the 9th Cavalry between 1870 and 1891; but Jim Crowism had become complete by 1918. As the South was left to "reconstruct" itself and the North turned to industrialism and political consolidation, the American military followed suit. The four veteran black units were prevented from seeing overseas service, and despite the almost desperate desires of young blacks to volunteer, caution was the rule. To make both the world and the United States safe for democracy was a peculiar mission of devoted blacks, a mission with a warrior heritage; but American policy in the military became one of proscription, a policy reinforced by the request of the British Government that the blacks not be sent to Europe. General John Pershing, Commander of the A.E.F. in World War I and perhaps the most modest and intelligent of American officers on the scene, saw black men as American citizens against whom he personally would not discriminate; however, he too believed that the traditional policy of having white officers leading black troops should have remained the rule.[20]

But despite harassments and resentments, black soldiers of the 369th, 370th, 371st and 372nd Regiments proved the fraud of discrimination. In the area of Champagne, the Meuse Argonne, near St. Mihiel, and in the Oise-Aisne offensive, blacks weathered the onslaught of the Central Powers, suffering nearly three thousand casualties in less than two hundred days of fierce fighting. The 369th alone lost 851 men in five days and could boast when the final shot was fired that they had not given up one inch of ground or lost a single man as a prisoner. Of the two hundred thousand men who had gone to France, 42,000 had seen combat and had received hundreds of decorations. Two black infantrymen, Henry Johnson and Needham Roberts, became the first Americans to win the French Croix de Guerre.[21]

Between the wars, demobilization was again the rule of the services, but for the blacks it was a return to the military policies of 1916. The attitudes of the new South became that of the military. Bitter irony again ruled when, during the attack of the Japanese on Pearl Harbor, a black sailor on the U.S.S. *Arizona* won the Navy Cross for taking over an anti-aircraft gun following the deaths of the regular gunners. The Navy since 1900 had taken on black men solely as messmen, and only six months after

Pearl Harbor did policies change. Judge William H. Hastie, a black aide to Secretary of War Henry Stimson, encouraged the integration of black soldiers but he met with resistance. The demands of broad-scale war, however, demanded men by the millions; and of the numbers who saw overseas service, nearly 500,000 were blacks. Twenty-two black units fought in Europe, receiving many commendations. Finally, in 1945, an attempt at integrating blacks and whites at platoon level proved successful. In the Air Force, the 99th Pursuit Squadron and the 332nd Fighter Group both fought magnificently in the Mediterranean area and eastern Europe. The Marines also, for the first time, took black enlistees and their service in the Pacific was superb. In every facet of wartime service blacks did their part well and were an integral part of the American war machine.[22]

The quality of black service in World War II and the continuing need for occupation forces following 1945 precipitated the intelligent decision of President Truman to guarantee integration and equality of treatment in the military. Since 1948 the dedicated service of blacks in the American forces has been clear. In 1962 blacks represented 8.2% of all military personnel while comprising only 11% of the total population. And in the Army alone, blacks made up 12% of the force. The problem of black men in the officer ranks remained the same, both due to discriminatory practices within the services and more specifically to the fact that officers are taken from the college-graduate pool of eligible men. By 1963, 3.2% of Army officers were black, of which only 1% had 20 or more years of prior service. Of these officers only one, Benjamin O. Davis Jr. of the Air Force, held General's rank. His father, Brigadier General Benjamin O. Davis, had been the first black officer to attain that level following World War II.[23] President Truman had thrown down the gauntlet to the defecting South in 1948, and the black military men held their own and then some through Korea and into the woeful political turmoil of Vietnam.

THE BLACK SOLDIER IN SOUTH AMERICA

The abilities of blacks in military affairs, indeed in the whole spectrum of national life in the Western world, is perhaps more pronounced in the development of the South American republics.

344

Brought originally as victims of exploitation, blacks remained to become heirs and managers of a new society. In Latin America the Negro became first a citizen and secondly a member of another race; the process of acculturation, therefore, was readily accomplished. Spaniards and Portuguese, unlike their North American counterparts, brought few women to their colonies; further, stratification of labor among blacks existed by virtue of establishment of classes of workers. More significantly, the blacks were regarded first as human beings, and policies implemented gave priority to the human condition. The difference between slave and Negro was significant, a significance especially important where the free black man was concerned. In North America, slave and Negro were one and the same to Anglo-Saxons, a concept which dictated the arbitrary attitudes to all blacks. The civil relationship of blacks to whites in the Latin continent was one of mutual concern and respect and race divisioning did not consume their energies.[24]

In South America the blacks were truly shapers of their destiny, and their remarkable talents as soldiers hallmark the history of the continent. In almost every endeavor for independence, the black man exercised his considerable talent, aggressiveness and managerial expertise. In Brazil, Haiti, Santo Domingo, and with the armies of St. Martín and Bolívar, blacks displayed the warrior skills of their African forefathers. Despite the comparatively "open" conditions of Latin slavery, blacks did maintain a disposition to be free. They continually challenged European controls, as can be seen in the flight of thousands of blacks to the frontier and away from Western world domination. Fugitives settled their own "colonies" in the interior territories.

Many blacks organized themselves into settlements; one such grouping in the 1620's formed the Republic of Palmares in northeast Brazil in the state of Algôas. There, for sixty-seven years they maintained a society based on African origins with a venerated king, legislatures, ministers of justice and a cooperative economic and social structure. A quite significant achievement of blacks was the Bahia uprising in the eighteenth century led by Moslem Negroes. Another notable warrior for freedom was Chico Rei of the state of Minas Gerai, who, after purchasing his freedom, became the first Negro abolitionist in Brazil as he organized other freedmen in the struggle to liberate his people.

Another Brazilian, Luiz Gama, used his pen as a sword to become a leader of abolition; and in this same line there was José de Patrocino who became the articulate leader of the crusade which finally brought an end to slavery in 1888. In Brazil, too, Henrique Dias, a black, stands as one of two national heroes of the colonial era.[25]

The most redoubtable black soldier in South America was certainly Toussaint L'Ouverture, slave grandson of an African king, who was to be both physical and spiritual leader of his Haitian people. Born a slave in 1743, L'Ouverture through considerable acumen and aided by the generosity of his master, became wealthy. Because of the severe class strife in Saint Domingue he joined his fellow blacks against Mulattoes and whites. In 1791 he became the first leader of disjointed guerilla bands and then of a mass, straggling army bent on liberation. With knife and machete and few munitions and other supplies, his forces lived off the land, struck the French at every opportunity and utilized their superior knowledge of the island to avoid retaliation. By the turn of the century he controlled all of modern Haiti and also Santo Domingo, which in 1795 had been ceded to Spain. L'Ouverture emanicipated the indigenous slaves and, oddly enough established a constitution allowing for a new slave trade with Africa. Napoleon I, nevertheless, was outraged at the black victory and dispatched 54 ships and 23,000 professional soldiers to defeat the Haitians. The victory over L'Ouverture was shortlived, however, as an aging, illiterate and brutally self-sacrificing former slave, Jean Jacques Dessalines, assumed command of the bedraggled black forces and proceeded to slaughter and hound the now-43,000 man French army. In 1804 only 8,000 French soldiers escaped the disease and holocaust that Haiti came to represent.

Leader of a black nation whose eternal purpose was to rid the island of every connotation of slavery, Dessalines proved unable to consolidate his successes democratically and Haiti failed to prosper. Upon his death in 1806 the island divided, and the northern portion fell under the rule of Henri Christophe, an exslave who had been one of the volunteers who fought with Lafayette in the American Revolution and who had been an indispensable soldier in Haiti's own struggle for independence. Possessing aristocratic pretensions, Christophe ruled as a Caesar, crowned himself King Henri I, and situated himself in the palace he had built at Sans Souci. Among the masses he instituted an iron military discipline designed to bring economic glory. Though ignorant himself, Christophe encouraged foreign intellectuals to come to Haiti; and his military astuteness brought security to his country. However, the unification of the island did not come with Christophe, who killed himself in 1820 after a dozen years of rule. The more democratic southern half of the island was governed by a Mulatto, Alexandre Pétion, who indulged his people to the detriment of the economy and his rule. In 1815 he gave asylum to Bolívar and provided arms and food in return for the promise that Bolívar would abolish slavery. It was not until 1820 that the island was united under Jean Pierre Boyer, a Mulatto who proved unable to provide Haiti with social and economic stability.[26]

The story of the black soldier in Haiti is of special interest in that the former slaves of this country had come largely from the African empire of Dahomey—blacks who were generally regarded as "bad slaves," who were moody, nostalgic and often suicidal. The French were partial to Dahomeian slave importation while the British sought their chattel from the Gold Coast and the Portuguese and Spanish preferred Yorubans from western Nigeria. During the later Colonial era, blacks from nearly every section of Africa came and as available supplies of slaves diminished, less vigorous and alert Africans were sought for export. In Haiti, for example, Congo Negroes were regarded contemptuously by their proud fellows because of their complacency and too-ready acceptance of bondage.[27]

THE WARRIOR TRADITION IN AFRICA

A study of African blacks is a study of basic soldierdom, qualities of which were carried by their countrymen to other lands. Native Africans had always been a proud people within the confines of their isolated continent, and the status of warrior was basic to every male. Tribal survival transcended every other exigency and became a continuing, often religious trial. Even in individual combat there is no substitute for expertise, and the blacks of Africa pursued military sophistication devotedly. In this regard there was no tribe which could match the brilliance of the Zulus and their resolute captain, Chaka.

From what is known of tribal warfare prior to 1800, the Nguni warriors of what is now Zululand settled their disputes in an orderly manner. Rival tribes drew lines some 100 yards apart, each carrying five-foot shields and two or more light javelins. The oval shields of leather were hardened by water-curing, which made them impenetrable at even close distances. Facing each other, the tribes would dispatch select warriors to within fifty yards. After shouting insults, they would throw their spears; this would in turn draw more tribesmen into the fray while other members of the tribe, male and female, would cheer them on from the rear. The retreat of one side meant victory, and should the fleeing enemy drop their spears—complete surrender. The conquering tribe would then rush forward wildly to take prisoners and cattle. Casualties were generally few and wounds seldom fatal.

This was the mode of Zulu warfare when Chaka, illegitimate son of a Zulu chieftain, joined the army of Dingiswayo, who ruled the Mtetwa tribe. Dingiswayo had achieved status through his military prowess, which consisted of organizing his military by age groups, which in turn developed discipline, a necessary ingredient in warfare. Between 1806 and 1809 the Mtetwas had conquered over thirty other tribes with a minimum of fatalities. To consolidate his victories, Dingiswayo would allow the defeated enemy to select a chieftain from the remaining ruling family while he incorporated their available youth into his own army. This practice insured respect, as he had not dishonored the vanquished; plus, it weakened any future military potential by exhausting their pool of available warriors.

While serving the Mtetwas, Chaka became a precocious student of warfare and he proceeded to develop techniques of his own. He was able to combine the confrontation and rushing strategies into a single charge. Further, he discarded the spear in favor of a short, broad-bladed, swordlike weapon and exploited the possibilities of using the shield as an offensive weapon to hook away the protection of his opponent, thereby exposing a vital target for the thrust of the blade. Sandals, too, were discarded to enable greater speed and mobility. Chaka also diversified his tactics from a pell-mell rush to a classic horn-shaped offensive formation by arranging his men in tight attacking groupings, with each company of 100 men forming a horn, the flanks turned toward the enemy thereby allowing for feints or attacks at any time at the flanks of the opposition while the main forces remained ready toward the rear. Dingiswayo, Chaka's commander, however, declined to use this strategy since high casualties were the rule. But fortune was with Chaka when, with his leader's aid, he became Chief of the Zulus. He immediately put his plans to use with startling success and in 1818 he combined with Dingiswayo against the Ndwandas, who captured and killed the old commander. Chaka assumed command, retreated, then counter-attacked for victory. Shortly thereafter Chaka, now leader of the consolidated tribes, again defeated the Ndwandas and launched a series of campaigns of expansion and in search of booty. By 1822 his empire stretched to 80,000 square miles controlled by an army of 30,000.[28]

The modes of warfare adopted in Africa by blacks were generally suited to the terrain to be covered and the kinds of attacks to be defended against. Hugh Clapperton, travelling in north and west central Africa, found soldiers traveling in combinations of cavalry and infantry. Foot soldiers carried a bow and arrows, a straw canteen and a triangular rations bag while the horsemen held shields and swords and spears. Several camels covered with heavily quilted cotton armor served as a kind of armored unit which protected the advance and retreat of the infantry men who fired their arrows from between the animals.[29] Some tribes displayed genius in laying out their cities to take advantage of natural defenses. The city of Jenne, lying south of Timbuktu, was built behind a network of streams and waterways and surrounded by natural moats of swampland, all of which provided safety for over 800 years until it fell to Sonni Ali of Songhai after a relentless siege. Still another defensive stratagem was that of wall-building. The Hausas of Hausaland in Nigeria built an earthen wall sixty feet high and thirteen miles around to protect and house their people. The large size was to provide against possible sieges, for the people could engage in subsistence farming within the walls. Twelve gates provided entry, each gate garrisoned by a group of soldiers whose huts were built just inside. Directly in front of the wall a broad ditch planted with long-thorned briars discouraged all but the most willful of invaders.[30]

No study, however brief, of blacks as soldiers in Africa would

349

be acceptable without mention of the valiant soldiers of Menelik and Haile Selassie and of the fanatical dedication of the Mahdi's followers at Khartoum. The campaigns of Menelik resulted in the first defeat of a European army by Africans. Following an Ethiopian treaty with Italy in 1882, the Italians, seeking colonies in Africa, occupied towns in Eritrea, including the port of Massawa, and were moving toward Tigre until they were decimated by 20,000 Abyssinians. Undaunted, the Italians turned to Menelik of Ethiopia for aid against the Abyssinians, led by John IV who was soon to be killed accidentally. Menelik thus became heir to the throne of Christian emperors stretching back to Solomon. The Treaty of Uccioli, signed with the Italians in 1889, provided Menelik with 28 pieces of artillery and 38,000 rifles while the Italians comforted themselves with the mistaken notion that they had secured a protectorate. They proceeded to advance into Eritrea, forcing Menelik to accept two million rounds of ammunition, to pay back an earlier loan, and to renounce his earlier treaty, all to the dismay of the Italians. When Menelik proceeded to negotiate with France and Great Britain, the Italians under General Barateri moved 14,500 men against Adowa, capital of Tigre, in three columns. One of these columns, under General Albertone, had the furthest to go, and following a miserable march in the rain at night he found himself out of contact with the other columns. He nevertheless continued his march to within sight of the city, whereupon Menelik's forces, which had observed the straggling column's every move and had prevented Italian scouts from keeping contact, fell on the flanks, surrounded the hapless Latins and killed 8,000 whites and 4,000 of their native allies.[31] The effects of this disaster remained with Italy until 1935 when, with poison gas and flame, they sought to avenge themselves, this time against the forces of Haile Selassie.

By 1935 Selassie had tried to modernize his armies. Swedish officers supervised officer training, and he created an academy for professional soldiers. When the Italian attacks began, his army adopted khaki in place of white uniforms for concealment. Selassie called upon tribal chieftains to turn to guerilla tactics; and, as his forefathers before him, he took personal command of his forces. He insisted on the strictest discipline, which was enforced by brutal punishment. Officers in the field and their men were admonished not to falter upon losing their commanders. One officer continued at an anti-aircraft emplacement for two days, though severely wounded, because he feared his men would panic if he fell. When gangrene took hold, his men pulled him from his station and rushed him 150 miles for medical aid, only to see him die on the way. The immediate subordinate was ordered executed, but Selassie commuted his sentence to taking away all his property, 30 lashes, and two stabs in the back with a bayonet. The Lion of Judah tolerated no disregarding of his orders.[32] Courage and discipline, however, could not defeat superior technology, and Ethiopia became the gravestone of the League of Nations.

In Africa, the combining of strategy, tactics and troop management by blacks reached a high point under Mohammed Ahmed, a Congolese who proclaimed himself Mahdi, successor to the Prophet. In 1881 he assembled a mass of 200,000 people, imparting a consuming religious zeal and holy mission. His purpose was to purge the religion of Islam of Turkish corruptions. Despising the weak Egyptian administration of the Sudan, the Mahdi and his armies took to the field and destroyed a 10,000 man force led by a British Colonel. He then began a march on the fortress at Khartoum. From each of his followers he demanded an oath: ". . . we swear to renounce the world and (look only) to the world to come, and that we shall not flee from the religious war [Jehad]." Each day began with the pounding of a huge war drum called El Mansura; those who declined to continue the drive were declared legal prey. On the move, the Mahdi's forces marched in three separate movements. An intense religious atmosphere prevailed, with feasts, prayers and sermons. They dispatched into Khartoum spies and infiltrators who terrorized the British and the citizens. The city, lying at the junction of the White and Blue Nile, was the administrative center of British power in the Sudan and was commanded by the reactivated, eccentric General George Gordon. Gordon had miscalculated the religious zeal of the Moslems, hoping that minor concessions would dissolve the uprising. The Mahdi's forces marched relentlessly onward, constantly beating war drums, laying down harassing fire, cutting off supply and communications lines, and neutralizing the river travel. The army exhibited exemplary skill and discipline; they learned to conceal their horses until the opportune moment for the attack, when they would rise in three phalanxes, move forward in even advance, swing to the right and into the defensive square of the opposition, plant their banner, pray, then hit and drop back, hit and withdraw. Khartoum, isolated and thoroughly demoralized despite the resolve of General Gordon, proved no match for the blacks of Islam.[33]

In the present era the blacks of Africa, and indeed the world, are relying increasingly on guerilla tactics to thwart advanced technological warfare. Revolutionary blacks have returned to the basics of survival by knowing and exploiting terrain, avoiding decisive encounters, propagandizing the settlers, encouraging quasi-religious emotionalism, forcing discipline through terror techniques, denying the existence of such a thing as a defensible strategic position, even to themselves, being constantly on the move, exploiting the divisions within their own elements, simplifying complex causative factors, constantly forcing the superior enemy to *react* rather than force a reaction, and playing on diverse political and world opinion to bring favor to their cause. A case in point was that of the Algerian struggle against the French, and more immediately, perhaps, the Biafran struggle to secede from Nigeria.[34]

The black man, then, has always been a soldier, a warrior in pursuit of recognition and in defense of his status as a human being. No matter where he found himself his indomitable will persevered. His life has been one of danger and confrontation with physical and psychological obstacles which have left scars but failed to crush his spirit. The implacable soldierly skill and devotion of the Zulus, the fanatical dervishes at Khartoum, the canny warriors at Adowa, the resolute shapers of Latin American destiny, the solitary, rebellious black knights of North American slavery, and the regimented contributors to democracy testify to the abilities of blacks as universal freedom fighters.

From the earliest times black soldiers have been natural and skillful masters of the craft of warfare. Stealth, speed of movement, employment of sophisticated maneuvers, psychological terror techniques, technology, terrain exploitation, and counter-intelligence were but a few of the components of survival warfare used by blacks throughout history. When it came to deployment and implementation of the individual soldier, there was little left untried. Europeans recognized the talents of blacks as they penetrated Africa from the fifteenth century onward and were ready to employ them as spearheads of imperialism. Every imperial power turned to the blacks for military resources. In the United States, blacks fought courageously in every struggle where freedom was a primary issue.

Wars for freedom are emotional wars. The demands placed upon soldiers in such causes can often be borne only by the most dedicated. In effect, those soldiers with the highest anxiety quotients tend to become the most daring and skillful instruments of war, especially in situations demanding instinctive reactions and individual responses. The totally committed identifies himself completely with his mission, seeing himself as being the primary gainer from victory and thereby personalizing the ends of war. In this context, dedication to victory has religious and fanatical overtones. For the blacks, such personal involvement in wars involving the concept of liberty was natural, and their successes outnumber their defeats.

SELECTED BIBLIOGRAPHY

BOOKS

Aptheker, Herbert, *Essays in the History of the American Negro*, New York: International Publishers Co., Inc., 1964. This book of provocative essays deals succinctly with the American Negro experience in politics, war, and social involvement to 1860.

Barnett, Donald, and Njami, Korari, *Mau Mau From Within*, New York: Monthly Review Press, 1966. An "inside" story of the workings of the terrorist African movement, much of it unverifiable.

Cashin, Herschel U. *Under Fire*, New York: F. Tennyson Neeley, 1899. Cashin's study is especially relevant to black soldier participation in the Spanish-American War.

Cornish, Dudley Taylor, *The Sable Arm: Negro Troops in the Union Army, 1861-1865*, New York: W. W. Norton and Co., 1966. No study of the total Civil War experience is complete without a reading of this book.

Davis, John P., Ed., *The American Negro Reference Book*,

Englewood Cliffs: Prentice-Hall, 1966. Unlike most reference studies, this valuable work by Negro scholars is a readable study of Black Americans in politics, religion, the military, and economics. It is a valuable addition to any library.

Fagg, John Edwin, *Cuba, Haiti and the Dominican Republic,* Englewood Cliffs: Prentice-Hall, Inc., 1965. This provides a perhaps too-brief, though concise review of these republics.

Fanon, Frantz, *The Wretched of the Earth,* Constance Farrington, Trans., New York: Grove Press, Inc., 1968. A disturbing, often shallow study of Black nationalism which presently is used as a kind of liturgy by Black revolutionary movements.

Greenfield, Richard, *Ethiopia, A New Political History,* New York: Frederick Praeger, 1965. This is a large, readable study which is a standard political history of one of the most unique and durable of African nations.

Herring, Hubert, *A History of Latin America,* New York: Alfred A. Knopf, Inc., 1967. The most complete study of all of South America.

Mandelbaum, David G., *Soldier Groups and Negro Soldiers,* Berkeley: U. of California Press, 1952. With regard to Blacks in the American military, this is an intriguing study of primary group relations.

McClellan, George B., *McClellan's Own Story,* New York: Charles L. Webster Co., 1887. Though often regarded solely as an apologia, this work is a valuable reference book on the high command and the first three years of America's Civil War.

McPherson, James M., *The Negro's Civil War,* New York: Pantheon Books, 1965. This is a very readable volume on Negroes' views of events of the period, 1860-65.

Muffett, David J. M., *Concerning Brave Captains,* Ontario: Don Mills, 1964. This is a fascinating study of the resistance of the Fulani to Lord Lugard in his conquest of Hausaland.

Niven, Rex, *Nine Great Africans,* New York: Roy Publishers Inc., 1964. A very sophisticated, often witty and urbane book dealing with outstanding religious, military, and political leadership.

Perham, Margery, *Ten Africans,* Evanston: Northwestern U. Press, 1963. This is an intelligent and illuminating compilation of contemporary accounts by African leaders who have revealed their feelings on western civilization as it was related to their people.

————, and Simmons, J., *African Discovery: An Anthology of Exploration*, Evanston: Northwestern U. Press, 1963. This is a collection of views of English travelers and explorers in Africa during the primary period of British imperial penetration.

Pershing, John J., *My Experiences in the World War*, New York: F. A. Stokes, 1931. General Pershing's autobiography reveals the truly professional military mind during a period of tense racial relations.

Randall, James G., and Donald, David, *The Civil War and Reconstruction*, Boston: D. C. Heath and Co., 1966. This second edition of the standard account of the American Civil War contains much dealing with Negro participation in the total war effort.

Rosenbaum, Robert A., *Earnest Victorians: Six Great Victorians Portrayed in Their Own Words and Those of Their Contemporaries*, New York: Hawthorne Books, Inc., 1961. This book has an especially good account of General Charles Gordon's activities in the Sudan.

Salk, Erwin A., *A Layman's Guide to Negro History*, New York: McGraw-Hill Book Co., 1967. Though lacking any narrative and footnotes, this almanac-type account of Black contributions is worth looking through for leads and ideas on often "forgotten" American Negroes.

Schiffers, Heinrich, *The Quest for Africa*, New York: G. P. Putnam's Sons, 1957. This is a necessary study of the European drive for African acquisition and the relations with native Africans.

Schoenfeld, Seymour J., *The Negro in the Armed Forces*, Washington: The Association Publishers, 1945. Written by a Navy Reserve Lt. Commander, this very short book provides an insight into the negative military practices of the United States in the utilization of black manpower.

Scott, Emmett J., *Scott's Official History of the American Negro in the World War*, L. L. Walters Co., 1919. The controversies surrounding Negro contributions in the First World War take on new dimensions in this provocative inside study.

Sherman, W. T., *Memoirs of Gen. W. T. Sherman*, New York: Charles L. Webster Co., 1891. This is especially important concerning General Sherman's activities during his "March to the Sea" when thousands of freedmen turned to his army for aid.

Strachey, Lytton, *Eminent Victorians,* New York: Harcourt Brace, 1918. This articulate work on Victorian minds and actions is valuable for its revelations concerning imperialism and British government thinking.

Tannenbaum, Frank, *Slave and Citizen: The Negro in the Americas,* New York: Alfred A. Knopf Co., 1946. Professor Tannenbaum's seminal study on comparative slave systems is the most provocative book of its kind. The works of Stanley Elkins and David Brion Davis are testaments to the ground this seminal study has broken.

Whitman, S. E., *The Troopers,* New York: Hastings House, 1962. This is an exciting account of Black soldier participation in the plains campaigns following 1865.

Williams, George Washington, *The Negro in American History,* 1619-1880, 2 Vols., New York: G. P. Putnam's Sons, 1888. Mr. Williams, a Negro participant in the American Civil War, wrote this outstanding early treatise on Negro developments in America. It is basic to understanding early Black history in the United States.

Woodward, C. Vann, *The Strange Career of Jim Crow,* New York: Oxford U. Press, 1964. This potent little book examines the developing racial separatism in America following the close of reconstruction. Along with his *Origins of the New South,* it is a significant volume contributing to understanding the completion of reunification of the nation.

ARTICLES

Davenport, Roy K., *"The Negro in the Army—A Subject of Research",* *Journal of Social Issues,* Vol. XII, No. 4, 1947, PP. 32-40. This article contains a brief resume of the practices of the military in utilizing Black personnel.

Davis, John P., "The Negro in the Armed Forces of America" in *The American Negro Reference Book,* John P. Davis, Ed., Englewood Cliffs: Prentice Hall, 1966, PP. 590-661. This chapter is a very good review of Negro participation in America's military history and is at times, argumentative, especially on derogatory comments regarding the Negro effort.

Document 282, U.S. House of Representatives, 27th Congress, 2nd Session. This is pertinent to the fractional distribution of Negroes among United States Navy crews during the Jacksonian era.

Document of the War Collected by W.E.B. DuBois, *The Crisis*, Vol. XVIII, 1919. PP. 19-23. This particular issue of DuBois' *The Crisis* details Black roles in World War I. His "An Essay Toward a History of the Black Man in the Great War," in the June, 1919, copy is also very worthwhile.

Hartgrove, W. B., "The Negro Soldier in the American Revolution," *The Journal of Negro History*, Vol. 1, No. 2, 1916, PP. 110-131. A basic understanding of Negroes and the Revolution begins with the reading of this essay in the most credible of periodicals devoted to Negro history.

Ibrahim, Mustafa B., "The Fulani—A Nomadic Tribe in N. Nigeria," *African Affairs, A Journal of the Royal African Society*, Vol. 65, No. 259, April, 1966, PP. 171-178. This article provides insight to the economic, physical, and social characteristics of the Fulani of Hausaland which fought the British and played a part in the drive for freedom in Brazil.

Lang, Kurt, "Technology and Career Management in the Military Establishment," in *The New Military*, Morris Janowitz, Ed., New York: Russell Sage Foundation, 1964, PP. 57-65. Professor Lang provides statistical information on Negroes in the American military and the traditions limiting them.

Oliver, Roland, "Bantu Genesis: An Inquiry into some Problems of Early Bantu History," *African Affairs*, Vol. 65, No. 26, July, 1966, PP. 245-247. This is a too-brief study of Bantu origins and culture.

Otterbein, Keith, "The Evolution of Zulu Warfare," in *Law and Warfare*, Paul Bohann, Ed., New York: Natural History Press, 1967, PP. 352-357. The military developments within the Zulu nation receive a detailed and technical treatment in this good chapter.

Wasserman, B., "The Ashanti War of 1900: A Study in Cultural Conflict," *Africa, Journal of the International African Institute*, Vol. 31, No. 2, April, 1961, PP. 167-169. This is an examination of the evolution of Anglo-Ashanti conflicts relating to the incursions on Ashanti leadership.

JACK J. CARDOSO took his baccalaureate from Pennsylvania State College, East Stroudsburg, Pa., his M.A. from Lehigh University, and his Ph. D. from the University of Wisconsin. He did further graduate work at the University of Pennsylvania, as a Voelkers Fellow at Claremont (Calif.) Graduate School, a History Fellow at the University of Wyoming, and he held a Coe Fellowship at Stanford University. He has published reviews for the *Journal of American History, The North Carolina Historical Review, Military Affairs,* and *Civil War History.* His article: "Lincoln, Abolitionism and the Patronage, the Case of Hinton R. Helper" appears in the *Journal of Negro History* (April, 1968); another article, "Postscript to California Gold: A Yuba River Venture" appears in the California *North State Review* (Winter, 1968). He also presented a paper on "The Southern Reaction to the Impending Crisis" at the 1967 meeting of the Pacific Coast Branch of the American Historical Association. Presently he is finishing a biography of Hinton Rowan Helper and doing a study of negrophobia in American life. He is Associate Professor of American History at State University College at Buffalo, New York.

NOTES

1. Frank Tannenbaum, Slave & Citizen, *The Negro in the Americas,* Vintage ed., New York: Alfred A. Knopf, Inc., 1946, pp. 88-95, 119-122.
2. *Ibid.,* pp. 42-62, 90-1; Hubert Herring, *A History of Latin America,* 3rd ed., New York: Alfred A. Knopf, Inc., 1967, pp. 112-116.
3. Herbert Aptheker, *Essays in the History of the American Negro,* New York: International Publishers Co., Inc., 1964, pp. 1-70.
4. W. B. Hartgrove, "The Negro Soldier in the American Revolution," *The Journal Of Negro History,* Vol. 1, No. 2, 1916, pp. 116-119.
5. *Ibid.,* p. 116.
6. *Ibid.;*John Hope Franklin, *From Slavery to Freedom: A History of Negro Americans,* New York: Alfred A. Knopf, Inc., 1967, p. 136.
7. *Ibid.,* pp. 136-8; W. B. Hartgrove, *op. cit.,* pp. 116-128.
8. John P. Davis, "The Negro in the Armed Forces of America," in *The American Negro Reference Book,* John P. Davis, Ed., Englewood Cliffs: Prentice Hall, 1966, p. 598.

9. George Washington Williams, *The Negro in American History* 1619-1880, New York: G. P. Putnam's Sons, 1888, Vol. II, p. 27.

10. John Hope Franklin, *op. cit.*, p. 170.

11. John P. Davis, *op. cit.*, p. 598.

12. *Ibid.*, pp. 603-4.

13. Dudley Taylor Cornish, *The Sable Arm: Negro Troops in the Union Army, 1861-1865*, New York: W. W. Norton and Co., 1966, pp. 111-5, 132-3, 288.

14. George B. McClellan, *McClellan's Own Story*, New York: Charles L. Webster, 1887, pp. 34, 253-4.

15. W. T. Sherman, *Memoirs of Gen. W. T. Sherman*, New York: Charles L. Webster, 1891, pp. 244-250.

16. *Ibid.*, p. 251; John P. Davis, *op. cit.*, p. 610.

17. W. T. Sherman, *op. cit.*, pp. 249-251.

18. Erwin A. Salk, *A Layman's Guide to Negro History*, New York: McGraw-Hill Book Co., pp. 62-3. Attempts by the author to verify these totals has proved futile. They are not compatible with those of Cornish.

19. S. E. Whitman, *The Troopers*, New York: Hastings House, 1962, provides a sweeping account of activity by blacks on the plains.

20. Herschel V. Cashin, *Under Fire*, New York: F. Tennyson Neeley, 1899, pp. 145-147; also, John P. Davis, *op. cit.*, p. 615; C. Vann Woodward, *The Strange Career of Jim Crow*, New York: Oxford U. Press, 1964. This seminal work on segregation and the completion of reconstruction is necessary to understanding the period following 1877. John P. Pershing, *My Experiences in th World War*, Vol. II, New York: F. A. Stokes, 1931, pp. 44-5; John P. Da s, *op. cit.*, p. 616.

21. Documents of the War Collected by W.E.B. DuBois, *The Crisis*, Vol. XVIII, 1919

22. *Ibid.;* Erw A. Salk, *op. cit.*, p. 63; John Hope Franklin, *op. cit.*, pp. 455-70.

23. Kurt Lang, "Technology and Career Management in the Military Establishment," in Morris Janowitz, Ed., *The New Military*, New York: Russell Sage Foundation, 1964, pp. 59-61.

24. Frank Tannenbaum, *op. cit.* This little book must be read in its entirety to get the full impact of institutional concepts of slavery. John Hope Franklin, *op. cit.*, 122-3.

25. Frank Tannenbaum, *op. cit.*, pp. 90-1; Hubert Herring, *op. cit.*, pp. 114-116.

26. John Edwin Fagg, *Cuba, Haiti and the Dominican Republic*, Englewood Cliffs: Prentice-Hall, Inc., pp. 120-26; Hubert Herring, *op. cit.*, pp. 426-29.

27. *Ibid.*, p. 111.

28. Rex Niven, *Nine Great Africans*, New York: Roy Publishers, Inc., 1964, pp. 78-103; Keith Otterbein, "The Evolution of Zulu Warfare," in Paul Bohann, Ed., *Law and Warfare*, New York: Natural History Press, 1967, pp. 352-4.

29. Margery Perham and J. Simmons, *African Discovery: An Anthology of Exploration*, Evanston: Northwestern University Press, 1963, pp. 89-90.

30. Rex Niven, *op. cit.*, pp. 108-113.

31. *Ibid.*, pp. 50-3; Richard Greenfield, *Ethiopia, A New Political History*, New York: Frederick Praeger, 1965, pp. 122-5.

32. *Ibid.*, pp. 173, 199-201, 205.

33. Robert A. Rosenbaum, *Earnest Victorians: Six Great Victorians Portrayed in Their Own Words and Those of Their Contemporaries,* New York: Hawthorne Books, Inc., 1961, pp. 312, 322, 326-7; Lytton Strachey, *Eminent Victorians,* New York: Harcourt Brace, 1918; see the chapter on Charles Gordon.

34. Frantz Fanon, *The Wretched of the Earth,* Constance Farrington, Trans., New York: Grove Press, Inc., 1968, pp. 130-143. This disjointed and existential work involves fact and fancy in postulating the theory of black revolution.

THE BLACK AMERICAN CONTRIBUTION
TO LITERATURE*

ABRAHAM CHAPMAN

Wisconsin State University (Stevens Point, Wisconsin)

A rich and varied body of literature has been created by black Americans that has become an organic part of the literature of the United States.

The black Africans, torn away from their native languages and cultures and transported to Colonial America, began to use English as a written language of literary expression more than 220 years ago. A slave girl named Lucy Terry, in Deerfield, Massachusetts, was the first American Negro poet, as far as we know. In 1746 she wrote "Bars Fight," a verse account of an Indian raid. Jupiter Hammon, a Long Island slave, is recognized as the first Afro-American poet to be published: an eighty-eight line religious poem printed as a broadside in 1760. In 1773, Phillis Wheatley, a Boston slave, was the first Negro in America to publish a volume of verse: *Poems on Various Subjects, Religious and Moral*, 124 pages, printed in London.

Of earlier and far greater literary significance than these first published poems is the great Afro-American folk literature in English created by the slaves in the plantation South. The folk poetry, with its striking imagery and metaphors, is wedded to the music of the spirituals and secular songs which proved to be the cradle of the most distinctive American music. The lyrics of these songs were only one literary manifestation of the Afro-

---

* Condensed and edited by the author from his Introduction to *Black Voices: An Anthology of Afro-American Literature*, New York: The New American Library (Mentor), 1968.

American imagination. The profusion of oral narratives and folk tales was another. Professor Richard M. Dorson, a scholarly authority on American folklore, has written:

> One of the memorable bequests by the Negro to American civilization is his rich and diverse store of folktales . . . Only the Negro, as a distinct element of the English-speaking population, maintained a full-blown storytelling tradition. A separate Negro subculture formed within the shell of American life, missing the bounties of general education and material progress, remaining a largely oral self-contained society with its own unwritten history and literature.[1]

It was only in the 1880's, with the publication of the *Uncle Remus* stories by Joel Chandler Harris, that the American reading public began to get its first inklings of a small portion of this very rich literature—as told by a white Southern journalist. And it was not very much earlier, in the 1860's, that some of the old spirituals and slave songs were published for the first time.

The poetic and rhythmic qualities of the spirituals and the dramatic qualities of the folk tales were blended with added qualities of emotional intensity and psychological suggestiveness in the creation of still another current of oral literary expression: the sermons of the Negro preachers.

The rich variety of Afro-American folk imagination and expression made its impact on the consciousness and sensibility of both black and white American writers and has entered the written literature of the United States in many different shapes and ways. This incomparable cultural harvest of the black man's experience, anguish, humor, and creativity in the United States remains a viable and potent source of folk and shared emotional experience which Negro writers in the twentieth century as varied as James Weldon Johnson, Langston Hughes, Sterling Brown, Margaret Walker, and James Baldwin, have drawn upon in accordance with their individual needs, talents and literary visions.

The earliest published prose writing by an Afro-American, as far as we know, also dates back more than two centuries. In 1760, the same year that witnessed the publication, in Hartford, of Jupiter Hammon's first broadside in verse, another slave with the same surname, Briton Hammon, published a narrative in Boston. It was an autobiographical pamphlet, entitled *A Narrative of the Uncommon Sufferings and Surprising Deliverance of Briton Hammon, a Negro Man.* Of historical rather than literary interest, this pamphlet unwittingly fore-shadowed a fact of Afro-American literary history: autobiographical narratives were to become the first genre of prose writing of literary importance.

From the 1780's to the end of the Civil War there was a steady flow of a literature outlawed before its birth, a literature "in spite of," created in defiance of the laws making literacy for slaves a crime. It consisted of autobiographies and narratives written, and sometimes told, by slaves who had escaped slavery. One of the earliest important works of this type is *The Interesting Narrative of the Life of Olaudah Equiano, or Gustavas Vassa, the African.* Vernon Loggins, in his book *The Negro Author in America,* affirmed: "At the time it was published, in 1789, few books had been produced in America which afford such vivid, concrete, and picturesque narrative."[2] Nineteenth-century peaks of this literary form are the narratives by Frederick Douglass, William Wells Brown and Samuel Ringgold Ward, leading Negroes in the antislavery movement.

Another current of prose writing developed simultaneously with the slave narratives—protests against slavery and antislavery expository writing. The first noteworthy work in this field, an essay of unmistakable intellectual and stylistic importance, was "An Essay on Slavery" signed by "Othello," a Free Negro. This essay apeared in 1788 in two installments in the November and December issues of *American Museum,* one of the four major magazines founded in the United States after the American Revolution. From 1791 to 1796 Benjamin Banneker, the Negro of many talents who was appointed by Thomas Jefferson to the commission which laid out the plans for the city of Washington, published his widely circulated annual *Almanacks.* On August 19, 1791, Banneker sent a letter to Jefferson, who was then Secretary of State, condemning the degradation and barbarism of slavery and arguing for recognition of the human worth and equality of "the African race." This letter was published in Philadelphia in 1792 and, until the Civil War, was reprinted countless times as a classic of Negro-American protest against slavery. Some believe that Benjamin Banneker was the author of the anonymous "Othello" essay.

From the first decade of the nineteenth century the protest writings of Lemuel Haynes and Peter Williams are remembered. In 1829, David Walker's famous abolitionist pamphlet *Walker's Appeal* was published in Boston and became, in the words of Vernon Loggins, "the most widely circulated work that came from the pen of an American Negro before 1840."[3]

In 1827, *Freedom's Journal,* the first Negro newspaper in the United States, began publication in New York City, four years before the birth of Garrison's famous Abolitionist organ *The Liberator.* The opening editorial in the first issue of the first Negro newspaper (March 16, 1827) declared: "We wish to plead our own cause. Too long have others spoken for us. Too long has the public been deceived by misrepresentations, in things which concern us dearly . . ."[4]

A group of articulate writers, speakers and fighters against slavery contributed to *Freedom's Journal,* including Samuel Ringgold Ward and William Wells Brown, who attracted public notice with their narratives. Poems by early Negro poets and versifiers were published in *Freedom's Journal* and in *The Liberator.*

We can detect a pattern in the development of Afro-American expression very similar to the general line of development of American writing. The real achievements in imaginative writing follow an initial period of expository, autobiographical, religious and political writing. Significantly, the first fiction and first play by a Negro came from an active abolitionist who contributed to *Freedom's Journal.* William Wells Brown, author of many important antislavery articles and books, also wrote the first novel by a Negro in the United States. The book, *Clotel,* was first published in London in 1853. A revised version was printed in the United States in 1864. William Wells Brown also wrote the first play by an American Negro: *The Escape; or, A Leap for Freedom,* published in 1858. Both his novel and play are of slight literary merit, but it is interesting that the Negro antislavery writings spill over into the first works of fiction and drama. Professor Alain Locke noted in an article he wrote for *New World Writing* (1952):

If slavery molded the emotional and folk life of the Negro, it was the anti-slavery struggle that developed his intellect and spurred him to disciplined, articulate expression. Up to the Civil War, the growing anti-slavery movement was the midwife of Negro political and literary talent.

The modern period of literature by Negro authors, marked by the mastery of literary craftsmanship, achievements in form, and the critical definition of specific literary and cultural problems of Negro Americans within American culture, opens with the 1890's. Paul Laurence Dunbar, Charles Waddell Chesnutt and W. E. B. DuBois loom large in these literary beginnings.

Very much of the literature created by black American writers in the twentieth century is unknown to the general reading public and little known even to students of American literature. Before any meaningful debate can take place on conflicting critical approaches and interpretations and on analyses of distinctive forms, structures, images and themes, the literature itself will have to become better known. All too often, and for far too long, it has been a spurned or neglected part of our literary heritage.

The climate of indifference, neglect or rejection in which this literature has developed is easy to document. Many important books in this field have long been inaccessible and out of print (only in late 1968 and 1969 did we witness the beginnings of change in this traditional and predominant picture, with the publication of new edition, old works and new studies, as part of the slow academic response to the pressures for recognition of Afro-American studies as a vital and significant field of study). One of the finest collections of Negro literature in the world, the Schomburg Collection—which is part of the New York Public Library in Harlem—does not have the budget to properly maintain itself and its rare books and manuscripts. Many public and college libraries have but the sparsest sprinkling of imaginative literature by black Americans. In American literature courses in most high schools and colleges, the voices of the black writers have been unheard and unknown.

I have taught a special course on the Negro in American literature to urban high school teachers from all over the country. These teachers maintain that there are school authorities in the urban centers who insist the teachers be very wary of, or ignore, works by black writers, because these writings are too disturbing, or too realistic, or too angry, when there are already enough "problems" with the ghetto students! This constitutes a kind of literary or cultural segregation, a stifling of the black literary voices, in addition to being wrong in educational principle. The black students know the confining and frustrating realities of ghetto life from experience and need not turn to books for that. But literature by black writers can give the black students a meaningful ordering and illumination of the black experience in this country; it can show them the creative and imaginative power and achievements of the black man and can prove very important psychologically.

As a result of the various walls standing between many black writers and the reading audience, large numbers of literate and cultured Americans, including a high proportion of English majors and students of literature in the colleges and most teachers of English in the schools, are not aware that many meaningful literary works have been created by black Americans and are an organic part of the American literary heritage. Unfortunately we still have to contend, in our study of American literature, with the long and harsh tradition of the rejection of the Negro in our society and the historically built-in tendencies in American culture to ignore or play down the importance of the black Americans as creators of cultural values and aesthetic forms in the United States.

This is not unexplored territory. Many important studies, anthologies, and specialized collections of writings have been published over the years—predominantly but not exclusively by Negro scholars, critics, writers and poets. But symptomatic of the long resistance to the proper recognition of the literary works created by black Americans is the fact that, even today, you will search in vain in definitive, up-to-date American literary histories for some of the elementary facts about black American writers and writing. You will search in vain, in almost all of the standard-American literary reference works of today for the "Negro Renaissance" or "Harlem Renaissance," interchangeable terms widely used by students of the Negro in American literature to denote the extensive literary output of the New Negro movement that arose in the 1920's. This was the literary explosion that brought into American literature the early works of such writers as Langston Hughes, Alain Locke, Jean Toomer, Claude McKay, Countee Cullen, Sterling Brown, Arna Bontemps, and others. But our literary histories, with very rare exceptions, simply do not recognize the existence of any flowering of Negro expression, or any specific literary movement of black Americans as being worthy of special notice.

This is clear evidence of how much remains to be done to become aware of the full diversity and scope of American literature, to open our ears and eyes to the voices and imaginative creations of black humanity in our midst.

I have no special thesis about Negro American literature to advance or prove. If there is anything I would like to emphasize, it is the individuality of each and every black writer, the diversity of styles and approaches to literature, the conflict of ideas, values, and varying attitudes towards life, within black America. In my reading and experience I simply have not found any such thing as "the Negro."

Even the name "Negro" is today the subject of intense debate among black people. The question has been posed as to whether or not the word "Negro" should be abandoned and replaced by the words "black" or "Afro-American." Lerone Bennett, Jr., in a lengthy and interesting article on this problem in *Ebony* in November, 1967 wrote:

> This question is at the root of a bitter national controversy over the proper designation for *identifiable* Americans of African descent. (More than 40 million "white" Americans, according to some scholars, have African ancestors.) A large and vocal group is pressing an aggressive campaign for the use of the word "Afro-American" as the only historically accurate and humanly significant designation of this large and pivotal portion of the American population. This group charges that the word "Negro" is an inaccurate epithet which perpetuates the master-slave mentality in the minds of both black and white Americans. An equally large, but not so vocal, group says the word "Negro" is as accurate and as euphonious as the words "black" and "Afro-American." This group is scornful of the premises of the advocates of change. A Negro by any other name, they say, would be as black and as beautiful—and as segregated. The times, they add, are too

crucial for Negroes to dissipate their energy in fratricidal strife over names. But the pro-black contingent contends . . . that names are of the essence of the game of power and control. And they maintain that a change in name will short-circuit the stereotyped thinking patterns that undergird the system of racism in America. To make things even more complicated, a third group, composed primarily of Black Power advocates, has adopted a new vocabulary in which the word "black" is reserved for "black brothers and sisters who are emancipating themselves," and the word "Negro" is used contemptuously for "Negroes" who are still in Whitey's bag and who still think of themselves and speak of themselves as Negroes.

In a deeper sense the new challenge to the name "Negro" is a reflection of the challenge to the racist conditions of life identified with the reality of being a Negro in America. It is a part of the fight for new identities and new realities of life for black Americans. *Ebony* and other Negro publications have initiated polls of their readers as to which name they prefer and the first choice is for "Afro-American," second choice for "black," and third choice for "Negro."

Because life in the black American community, as in every human community, is characterized by diversity, divisions and conflicts, there can be no single approach to Negro life, the black experience, or the literature and culture created by Afro-Americans. We would consider America as a whole a very static, drab and regimented country without the very deep and fundamental differences of opinion which mark our national and cultural life. We would reject any single thesis or sweeping generalization to define the literature or culture of the United States. I don't know why the vigorous debates and sharp political and cultural differences within the black communities should evoke surprise and wonder. Conflict of opinions and values is the way of life of every thinking and human community. The great debates in the black communities of America today only confirm again what needs no confirmation—that the black communities are as human, argumentative and divided in opinions as any thinking community.

American literary criticism largely ignores most of the works by the Afro-American writers. In the last few decades, a few individual Negro writers, namely, Ralph Ellison and James Baldwin, have won critical recognition and acclaim as major American authors. To a lesser degree the critical spotlight has also shone on Richard Wright, frequently in terms of his power, drive and searing anger—but quite often as a negative example, as the archetypal author of the "protest novel," which has been frequently dismissed as a subliterary species.

Rarely are Wright, Ellison and Baldwin seen and treated, in our general American literary criticism, as part of a bigger and older current of literary expression—a literary tradition created by Americans of African descent, a literary reality which is organically American, created on American soil in the American language, with the same rights to recognition for its American authenticity as the literature created by the descendants of the immigrants from England and Europe. Rarely is this literature of the Afro-Americans seen by our general literary criticism in its full light and complete complexity. On the one hand it is part of a literature and culture shared with white America as a whole, inevitably shaped in significant part by the dictates of the American language itself and by the forms of literary expression developed in the United States. At the same time, it is also a distinct and special body of literature, in the sense that the historical memories and myths, experiences, and conditions of life of the black Americans have been deliberately kept separate and apart, for generations, from the priority of conditions and values established for white Americans.

There is little general critical recognition of the fact that central metaphors and concepts of Ellison and Baldwin, like "the invisible man" and "nobody knows my name"—the invisibility and denial of identity, the facelessness and namelessness, which are associated with the Ellison and Baldwin dramatizations of the alienated Negro in America—are actually deeply rooted in the group or folk consciousness of black America and were given literary expression long before Ellison and Baldwin ever appeared on the literary scene.

In the dawn of this century, in *The Souls of Black Folk* (1903), a classic literary expression of the sensibility, consciousness and dilemmas of a black American intellectual, W. E. B. DuBois wrote:

After the Egyptian and Indian, the Greek and Roman, the Teuton and Mongolian, the Negro is a sort of seventh son, born with a veil, and gifted with second-sight in this American world—a world which yields him no true self-consciousness, but only lets him see himself through the revelation of the other world. It is a peculiar sensation, this double-consciousness, this sense of always looking at one's self through the eyes of others, of measuring one's soul by the tape of a world that looks on it in amused contempt and pity. One ever feels his twoness—an American, a Negro; two souls, two thoughts, two unreconciled strivings; two warring ideals in one dark body, whose dogged strength alone keeps it from being torn asunder.[5]

Many years later, in his book *Dusk of Dawn* (1940), Du Bois described the psychological impact of caste segregation in the following words:

It is as though one, looking out from a dark cave in a side of an impending mountain, sees the world passing and speaks to it; speaks courteously and persuasively, showing them how these entombed souls are hindered in their natural movement, expression, and development; and how their loosening from prison would be a matter not simply of courtesy, sympathy, and help to them, but aid to all the world . . . It gradually permeates the minds of the prisoners that the people passing do not hear; that some thick sheet of invisible but horribly tangible plate glass is between them and the world. They get excited; they talk louder; they gesticulate. Some of the passing world stop in curiosity; these gesticulations seem so pointless; they laugh and pass on. They still either do not hear at all, or hear but dimly, and even what they hear, they do not understand. Then the people within may become hysterical.[6]

The sense of duality, powerlessness, and rejection by a hostile society and environment, as expressed by Du Bois, comes from the core of the consciousness of black America and is reiterated time and again, in a multitude of ways, by black American writers.

James Weldon Johnson published an article entitled "The Dilemma of the Negro Author" in *The American Mercury* in

December, 1928. The title of the article itself sounds the note of duality we heard earlier in Du Bois. Observing that the Negro author faces all of the difficulties common to all writers, Johnson went on to say that "the Afroamerican author faces a special problem which the plain American author knows nothing about—the problem of the double audience. It is more than a double audience; it is a divided audience, an audience made up of two elements with differing and often opposite and antagonistic points of view. His audience is always both white America and black America." The theme is insistent: two worlds, two Americas, two antagonistic points of view.

Langston Hughes voiced this sense of division in an early poem "As I Grew Older":

> It was a long time ago
> I have almost forgotten my dream
> But it was there then,
> In front of me,
> Bright like a sun—
> My dream.
>
> And then the wall rose,
> Rose slowly,
> Slowly,
> Between me and my dream.
> Rose slowly, slowly,
> Dimming,
> Hiding,
> The light of my dream.
> Rose until it touched the sky—
> The wall.[7]

We hear the motif again in a late essay by Richard Wright, "The Literature of the Negro in the United States," articulated this way:

Held in bondage, stripped of his culture, denied family life for centuries, made to labor for others, the Negro tried to learn to live the life of the New World in an atmosphere of rejection and hate. . . . For the development of Negro expression—as well as the whole of Negro life in America—

371

hovers always somewhere between the rise of man from his ancient, rural way of life to the complex, industrial life of our time. Let me sum up these differences by contrasts; entity vs. identity; pre-individualism vs. individualism; the determined vs. the free. . . . Entity, men integrated with their culture; and identity, men who are at odds with their culture, striving for personal identification.[8]

Wright expressed the duality and the sense of twoness as a "versus" and identified the search for personal identity with being at odds with the prevailing culture in the United States.

In a symposium of prominent Negro writers broadcast by a New York City radio station in 1961, the moderator, Nat Hentoff, asked the late playwright Lorraine Hansberry the following question:

Miss Hansberry, in writing *A Raisin in the Sun,* to what extent did you feel a double role, both as a kind of social actionist "protester," and as a dramatist?[9]

Lorraine Hansberry answered:

Well, given the Negro writer, we are necessarily aware of a special situation in the American setting . . . We are doubly aware of conflict, because of the special pressures of being a Negro in America. . . . In my play I was dealing with a young man who would have, I feel, been a compelling object of conflict as a young American of his class of whatever racial background, with the exception of the incident at the end of the play, and with the exception, of course, of character depth, because a Negro character is a reality; there is no such thing as saying that a Negro could be a white person if you just changed the lines or something like this. This is a very arbitrary and superficial approach to Negro character. . . . I started to write about this family as I knew them in the context of those realities which I remembered as being true for this particular given set of people; and, at one point, it was just inevitable that a problem of some magnitude which was racial would intrude itself, because this is one of the realities of Negro life in America. But it was just as inevitable that

372

for a large part of the play, they would be excluded. Because the duality of consciousness is so complete that it is perfectly true to say that Negroes do not sit around twenty-four hours a day, thinking, "I'm a Negro."[10]

And Chester Himes, in an essay entitled "Dilemma of the Negro Novelist in U.S." published in 1966, wrote:

From the start the American Negro writer is beset by conflicts. He is in conflict with himself, with his environment, with his public. The personal conflict will be the hardest. He must decide at the outset the extent of his honesty. He will find it no easy thing to reveal the truth of his experience or even to discover it. He will derive no pleasure from the recounting of his hurts. He will encounter more agony by his explorations into his own personality than most non-Negroes realize. For him to delineate the degrading effects of oppression will be like inflicting a wound upon himself. He will have begun an intellectual crusade that will take him through the horrors of the damned. And this must be his reward for his integrity: he will be reviled by the Negroes and whites alike. Most of all, he will find no valid interpretation of his experiences in terms of human values until the truth be known.

If he does not discover this truth, his life will be forever veiled in mystery, not only to whites, but to himself; and he will be heir to all the weird interpretations of his personality.[11]

Afro-American literature takes us into the hearts and minds, into the inner worlds of black Americans. Literature as a way of knowing and perceiving probes beyond the conscious, the fully known, and the fully thought out. With contrast and analogy, imaginative ways of ordering images and values, with metaphor and symbol which suggest and imply the shapes and intimations of things and conditions sensed and known in the psychic subsoil, literature searches and captures human hopes and fears, dreams and nightmares, aspirations and frustrations, desires and resentments, which do not register on computer punch cards, statistical surveys and government reports. If America had only done something about the truths and literary revelations contained in Richard Wright's *Native Son*, published in 1940, with its profound psychological illumination of how the prison box of the big city ghetto was generating violence and destruction as the only language and means of action that had any validity for the hemmed in Bigger Thomas, living in a world without viable alternatives, moving in an incomprehensible mausoleum of dead dreams and hopes—then our past summers of discontent might have been very different.

There is still another special insight into American life that we get from black writers: the look and the feel and the psychological texture of the behavior of white Americans as it is manifest to black Americans. Here, too, we have an area of great human complexities, of codes of behavior and hidden emotional recesses, of cruelty and guilt, of cold calculation and the irrational, crime and conscience, hate and love. Here we find further illumination of a major concern of modern literature, the walls that isolate and separate man from man and the barriers to human connection and communication, with particular attention to what the "curtain of color" does to people on both sides of such a curtain. If, in addition to aesthetic delight, we turn to literature for its power of human illumination, both as mirror and lamp, then certainly the mirrors and lamps created by the black writers have a special value for America—if we are ready to look at the truths they expose.

A long time ago in the literary history of the United States, when the great debate was unfolding on whether and when and *how* a distinctively American literature would develop on this continent, the question of the Negro in American literature was an organic part of the whole discussion. Some of the highly original and nonconformist writers of that day, seeking to probe the uniqueness of America, thought that the United States differed most from England and all other countries in its human composition and evolution, its absorption of people from all the continents, races and regions of mankind. A truly American literature, these writers believed, would somehow express the new fusion of peoples and races in the new continent, the new human realities and conditions of life in the United States.

This conception was clearly voiced in the dawn of the "Golden Age" of American literature by Margaret Fuller, first editor of the Transcendentalist journal *The Dial*, who later joined the staff of the New York *Tribune* as the first professional book reviewer in America. In her landmark essay "American Literature: Its Position in the Present Time, and Prospects for the Future (1846)", a composite of reviews she had first written for the *Tribune*, later published in her two-volume collection of writings *Papers on Literature and Art*, Margaret Fuller wrote:

> We have no sympathy with national vanity. We are not anxious to prove that there is as yet much American literature. Of those who think and write among us in the methods and of the thoughts of Europe, we are not impatient; if their minds are still best adapted to such food and such action. . . . Yet there is often between child and parent a reaction from excessive influence having been exerted, and such a one we have experienced in behalf of our country against England. We use her language and receive in torrents the influence of her thought, yet it is in many respects uncongenial and injurious to our constitution. What suits Great Britain, with her insular position and consequent need to concentrate and intensify her life, her limited monarchy and spirit of trade, does not suit a mixed race continually enriched with new blood from other stocks the most unlike that of our first descent, with ample field and verge enough to range in and leave every impulse free, and abundant opportunity to develop a genius wide and full as our rivers . . . . That such a genius is to rise and work in this hemisphere we are confident; equally so that scarce the first faint streaks of that day's dawn are yet visible. . . . That day will not rise till the fusion of races among us is more complete. It will not rise till this nation shall attain sufficient moral and intellectual dignity to prize moral and intellectual no less highly than political freedom. . . .[12]

A decade later, in the high tide of the American Renaissance, Walt Whitman wrote in his Preface to the first (1855) edition of *Leaves of Grass*:

> Here is not merely a nation but a teeming nation of nations. . . . The American poets are to enclose old and new for

America is the race of races. Of them a bard is to be commensurate with a people. To him the other continents arrive as contributions. . . . he gives them reception for their sake and his own sake.[13]

Almost a century later, the American poet William Carlos Williams, in his prose volume of poetic insights and interpretations of the American heritage, *In the American Grain,* wrote:

The colored men and women whom I have known intimately have a racial character which has impressed me. I have not much bothered to know why, exactly, this has been so—

The one thing that never seems to occur to anybody is that the Negroes have a quality which they have brought to America . . . Poised against the Mayflower is the slave ship—manned by Yankees and Englishmen—bringing another race to try upon the New World . . . . There is a solidity, a racial irreducible minimum, which gives them poise in a world in which they have no authority.[14]

The hopeful vision of Margaret Fuller, Walt Whitman, and many others—that the United States would realize the promise and potential of its genius by transcending racial exclusiveness and welcoming the contributions and qualities brought to this continent by all races and continents—clashed, and clashes to this day, with a tenacious, strong and contrary current in American culture. It is in conflict with a cultural attitude and posture which Professor Horace M. Kallen, in his book *Cultural Pluralism and the American Idea* (1956), has designated as "a racism in culture":

It claimed that the American Idea and the American Way were hereditary to the Anglo-Saxon stock and to that stock only; that other stocks were incapable of producing them, learning them and living them. If, then, America is to survive as a culture of creed and code, it can do so only so long as the chosen Anglo-Saxon race retains its integrity of flesh and spirit and freely sustains and defends their American expression against alien contamination.[15]

The famous Gunnar Myrdal study of the American Negro problem, published in 1944, dealt with this same reality in a strictly sociological context, and called it "the anti-amalgamation doctrine." This doctrine is the opposite of the "melting pot" theory, which envisaged the assimilation and amalgamation of the various streams of white immigrants to this country into an American synthesis. The "anti-amalgamation doctrine" works in reverse and is described as follows in the Myrdal report:

> The Negroes, on the other hand, are commonly assumed to be unassimilable, and this is the reason why the Negro problem is different from the ordinary minority problem in America. The Negroes are set apart, together with other colored peoples, principally the Chinese and Japanese. While all other groups are urged to become Americanized as quickly and completely as possible, the colored peoples are excluded from assimilation.[16]

We can detect signs and echoes of this "racism in culture," this "anti-amalgamation doctrine," which is rooted so deeply in the American consciousness and American social practices, in white America's critical aproaches to the Negro in American literature. I hasten to make clear that I am not saying that all American critics, writers and readers are racists. What I am saying is that it is very difficult to maintain, in theory and practice, that the Negro is unassimilable, so different and inherently incapable of fitting into America like other people that he must be kept separate and apart, and at the same time see that this despised Negro has been, and is, a real and significant creator of American cultural values and esthetic forms. Racism and currents of conflict with racism, including the resistance to racism of black America, are organic elements in the dynamics of American culture. And, since the pressures of racism in American life and thinking remain more powerful and pervasive than the significant but weaker currents of antiracism, inescapably racist attitudes often spill over into the literary domain and blur America's literary and critical vision.

Evidence of how the pressures of racism penetrate literature can be found in the crowded gallery of stereotyped Negro characters in American fiction and drama—certainly not all Negro characters by white writers, but quite predominantly: the servile Negro, the comic Negro, the savage Negro. The opening lines of Sterling Brown's book *The Negro in American Fiction* (1937) declare bluntly: "The treatment of the Negro in American fiction, since it parallels his treatment in American life, has naturally been noted for injustice. Like other oppressed and exploited minorities, the Negro has been interpreted in a way to justify his exploitation."[17]

Ralph Ellison, in an early essay, wrote: "Thus it is unfortunate for the Negro that the most powerful formulations of modern American fictional words have been so slanted against him that when he approaches for a glimpse of himself he discovers an image drained of humanity."

The racist attitudes and feelings which have spawned the well-exposed stereotypes of Negro character in American imaginative literature, have also been responsible for distortions of critical criteria and for the double standards and special criteria we often encounter in American literary criticism when the works of Afro-American writers are discussed. Whether it stems from a fear of looking at the blackness of the black experience in America and the human consequences of American racism or whether it stems from some cultural variation of the doctrine of the "unassimilability" of the Negro, the fact is that we do encounter in American literary criticism various forms of rejection and negation of the meaning and value of the human experience of the Afro-American.

I shall later offer the evidence on which I base this assertion, but first I want to contrast the very common sympathetic approaches of modern literary criticism to the particularity and otherness of regional and ethnic individuality, as primary proof of why I think there is a reverse tendency in American criticism, a tendency to reject the unique value of the ethnic individuality of the Negro. What seems to be frequently reversed when the Negro enters the picture are the critical criteria—commonly accepted by more than one school of modern literary criticism— that literature is the art of the particular and individual, that the universal in literature is most fully achieved in the depth and completeness with which the uniqueness of the individual is portrayed, and that human freedom is a valid subject for artistic and literary exploration.

Let us see how some modern critics and writers approach and appreciate the particular ethnic and regional literary worlds of writers who are not Negro.

Albert Camus, the French writer of Algerian birth, declared: "No one is more closely attached to his Algerian province than I, and yet I have no trouble feeling a part of French tradition. . . . Silone [the Italian writer] speaks to all of Europe, and the reason I feel so close to him is that he is also so unbelievably rooted in his national and even provincial tradition."[18]

William Faulkner declared in his well-known *Paris Review* interview: "Beginning with *Sartoris* I discovered that my own little postage stamp of native soil was worth writing about and that I would never live long enough to exhaust it . . ."[19]

Isaac Bashevis Singer, the Jewish writer who came to the United States from Poland in 1935, writes in Yiddish and has been widely hailed as a significant figure in the contemporary literary scene since his works began appearing in English in the 1950's. He wrote in an article published in *Book World* early in 1968: "But the masters of literary prose have seldom left their territorial and cultural frontiers. There is no such thing as the international novel or international drama. Literature is by its very nature bound to a people, a region, a language, even a dialect."

James Joyce, writing outside his native Ireland, created his entire fictional world out of Dubliners, and this was no bar to his universal recognition as a giant of modern fiction.

W. B. Yeats, recognized as a major poet of the twentieth century, is not dismissed by any critic as "not universal" because he gave full expression to his Irish self; nor is he dubbed a "protest" propagandist by any serious critic because he stressed the thematic literary inspiration he derived from the Irish freedom movement. Yeats shed much light on the question I am now trying to examine in his essay "A General Introduction For My Work," written in 1937 for a complete edition of his works which did not appear, and later incorporated into his book *Essays and Introductions* (1961). Stating as his "first principle" that "a poet writes always of his personal life, in his finest work out of its tragedy, whatever it be, remorse, lost love, or loneliness," Yeats went on to say that he found his subject matter in the Irish resistance movement. He stated it in a very personal way: "It was through the old Fenian leader John O'Leary I found my theme." He speaks of O'Leary's long imprisonment, longer banishment, his pride, his integrity, and his dream—the dream of Irish freedom—that nourished and attracted young Irishmen to him and attracted the young Yeats too. He recalled that at the time he read only romantic literature and the Irish poets, some of which was not good poetry at all, and he added: "But they had one quality I admired and admire: they were not separated individual men; they spoke or tried to speak out of a people to a people; behind them stretched the generations."[20]

This is a quality we also find, in a different way, in the works of the Afro-American writers in which we can also feel this sense of a people speaking out to a people, with a sense of the generations behind: mythic memories of the remote African past, memories of slavery and common experiences in America.

Yeats, of course, as an artist, voiced his strong hatred of didactic literature but at the same time took pains to disavow any idea that his Irish self separated him from world literature and humanity as a whole. Later in this same essay Yeats wrote:

> I hated and still hate with an ever growing hatred the literature of the point of view. I wanted, if my ignorance permitted, to get back to Homer, to those that fed at his table. I wanted to cry as all men cried, to laugh as all man laughed, and the young Ireland poets when not writing mere politics had the same want, but they did not know that the common and its befitting language is the research of a lifetime, and when found may lack popular recognition. . . . If Irish literature goes on as my generation planned it, it may do something to keep the "Irishry" living. . .[21]

In his poetic approach, Yeats united three components which to others may seem irreconcilable or incompatible: to express the personal and private self, to express the common humanity the individual shares with all men, and to express the ethnic or racial self with its particular mythology and cultural past. If for "Irishry" we substitute black or Negro consciousness we can see that the best of the Afro-American writers have been struggling to express and blend the three components Yeats speaks of, and a fourth as well, which has made the situation of the black writer in America even more complex: their personal selves, their universal humanity, the particular qualities and beauty of their blackness and ethnic specificity, and their American selves. These are not separate and boxed off compartments of the mind and soul, but the inseparable and intermingled elements of a total human being, of a whole person who blends diversities within himself. This is the rich blend we find in the best of the Negro American artists.

The significance of Yeats' experience and point of view for an understanding of certain aspects of American literature is stressed, in a different way and in another context, by Cleanth Brooks in his book *William Faulkner: The Yoknapatawpha Country*. Brooks writes:

> Any Southerner who reads Yeats' *Autobiographies* is bound to be startled, over and over again, by the analogies between Yeats' "literary situation" and that of the Southern author: the strength to be gained from the writer's sense of belonging to a living community and the special focus upon the world bestowed by one's having a precise location in time and history.[22]

Certainly the Afro-American writer has this "sense of belonging to a living community" which should be appreciated as a source of strength. But the Negro writer and Negro community in the United States have historically been denied the advantages "bestowed by one's having a precise location in time and history." The Negro in America has been denied a proper location and place, has been in perpetual motion searching for a proper place he could call home. During slavery, the flight to freedom was the goal—the search for a home, a haven, the search for a possibility of secure belonging. After the Civil War, and to this day, this historical reality has expressed itself in the great migration from the South to the North and the patterns of flight and migration which are inherent in the spatial and plot movements in the novels of Richard Wright, Ralph Ellison, and James Baldwin. This opposite reality, of uprooting and dislocation, gave the Negro writer, to use the language of Brooks, a different "special focus upon the world," a focus of *denial* of a place, which we hear so clearly in the spirituals.

Here is how this theme is expressed time and again in lines chosen at random from different spirituals.

I'm rolling through an unfriendly worl'.

Sometimes I feel like a motherless child,
A long way from home . . .

Swing low, sweet chariot,
Coming for to carry me home . . .

I got a home in dat rock,
Don't you see? . . .
Poor man Laz'rus, poor as I,
When he died he found a home on high,

He had a home in dat rock,
Don't you see?

Deep river, my home is over Jordan.

I am a poor pilgrim of sorrow . . .
I'm tryin' to make heaven my home.

Sometimes I am tossed and driven.
Sometimes I don't know where to roam.
I've heard of a city called heaven.
I've started to make it my home.

American literary criticism has still not come to terms with the "special focus upon the world" that the realities of being a black man in America have created for the Afro-American writers. And all too often the critical assumptions articulated by Camus, Faulkner, Singer and Yeats are reversed into some kind of special critical doctrine for the black writer which seems to say or imply that to be meaningful for America, to be universal, the black writer has to be *other* than Negro, *other* than racial, *other* than what he actually and truly is.

What about the evidence for this statement? Let me begin with Louis Simpson, a fine contemporary American poet with a liberal and humane sensibility. When *Selected Poems* by Gwendolyn Brooks was published, he reviewed it among a group of new volumes of verse, in *Book Week* (October 27, 1963). Simpson wrote:

Gwendolyn Brooks' *Selected Poems* contain some lively pictures of Negro life. I am not sure it is possible for a Negro to write well without making us aware he is a Negro; on the other hand, if being a Negro is the only subject, the writing is not important . . . Miss Brooks must have had a devil of a time trying to write poetry in the United States, where there has been practically no Negro poetry worth talking about.

Why is writing about "being a Negro" a subject which "is not important"?—why, unless you somehow feel or believe that being a Negro is not important or that Negro life doesn't have values or meanings that are important? And why should there be anything wrong with our being aware of the Negro as author, anymore than it is wrong for us to be aware that Yeats is Irish and that Isaac Bashevis Singer is Jewish and that Ignazio Silone is Italian and that Dostoyevsky is unmistakably Russian and that Faulkner is very much of a Mississippian? And why so cavalierly dismiss practically all of Negro poetry in the United States with one fell swoop?

Or take another example, this one from academic criticism by Marcus Klein, a member of the Barnard College faculty. In his book *After Alienation: American Novels in Mid-Century*, he devotes two chapters to Ralph Ellison and James Baldwin and considers them very seriously. He writes:

> But what seems characteristic of major Negro literature since mid-century is an urgency on the part of writers to be more than merely Negro . . . The time has seemed to urge upon him [the Negro writer], rather, a necessity to discover his nonracial identity within the circumstances of race.[23]

Why this emphasis on being more than "merely Negro" and "non-racial identity"? Perhaps the clearest answer is provided in a critical statement by William Faulkner. In the rich and complex fictional world of Faulkner we encounter many Negro characters, ranging from Negro stereotypes tainted by the racism of their Mississippi origin to Negro characters of great artistic stature, with depth and dignity and profound symbolic meaning, like Sam Fathers and Lucas Beauchamp in *Go Down, Moses*. As man and critic, Faulkner, on numerous occasions, expressed the basic racist assumptions and attitudes of his society and his Mississippi environment, which Faulkner, the artist—at his best, but not always—succeeded in transcending. Let us look at one of his public nonliterary statements. In a speech delivered at the University of Virginia (February 20, 1958) and published in his book *Essays, Speeches and Public Letters,* Faulkner said:

> Perhaps the Negro is not yet capable of more than second class citizenship. His tragedy may be that so far he is competent for equality only in the ratio of his white blood. . . .For the sake of argument, let us agree that as yet the Negro is incapable of equality for the reason that he could not hold and keep it even if it were forced on him with bayonets; that once the bayonets were removed, the first smart and ruthless man black or white who came along would take it away from him, because he, the Negro, is not yet capable of, or refuses to accept, the responsibilities of equality.
>
> So we, the white man, must take him in hand and teach him that responsibility. . . . Let us teach him that, in order to be free and equal, he must first be worthy of it, and then forever afterward work to hold and keep and defend it. He must learn to cease forever more thinking like a Negro and acting like a Negro. This will not be easy for him.[24]

Here we have the crux of the problem: the rejection by powerful forces in American life and thought of any positive qualities and values in Negro life—the negation by cultivated people, by artists and poets, of the worth of "being a Negro" and "thinking like a Negro" and "acting like a Negro." In short, the repudiation of Negro identity and the vicious circle: on the one hand, the pressure to blot out the blackness of the black man, the pressure to make him like a white man—and, at the same time, the unrelenting pressure to slam the door of white society in his face and say: "Negro, keep out!"

These approaches to Negro life and literature by Negro authors contradict the critical premises voiced by T. S. Eliot in his famous review of James Joyce's *Ulysses,* which became axiomatic for much of modern criticism.

Eliot declared that "in creation you are responsible for what you can do with material which you must simply accept. And in this material I include the emotions and feelings of the writer

384

himself, which, for that writer, are simply material which he must accept—not virtues to be enlarged or vices to be diminished." Too much of American literary criticism is still not simply *accepting* the materials of the Negro writer—his subject matter and feelings and emotions, which are part of his material —and, in violation of well-established critical principles, is arguing with the material rather than addressing itself to how the writer has made artistic use of his particular material.

The underlying assumptions of Simpson, Klein and Faulkner are the antitheses of the premises long held by Negro American writers.

Participating in a radio symposium in New York City in 1961, Langston Hughes said:

> My main material is the race problem—and I have found it most exciting and interesting and intriguing to deal with it in writing, and I haven't found the problem of being a Negro in any sense a hindrance to putting words on paper. It may be a hindrance sometimes to selling them. . . .
>
> Well now, I very often try to use social material in a humorous form and most of my writing from the very beginning has been aimed largely at a Negro reading public, because when I began to write I had no thought of achieving a wide public. My early work was always published in *The Crisis* of the *N.A.A.C.P.*, and then in the *Opportunity* of the Urban League, and then the Negro papers like the Washington *Sentinel* and the Baltimore *Afro-American*, and so on. And I contend that since these things, which are Negro, largely for Negro readers, have in subsequent years achieved world-wide publication—my work has come out in South America, Japan, and all over Europe—that a regional Negro character like Simple, a character intended for the people who belong to his own race, if written about warmly enough, humanly enough, can achieve universality.
>
> And I don't see, as Jimmy Baldwin sometimes seems to imply, any limitations, in artistic terms, in being a Negro. I see none whatsoever. It seems to me that any Negro can write about anything he chooses, even the most narrow problems: if he can write about it forcefully and honestly and truly, it is

very possible that that bit of writing will be read and understood, in Iceland or Uruguay.[25]

Hughes was consistent in his position over a long period of years, a position which is really no more than not applying a reverse critical standard to the Negro writer. Some thirty-five years earlier, in his famous article "The Negro Artist and the Racial Mountain" published in *The Nation* (June 23, 1926), Hughes wrote:

> One of the most promising of the young Negro poets said to me once, "I want to be a poet—not a Negro poet," meaning, I believe, "I want to write like a white poet," meaning subconsciously, "I would like to be a white poet," meaning behind that, "I would like to be white." And I was sorry the young man said that, for no great poet has ever been afraid of being himself.[26]

In one of his interesting essays, "The Literature of the Negro in the United States," which is included in his book *White Man, Listen!*, Richard Wright stated his views this way:

> Around the turn of the century, two tendencies became evident in Negro expression. I'll call the first tendency: The Narcissistic Level, and the second tendency I'll call: The Forms of Things Unknown, which consists of folk utterances, spirituals, blues, work songs, and folklore.
>
> These two main streams of Negro expression—The Narcissistic Level and The Forms of Things Unknown—remained almost distinctly apart until the depression struck our country in 1929. . . . Then there were those who hoped and felt that they would ultimately be accepted in their native land as free men, and they put forth their claims in a language that their nation had given them. These latter were more or less always middle class in their ideology. But it was among the migratory Negro workers that one found, rejected and ignorant though they were, strangely positive manifestations of expression, original contributions in terms of form and content.
>
> Middle class Negroes borrowed the forms of the culture which they strove to make their own, but the migratory

Negro worker improvised his cultural forms and filled those forms with a content wrung from a bleak and barren environment, an environment that stung, crushed, all but killed him. . . .

You remember the Greek legend of Narcissus who was condemned by Nemesis to fall in love with his own reflection which he saw in the water of a fountain? Well, the middle class Negro writers were condemned by America to stand before a Chinese Wall and wail that they were like other men, that they felt as others felt. It is this relatively static stance of emotion that I call The Narcissistic Level. These Negroes were in every respect the equal of whites; they were valid examples of personality types of Western culture; but they lived in a land where even insane white people were counted above them. They were men whom constant rejection had rendered impacted of feeling, choked of emotion. . . .

While this was happening in the upper levels of Negro life, a chronic and grinding poverty set in the lower depths. Semi-literate black men and women drifted from city to city, ever seeking what was not to be found: jobs, homes, love—a chance to live as free men. . . .

Because I feel personally identified with the migrant Negro, his folk songs, his ditties, his wild tales of bad men; and because my own life was forged in the depths in which they live, I'll tell first of the Forms of Things Unknown. Numerically, this formless folk utterance accounts for the great majority of the Negro people in the United States, and it is my conviction that the subject matter of future novels resides in the lives of these nameless millions.[27]

Wright affirmed not only the distinctive literary values and the rich forms and content forged in the depths and lower depths of urban Negro life, he also insisted on its value to America. Later in this same essay, Wright declared: "We write out of what life gives us in the form of experience. And there is a value in what we Negro writers say. Is it not clear to you that the American Negro is the only group in our nation that consistently and passionately raises the question of freedom?"[28]

More recently, at the American Academy Conference on the Negro American which took place in 1965 and resulted in the two special issues of *Daedalus* devoted to "The Negro American," Ralph Ellison participated in the discussions and said:

> One concept that I wish we would get rid of is the concept of a main stream of American culture—which is an exact mirroring of segregation and second class citizenship. . . . The whole problem about whether there is a Negro culture might be cleared up if we said that there were many idioms of American culture, including, certainly, a Negro idiom of American culture in the South. We can trace it in many, many ways. We can trace it in terms of speech idioms, in terms of manners, in terms of dress, in terms of cuisine, and so on. But it is American, and it has existed a long time, it has refinements and crudities. It has all the aspects of a cultural reality. . . .
>
> The feeling that I have about my own group is that it represents certain human values which are unique not in a Negritude sort of way, but in an American way. Because the group has survived, because it has maintained its sense of itself through all these years, it can be of benefit to the total society, the total culture.[29]

John Oliver Killens, novelist and writer in residence at Fisk University, states another important view of a black writer in this way, in his volume of collected essays, *Black Man's Burden*:

> And now, in the middle of the twentieth century, I, the Negro, like my counterparts in Asia and Africa and South America and on the islands of the many seas, am refusing to be your "nigger" any longer. Even some of us "favored," "talented," "unusual," ones are refusing to be your educated, sophisticated, split-leveled "niggers" any more. We refuse to look at ourselves through the eyes of white America.
>
> We are not fighting for the right to be like you. We respect ourselves too much for that. When we advocate freedom, we mean freedom for us to be black, or brown, and you to be white, and yet live together in a free and equal society. This is the only way that integration can bring dignity for both of us. . . . My fight is not for racial sameness but for racial equality and against racial prejudice and discrimination. I

work for the day when black people will be free of the racist pressures to be white like you; a day when "good hair" and "high yaller" and bleaching cream and hair straighteners will be obsolete. What a tiresome place America would be if freedom meant we all had to think alike or be the same color or wear that same gray flannel suit. That road leads to the conformity of the graveyard![30]

Black writers today not only take for granted the value and distinctness of their blackness but many affirm a "black aesthetic" in literature and culture. Very revealing of the divergent and new currents of thinking among black writers today is the issue of the magazine *Negro Digest* for January, 1968. A large part of the magazine is devoted to a survey of the opinions of black writers, which is introduced in the following way by Hoyt W. Fuller, Managing Editor of the publication:

> There is a spirit of revolution abroad in the shadowy world of letters in black America. Not all black writers are attuned to it, of course, and some are even opposed to it which is to be expected also, one supposes. . . . There is, therefore, a wide divergence of opinion among black writers as to their role in society, as to their role in the Black Revolution, as to their role as artists—all these considerations tied into, and touching on, the others. *Negro Digest* polled some 38 black writers, both famous and unknown. . . . The questions elicited from the writers opinions relative to the books and writers which have influenced them, the writers who are "most important" to them in terms of achievement and promise, and what they think about the new movement toward "a black aesthetic" and the preoccupation with "the black experience," aspects of the larger Black Consciousness Movement.

Laurence P. Neal, a young black nationalist writer, expressed this view in the *Negro Digest* poll:

> There is no need to establish a "black aesthetic." Rather, it is important to understand that one already exists. The question is: where does it exist? . . . To explore the black experience means that we do not deny the reality and the power

of the slave culture; the culture that produced the blues, spirituals, folk songs, work songs, and "jazz." It means that Afro-American life and its myriad of styles are expressed and examined in the fullest, most truthful manner possible. The models for what Black literature should be are found primarily in our folk culture, especially in the blues and jazz. . . .

Strictly speaking it is not a matter of whether we write protest literature or not. I have written "love" poems that act to liberate the soul as much as any "war" poem I have written. No, it can't simply be about protest as such. Protest literature assumes that the people we are talking to do not understand the nature of their condition. In this narrow context, protest literature is finally a plea to white America for our human dignity. We cannot get it that way. We must address each other. We must touch each other's beauty, wonder, and pain.

Other Negro writers, like Saunders Redding and Robert Hayden, rejected the idea of a "black aesthetic." Redding asserted that "aesthetics has no racial, national or geographical boundaries," and Robert Hayden voiced sharp disagreement with the cultural black nationalism of LeRoi Jones. Poet and novelist Margaret Walker, on the other hand, wrote:

The "black aesthetic" has a rich if undiscovered past. This goes back in time to the beginning of civilization in Egypt, Babylonia, India, China, Persia, and all the Islamic world that precedes the Renaissance of the Europeans. We have lived too long excluded by the Anglo-Saxon aesthetic. . . . Where else should the journey lead? The black writer IS the black experience. How can the human experience transcend humanity? It's the same thing.

The contemporary black writers polled by *Negro Digest* were asked who, in their opinions, was the most important black writer. Richard Wright headed the choices, with Langston Hughes and James Baldwin in second and third place and Ralph Ellison trailing Baldwin.

In reply to the question on "the most important living black poet," LeRoi Jones came out first, with Robert Hayden and

Gwendolyn Brooks in second and third place and Margaret Walker in fourth.

This is a time of great liveliness, controversy, and creativity in the black literary world in the United States. The pages of *Negro Digest* in Chicago, *The Journal of Black Poetry* in San Francisco, the older Broadside Press in Detroit which publishes individual poems as broadsides and volumes of poetry, the numerous booklets of verse issued independently by little black publishing houses throughout the country, and the growth and development of the black theatre and drama, attest to the new vitality, dimensions and scope of black literature in the United States today.

SELECTED BIBLIOGRAPHY

A complete bibliography of poetry, fiction, drama, autobiography, essays and literary criticism by Afro-American writers would constitute a volume in itself. The following bibliography is divided into two parts: Anthologies of Literature from the period of the Harlem Renaissance in the 1920's to today, and selected books of Literary History and Criticism.

I: ANTHOLOGIES OF LITERATURE

Adoff, Arnold, Ed. *I Am the Darker Brother: An Anthology of Modern Poems by Negro Americans.* New York: The Macmillan Co., 1968.

Alhamisi, Ahmed and Harun Kofi Wangara, Eds. *Black Arts: An Anthology of Black Creations. Detroit:* Broadside Press, 1969.

Bontemps, Arna, Ed. *American Negro Poetry.* New York: Hill and Wang, 1963.

Brawley, Benjamin, Ed. *Early Negro American Writers, Selections with Biographical and Critical Introductions.* Freeport, N.Y.: 1968. (Reprinted from original edition published by The University of North Carolina Press, 1935).

Breman, Paul, Ed. *Sixes and Sevens: An Anthology of New Poetry.* London: Paul Breman, 1962.

Brown, Sterling, Arthur P. Davis, and Ulysses Lee, Eds. *The Negro Caravan.* New York: Dryden Press, 1943.

Bullins, Ed, Ed. "Black Theatre," a Special Issue of *The Drama Review,* Vol. 12, No. 4, Summer 1968.

Calverton, Victor F., Ed. *Anthology of American Negro Literature*. New York: The Modern Library, 1929.

Chapman, Abraham, Ed. *Black Voices: An Anthology of Afro-American Literature*. New York: The New American Library, 1968.

Clarke, John Henrik, Ed. *American Negro Short Stories*. New York: Hill and Wang, 1966.

Counch, Jr., William, Ed. *New Black Playwrights*. Baton Rouge, La.: Louisiana State University Press, 1968.

Cullen, Countee, Ed. *Caroling Dusk: An Anthology of Verse by Negro Poets*. New York and London: Harper & Brothers, 1927.

Cuney, Waring, Langston Hughes, and Bruce Wright, Eds. *Centennial Anthology—Lincoln University Poets*. New York: The Fine Editions Press, 1954.

Dorson, Richard M., Ed., *American Negro Folktales*, Greenwich, Conn.: Fawcett Publications, 1967.

Dreer, Herman, Ed. *American Literature by Negro Authors*. New York: Macmillan, 1950.

Emanuel, James A. and Theodore L. Gross, Eds. *Dark Symphony: Negro Literature in America*. New York: The Free Press, 1968.

Hayden, Robert, Ed. *Kaleidoscope: Poems by American Negro Poets*. New York: Harcourt, Brace & World, 1967.

Hill, Herbert, Ed. *Soon, One Morning: New Writing by American Negroes, 1940-1962*. New York: Knopf, 1963.

Hughes, Langston, and Arna Bontemps, Eds. *The Poetry of the Negro 1746-1949*. Garden City, N.Y.: Doubleday, 1949.

————, and Arna Bontemps, Eds. *The Book of Negro Folklore*, New York: Dodd, Mead, 1959.

————, Ed. *New Negro Poets U.S.A.* Bloomington, Ind.: Indiana University Press, 1948.

————, Ed. *The Book of Negro Humor*. New York: Dodd, Mead, 1965.

————, Ed. *The Best Short Stories by Negro Writers*. Boston: Little, Brown, 1967.

Johnson, Charles S., Ed. *Ebony and Topaz*. New York: Opportunity Press, 1927.

Johnson, James Weldon, Ed. *The Book of American Negro Poetry*. New York: Harcourt, Brace & Co., 1931.

Jones, LeRoi, and Larry Neal, Eds. *Black Fire: An Anthology* of *Afro-American Writing*. New York: William Morrow & Co., 1968.

Kerlin, Robert T., Ed. *Negro Poets and Their Poems.* Washington, D.C.: Associated Publishers, 1923.

Locke, Alain, Ed. *The New Negro.* New York: Alfred and Charles Boni, 1925. Reprinted, New York: Arno Press and The New York Times, 1968.

————, Ed. *Four Negro Poets.* New York: Simon and Schuster, 1927.

————, Ed. and Montgomery Gregory, Eds. *Plays of Negro Life: A Source Book of Native American Drama.* New York: Harper & Brothers, 1927.

Major, Clarence, Ed. *The New Black Poetry.* New York: International Publishers, 1969.

Patterson, Lindsay, Ed. An *Introduction to Black Literature in America. From 1746 to the Present.* New York: Publishers Company, Inc. 1969.

Pool, Rosey E., Ed. *Beyond the Blues: New Poems by American Negroes.* Kent, England: The Hand and Flower Press, 1962.

Randall, Dudley and Margaret G. Burroughs, Eds. *For Malcolm: Poems on the Life and Death of Malcolm X.* Detroit: Broadside Press, 1967.

Randall, Dudley, Ed., *Black Poetry. A Supplement to Anthologies Which Exclude Black Poets.* Detroit: Broadside Press, 1969.

Richardson, Willis, Comp., *Plays and Pageants from the Life of the Negro.* Washington, D.C.: Associated Publishers, 1930.

————, and May Miller, Eds. *Negro History in Thirteen Plays.* Washington, D.C.: Associated Publishers, 1935.

Schulberg, Budd, Ed. *From the Ashes: Voices of Watts.* New York: The New American Library, 1967.

Shuman, R. Baird, *Nine Negro Poets.* Durham, N.C.: Moore Publishing Co., 1968.

Troupe, Quincy, Ed. *Watts Poets: A Book of New Poetry &* *Essays.* Los Angeles: House of Respect, 1968.

Turner, Darwin T., Ed., *Black American Literature: Fiction.* Columbus, Ohio: Charles E. Merrill Publishing Co., 1969.

———— Ed., *Black American Literature: Essays.* Columbus, Ohio, Charles E. Merrill Publishing Co., 1969.

———— Ed., *Black American Literature: Essays,* Columbus, Ohio, Charles E. Merrill Publishing Co., 1969.

Watkins, Sylvester C., Ed. *Anthology of American Negro Literature.* New York: The Modern Library, 1944.

White, Newman Ivey, Walter Clinton Jackson, and James Hardy Dillard, Eds. *An Anthology of Verse by American Negroes.* Durham, N.C.: Trinity College Press, 1924. Reprinted, Durham, N.C.: Moore Publishing Co., 1968.

Williams, John A., Ed. *The Angry Black.* New York: Lancer Books, 1962.

————, Ed. *Beyond the Angry Black.* New York: Cooper Square Publishers, 1966.

II: LITERARY HISTORY AND CRITICISM

The American Negro Writer and His Roots. (No ED.) Selected Papers from the First Conference of Negro Writers, March, 1959. New York: American Society of African Culture, 1960.

Baldwin, James, *Notes of a Native Son.* Boston: Beacon, 1955.

————, *Nobody Knows My Name.* New York: Dial, 1961.

Berrian, Albert H. and Richard A. Long, Eds., *Négritude: Essays and Studies.* Hampton, Va.: Hampton Institute Press, 1967.

Bond, Frederick W. *The Negro and the Drama.* Washington, D.C.: Associated Publishers, 1940.

Bone, Robert A. *The Negro Novel in America.* New Haven, Conn.: Yale University Press, 1958. Revised ed., Yale University Press, 1965.

Brawley, Benjamin, Ed. *The Negro Genius: A New Appraisal of the Achievement of the American Negro in Literature and the Fine Arts.* New York: Dodd, Mead, 1937.

Bronz, Stephen. *Roots of Negro Racial Consciousness: The 1920's: Three Harlem Renaissance Authors.* New York: Libra, 1964.

Brown, Sterling. *The Negro in American Fiction.* Washington, D.C.: The Associates in Negro Folk Education, 1937.

————, *Negro Poetry and Drama.* Washington, D.C.: The Associates in Negro Folk Education, 1937.

Butcher, Margaret Just. *The Negro in American Culture.* New York: Knopf, 1956.

Cruse Harold, *The Crisis of the Negro Intellectual,* New York: Wm. Morrow & Co. 1967.

Ellison, Ralph. *Shadow and Act.* New York: Random House, 1964.

Emanuel, James A. *Langston Hughes.* New York: Twayne Publishers, 1967.

Farrison, William Edward. *William Wells Brown: Author and Reformer.* Chicago: The University of Chicago Press, 1969.

Ford, Nick Aaron. *The Contemporary Negro Novel: A Study in Race Relations.* Boston: Meador Publishing Co., 1936.

Gayle, Jr., Addison, Ed. *Black Expression: Essays by and About Black Americans in the Creative Arts.* New York: Weybright and Talley, Inc., 1969.

Gloster, Hugh M. *Negro Voices in American Fiction.* Chapel Hill: University of North Carolina Press, 1948.

Gross, Seymour L. and John Edward Hardy. *Images of the Negro in American Literature.* Chicago and London: The University of Chicago Press, 1966.

Hill, Herbert, Ed. *Anger and Beyond: The Negro Writer in the United States.* New York: Harper & Row, 1966.

Hughes, Carl Milton. *The Negro Novelist: A Discussion of the Writings of American Negro Novelists, 1940-1950.* New York: Citadel, 1953.

Isaacs, Edith. *The Negro in the American Theatre.* New York: Theatre Arts Books, 1947.

Johnson, James Weldon. *Black Manhattan.* New York: Knopf, 1930.

Jones, LeRoi. *Home: Social Essays.* William Morrow & Co., 1966.

Logan, Rayford W., Eugene C. Holmes, and G. Franklin Edwards, Eds. *The New Negro Thirty Years Afterward.* Washington, D.C.: Howard University Press, 1955.

Loggins, Vernon. *The Negro Author: His Development in America to 1900.* New York: Columbia University Press, 1931. Reprinted, Port Washington, N.Y.: Kennikat Press, 1964.

Margolies, Edward. *Native Sons: A Critical Study of Twentieth-Century Negro American Writers.* Philadelphia: Lippincott, 1968.

Mitchell, Loften. *Black Drama: The Story of the American Negro in the Theatre.* New York: Hawthorn Books, 1967.

Redding, J. Saunders. *To Make A Poet Black.* Chapel Hill: University of North Carolina Press, 1939.

Whiteman, Maxwell. *A Century of Fiction by American Negroes,* 1853-1952. Philadelphia: Maurice Jacobs, 1955.

Wright, Richard. "The Literature of the Negro in the United States" in *White Man, Listen!* Garden City, N.Y.: Doubleday, 1957.

NOTES

1. Richard M. Dorson, *American Negro Folktales*, Greenwich, Conn.: Fawcett Publications, Inc., 1967, p. 12.
2. Vernon Loggins, *The Negro Author: His Development in America to 1900*, Port Washington, N. Y.: Kennikat Press, Inc., 1964, p. 41.
3. *Ibid.*, p. 85.
4. Herbert Aptheker, Ed., *A Documentary History of the Negro People in the United States*, New York: The Citadel Press, 1951, pp. 82-83.
5. W. E. Burghardt DuBois, *The Souls of Black Folk*, Greenwich, Conn.: Fawcett Publications, Inc., 1964, pp. 16-17.
6. Cited in Kenneth B. Clark, *Dark Ghetto*, New York: Harper & Row, 1967, p. ix.
7. Langston Hughes, *Selected Poems*, New York: Alfred A. Knopf, 1968, p. 11.
8. Richard Wright, *White Man, Listen!* Garden City, N.Y.: Doubleday & Co. (Anchor), 1957, pp. 71, 72, 75.
9. Mathew H. Ahmann, Ed., *The New Negro*, Notre Dame, Ind.: Fides Publishers, 1961, p. 110.
10. *Ibid.*, pp. 110-111.
11. John A. Williams, Ed., *Beyond the Angry Black*, New York: Cooper Square Publishers, 1966, p. 53.
12. Perry Miller, Ed., *Margaret Fuller: American Romantic. A Selection from Her Writings and Correspondence*, Garden City, N.Y.: Doubleday & Co. (Anchor), pp. 230-231.
13. Harold W. Blodgett and Sculler Bradley, Eds., *Leaves of Grass*, Comprehensive Reader's Edition, New York: New York University Press, 1965, pp. 190-191.
14. William Carlos Williams, *In the American Grain*, New York: New Directions, 1965, p. 208.
15. Horace M. Kallen, *Cultural Pluralism and the American Idea*, Philadelphia: University of Pennsylvania Press, 1956, p. 82.
16. Arnold Rose, *The Negro in America. The Condensed Version of Gunnar Myrdal's An American Dilemma.* New York: Harper & Row, 1964, p. 21.
17. Sterling Brown, *The Negro in American Fiction*, Washington, D. C.: The Associates in Negro Folk Education, 1937.
18. Albert Camus, *Resistance, Rebellion and Death*, New York: Alfred A. Knopf, 1960, pp. 185-186.
19. Malcolm Cowley, Ed., *Writers at Work: The Paris Review, Interviews*, New York: The Viking Press, 1968, p. 141.
20. W. B. Yeats, *Essays and Introductions*, New York: Macmillan, 1961, pp. 509-510.
21. *Ibid.*, pp. 511 and 517.
22. Cleanth Brooks, *William Faulkner: The Yoknapatawpha Country*,

New Haven, Conn.: Yale University Press, 1966, pp. 2-3.

23. Marcus Klein, *After Alienation: American Novels in Mid-Century*, Cleveland, Ohio: World Publishing Co., 1963, p. 79.

24. William Faulkner, *Essays, Speeches and Public Letters*, Ed. by James B. Meriwether, New York: Random House, 1965, pp. 155-157.

25. Mathew H. Ahmann, Ed., *op. cit.*, pp. 112 and 122-123.

26. Francis L. Broderick and August Meier, *Negro Protest Thought in the Twentieth Century*, Indianapolis, Ind.: The Bobbs-Merrill Co., 1965, p. 92.

27. Richard Wright, *op. cit.*, pp. 83, 84, 85-86.

28. *Ibid.*, p. 101.

29. "Transcript of the American Academy Conference on the Negro American," *Daedalus*, Vol. 95, 1. Winter, 1966, pp. 287-441.

30. John Oliver Killens, *Black Man's Burden*, New York: Trident Press, 1965, pp. 12-13.

ABRAHAM CHAPMAN is Professor of English and Chairman of the American Literature survey courses at Wisconsin State University-Stevens Point. He has had a life-long interest in black American literature, has written and lectured extensively on the subject, and initiated and developed the first course on the Negro in American literature taught as a regular credit course in the Wisconsin university system. He is the author of *The Negro in American Literature*, published in 1968, and editor of *Black Voices: An Anthology of Afro-American Literature* (1968) which has been adopted as a text in colleges throughout the United States and has been introduced in the American literature curriculum in many high schools. Professor Chapman has contributed articles and book reviews to *Saturday Review, Yale Review, Wisconsin Studies in Literature, CLA Journal,* and other periodicals and has delivered papers at numerous scholarly meetings. In 1968 he received the biennial College Language Association Creative Scholarship Award for his study *The Harlem Renaissance in Literary History*, published in *CLA Journal*. In 1967 Professor Chapman taught a special course on the Afro-American in the literature of the United States for high school teachers from metropolitan centers throughout the country at the NDEA Institute in English at The University of Wisconsin-Milwaukee and for the 1968-69 academic year served as Visiting Professor at Texas Southern University, one of the leading black universities. He is currently working on a study of the Afro-American slave narratives.

BLACK AMERICAN CONTRIBUTIONS TO WESTERN CIVILIZATION IN PHILOSOPHY AND SOCIAL SCIENCE

FRANK T. CHERRY

State University College (Buffalo)

Three themes have run through the writings of black social scientists. One can detect in the writings of these black professionals—and to some extent it is still present in the most contemporary writings—a compelling need to convince the reader that the black man was a legitimate member of the human race; that he occupied a respectable position in evolutionary progression; that he was not, and is not, in short, an ape. This respectability or recognition theme can be found particularly in the writings of the historians who attempt to reconstruct the African background, but it is present in the writings of the other black social scientists as well.

The second theme, or focus of interest, is that blacks differ; that once you have seen one black you have not seen them all; that blacks do not all look alike, or behave alike. The internal differentiation of the group is, therefore, the second issue.

Black writers have a third concern, which can be referred to as the "my-fair-lady-hypothesis," i.e., that the behavior of the black man must be referred back to the social conditions, the environmental circumstances which have impinged upon the group; not to the innate qualities, nor constitutional attributes of the individual himself.

As for black philosophy, it seems relevant to observe that black philosophy, interestingly enough, has not been an armchair philosophy. This is because, ordinarily, the philosopher has also been an activist engaged in carrying out the philosophy of his choice; and, therefore, subjecting it to empirical test as he speculated.

Nonetheless, black philosophy can be reduced to a few issues, as can the writings of the other social scientists. There has been, since the earliest and without let-up, a concern with the nature of the black-white detente: a fusion or a stand-off. Shall blacks diffuse throughout the society, absorbing and assimilating, or shall they remain apart, being of the system but not of it? There are, it should be recognized, two ways to absorb and become assimilated. One group may play a passive role, allowing the other group to absorb it, with the result being a maintenance of the nature of the active group, its qualities intact. On the other hand, each group may give a little, take a little, so that the resultant is a third element, quite different from both but possessing characteristics of both. Black philosophers, in short, have had visions of the shore dimly seen but they have not always seen the same shore.

Related to the above is the second issue, one of individuation or self-interest. The second issue is produced by two peculiarities of the Western market economy. On the one hand, there is a stress upon individuation or pursuit of self-interest. On the other, there is a hierarchical structure or ranking system in which individuals find a place. This second issue is so intricate (and basic) that one is hard put to find a black leader (or follower, for that matter) who is not ambivalent about it. The matter can be put simply: if talented and skilled members of the group orient themselves in the direction of self-interest and individuation, their talents and their competence are lost to their less-talented and less competent fellow members. But if they orient themselves to the uplift of the group in an all-for-one and one-for-all code of conduct, they repudiate the American way of individual achievement and deny the very rationale for the struggle in the first place.

It should be a caution that the above looks at the matter and sees it as an issue, or dilemma, from the point of view of a member of an ethnic group (members of groups other than blacks have a similar problem). From the point of view of the society it is not a problem, issue, or dilemma. It is an asset. The conditions which give stability to a political regime and deter revolution, of course, spell the difference between the preservation and smooth perpetuation of a social system and regimes which are continually being toppled. In short, the stress on individuation in a Western market economy prevents or staves off revolution. It works against common cause.

In the pages that follow black philosophers will be seen taking a position on this matter. It will become evident that it is a problem of no mean proportions, especially to activists who are concerned with bringing off revolution or reform. What does one do, in other words, when one is interested in carrying out a social movement and finds that those members of the oppressed group who are best qualified to help have filtered up into the status hierarchy and are unable or unwilling to look back? How can they be impressed with the idea that they have, perchance, been brought to the kingdom for such a time as this?

It should come as no surprise, in view of the above two issues, that black philosophers face up to the two mutually exclusive issues of (a) violent or peaceful confrontation; and, (b) reform or revolution, for such a coming-to-terms with issues is inherent in the nature of things, as any cursory examination of the history of movements to relieve oppression will affirm. Any people having grievances will have to give concern to whether it is practicable or possible to attain relief within the legitimately-sanctioned system or whether they must circumvent the law. Any oppressed people seeking relief will also have to decide whether they must strike out for a complete change in the system which oppresses them or only for minor alterations.

Finally, there remains the nature of New Jerusalem. Only the most visionary of philosophers would attempt a description. Only the most philosophical of followers would require one. When one has pain the physician need not describe in detail how one will feel after the pain is removed. It is enough that the services of one who, presumably, can relieve pain have been secured and are on the job. It is, therefore, unnecessary to go to seek whether the philosopher has a dream. The burden of his role is, perhaps, the spelling out of the means of relieving the nightmare.

In the pages that follow, concern will be given to four persons selected as representative of the philosophical positions that have been taken on the four issues raised above. These persons have been selected and juxtaposed. There are two moderns or contemporaries and two "ancients." The two ancients are not really very ancient, having lived and worked in the twentieth century. We might think of them as pre-sit-in philosophers and post-sit-in philosophers. They are DuBois and Washington, as pre-sit-in philosophers and Malcolm X and Martin Luther King, Jr. as post-sit-in philosophers. One might remark that such a selection is hardly inclusive, hardly complete. This must be granted, with the comment that the aim was not to include every black leader who had ever uttered a thought but to choose black men of prominence whose public utterances had been extensive enough to cover the issues with some degree of completeness. Marcus Garvey is missing, as is Elijah Mohammed, as is Frederick Douglass. The position is that Garvey's philosophy does not vary radically from Malcolm's; Malcolm's not radically from Mohammed's; and, Douglass' not radically from DuBois'.

PHILOSOPHY

King conceives of an end comprised of brotherhood under God the father.[1] All men are God's children, even the erring ones. These erring ones, although manifesting evil and ungodlike works, are not to be discounted. They are still God's children, should be loved and forgiven, and persuaded through the martyrdom-like behavior of the oppressed to forsake their evil ways, repent and join the heavenly band. Hate is to be avoided, not only because of what it does to the object, but what it does to the initiator. King has seen the hate in the eyes of the Bull Connors and the Sheriff Clarks and would weep for his people if they came to that end, that sickness.[2]

Why the confrontation? A man owes it to his conscience to disobey an unjust law, to oppose injustice wherever practiced. In fact, he commits sin by failing to act when he observes injustice.[3]

Malcolm, on the other hand, feels that brotherhood should not be extended to the unappreciative.[4] Malcolm is closer to the Hammurabi Code of justice which requires a *quid pro quo* response pattern. Racism should be fought wherever found. It should be fought bitterly. One should not forget his mistreatment at the hands of the oppressor. There is the suggestion in Malcolm's thought that any people who allow themselves to be victimized deserve to be. Victims should respond violently to violent intimidation or terrorism. One should be a peace-lover, but resort to war when that peace is threatened. One should behave in the way people understand.

The philosophy of Malcolm and King come together much more closely when non-confrontation is brought into focus. In the language of the Booker T. Washington era, self-help activities are similar in both philosophies, King's and Malcolm's. There is an interest and concern for voter education and registration. Their theory of reform is similar, but their theory of revolution differs.

This recalls the Washington-DuBois dispute.[5] Washington and DuBois did not disagree on the self-help activities of blacks. There are at least two bases for such a statement. First, early speeches of DuBois can be examined which converge quite closely with what has come to be called the ideology of Washington.[6] Secondly, persons who knew DuBois personally and had many confidential conversations with him on this and other issues indicate that DuBois and Washington were like-minded on self-help and vocational education, but that they used these as public issues to cloak a cleavage based on a private experience. Not being free to disclose the private experience, what follows is a discussion of the public issue.

Washington felt, and rightly so, that whites were in control of the market and that blacks were peripheral or left out of it.[7] He reasoned that salvation, a secular salvation, lay in securing a place in that market. Securing such a place—and Washington feels that blacks must be realistic concerning their selection of that place, i.e., not being so wild-eyed and irrational as to think that the sky's the limit—was to be achieved through the mastering of the manual arts and the acquisition of economic security. The result: a detente, which resembles King's heavenly city where there will be produced a stability in which whites will see blacks as useful, functionally contributing to the on-going smooth process of commercial and industrial exploitation; in the ensuing period race will wither away. Such a construction probably reveals a basic misconception of the foundations of capitalism.[8]

On the other hand, DuBois contends that Washington is de-emphasizing the importance of the mental experience. DuBois seems to believe that developing a lunch-pail race is an evil of itself, an insult to the sanctity of the human spirit. It is almost as if DuBois were saying that even if race withered away via the Washington philosophy it would still be undesirable because its method would have violated a value more important than racial harmony. Thus we would have substituted one evil for a lesser one. For DuBois, there must be total life and anything short of that is an unjustifiable compromise.

In one sense Malcolm's position coincides with DuBois'.[9] It appears that Malcolm would reject King's heavenly city even if it became a manifest fact. Malcolm seems so opposed to the method of King that he would find any good, or utopian, or optimum outcome despicable and insufferable. A man should manifest manhood. Anything gained through less than full assertion of that manhood is reprehensible.

But is not cheek-turning a manifestation of manhood? Is not that power? For King, yes; for Malcolm, no.

King's basis for rejecting Black Power was that it was poor strategy.[10] It was King's strategy to prick the conscience of the silent sympathizer to such an extent that pressure is exerted thereby on the power structure. It was King's considered opinion that any militancy would harden the hearts of the silent sympathizers and leave matters about where they were at first, or worse.

One notes in both King's and Washington's thought a recognition that the white man's sentiments and sympathies are quite crucial and should be appealed to. This is conspicuously absent in the thinking of Malcolm and DuBois.

The emotional reaction of white men to the black's struggle for his rights is to DuBois and Malcolm an issue about which they could not care less.[11] But to King and Washington they have a central place. "Whether you like it or not, we are going to pursue our freedom and justice in this society by legal means," says DuBois of the Niagara Movement and NAACP. "By any means," says Malcolm of no particular organizational structure. "You have no need of fear nor anxiety," say Washington and King, "we are going to pursue our freedom and justice; but in a way that is not violent, nor very unsettling of the status quo; and with a conviction that the result will be mutually beneficial."[12]

Withdrawal or return? There is no withdrawal in King's philosophy. King's is the politics of confrontation. Malcolm's too, but not on the middle-class level of the March on Washington, etc. Malcolm feels that the confrontation should be an indigenous movement composed of down-and-out blacks who use the occasion to assert manhood by venting their wrath on the whites to show their anger and to retaliate for years of oppressive victimization.

Alienation or belonging? The black as American is unthinkable in Malcolm's philosophy. The black man's hands are across the sea and he should look homeward. The blacks are aliens in a strange land and their presence here is only a makeshift, temporary measure. Next year in Jerusalem for the blacks; but their Jerusalem is Africa. There is no such across-the-sea perspective in King's thought. The earth is the Lord's and God's children will inherit the land. Neither should blacks look to Africa for support in the struggle for justice in America. African countries are caught up in their own problems and there are no resources from those quarters that can aid blacks here.

Indigeneous or elite? DuBois stands alone. Anticipating Toynbee, DuBois sees civilization as a result of the efforts of a cadre of elite, a vanguard leading the way, lighting the path for the masses. The talented tenth should be developed and given their charge as pilots for the mass of black followers. Not so for Washington. There is in Washington's philosophy a hint that the manual worker is the salt of the earth (an anticipation of Veblen) and the professional a parasite. "Learn a trade," says Washington. "Greek and Latin are all right in their place; but later for these." "I have a dream," says King. The rank and file black looms large in this dream. Awaking the professional is a task King realizes lies ahead. For the rank and file the awakening is already a material manifestation.

Malcolm's contempt for the professional, educated black is nowhere concealed. The genuine movement, Malcolm believes, excludes them *ipso facto.*

HISTORY

DuBois, Woodson, Logan, Brawley, Epps, Franklin, Quarles,

405

Reddick, Bennett—these are the names associated with the writing of black history.[13] These are not all, of course, and in this section only one will be treated in any detail. One could make a case, however, for including and discussing them all in a book of this kind, on the basis of the fact that where gaps occur in the knowledge of the Western world any correction is a contribution. The absence of black events in the traditional history texts is at present a central issue. All of the black history writers have contributed toward alleviating that condition. Having stated this, it becomes necessary to make a more selective and perhaps unfairly discriminatory presentation.

It appears that one way of classifying black history is that of categorizing it as genuine or special. By general history one indicates those works which attempt to cover the total black experience in America.[14] The pioneer work here is Carter G. Woodson's *The Negro in Our History*. Perhaps, the most referred to is John Hope Franklin's *From Slavery to Freedom*.[15]

A second category may be called special histories: histories which treat a relatively short time span, e.g., the Reconstruction period, or a specific person, e.g., Frederick Douglass. An example of a special history is Benjamin Quarles' *Frederick Douglass,* considered the definitive work on Douglass.[16] Another special history is that of DuBois: *The Suppression of the African Slave Trade to the United States: 1638-1870*, a pioneer special history done by DuBois while a young Ph.D. student at Harvard.[17]

Although often in the writings of these black historians it is not made explicit, it can be inferred that their writings speak to some accusation or address some unspoken issue.

One can note in Carter G. Woodson's *The Negro in Our History* an effort to deal with the accusations that the black man has no past and that his behavior in Africa was sub-human.[18] Bennett in *Before the Mayflower* is making an attempt to establish the black man's right to a place in the world and America and to show his contributions.[19] Franklin's approach comes closer to the my-fair-lady hypothesis mentioned earlier. Franklin is quite environmental and institution-conscious, and for that reason his treatment is located closer to the sociological works of Davis, Drake, Johnson and Frazier, who will appear below. To Franklin, behavior patterns are central. He addresses himself to the question: why has the search for the good life been a futile and illusive one? It appears that Franklin is attempting to document the journey, the plight, the predicament of a wayfaring people traveling along a lonesome road. This can be illustrated by examining a recent paper by Franklin, "The Two Worlds of Race."[20]

"The Two Worlds of Race" brings the struggle of the black man in American life into sharp focus. Franklin gives a perspective of history which extends from the arrival of blacks on the American continent to the contemporary direction of the youth of today. His frame for this presentation is the separation of blacks and whites, which he refers to as the "two worlds of race." Accordingly, there is an examination of the historical forces which have influenced the juxtaposition of the ideal society with liberty and justice for all, and the racist society which allocates differential rewards based on color.

His treatment is institutional. He very subtly shows that governmental fiat and policy making have cuddled and cradled the racial myths and contributed to their preservation. On the other hand, counter forces in the society have taken up the mantle in the name of freedom (somewhat inconsistently, he shows) and struggled to defeat efforts to perpetuate the two worlds of race. The caution one must take is that liberal forces have not been without their departures and dilatoriness in regard to equality of the black. After Reconstruction, abolitionists despaired of the fight for black equality and pushed for separateness in a compromise with the status quo.

Reinforcing his institutional argument, Franklin examines the role of the church, school and market place in supporting the effort to prevent full manhood among blacks. Neither does the world of letters escape attention. Intellectuals, he reminds us, have lent their prestige and research to the perpetuation of racial myths in support of the status quo.

Franklin's assessment is dynamic. At the base of his treatment is an assumption that irrepressible forces are inherent in society which bombard the recalcitrant status quo ambivalences and force a future which portends one society, equitable and just. The signs of this development, Franklin states, are already visible. Among these signs are the recognition that the two worlds of race are an economic handicap, the promulgation of liberal laws, the shift in public opinion in the direction of black equality. The second, Franklin believes, is the most significant of the three.

Three ideas appeared to inform the orientation taken by the research group commissioned by the American Council on Education in 1939.[21] First, given a society structured along the axis of race, growing up black, conceivably, is not likely to be a wholly gratifying experience. Second, variation along regional lines should be expectable in view of pattern variation among regions. Third, some consequence for the life processes are rooted in the regional.

Out of respect to these impingements, a series of studies were commissioned. The study of growing up black in the deep South was assigned to Allison Davis; in the middle South to Charles S. Johnson; in the border states to E. Franklin Frazier; and, in the North to W. Lloyd Warner, Buford Junker and Walter A. Adams. Further differentiation was manifested in assigning Johnson the rural South, and Davis the urban South. Thus, Davis studied New Orleans and Natchez; Johnson studied counties in Tennessee, Mississippi, Alabama, Georgia and North Carolina. Frazier focused on Washington, D. C. and Louisville and Warner and his group studied Chicago. Material collected by the staff from New York City, Greensboro, North Carolina, Galesburg, Illinois and Milton, Pennsylvania, were also used. An overview of the U.S. was given by Ire DeA. Reid and the project was summarized in a book by Robert L. Sutherland.[22]

There is, of course, in the design of these works an assumption that behavior patterns have their roots in the social process and that the attitudes, values and self-concepts are an outgrowth of the environmental context within which one lives and has his being.

Two important assertions seem to emerge from these studies. First, an understanding of blacks requires that the group be internally differentiated methodologically. Thus it is not accurate to generalize about the behavior and human nature of black youth. On the contrary there must be a recognition that relative access to the goods, services and facilities of the society vary among blacks, and personality development varies accordingly. The second assertion is that no matter how close one gets to the facilities and resources of society, or no matter how far away one is from them, being black is an important desideratum which has its impact upon personality. A special tax is enacted from all black youth regardless of the relative well-being of their home situations. Remoteness of access, however, requires that a poor black youth pay a heavier tax. Thus, black youth having the good fortune to be born in the homes of professional parents emerge relatively unscathed. In no case, however, can the black tax collector be completely bypassed.

The recognition of these considerations goes far toward explaining why professional blacks make "common cause" with the Ghetto. They also serve to explain why failure to make common cause is designated by one black writer as "the world of make-believe."[23]

PSYCHOLOGY

Color Preferences. Quite pertinent in the context of color and the black tax is an effort on the part of Professor and Mrs. Kenneth B. Clark, in the '40's, to study in an experimentally contrived situation the relative attractiveness white skin color had for black children.[24] Clark's study is so closely allied that one feels justified in sandwiching it in between two groups of sociological studies. In general, there was a tendency on the part of black children to identify and prefer whiteness (white dolls were used) but not explicitly on the basis of a black tax (which has economic overtones). Rationalizations for choosing white skin took the form of "prettier" or "cleaner". Thus, it appears that although the observation has been made that blackness requires that one pay a unique tax, it is not rejected by black children on this basis. They reject it because it falls short of measuring up to the standards of beauty which they have learned in a society in which whiteness is dominant. Although sociologists might objectively produce findings to show that society exacts a tax for one's blackness, our black writers have not documented the age at which this fact enters the black child's consciousness.

Also in the '40's, the father of them all was produced. The moral dilemma confronting the American was documented in what is referred to as the outstanding landmark in the study of race relations.[25]

THE MYRDAL GROUP

An American Dilemma was the result of a collaboration between black and white American social scientists and the Swedish economist, Gunnar Myrdal. There were contributions of advice and memoranda from black and white, and it is impossible to assign the proper weight to each contribution. Myrdal, at one place in the preface, states that he drew heavily on the works of Ralph Bunche and St. Clair Drake.[26] It is, perhaps, not relevant to ask: Is *An American Dilemma* a black contribution, or how much of American Dilemma is black achievement? It will suffice to say that blacks made significant contributions to *An American Dilemma*, which stands alone in a class by itself as the most ambitious and successful effort to make a comprehensive and unbiased statement about the black-white stand-off in America.

More interesting, perhaps, than the content of *An American Dilemma* is the thought which underlay the selection of Gunnar Myrdal as the senior director of the project. All persons concerned were aware of the incendiary nature of the race issue. They were further aware that the influence of the prevailing racial myths was so far-reaching as to make escape by the most fleet of foot impossible. It was reasoned that the credentials needed by a director of such a project be that: (a) he should be beyond the influence of the racial myth; (b) he should be, preferably, from a country which had no racial problem; (c) he should be a technically competent and well-trained scholar of reputation. It was in the context of these presumptions that Myrdal was selected and *An American Dilemma* was written.

Myrdal asserts that the final presentation is a product of his own thinking.[27] But he acknowledges help from myriad sources. In his preface one encounters the names of the black social scientists of that and the present day. In addition to Ralph Bunche and St. Clair Drake, there are Doxey Wilkerson and

Sterling Brown, E. Franklin Frazier and Charles S. Johnson, Allison Davis and Kenneth B. Clark, Abram Harris and Alain Locke, Walter White and W. E. B. DuBois.

Myrdal cites specific writings done for the study by Brown, Davis, Drake, Frazier, Wilkerson and Reid.[28] It appears that these manuscripts were drawn upon by Myrdal as source material for the various chapters in the body of the work. Myrdal also acknowledges his debt to the already published works of blacks. It might be safe to say that America acknowledged its debt to the Myrdal Group by citing it as evidence in the court case that overthrew the separate-but-equal doctrine and made the moral dilemma which the Myrdal group tried to expose more manifest.

BLACK METROPOLIS

In *An American Dilemma* Drake and Cayton show that Chicago is composed of a black population which carries out the round of life at different levels of the economic spectrum.[29] They treat these performances as styles of life. Among the black community in Chicago there are several strata with corresponding and mutually exclusive interests, aspirations, values, sentiments, attitudes, thoughts and morality.

De-mything the notion of the black community as an undifferentiated mass was both the aim of this work and its end product. The work is a culmination of a WPA arrangement which had as its aim the creation of employment for idle workers as well as the creation of a body of data about the community assembled by the rank and file members of the community and supervised by professional social scientists.

The presentation, of course, is theoretical in that it tries to relate these styles of life, not only to one's length of residence in Chicago and points of origin, but also to the skills, abilities and socially useful tools one acquires, such as formal education, solidarity, family structure and means of earning a living. There appears to be implied, then, that the black community is a creation of the social structure of the larger society and that the differentiation cannot be explained racially, since race is constant but style of life varies. In other words, if style of life is a

411

function of race, how does one explain three different styles of life in only one race?

E. FRANKLIN FRAZIER

In the early 30's E. Franklin Frazier turned his attention to the arrival of black families in Chicago.[30] *The Negro Family in Chicago* addresses itself to two of the issues which have been the preoccupation of black writers: (1) moral behavior; and, (2) environmental influence. Frazier treats the third issue (internal differentiation) in his *The Negro Family in the United States.*[31]

In *The Negro Family in Chicago* Frazier faces up to the moral issues of illegitimacy, sexual casualness and family breakdown. He shows that such behavior is related to the loosening of bonds in the Northern cities and he interweaves this with a history of the bondsman in the pre-Civil War South. He shows that the breakdown or disorganization of the Chicago black family is an expectable outgrowth of two eras of American history: the period of slavery and the period of urbanward migration.

Frazier makes use of skin color to explain the differential solidarity of the black families and goes further to relate this to the different economic leverages of the family.

In *Black Bourgeoisie* Frazier turns to analysis of variables.[32] He exposes in broad strokes both his theoretical notions of society and his psychological conceptions of a particular sub-group of blacks to which he gives the name "black bourgeoisie."

There is implied in the work a continued allegiance to the Park "race relations cycle." Frazier seems to say in this work that Park's theoretical conception of the progressive and irreversible developmental stages of blacks is true. It is just that the blacks, particularly the black bourgeoisie, have not obeyed the rules. To illustrate, one example of rule-breaking is found in the current generation's orientation to college education which departs radically from the serious and puristic motivation of the black pioneers who loved learning for its own sake and sought it with missionary zeal. The implication is that the heavenly city of assimilation would have been a consummated dream but for the default of the Ebony-like blacks who departed into an ephemeral world of myth and make-believe. The fact that this dream of assimilation has not been fulfilled turns out to be topical to the extent of returning the current black movement to the philosophy of Garvey. With a difference, however: black power rather than black nationalism.

Frazier's contribution might lie in his depiction of the perseverance of black families under the yoke as well as their ingenuity in making out in a crushing and hostile environment and in inventing means of survival much like those used by persons who survive concentration camps.

OLIVER C. COX

Other writers had related the economic system to race relations (Frazier, Drake, Davis and Johnson). When one asserts that job loss can lead to desertion he is relating the economic system to race insofar as unemployment of black men is related to fatherless black families. Cox's presentation is unique in that he wishes to make it quite clear that the connection is closer than that.[33] Capitalism and modern race relations are inextricably-bound. The other authors give no basis for deriving such an inference from their works in spite of the fact that they show that the conditions of blacks would be much more sanguine if they (blacks) had a more favorable relation to the market place. Cox writes three books to document his hypothesis which is set down in *Caste, Class and Race.*[34] These are *Foundations of Capitalism, Capitalism and American Leadership* and *Capitalism as a System.*[35]

One of the notable differences between Cox's work and the other black sociologists is that in Cox one finds no hint of self-hatred. A second characteristic which makes Cox's work unique is that it is devoid of the "status-quo" orientation which Myrdal attributes to many works on race. As for the three preoccupations, Cox does not deal with the question of the black man's humanity; nor does he pay much attention to differentiation. He reserves the full force of his energy and interest for the environmental problem. One might say that he is the most environment-conscious of them all. The problem of blacks has been created by a manipulation of the environment; solution lies in further manipulation of that environment.

413

African writings may be separated along three dimensions: there are the African personality writings, writings which attempt to describe the unique features of African attitudes, thoughts, feelings and behavior and to relate these to African culture and social structure.[36] Second, there are the writings on the push for political autonomy, writings which analyze the power relations in Africa and the world and attempt to suggest blueprints for the struggle for political independence and economic viability.[37] Third, there are the empirical writings of a sociological or anthropological nature.[38]

The necessity of being black but proud is not limited to just one continent. The concept of negritude is an emergence which tries to deal with the problems of having one's personality shattered under the impact of galloping Westernization. The idea is that emulating the Westerner is a mistake, and cannot lead toward an integrated self. The African must look to his own roots for his soul and rethink the white writings which have made invidious comparisons between Western and African values.

On political independence, there is a strong feeling among African writers that Africans cannot look West in this area either. There are others who contend that the African future does not allow an emulation of either East or West. The African must find a third alternative. Current problems in Ghana and Nigeria turn on these issues and have led to internal strife.

Empiricism is a luxury Africa cannot afford, and this is reflected in the scarcity of works like Busia's *The Position of the Chief in the Modern Political System of Ashanti,* and Kenyatta's *Facing Mount Kenya.*[39] These writings, like those in American sociology and anthropology, attempt to relate behavior patterns to the cultural base and show the connection of both with the social structure out of which they emerge and in which they make sense.

DU BOIS, THE CONSUMMATE CONTRIBUTION

At 15, Du Bois was making a compilation of his own collected works and probably had an easier time of it than a present day scholar might.[40] Du Bois' original notion was to inundate the world with scientific research on the black man in America, which would set the record straight and convince the ignorant oppressors of the errors of their ways, thus bringing about a humane community much like the small town in Massachusetts in which he himself had grown up, in a cocoon as it were. After Fisk, Harvard and Berlin, therefore, Du Bois made his initial effort at the University of Pennsylvania (*The Philadelphia Negro*), producing a survey of a city at a time when most persons calling themselves social scientists were still speculating from the armchair in the ivory tower. The ink on Booth's study of London was still wet. There followed the Atlanta University studies which have been negatively evaluated as discrete facts unrelated to theory. Reality came to Du Bois in the nature of a lynching and he filed away his plans to be a scholar and entered the arena of action.

Du Bois was once asked by a young student why he had never compromised his principles, to which he replied, "Someday, young man, you will learn the difference between being able to obtain a cup of coffee because you have money and being able to obtain a cup of coffee because you stand for something." Miss Eartha Kitt expressed the same idea when she was asked whether she had lost money as a result of her statements at a Washington luncheon of Mrs. Lyndon Johnson. Her reply was, "Yes, I have lost money, but I have not lost my soul." Of such are made the Afro-American contributions to Western Civilization.

SELECTED BIBLIOGRAPHY

BOOKS

Davis, Allison, and Dollard, John, *Children of Bondage,* Washington, D.C.: American Council on Education, 1940. Studies the differential personality development among black youth in Natchez and New Orleans.

Drake, St. Clair, and Cayton, Horace R., *Black Metropolis,* New York: Harper & Row, 1962. Focuses on life styles among an urban black population.

Du Bois, W. E. Burghardt, *The Philadelphia Negro*, New York: Benjamin Blom, 1967. A social survey of the black population of Philadelphia.

————, *Dusk or Dawn*, New York: Harcourt, Brace & Co., 1949. An autobiography of Du Bois.

Epps, Archie, *The Speeches of Malcolm X at Harvard*, New York: William Morrow & Co., New York, 1968. Four speeches delivered by Malcolm X at Harvard with a commentary by Epps.

Frazier, E. Franklin, *Black Bourgeoisie*, Glencoe, Ill.: Free Press, 1957. An examination of the black middle class in the U.S.

————, *The Negro Family in Chicago*, Chicago: University of Chicago Press, 1932. An empirical study of the adjustment process of rural Negroes in Chicago.

————, *The Negro Family in the United States*. Chicago: University of Chicago Press, 1939. An examination of the emergence of the Negro family in the U.S. from African roots.

————, *Negro Youth at the Crossways*, New York: Shocken Books, 1967. A study of the socialization of black youth in Washington, D.C. & Louisville.

Johnson, Charles S., *Growing Up in the Black Belt*, Washington, D. C.: American Council on Education, 1941. An empirical study of the process of socialization of black rural youth in deep south communities.

Kenyatta, Jomo, *Facing Mount Kenya*, New York: A. A. Knopf, 1951. An anthropological treatment of the Kikiyu Tribe.

King, Martin L., Jr., *Where do We go From Here: Chaos or Community?* New York: Harper & Row, 1967. An analytical approach to the structure of race relations, the black movement and social thought.

Reid, Ire De A., *In a Minor Key*, Washington, D.C. American Council on Education, 1940. A summary of the status of black youth in the United States revealed by census materials.

Senghor, Leopold S., *On African Socialism*, New York: F. A. Praeger, 1964. A theoretical argument to support the strategy Africa should take to achieve autonomy and self-respect.

Sutherland, Robert L., *Color, Class, and Personality*, Washington, D.C.: American Council on Education, 1942. Summarizes the findings of the Youth Study done by Frazier, Davis, Johnson and Warner.

Clark, Kenneth B. and Mamie P. Clark, "*Racial Identification And Preference in Negro Children*," in Newcomb, Theodore M. and Eugene L. Hartley, *Readings in Social Psychology*, New York: Henry Holt & Co., 1947, pp. 169-178. Creates an experimentally contrived situation which tries to ascertain variables involved in the problems of identity for young black children.

Cox, Oliver C., "*Leadership Among Negroes in the United States*," in Gouldner, Alvin W., Ed., *Studies in Leadership*, New York: Russell and Russell, Inc., 1965, pp. 228-271. Treats the controversy which prevailed during the Washington-Du Bois period.

Drake, St. Clair, "*Negro Americans and the Africa Interest*," in Davis, John P., Ed., *The American Negro Reference Book*, Englewood Cliffs, New Jersey: Prentice Hall, Inc., 1966, pp. 663-705. Discusses the factors affecting the identification of the blacks in America with Africa. Discusses Du Bois' role in the Pan African Movement. Also discusses the Du Bois-Washington controversy.

Drake, St. Clair, "*The Social and Economic Status of the Negro in the United States*," in Parsons, Talcott & Kenneth B. Clark, Eds., *The Negro American*, Boston, Massachusetts: Houghton Mifflin Co., 1965, pp. 3-46. Treats class, caste, status, life style and power with particular reference to blacks in the United States. Also treats the stand off-fusion dilemma.

Franklin, John Hope, "The Two Worlds of Race," in *University of Chicago Magazine*, LVIII, December 1965, pp. 6-11 and LVIII, January, 1966, pp. 12-18. Investigates the social conditions which have underlain the emergence of racial duality and duplicity in the American nation from its infancy to the present.

————, "A Brief History of the Negro in the United States," in Davis, John P., Ed., *The American Negro Reference Book*, Englewood Cliffs, New Jersey; Prentice Hall, Inc., 1966, pp. 1-95. Details the social, economic and political developments as they apply to the black man from the beginning of the slave trade to the Civil Rights Act of 1964.

————, Rayford W. Logan and Sterling A. Brown, "American Negro," in *Encyclopedia Britannica*, Chicago: William Benton, Publisher, Encyclopedia Britannica, Inc., Vol. 16, pp. 188-

201. Contains section on Du Bois-Washington controversy as well as a rather well selected bibliography.

Hare, Nathan, "Black Invisibility of White Campuses," in *Negro Digest*, Vol. XVIII, March 1969, pp. 39-43 and 91-94. Treats certain factors which both determine and inhibit the contribution of Afro-Americans to Western Civilization.

Johnson, Charles S., "Negro in America," in *The Encyclopedia Americana*, New York: Americana Corporation, Int., Encyclopedia Americana, Vol. 20, pp. 65-74. Discusses the black man as a product of the peculiar forces he has encountered in the American social milieu.

NOTES

1. Martin L. King, Jr., *Where Do We Go from Here: Chaos or Community?* New York: Harper & Row, 1967, p. 37.
2. *Ibid.*, p. 33.
3. Martin L. King, Jr., "Letter from a Birmingham Jail," in *Why We Can't Wait*, New York: Harper & Row, 1963.
4. Archie Epps, *The Speeches of Malcolm X at Harvard*, New York: William Morrow & Co., 1968, pp. 48-64, 164.
5. W. E. B. Du Bois, *Dusk or Dawn*, New York: Harcourt, Brace & Co., 1949, p. 80.
6. W. E. B. Du Bois, *Souls of Black Folk*, Chicago: A. C. McLurg, 1933.
7. Emmet J. Scott and Lyman B. Stowe, *Booker T. Washington*, Garden City, N.Y.: Doubleday & Co., 1918, pp. 185-221.
8. Oliver C. Cox, *Foundations of Capitalism*, New York: Philosophical Library, 1959, pp. 13-24.
9. Du Bois, *Dusk or Dawn*, p. 92.
10. Martin L. King, Jr., *Where Do We Go From Here* . . . , pp. 23-66.
11. Archie Epps, *op cit.*, *pp.* 170-180; Du Bois, *op. cit.*, p. 90.
12. Emmett J. Scott and Lyman B. Stowe, *op. cit.*; Martin L. King, Jr., *op. cit.*
13. Kenneth B. Clark and Mamie P. Clark, "Racial Identification and Preference in Negro Children," in Theodore M. Newcomb and Eugene L. Hartley, *Readings in Social Psychology*, New York: Henry Holt, 1947, pp. 169-178.
14. Gunnar Myrdal, *An American Dilemma*, New York: Harper & Bros., 1944.
15. *Ibid.*, p. xv.
16. *Ibid.*
17. *Ibid.*
18. Carter G. Woodson, *The Negro in Our History*, Washington, D.C.: Associated Publishers, 1962.
19. Lerone J. Bennett, *Before the Mayflower*, Chicago, 1962.

20. John H. Franklin, "The Two Worlds of Race," in University of Chicago *Magazine*, Vol. LVIII, Dec. 1965, pp. 6-11, and LVIII, January, 1966, pp. 12-18.

21. Charles S. Johnson, *Growing Up in the Black Belt*, Washington, D.C.: American Council on Education, 1941; Ira de A. Reid, *In a Minor Key*, Washington, D.C.: American Council on Education, 1940; E. Franklin Frazier, *Negro Youth at the Crossroads*, New York: Shocken Books, 1967 (American Council on Education, Washington, D.C., 1940); Allison Davis & John Dollard, *Children of Bondage*, Washington, D.C.: American Council on Education, 1940.

22. Robert L. Sutherland, *Color, Class, and Personality*, Washington, D.C.: American Council on Education, 1942.

23. E. Franklin Frazier, *Black Bourgeoisie*, Glencoe, Ill.: The Free Press, 1957.

24. Clark and Clark, *op. cit.*, pp. 169-178.

25. Myrdal, *op. cit.*

26. *Ibid.*, p. xv.

27. *Ibid.*, p. xviii.

28. *Ibid.*, pp. xii-xiv.

29. St. Clair Drake and Horace Cayton, *Black Metropolis*, New York: Harper & Row, 1962.

30. E. Franklin Frazier, *The Negro Family in Chicago*, Chicago: University of Chicago Press, 1932.

31. E. Franklin Frazier, *The Negro Family in the United States*, Chicago: University of Chicago Press, 1939.

32. Frazier, *Black Bourgeoisie*, 1957.

33. Oliver C. Cox, *Caste, Class, and Race*, New York: Monthly Review Press, 1959.

34. *Ibid.*

35. Oliver C. Cox, *Foundations of Capitalism*.

36. Leopold S. Senghor, *On African Socialism*, New York: F. A. Praeger, 1964, pp. 74-84.

37. Kenneth Kaunda, *Zambia Shall Be Free*, New York: F. A. Praeger, 1963; Tom Mboya, *Freedom and After*, Boston: Little, Brown, 1963.

38. Jomo Kenyatta, *Facing Mount Kenya*, New York: A. A. Knopf, 1956; Kofia A. Busia, *The Position of the Chief in the Modern Political System of Ashanti*, London: F. Cass, 1951.

39. *Ibid.*

40. Du Bois, *op. cit.*

FRANK T. CHERRY, Professor of Sociology, State University of New York, College at Buffalo, is currently engaged in teaching in the S.E.E.K. program of the State of New York (an experimental academic program for the disadvantaged), and is consultant and research associate to a three-year study of the federally-financed Model Cities Program. He has been Exchange Professor, University College of Ghana; Ford Interne, under the Ford Foundation, Internship in College Teaching, at University of Chicago, supported by Fund for the Advancement of Education, 1953-54; and Visiting Professor at Roosevelt University, Chicago, 1964. He has also worked as a research consultant with Leo Burnett, Inc., Leo Shapiro, Associates, Social Science Research, Inc., Chicago Commission on Human Relations and National Opinion Research Center. His background includes many instructive and rewarding teaching experiences in such predominantly black Southern colleges as Dillard, Grambling, Albany State, Norfolk State and Tennessee A & I State.

THE MOORISH IMPACT ON WESTERN EUROPE

PHILIP S. COHEN and FRANCESCO CORDASCO

Montclair State College, (Montclair, N. J.)

"Ichabod, the glory hath departed." The names Córdoba, Granada, Toledo, Seville, the Alhambra still evoke images of resplendent cities with commanding towers, graceful archways, sheltered courtyards and shimmering fountains surrounded by a majestic alcazar. The mention of Moorish civilization still summons forth in the modern mind a confusion of vitality and languor. But, writing in 1896, Major Albert Gybbon-Spilsbury, an Englishman on a commercial expedition among the Sus of southern Morocco, lamented the intellectual and material decline of a people who, for nearly eight centuries from the early Middle Ages to the high Renaissance, maintained varying degrees of political power in Spain and held cultural preponderance over much of southwestern Europe.

I lived in Spain many years and took the greatest interest in the history of that marvellous country, as read in its ruins and the traces of its past grandeur, but I confess that I never really understood the story of these ruins until I had been through Morocco, and seen there the origin, the inception of every trace of the Moor in the Peninsular . . . The works of the Saracen in Spain vie with those of old Rome in artistic conception, solidarity of construction, and yet, thrust back from Europe, they have fallen into the lowest state of degradation, and lost every trace of that learning and creative power which at one time seemed to fit them for the highest place among the nations.[1]

This doleful note is most frequently struck during the two decades prior to World War I by German, French and British writers. Though it is conjecture, it is not unlikely that the sadness over vanished Saracenic splendor was stimulated by renewed interest in North Africa as a result of imperialist rivalries from which France emerged as the temporary victor. In general, however, the literature of that period recounts, uncritically, Moorish history from the first invasion of Spain by the Berber, Tāriq, in 711 to the *reconquista* in 1492. Moor, Arab, Saracen, Berber, Mussulman are all interchangeable.

In the literature of the 1930's there is a discernible shift of emphasis towards a more precise definition of Moorish ethnicity as well as a more careful weighing of the impact of Islamic influence on Spanish history.

Since 1945, there has been relatively little new writing on the subject of Moorish influence in the West. Post-war research, more anthropological than historical, has tended to reflect the cross-cultural approach. Moreover, the interaction between Islam and the West is considered within a context that is implicitly contemporary. But at the same time Islam and the West are dealt with as concepts, each of them phenomenalized into related but distinct social, philosophic and religious organisms investing a number of eras and areas.

Generalizations are, by definition, broad and these observations about the changing focus of interest in the relationship between Moorish and European civilization are generalizations. Exceptions may be found to any and all of the categories, and one can go back to well before the turn of this century to find some of the most pertinent writing on the subject.

As long ago as 1811, Thomas Bourke made some remarkably modern judgments as to the validity and bias of certain types of sources when he set out, as did many after him, to present a fair and balanced view of Moorish history in Spain. Rejecting the excessive claims and accusations of Moslem as well as Spanish writers, Bourke attempted to correct the myth, largely perpetuated by the Spanish, of the Moors as a blood-thirsty and barbarous people. But it becomes obvious that such calumny was motivated by religious hatred rather than by any objective assessment of how Spanish development was subsequently affected by the establishment of the kingdom of *Andaluz.*[2]

A narrative that portrays in fairly typical fashion the hostility between the two groups is the story of *Moors and Christians— a Tale.* It concerns a document found among the ruins of an old Moorish town in Sierra Nevada. The rich but illiterate land-owner, convinced that he has come upon the secret to a treas-ure, looks for a trustworthy translator. The circumstances of the story require that the document be passed from hand to hand, from Spaniard to Moor, each deceiving the other. Treasure is indeed indicated, but the parchment also enumerates a series of curses, the substance of which expose the deep-rooted bitter-ness of their author towards his enemies. Curses are heaped upon the Christians by the Moor who had once owned the land and whose ancestors were forcibly converted along with other Moslems, upon the Moors of Valencia for not having risen to the aid of the Moors of Granada—though they will have to answer to Allah, and upon Don Juan of Austria. The heaviest curse is reserved for that person, Christian, Jew or Moor, who disturbs the land or the treasure. These belong to Hassan-ben-Youssef who has added prophecy to anathema by foretelling the return of the Moors to Granada and the repossession of all their rights and property.

In the end, the treasure remains elusive, and human avarice is thwarted. But the greatest frustrations and indignities are suffered by the Christians for dealing with the enemies of the Church.[3]

Underpinning much of the belletristic literature is this theme of Moslem-Christian coexistence, which in the best of circum-stances, is fraught with difficulties and which, in the end, leads inexorably to conflict and death. Loyalty is repaid with perfidy, nobility with baseness, and love with scorn, and not infrequently, the Moor is the wronged one, thus making it clear that it would have been better if Othello had never met Desdemona and the Prince of Morocco had never met Portia. Only when the Moors have been expelled does Spain go on to national unification and international distinction.[4]

One cannot ignore these feelings as part of the Moorish legacy which, in turn, is part of the legacy of the Crusades even though the seeming inability of "pagans" and "polytheists" to understand each other expressed itself through warfare long before Christian efforts to regain the Holy Land. The point is made that cultural diffusion can be both a cause and a result of conflict as demonstrated by the clash of Moslem and Christian cultures at either end of the Mediterranean.

It is difficult to make a judgment as to whether the literature, with the exception of fiction, views the era of Moorish ascendancy as part of Spanish or Islamic history, but interesting only as an example of the kind of history that was once appealing to the West, *e.g.*, Jean Pierre Calris de Florian's, *The Moors in Spain*, an 18th century work published in the United States in 1910 and again in 1917. Imbued with romanticism, it presages the standard account of that segment of history which is under discussion here.

There is little question, however, that the most influential work of the pre-World War I Period, and not without influence in later periods if only to be refuted in some of its conclusions is *Spanish Islam* by R. P. A. Dozy. Still highly regarded as a reference source, Dozy's book continues to appear in new and expensive editions because, along with Stanley Lane-Poole's *The Moors in Spain*, it is among the first comprehensive and scholarly efforts to deal with the paradoxical relationships, symbiotic and antagonistic at one and the same time, of two nationalisms and two faiths.

Lane-Poole's volume is somewhat conformist in its esteem for the past and distress over the present. The arid country of the Moors and squalid lives of the people compel him to examine how they could have once been the conquerors of Spain; the then-and-now aspects of the Moorish homeland move him to review the centuries when the Moors were preëminent in the arts of peace and war. From their position as guardian and disseminator of Greek and Islamic culture to the subjugation of Granada and then the Inquisition, he traces the brilliancy of Moorish achievements until their dimming in Spain and their ultimate extinction in North Africa.

Again, one cannot help but feel that inherent characteristics of 19th century imperialism-romanticism, exoticism, and an evocation of the past—pervade the historicism of writers such as Lane-Poole. Introducing his subject, he says:

For a brief while, indeed, the reflection of the Moorish splendour cast a borrowed light upon the history of the land which it once warmed with its sunny radiance. The great epoch of Isabella, Charles V, and Philip II, of Columbus, Cortes, and Pizarro, shed a last halo about the dying moments of a mighty State. Then followed the abomination of desolation, the rule of the Inquisition, and the blackness of darkness in which Spain has been plunged ever since.[5]

But despite his affection for Andalusia, Lane-Poole expresses relief over the fact that Islamic expansion was stopped before it could spread across the northern shores of the Mediterranean. Charles Martel, he writes, defeated the Moslems on the seventh day of battle and "saved" western Europe.[6] Much of his account of Roderick, and the Visigoths is based on Washington Irving's, *The Conquest of Granada*. Tariq's invasion of Spain in 711 assumes legendary proportions, and the wise and just rule of the Moors is contrasted to the corrupt and sinful rule of the Visigoths.

In the two-thirds of the peninsula thus marked off by nature for their habitation, which the Arabs always called 'Andalus,' and we shall call Andalusia, to distinguish it from the entire peninsula, the Moors organized that wonderful kingdom of Cordova which was the marvel of the Middle Ages, and which, when all Europe was plunged in barbaric ignorance and strife, alone held the torch of learning and civilization bright and shining before the Western world.[7]

Coming out of the desert and being warriors did not prevent the Moors from developing a fair and equitable administration. The people of Spain were content with their new governors and, at least at the beginning, the difference in religion was not a factor. Moorish tolerance is stressed in Lane-Poole's description of the freedom of worship and freedom from forced conversion enjoyed by Jews and Christians. Conversion was widespread, however, and slaves were manumitted if they accepted Islam. According to Lane-Poole, slavery was incompatible with the tenets of Islam, but because it could not be eliminated, it was softened as a social institution.

Factionalism, fanaticism, and the distractions of an increasingly worldly environment eventually weakened the rule of the Moors in Spain. Antagonisms between the Arabs and Moors soon developed, and whatever the similarity in life-styles, social organization and military prowess between the two, it was acquiescence and not submission that accounted for the former's domination. The Moors deviated in some of their religious practices. They also managed to retain a high degree of political independence in North Africa that was not matched by the situation in Spain.

If factionalism was kept to a minimum under Abd-el-Rahman, it reached its height under the Almorávides who came to the caliphate in 1086. Moslem rule was finally crushed by the counter impulse of Catholic fanaticism unleashed by the Church Militant.[8]

By and large, Lane-Poole's book is a political and military history of the rise and fall of Moorish Spain. Scientific, philosophic and artistic accomplishments are dealt with only in the aggregate. More is said about them in the third important work of the period, Bernhard and Ellen Whishaw's, *Arabic Spain*.

This volume is in some ways a more tendentious and limited book than the other two. At the very beginning, the Whishaws assert that:

> The Moors in Spain had no architecture and no art of their own. All the arts and crafts and architecture miscalled Moorish are Arabic, inasmuch as they were borrowed by the Arabs of Spain (not by the Moors) from the Greeks, the Romans, the Copts, or the Persians, and their rise and decline can be traced step by step in Spain, just as they can in Syria and Egypt, which were certainly free from Moorish influence.[9]

Mudejar art owed its origins to the Arabs, Copts and Yemenites say the authors, a claim which assigns to the Moors the role of craftsmen and technicians rather than that of innovators and creators.

In the main, the Whishaws are more concerned with various influences on Spanish art and history and there is little that relates to Moorish impact on the West. If they are denied the inventiveness that is generally attributed to them, the Moors are still granted the reputation of enlightened and tolerant rulers. The Christians fared well religiously and politically under their regime, and the Catholic Church prospered. But, quoting Dozy for substantiation, the Whishaws disagree with Lane-Poole on the nature of the Gothic rule of three centuries. During that time, they believed, the Goths absorbed and adapted the Roman Civilization they had conquered. They emerged from barbarism to develop a civilization that built bridges and cities which impressed the Arabs.[10]

In *The Legacy of Islam*, the scope of Islamic contributions to early European Civilization is compressed into a series of essays beginning with the Berber or Moorish sweep into Spain and Portugal, and ending with a chapter on Astronomy and Mathematics. At the outset, Alfred Guillaume, the editor of the volume and author of the chapter on Philosophy and Theology, makes the following observation with respect to the essence of Islam and the quality of its influence:

> The nearest parallel is the Legacy of Israel. But whereas it is from the religion of the Jews that the complexion of the Legacy of Israel is derived, in the Legacy of Islam we do not treat of the religion of Mohammad *qua* religion; the reader will learn from this book that there is little that is *peculiarly* Islamic in the contributions which Occidental and Oriental Muslims have made to European culture. On the contrary, the legacy has proved least valuable where religion has exerted the strongest influence, as in Muslim Law. But Islam is the fundamental fact that made the Legacy possible. It was under the protection and patronage of the Islamic Empire that the arts and sciences . . . flourished.[11]

Yet there is the point of view expressed by many Spanish writers to the effect that the Moors distorted and diverted the development of Spain from its true destiny.[12] Had not the Spanish been forced to deal with the Moorish challenge, they might have pursued the same path as that of France, Germany, England, and Italy, or perhaps even been first among them. What happened instead was that Moorish occupation stimulated Iberian particularism, resistance to the invaders arousing the self-consciousness of the people. From these cores of resistance

427

evolved the little kingdoms and counties of Spain. When the Islamic wave receded more than 700 years later, the states, which had developed different traditions and dialects, fought each other.

Spain found itself behind the rest of Europe. As the *reconquista* moved south, the Spaniards lived off the resources of the Moslem lands and people, with the Moors as laborers and the Christians as a kind of military élite. They felt no urgency to develop their own economy.

> Among the 'Old Christians' there was no impulse towards economic activity; the reconquest, whether it was a conscious ideal or not, absorbed all men of action in military adventure. When the reconquest was interrupted, as it was from the middle of the thirteenth century until the fifteenth, the spirit of adventure led Aragon to seek hegemony in Italy and the East, and Portugal to exploration in Africa and the Atlantic, while Castille, having no outlet to the sea, consumed its energies in dynastic quarrels and barons' wars.[13]

Almost simultaneously, the fall of Granada and the discovery of America followed the union of Aragon and Castille. Again there was competition for the talents of the most vigorous, and America won. Expulsion of the Moors deprived Spain of agricultural labor and skilled craftsmen. Thus was its decline made ineluctable.

Those who had lived in close contact with the Moslems, a small educated group, learned a tolerance not generally found elsewhere in medieval Europe. Ferdinand and Isabella, however, were pawns of ecclesiastical fanaticism. "In no country in Europe did the clergy reach a position of power and influence comparable with that achieved in Spain; and the country came to be governed by an ecclesiastical minority with whom the true interests of Spain took second place." The old toleration gave way to a drive for unity, but it was a religious unity rather than a political one and the successors of Ferdinand and Isabella, especially Philip II, completed Spain's destruction.

What was destroyed? Nothing less than "a splendid civilization and an organized economic life" that contrasted sharply with the agony and chaos in the rest of Europe.

Córdoba was, in the tenth century, the most cultivated city in all the West. Ironically, Moorish culture was most effectively made available to other parts of Spain through emigration and conquest. When persecution under the Almorávides and Almohades sent the Mozarabes from Valencia to Castille, they took Moslem customs and styles with them. But the major form of diffusion was through Christian conquest.

The way to Muslim learning had been thrown open to the whole of Europe by the capture of Toledo (1085) and with the fall of Córdoba (1236) and Seville (1248) it spread rapidly. With the conquest of Granada (1492) the legacy might be said to come to an end, except for pottery and some of the minor arts.[14]

Also, ironically, this period of great intolerance, from the mid-eleventh to the mid-thirteenth century coincided with some of the most important religious, scientific, philosophic and artistic advances in Spain.

The architecture of Moorish Spain still presents a superb and arresting example of the artistry of its craftsmen. Aside from their more popularly known constructions, the Moors developed a system of vaulting that preceded the vaulting of Gothic architecture by two centuries. Mudéjar workmen built brick towers and coffered ceilings, hung inlaid doors and set colored tiles in geometric designs or with calligraphic inscriptions. Their lustre pottery is considered second only to Chinese porcelain. Mudéjar products were in demand by Popes and patrons in Spain, Italy, France and Portugal. Hispano-Moresque silks of recognizable patterns were used in Canterbury Cathedral.

Prior to the coming of the Moors, the vernacular in Spain was a Romance dialect which evolved from Low Latin. The Christians, and more than a few Moslems, continued to use this tongue, and still being in a fluid and formative state, the language borrowed heavily from Arabic, particularly in the use of nouns and, of course, place names.

By the tenth century the whole basis of life throughout Spain was profoundly influenced by Islam; with the capture of Toledo that influence spread to the rest of Europe. Since the destruction of Córdoba by the Berbers at the beginning of the eleventh century, Toledo had gradually become the centre of Muslim learning in Spain, and it maintained that position after the Christian conquest in 1085.[15]

The court of Alfonso VI was Christian, but showed strong Moslem influence. This was also true of the court of Frederick II at Palermo, 200 years later. Alfonso X, King of Castille and León in the thirteenth century, was another sponsor of Moslem learning. In addition to his collection of poetry and musical notations based upon Moslem sources, he was the first to describe the game of chess in a European language. The game, which came to the West from India and Persia *via* the Moslems, is explained in an Escorial manuscript attributed to Alfonso X (*el Sabio*) and contains an illustration of considerable relevance to the racial identity of the Moors.[16] Seated at a chess-board are two black and bearded Moors. Their turbans and robes are of obviously costly materials. At one side is a young servant playing on a lyre-like instrument, while at the other side are two women carrying refreshments. The drawing is, thus, far more than a depiction of a chess problem. It is a commentary on color and status in a pluralistic society.

It is the contention of J. B. Trend, writing in *The Legacy of Islam*, that Moorish Spain's most significant contribution to Europe was in the field of philosophy.

> Though they had adopted the narrowest and most orthodox forms of Muslim theology, they gave free rein to philosophic speculation; and although the Berber rulers—Almorávides and Almohades were inclined to fanaticism, they not only tolerated the speculations of the philosophers but even encouraged them, with certain reservations, so that the philosophers were left free and unhampered in their work of teaching, provided that their teaching was not spread abroad amongst people in general.[17]

But philosophy and theology could not remain separated, nor could their teachings, though hardly revolutionary, be confined.

The best work was actually done during a period of political instability, after the Córdoba caliphate but long before the

Renaissance. The Arabs had rediscovered the Greek philosophers (but not their historians or dramatists) and transmitted their learning to Africa and Spain. It was subsequently transmitted, largely through Jewish intermediaries, to European scholars. There is no question but that it is to the Moslems that Europeans are indebted for the revitalization of Greek learning. Interest in Aristotle was especially awakened by the writings of Averröes, who was so closely identified with his theories that in the minds of many it was difficult to extricate the ideas of one from the other. "His [Averröes'] system, which was extremely popular among the Jews, had penetrated Christian thought so deeply as to become a menace to the doctrines of the Church, and to St. Thomas especially belongs the merit of separating Aristotle from his commentator, and of criticizing the Arabian interpretation."[18]

The classical tradition, therefore, returned to Europe under the aegis of Islam, and while the precise relationship between Greek and Moslem interpretations of Faith and Reason, Predestination and Free Will remains a philosophical and theological tangle, a second level of debate, this time between Moslem and Christian thinkers, was created that is abundantly clear in its implications. Because of it a heritage was restored that enabled Western civilization to enter, unimpeded, one of its most exciting humanist eras.

> Had the Arabs been barbarians like the Mongols, who stamped out the first fire of learning in the East so effectively that it never recovered, and possibly never will recover, from the loss of its libraries and literary tradition, the Renascence in Europe might well have been delayed more than one century.[19]

Scholars from all over Europe, stimulated by the renewed contact with Arab and classical thought came to the schools of Toledo. Among them were Robert Anglicus, the first to translate the Koran, Adelbard of Bath, Michael Scot, and Daniel Morley. Latin translations of the works of Aristotle, Euclid and others were exceedingly hard to come by, and making them more available was, in fact, one of their major objectives.

In Moorish Spain, the intellectual climate was such that it was almost natural for the Moslem philosophers to function as a liaison between the Hellenic and Christian worlds. When Christianity itself had lost touch with philosophy, Islam was in the throes of philosophical dispute that was not unlike the controversies that had engaged the Greeks. Since Moorish Spain was a reflection of Oriental and African Islam in terms of theological inquiry, its own intellectual ferment could not help but stimulate Christian minds, waiting to be aroused.

Perhaps more Arab than Muslim, new doctrines concerning the essence of God and new concepts of Being raged within the Moorish community, introducing eventually to Moslem Spain the Mu'tazilite heresy, the doctrines of which are less important here than its insistence on submitting theology to reason. Thus, its challenge to Koranic orthodoxy presented men like Duns Scotus with a methodology for questioning Catholic orthodoxy.

Much of what the Christian West came to know of Aristotle was due to the efforts of the twelfth century Archdeacon of Segovia, Dominic Gundisalvus, through his translations of Moslem commentaries. In a similar vein, the role of two other Spaniards become prominent insofar as they provided a link between Moorish and Christian civilization. Raymund Lull's philosophy is generally considered to lie between Moorish and Augustinian bounds. Lull, who was fluent in Arabic, founded a School of Oriental Studies and achieved martyrdom in 1315 in his attempt to bring Christianity to the Arabs of North Africa. The earliest School of Oriental Studies to be founded in Europe was established at Toledo in 1250 by the Order of Preachers. Its most eminent scholar was Raymund Martín, a contemporary of St. Thomas Aquinas and an Arabist with an intimate knowledge of the Koran as well as Arab philosophers from al-Farabi to Averröes. The curriculum of Arabic and Rabbinical studies was to prepare students for missionary work among the Arabs and Jews. It was the General Order of Preachers which commissioned both the *Summa contra Gentiles* and the *Pugio Fidei adversus Maures and Judaeos*.[20]

According to Guillaume:

The resemblances between Averröes and St. Thomas are so numerous that they must be traceable to something firmer than mere coincidence. A common desire to reconcile philosophy and theology is not of great significance, but when the plan is worked out on parallel lines it is only natural to conclude that Averröes has bequeathed something more than a commentary on Aristotle to Christian scholarship. . . .

From the year 1217 onwards, the commentaries of Averröes were made available to the western schools by Michael Scot in Toledo. Many of Averröes' ideas were incorporated in Maimonides' great work which St. Thomas sometimes quotes.

Dour students like Ibn Hasm of Córdoba could sit down and compose Europe's first comprehensive *Religionsgeschichte* and the first systematic higher critical study of the Old and New Testaments. Phantasy could mix with fact and imagination gild the common metal of life until men like Ibnu-l-'Arabi produced their astonishing prototypes of the *Divina Commedia*.

The barrier of language decreed that our forefathers could only savour a fragment of this rich and varied line, and so, when the Muslim empire in Europe came to an end, all the knowledge that had not already been assimilated was banished with the defeated Moors. But even so East and West were intellectually much more closely aligned in the thirteenth century than they have ever been since.[21]

"The name of Moorish Spain," writes Rom Landau, "filled Europeans with as much wonder as did those of Baghdad and Constantinople."[22] But more than its awesome cities and unique ambiance, there was the stimulation of its intellectual activities, much of which, in turn, was stimulated by Islam's Hellenistic inheritance. The Moors, as part of Islam, played a supremely significant role in transferring this bequest to Europe. Less remote, at least in time, than the Greeks, the conquerors of the Mediterranean world presented a more accessible and willing source of the knowledge that an eager Europe was seeking. It is possible that what appealed to Europeans, on the threshold of the Renaissance, was the universalism of both Greek and Moslem learning. But Europe was spendthrift of its estate and the spirit that men like Leonardo da Vinci came to stand for was soon wasted. Western sciences, by and large, went on to pursue their aims independently of each other and independently of moral and religious considerations.[23]

Landau, like others, points out the similarities between the doctrines and writings of Averröes and St. Thomas Aquinas. The Córdoban philosopher exerted an important influence on medieval Scholasticism and was widely read, especially in Italy, until the sixteenth century. The Universities of Bologna and Padua were centers of Averroist influence, and from there it spread out to Venice, Ferrara, and other cities. In northeastern Italy Moslem Theology assumed an anti-ecclesiastical posture that foreshadowed the Renaissance. He held more of an authoritative position in the West than in Islam and his writings are preserved more in Latin than in Arabic. Landau is equally emphatic about the marked similarities between the cosmology of the twelfth century mystic and philosopher, Ibn Arabi (Ibnu-'l-Arabi) and that of Dante. Mysticism was an important branch of theology and among its influential schools, Sufism made perhaps the deepest impact on Western thought. Ibn Arabi and Ibn Masarra, both from Moorish Spain, were its leading exponents.

Raymund Lull was the most receptive and sympathetic interpreter of Islamic mysticism and, according to Landau, in recent years various aspects of Sufism have aroused the interest of modern Orientalists such as Louis Masignon of France, Asin y Palacies in Spain, and A. J. Arberry and R. A. Nicholson in England.[24] Nicholson, in his contribution to the volume on *The Legacy of Islam*, devotes a considerable part of his chapter on Mysticism to the work of Arabi as well as to the parallels with Dante.

Developments in astronomy and navigation were affected by religion, says Landau. Moslems needed to know the direction of Mecca even though in Spain, France or Italy. But searching the heavens led to more far-reaching results than locating the Holy City of Islam, and the building of the Maragha observatory in 1259 was one of them. Religion also led to the development of the astrolabe as another means of locating the precise direction of Mecca and indicating the precise hours for prayer. Its values as a navigational instrument came later but it was used by the West for this purpose through the seventeenth century. Al-Sarkali (Arzachel), who lived in the eleventh century, invented an improved astrolabe and wrote a treatise on it which, translated into Latin and Spanish, had a profound effect on the whole field of astronomy during the Middle Ages. The treatise is quoted by Copernicus in *De Revolutionibus Orbium Celestium*.[25]

Geographic knowledge was broadened by religion in much the same way as astronomy. The need for pious and observant Moslems to find their way to Mecca from any part of the empire encouraged travel. Where the pilgrim went, he recorded his observations about the climate and vegetation. A practical man and scholar, he also set down whatever scientific, artistic and historical data he could gather.

It is significant that when one of the great Christian princes, the Norman King, Roger II of Sicily, needed a compendium of the known world, he entrusted the work to an Arab. His choice fell on Idrisi from Ceuta in Morocco (1100-1166). The main value of Idrisi's work resides in his series of seventy maps which represent the most accurate picture of the world as it was then known. At a time when the earth was generally held to be flat, Idrisi drew it as spherical. His maps also show the sources of the Nile which are usually said to be a discovery of the nineteenth century.[26]

It is from Ibn Battuta, a native of Tangiers, that we get a thirteenth century voyager's impression of North Africa, the Middle East, and parts of southern Asia and Africa. Europe received most of its information about Africa, however, from Lee Africanus, known originally as Hassan al Wazzazi. Having traveled to many parts of that continent, he was brought to Rome after his capture by European pirates. Converted and baptized by Leo X, he wrote an account of his travels under the sponsorship of the Pope who was also the patron of Raphael and Michelangelo. The work was published under the title, *A Geographical Historie of Africa, written in Arabiche and Italian, by Iohn Lee a More, borne in Granada and brought up in Barbarie,* and went through 14 different editions. Later in his life, Lee Africanus returned to Morocco and Islam.

"Andalusian literature inevitably expressed a culture that was both Spanish and Arabic." Moorish poetry was popular at the courts of Frederick II of Sicily and Alfonse the Wise of Castille. Prose writings ultimately provided inspiration for some of the West's greatest authors. Arab influences can be detected in Cervantes' *Don Quixote,* Beckford's *Vathek,* Samuel Johnson's *Rasselas,* Defoe's, *Robinson Crusoe* and Goethe's *Westoestlicker*

435

Divan. Shakespeare's Christians are possessed of no greater dignity than are his Moors.[27] *The Song of Roland* remains one of the finest epic poems of all medieval literature.

The dissemination of Arabian music through Europe was accomplished mainly by the wandering medieval minstrels, echoes of whose music have survived for many centuries in Gypsy music. Even the English Morris dancers owe a debt to them. Their very name derives from that of their original Moorish mentors (Morisc). In Spanish particularly, many musical terms are of Arab origin, *e.g.* Zamra, zarabanda, huda, nourisca, and so on. . . . As we should only expect, the troubadours, whose poetry owed so much to the Arabs, introduced elements of Arab music as well as Arab instruments into Europe.

While the direct influence of Arabic music in Europe may have been limited, its spirit lived on in the West long after the end of the great Islamic Empire. Arab themes have continued to haunt Western composers right up to the present day. Anyone acquainted with the music of Morocco, who listens to Spanish Flamenco—especially in their purer *cante jondo* or *cante andaluz*—will instantly recognize the Moorish influence.[28]

Fairly numerous are the descriptions of the almost legendary beauty of Moorish Spain, but J. W. Draper offers a few statistics to surprise the reader who might have thought of its cities as compact areas in which all the intellectual and commercial activity was concentrated within a relatively small compound. It is, therefore, somewhat startling to learn that Córdoba was a sprawling urban center with over 200,000 homes and a population of over 1,000,000 people. Public lamps illuminated a thoroughfare that led along a straight line for a distance of 10 miles. "Seven hundred years after this time, there was not so much as one public lamp in London."[29]

Polished marble, balconies, hanging gardens, courts and cascades of water adorned palaces in Granada, Seville and Toledo, reflecting the fact that "the Spanish Mohammedans had brought with them all the luxuries and prodigalities of Asia."[30] Precious and semi-precious materials, mosaics, perfumes and spices were the staples of Moorish affluence. Because religion forbade the reproduction of the human form, certain aspects of art were obviously never developed. But, Draper observes, the khalifs who loved calligraphy and collected exquisite illuminated manuscripts were akin to the Popes of Rome who collected paintings and sculptures.

The taste for luxury extended to individual attire, but unlike their European counterparts, the beauty of their raiments did not conceal an indifference to personal cleanliness and hygiene. "No Arab who had been a minister of state, or the associate or antagonist of a sovereign, would have offered such a spectacle as the corpse of Thomas à Becket when his haircloth shirt was removed."[31]

As has been stated, the Moslem penchant for Greek Scholarship did not apply to history or drama. Neither did it apply to classical mythology which was rejected as licentious and idolatrous. But caution toward classical poetry, including that of Homer, did not impoverish their own poetic imagination nor did their prim attitude towards mythology prevent them from writing ribald songs.

> Notwithstanding this aversion to our graceful but not unobjectionable ancient poetry, among them originated the Tensors, or poetic disputations, carried afterward to perfection among the Troubadours; from them also, the Provencals learned to employ jongleurs. Across the Pyrenees, literary, philosophical, and military adventurers were perpetually passing; and thus the luxury, the trade, and above all, the chivalrous gallantry and excellent courtesies of Moorish society found their way from Granada and Cordova to Provence and Languedoc.[32]

And along with the tradition of Moorish gallantry and gaiety, polite literature and love songs, the European nobility acquired a taste for the more athletic pastimes of hunting, falconry and horseback riding.

Moorish Spain was tied to Europe by trade as well as by culture. Almeria, for example, was part of the commerce in gold and silk that went back and forth between Spanish ports and others such as Marseilles, Genoa and Palermo. The love for soft living, however, was inseparable from a love for learning. Both were derived from Islam's connection with the Orient and the ancient world. The region of Languedoc, probably more than any other place in Europe, reflected similar origins and helped keep them alive until religious and dynastic turmoil brought them to ruin.

What, in the final analysis, did bind Moorish civilization to Europe? "Since Europe, less self-contained than its adversary, never quite ceased to look south and east, the powerful presence of the Islamic world always loomed large in the Western mind."[33] Of course, Europe was selective and took what it needed to fill out the Hellenic-Germanic foundations, keeping Islam at arm's length at the same time. Yet, separated from Europe, Moorish Spain was still near enough to whet Europe's curiosity about its tantalizingly provocative culture. Thus, it did not matter that for a long time Spain, and Sicily, were not a part of Europe. Its political development was not affected and the cultural stimulation was there anyway.

Christianity was more concerned with Islam than the reverse. The concern was born of fear and suspicion of the unknown. Christianity never understood the Islamic world, and this lack of comprehension over its appeal to millions, despite the manifest errors of its faith, merely intensified that fear and suspicion. John of Damascus held Islam to be a Christian heresy and Mohammed a false prophet. Much of the Christian West confused Mohammed with Allah. Ironically, the Crusades helped provide more accurate knowledge, if only to better fight the enemy.

Such, indeed, was the purpose of the first translation of the Koran by Peter of Cluny in 1141. Even Raymund Lull considered the study of languages necessary in order to preach the gospel, reconquer the Holy Land, and refute Averröes. Colleges for the study of Hebrew, Chaldean, and Arabic were founded in Rome, Bologna, Paris, Oxford and Salamanca. Von Grunebaum attributes Lull's arrest by the Moors in 1307 to his superior performance in public disputations with Moslem theologians. But opponent of Islam or not, "no medieval Christian ever matched his understanding of the Muslims."[34]

Moorish civilization was very attractive to non-Moslems; its cities hypnotized them. The tenth century nun, Hrosvitha of

Gandersheim wrote of such things in *Passion of St. Pelagius.* St. Pelagius was martyred in the reign of Abdarrahman III (912-61). The Spanish Christians of the ninth century preferred Islamic culture to classical culture, a situation which was deplored by Alvaro, a Christian zealot who sensed that their motive was not to refute but to absorb. Furthermore, a popular belief in the early Middle Ages held that civilization tended to move from East to West. Learning had flowed from Egypt to Babylon, to Greece and Rome, to Italy, Gaul and Spain. What other conclusion then, but that, having reached the end of the movement, civilization, and therefore mankind, were close to the end.[35]

But the doom of mankind was not the final judgment. By 1500 such forebodings were fancied only by the most unenlightened. The West, in opting for a temporal society, made the conscious choice for a world in which concepts of individualism and nationalism were to be raised to exalted levels. In rejecting a universalist approach for itself, Christianity assured that Islam would also fail in its universalist quest. Each went its own way, and while the Western tradition was enriched in many areas by its contacts with Islam, it was least touched in its spiritual identity.

And it may simply be that the answer to the relationship between Moorish and Western civilization can be found by tracing the threads that lead both back to the Orient and the ancient world.

> ... The profound resemblance between medieval Christendom, both Latin and Greek, while heightened by political contacts and an intensive exchange of ideas, are due to community of origin rather than to an adjustment of any one unit to the impact of outside influence.[36]

SELECTED BIBLIOGRAPHY

Abu-Lughod, Ibrahim A. *Arab Rediscovery of Europe: A Study in Cultural Encounters.* Princeton: Princeton University Press, 1963. Representative of modern Arab scholarship.

Alarcón, Pedro Antonio de. *Moors and Christians and Other*

Tales. Mary J. Serrano, trans. New York: Cassell, 1891. Essentially, a literary source book. See Carl Brockelmann, *Geschichte Der Arabischen Literatur* (Leiden: E. J. Brill, 1943-49).

Arnold, Thomas Walker and Alfred Guillaume, eds. *The Legacy of Islam.* Oxford: Clarendon Press, 1931. A composite of modern scholarship with provocative and divergent viewpoints.

Arqués, Enrique. *Tierra De Moros: Estampas De Folklore.* Instituto General Franco de estudios e investigación hispano-árabe, Ceutá, Imp. "Africa," 1938, 2 vol. Ethnographic and detailed sourcebook.

Bourke, T. *A Concise History of the Moors in Spain.* London: John Murray, 1811. An old, but still valuable history which influenced most early 19th century historiography.

Brockelmann, Carl. *Geschichte der Islamischen Volker Und Staaten.* Munich: R. Oldenbourg, 1939. A political history, with sketches of cultural and intellectual life. English translation (1944) by Joel Carmichael and Moshe Perlmann.

Castro, Américo. *España En Historia: Cristianos, Moros Y Judios.* Buenos Aires, 1948. English translation by E. L. King, Princeton, 1954. A history which is more congenial to the Islamist which sees no continuity between Visigothic Spain and later Christian Spain, but something new which developed under the Muslims. Antithetic to the position of C. Sanchez Albornoz.

Clarke, Henry Butler. *The Cid Campeador and the Waning of the Crescent in the West.* New York: G. P. Putnam's Sons, 1897. Somewhat unreliable, except for notices of the literature. Influenced by Bourke.

Dozy, Reinhart Pieter Anne. *Spanish Islam: A History of the Moslems in Spain.* F. G. Stokes, trans. London: Chatto and Windus, 1913. First published in Leiden in 1861 (*Histoire Des Musulmans D'Espagne*). Levi-Provençal brought out a revised edition in 1932.

Draper, J. W. *History of the Intellectual Development of Europe.* 2 vols. London: John Murray, 1861. A classic history with a panoramic view of the history of Europe.

Encyclopaedia of Islam. 4 vols. Leiden: E. J. Brill, 1913-42. Revised ed., Leiden: E. J. Brill, 1960-continuing. Many articles on Islamic Spain containing material not otherwise available in European languages.

Florian, Jean Pierre Claris de. *The Moors in Spain*. Akron: Superior Printing Co., 1917. A neglected work of continuing value.

Grunebaum, Gustave Edmund Von. *Islam: Essays in the Nature and Growth of A Cultural Tradition*. London: Routledge and K. Paul, 1955. Cultural history, representative of the new scholarship. Influenced by Américo Castro.

————. *Medieval Islam: A Study in Cultural Orientation*. Chicago: University of Chicago Press, 1953. A collection of papers, largely interpretative.

————. *Islam: The Search For Cultural Identity*. Berkeley: University of California Press, 1962. Modern history with some notices of the earlier periods.

————. *Studies in Islamic Cultural History*. Menasha, Wisconsin: American Anthropological Association Memoirs, No. 76, 1954. Essentially in the modern tradition of cultural history, clearly in the tradition of Américo Castro.

Gybbon-Spilsbury, Albert. *The Tournaline Expedition*. London: J. M. Dent and Co., 1906. An historical sourcebook. Indebted to Bourke.

Hole, Edwyn. *Andalus: Spain Under the Muslims*. London: R. Hale, 1958. Largely derives from Levi-Provençal.

Imamuddin, S. M. *A Political History of Muslim Spain*. Dacca: Najmah, 1961. Work of a Pakistani scholar based on Levi-Provençal.

Landau, Rom. *Arab Contributions to Civilization*. San Francisco: American Academy of Asian Studies, 1958. Some nationalistic emphases, but valuable for modern history.

Lane-Poole, Stanley. *The Moors in Spain*. London: T. F. Unwin, 1893. Appeared originally in 1888; advances thesis that Spain's decadence began when she expelled the Moors. Largely in the tradition of literary history.

Levi-Provençal, Évariste. *Histoire De L'Espagne Musulmane*. 3 vols. Leiden: E. J. Brill, 1950-53. Reissued 1967. A monumental work, left unfinished, which takes the history down to 1031. See also his *La Civilisation Arabe En Espagne* (Paris, 1948).

O'Leary, De Lacy. *Arabic Thought and Its Place in History*. New York: E. P. Dutton and Company, 1939. An interpretative study in intellectual history.

441

Peters, F. E. *Aristotle and the Arabs.* New York: New York University Press, 1968. A specialized monograph on scientific and philosophic thought.

Terrasse, Henry. *Islam D'Espagne: Une Rencontre De L'Orient et de L'Occident.* Paris: Alcán, 1958. Essentially, the views of Américo Castro.

Watt, W. Montgomery and Pierre Cachia. *A History of Islamic Spain.* Chicago: Aldine, 1965. The best brief history available.

Whishaw, Bernhard and E. M. Whishaw. *Arabic Spain: Sidelights on Her History and Art.* London: Smith, Elder and Company, 1912. A composite literary and art handbook, somewhat dated. *Cf.* Terrasse.

NOTES

1. Albert Gybbon-Spilsbury, *The Tourmaline Expedition*, p. 33.
2. Thomas Bourke, *A Concise History of the Moors in Spain.* In his preface, the author states that his purpose in writing is "to give such an insight into their laws, customs, manners and exploits as may raise them to just estimation by removing some part of the obloquy too often cast upon them by the Spanish Historians."
3. Pedro Antonio de Alarcón, *Moors and Christians and Other Tales.*
4. This theme not only appears in the works of Washington Irving and Henry Butler Clarke's *El Cid Campeador and the Waning of the Crescent in the West*, but is also implicit in the political histories of medieval Spain.
5. Stanley Lane-Poole, *The Moors in Spain*, p. viii.
6. *Ibid.*, p. 30.
7. *Ibid.*, p. 43.
8. *Ibid.*, p. 270.
9. Bernhard Whishaw and E. M. Whishaw, *Arabic Spain: Sidelights On Her History and Art*, p. 3.
10. *Ibid.*, p. 381.
11. Thomas W. Arnold and Alfred Guillaume, eds., *The Legacy of Islam*, p. v.
12. This is the view best represented by C. Sanchez Albornoz in "España y Islam," *Revista De Occidente*, vol. VII, (April 1929). J. B. Trend points out that the surname is an hispanicization of the arabic name, al-burnusi, man with the burnous.
13. J. B. Trend, "Spain and Portugal," in *Legacy of Islam*, p. 3.
14. *Ibid.*, p. 11.
15. *Ibid.*, p. 15.
16. *Ibid.*, p. 33.
17. J. B. Trend, *op. cit.*, p. 28.
18. Alfred Guillaume, "Philosophy and Theology," in *Legacy of Islam*, p. 247.
19. *Ibid.*, p. 241.
20. *Ibid.*, p. 273.
21. *Ibid.*, p. 279 ff.

22. Rom Landau, *Arab Contributions to Civilization*, p. 12.
23. *Loc. cit.*
24. Rom Landau, *op. cit.*, p. 27.
25. *Ibid.*, p. 37.
26. *Ibid.*, p. 39.
27. *Ibid.*, p. 56.
28. *Ibid.*, p. 62. The subject is also dealt with by Gustave E. Von Grunebaum in his *Medieval Islam: A Study In Cultural Orientation*, p. 341.
29. J. W. Draper, *History of the Intellectual Development of Europe*, Vol. I, p. 31.
30. *Loc. cit.*
31. *Ibid.*, p. 33.
32. *Ibid.*, p. 35.
33. Gustave E. Von Grunebaum, *op. cit.*, p. 34.
34. *Ibid.*, p. 52.
35. *Ibid.*, p. 62.
36. *Ibid.*, p. 343.

DR. PHILIP S. COHEN received his Ph.D. from New York University, and pursued graduate studies at the University of Paris. He has taught at New York University, Upsala College, and is Professor of History and Chairman, Department of History at Montclair State College, teaching courses in Russian and Soviet History and The Middle East. He has held an NDEA Fellowship in Far Eastern Studies, and is the author of a textbook on World History and many articles on International Education. He also has been awarded a U.S. State Department grant for travel in India to study teacher education programs.

DR. FRANCESCO CORDASCO received his B.A. from Columbia University, and his M.A. and doctorate from New York University, with further study at the Universities of London and Salamanca. An educational sociologist and historian, he is presently Professor of Educational Sociology at Montclair State College, and has also taught at Long Island University, New York University, City University of New York, and the University of London. The author of many articles in scholarly journals, Dr. Cordasco has also written *A Junius Bibliography; The Shaping of American Graduate Education; Adam Smith: A Bibliographical Checklist;* and has written on the expatriation of the Jesuits from eighteenth-century Spain, and on other facets of eighteenth-century Spanish history.

AFRICA'S RELEVANCE TO MODERN CIVILIZATION: PAST INFLUENCES AND FUTURE TRENDS

ALI A. MAZRUI

Makerere University College (Kampala, Uganda)

The origins of modern civilization include influences from Africa. The coming changes in modern civilization might also bear the stamp of Africa's cultural models. On balance it was Africa north of the Sahara which had the most direct impact on European intellectual history in the past. In the coming years it is likely to be Africa south of the Sahara which will afford alternative models to the present crisis of confidence afflicting modern civilization.

These are of course generalizations. Sub-Saharan Africa was bound up with North Africa's cultural evolution from very early times; and the future impact of Africa is bound to include a role for North Africa. But the essential point to grasp is that Africa's relevance to modern civilization includes both an ancestral contribution to the very origins of that civilization on the one hand, and on the other hand, a unique offer of a way out extended to a world in a moment of traumatic reappraisal here and now. This essay will address itself to both parts of this thesis.

AFRICA AND THE GENESIS OF MODERN CIVILIZATION

A Ghanaian intellectual, Michael Dei-Anang, once wrote the following poem:—

Dark Africa?
Who nursed the doubtful child
Of civilisation
On the Wand'ring banks
Of life-giving Nile,
And gave the teeming nations
Of the West
A Grecian gift?[1]

Few would today seriously dispute that there was an Egyptian influence on at least the earlier phases of the Hellenic Civilization. In the words of Christiane Desroches-Noblecourt:—

> Egypt is the cradle of Mediterranean civilization and the archeologist's living book of history. . . . No effort should therefore be spared to find and preserve all the vestiges which may throw light on the history of our forebears, for was this not the crucible in which the basic elements of Western civilization were forged?[2]

And the American historian, Henry Bamford Parkes, has also affirmed that: "The Euphrates and the Nile valleys were the original sources of the civilization of Western man."[3]

Cultural historians in modern Africa have sought to emphasize that Ancient Egyptians were indeed Africans. There seems to be little reason to doubt this point. But were Ancient Egyptians of Negroid stock? Logically there is no reason why a people should not be natives of Africa without being *black*. The idea that all the people of each continent ought to be of one color is a dogma which has completely ignored the example of multi-colored Asia. The yellow peoples of China and Japan, the dark Tamils of Ceylon, the brown Gujerati in India, are all today part of the Asian continent. The ancient Egyptians did not therefore have to be black in order to qualify as natives of Africa.

And yet, if they can be shown to have been black, their links with sub-Sahara Africa would be easier to take for granted. There is evidence that at least a section of ancient Egyptians were Negroid. Basil Davidson, in his romanticism, sometimes over-argues the vision of the glorious African past. But he is probably well within the evidence available when he tells us the following:

An analysis of some 800 skulls from pre-dynastic Egypt—from the lower valley of the Nile, that is, before 3000 B.C.—shows that at least a third of them were Negroes or ancestors of the Negroes whom we know; and this may well support the view, to which a study of language also brings some information, that remote ancestors of the Africans today were an important and perhaps dominant element among populations which fathered the civilization of ancient Egypt.[4]

Whether the Negro element among the ancient Egyptians was only a third, or more, or less, the fact that it was there has become understandably part of Africa's cultural nationalism in our own day. As one cultural historian, Cheikh Anta Diop of Senegal, put it: "It remains . . . true that the Egyptian experiment was essentially Negro, and that all Africans can draw the same moral advantage from it that Westerners draw from Graeco-Latin Civilization."[5]

What makes Cheikh Anta Diop's position extreme is not his Africanization of the Pharaohs. It is not even the simple claim that ancient Egypt influenced the Hellenic civilization—a claim which few scholars would dispute. Anta Diop's extremism is perhaps in the magnitude he assigns to that Egyptian influence. At his most reckless, he virtually credits ancient Egypt with all the major achievements of the Greeks. But even when he does not go quite so far, he at least claims that Egypt was to the Greeks what the Western impact has been to Africa in our own times. To use his own words: "From Thales to Pythagoras and Democritus, Plato and Eudoxus, it is almost evident that all those who created the Greek philosophical and scientific school and who pass for universal inventors of mathematics . . . were disciples educated at the school of the Egyptian priests."[6]

Diop goes on to assert that if Plato, Eudoxus and Pythagoras had remained in Egypt for 13 to 20 years, "it was not only to learn recipes." He then draws the telling analogy in the following terms:

The situation is similar to that of underdeveloped countries in relation to their ancient metropolises. It does not occur to a national of those countries, whatever his nationalism, to dispute the fact that modern technique has been spread from Europe to the whole world. The rooms of the African students at the *Cités Universitaires* in Paris, London, etc. are comparable from all points of view to those of Eudoxus and Plato at Heliopolis, and they may well be shown to African tourists in the year 2000.[7]

Not everyone need command the same degree of confidence and optimism as Diop. But there is enough evidence to justify the claim, not only that ancient Egypt made a contribution to the Greek miracle, but also that she in turn had been influenced by the Africa which was south of her.

Ancient East Africa was indeed an extension of the classical world known by the Greeks. Sir Mortimer Wheeler has put East Africa alongside Mediterranean Africa as the two parts of the continent which, on present evidence, have had the longest intercourse with the outside world. To use Sir Mortimer's own words: ". . . two regions of Africa . . . have long looked outwards towards worlds across the seas. The first of these is the Mediterranean coastland which has always been inclined to share its ideas with Europe. The second is the East African coastline, the coastline of what we know as Somalia, Kenya and Tanganyika which has long shared its life with Arabia and India and continues to do so today."[8]

Later on, the Middle East exerted a different kind of cultural influence on Eastern Africa, particularly with the coming of Islam in coastal settlements. And even late in the Christian era there were areas of Europe which were no more closely integrated with Mediterranean Europe than the East African coastline was integrated with the Middle East. In the nature of the relationship between these areas, Roland Oliver might be exaggerating when he says: "Certainly Islam's African fringe can bear comparison with Christendom's northern European fringe at any time up to the late sixteenth century."[9]

But the exaggeration lies in the dateline he chooses. Well before the sixteenth century Europe had already become more closely integrated as part of Christendom than the East African coast was integrated with the southern sector of the Middle East. But Oliver is at least right in asserting that the integration of Europe was completed well after Islam had come to East Africa.[10]

What we should not overlook is that the Islamization of the East African coast was only a new manifestation of an older phenomenon—the phenomenon of East Africa's contacts with certain parts of the classical world. Later developments had their genesis in the general cultural inter-relationship within the classical world as a whole. As Marshall G. S. Hodgson has pointed out in a stimulating article on "The Inter-relations of Society and History":

> The Mediterranean basin formed a historical whole, not only under the Roman Empire but before and since . . . the core of the Middle East was the Fertile Cresent and the Iranian Plateau to which lands north and south from Central Eurasia to Yemen and East Africa looked for leadership, as did increasingly even Egypt, despite its distinct roots in its own past.[11]

THE UNITY OF THE NILE VALLEY

But East Africa's links with this world were not merely through its historical intercourse with the Middle East proper. They were also through its primeval relationship with the Nile Valley as a distinct subsection of the classical world. This relationship, though as yet only vaguely understood, is giving rise to challenging hypotheses. Fifty years ago a towering British scholar and archeologist, Sir Ernest Wallis Budge, put forward a hypothesis which, by 1954, was getting incorporated into the movement of historical Negritude. In his book on Negro civilizations, Dr. J. C. DeGraft-Johnson of Ghana cited testimony of Sir Ernest Budge that ancient Egyptians might have been, in part, Ugandans. DeGraft-Johnson quotes the following passage from Budge:

> There are many things in the manners and customs and religions of the historic Egyptians, that is to say, of the workers on the land, that suggest that the original home of their prehistoric ancestors was a country in the neighborhood of Uganda and Punt.[12]

449

Elsewhere Budge argues that Egyptian tradition of the dynastic period held that the aboriginal home of the Egyptians was Punt. But where was Punt? Budge answers in the following terms: "Though our information about the boundaries is of the vaguest character, it is quite certain that a very large proportion of it was in central Africa, and it probably was near the country called in our times 'Uganda'."[13]

Our information about the boundaries of Punt is still vague and controversial. And Budge was sometimes rash. But whatever the accuracy of speculations such as his, there is enough evidence to indicate significant primeval contacts down the Nile Valley, and movements of peoples in both directions. "It is to the Nile Valley that we look for the original link between Egypt and all south of it," one historian has asserted.[14]

And two other historians traced back to Egypt an ancient ceremony in Western Uganda on the accession of an Omukama of Bunyoro.[15]

There is also the conviction of a Bishop of Uganda earlier in the century—Bishop Alfred Tucker of the Church Missionary Society—that there were aspects of Kiganda culture which "must" have been of Egyptian origin.[16]

The distribution of the Nilotes along the Nile valley is another aspect of interest in trying to determine the degree of contact along the valley. An essay on ancient Egypt in the 1953 edition of *Encyclopedia Britannica* claims that there was a significant Nilotic element in the ethnic composition of early Egypt. The evidence for such claims is questionable. But the speculations partly arise out of the apparent cultural diffusion along the Nile Valley as a whole, and among populations descended from or affected by the Nilotes and Nilo-Hamites. One line of interpretation is to see Egypt as a recipient of certain influences from the south of her. The other is to see Egypt as the ultimate source of certain cultural elements discerned in the lives of people elsewhere in the continent. "That certain ritual practises and beliefs found in Equatorial Africa are of Egyptian origin need not reasonably be doubted," G. W. B. Huntingford has asserted. And he too turns to the Banyoro of Uganda to illustrate his thesis.[17]

There is much in the history of the Nile Valley that we have yet to discover. And in any case some of the cultural influences were carried up or down the valley long after the glories of classical times. But the evidence of primeval contact down the Nile Valley, and of significant movements of populations, is already persuasive enough. It is these contacts along the Nile, *plus* the intercourse through the Indian Ocean and the Red Sea, which converted at least some ancient East Africans into more meaningful members of the more classical world than, say ancient Britons could claim to be.[18]

What is being asserted here in this part of the chapter is, firstly, that Greek civilization, which is the fountain head of much in modern civilization, was significantly influenced by Egypt; secondly, that the Egyptian civilization was African in a meaningful sense, including the infusion of significant Negroid blood; and thirdly, that there was in any case an interplay of influences down the Nile Valley and between the East African coast and the Middle East important enough to make sub-Saharan Africa an integral part of the origins of ancient civilization.

On balance however, the more immediate influences from Africa onto Mediterranean and European cultural developments came from Africa north of the Sahara—though the North in turn owed a lot to what lay to the south of it.

But a new wave of influence may be starting in the second half of the twentieth century, partly in response to a period of confusion to which modern civilization has now drifted. The fine arts from Africa south of the Sahara are playing their part. English army officers and a few French painters were cast by history into the role of aesthetic discoverers within Africa. General Pitt-Rivers, Torday, Picasso, and Les Fauves were among the participants in this new exploration. Paul Bohannan has warned us:

No one should jump to the idea that Picasso's women who look two ways at once, or anything else about his work, is a copy of something he discovered in African art. There was little direct, stylistic influence, although some can be discovered by latter day critics. Rather, what happened was that with the discovery of African and other exotic art, the way was discovered for breaking out of the confines that had

451

been put on European art by tradition—perspective, measured naturalism, and anti-intellectual sentimentality.[19]

Bohannan continues to argue that African figurines could give the "modern" artist courage to foreshorten, to emphasize by changes of scale, to adjust scale to message.

> Looking at African art made such artists see what some of the earlier great painters had already known—El Greco stretches his human figures—that one sees passionately quite differently from the way one sees mensuristically. To get inside the vision it was necessary to get outside the inherited canons of art. And African . . . art was one means of taking such a journey.[20]

Breaking out of the European past by way of African traditions does bring us precisely to the present crisis of Western civilization and the agonizing quest for a new relevance. It is to this crisis of relevance confronting the value patterns of the modern world that we must now address ourselves, and trace the contours of Africa's offer of alternative pathways.

AFRICA AND THE NEW CRISIS OF RELEVANCE

One of the striking features of world trends in the 1960's has been the emergence of relevance as a moral imperative. This revolutionary fervor for relevance has been most dramatically illustrated in the students' movement. From Berlin to Berkeley, from Tokyo to Timbuktu, the demand of youth for greater relevance has been part of a fundamental re-examination of the values of modern civilization.

The heritage of traditional Africa may, in the wake of this militant quest for relevance, find a new vindication in the value patterns of the future. And the demands for Black Studies in the United States, taught preferably by Black teachers and studied by Black researchers, may provide one point of entry of African values to the mainstream of modern civilization. The demand for Black Studies seems to be a demand for courses more immediately pertinent to the understanding of the Black man's place in the civilization of the Western hemisphere and the Black man's heritage from where he springs. Here again is one meeting

452

point between a crisis of identity among Black people in the Western hemisphere and the crisis of relevance as a moral basis of intellectual values.

But what is relevance in this mix of seething unrest and fluidity of values? There are several criteria of relevance. These are not necessarily alternative criteria, but are often reinforcing ones. One criterion of relevance hinges on how big a gap exists between the spiritual world and the material world. In this area of relevance, one might say that the revolution started not with 20th century unrest, but with economic materialism as a social theory in the 19th century. When Karl Marx said he was putting Hegel on his feet the right way up, Marx was in fact asserting a doctrine of material relevance. The whole system of ideas which put economic motivation as the spring of psychological behavior, and made ideas a reflection of the material world instead of the other way around, and asserted economic equality in the world here and now as the paramount moral imperative, was indeed an ideology which was attempting in a drastic way to bridge the gulf between the world of spiritual ideals and the world of material needs.

Leopold Senghor, the poet-president of Senegal, once asserted that Marxism was basically alien to the African temperament because Marxism was atheistic and materialistic whereas the African had a profound spiritual propensity.[21]

It might be true that by being atheistic Marxism has made itself somewhat alien to African traditional values. But by being materialistic Marxism might have attempted to reduce the gap between itself and African tradition. Senghor and others like him have sometimes confused atheism with materialism. The two elements may indeed be inter-related but they are far from being identical. Marxist atheism is an attempt to deny the presence of a spiritual world at all. And yet Marxist materialism, particularly in view of its moral commitment to economic equity and social equality, reintroduces the world of the spirit—but in a way which emphasizes its links with the material world in a fundamental way.

African beliefs have been similarly insistent on an inter-penetration between the material and the spiritual worlds. The Christian doctrine of "My kingdom is not of this earth" would sound even more distant to most African traditionalist belief systems than Marxism is. Physics and metaphysics are inextricably intertwined. Even the dead are not up there in Heaven or Purgatory but continue to form a part of the lives of the living. Indeed, the dead in some African traditional religions have actually been called "the living dead."[22]

Of course the fact that Africans believe in ancestors who continue to be socially participant is a major difference between African traditional religions and Marxism. After all the African does remain theistic while historical materialism is atheistic. But the continuing interaction between ancestors and their descendants, between the world of the living and the world of the dead in African belief systems is itself a bridging of the gulf between the spiritual world and the material world. Even prayer in traditional religion is not simply a matter of phraseology, or of a shutting of one's eyes, or of attempted withdrawal from the world of physical being to the world of spiritual meditation. The physical and the spiritual are fused in African religious ritual by using the body to express the yearnings of the soul. The dance which leads to a trance and to spiritual elevation becomes part of a total religious experience. R. R. Marett has even gone as far as to assert that what he calls "primitive religion" is "not so much thought out as danced out."[23] African writers have often used the symbol of the African dance and the response to the drum as intimations of the ancestral spirit of Africa. In the words of David Diop:

> Negress my warm ruler of Africa
> My land of mystery and my fruit of reason
> You are the dance by the naked joy of your smile
> By the offering of your breasts and secret powers
> You are the dance by the golden tales of marriage nights
> By new temples and more secular rhythms. . . .
> You are the idea of All and the voice of the Ancient
> Gravely rocketed against our fears
> You are the word which explodes
> In showers of light upon the shores of Oblivion.[24]

And Senghor has sometimes sung about "the leader of the dance [making] fast his vigour to the prow of his sex."[25]

The impact of African modes of prayer is discernible among

Black people in the Western hemisphere at large. The tendencies of Black people to physicalize their emotions, through tears or trance, wail or dance, is part of this refusal to differentiate the material world from the world of the spirit, the body from the soul, physics from metaphysics.

Sometimes newly Westernized Africans have been known to feel embarrassed by this tendency of fellow Black people to physicalize their innermost feeling. Among the earliest church services attended by the youthful Kwame Nkrumah on his arrival in the United States in the 1930s was a Negro service at the Abyssinian church in New York. Nkrumah tells us about the minister's "dramatization" of the story of Jesus carrying the cross to Calvary. Before long the women in the congregation were overawed and began to weep and to shout. "It is Jesus! Have Mercy! Halleluiah!" The response of the audience as a whole had become loudly emotional.

Nkrumah was embarrassed. But he was embarrassed because he was accompanied by a European friend he had met on board a ship from Liverpool. With the stereotyped "stiff upper lip" British culture for a background, Nkrumah had apparently assumed that all Europeans despised displays of emotions. He was therefore ashamed of that "black emotion" in the Abyssinian Church because there was a white man there to witness it. Nkrumah tells us: "It was very embarrassing. Here was a European witnessing a most undignified Negro service. As we left the church I tried to apologize. . . ."[26]

But the young Dutchman who had come back to America to complete his theological studies at the Harvard Divinity School was apparently taken aback by Nkrumah's apology. He told Nkrumah that the service at the Abyssinian Church was the most beautiful thing he had seen in any church. "It was my turn to be astonished," Nkrumah relates.[27]

Among the Africanisms which have been discerned in the life-styles of Negroes of the New World, must in fact be included this tremendous capacity first to emotionalize spiritual experience, and then to physicalize those emotions in concrete bodily movements. The most striking examples may lie in places like Haiti, but similar Black tendencies have been observed elsewhere.[28]

This reduced gap between the spiritual and the material

455

becomes also a reduced gap between the spirit and the body. The body has a special meaning in much of Negro modes of self identification. James Baldwin tells us about how he stopped hating Shakespeare. At first Shakespeare had stood for him as a symbol of the oppression which had imposed on Baldwin an alien language as a mode of mental experience. But then, particularly as he was reflecting on these issues in France away from the hub of English speaking activity, Baldwin re-evaluated Shakespeare. He was particularly drawn towards the bard by Shakespeare's bawdiness. Baldwin regards Shakespeare as the last bawdy writer in the English language, and he found this a bond between him and Shakespeare precisely because he associated bawdiness with Shakespeare's unabashed preoccupation with things of the flesh.

Baldwin had seen this kind of bawdiness before—in things like jazz and its suggestions of sensuality. He felt that most Americans had lost contact with some of these areas of sensibility.

Baldwin was here grappling with the old problem of art, its medium, and its relationship to the realities of physical experience. As we indicated, he was convinced that the English language as an artistic medium, could be made to bear "the burden of any experience," no matter how removed from the areas of propriety of contemporary Anglo-Saxon society.

> In support of this possibility, I had two mighty witnesses: my Black ancestors who evolved the sorrow songs, the blues and jazz and created an entirely new idiom in an overwhelmingly hostile place; and Shakespeare who was the last bawdy writer in the English language. . . . Shakespeare's bawdiness became very important to me since bawdiness was one of the elements of jazz and revealed a tremendous loving, and realistic respect for the body, and that ineffable force which the body contains, which Americans have mostly lost, which I had experienced only among Negroes, and of which I had been taught to be ashamed.[29]

The crisis of relevance in the modern world now, especially in the arts, is partly a quest to re-establish contact between aesthetics and sensuality. The most dramatic example is in fact in modern drama and the groping for sexual candor on the stage. Other branches of literature seem to be also groping for a point of fusion between aesthetic appreciation and sensual responsiveness. This quest partly manifests itself in the themes which are treated and the erosion of taboos about subjecting sex to artistic treatment. But there is also experimentation in sensual styles as well as sensual themes.

There was a time in Africa's recent experience when the authority of the Christian missionaries was used to cast a cloud of disapproval on certain kinds of African dancing. Okot p'Bitek, when he was director of the National Cultural Center in Uganda, complained in many a public utterance about the tendency of colonial and Christian discouragement of certain African dances. And yet the dances were in fact major examples of fused aesthetic sensuality.

The bawdiness which James Baldwin observed in Shakespeare's plays, in jazz, and in the universal attitudes of the average American Negro, was all there in depth in some of those African dances.

The crisis of relevance in the Western world has now abolished the Lord Chamberlain in England, an institution which had served for many generations the purpose of censoring the English stage. In 1968 London could at last see, without the red pencil of the Lord Chamberlain, displays of the human body in all its nakedness in such presentations as the American play *Hair*. And African dancers themselves, from countries like Guinea and Uganda, found acclaim for their sensual movements in previously stuffy theaters of the Western world. Occasionally the women dancers from Africa were mistakenly called upon to cover their breasts, but on the whole, the entire international mobility of bodily performances previously regarded as immodest has been one of the great revolutions in assessing the place of the body in the arts. On the utilization of the body in performed art, Bob Leshoai, a South African literary figure, talks about the potential of folk-tales as material for African drama.

Great portions of the story can be told simply in mind action and music and dance. The body, in African dancing, is capable of being used to express and convey ideas that would be quite difficult to express adequately in speech. For exam-

457

ple, swaying of the hips, movement of the shoulders, the tempo of the stamping feet and the twitching of the nostrils can say so much to an infatuated suitor as to leave no doubt in his mind about the girl's attitude to him. This is a combination of movements which speak more fluently, adequately and unequivocally than the spoken word. Body movement in African dances is as important as hand movement in the Indian dance.[30]

Here again the gap between aesthetics and sensuality, art and the body, is narrowed.

Sometimes the narrowing takes the form of utilizing more than one of the five physical senses in art appreciation. Paul Bohannan has lamented the inevitable reluctance of American museums to let African specimens be handled. Bohannan points out that tactile sensations are as important in learning about African sculptures as are visual sensations. He suggests that it is easiest to learn if one can get the work into one's hands.

The memory of it, like the sensation of it comes through the muscles and the sense of touch as well as through the eyes. Dahomean brass sculpture is tactilely sinewy and tough and not at all delicate as it appears to the visual sense: actually of course, the combination tells a great deal about Dahomean culture. Some African wood carving is in heavy earth-bound wood; other is in wood so porous and so light as to seem almost spiritual. To make such remarks is *not* so much to interpret African art [which they do not] as to prepare one for the fact that there is more in it than the artist put there and the something more is derivative of the cultural view of the human condition.[31]

Sculpture had for long been permitted in Western civilization certain liberties of revelation in portraying the human body in naked frankness. But the other Western arts had remained relatively inhibited, until the gulf between arts and sensuality became so great that it was swept into the crisis of relevance currently afflicting Western civilization.

The old images of the African in Western romantic thought are now reasserting a new meaning for Western civilization itself. The African has indeed often been conceded a nearness to nature. But in the context of modern problems, and the unrest which is afflicting intellectual values in universities from Canada to Japan, this old policy now possesses a new pertinence. To use the words of Jean-Paul Sartre, the French philosopher: "In concerning himself first with himself, the Negro proposes to gain nature in gaining himself." Sartre then proceeds to cite the poet who said, "They abandoned themselves, possessed to the essence of all things ignoring surfaces but possessed by the movement of all things."

The nearness to nature which is attributed to the Negro becomes associated with spontaneity; spontaneity finds expression sometimes in responsive sexuality; and sexuality connotes the nakedness of things. The entire life style of the Negro is romanticized into one constant work of natural creation. To quote Sartre again, "techniques have contaminated the white worker, but the black remains the great male of the earth, the sperm of the world. His existence—it is the great vegetal patience; his work—it is the repetition from year to year of the sacred coitus. He creates and is fertile because he creates. The sexual pantheism of these [black] poets is without doubt that which first strikes the reader. To labor, to plant, to eat, is to make love with nature. . . ."

Behold yourself
Erect and naked
Shaft you are, and you remember.
But you are in reality the child of this fecund shadow
Which feeds of the milk of the moon.
Then you slowly shape yourself into a rock
On this low wall entwined by the dreams of flowers
And the perfume of the idle summer.[32]

If the Negro is sometimes conceived as the symbol of masculinity, Africa is sometimes conceived in decidedly feminine terms. But in both conceptions, the theme of nakedness is again recurrent. Leopold Senghor thinks of his part of Africa in such feminine terms. In the words of his famous poem:

Naked woman, black woman
clothed with your color which is life,

with your form which is beauty!
In your shadow I have grown up;
The gentleness of your hand was
laid on my eyes. . . .
Naked woman, black woman
I sing your beauty that passes,
the forms that I fix in the Eternal
Before jealous Fate turns you to ashes
To feed the roots of life.[33]

THE QUEST FOR SOCIAL INVOLVEMENT

Linking the body to art is in this instance linking art to the human person. But another way in which Africa has pertinized or made relevant artistic experience has been to link art not only to the human person but also to human society. In comparing Africa's artistic experience with experience in his own country, the United States, Professor Paul Bohannan has had occasion to say the following:

> In order to appreciate the African aesthetic, then, we must first recognize a few points in our own. Probably the most important one to note is that even in the mid-twentieth century, Americans have an unshakable conviction that 'art' is something special—a little off to the left of life. Art is, we are taught, a separate world; it is done only by special kinds of people who are not very 'practical'. Such an opinion cannot be held by a people who have no word for 'art' and none for 'society' or 'reality'. . . . Art permeates African culture, which in turn permeates African art. Art is not set aside from 'real life'—it cannot be among a people who do not make such distinctions.[34]

Much of African art serves social functions, and the relevance gap is narrowed by the sense of immediacy between the artist and the social purposes his creativity is called upon to serve.

In the history of Western art too, there was a time when the immediacy of the society was quite close. Shakespeare had his patrons and was sensitized to the social functions of the theater in his own time. There was of course a risk in this kind of situation—lest excessive control over the artist be exerted. But the risk would usually only arise in a scale of values which put individual privacy above social relevance as an aethetic imperative.

The desocialization of art in much of Western civilization came at precisely the moment when art was beginning to depend for its survival more on mass impersonal audiences than on individual aristocratic patrons. Mass impersonal audiences for the artist afforded privacy. The artist was not called upon to be sensitive to any discernible school of social opinion and certainly not to any particular individual patron as a link. The relative dependence inherent in specified patronage was itself a way of socializing the artist and preventing him from cutting totally loose into social distance.

To be dependent on specified individuals was a reduction in autonomy, but to be dependent on a number of individuals large enough to become a mass-market was often to enjoy a degree of individualism not adequately consistent with social involvement.

A tendency in Western society has therefore been for the artist to rebel against society, either by conviction or as an aesthetic stance. To rebel against particular norms in society is not necessarily a form of social withdrawal but could indeed be a form of social involvement if the purpose is a commitment to reform. But much of the withdrawal of the artist in the Western world from Western values is inspired by a haughty rejection of the dominant norms in his society, rather than by angry commitment to social transformation. In the words of Joseph Bensman and Israel Garver,

> In modern society, where artists have engaged in social commentary, they have more often than not rejected dominant social values. Serious art has generally been hostile or indifferent to industrialism and the middle-class way of life. This rejection has not necessarily been programmatic, utopian or revolutionary, but rather critical of the philistinism and shoddiness of materialistic society.[35]

But in Africa the artist, even when critical of what is happening in his society, has traditionally been the critic from the

461

inside. The idea is not to withdraw from that which the artist despises, as has tended to be the case in the behavior of artists in modern Western civilization. In Africa it has been a case of social engagement in preserving or in modifying what is going on. The African artist either conformed or sought to reform. In the words of Wole Soyinka, the Nigerian playwright:

> The artist has always functioned in African society as the record of the mores and experience of his society, *and* the voice of vision in his own time. It is time for him to respond to this essence of himself.[36]

This is a conception of the artist as a sage or teacher. Wole Soyinka sometimes talks as if this particular conception of the role of the artist in Africa is now endangered by demands that the artist should follow "the mass direction"—that is, he must always conform with the masses even when he is compelled to seek to reform them. And yet in reality the ordinary people still look on the African writer today in the way most of novelist Chinua Achebe's readers in Nigeria looked to him—as a kind of "teacher." The teacher in African society often had a mystique. That is one reason why President Nyerere of Tanzania is still respectfully referred to in his country as *Mwalimu*. He has become president of his country. Yet the title of teacher is still a contribution to his stature rather than a detraction therefrom.

The prestige of the teacher becomes in the modern period in Africa intertwined with the prestige of the printed word. The art of writing and its newness commands a sense of awe among much of the population. Again, African creative writers seem to have captured the spirit and the obligation either of involved conformity or involved reform. In the words of Chinua Achebe again, Africa's leading novelist in the English language:

> The writer cannot expect to be excused from the task of re-education and re-generation that must be done. In fact, he should march in front. . . . Perhaps what I write is applied art as distinct from pure. But who cares?[37]

In this simple statement is captured a whole new world of civilized engagement. Africa's traditional value patterns might well constitute a critically pertinent road-sign for the travellers in search of new social bearings.

The African continent, partly through ancient Egypt, helped to release the forces of rationality by contributing to the Greek intellectual miracle. Out of that Greek rationality there gradually evolved a Western rationalism, then a Western secularism, then a Western individualism, and finally a sense of anomie at the heart of Western civilization. The cure might well lie back in the villages of Africa again. The Eurafrican Wheel has perhaps come full circle. Sub-Saharan traditions of fusion between ideals and materialism, between the naked body and the soul of man, between art and sensuality, between the individual and society, could now take over where ancient Egypt left off—and put Africa once again in the mainstream of relevant civilized values.

NOTES

1. From his poem "Africa Speaks." Immanuel Wallerstein uses these as opening lines for his book *Africa: The Politics of Independence*, New York: Vintage, 1961.

2. Christiane Desroches-Noblecourt, Curator, Department of Egyptian Antiquities, Musée du Louvre, Paris, *The UNESCO Courier*, February, 1960.

3. Parkes, *Gods and Men: The Origins of Western Culture*, New York: Alfred A. Knopf, 1959, p. 52. See also a popular commentary entitled *The Ancient Kingdoms of the Nile* by Walter A. Fairservis, Jr., New York: The New American Library of World Literature, 1962.

4. Davidson, *Old Africa Rediscovered*, London: Victor Gollancz, 1961, p. 28.

5. For a brief version of his views on this, see Cheikh Anta Diop "The Cultural Contribution and Prospects of Africa," proceedings of the first International Conference of Negro Writers and Artists, *Présence Africaine*, special issue, June-November 1956, pp. 347-54.

6. Cited by Erica Simon, Negritude and Cultural Problems of Contemporary Africa, *Présence Africaine*, Vol. 18, No. 47, Third Quarter, 1963, p. 140.

7. *Ibid.*, p. 140. See DeGraft-Johnson, *African Glory: The Story of Vanished Negro Civilizations*, London: Watts & Co., 1954.

8. See the chapter by Wheeler in *The Dawn of African History*, edited by Roland Oliver, London: Oxford University Press, 1961, p. 2.

9. See Oliver's concluding chapter *ibid.*, p. 97.

10. See also Roland Oliver and J. D. Fage, *A Short History of Africa*, Penguin, 1962, especially Chapter 8. These points are also discussed in Mazrui, *Ancient Greece in African Political Thought*, an inaugural lecture, Nairobi: East African Publishing House, 1967.

11. *Comparative Studies in Society and History*, Volume V, No. 2, January 1963, pp. 233-232.

12. DeGraft-Johnson, *African Glory, op. cit.*, p. 8.

13. Budge, *A Short History of the Egyptian People,* London: J. M. Dent, 1914, p. 10.

14. A. J. Arkell, "The Valley of the Nile" in the *Dawn of African History, op. cit.*, p. 12.

15. The ceremony was that of "shooting the nation" by firing arrows at the four points of the compass. Roland Oliver and J. D. Fage link this with the concept of divine kingship, "Egypt's eventual legacy to so much of the rest of Africa." See their book *A Short History of Africa, op. cit.*, p. 37. For a different interpretation of the concept of divine kingship in Uganda see Merrick Posnansky, "Kingship, archeology and historical myth," *Uganda Journal*, Vol. XXX, No. 1, 1966, pp. 1-12.

16. Alfred R. Tucker, *Eighteen Years in Uganda and East Africa,* London: Edward Arnold, 1908, Vol. 1, p. 86 ff.

17. See Huntingford, "The Peopling of the Interior of East Africa by its Modern Inhabitants" in *History of East Africa,* Vol. 1, edited by Roland Oliver and Gervase Mathew, Oxford: Clarendon Press 1963, pp. 88-89.

18. Mazrui, *Ancient Greece in African Political Thought, op. cit.* For this part of the chapter I have borrowed heavily from my inaugural lecture.

19. Bohannan, *Africa and Africans,* Garden City, N.Y.: The American Museum of Natural History, 1964, p. 156.

20. *op. cit.*

21. Among other places Senghor said this in his lecture at Ibadan University in Nigeria in September 1964.

22. The term is John Mbiti's, Professor of Religious Studies at Makerere University College, Kampala, Uganda.

23. See Marett, *Threshold of Religion* [London, 1909] page xxxi, see also Sundkler, *Bantu Prophets.*

24. Diop, "To a Black Dancer" in *Modern Poetry From Africa,* edited by Gerald Moore and Ulli Beier, Penguin African Library, 1963, pp. 59-60.

25. See "Congo," *Prose and Poetry of Senghor,* translated by John Reed and Clive Wake, London: Oxford University Press, 1965, p. 141.

26. See Nkrumah, *Ghana: Autobiography of Kwame Nkrumah,* New York and Edinburgh: Nelson, 1957, p. 28.

27. *Ibid.*

28. See Melville Herskovits, *The Myth of the Negro Past,* Boston: Beacon Press, 1941.

29. Baldwin, "Why I Stopped Hating Shakespeare," *Insight,* No. 11, Ibadan: British High Commission, n.d., 1964.

30. See Leshoai, "Theater and the Common Man in Africa," *Transition* No. 19, 1965, p. 26.

31. Bohannan, *Africa and Africans, op. cit.*, pp. 156-157.

32. See Sartre, *Black Orpheus,* Paris: Présence Africaine, pp. 45-47.

33. See Senghor, *Prose and Poetry, op. cit.* pp. 105-106.

34. Bohannan, *Africa and Africans, op. cit.* pp. 152, 150.

35. Bensman and Garver, "Art and the Mass Society," *Social Problems,* Vol. 6, Summer 1958, pp. 4-10. Reprinted in Ephraim H. Mizruchi, *The Substance of Sociology,* New York: Appleton-Century-Crofts, 1967, p. 533.

36. See Soyinka, "The African Writer in the Modern State," *Transition,* Vol. VI, No. 31. Kampala, 1967.

37. Achebe, "The African Novelist as Teacher," *New Statesmen,* London, January 29, 1965.

ALI AL'AMIN MAZRUI was born in Kenya in 1933. He earned his Bachelor and Master degrees at the University of Manchester (England) and Columbia University (New York) respectively, and studied for a Ph. D. at Nuffield College, Oxford. The author of five books on Africa and many published articles and papers, Professor Mazrui has also worked in journalism, broadcasting and diplomacy. He is currently Professor and Chairman of the Department of Political Science in Makerere University College, Kampala, Uganda.

AFRICAN ART FROM PREHISTORY
TO THE PRESENT

JAMES A. PORTER

Howard University
(Washington, D.C.)

As the title of this essay suggests, the chronological and
geographical range of African Negro art is greater than what is
usually assumed by most writers who are concerned with its
character and history. It is not enough, and scarcely accurate,
to divide one's discussion of the art into "traditional" and "modern" or "tribal" as opposed to "contemporary" phases; for to
Western eyes the very strangeness of African Negro art may
inhere in its remarkable "anticipation" of much that is new in
Western art, or equally in its sometimes puzzling affinity in some
wise to aspects of Oriental art. The application of the term "traditional" to African art as a means of avoiding use of the term
"primitive" is to ignore the great variety of styles which make
up its corpus, or, at least to gloss over their regional or local
differences. It must also be borne in mind that it has its "secular
forms" as well as its religious or spiritual connotations, and that
both are an undeniable ingredient in that which makes for the
continuity of traditional themes in tribal styles, some of which
have retained significance until today.

PREHISTORY AND ANTIQUITY

The foregoing considerations are indeed paramount since the
origins of the arts of black Africa are now sought in prehistory.
The arts of Africa as here considered will therefore embrace
not only certain phases of the Neolithic past as documented by

discoveries in the Sahara and prehistoric Nigeria, but will also include a synoptic treatment of art production in black Africa's classical and feudal ages, as noted in the civilizations of Cush and Nubia, of the Western Sudan and of medieval Nigeria.

We owe our knowledge of the vast accumulation of rock engravings and rock paintings that dots the Saharan and Libyan desert and which also enlivens the Nigerian Sahel to the assiduous and patient labor of many scientists as well as talented laymen. Obviously the reports and interpretations of these materials supplied by such men as Frobenius and the Abbe Breuil, by Marcel Griaule, Obermaier, Mauny and that brilliant Frenchman, Henri L'Hote, are of the highest value to the art historian who must consult their data and conclusions. However, it would be of little use to provide an extensive list of their names and discoveries in this place.

The published report of Henri L'Hote's explorations and discoveries of rock-painting sites in the Saharan Tassili n'Ajjer throws much light on the nature of human occupation as well as animal life in Saharan prehistory. Here is no speculative or schematic reconstruction of the human phases of desert life, but a marvelously rich and instructive pictorial catalogue of teeming cultures and diversified racial stocks together with endless renderings of matchless skill of an abundant wild life! What astonishing gifts of observation and what sensitive projections of fantasy are displayed!

According to L'Hote, important phases of this art are attributable to Negroids or black men; for Negro types do appear in significant numbers in the pictures. The productions run through the several time-phases of the early Neolithic, the Neolithic, the Protohistoric, and the period of horse and camel. But so numerous are the paintings and so varied their subjects that L'Hote prefers to concentrate his discussion of them under the headings "ancient phase," "evolved phase" and "special styles."

Curiously, however, the number of main styles is so great (18 in all), that one is tempted to believe that period or racial overlap notwithstanding, some continuous evolution of subject and style may ultimately be described. Indeed, in all these "phases" of rock painting the hand of the Negro artist is detectably present either by representative style or by admixture with hybrid forms supposedly proto-Egyptian. In the foreword of his book, *The Search for the Tassili Frescoes,* the author, L'Hote, writes as follows:

> Two main art-styles stand out from the mass of paintings. One is symbolic in character. It is the more ancient and is apparently the work of Negro artists. The other is more recent. It is frankly naturalistic and its influences from the Valley of the Nile are discernible . . . the most archaic of the Tassili pictures belong to a school known up to now and one that apparently was of local origin. The pictures of this latter phase afford us the most ancient data that we have concerning Negro art.

Among the numerous probable links with a later phase of black African tribal life suggested in these pictures perhaps the most amazing are the paintings of mask-wearing individuals whose ritual paraphernalia is definitely similar to certain zoomorphic masks (Banda and Firespitter) which are still made and worn by the Baga and Senufo of the Guinea and the Ivory Coast respectively! Such arresting figurations of the human form added to those of the pre-dynastic phase described by L'Hote as harboring a "Negro-Egyptian complex" must inevitably be combined with existing proofs of the presence and persistence of a Negro ethnic component among the founding races and the builders of early Egyptian civilization.

THE CLASSICAL AGE OF AFRICAN ART

The formation of the civilizations of ancient Cush and Meroë in the Nile Valley to the south of Egypt result from the presence and the assimilative hardihood of Negro peoples who ultimately amalgamated with such Caucasoids as the pastoral Beja and with Egyptians while receiving fresh reinforcements of Negroes from the eastern Sudan. The rise of this close-knit culture at the end of the third millennium B.C. placed a strong cultural entity on Egypt's southern border that in time took on features of parallel development to the dominant civilization.

Ancient Cush offers one of the primary examples in Africa of the rise of an urban and agricultural civilization in the midst of minimal support from an industrial technology. In point of religion as well as social formation it was a coherent culture founded on the conception of divine kingship, as in Egypt, at the head of a polytheistic religion. Internally, Cush was caught up in the nurture and conservation of its own culture, though subordination to Egypt and early intercourse with other nations undoubtedly encouraged the growth of urban centers surrounding the nuclei of shrines and temples. Her proud monarchs, who evidently wished to share the practical benefits of adherence to Egypt's all-pervading Cosmogony, also erected tombs for themselves and relatives in the hope thus to gain eternal life. At their behest, palaces, temples and streets were made, and the ruins of such monuments can still be seen at the sites of Amara, Kerma, Kawa, El Kurru, Gebel Barkal (Napata), Meroë, Musauwarat el-Sofra and Naga.

Explorations and archeological digs undertaken in those ruins by G. Reisner, Dunham and Jansen, Chapman, Chittick, Shinnie and others clearly reveal both the indigenous and the borrowed merits of Cushite art. Such finds include gold and silver castings, jewelry of a refined facture, excellent pottery (Kerma), tiles, sculpture in stone, and parts of furniture which have been removed to enrich the museums of Khartoum, Europe and the United States. It has been disclosed that occasionally statues in the round in addition to flat decorative carvings on temple ruins seem to partake of the Egyptian canon of figural design while still conserving proportion and facial features that memorialize the taste of the Negro.

CHRISTIAN NUBIA

With the introduction of Christianity in 545 A.D., Meroë (renamed Nubia by the Christians), gave rise to the strong kingdom of Dongola which was actually a union of two states. This Christian kingdom and its allies farther South in the locality of Khartoum, not only resisted the incursions and strategies of attrition of Islam and other inimical forces, for generations that were co-eval with the western early Middles Ages, but also served as a center for the propagation of the faith to southward and northward, i.e., to Ethiopia and to Libya. It had the strength to promote the founding of monasteries and the courage and resourcefulness to build churches (often magnificent) in the Byzantine style.

It is a certainty that medieval Nubia was at least in part the creation of black descendants of Sudanese and Cushites. Looking at some of the church frescoes and mosaics that have been recovered from the ruins one has the feeling that a Negro-African aesthetic could not be denied.

NOK IRON AGE ART

The identification of hundreds of terra-cotta and pottery fragments and of iron and stone implements as the debris of a prehistoric culture in Nigeria has pushed the time span of Negro art in that country back to the first millennium B.C. The uncovering of these materials through the activities of tin mining on the Jos Plateau attracted expert appraisal by the British archeologist, Bernard Fagg who identified it as an iron-age culture and named it for the village of Nok where the first artifacts were found. While the estimated age of this culture has been ascertained to be somewhere in the neighborhood of 2000 B.C. the terra-cotta fragments of themselves belong to an art industry that falls between 500 B.C. and 200 A.D.

Nok art consists of human and animal figures chiefly in fragmented condition; and the aesthetic range of the same falls between naturalism and a sort of geometric abstraction in both figures and heads. As a matter of fact, it exhibits rather remarkable stylistic variance for so early a period; and on this head William Fagg, ethnologist and brother of Bernard Fagg, comments as follows:

> . . . Many illustrations would be needed to suggest the extra-ordinary range of sculptural forms in which the Nok artists conceived the human head, the simplest of these being the sphere, the cone (most often inverted) and the cylinder (used with extreme boldness in a head from Katsina Ala) . . . Wherever there is evidence to guide us, the heads appear to have been related to their bodies in what I call "African proportion," that is, one-third to one-quarter of the total height as opposed to the natural proportion of one-sixth to one-seventh. Thus the tendency to emphasize the head presumably as the principal seat of the life-force—which is general in more recent African art, was already established more than 2000 years ago, and this fact helps to refute the

471

not uncommon view that the 'distortions' of recent African sculpture are the result of degeneration from some naturalistic golden age before the white men came.

While a hiatus of several centuries prevails between the end of Nok art and the emergence of Ifé, there are yet many features of the former which lead us to suspect that it could have been influentially antecedent to that of Ifé. Speculatively, this relationship rests mainly but not exclusively on grounds of medium and technique. Our discussion of the art of Ifé to follow will make this clear. F. Willet and other scholars seem almost inclined to regard Nok art as the primitive phase of Ifé, but of course are careful not to make that a firm conclusion in the absence of evidence to bolster such surmise.

EMPIRES AND ARTS OF THE WESTERN SUDAN

From reports and histories written by early Arab geographers, explorers and historians, the world has learned much of the great feudal empires that rose and then declined in succession in the Western Sudan from a few generations before Mohammed until the late nineteenth century. These territorial empires were formed predominantly upon a nuclear ethnic component of black peoples in every case, though other racial stocks such as Berber, Arab, Jew, Touareg and Fulani brought formative and sometimes destructive influences to bear.

The earliest of the Sudanese empires was that of Ghana. Enjoying a phenomenal span of autonomous life since its founding in the third or fourth century A.D., this state was first devastated by the advance military religionists of Berber and Arab civilization and finally destroyed through the rebellious uprisings of other black races within her own borders or living contiguous thereto in southern and western Sudan. Ghana was utterly destroyed in 1240 by Sundiatia, the Mandingo ruler of Kangaba.

The French explorer, Bonnel de Mézières, believing the actual location of the ancient capital of Ghana to have been the site of the dusty village of Kumbi Saleh lying 200 miles north of Bamako, undertook to excavate the site in 1914. His results were interesting though not conclusive. Nevertheless, his work helped to define Ghana as a state that drew strength from an

472

iron-working industry and which also functioned as a vast commercial empire whose lifelines secured the passage of gold and of slaves from districts of the lower Sudan, that is, the savannah and the forest, northward to Algeria and Tunisia and Morocco.

Renewal of archaeological work at the site in 1949 by Mauny and Thomassey brought out other interesting facts; namely, that Kumbi had indeed been a great city probably very similar to old Kano as Heinrich Barth saw it in the 1850's. Indeed it might be characterized as having been a "twin city" with one huge section reserved to the residence of the king, the court and all permanent residents separated by a middle district six miles wide, though covered more or less with the huts of slaves, from a kind of *sabun gari* or market city reserved to visiting tradespeople, their animals of transport and subsistence, and to their servitors.

In summarizing the kinds and quality of finds reported by Mézières and his continuators at Kumbi Saleh, Basil Davidson writes as follows:

> . . . Among many large dwellings and a mosque, two mansions excavated by Thomassey suggest something of its scale and comfort. One of these was about sixty-six feet long and forty-two feet wide, and had seven rooms opening out of one another on two stories connected by an efficient staircase. The other was still larger, and had nine rooms. Built mainly in blocks of slatelike schist cemented with banco, their interior walls had been decorated with a yellow plaster of which a little is still preserved. No objects in silver or gold were found, but a large store of objects in iron . . . (and) among these iron objects were lances, knives, arrowheads, nails, a varied collection of farming tools, and one of the finest pairs of scissors of early medieval date ever to be found in any country. A large quantity of glass weights, evidently for weighing gold, were recovered; many fragments of pottery of Mediterranean provenance; and seventy-seven pieces of painted stone, of which fifty-three bore verses of the Koran in an Arabic script, while twenty-four others had decorated motifs.

Apart from the casual descriptions of the use of gold orna-

473

ments, of golden ceremonial staves and other paraphernalia of court receptions, there is little else in the category of creative arts which can be reported as distinguishing the empires of Mali and Songhay which rose upon the ashes, so to speak, of Ghana and the enforced submission of lesser tribes and kingdoms. This observation does not apply, however, to their architecture. Whatever the nature of Ghanaian architecture might have been, it is to be assumed that as a style it too was lost with the destruction of the empire. But the "Sudanese style" of building as we know it was probably derived and formulated from the building practices of the Mandingo and the Songhay peoples of the Sudan through several early generations.

This unique style of building, the so-called "mud architecture" of the western Sudan, has in the course of centuries greatly influenced modes of building to the south, for example, in northern and central Nigeria and even northern Ghana and Togo. While legend says that the mosques and palaces of Gao and Djenné and of Timbuctoo were rebuilt in an original style by a visiting poet-architect from Granada, Spain, who returned with the Emperor of Mali from Cairo, it would seem doubtful, given the strong affinity which that style bears to structural idioms in Mauretania, Tunisia and southern Algeria, that it could be thus blithely attributed to the brief intervention of a poet-architect who probably worked without plans or sketches, that is to say, more or less by verbal command. However that may be, it is the extraordinarily adaptable and manipulable style of the Sudanese mosque and indeed of the typical large palace and dependent buildings which represents the chief contribution of the civilizations of Mali and Songhay to the arts and crafts of the Sudanic civilizations.

TRIBAL ARTS OF THE SUDAN AND OF UPPER GUINEA

Of the numerous peoples of these areas, the Dogon and the Bambara, the Baga, the Senufo, Mossi and Bobo are well-known for the high quality and variety of their sculpture in wood. The *Dogon* who live in Mali possess a thoroughly distinctive concept of the universe which influences every aspect of their lives from birth to death. More than an ontology, it is also a theory of the genesis of the world, involving the inter-action of sky and earth deities,—in short, a collection of myths of creation which also explains nature's rhythmic energies of increase and the actions, purposes and destiny of mankind. They are the makers of several types of ancestor figures embracing both male and female partners in dyadic form. They also make a great variety of masks many of which are employed in connection with the rites of passage; while others are employed in fertility rites, and still others in the implorative ceremonies of hunting.

Bambara culture, like the Dogon, is largely controlled by priests and headmen who are the cult leaders of powerful secret societies. However, in their art, at least, the Bambara show some of the effects of the anti-figural bias of the Muslim religion to which they have been only partial converts. The influence is visible in the use of linear surface decoration and in the reduction of otherwise plastic forms to a kind of filigree or alternation of open and closed spaces as in the famous *Chi' Wara* image or antelope deity which they make. Many types of masks are made by the Bambara, but among those of most prominent interest are the horned variety called *n'tomo* for the secret society of uncircumcised youth; the *komo* mask produced for an association whose membership is only for the circumcised, and the *koré-ku,* a mask worn for the ancestors in the ritual performances of the Koré society which is responsible for the fertility of the fields.

The Bambara are also not without their "ancestor figures," and in fact, can be credited with having evolved or created an unique type of that class of sculpture, in that variety usually referred to as "the chain of ancestors." This type is supposed to signify the importance of descent groups or tribal lineage among them, and its general characteristics are as follows: Large well modelled heads whose features adhere nevertheless somewhat rigidly to a type. Wherever the full figure is used the stance or posture is more or less hieratically rendered. The same may be said to be a consistent aspect of the ancestor chain which briefly is a collection of superposed busts or heads, one emerging from the other in a pattern that seems generally to respond to an enclosing semi-circle.

The Baga are also a lower Sudanese group whose migratory habit has in recent times brought them in numbers to the coastal region of modern Guinea. They are the creators of two very spectacular masks of monumental size. The larger, and more important perhaps is the *nimba* or "Mother" mask of enormous size. Its form is limited to a bird-like head with decorative and contrasting raised hatchings forming a striated effect resembling a cicatrice design. The *banda* mask is entirely different. Its total effect is zoomorphic, resulting from a combination of parts borrowed from the boar, the crocodile and also imitated from the features of the human face. It is also made distinctly decorative though at the same time fearsome by clever additions of bright color. While the Baga do make other images their fame as artists might well rest on these two unique forms.

The *Senufo* or *Siena* are spread over a vast territory extending northward into southern Mali and southward to the very center of the Ivory Coast. They live in a loose confederation and have never, it seems, as a tribal group, sought to re-organize themselves into statehood. But as artists the Senufo are among the most productive of west coast groups, and at the same time have a most varied repertory of forms. While certain of their masks show great subtlety of design and facture, other forms, including entire figures, exhibit a wonderful boldness of design combined with an energetic rhythmic accent. This is equally the case with the famous "firespitter" masks and their celebrated statues whether "Deble" (rhythm pounders) or equestrian ancestor figures. Occasionally, their engaging mystical conception of "Katioléo," the great Mother Goddess, is given a monumental form.

Their art is also related more than superficially to the refined harmonious sculpture of certain tribes of the Ivory Coast such as the *Baulé* and the *Guro* to whom they are neighbors. But the sharing of preferences here is not extended as well to the Ivory Coast representatives of the Mande-speaking groups such as the *Dan, Kran, Guerzé* whose more numerous branches extend deep into Sierra Leone and Liberia. Some elements of the Senufo, like these tribes, are members of the great PORO Society which exercises such strict social control among its adherents in the states cited.

The Dan masks and those created by the Baulé and Guro are generally acknowledged and sought after for their beauty of form and patination and exquisite facture. Few sculptural figures, however, can equal the ancestor carvings for which the

Baulé, whose culture Delafosse has attempted to connect with ancient Egypt, are justly famous.

SCULPTURE OF UPPER VOLTA, GHANA AND DAHOMEY

In these national areas we find an art that is more definitely sustained by the ruling class of society. Its major trait is clearly that of a court of art such as developed by the *Ashanti* in *Ghana,* by the *Mossi* in Upper Volta, the *Fon* and *Ewes* in Dahomey, and by the western Yoruba in Dahomey. Like the Baulé, the Ashanti nation to whom they are related have acquired great skill in the making of gold ornaments and implements. A similar command of casting techniques is exhibited in their famous gold weights which though mainly of brass were formerly used as weights or counters for the weighing of gold dust. Important ritual vessels of brass and bronze were also cast by the Ashanti smiths. Their art is usually classified as a superior handicraft but it also includes the carving of wooden images such as the *Akua' Ba* fertility dolls, the making of funerary pottery and funerary figures of almost equal interest.

On the basis of the great variety of forms and techniques which the traditional arts of *Dahomey* now gathered into the royal museum at Abomey and in the museums of the world exhibit, one may conclude that only the patronage of the princely court of Dahomey could have made possible such a high level of achievement, and especially now that some of the erstwhile arts of the court have definitely declined or disappeared. Nevertheless, it is still possible to see in Dahomey exceptionally fine examples of brass casting and calabash carving in addition to colorful appliqué embroideries or banners of exemplary vigor of design and decorative beauty.

ART IN NIGERIA, IN THE CAMEROONS AND GABON

Perhaps the most impressive instances of an art nurtured, supported and protected by a ruling caste or court life in all Africa are to be found in Nigeria where the traditional arts of Ifé and Benin once flourished under the patronage of priest-kings and warrior kings. It is thought that the terra-cotta images and bronze idealized portraits which are the main body of Ifé art memorialize an artistic enterprise initiated at least as early

477

as the twelfth century A.D. The repertory of this art (subjects, of course) is even more diversified than that of Nok while in its technical effects and to a slight degree even in subject matter it suggests morphological links with Nok.

It was from Ifé that the artisans of Benin learned to cast works in brass and bronze by the "lost-wax" process. It is logical, therefore, to expect that the bronzes of Ifé with which we are familiar represent a most skillful attainment in the art of bronze casting; and to a large extent comparisons made by experts seem to substantiate this expectation. However that may be, the bronzes of Ifé adhere far more closely to a canon of idealized realism than do even the earliest and best of the Benin portrait heads which in the course of time finally declined to a static formularized symbolic portraiture in later generations.

A complete survey of these two tribal styles would reveal an astonishing richness of material and technical resources mastered by their artists. Ifé artists, were also expert in the carving of such hard materials as quartzite as their royal stools still preserved to us indicate, also granite and the softer material of steatite. The making of glass beads and the shaping of stone units for necklaces led in both cultures to mastery of the working of coral and jasper. Benin art, as shown by William Fagg, also includes a popular style which along with the numerous works in ivory, wood and terracotta that may be classified as handicraft, exerted a transforming influence on the lesser arts of neighboring peoples. Fagg has chosen to call the collection of works representing the latter activity the *Lower Niger Bronze Industry.*

No African art style affords us a more complete illustration of the life and symbolic forms and religious, artistic and ceremonial uses of a court. It is interesting to note that with the arrival of Europeans in Benin, particularly the Portuguese, there began a tentative patronage of Benin craftsmen by European missionaries as well as merchants. Examples of this "Afro-European" phase of their production are still to be seen in a few museums of Europe and the United States.

Of almost as great interest and variety are the works of Yoruba artists. Great quantities of masks and statuettes representing Yoruba regional styles are known. *Ibo* and *Ibibio,* and Niger

Delta tribes such as *Ijo* and *Ekoi* are also prolific carvers of masks and figures.

While the bronze plaques made by the Bini to be affixed to the pillars of the royal buildings in the king's compound could hardly be termed "architectural sculpture," the greater part of the religious and ceremonial art produced by the dominant tribal groups in Cameroons—the *Bamiléké, Bali, Bafut, Bamenda* would appear to fit that description perfectly. Sculpture is used for both magical and decorative purposes on the supporting pillars and door frames of Cameroons huts which, be it noted, are given an unique form among the Bamiliké particularly. In plan and profile the *Bamiléké* hut is both quadrangular and conical; while the use of bamboo and rattan as the principal material of its composition results in an excellent background for the bold forms and rhythmic patterns with which the architectural sculpture of the Cameroons is endowed.

It is in the Cameroons that we first meet the Bantu culture, which from that area spreads southward and eastward to Gabon and throughout the Congo Basin, the Central Congo and to the East as far as Lake Tanganyika.

Among the unique forms of sculpture and carving produced in Gabon are the *Bieri* of the Fang, a general descriptive term that designates both the cryptic mortuary heads and the powerful statues which have the same function, both in hardwood. The remarkable *Nbulu-Ngulu* figures of the Kota which are placed in mortuary baskets as guardians of the ancestral reserve and which combine metal laminations over a carved wooden core are universally admired as "proto-cubist" in design. But few African carvings combining lamination in metal over a spare wooden form approach more closely the concept of a disembodied spirit or to the sculptural form which supposedly is its habitation. Surprising variations on human features are likewise played by several peoples of Gabon who may share the same iconographic image; as in the so-called M'Pongwe or Pahouin mask which to many observers seems to have an "oriental" or Japanese cast of features.

ARTS OF THE CONGO

It is well known that the coastal strip of the Congo region

usually referred to as *Bas-Congo* (Lower Congo) was first visited by European Navigators and explorers late in the fifteenth century and in the early sixteenth century. The presence of Jesuit missionaries and representatives of Christian religious orders was especially influential in the seventeenth century. The effects of European contact have been interestingly perpetuated in brass crucifixes and other liturgical vessels developed by the artists of that region under the inspiration, not to say, urgency, of the European missionaries. In general, however, such evidence as we have in extant items in which the European is visibly portrayed can be classified as "secular" or profane rather than religious and can scarcely be dated earlier than the mid-nineteenth century in most cases.

Not all Congo art reflects a direct concern with the imagery of realism, but it should be noted that among tribal groups of that region which in the traditional past have produced forms displaying a mastery of the human figure in both single and combined forms are those that we know under the generic Bantu name of *BaKongo*. This name in its plural form refers to such peoples as the Mayombe and Bavili, the Bawoyo in the enclave of Cabinda, the Bankanu and Bazombo. As William Fagg in his *African Tribal Sculptures* has noted, ". . . The decorative style [of these groups] shows many traces of the old splendours of the Kingdom of Kongo which was flourishing among their ancestors when the Portuguese first reached West Africa." In contrast thereto, their modern sculpture, particularly, shows a high degree of naturalism as well as surface delicacy.

Among the strikingly emotionalized figural forms produced in the area of Lower Congo, one must mention the funerary figures of soft stone known as *mintadi*, and the "magical" images known as *kondé*, the latter, supposedly, being the implements of the fetisher, which seem to anticipate the aesthetic purposes of "found" sculpture or "assemblage," if you will, as practiced in Europe and America.

Throughout the Congo, the types of masks employed by various tribal cultures, at least in the past, appear to represent not only the vital gift of inventiveness, but also of a brilliant technical skill in suiting form to intention as well as to the ultimate function of the object. Tribal styles of the Pende, the

Yaka, Bembé, Bena Lulua and numerous other groups, illustrate this observation in the variety of their production.

Several great cultures in the Central, South and East Congo regions are distinguished as much for the unique artistic forms of their masks as for the beauty and power, and often high decorative character of their ancestor figures or commemorative images of their departed kings. Some connection in point of shared artistic tradition has been suggested as once effectual between the *Kuba*, who formerly were both culturally and artistically preeminent in the Central Congo, and the West Coast tribes of Bambala and Bakongo. But in the course of time it seems that they themselves must have "Kuba-ized" a number of their neighbors in terms of shared art forms and customary ways since significant aspects of Kuba taste or preference show up in the masks and figures of the Pende, the Dengese and the Lulua. But as a matter of fact, it is Kuba art in some of its most conspicuous phases which most nearly approaches in type as well as range of decorative form the originality and confident facture already noted as marking the great court arts of Benin. Interesting comparisons, therefore, might be made between their marvelous series of 18 portraits of kings whose names, for the most part are actually known, and Bini conceptions of royalty as preserved for us in their numerous bronze portrait heads and other symbolic royal imagery.

In the Katanga Province, which lies to the East and South of the territory occupied by the Kuba and their neighbors, are the interesting tribal cultures of the *Luba, Songye, Yaka* and *Chokwe* which to some slight degree display interrelatedness of artistic traits. Luba art, the predominant art in the province, is both subtle and self-contained; and so far as the consistency of stylistic traits is concerned has exhibited that quality most usually in their application of figural forms of symbolic meaning to ceremonial or ritual furniture and implements of many kinds. In other words, the magisterial forms which appear in masks and large figures are also used imaginatively though in smaller scale on the classes of objects indicated. Among their best-known works are the famous Caryatid stools known as *buli* of which there are at least two distinct styles.

In Northeastern Congo live the *Léga* whose delicate and virtually esoteric carvings in ivory and bone introduced a facet of whimsy, one might say, into the otherwise overpoweringly noble and imposing forms of the Eastern and Northern Congo.

Finally, we have to mention the self-mirroring arts of the Mangbetu whose practice of head deformation on their children has been interestingly transmitted through their art as an element of style. Material evidence of this is seen in their anthropomorphic honey boxes, their harp-like musical instruments, and especially their beautifully formed palm-wine and water jugs.

As this essay doubtless makes clear, the range and complexity of African sculptural and handicrafts is enormous. There is not space to consider, for example, the mask forms and craft arts of such groups in Northeast Congo as the Azande, or the many aspects of art and crafts which have dazzled western visitors among such tribes as the Wakerewe near Lake Victoria, or the Makonde, in Tanzania, in earlier days makers of "surrealist" masks, but today, of wooden figures which seem by turns grotesque and fanciful.

CONTEMPORARY AFRICAN ART

In some black African countries the emergence of a significant contemporary art has had to wait on the achievement or the arrival of national political independence. This alone, however, has not brought freedom to the artist or new directions for art in every case. The economic question, that is to say, conscious commitment to the support of the arts (not always visible in all the independent states) which is tied to "traditionalism" on the one hand and conservative factors of historical and social origin on the other, may be said to be one of the "brakes" which have acted against the swift emergence of a new art consciousness in black Africa. It is necessary to realize, nevertheless, that the lack of good teachers or wise counsel, or art criticism has in many instances abetted the proliferating effect of the workshop conditions from which "airport" art has developed. Nor can we ignore the effects of "cultural drying up" wherever religious and social customs that once nourished the artist or provided him with both themes and a reason for creating, have declined or died out.

It must be admitted that the relative infertility of African art is most disheartening at present in those places where moribund or dead tribal traditions have scarcely been replaced with a contemporary cultural vigor. One also notes in many places the absence of such institutions as might be formed to assure public nurture of art and culture. In some places where they do exist, at least in terms of name and physical location, underbudgeting and understaffing effectually nullify the projected programs. There are of course, and happily, a few bright exceptions to this state of things.

Nigeria and Ghana are among the most art- or-culture-minded of all the black independent countries. As one would expect, it is in those countries where the introduction or development of culture centers like *MBari* or the Ghana Theatre and its cultural organ *Okyeame* and the forming and encouragement of art associations or clubs in colleges and universities have been purposeful that we observe a largely successful stimulation to art activities and to an incipient cultural re-integration. In these countries and in Ivory Coast and Senegal, all this has been done with some government assistance if not direct sponsorship.

Despite all such efforts, however, and even in the face of the most expert counsel at times, that decline of art activity which has been noted and deplored both inside and outside Africa has not yet been arrested. Indeed, no matter how many words of praise have been poured out for the work of the Belgian "academies" in the Congo, and the fruitful philosophies which have been put to use at Makerere College, or for the cultural nationalism undergirding a recrudescent culture in Zambia and Kenya, one senses that the difficulties encountered by the leadership are nothing if not laborious or even exhausting.

As in Nigeria and the Congo, one observes that some traditional art persists. One also observes that the gap between old and new in terms of art at least is widening, not closing, for the reasons already given. Strange to say, it is this inherent split in art culture which has persuaded some artists that it is to their advantage to work in at least two styles,—one that has traditional form as well as content; the other novel, or at least typically contemporary. Though such a procedure does represent a compromise on the part of the artist, it is not entirely born of expediency since the number of those artists who can satisfy both the native or indigenous patron and the foreign tourist patron is not great. Opposed to such practice which at bottom is a thing of individual or personal preference, is the encouragement of "schools" or collective studios by very capable and sympathetic Europeans such as Frank McEwen where the basic personal idiom of the artist is "led out" and encouraged.

But in point of patronage as well as instruction, it is clear that there are efforts afoot to relieve the African painter or sculptor of the burdens of traditional precedent as well as those of disciplined learning. The "School of Oshogbo" artists under the leadership of Suzanne Wenger and Ulli Beier has been moving under this definitive objective: While the young student is encouraged to derive his subjects from tribal background including religion or mythology, he is also encouraged to express himself freely and inventively and to ignore so far as possible the trammels of a disciplined technique. Back of this there is also an architectural interest in mural displays connected with Yoruba shrines but also with experimental theatre and a few business enterprises. Similarly, in East Africa, with the School of *Paa Ya Paa* in Kenya, which is presided over, I might say, by the outspoken artist Emilio Njau, the insistence on African originality and cultural perspectives almost to the exclusion of outside influences or directions is leading to a new conception of the possibilities and the purposes of African art. Other efforts of similar order are rising in Cameroons, the Democratic Republic of the Congo and in Senegal.

EUROPEAN INFLUENCE ON THE ARTISTS

African art having in the past deeply influenced Western art is now in some respects being influenced or even partly formed by European taste and, of course, modern art. Of those outstanding African painters and sculptors who today find their work admired and purchased by many Europeans and Americans both inside and outside Africa, the majority have studied art in Europe, though afterwards they may have returned to Africa. I do not, of course, bracket in this group the anonymous carver or even the wellknown master of a workshop, however excellent his small ivory carvings or carvings in wood may be. It should be brought out, however, that among the painters and sculptors with European training, several have managed to retain their African quality as practitioners. To be sure, they do, in some cases, revert to such "popularisms" as memory portraits of the Oba, or to "African Motherhood," "the palm-wine tapper," "the medicine man," etc., but these themes are still celebrated in Africa for what is thought to be their symbolic value.

It is therefore not inappropriate to mention here by name some of those African artists who have most decisively impressed their own fellow-countrymen as well as foreign patrons. It will not be possible to assess their contributions critically since there is not space to do so. Possibly just to mention them here is in a sense to commend the more original merits of their work to the interested reader.

Among Nigerian artists who have scored both at home and abroad are the new "old masters" like Ben Enwonwu who is both painter and sculptor, Felix Idubor, a prolific sculptor, the fine traditional sculptor, Lamidi Fakeye, as well as the young but very promising painters, Demas NWoko, Simon Okeke, Solomon Wangboje, and a few others. Many others have studied under British instructors in the several Universities in Nigeria.

Ghana has produced three important sculptors, one of whom was for years the leading art theorist and teacher of art in Ghana, Kofi Antubam who died in 1963. His compatriots, Vincent Kofi and Dr. Ampofo are well-known for their sculpture in wood.

Sudan and Ethiopia have also their quota of well-trained but very creative painters, such as Ibrahim Salahi of Khartoum. The leading painters of Ethiopia today, Afewerke Tekle, Skunder Bhogossian and Gebre Desta were all trained abroad but profess startlingly disparate ways of projecting their individual styles.

Similarly, Senegal has its Papa Ibra Tall, and Tanzania its Sam Ntiro; but of the many painters of the Congo, almost none have gone abroad to study, though many have visited and exhibited widely in Europe.

Among the most revealing events in recent years was the Dakar World Festival of Negro Arts held at Dakar in April, 1966 whose organizers sought to bring together from all over the world the work of living black artists with a view to achieving a survey of the inherent similarities and the superficial differences to be noted in black contemporary painting and sculpture. But few common denominators were found except among the representatives of those countries which could be considered neighbors and sharers of similar themes, motives or cultural conditioning. The most prevalent similarities among the Africans were the love of bright or plangent colors, of patterned rhythms, and a tendency to decoration rather than expression. Nevertheless, nothing that one might call a general African style came to the surface, though a number of artists could fairly be credited with having achieved an individual idiom or style. In view of what has already been written to emphasize the achievements of individual and influential artists in particular countries it would be gratuitous indeed to make any further comparisons here among African painters or sculptors.

If the great numbers of producing painters and sculptors and craftsmen now at work in Africa can mean anything it must suggest that the art spirit is not yet dead in that continent. It suggests further that a new consciousness of art is really emerging and that it can be credited largely to the indomitable and increasingly successful effort that a number of very talented artists with relatively small understanding on the part of their own countrymen have been making on behalf of all the others.

SELECTED BIBLIOGRAPHY

Arkell, Anthony J., "The Eastern Sudan, 'the land of the black men'," in *Encyclopedia of World Art*, New York, McGraw-Hill Book Company, 1967, pp. 655-659.

David, Basil, *The Lost Cities of Africa*. Boston and Toronto: Little, Brown and Company, 1959, Chapters II, III.

Davies, Oliver, *West Africa Before the Europeans*. London: Methuen and Company, 1967, pp. 256-258.

Desplagnes, Louis, *Le Plateau Central Nigérien, Une Mission Archélogique et Ethnographique au Soudan Français*, Paris: Emile LaRose, 1907.

Fage, J. D., *An Introduction to the History of West Africa* (Third Edition), Cambridge: At the University Press, 1962.

Fagg, William, *The Art of Central Africa*: *Sculpture and Tribal Masks*. New York: The New American Library, 1967.

—————, *Nigerian Images*. London: Lund Humphries, 1963, pp. 22-24.

Forman, W. and B., and Philip Dark, *Benin Art*. London: Paul Hamlyn, 1960.

Frobenius, Leo, *Historie de la Civilisation Africaine*. Paris: Gallimard, 1933.

Himmelheber, Hans, *Les Masques Africaines*. Paris: Press Universitaires de France, 1960.

Hintze, Fritz and Ursula, *Civilizations of the Old Sudan*: *Kerma, Kush, Christian Nubia*. Leipzig: Verlag fur Kunst v. Wissenschaft, 1968.

Leuzinger, Elsy, *Africa, The Art of the Negro Peoples*. (Art of the World Series.) London: Methuen, 1964, Chapters II, III, IV, V, VI.

Es-Sadi, Imran Ben Amir, *Tarikh es-Soudan* (Trans. O. Houdas), Paris: E. Leroux, 1900.

Torday, E. and T. A. Joyce, *Notes Ethnographiques sur Les Peuples Communé-Appelés Bakuba* . . . Bruxelles: Ministère des Colonies, 1911.

Born in Baltimore, Maryland, the son of a Methodist minister, James A. Porter received his basic education in the public schools of the District of Columbia. He received the B.S. degree in Art from the Fine Arts Graduate Center, New York University. Since 1953, Professor Porter has untiringly devoted much of his time and energies toward the administration of the Department of Art at Howard University. Since that time, he has served as Head of the Department and Director of the Gallery of Art. Professor Porter is a creative artist in his own right and has won several awards for his painting. He was recently honored by the White House at the 25th Anniversary Celebration of the founding of the National Gallery of Art along with 25 other artist-educators as "one of America's most outstanding men of the arts in 1965." He is well recognized as a leading authority on African and American Art and has also published several articles and pamphlets on the art of Americans of African descent. His celebrated book, *Modern Negro Art,* Dryden Press, has become a classic in this field.

CONTEMPORARY BLACK AMERICAN ART

JAMES A. PORTER

(*Howard University*)

The contributions of scientific research in this century to knowledge of the Negro have made invaluable evidence for the prolongation of African culture into the complex civilizations of the Western Hemisphere available to all who may be interested. If previously—say, as late as World War I—the greater part of the world had believed the American Negro to be merely an unhealthy graft upon the tree of American civilization, there is not now, nor has there been for more than two generations, any qualified excuse whatever to persist in that belief. Cognizant as we may well be of the breadth, complexity, and stratified depth of Western life and culture, objective study of the variety of cultural strands composing its fabric, including those contributed by the many tribal variants of the American Indian, constrains us to include as well that more direct heritage of the American Negro in which African characteristics predominate.

If this contemporary orientation towards the historic values of Negro culture is stimulating to contemplate, it is also sobering to reflect that it has been tardy in arriving. Prior to World War I, the number of white students of American culture or of the cultural potential of different social and ethnic groups in America creditable with a sound knowledge of Negro life and culture was very small. *Per contra*, there were such enlightened anthropologists and masters of objective historical method as Franz Boas, the historian Albert Bushnell Hart, and sociologists like the late W. E. B. DuBois, whose writings lifted the scales from the eyes of all who were willing to read them believingly. Yet, one wonders if our present disposition to weigh the deserts of the Negro in the light of a more perfect knowledge of his past could ever have been developed without the intellectual or scholarly and programmatic leadership of such great Americans as W. E. B. DuBois, Carter G. Woodson, Kelly Miller, Alain LeRoy Locke and the late E. Franklin Frazier.

It was also the sympathetic interest of scholars like the late anthropologist Melville J. Herskovits, the ethnographers D. Price-Mars, Morton Kahn and Leyburn, and such Negro philosophers and interpreters as Locke and Lorenzo D. Turner, which focused attention upon the persistent—as opposed to the latent—"Africanisms" in the culture of the southern United States, the Caribbean, and the several Guianas of South America, thus projecting a new realm of discourse that subsequently attracted increasing scholarly effort to the interpretation of Afro-American culture. Ultimately, their work precipitated an ever-broadening and apparently unending stream of essays and projects relating to the history and morphology of Negro culture.

Thus, it would be nonsensical to claim that the broadening appreciation of the Negro and his arts in the Western Hemisphere was entirely due to the activity of Negro scholarship or connoisseurship. As a matter of fact, the Negro scholar has often been supported in that connection by the cooperative as well as the collaborative assistance of white intellectuals who were sincerely enthusiastic to correct the record and to reveal the truth. For example, it is well to recall that the tardiness of white America to acknowledge wholeheartedly the Negro's contribution to popular music and especially to Jazz was first dealt a serious thrust by the knowledgeable published writings of European lovers of Jazz. And that re-assessment of American Jazz was certainly commenced prior to the synthetic use of "jazz" by George Gershwin and Paul Whiteman. In addition, it will be recalled that Anton Dvorak in his "New World Symphony" and Henry Krehbiel in his *Afro-American Folk-Songs* provided even the somewhat skeptical American Negro with sound reasons for accepting the Negro Spiritual as an art form.

It was not, however, until the advent of the "New Negro Movement" in the 1920's that the formative arts of painting, sculpture, of the print and of design also became the acknowledged province of the American Negro. Prior to that period, the impact of African art, as developed through the conscious use thereof made by Picasso, Matisse, Vlaminck, Derain and certain German Expressionist painters, had also been felt in the Americas. Yet, the significance of that event for Negro art in America was not defined until Alain Locke employed his astute critical powers and his ready pen to appraise the past performances of the Negro artist and to explain the connection with African art sustained by American Negroes within the framework of what he chose to call "The Ancestral Arts." Perhaps it is now quite certain that Locke's main contribution to our appreciation of modern Afro-American art was his interesting apology for the distinctive aesthetico-racial (but not the "primitive"), traits of African art; and second, his rather romantic advocacy of those characteristics as a point of departure for the young American Negro artist.

AFRICAN SURVIVALS

It is important to realize that evidence of African survivals in the earliest manifestations of Afro-American creativity in the United States demonstrably exists. The writer of this essay, in his book *Modern Negro Art*, published in 1943, devotes an entire chapter to supporting evidence for the conscious survival of African art forms and techniques in some parts of the Southern United States, notably in the States of Alabama, Louisiana, North and South Carolina, and Virginia. Architecture offers proofs of this cultural phenomenon in techniques of house construction and the making of wrought-iron supports and ornaments for balconies and porches in New Orleans, Louisiana, Mobile, Alabama, Charleston, South Carolina and parts of Virginia.

ANONYMOUS CRAFTSMEN

The crafts of weaving, wood carving and embroidery have also provided a way of retaining various African features; while that remarkable and challenging species of "plantation pottery" produced by slave craftsmen of North and South Carolina, as noted by Cedric Dover in his *American Negro Art*, bears unmistakable signs of African recollection in certain peculiarities of surface design. Apart from this, yet related thereto, is the pregnant fact that countless Negroes were engaged in earning money to buy

491

their freedom through skilled employment as sign painters, silver smiths, cabinet and coach makers, stucco ornamentalists, and even as shipwrights. There was even a very early Negro sculptor, Eugene Warbourg of New Orleans, whose principal work until he left New Orleans for the opportunity of study in Europe was the making of ornamental gravestones. To these we must add the early Negro portrait limners, and those Negro sailors as well whose contributions to the immense sum of "scrimshaw art," now to be seen in America's marine museums, must forever remain anonymous and unassigned.

Freedom was ever an incentive to the slave; and we must remember that the greater part of the burden of production in the industrial crafts of the South was borne by bondsmen. Yet it is certain that the slave was apt to strive as best he could to obtain for himself those privileges which he could not help but observe were enjoyed by many "free men of color." But though the slave were ever so talented, it was rarely artistic talent, but rather painfully acquired mechanical skills, unremitting labor, and, occasionally, thrift, which helped him most to buy his freedom. In general, the slavocracy brutally suppressed, wherever possible, all philanthropic effort to educate the slave. For this and other reasons we find that the Negro rarely emerged as an individual artist or even a privileged, self-employing artisan from the welter of southern industrial strivings.

EARLY INDEPENDENT BLACK ARTISTS

Even in the North, where opportunities for the talented Negro were more frequent, and repression of the Negro probably less severe, the traces of poverty and the shadow of repression tied the hopes of Negro art to an uncertain future; and such harsh and unfavorable social conditions were the very cause of the scarcity of production attributable to the early talented Negro. It is quite likely that the same set of social conditions made it inevitable that the majority of Negro artists should ape the residual European art techniques or modes of painting which underlay the American system of art practice and art apprenticeship of the time.

Such inimical influences were transcended, however, in the life and work of a handful of "free" Negro artists such as the

492

draftsman-engraver, Patrick Reason, the landscape and mural painter, Robert S. Duncanson of Cincinnati, the excellent portrait painter, William Simpson, and E. M. Bannister, painter of naturalistic landscapes and also one of the founders of the Providence Art Club.

Even though seemingly unsophisticated in aesthetics, these artists often produced work of a beguiling unpretentiousness that, nevertheless, possessed both dignity and supple grace. And there were others—all free men of the *antebellum* period—among whom I would cite the Negro Quaker, Robert Douglass, Jr., of Philadelphia, and Joshua Johnston of Baltimore, a painter of prim portraits who still remains a somewhat shadowy figure.

The career of Edmonia Lewis, the first Negro woman sculptress, begun prior to the Civil War, came to an end near the turn of the century. While the actual date of her death is not yet known, the many interesting details of her life and work which are known testify to a wonderfully courageous spirit. Her career was a steady and arduous climb to a place of honor and high reputation in Europe and, finally, in America as one of the foremost American exponents of the neo-classic style in sculpture. She resided in Rome from 1867 to 1884, but repeatedly sent her work to be exhibited and sold in the United States. Her most famous work, "The Death of Cleopatra," now lost, was exhibited at the Philadelphia Centennial Exposition of 1876. The only other Negro artist of the United States to have his work on view at the same exposition was Edward M. Bannister who sent a landscape entitled "Under the Oaks."

Negro America was largely ignorant of this brief professional triumph over prejudice and discrimination, for few Negroes in the last quarter of the Nineteenth century could have appreciated the gigantic labors that went into the making of Edmonia Lewis's success as an expatriate American sculptress. Perhaps few were aware that Bannister, a "Negro import" from Nova Scotia, had been challenged to become an artist in order to disprove the published assertion that while the Negro obviously possessed an appreciation for art, he had not shown a capacity to produce it.

A new interest in the American scene at this time had been awakened in the American artist of whatever color by the westward expansion of the country following the Civil War. The remarkable mid-western romantic-realist painter, Robert S. Duncanson, devoted a number of canvasses to western landscapes prior to his death in 1871. E. M. Bannister, by that time, had become one of the leading painters of bucolic scenes in the Northeastern part of the United States.

Worthy successors of these men were Henry Ossawa Tanner and William A. Harper. As an approach to painting, Harper's art illustrates a certain continuity from the work of Bannister. But this analogous relationship vanished rather quickly in the glow and splendor of Harper's landscapes after his adoption of an impressionist technique acquired in France and matured by trips to Mexico and the American West.

No American painter, probably not the great Winslow Homer nor even the eagle-eyed Thomas Eakins, could match that resplendent vision of a national American culture which had been proposed for them by the poet Walt Whitman in *O Pioneers* and in his celebrated political and literary document *Democratic Vistas*. In fact, only the most gifted among the white American artists of this period were able to escape the deadly dull mechanical routines of portrait painting and banal illustration, or the lofty, remote and classicizing sentiments learned by way of the warmed-over formulas of "beaux-arts" academies in Europe. All such preoccupations were too distant from the basic concerns of the Negro artists to be of any use. And so, turning away from such outworn traditions, the Negro artist wandered perhaps cheerless but alert into the pathless fields of the countryside towards the humble cabins in which he knew that the black freedman, still the backbone of the rural South, could be found and portrayed.

TRANSITIONAL ARTISTS

In just such an environment, Henry O. Tanner, during the years when he was still under the influence of his great American teacher, Thomas Eakins, strayed briefly in the 1880's and quickly fashioned therefrom a few fine landscapes and also some spellbinding portrayals of peasant Negroes in which we detect something of the sweet though melancholy lyricism that pervades the poetry of Paul Laurence Dunbar. Later, after his self-expatriation to France, Tanner became one of the foremost exponents of the "flight-to-religion" position, seeking in themes of biblical history and faith the broader canvas of human experience and aesthetic emotion.

Meta Vaux Warrick's early sculpture is a hymn to tradition expressed in forms which reflect the intense struggle of a soul with its own nature. In her work, which was clearly inspired by that of Rodin, she occasionally pushed her interpretations of humanity's sad plight to expressional extremes of despair, remorse, anger, and resignation. Certain of these moods were expressed with subtlety, and some awkwardly, but in the main, sincerely. In some ways, she seems to have been a continuator of the earlier Edmonia Lewis, although her brief sojourn in Europe resulted in the acquisition of "impressionist realism" as opposed to her predecessor's neo-classicism.

From 1900 to 1925, Negroes generally had to make their own opportunities in the fine arts. Aware of but little artistic tradition within the race and lacking a clear understanding of the issues confronting American art, Negro talent was forced to seek training or at least guidance in the schools and studios of reputable white artists who would accept them. Often, they were forced to beg for opportunities to study art in a serious way or to exhibit their work. Those who wished to exhibit their work usually had access only to the social rooms of churches, the vestibules and reading rooms of public libraries and Y.M.C.A. buildings, or to the class rooms of Negro public schools. Very little help came to them even through channels of race leadership or education, or from white patrons of means. Discouraging also, was the fact that but few knowledgeable interpreters of Negro art could be found among that day's Negro intellectuals. Apparently more concerned with the general problems of the Negro, race leaders did not too directly or seriously lend support to Negro art or the artist.

Through such vicissitudes arose the first group of "realist" painters and sculptors around 1915. Unable to support themselves by art alone, they were, despite that handicap, keen, if hindered observers of the realities around them. John Henry Adams, Jr., Lenwood Morris, W. O. Thompson, William E. Scott, T. E. Hunster, Edward Harleston, Laura Wheeler Waring and Alan

Freelon won praise for their interpretations of Negro character, and of regional life and landscape. None of them was a great artist, yet each did achieve results in some way comparable to the work of their better-known white contemporaries of the realist school, who had become derisively distinguished in the public mind by the sobriquet, "The Ashcan School" of painters.

In art, as in literature, science, education and other walks of life, the alert Negro had felt a compelling urge to defeat the theoretical, or fanciful, and often vicious misconceptions and prejudices entertained of his race by the white world. The struggle to do just that was most intense throughout the first twenty-five years of this century. Knowing this, we can understand why the Negro realists were dominated by an interest in factual renderings of the Negro. Later, they were to build on the materials thus discovered: Sculpture symbolizing the Negro's cultural and historical contributions, his aspirations, his sufferings, was created by Meta Warrick Fuller with enchanting power. Her younger contemporaries, May Howard Jackson, portrait sculptor, and Edward Harleston, in direct impressive portraiture of Negro leaders and in fine character studies, definitely enriched Negro art with dignified or with picturesque types. Yet, adverse circumstances kept these pioneer artists from utilizing their creative energies to the full.

The isolation of the American Negro artist of the middle period from the mainstream of culture is well illustrated by the fact that the great New York Armory Show of 1913 made little impression on him until the late 1920's. For fully fifteen years after its closing, young Negro artists were still preoccupied with academic realism or with a belated impressionism of manner, while all around them the old complacency of American art was losing ground.

NEW NEGRO MOVEMENT

Unemployment, labor strikes, conflicts and bad housing in the larger American cities throughout the 1920's were a consequence of industrial and social dislocations brought on by the first World War. But this social upheaval was also a harbinger of the great depression of the 1930's. Out of the effort to interpret and probably to exploit such mass disturbances and shifting economic conditions as they affected the Negro was born the intellectual and cultural ferment known as the "New Negro Movement." Then, for the first time in history was world attention focused on the cultural heritage and the living arts of the American Negro. An important book that took note of the Negro's achievements in art up to 1925 also pointed out ways in which he might go further. This was *The New Negro: An Interpretation*, edited by Alain LeRoy Locke.

The careful reader of that book will note that at least a few Negro artists had survived the rough artistic weather of the earlier decades; that indeed, their lack of popularity had been a test of their power of survival. The older artists of that period, Henry O. Tanner, May Howard Jackson, Harleston, Freenol, and Laura Wheeler Waring, Tanner, Meta W. Fuller, and May Howard Jackson were mentioned in Locke's book. They were mentioned critically but not by any means with dispraise. Their work was viewed, however, as representative of an earlier day, but not of the new day. This must be carefully borne in mind if we are to understand the nature of that artistic resurgence which marked Negro culture in the third decade of this century. May Howard Jackson, who died in 1939, and Malvin Gray Johnson, a most promising talent whose untimely death in 1934 was deeply mourned, were two artists of clear and solid objectives who had not time, however, to realize with equal success all the projects they attempted. In retrospect, the same characteristics of non-fulfillment mar our appreciation of E. A. Harleston who died in 1931.

Realism would appear to be as likely a part of the Negro heritage of art as any other acknowledged artistic tradition. Indeed, it is also an aspect of African Negro art, although it has been largely alienated from us through disparagements upon it by those who have made it their purpose to misinterpret or to minimize the double heritage of the conceptual and the real, the abstract and the concrete, the imaginative and the representational which are equally present therein. From black Africa's Middle Ages there has risen to challenge modern art and modern taste one of the world's most vigorous traditions of realistic art. The great bronze Ifé heads and the bold but extraordinarily poised creations of Benin and the Ashanti of the

Fifteenth and later centuries strike us as being an almost direct anticipation of the noble Baroque masterpieces of sculpture by the Eighteenth century Brazilian mulatto sculptor, Aleijadinho, or the powerful modeling of the painter-wood-engraver Charles White, whose monumental forms realistically projected in paint inevitably recall the diversified legacy of African realism.

It is a fact of rather curious interest that his older contemporary, Archibald Motley, one of the original "New Negro" talents, is another notable exponent of the same tradition. Also in line with this substantial tradition is the veteran expressionist painter, Beauford Delaney, "the amazing Beauford" of Henry Miller's unique biographical sketch. Indeed, the social commentary of Charles White is further inflected in the varied work of Charles Davis, Eldzier Cortor, and John Wilson, three young artists whose canvasses seem to brood over the slum and ghetto lands of the great Northern cities. But it is doubtful that Richmond Barthé's sculpture, particularly of the period 1940 to 1948, could be properly appreciated except in the light of that American new realism which enlivens and sometimes spiritualizes not only the work of certain American practitioners who were the "white regionalists" of the 1930's and 40's, but even that potent Mexican realism of the 1920's and 1930's.

INFLUENCE OF AFRICAN NEGRO ART

By 1933, the dehumanizing effect of cubist principles on form was beginning to modify Negro painting, sculpture and graphic art quite significantly. Zestfully introduced to Americans through the Armory Show, this style had first taken firm root in the paintings of the Americans Max Weber, John Marin, Alfred Maurer, Niles Spencer, and Preston Dickinson. A foretaste of the Negro artist's use of cubist forms had been seen in the book illustrations and earliest formal experiments of Aaron Douglas, James L. Wells, Hale Woodruff, and Malvin Gray Johnson. Its radical contrasts of form hardly affected the normative realism, however, of such sculptors as Barthé and Augusta Savage, unless it can be said that it influenced their work toward better structure and also economy of design and facture.

One of the sources of Cubism had been African Negro sculpture; and it was the recognition of the importance of this connection by Paul Guillaume and other French critics, and later by Albert Barnes and Alain Locke, which effectually attached the cubism of African forms to the new experimental growth of modern Negro art.

Happily, it is not yet possible to say with finality that the fructifying influence of African art on modern Afro-American art has diminished. Individually and separately, I am sure, there must be a very substantial number of American artists who still have recourse to its discipline, precisely as there are many American artists who still check their own native primitivism by the timeless traditions of American Indian art and American colonial art. But the earlier morphological transfer of geometric or crystalline shapes has now declined virtually to zero, while something more important, because more expressional as well as abstract, has replaced it.

An embarrassed self-consciousness has sometimes attended the experimental use which our artists have tried to make of either the African or the geometric forms of Cubism, as if the pattern into which the artist had chosen to cast his forms had met a recalcitrant medium. Nevertheless, it would be rewarding, if there were space to do so, to trace the gentle evolution of cubistic form in modern Negro art towards and finally into abstraction through the sculpture of Elizabeth Prophet and Augusta Savage, and the more youthful Selma Burke and John Rhoden, not forgetting, by any means, the gingerly rhythms of William H. Johnson's early expressionist cubism, or the surrealist and abstract qualities in the magical paintings of Harlan Jackson and Harper Phillips, or the bronzes of Barbara Chase and Richard Hunt.

It is unlikely that "racial" or "traditional abstraction" can be identified as a genre of Negro art, although the productions of certain Afro-American artists may seem to draw upon modalities extracted from the personal experience of race. We are aware, nevertheless, of a kind of conscious "atavism," deriving from the practice of subjectivized illustration of certain folkthemes used in the work of important Cuban, Venezuelan, Haitian and Brazilian artists. Emergent as far back as the 1940's, this phenomenon has persisted almost to the present. The best or at least the most effective instances are to be observed in the paintings of the great Wifredo Lam and his pupil, Roberto Diago who died untimely. Occasionally, the sculpture of Ramos-Blanco and Rita Longa, both Cubans, is similarly inspired.

NEGRO ART IN LATIN AMERICA

Many of the Haitian so-called "primitive" painters, among whom the most interesting are Philomé Obin, the late Hector Hippolyte, Louverture Poisson, and Rigaud Benoit to name but a few; or even their opposites, those intellectual and sophisticated students of Vaudou, who are the spiritual off-spring of Lucien Price, now deceased, have combined renascent African forms with an intense purity of vision that is quite astonishing. In the United States, a similar intensity of vision is remarked in the brilliant early gouaches of Jacob Lawrence, whose "symbolic narratives" are proclamations of color, or in Horace Pippin's folk-memory paintings which even manage to hold their own in juxtaposition to Romare Bearden's early compositional essays that were couched in disjunctive forms and raw color. Since 1955, Lois M. Jones's (Mrs. Pierre-Noël) almost annual visits to the "Magical Island" have resulted in watercolors and oils of enchanting landscapes, and harbor and market scenes with colors tempered to the mercurial moods of the Haitian atmosphere.

AFRO-AMERICANS IN AFRICA

It will not be inappropriate to mention here the visits in Africa which a few American Negro artists have made with a double purpose to learn more at first hand about contemporary African art and to gratify the irresistible impulse to view and to record the African scene. The first to make such a visit with an avowedly journalistic purpose in mind was Elton Fax, an outstanding New York illustrator. His book, *African Vignettes*, is the pictorial result of his travels in West Africa. As a kind of picture-diary, this book has won unusual popularity to the great satisfaction of the artist as well as his sponsors who were the American Society of African Culture. Fax's illustrations include portraits of Africans and swiftly sketched scenes of African street life.

Dr. John T. Biggers, Head of the Department of Art at Texas Southern University, was the next artist to visit in Africa. Biggers chose to focus his artistic tour on Ghana, a choice that no doubt afforded a better opportunity to achieve both unity and cumulative impact of subject content in his designs. It should be stressed that while some of Dr. Biggers' "painterly" drawings are of great size they were reduced to the compass of a folio volume and published most effectively under the title of *Ananse; The Web of Life in West Africa.*

Jacob Lawrence has been twice to Africa, the first time accompanying an exhibition of his own paintings in the hope of stimulating a free exchange of ideas with African artists in Nigeria. His second visit in June, 1964, was devoted to a painter's research of the African scene and resulted in a large exhibition of his work at Lagos, Ibadan and New York.

RECENT MURAL PAINTING

Mural painting and relief sculpture by Negro artists still reflect as previously in the days of the Roosevelt administration and the New Deal, the social and topical emphasis previously imposed by the now discontinued Government Works program for the Arts. Nevertheless, some significant progress was made by our mural painters through the Federal Arts Projects in the 1940's. Under that program, artists of lesser abilities were sometimes employed to decorate walls along with the best; and private patronage also encouraged many of the younger artists thus limelighted by official recognition. Almost without exception, Negro artists were assigned wall spaces in buildings largely in daily use by Negroes, such as schools, hospitals, libraries and community centers. Yet, it must be admitted that this obviously considered location for their work was in the last analysis good for the Negro clientele to whom their objective paintings were directed. It was in this way that underprivileged persons could view good works of art. Often they were inspired as well as instructed.

Thus, the historical paintings of Aaron Douglass and W. E. Scott, of Charles Alston—particularly the latter artist's mural series on cycles of Negro History still to be seen in the Harlem Hospital—and the several mural panels prepared by James Porter, Lois M. Jones, Charles White and Hale Woodruff would, if presented together in one grouping, relate the complete history of the Negro people in the United States. Indeed, with few exceptions, our mural painters of today still choose to work within the racial theme and scope. Between Aaron Douglass' Fisk University Murals and the huge paintings completed by Charles Alston and Woodruff for the Golden Gate Insurance Company in California, or the equally fine productions of Elmer Brown in Cleveland and Charles Stallings at Morgan College in Baltimore, there is scarcely a mural painting that does not have as its main content the episodic portrayal of Negro life and history.

In America, the racial double standard operates in the field of art as well as in other fields of endeavor. There is no Negro member, so far as I am aware in the National Society of Mural Painters; nor has the Associated American Artists yet taken in any appreciable number of Negro artists. Throughout the country there are art societies which reject Negro applicants on the basis of the local customs. However, there are material gains in the forms of prizes, awards, commissions, honors and sales of which some Negro artists, particularly those of wide reputation, have had their share.

BLACK "GRAPHICS"

Perhaps it is in the Negro's graphic art that one can see most clearly the future as concerns the basic goals of the Negro. Employing a noble and ancient medium which traditionally has been close to the people and sometimes the best interpreter of their hopes, the Negro artist is beginning to find eloquent and passionate voice in the media of the wood-cut and wood-engraving, the multiple forms of etching, the lithograph and the silk-screen print. The most important single reason for this trend is that it affords a short-cut to popular interest and consumption; since the print that results from these media is often of modest price as compared with the prices of paintings.

It is also important to note that agencies for the distribution of the print have sprung up to negotiate for the artist. Universities with art departments or galleries like those of Howard University and Atlanta University have long served the artist-printmaker in that way. In Chicago, the National Conference of Artists, and in Los Angeles, the Cultural Exchange Center, offer selected prints by contemporary Negro artists through the medium of portfolio publication and distribution and by review advertising in art and literature journals. In addition to the foregoing, there are several important galleries in New York and Washington, D. C. which serve the Negro artist and the would-be patron through programs intended to make the work of the Negro artist available on the same basis as the work of the non-Negro artist.

Technical mastery of the print medium through experimentation with novel materials, that is to say, with materials that were never previously used in techniques of engraving or etching, is clearly one of the goals of modern art. Yet, the Negro artist shows but little interest in technical facility for its own sake. While his instructors, the master printers or "professors" of print-making, of which there are several connected with various centers of academic learning, must be so concerned, it suffices the Negro practitioner to discover those possibilities of the print which best convey thought or feeling or both. Subtlety where needed, and complexity where it serves; but as for the rest, a bold and refreshing simplicity. That, I should say, sums up the Negro artist's conception of the print.

The number of artists who rise to that level of performance, however, is not large. Among the most interesting as well as competent are James L. Wells, long known as the "Dean" of Negro printmakers. There are also Charles White to whose powerful realism reference has already been made, and Norma Morgan who takes the inspiration for her engraved forms from her long sojourn in the moorland wilderness of Scotland. John T. Biggers has not only drawings but fine lithographs to his credit; and Mildred J. Thompson, now resident in Germany, has produced some of the most fanciful and yet arresting etchings and woodcuts that it has ever been the privilege of the writer to see. Excellent promise of even better things to come is embedded in the accomplished work of Ruth Waddy, Margaret Burroughs and David Driskell.

In an earlier paragraph the writer has stated that there were but few Negro intellectuals who deliberately concerned themselves either as critics or historians with Negro art in the 1920's. Indeed, the only accredited Negro art critic of that time was Alain Locke. In addition, Henry O. Tanner was the only Negro painter to enjoy consistent mention in the American press prior to the New Negro Movement; but even he was mentioned in but few books of serious criticism or history devoted to American art. In contrast to this, we note that today numerous announcements, reviews and criticisms of single works and group performances by Negro artists are scattered throughout the pages of American magazines and newspapers. A number of white writers, nearly all of whom are historians or trained critics of art, have recently been careful to include the contributions of the Negro artist in their general studies of American art as well as their revaluations of particular periods of art. Among these I would cite Oliver Larkin, Ralph M. Pearson, Winslow Ames, John I. H. Baur, Aline Loucheim, Leslie Ahlander and Frank Getlein.

It is certain that the double standard of appraisal and of employment that formerly discouraged the Negro artist is fast disappearing, especially so when we are able to name quite a significant number of Negro artists who are now teaching in college art departments or in schools of art which only yesterday had exclusively white faculties. In addition to that bit of progress, we note that Negro art patrons are appearing in ever-growing numbers, not just as occasional buyers, but as collectors who often purchase their art directly from art galleries established in such cities as Chicago, Washington, D. C., New York and San Francisco.

I conclude in the conviction that the American Negro is now moving with the great wave of creativity which is cresting in America. This, in fact, is a cultural upsurge of crucial importance, and it offers the artist and writer unprecedented opportunities for the development of mobility and independence of creative thought and imagery. The question is will the Negro artist continue to exploit his present opportunities in the realization that such an engagement is more than a test of sheer tenacity:

It is a challenge to all his capabilities; though the answer to the query actually rests with the Negro people as a whole, not specifically with their interpreters. Therefore, it is predictable that only the as yet unspent social and cultural drives of that people can unfailingly sustain the Negro artist as he embraces the broader opportunities of the future.

SELECTED BIBLIOGRAPHY

BOOKS

The Nineteenth Century

Arnold, John N., *Art and Artists of Rhode Island*. Providence, R. I.: Citizens Association, 1905.

Brawley, Benjamin G., *The Negro Genius*. New York: Dodd Mead, 1937.

Dover, Cedric, *American Negro Art*, Greenwich, Conn.: New York Graphic Society, 1960.

Freeman, Murray, *Emancipation and the Freed in American Sculpture*. Washington, D. C.: The Author, 1916, p. 21.

Larkin, Oliver W., *Art and Life in America*. New York: Holt Rinehart and Winston, 1966, pp. 279; 436-437.

Locke, Alain L., *The Negro in Art: A Pictorial Record of the Negro Artist and of the Negro Theme in Art*. Washington, D.C.: Associates in Negro Folk Education, 1940.

Porter, James A., *Modern Negro Art*. New York: Dryden, 1943.

————, "Robert S. Duncanson, Midwestern Romantic-Realist," (Monograph). *Art in America*, Vol. XXXIX, 3, October, 1951.

Rodman, Seldon, *Renaissance in Haiti: Popular Painters in the Black Republic*. New York: Pellegrini and Cudahy, 1948.

Taft, Lorado, *The History of American Sculpture*. New York: Macmillan, 1903, p. 212.

PERIODICALS

Bullard, Laura C., "Edmonia Lewis," *The Revolution*. New York: April 20, 1871.

Fauset, Jessie, "H. O. Tanner," *The Crisis*, April, 1924, pp. 255-258.

Porter, James A., "The Transcultural Affinities of African Negro Art," in *Africa Seen by American Negroes*, Dijon: Présence Africaine, 1958.

Smith, Lucy E., "Some American Painters in Paris," *The American Magazine of Art*, Vol. XVIII, 3, March, 1927, p. 134.